Contents

AQA A-level

Business

2 Third Edition

John Wolinski and
Gwen Coates

Approval message from AQA

This textbook has been approved by AQA for use with our qualification. This means that we have checked that it broadly covers the specification and we are satisfied with the overall quality. Full details of our approval process can be found on our website.

We approve textbooks because we know how important it is for teachers and students to have the right resources to support their teaching and learning. However, the publisher is ultimately responsible for the editorial control and quality of this book.

Please note that when teaching the **AQA A-level Business** course, you must refer to AQA's specification as your definitive source of information. While this book has been written to match the specification, it cannot provide complete coverage of every aspect of the course.

A wide range of other useful resources can be found on the relevant subject pages of our website: www.aqa.org.uk.

Orders: please contact Bookpoint Ltd, 130 Park Drive, Milton Park, Abingdon, Oxon OX14 4SE. Telephone: (44) 01235 827720. Fax: (44) 01235 400454. Email education@bookpoint.co.uk Lines are open from 9 a.m. to 5 p.m., Monday to Saturday, with a 24-hour message answering service. You can also order through our website: www.hoddereducation.co.uk

ISBN: 978 1 4718 3611 4

© John Wolinski and Gwen Coates 2015

First published in 2015 by
Hodder Education,
An Hachette UK Company
Carmelite House
50 Victoria Embankment
London EC4Y 0DZ
www.hoddereducation.co.uk

Impression number   10 9 8 7 6 5 4 3 2

Year   2019 2018 2017 2016

Cover photo © Rawpixel - Fotolia

Illustrations by Integra Software Services Pvt. Ltd., Pondicherry, India

Typeset in 11/13 pt ITC Berkeley Oldstyle Std Book by Integra Software Services Pvt. Ltd., Pondicherry, India

Printed in Dubai

A catalogue record for this title is available from the British Library.

Introduction

This textbook has been written specifically to meet the needs of students during the second year of AQA A-level Business. Along with the Year 1 book, it provides all of the materials needed for students taking the AQA A-level Business qualification. It provides comprehensive coverage of the subject content of the Year 2 AQA A-level specification, section by section, as it is laid out in the specification document. These sections are those that the AQA scheme of work suggests are covered during the second year of the A-level Business course.

Up-to-date examples and illustrations from actual businesses and situations are used throughout the book in order to help you to recognise the dynamic and changing nature of business and its relevance to society.

Structure

This book follows the order of the AQA A-level Business (7132*) specification. (*7132 is the AQA code used to describe the A-level award.) The Year 2 material builds on the Year 1/AS content (AS coded as 7131). You should ensure that you have studied the Year 1 book before reading this book.

The AQA A-level Business specification is divided into ten sections. Six of these sections constitute the A-level Year 1 (and AS). The Year 2 consists of four new sections.

The Year 1 (and AS) is designed to introduce the concept of business and the environment in which businesses operate.

- **Section 1: What is business?**

It then focuses on the working of the four main functional areas of business:

- **Section 2: Managers, leadership and decision-making**
- **Section 3: Decision-making to improve marketing performance**
- **Section 4: Decision-making to improve operational performance**
- **Section 5: Decision-making to improve financial performance**
- **Section 6: Decision-making to improve human resource performance**.

This Year 2 book moves the focus to the overall strategic management of businesses, incorporating detailed scrutiny of the internal and external environment within which businesses operate. It is divided into four sections, each of which is split into further parts – shown by the individual chapters in this book. The sections and chapters are summarised below:

- **Section 7: Analysing the strategic position of a business. Chapters 1 to 8**
  This section examines the mission and objectives of businesses. It examines how businesses and their objectives are influenced by the internal strengths and weaknesses of the business, and how external opportunities and threats affect different businesses. The section concludes with an examination of how strategic options can be analysed.
- **Section 8: Choosing strategic direction. Chapters 9 to 10**
  This section looks at how a business chooses its strategic direction (choosing which markets to compete in and which products to offer) and how it decides on its strategic positioning (how it chooses to compete).
- **Section 9: Strategic methods: how to pursue strategies. Chapters 11 to 14**
  This section provides an assessment of the merits and demerits of four different strategic approaches: changing scale; innovation; internationalisation and greater use of digital technology.
- **Section 10: Managing strategic change. Chapters 15 to 18**
  This concluding section examines how businesses manage their strategies. It looks at how businesses manage change and organisational culture. It concludes by studying strategic implementation and potential problems relating to the management of strategy.

Special features

This book contains several special features designed to aid your understanding of the requirements of the AQA A-level Business course.

Key terms

These are clear, concise definitions of the main terms needed for the course. Every term in the AQA Year 2 specification is included as a key term to enable you to develop a sound understanding of the concepts that are essential learning.

Authors' advice

Both authors have over 30 years' experience of teaching and have used this to provide snippets of advice that will help you to improve your understanding of topics that may provide certain challenges and to help you avoid potential pitfalls.

Fact files

Topical examples from the world of business are included at regular intervals to help you develop your understanding and application skills by showing how the business ideas you have studied can be applied to real-life situations. The fact files will also increase your awareness of current developments and practices.

Did you know?

These boxes are placed throughout the book; they provide useful insights into the ideas and concepts covered in the course and their use in businesses. The comments will help you to improve your understanding of business activities.

What do you think?

On occasions, facts or comments on business activity are presented in the form of a challenge – what do you think? There is often a range of possible solutions to business problems or many differing consequences to an action. These boxes will get you thinking about the possible alternative solutions or consequences.

Practice exercises and case studies

In the 18 chapters of this book, there are 50 different practice exercises that are provided to help you check your understanding of the topics you have covered in each chapter. Many of the questions in these exercises are geared towards assisting you in revising and testing your knowledge and understanding of the topics covered. Other questions will enable you to test your application skills, particularly where calculations are involved. Some questions will also test higher-level skills, such as analysis and evaluation.

In the book there are also 24 case studies to provide further practice of answering questions. Most of these case studies are based on real-life businesses and provide background information that is intended to help you to:

● develop further your understanding of the business world
● practise and develop your skills.

For shorter chapters the practice exercises and case studies are placed at the end of the chapter. This is to allow your understanding of the chapter contents to be tested immediately after completing the topics. However, some longer chapters cover a great deal of material and have been divided into identifiable topic areas. Consequently, some of the practice exercises and case studies in these chapters have been placed in the body of the chapter, at the point at which a particular topic area has been completed. As a result, you will be able to test your understanding immediately after completing that topic rather than waiting until the end of the chapter.

Assessment skills

The hierarchy of skills

Every mark that is awarded on an A-level paper is given for the demonstration of a skill. The following four skills are tested:

● Knowledge and understanding – demonstrating knowledge and understanding of the specified content of the course, such as knowing the definition of a business term or stating the advantage of a particular method.
● Application – relating or applying knowledge and understanding to a specific organisation or situation. An example might be advising a business to target a particular segment of consumers, based on recognising the most relevant consumers for that organisation.
● Analysis – using business theory to develop a line of thought in relation to the solution of a business problem. An example might be showing how improvements in the quality of a product may cause cash-flow problems in the short term but lead to more satisfied customers, and therefore more sales revenue, in the long run.

- Evaluation – making a judgement by weighing up the evidence provided and, possibly, recognising the strength, quality and reliability of the evidence before making a decision.

All questions are marked according to this hierarchy of skills, with knowledge being the easiest and evaluation being the most difficult.

Command words

To help you recognise the highest level of skill required in a question certain command words will be used. Some key command words are:

- **Calculate:** Work out the value of something, such as the percentage of labour turnover.
- **Describe:** Set out the characteristics of certain data, such as a trend in sales value.
- **Explain:** Set out purposes or reasons, such as the factors influencing a decision to expand capacity.
- **Analyse:** Separate information into components and identify their characteristics, such as showing how financial incentives for staff may affect motivation.
- **Evaluate:** Judge from available evidence, such as weighing up the pros and cons of a particular marketing strategy.
- **Justify:** Support a case with evidence, such as studying two possible options for a business and showing why a particular option is better than an alternative option.
- **To what extent:** Say by how much or how many, such as studying a business that is aiming to increase profits and assessing the degree to which a decision to decrease price might improve (or worsen) the business's profitability.

Assessment of AQA A-level Business

The **scheme of assessment** describes the format of the examinations and the methods of assessment — the A-level course is assessed 100 per cent by examinations. For the A-level qualification students take THREE examination papers. **Unlike previous qualifications all three of these papers must be sat at the end of the A-level course. These examinations are based on BOTH the AS (1st year) specification and the Year 2 specification and each examination paper can test any topic.** Thus a topic from a specific chapter might be tested in Paper 1, Paper 2 or Paper 3 of the A-level. The essential difference between the three papers is the style of assessment.

A-level Paper 1: 2 hours. Maximum marks: 100. All questions in Sections A and B are compulsory.

A-level Paper 1 consists of four sections:

- Section A – Multiple-choice questions. 15 questions. 15 marks
- Section B – Short-answer questions. Approximately 6 questions. 35 marks
- Section C – Essays. One essay from a choice of two essays. 25 marks
- Section D – Essays. One essay from a choice of two essays. 25 marks

A-level Paper 2: 2 hours. Maximum marks: 100. All questions are compulsory.

A-level Paper 2 consists of three sets of data response questions. One of these data response questions will be based on material that is predominantly numerical or graphical. The other two data response questions will be based on information that is literate or a combination of literate and numerate information.

The format of the questions set may vary but will be based on the following:

- Each set of data response questions will commence with a calculation (or two), short-answer or analytical question.
- Each set of data response questions will include a question testing analysis.
- Each set of data response questions will conclude with a question requiring evaluation.

Overall, the paper will include approximately 9 or 10 questions.

A-level Paper 3: 2 hours. Maximum marks: 100. All questions are compulsory

A-level Paper 3 consists of approximately 6 or 7 questions based on a single case study.

The format of the questions set may vary but will be based on:

- 2 or 3 analysis questions
- 3 or 4 evaluation questions.

Study advice

Keep up to date

This book contains many topical examples for you to use, but business is constantly changing. Although a textbook provides you with the theory, reading newspapers, magazines and internet articles will help you to keep pace with changes. One thing is guaranteed: the business environment will have changed between the beginning and the end of your A-level course, so there is no substitute for keeping an eye on the latest business news.

Build your own business studies dictionary

As you progress through this book, build up your own glossary/dictionary of terms. This will ease your revision and help to ensure that you can define terms clearly. Knowing the exact meaning of terms will also allow you to write relevantly on the other, non-definition questions.

Read each chapter thoroughly

On completion of each topic, make sure that you have read each page of the relevant chapter and use the questions at the end of each chapter to test yourself. If you adopt this approach for every chapter of the book, your revision will be just that: revising what you have already learned rather than learning material for the first time.

Complete the practice exercises and case studies

Tackle the practice exercises and case studies in each chapter, even if you are not asked to do so by your teacher. Completion of these exercises will help you to check that you have understood the basic ideas in the chapter. It will also help you to develop the best approach to answering business questions.

Develop your communication and data-handling skills

There is no need to have studied GCSE Business before starting the A-level course; the AQA AS and A-level specifications assume that you have no prior understanding of the subject. However, the courses do expect you to have already developed certain skills during your general GCSE programme. These skills are communication and the ability to use and interpret business data. You should be able to understand and apply averages (the mean, median and mode); prepare and interpret tables, graphs, histograms, bar charts and pie charts; and interpret index numbers.

Focus on the higher-level skills

It is tempting to focus chiefly on the facts when you are revising. Remember that it is important to consider the *depth* of your answers. Include scope for this in your revision so that you are able to succeed in analysis and evaluation. Try to think of ways to apply your learning.

Read the Chief Examiner's report

This report will alert you to the strengths and weaknesses shown by previous students and will help you to refine your approach. Along with previous examination papers and mark schemes, these reports are available in PDF format from the AQA website (www.aqa.org.uk).

We wish you well in your studies and examinations, and hope that this book helps to provide you with the understanding needed to succeed. Good luck!

1 Mission, corporate objectives and strategy

This chapter begins with a discussion about the influences on the mission of a business. It then considers the internal and external influences on corporate objectives and decisions, including the pressures for short-termism, business ownership and the external and internal environment. A distinction is made between strategy and tactics. The links between mission, corporate objectives and strategy are then explained. The impact of strategic decision making on functional decision making is considered. Influences on, and the importance of, competitive advantage are then reviewed. The chapter concludes with an explanation of SWOT analysis and a consideration of its value to business.

Influences on the mission of a business

Before an organisation can start to address the task of planning and setting objectives, it must have a clear understanding of its overall purpose. This is expressed as a **mission** and is communicated via a mission statement. The first half of Chapter 1 of AQA A-level Business Book 1 considered business mission in detail; ensure that you reread that chapter to refresh your understanding of the concept.

> **Did you know?**
> A mission statement is a qualitative statement of an organisation's aims that uses language intended to motivate employees and convince customers, suppliers and those outside the organisation of its sincerity and commitment.

> **Key term**
> **Mission** An organisation's aims or long-term intentions, its ultimate purpose; a business mission is sometimes the same as its corporate aims.

Some authors separate the idea of business vision and business mission; others see them as a single concept. Where they are separate concepts, the vision of an organisation is what it wants to become, while the mission is a reflection of the present and states what the business is and what it values.

Mission and vision statements are important because:

● They communicate the purpose and values of an organisation to its stakeholders. The better employees and other stakeholders understand an organisation's purpose, through its mission and vision, the better able they will be to understand its strategy (i.e. the plan about how it will achieve its vision and mission) and its implementation. (Strategy is explained in more detail later in the chapter.)
● They inform the strategy adopted by an organisation.
● They enable measurable goals and objectives to be identified, which allow an organisation to gauge the success of its strategy.

A range of factors influence the mission of a business. These include:

● The size of a business. A small local business may have a mission that reflects the personal interests of the owner, for example simply to make a living or to provide products of excellent quality to meet local needs. There is less likely to be employee involvement in determining the mission of a small business and the owner's own goals may be non-negotiable. As a business grows, its mission will change and may, for example, reflect the interests of a wider group of stakeholders or incorporate national or global aspirations about its activities.
● The range of activities undertaken by a business. A large organisation with a range of different activities or a business that produces a range of different products for different markets, may find it difficult to identify a single-sentence mission statement that encompasses all of its activities. For example, a supermarket with an original mission that was focused on value for money may have to rethink its mission if it moves into banking and financial services. To counter this, some companies produce mission lists, while others produce mission booklets. While these tend to cover all of a company's activities, they are less memorable than a single-sentence mission.
● The nature of owners and important stakeholders in a business. (Stakeholders were discussed in detail in Chapter 6 of Book 1.) The mission must be one that is understood and agreed upon by all stakeholders if it is to be effective in providing a common purpose and a collective view. Some mission statements fail to have any impact on company performance because they do not provide a clear signal as to how the purpose, values and strategy should guide employees' standards and behaviour. Involving employees in determining the mission may result in their greater commitment to the business and its mission. However, mission statements do not necessarily add value and can do serious harm if, for example, employees recognise that the values and behaviour standards mentioned in the statement are different from their own. For example, when a high-profile petroleum company issued a mission statement that included an appeal for a balanced home and work life, many of its employees ridiculed the document because it did not reflect their experience of working in the company.
● Changes over time. As the nature of a business and its goals change, its mission needs to be continually monitored and altered. For example, Microsoft, founded in 1975, originally supplied the operating system for a major mainframe provider. Its early mission was 'a computer on every desk and in every home'. Today, its range of activities has grown to encompass the internet and related technologies and its mission now is: 'Helping our customers realise their full potential'.

▲ A small local business is likely to have a different sort of mission statement to a multi-national

- The actual performance of an organisation. Mission statements need to match what is actually happening in an organisation and should be checked for any hidden meanings or negative implications before being placed into the public domain. This was clearly not the case when the former British Rail, which was known for delays and cancellations of train services, launched its famous 'We're getting there' mission statement.
- External factors, such as the level of competition, economic conditions and possible government regulation, may influence a business mission. Some of these factors were considered in Chapter 3 of Book 1 and there is further discussion of the external environment in Chapters 4, 5, 6 and 7 of this book.
- A business's strengths and opportunities. Its strengths are likely to be its distinctive competences, which are likely to become its competitive advantages. Competitive advantage refers to why one business outperforms its competitors because of particular features about, for example, its technology, image and brand name or employees. (Competitive advantage is discussed in detail in Chapter 10.) Taking this difference into account when determining a mission can mean that the mission becomes a recipe for success. This is because the mission defines an organisation's accomplishments and its competitive advantage, which differentiates it from everyone else. It also provides employees with directions to help them develop plans and look for opportunities for improvement.
- The extent to which a business demonstrates social responsibility in its actions can influence its mission. This is usually a reflection of the views and nature of founders and leaders of a business and also of its stakeholders. For example, the founder of The Body Shop, Anita Roddick, was very clear about reusing, refilling and recycling containers and packaging, and about the source and use of natural ingredients for the products sold.

▲ Social and environmental responsibility are very important to the Body Shop

Internal and external influences on corporate objectives and decisions

Corporate objectives are set in order to co-ordinate business activity and give a sense of direction to, and guide the actions of, an organisation as a whole. They act as a focus for decision making and effort, and as a yardstick against which success or failure can be measured. They also encourage a sense of common purpose among the workforce. A sense of common purpose makes it much easier to co-ordinate actions and to

Key term

Corporate objectives Goals of the whole organisation rather than of different elements of the organisation. They are set in order to co-ordinate the activities of, give a sense of direction to, and guide the actions of the whole organisation. They are dictated by the mission or corporate aims of an organisation.

Did you know?

Corporate aims are often provided in the form of a mission statement and give a general focus from which corporate and other objectives can be set. Aims determine the way in which an organisation will develop.

create a team spirit, which in turn is likely to lead to improvements in efficiency and a more productive and motivated staff. Corporate objectives govern the functional objectives or targets for each division or department of the business. See Chapter 1 in Book 1 for a detailed discussion about what business objectives are, why they are set and the difference between corporate and functional objectives and decisions.

Examples of **corporate objectives** include: maximising shareholder wealth; maximising sales revenue; focusing on a firm's core capabilities rather than venturing into risky diversification; social and environmental responsibility; adding value; and enhancing reputation through continuous technological innovation.

There are many influences on business objectives and decisions; the following include some of the most important ones. They are classified according to whether they are broadly internal or external influences.

Internal influences on objectives and decisions

- Business ownership: Whether an organisation is profit making or non-profit making will have a significant influence on corporate objectives and decision making. If profit making, whether the business is a sole trader, private limited company or public limited company will also have an important influence. The different forms of business ownership were discussed in detail in Chapter 2 of Book 1.
- The relative power of stakeholders: Stakeholders were examined in detail in Chapter 6 of Book 1. The relative power of individual stakeholder groups and their influence on objectives and decision making depends on the nature of the business. For example:
  - in some small family businesses, the interests of shareholders may be the major influence on objectives and decision making
  - for organisations whose location has a major impact on the local environment, local communities or environmental pressure groups may be powerful stakeholders that influence decision making and the setting of objectives and ability to meet objectives.

  Whether a business adopts a traditional (or shareholder value) perspective will influence its objectives and decisions. These issues were discussed in detail in Chapters 2 and 6 of Book 1.
- Ethics: A decision made on ethical grounds might reject the most profitable solution for a business in favour of one that provides greater benefit to society as a whole, or to a particular group of stakeholders, such as the local community or employees. The approach to ethics in a business, which is heavily influenced by its leaders and the culture that is present in the business, will be influential in the setting of objectives.
- Business culture: Culture is often described as 'the way that we do things around here', meaning the type of behaviour that is considered acceptable or unacceptable. Culture has a major influence on objectives and decision-making processes in an organisation, in particular in relation to how it responds to changes in the external environment. For example, the culture of an organisation will influence how resistant to change it is and thus the level of risk it is prepared to take in terms of decision making and will thus be an important influence on objectives. Culture is considered in detail in Chapter 16 of this book.

- Resource constraints: Resources can be financial, human or physical. The fact that all resources are scarce relative to the demand for them has a huge influence on a business's objectives and its decisions. Resource constraints mean that every decision about how to deploy limited resources will involve a consideration of opportunity cost. This is explained in more detail below:
  - Financial resources. If a company is unable to generate sufficient financial resources, this will affect its objectives and its decision making. For example, decisions about expansion or diversification will depend on a business having sufficient funds, or access to funds, to support these developments. Limited financial resources will mean a business must choose between alternatives, for example, whether to allocate a larger budget to its marketing activities or to improving the quality of its production facilities.
  - Human resources. The availability of human resources will influence an organisation's objectives and decision making. For example, whether a business decides to introduce a particularly complex piece of computer software might depend on whether it has sufficient trained staff, whether it will be able to recruit such trained and experienced individuals or whether it can provide appropriate training for unskilled, but otherwise suitable staff.
  - Physical resources. If a business has set an objective to expand its business in a particular geographical area, the availability of suitable sites at affordable prices is likely to influence the suitability and attainability of this objective.

▲ The availability of human resources will impact decision making

External influences on objectives and decisions

- Pressure for short-termism: this is where businesses focus on short-term profit objectives rather than long-term performance objectives. It is often the result of pressure from institutional investors seeking to maximise their funds and profits. Detailed discussion about public limited companies and the pressures they face from institutional investors to focus on short-term objectives were discussed in Chapter 2 of Book 1.
- The external environment: The external environment and its impact on business costs and the demand for goods and services were discussed in Chapter 3 of Book 1. That discussion indicates very clearly that the external environment is a major influence on objectives and decision making in business.
  - Changes in economic policy, such as an increase in interest rates, will influence business objectives and decisions about, for example, whether to delay expansion plans because the costs of finance become too high and consumers' discretionary income falls. On the other hand, improving economic growth may mean incomes are rising and this in turn might cause a business to look more favourably on plans for expansion if it believes higher incomes will mean more sales.
  - Environmental factors might influence objectives and decisions, for example about which method of waste disposal to adopt.
  - Demographic trends may influence objectives and decisions about the mix of products a business should provide in order to take advantage of, for example, the growing number of elderly people in the population.
  - The actions of competitors will also be a significant influence on objectives and decision making. For example, if a competitor brings

▲ Companies such as SAGA specialise in holidays for the over 50s.

out a new product, reduces the price of its existing products or establishes a new sales outlet nearby – each of these actions will influence the objectives and decisions a business makes about its own product, pricing and location strategies.

Long- and short-term influences on objectives and decisions

In practice, objectives are constantly modified in response to changes in the market, the external environment and opportunities available. Thus short-term objectives may vary from longer-term objectives. For example:

- A financial crisis is likely to encourage a firm to focus on short-term survival rather than, say, growth or market share. This does not mean that its long-term objectives in relation to growth or market share and relevant decisions about these have changed. However, in the very short term, contingency plans and alternative strategies may be required.
- A firm may have a long-term objective of improving profitability, but in the short term profitability might be sacrificed in order to try to eliminate a competitor. For example, in the short term, a firm might use very low pricing (sometimes known as destroyer or predatory pricing) in order to force a competitor from the market. This might mean losses being sustained in the short term in order to pursue growth and increase market share, which in turn should improve long-term profitability.
- In a recession, emphasis is likely to be placed on survival, whereas over the longer term and in a boom period, the potential for high profits may encourage other objectives, such as helping the environment or local community, or diversification.
- Changes in government policy may force a company to adopt different short-term priorities. For example, an increase or decrease in interest rates can have a significant impact on the borrowing costs of a business, and depending on the market it operates in, on consumer demand for its products. (Interest rates and their impact on business were discussed in detail in Chapter 3 of Book 1 and in Chapter 5 of this book.)
- Negative publicity from, for example, a faulty product or an environmental disaster, will cause a firm to focus on improving its image in the short term in order to re-establish itself in the market, regardless of its longer-term objectives. The Fact file on Nike in Chapter 3 of Book 1 illustrated this.

The distinction between strategy and tactics

Strategy

Objectives form the basis for decisions on strategy. **Strategy** is the medium- to long-term plan that will allow a business to achieve its objectives. Such plans include details about what is to be done and the financial, production and personnel resources required to implement the plans. Strategies should not be considered until corporate objectives have been agreed.

Corporate strategies are the general approaches that a company uses and the policies and plans it develops in order to achieve its corporate aims and objectives. Just as corporate aims and objectives are translated into more detailed functional objectives, corporate strategies are translated into more detailed functional strategies.

Corporate strategies are usually planned at board of directors level, but have an impact at functional levels within a business. They involve decisions about broad issues such as what precise market the business is in, who its competitors are, and how it intends to compete. Corporate strategies may also involve decisions on whether to diversify into new products and new markets.

In a multi-product business, corporate strategy will be concerned with how the various products fit together and contribute to the overall success of the business. If one of its corporate objectives is to increase market share, a firm's corporate strategies will focus on how this will be achieved, which might involve decisions on whether to expand, for example, into America or into Europe. If a corporate objective is to improve profitability and cut costs, a corporate strategy might be to outsource its backroom administrative activities to countries where labour is much cheaper. If a company has been hit by falling demand or a need to improve efficiency in order to compete more effectively, corporate strategies might involve reorganisation from a functional to a matrix structure or from a geographical to a product-based structure.

Tactics

While strategy tends to be decided at board of directors or senior leader level, **tactics** tend to be decided by functional heads of departments. Tactics are the means by which a strategy is carried out. A range of different tactics may be used as part of a single strategy. Tactics enable an organisation to reach the milestones or interim targets that have been set in order to achieve its overall objectives.

Sometimes the distinction between strategy and tactics is explained in terms of strategy being about 'what' an organisation is going to do and tactics being about 'how' it is going to do something. While strategy tends to be longer term and changes infrequently within the period set to achieve the organisation's objectives, tactics tend to be short term and change frequently in relation to market and external influences.

The following examples illustrate the distinction between strategy and tactics:

- A business may wish to improve its market standing; its strategy may be to improve its brand image in comparison to that of its competitors; the tactics that are used to do this might include television and online advertising and celebrity endorsements.
- A business may wish to improve the quality and skills of its employees in order to maintain or improve the quality of service provided to customers; the strategy might be to improve retention of its best-performing employees; tactics might be to provide them with the best rates of pay, best in-work benefits and/or involve them more in decision making.

> **Author advice**
>
> Just as any decision has an opportunity cost, so choosing one strategy rather than another involves an opportunity cost.

> **Key term**
>
> **Tactics** The means by which a strategy is carried out; a range of different tactics may be used as part of a single strategy.

The links between mission, corporate objectives and strategy

An organisation's mission will influence its corporate objectives. The organisation's strategy will be the plan that is designed to achieve these objectives and to ensure that the organisation's actions match its mission.

Aims and objectives start off broad at the corporate level and become more detailed at the level of each functional area, thus encouraging a

Author advice

Strategic analysis (also known as corporate planning) requires you to bring together many of the concepts and content covered elsewhere in the course – marketing, finance, people, operations.

Do not allow different terms to confuse you. In this area, many terms are used interchangeably and essentially mean the same thing. For example, corporate plan, strategic plan and corporate strategy all refer to the broad corporate-level plans that a business makes in order to achieve its objectives.

co-ordinated approach. The same approach is used in determining the corporate plan or strategy that will be put in place to achieve these aims and objectives. Functional strategies or plans will set out what the different functions of the business (including marketing, production, human resource and finance) will do to contribute to the overall corporate strategy or plan and hence the achievement of corporate objectives.

A corporate plan is a strategy detailing how a firm's aims and objectives will be achieved, comprising both medium- and long-term actions. It clarifies the role of each department in contributing to meeting the aims and objectives of the organisation. As a result, it allows for better co-ordination of activities within a business. In addition, it helps to identify the resources required by the organisation and so makes it easier to raise finance by providing a clear plan of action, indicating how and why investment is required. Its success depends on a number of issues, including whether it is the right plan for the business in its present circumstances, whether there are adequate financial, human or production resources to implement the plan, the probable actions and reactions of competitors, and how changes in the external environment are likely to affect the plan and the business.

The corporate or strategic planning process illustrates the strong links between mission, corporate objectives and strategy. It involves the following stages:

- **Mission statement**. This stage sets out the purpose of the organisation and its corporate aims (also discussed in Chapter 1 of Book 1).
- **Objectives**. This stage breaks down the corporate aims and indicates how they can be achieved in terms of corporate and functional objectives (discussed in Chapters 1, 7, 11, 16 and 20 of Book 1).

To produce a plan of action or strategy, the company needs to gather information about the business and its market. Such information comes from internal and external sources.

- **Internal environment**. This stage reviews the organisation's different functional areas, including marketing, finance, operations and human resources, in order to assess its core competences, what its key resources are and how successful it is in the markets in which it operates. It is through sensible resource utilisation and a focus on its core competences that a business is best able to take advantage of opportunities in its environment.
- **External environment**. This stage assesses the key changes that are taking place in the organisation's external environment and makes use of PESTLE analysis (discussed in Chapter 3 of Book 1 and in Chapters 4, 5 and 6 later in this book) and Porter's five forces analysis (discussed in detail in Chapter 7 of this book).
- **SWOT analysis**. This stage identifies the key internal strengths (S) and weaknesses (W) of the organisation and its external opportunities (O) and threats (T). It analyses what the organisation needs to do to counter threats, seize opportunities, build on its strengths and overcome its weaknesses (covered later in this chapter).
- **Strategic choice**. This stage identifies a range of options available to the organisation in order to gain a competitive advantage. A range of approaches to decision making can be used (covered in detail in Chapter 5 of Book 1) and Porter's generic strategies (considered in Chapter 10 of this book).

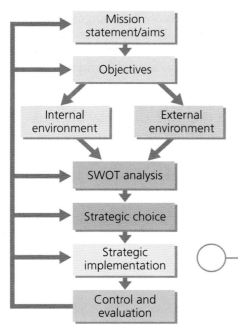

▲ **Figure 1.1** Map of the corporate planning process

Author advice

Note how almost all of these stages are covered in other areas of the A-level specification. Ensure that your knowledge and understanding of all of these areas is sound and that you can apply your understanding of corporate planning effectively, and in an integrated manner, to a given situation.

Key term

Strategic decision making
Concerns the general direction and overall policy of an organisation. Strategic decisions have significant long-term effects on an organisation and therefore require detailed consideration and approval at senior management level. They can be high risk because the outcomes are unknown and will remain so for some time.

- **Strategic implementation**. This stage puts a strategy into effect, creating a framework and responsibility for carrying out the strategy at the functional or departmental level. This is where strategies are translated into policies, rules, procedures and operational targets within the different functional areas.
- **Control and evaluation**. This stage monitors and reviews the success of the strategy and assesses actual performance against what was intended. It enables modifications to be made to the mission, objectives, SWOT analysis, strategic choices and implementation strategies. It is therefore not only a control device, but also a means of continuous improvement.

Figure 1.1 illustrates the whole process of corporate or strategic planning and demonstrates the links between mission, corporate objectives and strategy.

The impact of strategic decision making on functional decision making

Decision making in any business is very important and takes place at every level of the organisation. It varies from short term to long term and from corporate and strategic to functional and tactical. Decisions are usually constrained by both internal and external factors – for example, by the finance available, the skills of the workforce, competitor activity or government policy. Most decision making includes an element of risk and this is certainly the case with strategic decisions. However, just because something is risky does not mean that it should not be pursued. It does mean, however, that careful analysis of the balance of risk and reward should be carried out.

Strategic decisions often involve moving into new areas and this requires additional resources, new procedures and retraining. Strategic decisions might concern whether a business should consider expansion by acquisition or organic growth (considered in Chapter 11 of this book) in order to achieve its corporate goal of, say, market dominance. They might also be about how a business will compete in a way that distinguishes it from its competitors – for example, on the basis of quality and uniqueness or in terms of cost leadership and low prices.

Unlike strategic decisions, functional decisions can usually be calculated and their outcomes are usually more predictable. For example, if a product's sales are below target, functional decisions in the marketing departments may be taken to remedy this – for example, cutting the price of the product and/or running a sales promotion. Equally, there may be issues with the quality of the product, in which case, functional decisions in the operations department may be required to improve the product.

The following example illustrates the impact of **strategic decision making** on **functional decision making**.

Key term

Functional decision making Tends to be short to medium term and is concerned with a specific functional area rather than overall policy. Functional decisions are usually taken to support the implementation of strategic decisions and are usually made by middle management.

A corporate objective of improving the profits of a business might result in a strategic decision to increase the market share of an existing product. This corporate objective and strategic decision about how it is to be achieved will be translated into functional decisions to be taken by the marketing division. These may involve decisions about marketing objectives and marketing strategies and tactics such as trying to increase the market share of Product A by 20 per cent over the next two years using price discounts or predatory pricing strategies, advertising and promotion campaigns and product placements.

Practice exercise 1

Total: 55 marks

1. Explain the term 'mission' and give an example of a business mission from an organisation you are familiar with. *(5 marks)*

2. Identify and explain two influences on the mission of a business. *(6 marks)*

3. Explain how the following are likely to influence the corporate objectives of a business:
   a) the pressures for short-termism *(5 marks)*
   b) business ownership. *(3 marks)*

4. Identify and explain one other internal influence and one other external influence on the corporate objectives of a business. *(6 marks)*

5. Explain the term 'strategy' in a business context. *(3 marks)*

6. Distinguish between 'strategy' and 'tactics' in a business context. *(5 marks)*

7. What is the relationship between the strategy of a business and its mission and corporate objectives? *(6 marks)*

8. What is a corporate or strategic plan? *(4 marks)*

9. Identify the various stages involved in the corporate or strategic planning process. *(6 marks)*

10. Distinguish between strategic and functional decision making. *(6 marks)*

SWOT analysis and its value

A SWOT (strengths, weaknesses, opportunities and threats) analysis is a structured approach to assessing the internal and external influences on corporate strategies. It involves a consideration of the strengths and weaknesses evident in a business (i.e. internal influences) and the opportunities and threats it faces (i.e. external influences). In the earlier section of this chapter on the links between mission, corporate objectives and strategy, it was explained that a **SWOT analysis** forms part of an organisation's strategic planning process.

A SWOT analysis consists of an internal and an external audit of an organisation.

Key term

SWOT analysis A technique that allows an organisation to assess its overall position, or the position of one of its divisions, products or activities. It uses an internal audit to assess its strengths and weaknesses, and an external audit to assess its opportunities and threats.

Internal audit

Internal influences are determined by an internal audit, which involves looking at current resources, how well they are managed and how well they match up to the demands of the market and to competition. It needs to range across all aspects of each of the functional areas. An internal audit is essentially an assessment of the strengths and weaknesses of a business in relation to its competitors. These strengths and weaknesses are within the direct control of the business. (More detailed aspects of the internal position of a business are considered in Chapters 2 and 3.)

External audit

External influences are determined by an external audit, which involves looking at the possibilities for development in different directions in the future. One method of analysing these external factors is to categorise them according to a PESTLE analysis. An external audit is essentially an assessment of the opportunities and threats facing a business in the general business environment, that is the factors that have the potential to benefit the organisation and the factors that have the potential to cause problems for the organisation. Opportunities and threats are outside the direct control of the business. (More detailed aspects of the external position of a business are considered in Chapters 4, 5, 6 and 7.)

Once the internal and external audits have been carried out, all of the information obtained is presented in such a way as to assist decision making. This is presented in the form of a SWOT analysis. An example of a SWOT analysis for a hypothetical business is shown in Table 1.1.

> **Author advice**
>
> Strengths and weaknesses are about the present, but opportunities and threats are about the future. This introduces the issue of uncertainty into any analysis. Remember, therefore, that when considering external factors in a SWOT analysis, the future is uncertain.

> **Did you know?**
>
> Remember, PESTLE stands for political, economic, social, technological, legal and environmental factors.

▼ **Table 1.1** Example of a SWOT analysis

INTERNAL FACTORS	
Strengths	**Weaknesses**
<ul><li>excellent reputation for high-quality products</li><li>seen as innovative</li><li>highly skilled staff, selected through a well-organised recruitment and selection process</li><li>sound investment in fixed (non-current) assets and modern equipment and methods</li><li>an international leader in research and development in its field</li><li>an efficient, delayered company structure</li><li>very profitable in comparison to similar organisations</li></ul>	<ul><li>reputation as a poor employer</li><li>product portfolio has too many products in decline and growth stages, with a shortage of products in maturity</li><li>expertise in a limited range of market segments</li><li>limited provision of training for office staff and production-line workers</li><li>high levels of staff turnover and absenteeism</li><li>poor accessibility to location of main headquarters</li><li>communication difficulties between different divisions and subsidiaries</li><li>low level of liquidity; cash-flow problems in recent years</li></ul>
EXTERNAL FACTORS	
Opportunities	**Threats**
<ul><li>change in social attitudes towards environmental protection (e.g. green consumers)</li><li>low wages and high unemployment levels among local people with appropriate skills</li><li>main competitor experiencing financial difficulties</li><li>government economic policy encouraging more spending</li><li>recent legislation requires many companies to buy one of the firm's pieces of equipment</li><li>increase in skills-based training schemes</li><li>a fall in the exchange rate, helping exporters</li><li>new markets opening up in other parts of the world</li><li>social trends will encourage families to purchase more of certain products</li></ul>	<ul><li>downturn predicted in the business cycle</li><li>high levels of competition within the market</li><li>many new products are being released by new entrants into the market</li><li>technological changes mean that recent capital purchases will soon become obsolete</li><li>an ageing population will mean fewer sales of certain products</li><li>pressure group activity against the opening of a new factory</li><li>windfall tax on certain companies</li><li>increase in interest rates</li></ul>

The value of SWOT analysis

The value or advantages of SWOT analysis are as follows:

- A SWOT analysis provides a structured approach to assessing the internal and external influences on an organisation's performance.
- Undertaking a thorough internal and external audit of an organisation is an excellent basis on which to make decisions. Linking the present position and future potential of a business to the market in which it operates and the competitive forces that exist there, helps inform decisions about the strategy. An appropriate strategy will assist a business to achieve its objectives.
- Using the information in a SWOT analysis, leaders are able to analyse what needs to be done to counter the threats faced by their organisation, to seize the opportunities available to it, to build on its existing strengths and to overcome any weaknesses it has.
- One way of developing competitive advantage is for a business to use a SWOT analysis to find the best combination of relative strengths and the absence of critical weaknesses to use against competitors in the market in which it operates.
- Highlighting current and potential changes in the market and the external environment encourages an outward-looking approach.
- Comparing its SWOT analysis with that of a major competitor can help to identify the true strengths and opportunities for a business and for its competitor. For example, if a business' SWOT analysis identifies the same strengths as its competitor, it is possible that these are not actually strengths for either of them – but are simply requirements for competing in the market in which they both operate.

The disadvantages of SWOT analysis are as follows:

- A SWOT analysis can be time consuming and the situation, especially the external factors, may change rapidly. Thus organisations must use the results of a SWOT analysis with caution. What might have been a strength in the past may now be a weakness, or what was previously a threat may now be an opportunity.

Did you know?

All firms, whether large or small, will do something similar to a SWOT analysis, even if it is not as formalised as discussed here. A large firm will use a formal approach to establish and maintain competitive advantage. It needs the discipline of this approach to co-ordinate action and provide a focus for strategic analysis. A small firm, on the other hand, is likely to conduct a SWOT analysis in a much less formal and much more intuitive way.

Group exercise

1. Complete a SWOT analysis of your school/college. In doing so, consider how your school/college can attempt to:
   a) minimise the effects of the threats facing it
   b) take advantage of the opportunities available to it
   c) build on its strengths
   d) overcome its weaknesses.

2. On the basis of your SWOT analysis, discuss the possible strategies open to your school/college.

Practice exercise 2

Total: 35 marks

1. In relation to SWOT analysis, which of the following is a true statement?
   a) Strengths are part of the internal audit and look at the future.
   b) Weaknesses are part of the external audit and look at the present.
   c) Opportunities are part of the external audit and look at the future.
   d) Threats are part of the internal audit and look at the present. *(1 mark)*

2. Explain one example of a possible strength a business might have in relation to the work of its marketing function and one example of a possible strength of its operations management function. *(8 marks)*

3. Explain one example of a possible weakness a business might have in relation to the work of its finance and accounting function and one example of a possible weakness of its human resource function. *(8 marks)*

4. Explain one example of an opportunity in the external environment that might be available to a manufacturing business. *(4 marks)*

5. Explain one example of a threat in the external environment that might confront a business in the tourism sector. *(4 marks)*

6. Why might issues about uncertainty and time be important considerations in relation to a SWOT analysis? *(5 marks)*

7. Explain the value to any business of undertaking a SWOT analysis. *(5 marks)*

Case study: Halfords

Halfords is the UK's leading retailer of automotive and leisure products and the leading independent operator in garage servicing and auto repair. It has over 460 stores and over 300 autocentres in the UK and employs approximately 12,000 people.

Halfords' vision is: 'We help and inspire our customers with their life on the move.' It aims to maximise returns for its shareholders. To do this, its objective is to achieve sales in excess of £1 billion by the end of financial year 2016.

Its strategy to achieve its objective is to increase its market share in three specific segments, which it calls its three strategic pillars. These are:
● 'supporting drivers of every car'
● 'inspiring cyclists of every age'
● 'equipping families for their leisure time'.

In order to achieve growth in its three strategic pillars, Halfords is pursuing a strategy called *getting into gear*. This aims to improve customer experience by improving the quality of service in its stores; supporting the three main groups of customers – drivers, cyclists and families; improving its stores; improving its systems; improving its online sales provision and digital service facilities.

Each of its business units is required to achieve targets that link to its overall business strategy, which in turn link to its main objective.

Halfords suggests that it is uniquely placed to fulfil its first strategic pillar, '*supporting drivers of every car*'. It provides products to maintain and enhance vehicles as well as in-store, on-demand fitting services and full autocentre service and repair.

Its second strategic pillar seeks to extend its position in the fast-growing cycling market, which it sees as being driven by sporting heroes, health benefits, environmental concerns and pure enjoyment. '*Inspiring cyclists of every age*' means offering the most comprehensive ranges of cycles at the most attractive prices, backed up by expertise to build and service cycles and a comprehensive range of parts, accessories and clothing.

'*Equipping families for their leisure time*' aims to take advantage of a market that is generally fragmented with lots of different businesses providing different elements of what Halfords offers under one roof. This third pillar gives Halfords the flexibility to extend its range and introduce innovative products as appropriate.

➤➤➤

Halfords says that the vast majority of its focus will be on the first two pillars because these markets are significant and Halford believes that if it is successful, it can obtain a larger market share in these areas at the same time as the overall markets are growing.

Some of Halfords' potential strengths, weaknesses, opportunities and threats are listed in Table 1.2.

▼ **Table 1.2** Some of Halfords' potential strengths, weaknesses, opportunities and threats

INTERNAL FACTORS	
Strengths	**Weaknesses**
• Wide range of high-quality products with a competitive combination of price and service. The wide range of products means it is able to adapt what it offers and reposition itself if the business environment changes. • Levels of car-maintenance skills among the general public have been declining at the same time as the complexity of product design has been increasing. Halfords tries to match these changes by providing on-demand, seven-days-a-week services for fitting replacements such as bulbs and batteries to products customers have purchased, as well as full service and repair services at its autocentres. • 90% of the population is within a 20-minute drive of these stores and autocentres. • One of the UK's biggest retailers of cycling and motor parts • Successful online sales service • 24-hour free customer delivery system	• Post-sale customer service system not as good as it could be • Sales limited to the UK and Ireland • Distribution system limited to mainland UK
EXTERNAL FACTORS	
Opportunities	**Threats**
• Potential for online delivery outside of the UK and Ireland • Potential for expansion in developing countries where people focus more on car repair and maintenance rather than replacing old cars with new ones	• Intense competition from other service centres, particular those owned by the main car manufacturers • How sustainable the current popularity of cycling is and what the likelihood is that there will be a decline in customer demand for bicycles • What the likelihood is of a decline in customer income levels and disposable income due to another financial crisis • How likely it is that competitors will be able to provide equally good quality products and services at lower prices

Questions

1. Explain how Halfords' strategy might be translated into tactics for any one of its functional areas, that is for its marketing, operations, finance or human resource functions. *(4 marks)*

2. Using Halfords as an example, explain why broad corporate objectives and strategies need to be broken down into functional and tactical decisions if an organisation is to be successful in meeting its aims. *(4 marks)*

3. To what extent does the case study illustrate the importance to a business such as Halfords of ensuring a clear relationship between mission, objectives and strategy? *(16 marks)*

4. To what extent is a SWOT analysis a valuable approach to strategic planning for a business such as Halfords? *(16 marks)*

Analysing the existing internal position of a business to assess strengths and weaknesses: financial ratio analysis

Chapters 2 and 3 explain how the current internal position of a business can be analysed, in order to assess its strengths and weaknesses.

Chapter 2 focuses on the analysis of a business's financial position. This analysis commences by investigating company accounts, focusing on the balance sheet and income statement. The opening section shows how these accounts are constructed and how they can be used to show the strengths and weaknesses of a business's financial position. However, the main body of this chapter examines how the information in these accounts can be used to conduct financial ratio analysis in order to assess a business's financial performance. In this chapter, financial ratio analysis includes a focus on profitability (return on capital employed), liquidity (current ratio), gearing and the financial efficiency ratios of payables days, receivables days and inventory turnover. Interpretation of these ratios, using comparisons with other businesses and over time, is explained. The chapter concludes with an evaluation of the value of ratio analysis as a way of assessing business performance.

How to assess the financial performance of business using balance sheets, income statements and financial ratios

The financial performance of a business can be assessed in a number of ways. In general, the data for this assessment is obtained from two main documents: the balance sheet and the income statement. These two documents provide a valuable insight into financial strengths and weaknesses. More significantly, they provide the data for ratio analysis, which is the main management tool for the analysis of a business's financial performance.

Key terms

Balance sheet A document describing the financial position of a company at a particular point in time. It compares the value of items owned by the company (its assets) with the amounts that it owes (its liabilities).

Income statement An account showing the income and expenditure (and thus the profit or loss) of a company over a period of time (usually a year).

Both documents are based on historical data and show what has happened in the recent past.

Management accounting The creation of financial information for use by *internal users* in a business, to predict, plan, review and control the financial performance of the business.

Company accounts

Two key financial documents kept by firms are:

- the **balance sheet**
- the **income statement**.

These documents are required by law in order to show people the financial strengths and weaknesses of a company's recent performance and current situation. They can also be used to assess the potential of a company, particularly when trend analysis is used to estimate future performances based on recent history.

Purposes and users of company accounts

Accounting information serves many purposes and these depend on who is using the accounts. The main users and purposes are summarised in Table 2.1.

In AQA A-level Business Book 1, the main focus of Chapters 16 to 19 on 'Decision making to improve financial performance' was on **management accounting**, through examining breakeven analysis, sources of finance, cash-flow forecasting and budgeting.

This book provides a further focus on management accounting by examining investment appraisal in Chapter 8. However, there is greater emphasis on financial accounting. This chapter studies company accounts and their significance, building on 'How to analyse profitability' in Chapter 17 of Book 1.

▼ **Table 2.1** Purposes of accounting information

Users	Purpose
Internal users Managers	Managers use information to record financial activities, plan appropriate courses of action, control the use of resources, and analyse and evaluate the effectiveness of actions and decisions taken in financial terms.
Employees	Employees can assess the security of their employment and the ability of the firm to provide them with reasonable wages by examining the financial position of the business.
Owners and investors*	Investors want to compare the financial benefits of their investment with alternatives, such as shares in different companies or savings in a bank. Invariably, the financial benefits to owners and investors are closely related to the financial success of the business.
External users Government	The government wants to know that the business has met its legal requirements and that it has paid certain levels of tax. In addition, UK firms collect some taxes, such as VAT and the income tax payments of their employees, and pass them on to the tax authorities. Government also uses this information to assess the impact of its economic policies on the sales revenue and profits of businesses, and to plan future policies.
Competitors	Competitors are able to compare their performance against rival companies and benchmark their performances. Government encourages the publicising of results so that firms can learn from each other's strengths and errors.
Suppliers	Suppliers want information about a firm's financial situation before agreeing to supply materials. This may help them to decide if the firm is likely to continue operating. Closer scrutiny may help the supplier to identify the sort of payment terms that are being offered to other suppliers.
Customers	Customers want to know if the company is financially sound and that guarantees and after-sales servicing agreements are secure. Business customers want to establish whether it is advisable for them to draw up long-term supply contracts with this company.
The local community	The local community relies on businesses for employment and wealth creation. The local council may need to modify its housing or road-building plans if a local firm is getting into financial difficulties and is likely to close down or reduce staff. (It may also need to consider the possible consequences if a local firm is becoming very successful and wishes to expand.)

*Investors would be considered external users if they are considering whether to invest in a business, but have not yet invested.

Key terms

Assets Items that are owned by an organisation.

Balance sheet A financial statement that summarizes a company's assets, liabilities and shareholder's equity at a particular point in time.

Non-current assets Resources that can be used repeatedly in the production process, although they do wear out (depreciate) or lose value over time. These are often known as fixed assets. Examples are land, buildings, machinery and vehicles.

The main intangible asset is **goodwill**, which includes the value of a firm's brand names, patents and copyrights. The value of intangible assets is difficult to assess objectively, so it is customary to exclude them from the balance sheet.

Current assets Short-term items that circulate in a business on a daily basis and can be expected to be turned into cash within one year.

Financial Accounting The provision of financial information to show external users the financial performance of the business. It concentrates on historical data.

Analysing balance sheets

What is a balance sheet?

A balance sheet looks at the accumulated wealth of a business and can be used to assess its overall worth. It lists the resources that a business owns (its **assets**) and the amounts it owes to others (its **liabilities**).

In addition, it shows the **equity** (capital) provided by the owners (the shareholders in a limited company). Equity is provided through either the purchase of shares or the agreement to allow the company to retain or 'plough back' profit into the business, known as **reserves**, rather than using it to pay further dividends to the shareholders.

▲ Machinery counts as an asset

Elements of the balance sheet

In order to understand the layout of the **balance sheet**, it is important to understand the different elements listed in it.

Assets

Assets can be divided into two main categories according to time:

- **Non-current assets**. These assets tend to be owned by an organisation for a period of more than 1 year.
  - In general, non-current assets are purchased to allow a business to operate continuously. Land and buildings are acquired so that the business has the premises from which to operate. Machinery and equipment enable businesses to manufacture and/or sell their goods and services, and to administer their business. Vehicles are required for delivery and staff transport, as appropriate.
  - Non-current assets can be classified as:
    - Tangible assets, which are non-current (fixed) assets that exist physically.
    - Intangible assets, which are non-current assets that do not have a physical presence, but are nevertheless of value to a firm. The main intangible asset is *goodwill,* which includes the value of a firm's brand names, patents and copyrights. The value of intangible assets is difficult to assess objectively, so it is customary to exclude them from the balance sheet.
- **Current assets**. These assets tend to be owned for less than 1 year.

Examples of current assets are inventories {stocks}; receivables (debtors) – people who owe the business money, usually customers who have been given credit terms; cash and other cash equivalents (mainly the bank balance).

Inventories (stocks) consist of finished products, work-in-progress (partially completed goods) and raw materials. In order to meet the accounting concept of prudence, inventories {stocks} are valued at the cost paid, rather than the price they are expected to fetch. Firms regularly update the value of their inventories. If inventories have been damaged, have exceeded their sell-by date or have gone out of fashion, their value is reduced. Similarly, the value of **receivables** (debtors) is reduced if any receivable is behind schedule and unlikely to be paid. (Most firms value their receivables at slightly below their face value to allow for **bad debts**: that is, receivables that are not paid.)

▲ Inventories are classed as a current asset

Did you know?

The balance sheet only shows those non-current assets that are owned by the business. In 2009, HSBC sold its headquarters in Canary Wharf, London for £773 million to a South Korean investment group. As a consequence, HSBC's non-current assets fell by £773 million (but its cash reserves rose by £773 million). In 2007, HSBC had sold the building to a Spanish company for £1.09 billion, a record UK price for a building, and rented the property from the new owners for £43.5 million a year. However, financial difficulties for the Spanish company led to HSBC buying it back in 2008 for £840 million. This boosted HSBC's profit for that year by £250 million (the difference between the revenue HSBC received from selling the building and the cost it incurred in buying back the building).

Key terms

Liabilities Debts owed by an organisation to suppliers, shareholders, investors or customers who have paid in advance.

Total equity or total shareholders' equity (capital) Funds provided by shareholders to set up the business, fund expansion and purchase fixed assets.

Liabilities

Liabilities are classified according to time, in a similar way to assets:

● **Non-current liabilities** (long-term liabilities) are debts due for repayment after more than one year.
● **Current liabilities** are debts scheduled for repayment within one year.

Examples of **non-current liabilities** are debentures and long-term or medium-term loans. **Debentures** are fixed-interest loans with a repayment date set a long time into the future. *Loans* are usually provided by banks. These long-term liabilities must be repaid, but they mean that a company does not need to issue more shares to raise funds to purchase fixed assets.

Examples of **current liabilities** are payables (creditors), bank overdrafts, corporation tax owing and shareholders' dividends due for payment. **Payables** (creditors) are people or organisations that are owed money by the firm. Often these are suppliers awaiting payment, but they may be traders who have supplied services, such as gas, electricity and telephone systems. In the balance sheet, traders and suppliers are combined under the description 'trade and other payables'.

Equity

Equity takes two main forms:

● **Share capital** – the funds provided by shareholders through the purchase of shares.
● **Reserves and retained earnings** – those items that arise from increases in the value of the company, which are not distributed to shareholders as dividends, but are retained by the business for future use.

Most reserves arise because shareholders have voted at the annual general meeting to allow the company to keep some of the profit, rather than distribute it to shareholders as dividends.

Purposes of the balance sheet

The details provided in the balance sheet help stakeholders to assess the financial strength of a business. As with the income statement, the balance sheet should be studied over time and a comparison made with the balance sheets of competitors in order to draw valid conclusions.

Scrutiny of the balance sheet serves the following purposes:

● **Recognising the scale of a business**. Adding non-current assets to working capital (see Table 2.2) gives an overall view of the capital employed by a business and thus its overall worth.
● **Calculating the net assets of a business**. The balance sheet shows the overall worth of a business: its total assets minus its total liabilities. This figure (net assets) shows the value of the business to its shareholders.
● **Gaining an understanding of the nature of a business**. The structure of a business's assets may give information about the nature of the business. For example, businesses in the primary industries, such as agriculture and mineral extraction, often own large areas of land in comparison to other businesses, although high-street organisations may own expensive land. Shops tend to possess high levels of **inventories** (stocks), as they need to display their goods to attract customers. Low levels of receivables (debtors) are shown on the accounts of businesses providing personal and financial services, as there is a tradition of immediate payment rather than credit facilities being provided.
● **Identifying a business's liquidity position**. Comparing liquid or current assets (those that can be turned into cash quickly) with current liabilities (those that must be paid back soon) shows whether a business is going to be able to avoid cash-flow problems.
● **Showing sources of capital**. The balance sheet shows whether a business is raising its finance from retained profits or long-term loans.
● **Recognising the significance of changes over time**. Continual scrutiny of the balance sheet can identify any undesirable changes that take place.

▲ Companies in mineral extraction may own more land than other businesses

The layout of the balance sheet

The balance sheet allows the **net value** of a company (its **net assets**) to be calculated by working out the **total assets** (non-current assets and current assets) and subtracting **total liabilities** (current liabilities and non-current liabilities). Alternatively, net value could be obtained by adding **non-current assets** to **working capital** and subtracting **non-current liabilities**.

Author advice

Remember, reserves are not cash. Usually they are an entry in the accounts that shows how much profit the firm has retained, but invariably the purpose of this action is to purchase non-current (fixed) assets. Any cash held by the business is shown under current assets. Technically, reserves are included to recognise the fact that they are a liability owed to shareholders, not an asset. Reserves represent the sum that shareholders could have taken as dividends, but which was retained in the business for its own use.

The format also allows the **capital employed** (net assets plus non-current liabilities) to be calculated, by adding **non-current assets** to **working capital** or **net current assets** (current assets minus current liabilities), or by adding **total equity** to **non-current liabilities** (see Table 2.2).

Useful balance sheet formulae

current assets = inventories + receivables + cash and other cash equivalents

working capital (or net current assets) = current assets − current liabilities

net assets = non-current assets + current assets − current liabilities − non-current liabilities

net assets (or net worth) = non-current assets + working capital (or net current assets) − non-current liabilities

assets employed = net current assets + non-current assets

total equity = share capital + reserves

capital employed = total equity + non-current liabilities

assets employed = capital employed

The balance sheets below (Table 2.2) refer to a fictitious company called Rounded Figures plc. The company supplies food products and is famous for its cream cakes and doughnuts.

▼ **Table 2.2** Balance sheets of Rounded Figures plc, 30 June 2016 and 30 June 2015

	As at: 30.6.16 (£000s)		As at: 30.6.15 (£000s)	
Non-current assets (fixed assets)		890		750
Inventories (stocks)	60		50	
Receivables (debtors)	150		140	
Cash and other cash equivalents	300		310	
Total current assets		510		500
Payables (creditors)	(300)		(250)	
Current liabilities		(300)		(250)
Net current assets (working capital)		210		250
Non-current liabilities (long-term liabilities)		(200)		(280)
Net assets (net worth)		900		720
Share capital	300		280	
Reserves	600		440	
Total equity	900		720	
NB capital employed = non-current assets + net current assets =		1,100		1,000

Why the balance sheet always balances

The balance sheet balances because:

assets = liabilities + equity

In 2016, Rounded Figures plc has assets of £1,400,000 (£890,000 + £510,000).

It has liabilities and equity of £1,400,000 (£300,000 + £200,000 + £900,000).

Practice exercise 1

Total: 30 marks

1. Which one of the following is a current asset?
   a) inventory
   b) land
   c) machinery
   d) share capital *(1 mark)*

2. Which one of the following is a current liability?
   a) cash
   b) long-term loan
   c) payable
   d) receivable *(1 mark)*

3. Which one of the following is a non-current asset?
   a) bank overdraft
   b) cash
   c) inventory
   d) machinery *(1 mark)*

4. What is meant by the term 'balance sheet'? *(3 marks)*

5. What are the differences between assets, liabilities and equity? *(9 marks)*

6. Why is it important to distinguish between non-current assets and current assets? *(6 marks)*

7. Explain **three** uses of balance sheets. *(9 marks)*

Practice exercise 2

Total: 20 marks

Using the data in Table 2.3, calculate the following values:

1. Non-current assets (fixed assets) *(3 marks)*

2. Current assets *(3 marks)*

3. Current liabilities *(3 marks)*

4. Net current assets (working capital) *(3 marks)*

5. Non-current liabilities *(2 marks)*

6. Net assets (total net assets) *(3 marks)*

7. Total equity (capital) *(3 marks)*

▶▶▶

▼ **Table 2.3** Balance sheet data

	£m
Intangible assets	68
Cash and other cash equivalents	4
Payables (creditors)	23
Share capital	74
Receivables (debtors)	34
Bank overdraft	3
Bank loans (over 1 year)	16
Land and buildings	88
Inventories (stock)	19
Vehicles	11
Reserves	132
Plant and machinery	24

Classifying business expenditure

Business expenditure can be classified as either revenue expenditure or capital expenditure.

Revenue expenditure is spending on day-to-day items such as raw materials, inventories, wages and power to run the production process.

Capital expenditure exists when the spending is on an item that will be used time and time again (non-current assets), such as property, machinery, vehicles and office equipment. For accounting purposes, if the expenditure on an asset continues to help the business in future years, it is capital expenditure.

▲ Stationery and office equipment are non-current assets

The significance of the distinction between capital and revenue expenditure

When constructing accounts, accountants follow certain agreed principles. One of the basic rules of accounting is the **matching** or **accruals concept**. This states that, when calculating a firm's profit, any income should be matched to the expenditure involved in creating that income. What are the implications of this convention?

For revenue expenditure the implications are reasonably clear. Any wages paid to production-line workers and payments for raw materials are deducted from the income earned from selling the final product. It is assumed that the sales revenue and expenditure take place in the same financial year. Thus, wages and power are always treated as a cost in the year in which the payment is made. In general, payments for raw materials are treated in the same way. However, if there are some raw materials left over at the end of the year, the value of those raw materials is transferred to the next year's accounts, as that is when they will be used. This meets the requirements of the 'matching' principle, because raw material costs are matched to the time period in which the finished product is sold.

For capital expenditure the situation is very different. Fixed assets are used over a long period, so any capital expenditure needs to be spread over the lifetime of the fixed asset in order to 'match' the spending to the income that it creates. For example, a machine that costs £50,000 and lasts for five years could be deemed to cost £10,000 a year for the next five years, in the income statement (see later). It should not be charged as £50,000 in the year in which it is purchased because it will continue to create income in all five years.

Another accounting convention – that of **prudence** – states that accounts should ensure that the worth of the business is not exaggerated. This means that a firm must be careful and therefore slightly pessimistic in estimating the value of its assets.

These two conventions (matching and prudence) lead to a system that reduces the value of any fixed asset by a sum equal to the figure that has been agreed as the cost of the item for that year. In the above example, the value of the £50,000 asset will fall by £10,000 per year for five years, so that its value in the balance sheet after the end of the five years is zero. This process is known as depreciation. Depreciation usually occurs because non-current assets wear out over time, but it can also be caused by excessive use or obsolescence (where the asset has become out-of-date).

Analysing income statements

What is an income statement?

An income statement describes the income and expenditure of a business over a given period of time, usually a year. The income statement shows the profit (or loss) made by the business. The profit (or loss) is the difference between a business's income and its costs. For many organisations, making a profit is their main objective. Even if other aims are pursued, such as growth, image, workforce welfare and social responsibility, financial success is needed to fund these objectives. These objectives were explained in Chapter 1 of Book 1.

Purposes of the income statement

- Regular calculations of profit throughout the year help managers to review progress before the final end-of-year accounts are completed, while the final accounts allow managers to assess the success of their policies.
- It allows shareholders to assess whether their investment is beneficial.
- It enables people to see if profit is being utilised in a sensible way.

- To satisfy legal requirements, the Companies Act requires companies to publish their income statements.
- Publication allows stakeholders to see if a firm is meeting their needs.
- Comparisons can be made between different firms (inter-firm comparisons) in order to measure relative performance.
- Comparisons can be made over time (temporal comparisons) to see if a firm is improving its performance.
- Comparisons can be made within the business (intra-firm comparisons) to assess the effectiveness of different divisions or branches.
- The income statement can be used to show potential investors that a firm is successful and able to repay loans or provide a good return on investments.

> ### Fact file
>
> *Accounts and company legal structures*
>
> The details provided in the company accounts depend on the legal structure of the business. The government requires more detail from a public limited company than from a private limited company. Accounts of sole traders only need to meet the needs of the tax authorities.

▲ Production-line workers are included within 'cost of sales'

Structure of the income statement

The income statement is divided into sections, each of which provides useful information for users of the accounts.

Revenue and cost of sales

This part of the statement records the revenue (turnover or sales income) of the company and the 'cost of sales' (costs that can be linked directly to the provision of the product or service). 'Cost of sales' includes items such as raw materials and wages of production-line workers for a manufacturer, or the cost of purchasing stock and warehousing and transporting the stock to shops for a retailer. This section calculates the **gross profit**.

Expenses (overheads)

This part takes the gross profit and deducts those costs that are not directly related to producing the product or service, such as marketing expenditure, general administration costs, rent and depreciation. These costs are termed 'expenses' (overheads). This section calculates the **operating profit**.

> ### Key terms
>
> **Gross profit** Revenue minus cost of sales. The gross profit shows how efficiently a business is converting its raw materials or stock into finished products.
>
> **Operating profit** The revenue earned from everyday trading activities minus the costs involved in carrying out those activities. It is also gross profit *minus* expenses.

> ### Did you know?
>
> **Exceptional items** are items that have a one-off effect on profits. In 2014, Morrisons plc incurred exceptional administrative costs of £903 million, as a result of their selling of loss-making activities such as Kiddicare (its childrenswear business). This led to an operating loss of £95 million, but by separating it in the accounts it is possible to see that this was a one-off event rather than a recurring theme. Exceptional items are listed separately because they do not relate to the main focus of the business.

Finance income and finance costs

This element of the income statement includes information on any interest payments made by a company and any interest received on money lent or saved. This information is useful for shareholders in gaining an understanding of the company's liquidity and the extent to which it borrows or lends money.

After these two items have been calculated, the profit before tax is shown.

Tax paid on the profits made

The final profit is found by the following calculation:

profit for the year/period = profit before tax − tax on profit (or income)

For a public limited company, corporation tax is charged on profits, but for an unincorporated business, such as a sole trader, income tax is charged.

The income statement concludes by showing how much of this profit is attributable to shareholders (in many cases it will be all of the profit).

Reasons for the structure of the income statement

The first section (revenue and cost of sales) enables a business to see how efficiently it is turning materials into sales revenue. A high gross profit level suggests that costs of sales are being kept low or that the business is achieving a high **value added** by creating a product that fetches a high price.

The next section of the income statement (expenses) shows the efficiency of a firm in controlling its spending. If expenses are low, the firm should be able to secure a high operating profit.

The finance income and finance costs section gives an indication of how much the business borrows and lends money, and the efficiency with which it handles these financial operations.

What happens to profit?

The profit for the year is often described as 'earnings'. These 'earnings' are often converted to 'earnings per share', to show how much profit has been made for each share held in the company. A breakdown of the use of these earnings (profits) is of particular interest to shareholders. A business that is using most of its profits to pay high dividends will please shareholders looking for a quick return. However, shareholders with a long-term interest in the business may prefer to see higher retained profits, as these will be reinvested into the business to boost profits in the future.

The layout of the income statement

It is customary to publish the latest income statement alongside the income statement from the previous year (or the equivalent period from the previous financial year if the account covers less than one year). Typically, income statements are published for a period of a year, but it is not unusual for firms to publish six-month or three-month income statements.

Useful income statement formulae

gross profit = revenue − cost of sales

operating profit = gross profit − expenses +/− exceptional items

Author advice

Always remember to compare like with like when analysing a given profit or loss. The profit recorded may be the profit for the year or the operating profit, and it might be shown before or after tax. Comparing operating profit before tax with operating profit after tax would lead to an inappropriate conclusion.

Where there are no exceptional items:

operating profit = gross profit − expenses

profit before tax = operating profit + finance income − finance costs

profit for the year = profit before tax − taxation

Example of an income statement: Rounded Figures plc

Rounded Figures plc specialises in cream cakes and doughnuts.

Table 2.4 shows the income statements for Rounded Figures plc for the financial years ending in 2015 and 2016. Note that it is traditional to place the latest year on the left and the previous year on the right.

▼ **Table 2.4** Income statements for Rounded Figures plc

Years ending:	30.6.16 (£000s)	30.6.15 (£000s)
Revenue	2,500	2,000
Cost of sales	(1,150)	(1,050)
Gross profit	**1,350**	**950**
Expenses	(970)	(700)
plus (minus) Exceptional items	0	200
Operating profit	**380**	**450**
Finance income	50	70
Finance costs	(100)	(70)
Profit before tax	**330**	**450**
Taxation	(66)	(90)
Profit for year	**264**	**360**
Earnings per share	£0.88*	£1.29*
*Additional information:		
Number of shares issued (thousands)	300	280

Profit utilisation

It is common for a business to use its profit in one of two ways.

Dividends paid to shareholders

Every six months, public limited companies usually pay a dividend to their shareholders. This dividend payment represents the share of the profits allocated to shareholders.

Some shareholders depend on the dividend payment as a source of income. This is particularly the case for some retired people who have invested their savings or pensions in shares and therefore rely on their shares to provide a steady flow of income. These shareholders may have a greater interest in making sure that a high dividend is paid.

Retained profits

In order to fund expansion plans and capital investment, company directors may wish to keep some of the profits in the business. This avoids the need to pay interest on borrowed money or to sell more shares in order to finance expansion. Retained (or 'ploughed-back') profits help to increase the assets of a business and should therefore increase the value of the company. Furthermore, retained profits should help the business to increase its future profits (and thus increase future dividends). Consequently, shareholders often support requests to increase the level of retained profit. In practice, most firms will strike a balance between paying dividends and retaining profits.

On occasions, profit may be utilised in different ways. Shell recently used £2 billion of its profit to buy back shares from shareholders. In future years this means it will have to pay dividends to fewer shareholders.

Fact file

Profit retention at Rolls-Royce

Decisions to retain profit or pay dividends often depend on recent history and corporate aims. In the early years of the twenty-first century, Rolls-Royce's policies varied considerably. In 2002 it made a loss of £53 million but paid dividends totalling £133 million. This was possible because of retained profits from earlier years. Having drained some of the company's funds in 2002, shareholders agreed to a lower dividend in 2003 and received no dividend in 2004 when the company recorded a good profit level. In 2004 the company borrowed money to fund research and development. This investment paid off with record profits in 2007, which were then surpassed in 2009 and

2012. In more recent years, Rolls-Royce shareholders have accepted fairly consistent, but slightly increasing levels of dividend payouts, allowing the company to retain high levels of profit in good years. In 2010 Rolls-Royce had a relatively low profit of £543 million and gave 55% to shareholders; in 2013 only 16% of its record profit of £2,335 million was given as dividends, leaving it with almost £2 billion of retained profit, some of which was used to buy back shares.

UK companies are often accused of taking short-term decisions to satisfy the immediate needs of shareholders, but Rolls-Royce has shown that it can plan long term. Having increased its vulnerability in 2002, it has continued to reap the benefits of long-term planning for growth.

Practice exercise 3

Total: 30 marks

1. Revenue *minus* 'X' = Gross Profit. 'X' is:
   a) cost of sales
   b) expenses
   c) finance costs
   d) tax. *(1 mark)*

2. For a public limited company, which tax is deducted from 'profit before tax' to get the 'profit for year' figure?
   a) Business rates
   b) Corporation tax
   c) Income tax
   d) VAT *(1 mark)*

3. What is meant by the term 'income statement'? *(3 marks)*

4. Identify two purposes of an income statement. *(2 marks)*

5. What is the difference between operating profit and profit for the year? *(4 marks)*

6. Identify the two ways in which profit is utilised. *(2 marks)*

7. Using the figures below, calculate:
   a) the gross profit *(3 marks)*
   b) the operating profit. *(3 marks)*
   Show all of your working.

- Cost of raw material   £400,000
- Marketing expenditure   £125,000
- General administration   £200,000
- Sales revenue   £980,000
- Wages of production-line worker   £110,000

8. A company must pay tax of 30 per cent on its profit of £200,000. If it plans to use 60 per cent of its profits (after tax) to build an extension to its factory, how much of its profit will be paid to shareholders? *(4 marks)*

9. Why might shareholders allow a business to keep all of the profit for its own use? *(4 marks)*

10. Calculate the earnings per share based on the following data:
    Profit for year: £300,000
    Shares issued: 500,000 at 50p each. *(3 marks)*

Practice exercise 4   *Total: 10 marks*

Refer to the income statement for Rounded Figures plc for the year ending 30.6.16 (see Table 2.4 above).

1. Rewrite the income statement to take into consideration the following changes:
   Revenue: increases by 20 per cent
   Cost of sales: increases by £100,000
   Expenses: increase by £150,000
   Finance income and finance costs: no changes
   Corporation tax: equal to 20 per cent of profit before tax. *(8 marks)*

2. Based on these changes, calculate the amended earnings per share on the assumption that the number of shares remains the same as for 30.6.16. *(2 marks)*

Analysing data

When analysing accounting information it is difficult to draw meaningful conclusions from a single piece of data. When using financial data to analyse a company's situation, it is best to consider data that:

● allow comparisons with other businesses
● allow comparisons with a company's own performance over time.

Decision making that considers these two factors is likely to be more accurate than a single piece of data, which may be unrepresentative.

Types of comparisons

To interpret financial data, the data should be compared with other results, so that the company can be judged in relative terms. The main methods of comparison are as follows.

Inter-firm comparisons: comparisons with other businesses

A business should compare itself to rival businesses in order to assess its relative performance. Ideally, the business should select those competitors with which it has most in common, as any external factors that are helping (or hindering) the business should be having a similar effect on those competitors.

The balance sheet can be used to show the overall worth and therefore the scale of operations of different businesses. The income statement allows a business to compare its revenue and profit against those of its competitors. It also helps the business to discover whether it is controlling certain costs as efficiently as its competitors.

Comparisons over time: trend analysis

A business's data should be compared over time in order to register trends in efficiency and to allow for exceptional circumstances in a particular year. A business may take a long time to reap the benefits of a restructuring or to devise suitable strategies to fight off a new competitor. For these reasons, it is important to use data to identify trends in performance as well as the performance in one particular year.

▲ A modern shopping mall is filled with competing businesses

Intra-firm comparisons: comparisons within the business

The efficiencies of different divisions or areas of a business can be compared. Again, comparisons should be made between similar areas of the business. A retailer should compare stores in similar towns where the size of population and levels of competition are matched.

From the balance sheet it is worth comparing the net current assets (working capital) of different divisions or branches within the business. Income statement comparisons may enable the business to ascertain which of its branches is generating the most profit.

Comparisons to a standard

Certain levels of performance or standards are recognised as efficient within particular industries or the business community as a whole. A business can compare itself with these standards in order to assess its performance objectively. It is often easy to obtain comparable data from other businesses too, if such standards are widely used.

A business might use its balance sheet to compare its liquidity with the standard for that industry. It could also compare its performance with the performance of the economy as a whole.

Author advice

Remember that published accounts, such as the income statement and balance sheet, are historical: they show what has already happened. Consequently, they can be used to analyse the company's actual performance. However, in order to judge the potential of the business, these data need to be extrapolated into the future. External factors also need to be considered.

Taking Rolls-Royce as an example, its profit increased consistently until 2013, suggesting further increases in the future. However, cuts in government spending by many countries and falling commodity prices led to a decline in Rolls-Royce's profit in 2014. These trends are expected to continue in 2015, so Rolls-Royce is expecting a 13% fall in its profits in 2015, despite improvements in trading conditions for most other firms.

▲ A Rolls-Royce aircraft engine

Ratio analysis

Ratio analysis is based mainly on data extracted from the firm's financial accounting records – usually the balance sheet and income statement. However, for some ratios, information needs to be extracted from the management accounting information or other sources.

Key term

Ratio analysis A method of assessing a firm's financial situation by comparing two sets of linked data.

Fact file

What is a ratio?

A ratio is a comparison of a figure with another figure, where the relative values of the two numbers can be used to make a judgement. Ratios are expressed as, for example, 2.5:1. In this example, the first digit is two and a half times the second digit. In ratios, the second digit is always 1. Despite the name of this technique, most of the 'ratios' featured in ratio analysis are actually stated as percentages or raw numbers, and hence not presented in the format of the example above.

As indicated earlier in this chapter, different groups of people use the information provided in a company's accounts in order to judge a company's situation. Some actual figures in the accounts, such as operating profit, can be used to draw conclusions about a company's performance. However, much more meaningful conclusions can be drawn by comparing this figure with another. If a company has doubled its profit in the last decade, is this an indicator of success? Most people would conclude that this does show good performance, but what if the scale of the business has trebled in that time? Should its profits have trebled too? Ratio analysis allows us to compare two sets of data (in this case, profit and scale) in order to try to draw more meaningful conclusions.

Stages in using ratio analysis

If ratios are to prove useful, careful selection and organisation are needed. The following process will help businesses to take full advantage of ratio analysis:

1. Identify the reason for the investigation. Is the information needed to decide whether to become an investor, customer or a supplier, or is it being used by the organisation itself to improve its own efficiency?
2. Decide on the relevant ratio(s) that will help to achieve the purpose of the user(s).
3. Gather the information required and then calculate the ratio(s).
4. Interpret the ratio(s). What is the meaning of the results that have been obtained?
5. Make appropriate comparisons (such as comparison with another business and/or comparison over time) in order to understand the significance of the ratio(s).
6. Take action in accordance with the results of the investigation.
7. Apply the above processes again, to measure the success of the actions taken in stage 6.

Types of ratio

Ratios can be categorised under four headings, as shown in Table 2.5.

▼ **Table 2.5** The main types of ratio and their meanings

Type of ratio	Meaning of ratio type
Profitability ratios	These compare profits with the size of the firm. As profit is often the primary aim of a company, these ratios are often described as **performance ratios**.
Liquidity ratios	These show whether a firm is likely to be able to meet its short-term liabilities. Although profit shows long-term success, it is vital that firms hold sufficient liquidity to avoid difficulties in paying debts.
Gearing	Gearing focuses on long-term liquidity and shows whether a firm's capital structure is likely to be able to continue to meet interest payments on, and to repay, long-term borrowing.
Financial efficiency ratios	These generally concentrate on the firm's management of its working capital. They are used to assess the efficiency of the firm in its management of its assets and short-term liabilities.

Author advice

A wide variety of ratios can be used to judge a firm's performance. The intention of the AQA A-level specification is that students should understand the significance of ratio analysis and be able to interpret and apply sufficient ratios to draw valid conclusions about a firm's operations.

For these reasons, six specific ratios have been incorporated into the Year 2 specification, alongside the three profitability ratios included in Book 1. There are other ratios that can be used to assess a company. However, only those ratios that are identified in the AQA specification are considered in this chapter.

Figure 2.1 provides a summary of the types and classification of the ratios used.

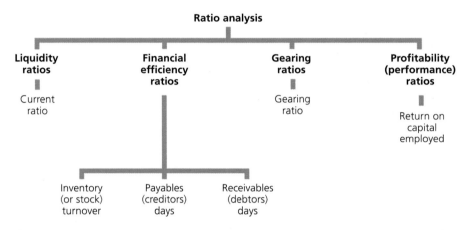

▲ **Figure 2.1** Classification of financial ratios

Please note that in Chapter 17 of Book 1, the following three profitability ratios were examined:

- gross profit as a percentage of sales revenue
- operating profit (profit from operations) as a percentage of sales revenue
- profit for year as a percentage of sales revenue.

Be prepared to use these profitability ratios in the A-level, particularly operating profit (profit from operations) as a percentage of sales revenue.

Users of ratios

Ratios serve a number of purposes, which will be outlined in detail later in this chapter as each ratio is examined. Different ratios meet the needs of a variety of users of accounts. Table 2.6 shows the main groups of users and their reasons for using ratio analysis.

▼ Table 2.6 Users and their reasons for using ratio analysis

Users	Reasons for using ratio analysis
Managers	To identify the efficiency of a firm and of its different areas, to plan ahead, to control operations and to assess the effectiveness of policies
Employees	To find out whether a firm can afford wage rises and to see if profits are being allocated fairly
Government	To review the success of its economic policies and to find ways of improving business efficiency overall
Competitors	To compare their performance against rival firms and discover their relative strengths and weaknesses
Suppliers	To know the sort of payment terms that are being offered to other suppliers, and whether a firm can afford to pay
Customers	To know if the future of a firm and therefore any guarantees and after-sales servicing agreements are secure
Shareholders	To compare the financial benefits of their investment with other alternatives, such as owning shares in a different firm or putting savings in a bank

Practice exercise 5

Total: 25 marks

1. What is meant by the term 'ratio analysis'? (*3 marks*)

2. Identify five different users of ratio analysis. (*5 marks*)

3. Select two of the five users identified in question 2 and explain the reasons why they might use ratio analysis. (*8 marks*)

4. Distinguish between comparisons over time and comparisons between businesses. (*4 marks*)

5. A business observes that one of its departments is better at cutting costs than the other departments. This is an example of comparison:
   a) over time
   b) to a standard
   c) between businesses
   d) within a business. (*1 mark*)

6. Identify the four main types of ratio. (*4 marks*)

Using ratios

The majority of ratios are based on information from the income statement and the balance sheet. Each of the six ratios explained in this book is calculated using the figures from the accounts of Rounded Figures plc, a supplier of doughnuts and cream cakes. Thus Tables 2.7 and 2.8 are identical to Tables 2.2 and 2.4 from earlier in this chapter. To allow comparisons over time, the accounts shown are from two successive years, the financial years ending on 30 June 2016 and 30 June 2015. Later in this chapter, *inter-firm* comparisons will be made with Rounded Figures plc's main rival, Doh! Nuts! plc.

▼ **Table 2.7** Balance sheets of Rounded Figures plc, 30 June 2016 and 30 June 2015

As at:		30.6.16 (£000s)		30.6.15 (£000s)
Non-current assets (fixed assets)		**890**		**750**
Inventories (stocks)	60		50	
Receivables (debtors)	150		140	
Cash and other cash equivalents	300		310	
Total current assets		**510**		**500**
Payables (creditors)	(300)		(250)	
Current liabilities		**(300)**		**(250)**
Net current assets (working capital)		210		250
Non-current liabilities (long-term liabilities)		**(200)**		**(280)**
Net assets (net worth)		900		720
Share capital	300		280	
Reserves	600		440	
Total equity	**900**		**720**	
NB capital employed = non-current assets + net current assets =		1,100		1,000

▼ **Table 2.8** Income statements for Rounded Figures plc

Years ending:	30.6.16 (£000s)	30.6.15 (£000s)
Revenue	2,500	2,000
Cost of sales	(1,150)	(1,050)
Gross profit	**1,350**	**950**
Expenses	(970)	(700)
plus (minus) Exceptional items	0	200
Operating profit	**380**	**450**
Finance income	50	70
Finance costs	(100)	(70)
Profit before tax	**330**	**450**
Taxation	(66)	(90)
Profit for year	**264**	**360**
Earnings per share	£0.88*	£1.29*
*Additional information:		
Number of shares issued (thousands)	300	280
Dividends paid (£000s)	100	200

Author advice

You will need to remember the formulae for each example of ratio analysis. The six required by AQA are explained in this chapter. However, it will also be useful to use the three profitability ratios explained in Book 1, if any of them are relevant to the analysis you are required to undertake.

The key skill that you will need is the ability to recognise which ratio or ratios need to be used. For example, if the question is about a company's cash flow or a liquidity problem, the current ratio will discover how serious the problem is. In contrast, if profitability is the main issue, the return on capital employed should be used to make a judgement, although the operating profit margin is very useful too.

It is vital that you understand the purpose of each ratio so that you can select an appropriate ratio or ratios to calculate.

Profitability and performance ratios

Most firms aim to make a profit. In order to assess the efficiency of a business in achieving this major objective, two **profitability (or performance) ratios** may be used: **the return on capital employed** and the operating profit margin (operating profit as a percentage of sales). The operating profit margin was covered in Chapter 17 of Book 1. This section will focus on return on capital employed as the key measure of profitability, but ensure that you are familiar with the operating profit margin as well.

Return on capital employed

The return on capital employed (ROC or ROCE) ratio shows the operating profit as a percentage of capital employed; capital employed equates to the value of the capital that a firm has at its disposal.

Operating profit is considered to be the best measure of performance, as it focuses only on a firm's main trading activities, whereas other measures of profit, such as profit for the year, can include items that are not a reflection of efficiency.

Profit *before tax* is used because tax rates vary between countries, so profit after tax is a less consistent measure of a firm's performance.

Capital employed is generally considered to be the best measure of a firm's size. It is calculated by adding the total equity provided by shareholders (in the form of purchases of shares and profits that shareholders have allowed

Key terms

Profitability (or performance) ratios Measure the efficiency with which a business makes profit, in relation to its size.

Return on capital employed Measures the profitability of a business by calculating its operating profit as a percentage of the capital that a business has at its disposal – that is, its capital employed.

the firm to retain) to any non-current liabilities (such as long-term loans and debentures). This is not a totally reliable guide as firms are tending to lease many assets rather than purchase them, but in general, capital employed is a good basis for comparing the scale of firms' operations.

Return on capital employed is measured as a percentage, using the following formula:

$$\text{return on capital employed (\%)} = \frac{\text{operating profit or profit before tax}}{\text{total equity + non-current liabilities}} \times 100$$

(Profit before tax should be used if both profit figures are available.)

Based on Tables 2.7 and 2.8, the ROCE for Rounded Figures plc is:

2015: $\frac{450}{1,000} \times 100 = 45\%$

2016: $\frac{330}{1,100} \times 100 = 30\%$

Conclusion: in 2015 Rounded Figures plc achieved an ROCE of 45 per cent, indicating a high level of profitability. In 2016 the ROCE decreased to 30 per cent. This is still a very good level of ROCE for most industries, but indicates that Rounded Figures plc did not perform as well in 2016 as it did in 2015. Over time the firm's profitability has worsened. However, profitability is high and so it is likely that a comparison with other businesses would give a favourable result.

NB: A closer study of the income statement indicates that in 2015 there was an exceptional item of £200,000 which boosted the operating profit for that year. For evaluation it would be worth noting that without this exceptional item, the ROCE in 2015 would have been much lower (25 per cent). Thus Rounded Figures plc's performance in 2016 could actually be an improvement on 2015.

Fact file

Benchmarking

Figure 2.2 shows the average ROCE for all UK companies in recent years. Companies can use these figures as a benchmark to see if they are making a good profit. These figures apply to *all* companies. However, the performance of manufacturing companies is generally lower than companies in the service sector. Therefore, Rounded Figures plc might wish to compare itself to the average ROCE for services, which averaged 14 per cent in this period.

It should also be noted that there are considerable variations in performance between industries. For example, the average return on capital was over 20 per cent in pharmaceuticals, but below 3 per cent in engineering and agriculture.

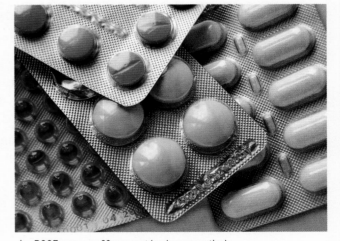

▲ ROCE was over 20 per cent in pharmaceuticals

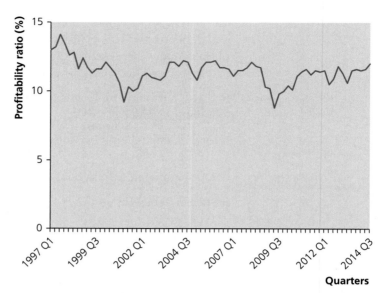

▲ **Figure 2.2** Profitability ratios for UK firms, 1997 to 2014
Source: ONS

Practice exercise 6 ### *Total: 20 marks*

1. Explain why return on capital employed is considered to be a good measure of a firm's performance. *(6 marks)*

2. Explain one reason why return on capital employed might *not* be a good indicator of a firm's success. *(6 marks)*

   Questions 3 and 4 are based on the following information, which is extracted from the accounts of ABF plc. This group is a diversified company that mainly specialises in food products, with brands such as British Sugar, Ryvita, Jordans, Kingsmill, Patak's and Twinings. It also owns Primark Stores.

Years ending:	13.9.2014 (£m)	13.9.2009 (£m)
Operating profit	1,080	625
Capital employed	7,788	6,573

3. Based on the information above, calculate the return on capital employed for the year ending 13 September 2014 and the year ending 13 September 2009. *(6 marks)*

4. In which year did ABF plc enjoy the best performance? Use the ratios calculated in question 3 to support your views. *(2 marks)*

Liquidity ratios

The AQA specification only requires one **liquidity ratio** to be studied. The **current ratio** is used in order to assess the ability of an organisation to meet its short-term liabilities.

Although profit is the main measure of company success, firms can be vulnerable to cash-flow problems, so the ability of a firm to meet its immediate payments (**solvency**) is a key test. Liquidity ratios concentrate on balance sheet information. Examination of a firm's short-term (current) assets and its current liabilities allows an observer to analyse a firm's ability to stay solvent in the short term.

It is estimated that as many as 30 per cent of all business failures can be attributed to insolvency. Consequently, liquidity ratios are vital in analysing a firm's financial position.

Current ratio

In order to meet its liabilities, a firm can draw on its short-term (current) assets. Cash and bank balances are the most liquid current assets. However, receivables (debtors) will be paying their debts to the company, thus providing a steady source of cash. Similarly, inventories (stock) will be sold continually, providing the business with an additional means to pay its current liabilities.

The ratio is calculated as follows:

current ratio = current assets:current liabilities

If a company has between £1.50 and £2 of current assets for every £1 of current liabilities, it is unlikely to run out of cash. Therefore, the 'ideal' current ratio is between 1.5:1 and 2.0:1.

It should be noted that a maximum as well as a minimum ratio is recommended. The opportunity cost of holding too many current assets is the lost opportunity to purchase non-current assets such as machinery. The non-current assets are needed to produce the goods that provide the company's profit. Consequently, a high current ratio may be an advantage in the short run but will inhibit the long-term profitability of a company.

Based on Table 2.7, calculation of these ratios for Rounded Figures plc gives the following results:

June 2016:   510:300   1.7:1

June 2015:   500:250   2.0:1

Conclusion: In 2015 the current ratio was at the upper level of the 'acceptable' range. In 2016 it was lower, but comfortably in the middle of the 'acceptable' range. Rounded Figures plc would appear to be removing some of the liquidity that it had in 2015, taking it into the middle of the 'acceptable' range. Thus these changes could be seen as an improvement in its liquidity.

What do you think?

The 'ideal' levels of the liquidity ratios are based on historical research. Some years ago, an examination was undertaken of the balance sheets of leading companies over a period of years. It found that a number of businesses whose liquidity ratios were below the advisable (ideal) levels went into liquidation. Similarly, those with excessive liquidity tended to make less profit over time because they were not putting enough money into non-current assets.

'Ideal' ratios were set as a result of these observations, but do they still apply today? With businesses using just-in-time inventory control, and having much easier access to funds, many accountants feel that these 'ideal' levels are too high. Retailers that benefit from a constant flow of cash receipts can survive with very low levels of liquid assets. Based on data from the year 2014, W.H. Smith has a current ratio of 0.80:1. In comparison, Tesco's current ratio is only 0.73:1 and Morrison's current ratio is 0.50:1. These ratios are well below the minimum 'ideal' levels of 1.5:1, but none of these businesses appear to be at risk of insolvency (although Morrison's low ratio may well have been affected by recent low profits).

Data on the average current ratio of UK companies since 2000 shows that it has steadily increased from 1.2:1 in 2000 to over 1.4:1 in 2014, but this average is below the 'recommended' minimum level of 1.5:1.

In the light of these data we might wish to reassess the liquidity of Rounded Figures plc. If 'standard' current ratio targets are excessive for modern retailers, then Rounded Figures appears to have too much liquidity, which might be adversely affecting its profits.

Practice exercise 7

Total: 20 marks

1. In theory, the current ratio should be ideally between x:1 and y:1, where x and y are numbers.
   a) What is the ideal value for x? *(1 mark)*
   b) What is the ideal value for y? *(1 mark)*

2. Why should a firm try to avoid a low current ratio? *(4 marks)*

3. What is the disadvantage of a high current ratio? *(4 marks)*

   The following information is extracted from the accounts of ABF plc.

   Extracts from balance sheets of ABF plc

Values as at:	13.9.2014 (£m)	13.9.2009 (£m)
Current assets	3,626	3,015
Current liabilities	2,684	2,460

4. Based on this information, calculate the current ratios for the years ending 13.9.2014 and 13.9.2009. *(4 marks)*

5. In the light of the table and your calculations in question 4, analyse how well ABF plc has managed its liquidity. *(6 marks)*

▲ Twinings tea is part of ABF plc

Gearing

Gearing examines the capital structure of a firm and its likely impact on the firm's ability to stay solvent in the long run. There is one relevant measure of gearing, known as the **gearing ratio** (or capital gearing).

The gearing ratio is measured by the following formula:

$$\text{Gearing (\%)} = \frac{\text{Non-current liabilities}}{\text{Total equity + non-current liabilities}} \times 100$$

Non-current liabilities normally take the form of loans, such as debentures or long-term loans from the bank.

High and low gearing

If the gearing ratio is greater than 50 per cent, the company is said to have *high* capital gearing. If the gearing ratio is below 25 per cent, the company is said to have *low* capital gearing. Usually, capital gearing between 25 per cent and 50 per cent would be considered to be within the normal range, but the interpretation of 'high' and 'low' gearing can vary over time. For example, the current (2015) record low interest rates have encouraged firms to borrow money, rather than raise finance through share (equity) capital. Consequently, more firms at present tend to have high capital gearing ratios.

A high capital gearing ratio shows that a business has borrowed a lot of money in relation to its total capital. A low capital gearing ratio indicates that a firm has raised most of its capital from shareholders, in the form of share capital and retained profits.

Based on Table 2.7, the gearing ratios for Rounded Figures plc for 2015 and 2016 are:

2016: $\dfrac{200}{1,100} \times 100 = 18.2\%$

2015: $\dfrac{280}{1,000} \times 100 = 28.0\%$

Conclusion: the gearing ratio for Rounded Figures plc has fallen from a 'normal' level to a 'low' level. The ratios in both 2015 and 2016 suggest that Rounded Figures plc is unlikely to come under any pressure from having to repay loans or pay interest on borrowed money. Furthermore, the lower figure in 2016 shows that there is a reduction in any pressures of this nature.

Fact file

UK gearing ratios

The average gearing ratio in the UK has increased in recent years. If interest rates are low and the economy is growing steadily, businesses will be eager to take advantage of the opportunity to borrow money at low rates of interest and lenders will be eager to lend, confident that businesses will repay any money that is lent. However, the recent low interest rates have coincided with both recession and low liquidity for banks, because of their financial losses through 'bad debts'. As the UK emerged from recession there were slight increases in bank lending, but mainly to large firms who were deemed to be less risky. As a consequence, gearing ratios for small firms have decreased, because owners have needed to put in more finance (or attract new shareholders) to compensate for the lack of loans available.

Benefits of high capital gearing

High capital gearing offers several benefits:

- There are relatively few shareholders, so it is easier for existing shareholders to keep control of a company.
- The company can benefit from a very cheap source of finance when interest rates are low.
- In times of high profit, interest payments are usually much lower than shareholders' dividend requirements, allowing a company to retain much more profit for future expansion.

Benefits of low capital gearing

Low capital gearing also has advantages:

- Most capital is permanent share capital, so with low gearing a company is at less risk of payables (creditors) forcing it into liquidation.
- A low-geared company avoids the problem of having to pay high levels of interest on its borrowed capital when interest rates are high.
- A company avoids the pressure facing highly geared companies that must repay their borrowing at some stage.

We can conclude that there is no ideal gearing ratio. The best gearing percentage will depend on circumstances.

- A highly profitable company will prefer high gearing, as its dividend payments usually exceed its interest payments on loans. High gearing is also advantageous if interest rates are low and if the owners of a business want to limit the number of new shareholders.
- Low gearing tends to exist if companies are less profitable, if interest rates are high and if a company is prepared to expand the number of its shareholders. Companies that have retained high levels of profit in the past tend to have low levels of gearing.

Practice exercise 8

Total: 40 marks

1. Capital gearing is considered to be 'high' if it exceeds what percentage? *(1 mark)*
2. Capital gearing is considered to be 'low' if it is below what percentage? *(1 mark)*
3. Explain two possible disadvantages of high capital gearing. *(8 marks)*
4. Explain two possible advantages of high capital gearing. *(8 marks)*
5. Explain why high levels of capital gearing are likely to coincide with the lowest levels of interest rates in the UK. *(5 marks)*
6. Explain one reason why a firm's gearing levels might be low during a period of recession. *(5 marks)*

   The following information is extracted from the accounts of ABF plc.

Values as at:	13.9.2014 (£m)	13.9.2009 (£m)
Balance sheet:		
Capital employed (total equity plus non-current liabilities)	7,788	6,573
Non-current liabilities/loans	1,035	1,329

7. Based on this information, calculate the gearing ratios for the year ending 13 September 2014 and the year ending 13 September 2009. *(6 marks)*

8. In which year did ABF plc have the best gearing ratio? Justify your view. *(6 marks)*

Financial efficiency ratios

Financial efficiency ratios measure the efficiency with which a business manages specific assets and liabilities. They allow a business to scrutinise the effectiveness of certain areas of its operation. This section analyses the three financial efficiency ratios included in the AQA A-level Business specification: payables days, receivables days and inventory turnover.

Payables days

This ratio shows the number of days that it takes to pay back any payables owed by a business. As payables are sometimes referred to as 'creditors', it is also known as 'creditor days'. As noted in the calculation of inventory turnover (explained later in this section), the cost of sales is the best estimate of what a firm pays to its suppliers. Therefore, this figure is used to represent the total costs of supplies in a year.

$$\text{Payables days} = \frac{\text{Payables}}{\text{Cost of sales}} \times 365$$

> **Did you know?**
>
> The ratio 'payables (or creditors) days' is also known as 'the average age of payables (or creditors)'.
>
> Firms that receive long-term credit from their suppliers may expect a high figure for payables days, but companies that pay suppliers in cash will have a low figure.
>
> In general terms, a firm will want to have as high a value as possible, meaning that payables are not being paid quickly. In effect, this means that the business is holding another organisation's money. However, if a business has a high payables days figure because it has not paid a debt on time, this would not be a good sign.

> **Fact file**
>
> *Sale or return*
>
> Some shops purchase inventories on a sale or return basis. This means that they do not have to pay their suppliers until they have sold the product. Consequently, they may have a high payables days figure. However, suppliers that offer these terms tend to charge a higher price to the buyers because it is the supplier that takes the risk if the product is not sold.

Firms will hope for a payables days figure that exceeds their receivables days figure (see next section), as this will help cash flow.

The calculations for Rounded Figures plc based on Tables 2.7 and 2.8 are:

2016: $\dfrac{300}{1,150} \times 365$ = 95.2 (95) days

2015: $\dfrac{250}{1,050} \times 365$ = 86.9 (87) days

Conclusion: these figures show that Rounded Figures plc has a very high figure for payables days, so it is likely to be able to hold high levels of cash. The company does not appear to be short of cash, so it is probable that these high figures exist because the company's suppliers offer Rounded Figures plc generous credit terms.

Receivables days

This ratio shows the number of days that it takes to convert receivables into cash. As receivables are often known as debtors this ratio is also known as 'debtor days'.

$$\text{Receivables days} = \frac{\text{Receivables}}{\text{Revenue (annual sales)}} \times 365$$

Firms that provide long-term credit for their customers, such as Freemans catalogue, may expect a high figure, but companies that deal mainly in cash transactions, such as Papa John's Pizza, will have a low figure for receivables (debtor) days.

Did you know?

The ratio 'receivables (or debtor) days' is also known as 'the average age of receivables (or debtors)'.

Standards vary between industries, but in general terms a firm will want to have as low a value as possible, meaning that receivables are paying promptly. Although the finance department will wish for prompt payment, the marketing department may want to offer generous credit facilities to attract customers. Retailers of furniture traditionally offer long credit terms, so high receivables days may be a feature of that trade. Car manufacturers provide garages with credit to encourage them to display a wide range of stocks, leading to high receivables days.

The calculations for Rounded Figures plc based on Tables 2.7 and 2.8 are:

2016: $\dfrac{150}{2,500} \times 365$ = 21.9 (22) days

2015: $\dfrac{140}{2,000} \times 365$ = 25.6 (26) days

Conclusion: these figures are reasonable, given the fact that many businesses offer 28 or more days to pay receivables. However, they appear to be high for a business dealing with fresh products that are sold on a daily basis, so the reasons for this should be investigated. Rounded Figures plc will be pleased that the 2016 figure is lower than the 2015 result, because this means its receivables are being turned into cash more quickly in 2016 than in 2015.

Fact file

Payables and receivables

Firms tend to compare payables days with receivables days. In general, a firm trying to remain solvent will benefit from a situation whereby its payments to payables (its suppliers) take longer to make than the time it takes to receive payment from its receivables (its customers). Ideally, its payables days should exceed its receivables days.

Subtracting the 'receivables days' from the 'payables days' gives the following results:

2016: 95 days – 22 days = 73 days

2015: 87 days – 26 days = 61 days

These figures show that Rounded Figures plc is currently taking approximately 70 days longer to pay its debts than it is taking to receive money owed to it and that the figure increased by 12 days between 2015 and 2016. This means that the business should be able to benefit from possessing high levels of cash (for example, earning interest from the bank and having a healthy cash flow). However, the business needs to be aware of the possible problems it will face if its payables start to demand payment more quickly.

Did you know?

Many firms that provide credit for their customers 'factor' their receivables to a specialist bank. Banks such as Barclays Partners and GE Capital thus 'own' the debts. Consequently, retailers such as SCS and Currys will not have as high levels of receivables as might be expected.

Inventory turnover

This measure of financial efficiency indicates how quickly inventory (stock) is converted into sales. It is also referred to as 'stock turnover'. A high figure means that stock is sold quickly, thus bringing money into the business more rapidly.

$$\text{Inventory turnover} = \frac{\text{cost of goods sold}}{\text{average inventories held}}$$

Sales are valued at cost to provide a fair comparison, as inventory values in the accounts are based on the cost paid for them rather than the price at which they will be sold.

The inventory turnover figure represents the number of times in a year that a business sells the value of its inventory. A value of 3 means that it sells its inventories three times a year (that is, once every four months). Thus it will take four months, on average, to convert inventory into cash (if no credit is given). A value of 26 means that the business converts inventories into cash every two weeks. The higher the figure, the better it is for a business's cash flow.

Factors influencing the rate of inventory turnover

The main influences on inventory turnover are:

- **The nature of the product**. Perishable products or products that become dated, such as newspapers, have very high rates of inventory turnover. In contrast, some products, such as antiques, sell slowly and so have a low rate of inventory turnover.
- **The importance of holding inventory**. Some businesses, such as clothes retailers, need to hold high inventory levels to encourage shoppers.
- **The length of the product life cycle/fashion**. Fashionable products are expected to sell quickly and products with very short life cycles (such as computer games) must also have a rapid turnover.
- **Inventory management systems**. Companies that use just-in-time inventory control have very low inventory levels, so their rate of inventory turnover is high.
- **Quality of management**. Poor market research may lead to inappropriate inventory being displayed and therefore low rates of inventory turnover being achieved.
- **The variety of products**. An organisation with 20 varieties of a product will inevitably be holding higher inventory levels overall than an organisation with only one version of a product.

▲ Perishable goods such as fresh fruit and vegetables at a greengrocers will have a high rate of inventory turnover

Author advice

It is not possible to calculate the inventory turnover figure accurately from published accounts. For a manufacturing company, the cost of goods sold will include production costs in addition to purchase of inventories. Thus 'cost of goods sold' will exaggerate the amount of inventories sold. However, the 'average inventories held' figure may also be an exaggeration, as inventories may be raw materials rather than finished products. These two effects may cancel each other out.

If you are required to calculate and interpret the inventory turnover figure, use the formula provided. However, you may wish to comment on the limitations of this calculation in your overall evaluation.

Based on Tables 2.7 and 2.8, the inventory turnover figures for Rounded Figures plc for 2016 and 2015 are:

2016: $\dfrac{1,150}{60} = 19.2$

2015: $\dfrac{1,050}{50} = 21.0$

These results suggest that Rounded Figures plc took 365/19.2 = 19.0 days to turn over its inventory (stock) in 2016. In 2015 it took 365/21.0 = 17.4 days. Although the figure has worsened slightly from 2015, this change is relatively minor.

Practice exercise 9

Total: 55 marks

1. Financial efficiency ratios assess the financial efficiency of:
   a) a business's overall profitability
   b) specific aspects of a business's activities, such as inventory control
   c) a business's cash flow
   d) the accuracy of a business's budgeting. *(1 mark)*

2. Explain one advantage and one disadvantage to a business of having a high value for receivables days. *(6 marks)*

3. Outline one possible benefit and one possible problem to a business whose receivables days are higher than its payables days. *(6 marks)*

4. How would the introduction of just-in-time inventory control affect the value of the inventory turnover rate of a business? *(4 marks)*

5. Explain two other factors that influence the rate of inventory turnover of a product. *(6 marks)*

6. Explain one benefit of a high rate of inventory turnover. *(4 marks)*

7. The following information is extracted from the accounts of ABF plc.

Years ending/as at:	13.9.2014 (£m)	13.9.2009 (£m)
Income statement		
Sales revenue (turnover)	12,943	9,255
Cost of sales	11,865	8,639
Balance sheet		
Receivables	1,293	1,121
Payables	2,046	1,413
Inventories (stock)	1,631	1,262

Based on this information, calculate the following ratios for the years ended 13 September 2009 and 13 September 2014:
   a) payables day *(4 marks)*
   b) receivables day *(4 marks)*
   c) inventory turnover. *(4 marks)*

8. Based on your answers to question 7, and any other information, compare and discuss the financial efficiency of ABF plc in 2014 and 2009. *(16 marks)*

Practice exercise 10 (below) provides the opportunity to conduct comprehensive ratio analyses of all six ratios for a particular business.

Note: This chapter has introduced the formulae for all six ratios on the AQA Year 2 Business specification. These have each been described separately in this chapter. For ease of reference, these six ratios are summarised as an appendix to this chapter. In order to answer the questions in Practice exercise 10, you are advised to refer to this appendix.

Practice exercise 10

Total: 20 marks

This is a self-assessment exercise. The answers to the questions below can be found in Case Study 1 towards the end of this chapter.

Doh! Nuts! plc is the main rival of Rounded Figures plc. Although Doh! Nuts! plc has based its reputation on the quality of its doughnuts, it has started to diversify into the market for cream cakes.

▼ **Table 2.9** Balance sheet for Doh! Nuts! plc, 30 June 2016

As at: 30.6.16	(£000s)	(£000s)
Non-current assets (fixed assets)		**1,250**
Inventories (stocks	150	
Receivables (debtors)	25	
Cash and other cash equivalents	25	
Total current assets		**200**
Payables (creditors)	(250)	
Current liabilities		**(250)**
Net current assets (working capital)		**(50)**
Non-current liabilities (long-term liabilities)		**(600)**
Net assets (net worth)		**600**
Share capital	400	
Reserves	200	
Total equity		600
NB capital employed = non-current assets + net current assets		1,200

▼ **Table 2.10** Income statement for Doh! Nuts! plc

Year ending:	30.6.16 (£000s)
Revenue	2,000
Cost of sales	(1,200)
Gross profit	**800**
Expenses	(760)
plus (minus) Exceptional items	60
Operating profit	100
Finance income	50
Finance costs	(50)
Profit before tax	**100**
Taxation	(20)
Profit for year	**80**
Earnings per share	£0.20

Based on the balance sheet and income statement (Tables 2.9 and 2.10), calculate the following ratios for Doh! Nuts! plc for the financial year ending 30 June 2016:

1. Return on capital employed (%)   *(4 marks)*

2. Current ratio   *(3 marks)*

3. Gearing (%)   *(4 marks)*

4. Payables days   *(3 marks)*

5. Receivables days   *(3 marks)*

6. Inventory turnover   *(3 marks)*

The value of financial ratios when assessing performance

Ratio analysis is an excellent way of assessing the performance of a business. Each ratio provides a different insight into the strengths (or weaknesses) of a business's performance. Overall, scrutiny of the balance sheet and income statement, accompanied by the calculation and analysis of the six ratios described in this chapter, provide an excellent overview of a business's **financial** performance. The three profitability ratios from Chapter 17 of Book 1 also add further insight into the business's performance. Table 2.11a summarises the main purposes and value of each ratio. Table 2.11b summarises the main purposes and value of the ratios covered in Chapter 17 of Book 1.

▼ **Table 2.11a** Purposes and value of performance ratios covered in this chapter

Ratio	Main purpose
Return on capital employed (%)	• To assess whether a business is making a satisfactory level of profit from the capital that it has available to it.
Current ratio	• To see if a business is likely to run short of liquid assets in the short term.
	• To ascertain whether a cash-flow problem might occur in the short term.
Gearing (%)	• To measure how reliant a business is on borrowed money.
	• To study the likely impact on the costs of a business if there are changes in interest rates.
	• To gauge whether a business may be vulnerable from having to repay loans in the next few years.
Payables days	• To discover the time taken for a business to pay its debts to its payables.
	• To assess whether a business is in danger of defaulting on the debts it owes.
Receivables days	• To discover the time taken for its receivables to pay their debts to a business.
	• To assess whether individual receivables are possibly going to become bad debts.
Inventory turnover	• To calculate how many times a year a business is able to sell its inventory (stock).
	• To measure the speed at which a business is able to convert its inventories into sales.

▼ **Table 2.11b** Purposes and value of performance ratios covered in Chapter 17 of Book 1

Ratio	Main purpose
Gross profit margin (%)	• To assess whether a business is adding value when converting its raw materials or inventories into something that is valued by its customers.
Operating profit margin (%)	• To assess whether the overall performance of a business is efficient in terms of creating profit from its main operations.
Profit for year margin (%)	• To ascertain the extent to which owners / shareholders will benefit financially from their investment in a business.

The value of ratio analysis is illustrated in Practice exercise 11. Each of the ten questions can be answered by using a suitable ratio.

Practice exercise 11

Total: 20 marks

Which ratio would you use to answer each of the following instances?

(For questions 1 to 9, each of the nine AQA ratios in Tables 2.11a and 2.11b above should be selected once. Question 10 requires one of the nine ratios to be used a second time.)

1. How effective inventory control in a business is. *(2 marks)*

2. Whether shareholders are likely to be happy with their share of the profit. *(2 marks)*

3. Whether a business is likely to be able to avoid a liquidity problem in the short term if it can convert all of its liquid assets into cash. *(2 marks)*

4. How effective a business is in turning its raw materials or finished goods into products with a much higher value. *(2 marks)*

5. Whether a business is likely to experience a liquidity problem in the long term. *(2 marks)*

6. How successful the business is in using its capital to generate profit. *(2 marks)*

7. How quickly a business is receiving money from customers who buy its goods on credit. *(2 marks)*

8. Whether a business is successful in generating profit from its usual business activities, in comparison to the sales revenue that it receives. *(2 marks)*

9. Whether suppliers are providing the business with good credit terms. *(2 marks)*

10. How vulnerable the business might be if there is a dramatic increase in interest rates. *(2 marks)*

Author advice

In strategic management it is rare for an issue to be based purely on one functional area, such as finance or human resource management. However, ratios and other analysis based on targets tend to give a definite view – a company's performance is either better or worse than its target. Consequently, judgements based on ratios/targets alone will have a limited focus. The usefulness of ratio analysis is influenced by the reliability of the information, the possible objectives of the business and the external factors that can influence performance.

Limitations of ratio analysis

Ratio analysis provides a scientific basis for decision making and is an excellent guide for assessing the strengths and weaknesses of a firm's existing financial position. However, firms have many different aims and objectives, so financial performance is not the only measure of a firm's success. Other, non-financial indicators (such as social audits) also have a part to play in assessing a firm's performance. Furthermore, each functional area of a firm will have targets that can be used to measure the strengths and weaknesses of a firm's overall performance. Ratio analysis should be used alongside these other indicators to assess a firm's success or failure. Some of the problems and limitations of ratio analysis are outlined below.

Reliability of information

The reliability of available information limits the usefulness of ratio analysis in several ways:

▲ How would a signal system for a disused railway line be valued?

- The data on which ratios are based may be unreliable.
- Some figures, notably asset valuation, are subjective to some extent. For example, how valuable is a railway line and signalling system to an organisation if it decides to close the route?
- Different accounting methods may be employed. For example, firms can use different methods for valuing non-current assets in their balance sheets.
- In recent years many businesses have encountered 'bad debts', where receivables have been unable to pay the money they owed. Although most firms reduce the value of their 'receivables' to allow for possible bad debts, it is impossible to place an exact figure on bad debts. During the recession many firms, particularly banks, made heavy losses because they underestimated the value of these bad debts.
- A firm's financial situation changes daily, and it may manipulate its accounts to provide a favourable view on the date on which they are prepared. This practice is known as window dressing.

Historical basis

The historical basis of published accounts affects ratio analysis for the following reasons:

- Accounts indicate where a company has been, rather than where it is going. Past performance is not necessarily a useful guide to the future. A number of former 'blue-chip' companies (i.e. companies recognised as excellent performers) have fallen behind rivals in recent years. In recent years, many long-established businesses, such as Phones4U, Habitat and JJB Sports, got into financial difficulties or went into liquidation.
- Accounts show *what* has happened, rather than *why*, and so they can only serve to point out potential problems.

Comparisons

Ratios rely on comparisons, but they always involve difficulties because no two firms or divisions face identical circumstances.

Corporate objectives

Ratio analysis only looks at financial measures, and relies on the assumption that maximising profit is the only aim of all firms. It ignores other objectives that may be more important to a firm:

- **Reputation**. A profitable firm that is seen to be exploiting its customers may suffer a considerable loss of goodwill.
- **Human relations**. A firm may experience a high rate of labour turnover and low levels of productivity if it does not meet the needs of its employees.
- **Relationship with suppliers**. Low prices paid for materials can help profits in the short term, but might upset suppliers.
- **Product quality**. This may be essential for long-term customer loyalty. Reducing quality as part of a cost-cutting exercise may increase profits in the short term, but in the long run this can lead to a decline in the number of customers.
- **Future profit**. It may pay a firm to make decisions that do not lead to, or produce, profit in the short term, in order to create profit for the future. Research and development (R&D) is an example of an activity that may reduce current profit in order to help future profit levels.

External factors

Company performance is very dependent on outside factors. A PESTLE analysis will show the external factors (opportunities and threats) that affect performance. Examples include:

- the stage of the economic cycle (for example, boom or recession)
- government legislation, which may add costs or create markets
- changes in taste – in favour of or against a firm's products
- new technology leading to new products or processes in a market
- the level of competition, which can affect the ability of a firm to make money.

It is vital that these and other factors are considered before conclusions are drawn.

Conclusion

Financial ratio analysis must not be ignored. It provides an excellent guide to performance. However, conclusions should be based on the specific circumstances, and the problems and limitations involved in financial ratio analysis should be taken into account.

Practice exercise 12

Total: 50 marks

1. Explain two factors that may cause the information used in a firm's ratio analysis to be unreliable. *(8 marks)*

2. State two types of 'comparison' used in ratio analysis. *(2 marks)*

3. Explain three reasons why comparisons of ratios may provide misleading results. *(12 marks)*

4. Identify two external factors that can affect company performance. Using a particular ratio, show how it might be affected by the two external factors that you have identified. *(8 marks)*

5. Analyse how changes in a car manufacturer's corporate objectives might influence the ways in which a car manufacturer uses ratio analysis. *(8 marks)*

6. 'Ratio analysis is of limited use because it shows the past, not the future.' To what extent is this statement valid? *(12 marks)*

Case study 1: Rounded Figures versus Doh! Nuts! The battle of the heavyweights

Table 2.12 summarises the ratio analysis calculations for Rounded Figures plc and Doh! Nuts! plc for the year ending 30.6.2016.

▼ **Table 2.12** Ratio analysis: Rounded Figures and Doh! Nuts!

Ratio	Rounded Figures plc	Doh! Nuts! plc
Return on capital employed (%)	30.0%	8.3%
Current ratio	1.7:1	0.8:1
Gearing (%)	18.2%	50.0%
Payables days	95 days	76 days
Receivables days	9 days	5 days
Inventory turnover	19.2	8.0

Question

Total: 20 marks

Based only on the ratios provided in Table 2.12, evaluate the main reasons why Rounded Figures plc would be seen as a better-performing business than Doh! Nuts! plc. *(20 marks)*

Case study 2: Dunelm and the homewares market

The UK homewares market consists of businesses offering items for the home, such as bedding, curtains, small electrical appliances, storage, pictures and crockery. The market is estimated to be worth over £11 billion a year. The nature of the products in this market is such that market growth is slow, but relatively resilient to economic downturns such as recessions.

The homewares market is unusual in that many firms that sell homeware items specialise in other products too. In recent decades, specialist 'homeware' firms experienced decline as supermarkets, DIY stores and department stores began to dominate. However, the last ten years have seen a resurgence in specialist homeware retailers, such as The Range and Dunelm. In 2013 Dunelm became the new market leader, overtaking the John Lewis Partnership – a department store – as the largest retailer of homeware products. The third largest retailer in this market is also a non-specialist – Argos (part of the Home Retail Group – HRG). Incidentally, the other division of HRG is Homebase, a DIY store whose range of products includes many homeware goods.

The market is very competitive, with only two stores (Dunelm and John Lewis) exceeding a 7 per cent market share. The largest ten firms have a combined market share of 50 per cent of the total market.

The key factors creating customer loyalty in this market are shown in Figure 2.3.

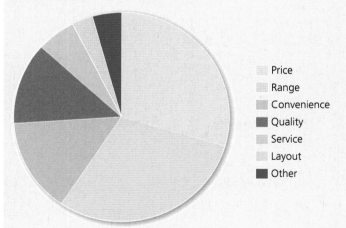

- Price
- Range
- Convenience
- Quality
- Service
- Layout
- Other

Dunelm has become the market leader because it provides a wide range, without the distraction of non-homeware goods, and offers a broad range of prices to suit individual customer preferences. With over 140 retail outlets and online ordering, Dunelm also offers convenience.

Dunelm's main corporate objective is growth. Because the market itself is not growing, this has to be obtained from increasing market share. This growth requires sound profit levels so that growth can be financed through the use of retained profits. Other key objectives are:

- Increase multi-channel sales, especially internet sales, which currently account for 6 per cent of company sales. The website has been updated, a mobile app developed and the product range extended to support this objective.
- Improve delivery time for online customers from five days to three days.
- Improve staff development and offer paid time off to support local community projects.
- Set targets to ensure that suppliers have good working conditions and appropriate environmental policies
- Increase recycled waste to 90 per cent of all waste and retain current achievement of zero waste to landfill sites.

Tables 2.13 and 2.14 show the latest (2014) financial accounts for Dunelm. For comparison over time, Table 2.15 shows the value of the six key ratios for Dunelm in 2010 and 2012. For comparisons with other businesses, Table 2.16 summarises the six key ratios for three of Dunelm's main competitors: John Lewis, Argos and Laura Ashley. It should be noted that Dunelm rents its properties and so owns relatively few non-current assets. Consequently, its capital employed is low in comparison to firms that operate on a similar scale, but using property that they own.

▲ **Figure 2.3** Factors influencing customer loyalty in the UK homewares market

▼ **Table 2.13** Balance sheet for Dunelm plc, 28 June 2014

As at: 28.6.14	(£ millions)	(£ millions)
Non-current assets		**165.9**
Inventories	115.5	
Receivables	19.5	
Cash and other cash equivalents	21.7	
Total current assets		**156.7**
Payables	(76.0)	
Other current liabilities	(16.4)	
Total current liabilities		**(92.4)**
Net current assets (working capital)		**64.3**
Non-current liabilities (long-term liabilities)		**(40.5)**
Net assets (net worth)		**189.7**
Share capital	44.5	
Reserves	145.2	
Total equity		**189.7**
NB capital employed = non-current assets + net current assets =		**230.2**

▼ **Table 2.14** Income statement for Dunelm plc, year ending 28 June 2014

Year ending: 28.6.14	(£ millions)
Revenue	730.2
Cost of sales	(368.9)
Gross profit	**361.3**
Expenses	(245.3)
plus (minus) Exceptional items	0
Operating profit	**116.0**
Finance income	0.5
Finance costs	(0.5)
Profit before tax	**116.0**
Taxation	(26.9)
Profit for year	**89.1**
Earnings per share	£0.44

▼ **Table 2.15** Ratio analysis: Dunelm plc, selected years

Ratio	2009–2010	2011–2012	2013–2014
Return on capital employed (%)	66.9%	46.0%	?
Current ratio	1.06:1	1.52:1	?
Gearing (%)	1.3%	1.5%	?
Payables days	100 days	114 days	?
Receivables days	8 days	10 days	?
Inventory turnover	4.2	3.6	?

▼ **Table 2.16** Ratio analysis for main competitors, 2013–14

Ratio	John Lewis Partnership	Home Retail Group plc	Laura Ashley plc
Return on capital employed (%)	11.3%	3.7%	12.5%
Current ratio	0.63:1	1.63:1	1.32:1
Gearing (%)	52.1%	10.9%	6.6%
Payables days	97 days	104 days	21days
Receivables days	9 days	46 days	45 days
Inventory turnover	10.8	4.3	3.2

Questions

Total: 65 marks

1. Use the data in Tables 2.13 and 2.14 to calculate each of the six ratios shown as question marks in Table 2.15. *(6 x 3 = 18 marks)*

2. Using Table 2.15 and your answer to question 1, evaluate the financial performance of Dunelm plc over the period 2009–10 to 2013–14. *(16 marks)*

3. Using Table 2.16 and your answer to question 1, evaluate the financial performance of Dunelm plc in the year ending 2014, in comparison to its three competitors shown in Table 2.16. *(16 marks)*

4. Analyse **three** non-financial factors that might be considered when making a judgement on whether Dunelm has performed well as a company in 2014. *(15 marks)*

Appendix: formulae for financial ratios in Year 2 of AQA A-level Business

1. Current ratio:

   current ratio = current assets:current liabilities

2. Return on capital employed (ROCE)

   $$ROCE(\%) = \frac{\text{operating profit}}{\text{total equity + non-current liabilities}} \times 100$$

3. Gearing

   $$\text{gearing (\%)} = \frac{\text{non-current liabilities}}{\text{total equity + non-current liabilities}} \times 100$$

4. Receivables (debtors) days
   *receivables = debtors

   $$\text{receivables'* collection period} = \frac{\text{receivables*}}{\text{revenue}} \times 100$$

5. Payables (creditors) days
   *payables = creditors

   $$\text{payables'* collection period} = \frac{\text{payables*}}{\text{cost of sales}} \times 100$$

6. Inventory or stock turnover

   $$\text{inventory (stock) turnover} = \frac{\text{cost of goods sold}}{\text{average inventories held}}$$

3

Analysing the existing internal position of a business to assess strengths and weaknesses: overall performance

This chapter examines non-financial ways of assessing a business's strengths and weaknesses, drawing on the objectives and data from other functional areas – human resources, operations management and marketing. It considers how this can be analysed over time and in comparison with other businesses. The concept of core competences is introduced and its importance explained. The contrast between the assessment of short-term and long-term performance of a business is considered, examining the tendency to use financial analysis for short-term assessment and non-financial analysis for long-term assessment. The chapter concludes by discussing the value of two specific measures of assessing business performance: Kaplan and Norton's Balanced Scorecard model and Elkington's triple bottom line.

How to analyse data other than financial statements to assess the strengths and weaknesses of business

Limitations of financial performance indicators

In Chapter 2 we examined how a business's financial performance could be measured. However, there are drawbacks to relying solely on financial performance measures:

- Backward looking. Financial measures tend to describe what has happened, rather than what is likely to happen in the future.
- Limited focus. Financial performance tends to reflect the wishes of shareholders rather than other stakeholders.
- Short term. Focusing on financial performance can encourage decisions that enable financial targets to be met even though this may have detrimental effects for the long-term success of the business.
- Internal perspective. The success of the business depends on its anticipation of external factors rather than just its internal operations; non-financial measures of achievement, such as customer satisfaction and quality, may be more relevant to the future success of the business.

Using non-financial data to analyse performance

Each of the functional areas of a business – finance, marketing, human resource management and operations management – has its own measurable objectives, which contribute towards the overall success of the business. Although some of these objectives, such as labour turnover and capacity utilisation, are focused specifically on a given area of the business, they all contribute to the overall success or failure of the business.

In Chapter 2, we analysed the internal position of a business in order to assess its financial strengths and weaknesses. Financial performance is of great significance to the success of most businesses. Indeed, some of the financial objectives dealt with in Chapter 2, such as the achievement of a high return on capital employed percentage, are recognised as overall business objectives rather than objectives related purely to the finance department of the business.

Nevertheless, all of the functional areas of a business contribute to business success. Consequently, the strengths and weaknesses of the other functional areas, measured by their ability to achieve their functional objectives, are important determinants of a business's success. Furthermore, businesses have many corporate objectives that are not specific to any one functional area.

These corporate and non-financial objectives were introduced in the AQA A-level Business Book 1. Business (corporate) objectives were introduced in Chapter 1; marketing objectives were explained in Chapter 7; operations management objectives were explained in Chapter 11; and human resource management objectives were explained in Chapter 20. In addition, Chapters 12 and 21 explained how to calculate and interpret operations management and human resource data respectively, in order to measure performance. (You may wish to revisit these chapters to familiarise yourself with these non-financial measures of business performance.) Table 3.1 summarises the non-financial objectives/measures of performance that were covered in Chapters 1, 7, 12 and 21 of Book 1. (Quality management was covered in Chapter 14 of Book 1.)

To measure business performance, whether financial or non-financial, businesses use **performance metrics**.

Key term

Performance metrics Measure a business's activities and performance. These measures should be suited to the needs of the stakeholders as a whole, rather than focus on the needs of shareholders and managers.

Author advice

In this context, the phrase 'non-financial' applies to the fact that the objective is not the responsibility of the finance function of the business. Thus some 'non-financial' objectives are measures of the financial efficiency of one of the functional areas of a business. For example, **unit costs of production** are a measure of the efficiency of the operations management function of a business.

▼ **Table 3.1** Non-financial objectives/measures of performance

Business objectives	Marketing objectives	Operations management objectives/ measures of performance	Human resource objectives/measures of performance
Growth	Sales volume/ value	Labour productivity*	Labour turnover
Survival	Market share (%)	Unit/average costs	Labour retention
Social objectives	Brand loyalty	Capacity utilisation	Labour productivity*
Ethical objectives		High quality	Employee costs as a % of turnover
			Labour costs per unit

*Labour productivity is used to measure the performance of both operations management and human resources.

The list of objectives above is very comprehensive and individual businesses will usually choose the objectives that they consider to be the most relevant to their particular circumstances.

In Chapter 2 we used ratio analysis to compare the strengths and weaknesses of the financial performance of two businesses – Rounded Figures plc and Doh! Nuts! plc. In this chapter we will assess their non-financial performance in order to assess their relative strengths and weaknesses. The list of non-financial objectives in Table 3.1 will be used to assess the strengths and weaknesses of the two companies and forms column 1 of Table 3.2 (below). To assist the comparison, both businesses will be assumed to have identical objectives. The specific objectives targeted by the two companies are shown in column 2 of Table 3.2. Columns 3 and 4 of Table 3.2 show the actual performances of the two companies in 2016.

▼ **Table 3.2** Non-financial performance of Rounded Figures plc and Doh! Nuts! plc in 2016

Business objectives	Specific objective/target for both firms	Rounded Figures – actual performance	Doh! Nuts! – actual performance
Growth	+ 5% p.a.	+25%	+8%
Survival	ROCE > 5%; Current ratio > 1.5:1	34.5% & 1.7:1	8.3% & 0.8:1
Social objectives	Cut waste products by 10% p.a.	Cut by 5%	Cut by 15%
Ethical objectives	Fairtrade products to grow by 10% p.a.	7% growth	13% growth
Marketing objectives			
Sales volume/value	+ 5% p.a. by value	+25%	+8%
Market share (%)	10%	12.5%	10.0%
Brand loyalty	Repeat customers > 60%	54%	75%
Operations management objectives/measures of performance			
Labour productivity	Target = 65 units per head	70 per head	64 per head
Unit/average costs	Unit costs < £0.40	36p per head	40p per head
Capacity utilisation	90% to 95%	99%	90%
High quality	Customer satisfaction rating > 8 out of 10	6.6	9.3

Business objectives	Specific objective/target for both firms	Rounded Figures – actual performance	Doh! Nuts! – actual performance
Human resource objectives/ measures of performance			
Labour turnover	Below 15%	30%	10%
Labour retention	Above 85%	80%	92%
Labour productivity	Target = 65 units per head	70 per head	64 per head
Employee costs as a % of turnover	Below 40%	38%	40%
Labour costs per unit	Labour costs per unit < £0.16	15p per head	16p per head

Analysis of data in Table 3.2

As with financial performance, non-financial data may be analysed over time or in comparison with other businesses. Table 3.2 focuses on the latter. The former approach would be conducted by taking a specific company and collecting and analysing data over the last few years, to establish whether it is showing an improvement or a worsening of performance.

Business objectives

In terms of growth and survival, Rounded Figures outperformed Doh! Nuts!. The latter's low liquidity might threaten its survival, but the sound profit level should enable it to overcome any short-term difficulties. For social and ethical objectives, Doh! Nuts! has exceeded its objectives, but Rounded Figures has missed its targets. Shareholders seeking financial returns might consider Rounded Figures to have the greatest strengths, because its first two objectives are likely to boost profits. However, ethical shareholders, society as a whole and certain stakeholder groups may consider the achievements of Doh! Nuts! to be more impressive, as it has met more of its targets and arguably satisfied a broader range of stakeholders.

Marketing objectives

Again, Rounded Figures' excellent growth is a major achievement and this has helped it to exceed its market share objective. However, this seems to have been achieved despite a failure to achieve its brand loyalty objective. It seems likely that the marketing function has succeeded in attracting many new customers, but there are issues that are leading to existing customers becoming less loyal. This could cause future problems.

Doh! Nuts! has just achieved its first two marketing objectives and performed well on repeat customers. This implies that customers are very satisfied, but suggests that there may be unfulfilled potential to attract new customers.

Operations management objectives

Rounded Figures has achieved very good labour productivity, a factor which would help the company to reach its unit costs target too. The high capacity utilisation also helps to reduce unit costs, but at 99 per cent it is above its target and this may mean that the business cannot fulfil orders in the future, especially if it continues to grow. The customer satisfaction rating is a serious issue and may well be the cause of the low level of repeat customers.

Doh! Nuts! is again showing a more even performance across its various objectives, but without surpassing them in the way that Rounded Figures does on occasions. Labour productivity is just under target, but the unit cost objective, which is more important for the company's success, has been achieved. Capacity utilisation is within the target range, offering both an efficient use of resources and some flexibility to cope with growth. The customer satisfaction rating is well above target and should help future success.

Human resource objectives

Good labour productivity for Rounded Figures helps it to meet its target objectives for employee costs as a percentage of turnover and labour costs per unit. However, the retention rate is below target and the high labour turnover suggests that there are problems. The two rates indicate that some employees must be leaving within their first year, because the 80 per cent retention rate means that 20 per cent of long-term employees have left. However, with a 30 per cent labour turnover this means that 10 per cent of the 30 per cent labour turnover were employees in their first year. These issues may create problems in the future.

Doh! Nuts! is close to its HR targets for productivity and costs. Its greatest strength appears to be in high retention and low labour turnover. These factors suggest a well-motivated and perhaps loyal workforce.

Conclusion

In Chapter 2 the financial analysis showed that Rounded Figures was superior to Doh! Nuts!. Very often, financial strength allows a company to devote resources to ensuring that non-financial objectives are achieved too. However, in this case the non-financial data suggest that Rounded Figures has some problems which may not yet have fully impacted on the company, but which may lead to future decline. These issues centre around under-achievement of social and ethical objectives, low brand loyalty and quality, and poor human resource management with respect to labour turnover and retention.

In contrast, while Doh! Nuts! does not have the outstanding successes of Rounded Figures, in terms of growth and profitability, it has achieved the vast majority of its objectives, with no single target significantly under-achieved.

Stakeholder mapping (see Chapter 6 of Book 1) might help to measure the overall achievement. It may be that the needs of shareholders' dominate Rounded Figures' strategic management, while Doh! Nuts!'s strategy is geared towards satisfying a broader range of stakeholders.

This example illustrates three major difficulties in the analysis of the strengths and weaknesses of a business:

- How can the relative importance of each objective be weighted?
- Are the objectives realistic or are some too challenging or too easy to achieve?
- To what extent is the achievement of objectives attributable to internal factors? Although this analysis is intended to measure the companies' internal strengths and weaknesses, the outcomes will be affected by external factors.

▲ While Rounded Figures' financial position was better than Doh! Nuts!, the latter performed better against its non-financial objectives

61

Fact file

Human resource objectives at AstraZeneca

The measures of performance outlined in Table 3.2 are indicative of the types of criteria that businesses use to measure their strengths and weaknesses. However, each company will choose its own measures to reflect the circumstances of the business and the priorities of its managers and other stakeholders.

AstraZeneca, the pharmaceutical company, uses HR objectives that differ significantly from those listed in Table 3.2. Examples of its performance against certain human resource management measures are summarised here.

Its objective to achieve equality for workers is measured as follows:

- percentage of workforce that is female: 50.4 per cent
- ratio of male wages to female wages: 1.15:1.0

Its objective to provide secure employment is measured as follows:

- percentage of workers with full-time contracts: 97.3 per cent
- percentage of workers with permanent contracts: 98.7 per cent.

Other HR measures include (2013 data):

- Labour turnover: 15.3 per cent per annum
- Reducing absences through accidents and illness by 25 per cent, from 2011 to 2015.

What do you think?

The fact file on AstraZeneca outlines the methods it uses to measure HR performance. These measures are very specific to AstraZeneca and mean that it is very difficult to compare its HR performance with that of its competitors or other businesses. In contrast, there are standardised measures of financial performance, such as ROCE and gearing, which allow direct comparison of financial performance.

Does this mean that non-financial measures of performance have very little practical use? What do you think?

Difficulties in using non-financial methods of performance

There are a number of difficulties in using non-financial measures of performance, which undermine its usefulness.

- There is no standardisation of measures to use (see Fact file on AstraZeneca).
- Where there is use of standardised measures, such as labour turnover, there is not always widespread agreement on what is considered a desirable level to achieve.
- Often, firms use non-financial measures that are qualitative, and so the measure of performance is likely to be a subjective opinion of a senior manager.
- Non-financial measures are often interdependent, and so the achievement of one measure automatically means that another measure is almost certain to be achieved. For example, there is a very strong link between labour productivity, unit costs and employee costs as a percentage of turnover.
- As with financial measures, they often reflect what has happened, rather than what will happen.
- The relative importance of different measures is very difficult to judge and may often change over time. For example, human resource measures

are likely to be seen as more important if there are HR difficulties in the business. If there are no issues with human resources, then HR measures might not be deemed to be very significant.

- Excessive use of monitoring and analysis of non-financial methods can divert resources away from factors that influence performance directly.
- The desire for objectivity may encourage firms to use quantitative measures when qualitative measures may actually be more useful, albeit harder to measure.

Despite these difficulties, there is a growing recognition of the usefulness of non-financial performance measures in order to assess the strengths and weaknesses of a business. Consequently, models of performance that incorporate both financial and non-financial methods have been developed. Examples of these measures, such as Kaplan and Norton's Balanced Scorecard model, are dealt with later in this chapter.

The importance of core competences

Core competences represent the unique strengths of a business that cannot be easily replicated by a competitor. They are the strengths that are critical to the success of the business. They are also described as core capabilities or distinctive competences. As with non-financial assessment of strengths and weaknesses, the concept became popular in the 1990s.

The thinking behind core competences is based on the belief that senior managers cannot effectively manage every business activity within a business. The aim of managers should be to concentrate on activities that are vital to the business aim of improving its competitiveness. A key strategy that has developed from the focus on core competences is outsourcing. Prahalad and Hamel suggested that business functions that are not enhanced by core competences should be outsourced to other companies, as long as this outsourcing is financially sensible. In this way businesses could focus on their strengths and, ideally, benefit from the strengths of other businesses. This could arise because functions that were outsourced would become the responsibility of other companies who had core competences, and therefore greater expertise, in that particular function. In this way the business would be able to focus on improving its internal efficiency, while also benefiting from core competences in those businesses to which it outsourced functions that were not among its own core competences.

What are core competences? Prahalad and Hamel outlined three ways of assessing whether something is a core competency:

- Does it make a significant contribution to the benefits that customers believe they are receiving from buying the end product?
- Does it help to provide potential access to a wide variety of markets?
- Is it difficult for competitors to replicate?

An example to illustrate core competence is that of Apple. Apple's core competence is generally recognised to be its ability to **design**. This competence has led to considerable levels of brand loyalty among Apple's customers, who eagerly await the latest new product development. This is enhanced by the fact that the design skills have been applied across a wide

Key term

Core competences (often known as core competencies) The unique ability or abilities of a business that enable it to achieve a competitive advantage.

Did you know?

The phrase 'Core Competences' was introduced into business management literature by C.K. Prahalad and Gary Hamel, who used it in some articles in the *Harvard Review* in 1990. These articles led to a book: *Competing for the Future*. Prahalad and Hamel believed that the key to success lay in business leaders identifying the company's core competences and using this knowledge to develop those competences in order to achieve growth.

63

▲ Competitors have found it hard to match Apple's core competency

range of products. This core competence has provided access for Apple into new markets. The strength of the design skills within Apple has allowed it to maintain this core competence throughout its history. Competitors have found it difficult to match or replicate these designs and Apple is able to prevent this replication through patents and copyright laws. Apple has a reputation for vigorously pursuing legal redress if there is any suggestion that another company has copied its ideas. Apple's financial strength can intimidate smaller businesses who would not be able to afford the legal proceedings, and has also caused difficulties for major corporations such as Samsung, which has been fined heavily (mainly in the USA) for breach of some of Apple's patents.

Businesses must not assume that core competences will remain as a permanent fixture. Their development and exploitation requires careful management and planning. Training of staff, investment in new resources, and takeovers of other businesses are all used by businesses to consolidate and extend their core competences.

Core competences are liable to change. In a dynamic business environment some core competences become less relevant, some companies find it difficult to maintain the quality of a core competence, while others develop other unique strengths that enable them to achieve success. Google's original core competence was its computer algorithm that transformed internet searches. **Innovation** is seen to be a core competence for Google. Some of its more recent products include Google maps – including street views, Google glass, intelligent machines and self-drive cars, and shopping express – a service that provides same-day delivery from both national and local retailers.

Core competences are vital in achieving added value, but it is important that businesses do not become complacent. In 2012, Sir Richard Broadbent, Chairman of Tesco plc, outlined Tesco's four major core competences:

- outstanding operational effectiveness
- understanding of how to serve customer needs
- a passion for staff development
- excellent management of a complex environment with great teamwork.

However, Tesco's market share fell by about 3 per cent in the aftermath of the recession. The company cut back on its economy range of products at the exact time that Aldi and Lidl were growing because of their low prices, and Tesco's management failed to manage the complex environment in which it had previously traded with great success. In 2014, the new Chief Executive, Dave Lewis, indicated that its core competences were:

- effective use of scale
- staff
- multi-channel leadership.

The concept of core competences has been widely criticised in recent years. Difficulties with the control and quality of outsourcing have undermined the effectiveness of businesses that focus just on their core competences. Excessive outsourcing has also led to businesses, such as Dell, losing their original core competences.

Assessing short- and long-term performance

The reasons for short-termism

A common criticism of financial performance indicators, such as ROCE% and the current ratio, are that they focus on the short term. By showing what has happened in the last year, they provide an excellent guide to recent performance and a reasonably good indicator of the near future. However, they are not reliable indicators of the long-term future of the business, because there is no indication of whether these results can be sustained in the future.

Considering the longer-term future of business activities is the main focus of businesses' corporate social responsibility (CSR). (CSR is considered in Chapter 6.) Most large businesses devote considerable attention to limiting the negative effects that their activities might have on future generations. However, performance indicators have traditionally done very little to enable a business to consider its long-term future prospects.

Short-termism is a common feature of both business and government activity. Business reporting has changed in recent years from annual reporting to quarterly reporting. These changes have been driven by the growing pace of change in society. Ironically, it is this growing pace of change that means that long-term planning is so important. Market circumstances can change so quickly that a business can become unsustainable much more quickly.

A major criticism of short-termism is its focus on short-term profits and shareholder value. Shareholders are now much more inclined to buy and sell shares in order to move money into businesses that appear to offer them short-term financial gains. In 1975, the average length of time that a shareholder owned shares was six years. In 2015, this figure had fallen to six months. In turn, this has put pressure on boards of directors to focus on ensuring that shareholders get good financial returns in the form of dividends or increasing share prices. Short-termism as an external influence on corporate objectives is covered in Chapter 1 of this book.

The pressure for short-termism is also connected to the reward system for many senior executives of businesses. Their reward systems are often based on the share price of the business. This leads to managers focusing on short-term strategies that will increase the share price regardless of the long-term consequences. In the UK, this has led to a lack of attention being paid to activities that tend to yield results over a long period of time, such as training staff (to improve labour productivity), investment in capital equipment (to reduce unit costs) and research and development (to improve new product development).

Focusing on the long term

The worldwide recession led to the demise of a number of very well established companies. Many of these companies performed well in the short term, but did not have the capability to deal with the change in the external environment that led to the recession. This has been one of the

> **Key term**
>
> **Short-termism** A tendency for businesses to prioritise current performance rather than the long-term sustainability of the business.

factors that has encouraged business leaders to look more to planning for the long term.

The growing pace of change has also led to growing risks, with uncertainty arising from factors such as climate change, growing population, increasing inequality and lower economic growth.

Business leaders, such as Sir Richard Branson, are calling on companies to take a much longer view when measuring their performance. These leaders recommend that businesses should prioritise people and planet, alongside profit. (This approach will be discussed later in this chapter.)

A leading exponent of long-term measures of performance is McKinsey & Company, a global management consultancy. McKinsey & Company suggests a much greater focus on non-financial measures, as many of these, such as research and development expenditure, are more likely to influence future value creation within a business. The consultancy advocates the use of 'health metrics' as a way of assessing future performance. These health metrics are similar to Kaplan and Norton's Balanced Scorecard approach, which is covered in the next section.

McKinsey & Company emphasises that metrics (measures of performance) need to be specific to the individual business, but propose some generic metrics that can be used to assess short-term, medium-term and long-term performance. These are summarised below.

1. Short-term metrics (measures)

These measures use historical performance to help indicate whether growth and return on investment for shareholders can be sustained, or whether they will improve or worsen:

- **Sales productivity measures**. These measures examine recent sales and include market share and the ability to add value. For retailers, sales per store and the change in the number of stores per annum would also be considered.
- **Operating cost productivity measures**. These measures focus on a firm's unit (average) costs. The breakdown of these costs can also be examined to detect areas of efficiency or inefficiency.
- **Capital productivity measures**. These measures focus on working capital, such as inventories, receivables, payables and non-current assets such as machinery and property. These measures show whether cash flow is likely to be satisfactory and can also measure how effectively a business is using its capital.

Overall, these measures – which combine financial ratios and non-financial measures of performance – indicate the current 'health' of a business.

2. Medium-term metrics (measures)

These measures project whether a business can maintain or improve its performance over the next few years. The time period is usually one to five years, but may be longer in businesses in which strengths can be maintained over a longer period of time. For example, a business that relies on patents may sustain its strengths for up to 20 years.

- **Commercial health measures**. These measures examine whether a business can maintain or improve sales revenue in the medium term.

Measures used include products in the pipeline (levels of new product development), brand loyalty, customer satisfaction and external risk, such as proposed legislation or competitors developing new products.

- **Cost structure health measures**. These measures assess whether there is scope to continue to reduce unit costs, relative to competitors.
- **Asset health measures**. These measure the extent to which non-current assets, such as buildings, are being maintained and improved, in order to avoid significant deterioration in their future usefulness.

Overall, these measures – which focus more on non-financial measures of performance – indicate possible changes in the 'health' of a business in the near future.

3. Long-term metrics (measures)

These measures show the ability of a business to sustain or expand on its current operations and its ability to identify and exploit new areas of growth.

These measures are much more qualitative (subjective) and require a business to look outside its own environment to a greater extent. Possible measures are:

- Anticipated changes in consumer tastes
- Recognition of new technologies
- Relevance of core competences to future markets
- Potential for joint ventures in order to utilise other firms' core competences
- Internally: the people, skills and culture of a business
- The company's share price. A value in excess of the worth of its assets suggests that investors have faith in the firm's ability to cope with future changes.

Source of section on metrics: Adapted from www.mckinsey.com and other sources

The value of different measures of assessing business performance

There is no widespread agreement on how to assess the overall performance of a business. Consequently, a number of models have been developed. In this section we will examine two of these models:

- **Kaplan and Norton's Balanced Scorecard** model.
- Elkington's triple bottom line (profit, people, planet).

Kaplan and Norton's Balanced Scorecard model

In the early 1990s there was a tendency to focus purely on financial measures of performance, even in instances where the vision or mission statement of the business implied that it had a wider spread of goals.

In 1992, Robert Kaplan and David Norton introduced the concept of the Balanced Scorecard. This was an approach that added non-financial measures of performance to the traditional measures of financial performance, so that business performance was assessed in a more holistic fashion.

Kaplan and Norton believed that the Balanced Scorecard would give managers a better understanding of the strengths and weaknesses of their

Key term

Kaplan and Norton's Balanced Scorecard A strategic planning and management system used to ensure that a business's activities are linked to its vision statement.

businesses and its future prospects. It consisted of a model that assessed a business's performance from four different perspectives:

- the financial perspective – how a business is regarded by its owners or shareholders
- the customer perspective – how customers perceive a business
- internal business processes perspective – how efficiently a business manages its operations
- learning and growth perspective – how a business can maintain improvement and continue to create value.

As a strategic management process, the Balanced Scorecard would involve the following steps for each of the above perspectives:

- decide on a set of aims for each of these perspectives
- translate each of these aims into measurable objectives
- design strategies (initiatives) to achieve these objectives
- measure actual performance against these objectives on a regular (usually annual) basis
- adapt strategies, and possibly the objectives, according to levels of success or failure and changes in the internal and external environment.

Figure 3.1 shows a template for planning and monitoring business strategy through the Balanced Scorecard. For each perspective, the objective and the way (or ways) in which it should be measured are agreed. Specific target levels are agreed and strategies (initiatives) are then planned in order to reach these targets. On a regular basis, the actual outcomes are compared to the targets and strategies, which are then updated, if necessary.

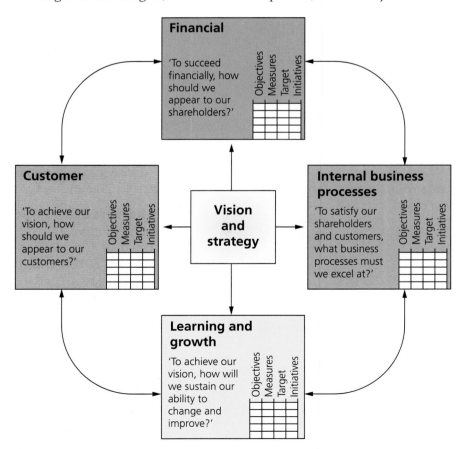

▲ **Figure 3.1** Kaplan and Norton's Balanced Scorecard

For each of the four perspectives, a business would choose its own objectives and measures of performance, to take into consideration the unique nature of each business. The list of objectives and measures below is an illustration of some of the objectives and measures that might be used:

- Financial perspective:
  - profitability; for example, a 15 per cent ROCE
  - liquidity; for example, a current ratio of 1.5:1
  - gearing; for example, a gearing ratio of less than 50 per cent
  - growth; for example, sales revenue growth in excess of 5 per cent per annum.
- Customer perspective:
  - marketing performance; for example, market share in excess of 10 per cent
  - customer satisfaction; for example, a 5 per cent reduction in customer complaints
  - customer loyalty; for example, a minimum of 60 per cent repeat customers
  - responsiveness; for example, 100 per cent of deliveries within two days.
- Internal business processes perspective:
  - productive efficiency; for example, a 5 per cent cut in unit costs
  - efficient use of capacity, for example, capacity utilisation above 90 per cent
  - loyalty of workforce; for example, annual labour turnover below 15 per cent
  - labour costs per unit cut by 5 per cent per annum.
- Learning and growth perspective:
  - new product development; an increase in the number of new products launched
  - research and development; R&D to exceed 5 per cent of sales turnover
  - employee engagement; increase in number of employee suggestions made
  - staff development; each member of staff to experience at least 15 days of training per annum.

▲ The customer's perspective is one of the measures considered in Kaplan and Norton's Balanced Scorecard

Advantages of the Balanced Scorecard approach

- It provides a broader view of the business's performance.
- It provides specific targets that can be monitored so that success or failure can be measured accurately.
- It links objectives more closely to strategy.
- It allows employees to see more clearly where their role fits within the vision and goals of the organisation.
- It acts as a motivator for employees who are given specific targets and who can be rewarded for their achievement.
- Constant monitoring allows potential weaknesses to be detected quickly and remedial action taken

Weaknesses of the Balanced Scorecard approach

- It can be difficult to quantify certain objectives and therefore some objectives may not be given the same level of priority as others.
- Excessive numbers of targets can cause confusion and distract workers from the key objectives.
- Getting the right balance between the four perspectives is difficult.
- Getting the right balance of objectives within each of the four perspectives is also difficult.

Key term

The triple bottom line
Describes a means of assessing business performance that considers three different factors: financial returns (profit), social responsibility (people) and environmental values (planet).

Elkington's triple bottom line (profit, people, planet)

John Elkington, who introduced the term, was the founder of a UK business consultancy called SustainAbility. Elkington advocated the use of **the triple bottom line** as a way to measure performance in a more balanced way, but also in a way that measures the future sustainability of business and communities.

The triple bottom line approach considers that a business's overall performance should be assessed by considering three different categories of factors:

- 'Profit': the traditional, financial measures of performance, such as ROCE% and capital gearing, to assess the short-term financial success of the business.
- 'People': assessing non-financial factors that measure the social responsibility demonstrated by a business, such as employee welfare, situation for suppliers and customers and support for local communities.
- 'Planet': measuring the extent to which a business's activities are environmentally friendly.

Elkington believed that 'the concept of triple bottom line demands that a company's responsibilities be to its stakeholders rather than shareholders'. (See Chapter 6 of Book 1 for more detail on stakeholders.)

The triple bottom line and sustainability

In the 1980s and 1990s there was a movement towards cost-cutting as the main priority for global businesses. Alongside the view of core competences, this led to the growth of subcontracting of activities to low-cost countries, such as Brazil, China and India. However, during this period, some businesses began to realise the problems that this was creating, mostly in the form of exploitation of labour and environmental damage, such as deforestation of the Amazon rainforest. This led to a desire to incorporate corporate social responsibility more fully into business objectives.

Elkington's view was that the triple bottom line measures the full cost to society of business activity. Its growth in popularity coincided with concerns about unethical business practices, particularly concerning the actions of suppliers in places such as Bangladesh, where workers rights are often overlooked. Businesses are now recognising that their responsibility to society does not end with their own direct actions. (The Fact file on Nike in Chapter 3 of Book 1 illustrated this point.)

According to the World Commission on the Environment and Development, **sustainable development** is development that meets the needs of the present, without compromising the ability of future generations to meet their own needs. Thus sustainability requires a balance between three main objectives:

- social progress, taking into account everyone's needs
- environmental protection and careful planning of the use of natural resources
- steady levels of economic growth.

These three objectives correspond to Elkington's triple bottom line. The triple bottom line recognises that it is vital for business sustainability that businesses create value for shareholders and customers. However, it also recognises that this wealth creation should take into consideration the needs of the communities and other stakeholders. Furthermore, the triple bottom line recognises the long-term sustainability of the world's resources, recognising that short-term growth may endanger the prosperity of future generations if it is achieved through depletion of resources.

▲ Elkington's triple bottom line assesses business performance not only on the basis of profit but also social and environmental responsibility

The two major problems with the triple bottom line are how to measure the non-financial categories and how to balance the needs of the three types of objective. The 'profit' element of the triple bottom line can be measured in financial terms, but the other two objectives are only measurable, on the whole, through qualitative factors. Because businesses have become more data driven in recent times, this can lead to a tendency for businesses to focus more on the profit element than on people and planet.

Fact file

The Body Shop

The Body Shop is recognised as a business that uses the triple bottom line approach. In 2006, the company was bought by L'Oréal, leading to fears that it would move away from prioritising its ethical and sustainable objectives. At the time, Anita Roddick, Body Shop's CEO, promised to use the Body Shop to try to influence L'Oréal to become more ethical. As a result, L'Oréal is now sourcing more of its ingredients from Fairtrade organisations, including some of the Body Shop's own suppliers. However, there is still one area of conflict. In China it is a legal requirement for cosmetics to be tested on animals before being marketed. Retailers, such as Body Shop, are banned from selling in China, but L'Oréal has accepted animal testing in order to enter the Chinese market.

Practice exercise 1

Total: 55 marks

1. Which one of these criticisms of the use of financial performance indicators is not true?
   a) They are based mainly on the needs of shareholders rather than stakeholders.
   b) They tend to focus on the short term rather than the long term.
   c) They tend to look forwards rather than backwards.
   d) They tend to ignore qualitative factors.   *(1 mark)*

2. Which one of the following might be a measure of operations management performance?
   a) market share   **c)** brand loyalty
   b) labour productivity   **d)** growth   *(1 mark)*

3. Which one of the following might be a measure of human resources performance?
   a) labour turnover   **c)** high-quality products
   b) unit costs   **d)** capacity utilisation   *(1 mark)*

4. Which one of the following is not an advantage of the Balanced Scorecard approach?
   a) It may allow employees to see how they can influence a business's success.
   b) It can motivate employees.
   c) It links objectives and strategy.
   d) It focuses solely on non-financial measures of performance.   *(1 mark)*

5. Explain the meaning of the term 'core competence'. *(3 marks)*

6. State the three elements of Elkington's triple bottom line. *(3 marks)*

7. State the four perspectives of Kaplan and Norton's Balanced Scorecard. *(4 marks)*

8. Explain, giving one example of each, the difference between short-term metrics (measures) and long-term measures of business performance. *(5 marks)*

9. Explain how a business might use the Balanced Scorecard to create a business strategy. *(6 marks)*

10. Explain how Elkington's triple bottom line can help a business to improve its performance. *(6 marks)*

11. Explain two difficulties that might arise from using non-financial data to measure business performance. *(8 marks)*

12. Explain two ways of assessing whether something is a 'core competence'. *(8 marks)*

13. Explain two possible reasons for short-termism by UK businesses. *(8 marks)*

Case study: BT's Better Future

In January 2015, the list of the Global 100 most sustainable corporations in the world was published. Eleven UK companies were placed in the top 100 world companies for sustainability. In 15th place was BT, making it the highest ranked of the world's telecommunication companies.

Research by BT revealed that customers value social responsibility. Its research showed that there was a strong statistical correlation between customer satisfaction and corporate social responsibility, with 84 per cent of consumers believing that sustainability was important.

Consequently, BT believes that using the triple bottom line not only yields future sustainability, but also provides short-term benefits in terms of greater customer satisfaction. BT's strategy is to quantify these objectives so that progress can be monitored. In many cases the objectives are long-term goals for 2020, split into annual targets for successive years. Some of the key examples of BT's 'people and planet' objectives are updated annually, and their performance against these objectives is summarised below:

▼ **Table 3.3** BT's Better Future performance indicators: 2013–14

Performance indicators	2013–14 target	2013–14 result
99% of UK to have access to high-speed internet	58%	66%
Cut waste to landfill sites	Cut by 30%	Cut by 57%
Customer service rating measured by – 'Right first time'	+ 4.0%	+ 1.5%
Employee engagement index	3.69/5	3.82/5
Sickness absence rate	<2.13%	2.10%
Ethical performance: measuring employees' awareness and training	4.19/5	4.29/5
Ethical trading – monitor high-/medium-risk suppliers within 3 months	100%	97%
Relations with suppliers rated 'good' or 'excellent'	89%	89%
% of pre-tax profit invested in sustainable activities	1.0%	1.01%

Source: BT

Questions

1. Which one of the following categories of objectives did BT **fail** to achieve?

   a) employee engagement index

   b) sickness absence rate

   c) ethical trading

   d) relations with suppliers *(1 mark)*

2. Explain **one** strength and **one** weakness of using quantitative data to measure a company's 'planet and people' performances. *(8 marks)*

3. Using the data in Table 3.3, and your understanding of business, answer the following question: To what extent does BT's performance in 2013–14 guarantee a sustainable future for BT plc? *(16 marks)*

4

Analysing the external environment to assess opportunities and threats: political and legal change

This chapter considers the impact of changes in the political and legal environment on strategic and functional decision making. In considering the political and legal environment, the chapter provides a broad review of the scope and effects of UK and EU law related to competition, the labour market and environmental legislation. It also discusses the impact of UK and EU government policy related to enterprise, the role of regulators, infrastructure, the environment and international trade.

The impact of changes in the political and legal environment on strategic and functional decision making

From a business perspective, the political environment is essentially the range of government policies and their impact on business. Similarly the legal environment is the range of legislation and regulation that has been passed and its impact on business. The AQA specification requires a focus on the impact of changes in the political and legal environment on strategic and functional decision making. The concepts of strategic and functional decision making were introduced in Chapter 1. To reiterate, strategic decision making concerns the general direction and overall policy of an organisation and tends to be long term, whereas functional decision making tends to be short to medium term and is concerned with specific functional areas rather than overall policy.

The scope and effects of UK and EU law

In general, law, in terms of the legislation and regulations introduced by government, is intended to protect those with weaker bargaining power. From a business perspective, it ensures that competition between firms is fair, that employees are treated fairly, that firms pay due attention to the impact of their actions on the environment, that consumers receive a fair deal and that products meet health and safety standards. In this sense, the law ensures a more ordered and predictable environment and one that is fairer for all parties concerned.

Did you know?

The legal system of the European Union takes priority over national legislation. EU regulations are directly binding on all member states without the need for national legislation to put them in place. European Union directives are instructions from the EU to member countries. These usually require each country to pass legislation through its own parliament so that there is 'harmonisation' (i.e. the same laws in each country). In practice, different countries do not always pass identical laws, as interpretation may vary.

▲ EU laws are interpreted in the Houses of Parliament and implemented in an appropriate way for the UK

The scope and effects of UK and EU law related to competition

In the UK two sets of competition rules apply. Anti-competitive behaviour, which may affect trade within the UK, is specifically prohibited by the Competition Act 1998 and the Enterprise Act 2002. Where the effect of anti-competitive behaviour extends beyond the UK to other EU member states, it is prohibited by the Treaty on the Functioning of the European Union (TFEU).

UK and EU competition law prohibit three main types of anti-competitive activity: anti-competitive agreements, abuse of a dominant market position and mergers that result in dominant positions

1. Anti-competitive agreements

Both UK and EU competition law prohibit agreements and arrangements that prevent, restrict or distort competition and which affect or may affect trade within the UK or the EU. The types of arrangement that are generally prohibited by UK and EU law include:

a) agreements that directly or indirectly fix purchase or selling prices, or any other conditions such as discounts or rebates

b) agreements that limit or control production, markets, technical development or investment, such as setting quotas or levels of output

c) agreements that share markets or sources of supply

d) agreements that apply different conditions to similar transactions so that one party is at a disadvantage compared to other parties.

2. Abuse of a dominant market position

Both UK and EU competition law prohibit businesses with significant market power unfairly exploiting their strong market positions. To be in a dominant position generally means where the market share of an individual business is at least 40 per cent. Being in a dominant position is not in itself a breach of competition law. It is the abuse of that position that is prohibited. (Note that this is a different measure to that used by the CMA when investigating whether potential mergers might reduce competition. In this case, one of the criteria for investigation is if the combined market share of the resulting merged firm is 25 per cent or more.) Examples of behaviour that could amount to an abuse by a business of its dominant position include:

a) imposing unfair trading terms, such as exclusivity, for example when only a particular supplier's products can be displayed

b) excessive, predatory or discriminatory pricing

c) refusal to supply or provide access to essential facilities

d) requiring a buyer who wishes to purchase one product to also purchase other products (known as 'tying').

3. Merger control

A merger, acquisition or joint venture can be subject to review by UK or EU competition authorities to assess whether it will reduce competition in the market to a significant extent. Mergers are considered in detail in Chapter 11 of this book.

Did you know?

Cartels are agreements between companies to limit competition. Cartel behaviour between competitors is seen as one of the most serious forms of anti-competitive behaviour and carries the highest penalties. A 'hardcore' cartel is one which involves price fixing, market sharing and limiting the supply or production of goods or services. Individuals prosecuted for a cartel may be liable to imprisonment for up to five years and/or the imposition of unlimited fines.

Fact file

Price-fixing cartel

In April 2011, the European Commission imposed penalties on Unilever (maker of detergent products such as Omo and Surf) and Proctor and Gamble (P&G, which owns Tide and the rights to the Persil brand in Britain), after finding that they had colluded over prices for more than three years. EU competition policy views cartels as anti-competitive activity. It believes that cartels enable businesses to extract higher prices from consumers than if companies compete fairly and on their own merits.

According to the Commission, the price-fixing cartel began in January 2002, when P&G and Unilever, together with the Germany company, Henkel, held talks over plans to implement an industry-wide programme to improve the environmental performance of detergents. The three companies agreed to reduce the amount of packaging they used

but, in order to maintain their market positions, they colluded to keep prices unchanged, and later to collectively raise prices. The arrangement lasted until March 2005 and involved products sold in Belgium, France, Germany, Greece, Italy, Portugal, Spain and the Netherlands.

Following the judgment, Unilever said that it had retrained managers across Europe so that they better understood European competition rules. P&G said it had strengthened its global compliance programme.

The fines amounted to €211.2m for P&G and €104m for Unilever. Both fines were reduced because the companies co-operated with the investigation and agreed to settle. The reductions were part of the Commission's attempt to speed up its investigations and to reduce the costs of investigation.

Source: adapted from information on europa.eu, the European Commission website

Key UK legislation in this area includes the following:

- **Fair Trading Act, 1973**: This set up the Office of Fair Trading (OFT), which had three main duties:
  - to consider whether takeover bids should be investigated by the Competition Commission on the grounds of being against the public interest
  - to investigate suspected anti-competitive practices, such as market-sharing agreements where firms agree not to compete with each other in areas of the market
  - to investigate existing monopolies.
- The OFT was merged with the Competition Commission to form the Competition and Markets Authority (CMA) in 2014.
- **Competition Act, 1998**: This legislation reformed and strengthened UK competition law by prohibiting anti-competitive behaviour and raising substantially the fines that could be imposed on offending companies. It brought UK competition law into line with European Union law. Responsibility for applying and enforcing the Act rested with the OFT until 2014, when the Competition and Markets Authority (CMA) was formed. Key features of the Act include:
  - prohibiting anti-competitive agreements such as cartels
  - prohibiting the abuse of a dominant market position (e.g. abuse by limiting production, by refusing supply, by restricting new technical development or by full-line forcing, that is, forcing retailers to take the whole of a product range rather than a single item)
  - allowing fines of up to 10 per cent of UK turnover.
- **The Competition Commission**: This government-funded organisation oversaw and enforced laws that attempted to eliminate anti-competitive business practices in the UK.
  The Competition Commission was merged with the OFT to form the Competition and Markets Authority (CMA) in 2014.
- **Enterprise Act, 2002**: The main provisions of this Act are:
  - more transparent and accountable decision making by competition authorities
  - criminal sanctions to deter cartels
  - greater opportunities for victims of anti-competitive behaviour to gain redress
  - strengthening consumer protection measures.
- **Competition and Markets Authority (CMA)**: This was formed on 1 April 2014 following the merger of the Office of Fair Trading and the Competition Commission. Its intention is to ensure more robust enforcement of the competition rules, with higher fines and more criminal prosecutions in appropriate cases.
- **The Financial Conduct Authority (FCA)**: From 1 April 2015, this organisation has similar powers to the CMA, but in relation to competition in the financial services sector.

Fact file

Payday lenders

The CMA has undertaken a lengthy investigation into payday lenders and found that the lack of competition between lenders was leading to higher costs for customers. As a result of the investigation, the CMA announced in February 2015 that payday lenders must make it easier for customers to compare the cost of credit by being required to publish clear and comparable information on the potential cost of their products. This will be listed on a regulated price comparison website. The measures to be introduced will make it easier for customers to shop around for loans and encourage lenders to compete on price, rather than on factors such as how quickly they could make funds available. They would also ensure that caps on the amount lenders can charge for a loan do not become the standard price for all loans.

Note: Payday lenders offer payday loans. These are loans for relatively small amounts of money (usually less than £1,000), taken out for short periods of time (often for less than a week, but up to about five months). Interest rates are high if the repayment date is missed and charges mount up rapidly. They are typically advertised as a means of funding unexpected purchases that arise a few days before the end of the month when people are more likely to be strapped for cash and waiting for payday.

Source: adapted from information on www.gov.uk/cma

Fact file

Reference pricing

In 2012, the OFT opened an investigation into whether a number of retailers within the furniture/carpet sector (with brands including Carpetright, DFS, Dreams, Furniture Village, Harveys, Bensons for Beds and ScS), were engaging in the use of misleading reference pricing.

Reference pricing refers to offers which aim to demonstrate to consumers that they provide good value by including a reference to another, typically higher past or future price. An example of reference pricing might be, 'Was £900, now less than half price at £400'.

The OFT took the view that misleading reference pricing was likely to deceive the average consumer, influence consumers' buying decisions and put other businesses at a competitive disadvantage. They said that consumers should be able to trust that the price comparisons made by businesses are fair and meaningful and that advertised 'savings' are genuine.

The OFT's view was that a genuine reference price was the price at which a retailer expected to, and usually did, sell a significant number of its products.

Following its monitoring of the retailers' pricing practices, the OFT considered that the reference prices used, displayed and advertised for some products were not genuine. Following the published outcomes of the investigation in March 2014, the retailers confirmed a commitment to the use of genuine reference prices and, without any admission of liability, made changes to their reference pricing practices. On the basis of their commitments, the OFT closed its investigations, although the CMA (which took over from the OFT in April 2014), will monitor pricing practices within the sector to check whether retailers are complying with their legal obligations.

Source: adapted from information on www.gov.uk/cma-cases/furniture-and-carpet-businesses-misleading-reference-pricing

The scope and effects of UK and EU law related to the labour market

UK and EU law related to the labour market, otherwise known as employment legislation, aims to ensure that employees and employers act fairly in dealing with each other by defining their rights and obligations.

What do you think?

Despite the existence of the Equality Act 2010 and previous anti-discrimination legislation going back to the 1960s, the difficulty of obtaining legal proof of discrimination means that discrimination still persists.

In relation to this issue and/or other issues of social responsibility, to what extent do you think the passing of laws can provide a substitute for ethical behaviour?

Equality Act 2010

The Equality Act 2010 simplified the law on discrimination by bringing together existing separate anti-discrimination legislation into a single act. It replaced the Equal Pay Act 1970, Sex Discrimination Act 1975, Race Relations Act 1976, Disability Discrimination Act 1995, Employment Equality (Religion or Belief) Regulations 2003, Employment Equality (Sexual Orientation) Regulations 2003 and the Employment Equality (Age) Regulations 2006. It mirrors the intentions of a number of EU Equality Directives.

The Act simplified, strengthened and harmonised previous legislation and provides Britain with a discrimination law that is intended to protect individuals from unfair treatment, promote a fair and more equal society and advance equality of opportunity for all. The Act requires equal treatment in access to employment as well as private and public services, and makes it unlawful to discriminate against someone with a 'protected characteristic'. The 'protected characteristics' identified by the Act are: age, disability, gender reassignment, marriage and civil partnership, race, religion or belief, sex, and sexual orientation.

Details of some of the legislation replaced by the Equality Act 2010, key features of which are now subsumed within that Act, are given below:

- **Race Relations Acts, 1976**: The Act made it unlawful to discriminate in the workplace against any person on grounds of skin colour, race, ethnic or national origin. Specifically, the Act made it unlawful to refuse employment, training or promotion on these grounds, or to select someone for dismissal on grounds of race. The Commission for Racial Equality was given the responsibility to ensure the effective implementation of the Act. Its key duties were to work towards the elimination of discrimination and to promote equality of opportunity.
- **Equal Pay Act, 1970**: The Act required employers to provide equal pay and conditions for those doing the same jobs, or work of equivalent difficulty.
- **Sex Discrimination Act, 1975**: The Act forbade discrimination in the workplace against either sex in relation to recruitment, terms and conditions, and access to training or promotion. It also set up the Equal Opportunities Commission to promote the ideas and practices required to eliminate sex discrimination in education, advertising and employment.
- **Disability Discrimination Act, 1995**: The Act forbade employers from treating those employees with disabilities less favourably than others. It

▲ It is illegal to discriminate against anyone on the basis of skin colour, race, ethnic or national origin, age, sex or disability

required employers to make reasonable adjustments in order to provide working conditions and an environment that helped to overcome the practical difficulties of disability.

● **The Employment Equality (Age) Regulations 2006**: The Regulations made it unlawful for an employer to discriminate against someone on the grounds of age.

▲ The Equality Act 2010 aims to end discrimination at work

Did you know?

By 2014, the average full-time pay gap between men and women was at its narrowest since comparative records began in 1997. According to the Office of National Statistics (ONS), the difference, based on median hourly earnings excluding overtime, was 9.4 per cent in April 2014 (a gap of about £100 a week) compared to a gap of 17.4 per cent in 1997.

Equality and Human Rights Commission

Prior to October 2007, there were three separate equality commissions: the Commission for Racial Equality, the Disability Rights Commission and the Equal Opportunities Commission. On 1 October 2007, these three equality commissions merged into a new Equality and Human Rights Commission. Its mandate is to challenge discrimination and to protect and promote human rights.

Fact file

Asda and the Equal Pay Directive

The European Union's Equal Pay Directive of 1975 established the principle of equal pay being given for work of equal value rather than simply for the same work. In 2014, an equal pay claim was brought against the supermarket Asda. Hundreds of female Asda shop workers claimed that they did work of equal value to staff in Asda's male-dominated and higher-paid distribution centres.

If the workers win, they could be entitled to six years' back pay for the difference in earnings. Asda and other supermarkets and retailers may therefore have to pay millions of pounds in higher wages and back pay to store staff, mainly women, if these test cases for equal pay are successful.

Individual cases against Asda were registered in different regions by individual staff, but their cases have been ordered to be consolidated into one case. At the time of writing, this claim had not been decided.

Most cases of job evaluation to establish whether jobs are of equal value have so far affected local councils. Birmingham, for example, has had to pay over a billion pounds in back-pay settlements to women – including cleaners, cooks, care workers and school lunch supervisors – who were denied bonuses and attendance allowances given to male road cleaners and refuse collectors.

Fact file

Etam and the Equality Act

Most cases of sex discrimination in the workplace concern discrimination against women. However, cases of discrimination against men do occur, as the following example illustrates.

There are times when it is a genuine occupational requirement that an employee be female. Such an occupational requirement would apply under the

Equality Act 2010 where, looking at the nature of the work, the employer shows that being of a particular sex is an occupational requirement, and the application of that requirement is an appropriate way of achieving a legitimate aim. However, this was not proven in the case of *Etam plc v Rowan*. In this case, it was found that the employer, Etam, had failed to show that a job as a sales assistant in a women's clothing store had to be done by a woman. It was judged that the store could have organised the work so that a man did not have to undertake duties in the fitting room.

In addition to the right not to be discriminated against in relation to the protected characteristics identified in the Equality Act 2010, UK and EU laws give employees other rights in relation to their employment. These include: how they are disciplined, dismissed or made redundant, how their grievances are handled, minimum wages, absences from work for sickness and holidays, maximum working hours, maternity and paternity leave, and the right to apply for flexible working. Employees who feel they have been denied their rights can take their case to an Employment Tribunal. About 200,000 claims are made each year in Employment Tribunals.

Other important examples of UK employment legislation include:

- **Employment Relations Act, 2004**: The Act identified employee rights in relation to trade union membership and claims for unfair dismissal, for example requiring an employer to recognise a union if 50 per cent or more of the workforce are members.
- **Employment Act, 2008**: The Act brought together, strengthened, simplified and clarified key aspects of UK employment law relating to dispute resolution in the workplace, the enforcement of the national minimum wage and trade union membership. In particular, it brought together key elements of UK government employment relations policy – that of increasing protection for vulnerable workers and of lightening the load for law-abiding businesses.

When the Conservative and Liberal Democrat coalition government came to power in 2010, it introduced an Employment Law Review. The overall aim of the review is to reduce the regulatory burden on business and introduce greater flexibility to the labour market. The review is due to complete its work during 2015. At the time of writing, a range of changes to employment law had been introduced. These include:

- **Children and Families Act**, which introduced shared parental leave and shared parental pay, and extended the right to request flexible working for all employees.
- **The Small Business, Enterprise and Employment Bill** (introduced in June 2014 and due to become law in 2015), which covers a wide range of issues, including clauses on:
  - zero hours contracts – aiming to provide better protection for employees on zero hours contracts by banning exclusivity clauses (see the Did you know? box on the left)
  - national minimum wages – higher penalties will apply to employers who fail to pay the national minimum wage
  - employment tribunals – penalties for employers who fail to pay tribunal awards and limits on tribunal postponement
  - apprentices – steps to increase the number of apprentices and to change the funding arrangements
  - whistleblowing – introducing annual reporting on whistleblowing disclosures (see the Did you know box? on the left).

EU labour law complements initiatives taken by individual EU countries by setting minimum standards. It does this by adopting laws (known as EU directives) that set minimum requirements for working and employment conditions and for informing and consulting workers. (Chapter 24 of Book 1 provided further detail on the EU recommended consultation processes.) Individual EU countries are free to provide higher levels of protection if they wish. For example, while the European Working Time Directive

Whenever a dispute before a national court raises a question of how to interpret an EU directive, the court can refer the issue to the European Court of Justice. The European Court then gives the national court the answers it needs to resolve the dispute.

The European Commission checks that EU directives are incorporated into national law and ensures through systematic monitoring that the rules are correctly implemented. When the Commission considers that an EU country has not incorporated a directive into national law correctly, it can take action against that country. In this way, it ensures that all the rights set out in the directives are available in national law. (The Commission cannot take action on behalf of individual citizens – that is up to the relevant national authorities.)

entitles workers to 20 days' annual paid leave, many countries have opted for a more generous provision for employees.

The scope and effects of UK and EU law related to the environment

'The environment' is generally considered to involve issues to do with air, water and land. The main regulatory bodies charged with responsibility for protection of the environment are the Environment Agency and local authorities. Environmental laws cover a huge range of issues, from those that are local, such as noise control, to those that are global issues, such as climate change control.

Since the UK joined the European Community in 1972, European environmental legislation, in the form of EU directives, has increasingly shaped domestic environmental laws. (See Chapter 3 in Book 1 for a discussion of the Waste Electrical and Electronic Equipment Directive [WEEE].)

The European Union has some of the highest environmental standards in the world. Its main priorities include: combating climate change, preserving biodiversity, reducing health problems from pollution and using natural resources sustainably.

UK legislation related to environmental protection includes:

- **Environmental Protection Act, 1990**: This Act was introduced to prevent pollution from emissions.
- **Environment Act, 1995**: This Act set up the Environment Agency and the National Park authorities. It also required the secretary of state to prepare a national air quality strategy and a national waste strategy, and to improve the protection of hedgerows.
- **The Waste and Emissions Trading Act, 2003**: This Act makes provision about waste and penalties for non-compliance with schemes for the trading of emissions quotas.
- **Climate Change Act, 2008**: Two key aims underpin this Act: to improve carbon management and help the transition towards a low-carbon economy in the UK; and to demonstrate strong UK leadership internationally, signalling that the UK is committed to taking its share of responsibility for reducing global emissions. A key provision is the introduction of legally binding targets for greenhouse gas and carbon dioxide emissions.
- **Energy Act 2013**: Makes provision for reforming the electricity market, encouraging low-carbon electricity generation and ensuring security of supply and storage.

Examples of the impact of changes in the legal environment on business and on strategic and functional decision making

1. Laws relating to competition

By improving the competitiveness of markets and reducing the opportunities for firms to engage in anti-competitive behaviour, legislation in this area is likely to make it easier for firms, including small firms, to compete on a level playing field. The implications of not complying with competition law are varied and include reputational damage and its consequences for sales and profits, and actual financial penalties and criminal convictions. As a result, such legislation is likely to influence a firm's decisions about the prices to charge customers, about the quality standards its products need to reach, about its relationships with its suppliers, customers and competitors, and whether to expand by merging with or acquiring other firms. There will be greater incentives for firms to seek competitive advantage through 'fair' rather than 'unfair competition'. This will influence both strategic decision making about the type of markets a firm should compete in and what its long-term corporate objectives and strategies are likely to be. It will also influence functional decision making, in particular in relation to its marketing, operations and finance activities.

2. Laws relating to the labour market

- Although employers incur additional costs in complying with legislation, they also benefit from the implementation of such legislation. A more regulated working environment where rights and responsibilities are understood and respected contributes in part to improved employer/employee relations and employee motivation. This may be reflected in increased productivity and in fewer working days lost to strike action and poor industrial relations. Equality legislation contributes to ensuring the 'best' candidates are recruited for jobs, which in turn improves efficiency and productivity. Laws relating to the labour market allow business to take strategic and functional decisions in a working environment that provides a clear framework of rights and obligations. For example, by ensuring that all relevant employment legislation is implemented, a business is more likely to be able to protect the health and well-being of its employees and retain its workforce over time. If expansion is being considered, a business that has a well-motivated workforce and a good reputation as an employer is more likely to be able to attract and recruit new employees of the right calibre. Equally such a business can confidently make difficult decisions related to dismissal or redundancy. (Chapter 22 in Book 1 discussed some of these issues in more detail.)

3. Laws relating to the environment

There is little doubt that to implement the requirements of environmental legislation, business costs are likely to increase. However, ensuring that strategic and functional decision making leads to sound environmental management of its processes and products is likely to help promote a company's products and services and improve its corporate standing. Environmental laws that are enforceable against a relatively small industry sector, for example, waste management, may have a direct impact on other sectors. For example, the ban on ozone-depleting CFCs (chlorofluorocarbons) will have had significant impact on functional decisions about operations and marketing and will have led to major changes to the design of products like fridges and aerosols.

Fact file

Consumer protection and health and safety legislation

Two other important areas of legislation not covered in the AQA specification are consumer protection and health and safety legislation.

Consumer protection legislation aims to safeguard consumers from exploitation or exposure to unsafe products or services. Legislation in this area can:

- increase costs of production: complying with the legislation may raise costs, which may affect price and profit margins. However, these should be balanced against the possible fines that might be incurred if an expensive legal case were successfully brought against a firm that was not complying with legislation.
- improve quality: complying with the legislation may improve the quality of a product or service, which in turn may enhance a firm's reputation and strengthen consumer loyalty.

- reduce waste: improved quality may lead to potential savings in relation to rejects and returns.
- reduce/improve UK competitiveness: higher costs of compliance need to be set against higher quality of products and services.

The aim of health and safety legislation is to provide a safe working environment for employees. Legislation in this area can:

- increase costs: for example, the introduction of safety measures, training and the employment of safety staff will increase costs and therefore might affect profit margins and prices.
- influence a firm's reputation: for example, a lack of safety could damage sales and hence profit levels. Equally, a good safety record could have a beneficial effect on recruitment, since potential employees will want to work for a firm with a good safety record.
- influence the motivation of employees: for example, security in the work environment is recognised as one of Herzberg's hygiene factors (see Chapter 23 of Book 1).

Author advice

When considering the impact of specific areas of legislation, or legislation in general, try to weigh up the arguments: that is, evaluate. There will always be constraints and additional costs or administrative burdens imposed on business in complying with legislation, but there will also be benefits for individual firms and consumers, and for the wider business community and the economy.

Practice exercise 1
Total: 40 marks

1. Explain the general purpose of legislation from the point of view of a business. *(4 marks)*

2. Explain two advantages to a business of legislation related to competition. *(6 marks)*

3. Using an example, explain how legislation related to competition might affect strategic or functional decision making in a business. *(4 marks)*

4. Explain two advantages to a business of legislation related to the labour market. *(6 marks)*

5. Using an example, explain how legislation related to the labour market might affect strategic or functional decision making in a business. *(4 marks)*

6. Explain two advantages to a business of legislation related to the environment. *6 marks)*

7. Using an example, explain how legislation related to the environment might affect strategic or functional decision making in a business. *(4 marks)*

8. Identify and explain two disadvantages to a business of the legislation discussed in this chapter. *(6 marks)*

▶▶▶

Essay question

Total: 25 marks

It is often suggested that legislation creates a level playing field for businesses to operate in. To what extent is this true or desirable? Justify your answer. (You may choose to answer this question by reference to a specific area of legislation, such as that related to competition, the labour market, the environment or by reference to legislation in general.)

(25 marks)

The impact of UK and EU government policy

In general, governments seek to have some control over the business environment in order to achieve a range of economic and social objectives and to establish an ordered, predictable and equitable (fair) environment. The range of policies used to achieve these objectives includes the provision of goods and services (such as education, healthcare and housing) by government, economic policies to regulate the economy, legislation, the provision of unemployment benefits and state pensions and the levying of taxes and the provision of subsidies.

The use of such policies is described as government intervention. Depending on the political values of a government, it may wish to introduce more or less government intervention and leave more or less business decision making to market forces, that is, to the forces of demand and supply.

The extent to which governments intervene in the economy varies from country to country and also changes over time. For example, governments in most Eastern European countries, under their previous communist regimes, were extremely interventionist in their approach. However, as a result of political changes, these economies are now mostly driven by market forces.

Most governments in the developed world provide a range of what are considered to be essential goods and services, including education, health and housing. The politics of the government of the day will determine the degree of intervention in the economy and hence whether a more extensive range of goods and services are provided by, or controlled by, government.

For example, before 1979 in the UK, a range of vital industries, known as nationalised industries, were under government control. These included coal, steel and the railways, and hence these goods and services were provided by government. The election of a Conservative government, led by Margaret Thatcher, in 1979, had a huge impact on the economy and the business environment, and significantly changed business conditions. The changes placed a much greater emphasis on the market, with the introduction of an extensive policy of privatisation and deregulation, and legislation to reduce the power of trade unions and 'free up the labour market'. Despite the election of a Labour government, which was in

Did you know?

The term 'free market' means an economy or sector of an economy where government intervention is minimal and where the market forces of demand and supply are expected to maximise business efficiency and consumer satisfaction.

power from 1997 to 2010, there was no return to the more interventionist government policy of Labour governments prior to 1979. The coalition government of Conservatives and Liberal Democrats that was in power from 2010 to 2015 did not alter this position either.

The impact of UK and EU government policy related to enterprise

Enterprise is an important concept that is being actively promoted by the government through, for example, its support for start-up businesses and its promotion of enterprise in the school curriculum. Television programmes, such as 'The Apprentice' and 'Dragons' Den', have encouraged a much wider interest in entrepreneurial activity.

▲ Richard Branson, Sarah Willingham and Alan Sugar have shown the kind of entrepreneurial spirit that the government hopes to inspire

Key term

Enterprise Almost any business or organisation can be called an enterprise, but the term usually refers to the process by which new businesses are formed and new goods and services created and brought to the market. Enterprises are usually led by an entrepreneur (see Did you know? box on the right). Increasingly, the term 'enterprise' is used when discussing the development of skills relevant to becoming a successful entrepreneur and establishing a successful business enterprise, including the importance of risk taking (see on the right).

Did you know?

In order to promote enterprise, discussion often centres on developing enterprise skills. These are skills that allow an individual or organisation to respond effectively to changing market situations. The definition of enterprise capability used by the Department for Business, Innovation and Skills (BIS) includes innovation, creativity, risk management, risk taking and a 'can do' attitude.

Linked to the term 'enterprise' is the concept of the 'entrepreneur'. Entrepreneurs are the individuals who have an idea that they develop by setting up a new business and encouraging it to grow. They take the risk and the subsequent profit that comes with success or the loss that comes with failure. The characteristics of successful entrepreneurs include:

- determination and persistence
- passion
- the ability to spot and take advantage of opportunities
- relevant skills and expertise
- vision, creativity and innovation
- motivation to succeed and not be daunted by failure
- willingness to take risks – possibly the most important quality of an entrepreneur.

Fact file

Innocent Drinks

Richard Reed co-founded Innocent Drinks, a smoothie and fruit drinks company, with two of his friends in 1999. Despite Reed having no experience of running his own business, no financial backing and a product with a very short shelf life, Innocent became an unexpected success story.

Reed took note of the advice of a colleague who said that in setting up a business he should make sure he knew the target audience. The only target audience he and his co-founders knew well was their friends and family, and what they identified was a need for something simple and healthy to consume, to combat the long working hours and relatively unhealthy lifestyles they led. So Innocent was conceived from the idea of making it easy for people to consume something healthy.

In the summer of 1998, Richard and his co-founders developed their first smoothie recipes but were still nervous about giving up their jobs. They bought £500 worth of fruit, turned it into smoothies and sold the smoothies from a stall at a music festival in London. They put up a large sign saying 'Do you think we should give up our jobs to make these smoothies?'

Two bins were set out: one reading 'yes' and the other reading 'no', and people were asked to put all their empty bottles into one of them. At the end of the weekend, the 'yes' bin was full and they decided to resign from their jobs.

Reed suggests that anyone starting their own business needs to have a clear idea of what they are selling, along with determination and passion. They must be focused, single minded and never lose sight of what they are trying to achieve. Reed suggests that successful entrepreneurs do not wait for external factors to develop the business; they use their initiative, ensure that things keep improving, and learn from what they do. He says, 'If you're not the kind of person who'll make an idea happen, you're not an entrepreneur.'

The government believes that an environment that encourages enterprise and supports people who take opportunities and risks is crucial for improving productivity. A strong entrepreneurial base is essential for encouraging growth and prosperity in a modern economy. New and more dynamic businesses increase competitive pressures in markets, and facilitate the introduction of new ideas and technologies and more efficient working practices.

A successful enterprise culture, in the form of small and medium-sized enterprises (SMEs), boosts an economy's productivity by increasing competitive pressure. This forces existing businesses to increase their efficiency in order to stay in the market. If existing businesses are unable to match the productivity of new or rapidly growing SMEs, either they are forced to leave the market or their market share is reduced. This then increases the productivity of the market as a whole. In addition, any

Did you know?

It was a 2012 report on growth by Lord Heseltine (*'No stone unturned: in pursuit of growth'*) which set out a comprehensive plan to improve the UK's ability to create wealth. The report made the case for a major rebalancing of responsibilities for economic development between central and local government, and between government and the private sector. The report recommended making Local Enterprise Partnerships (LEPs) the principle delivery vehicle for EU funding. The government accepted the report's recommendations in relation to the devolution of government spending to local areas and this led to the creation of LEPs.

Did you know?

Small firms are generally defined as businesses with fewer than 500 employees. In 2015, 95 per cent of businesses in the UK employed fewer than ten people. Firms employing fewer than ten people are known as microbusinesses. Since 2008, there are 600,000 more microbusinesses in the UK.

efficiency gains can be passed on to consumers through lower prices and greater choice.

The Department for Business, Innovation and Skills is responsible for promoting economic growth in the UK and for encouraging people to start and grow businesses. On 31 March 2012, Regional Development Agencies, which provided support and funding for businesses, were abolished. In their place, the government encouraged the setting up of Local Enterprise Partnerships (LEPs) between local authorities and businesses. There are 39 LEPs in England. They help determine local economic priorities and encourage economic growth and job creation in their area. LEPs can apply to become Enterprise Zones, which enable businesses in these zones to take advantage of a range of opportunities, including tax incentives and simplified planning regulations.

Lord Young, the Enterprise Adviser to Prime Minister David Cameron has published two recent reports on enterprise in the UK:

1. **Enterprise for All, 2014**: This report considers how education can foster an enterprising attitude, including the desire to become an entrepreneur, encouraging more people to enter self-employment or to start their own company. The report suggests that enterprise is about a can-do and positive attitude and about equipping people with the confidence to develop a career and vocational interests. Enterprise therefore supports the development of a wide range of work and professional skills and capabilities, including resilience, risk taking, creativity and innovation, as well as a self-belief that starting a business is a viable career choice

2. **Report on Small Firms 2010–15**: This report notes a record number of small firms in the UK in 2015 – 5.2 million, an increase of 760,000 since 2010. These small firms account for 48 per cent of employment and 33 per cent of private sector turnover. The report suggests that the main factor encouraging enterprise and growth in the number of small firms is the mass adoption of technology. It explains that technology has lowered the barriers of entry for people of all backgrounds and ages to make a business idea happen and to use mobile and digital devices to find customers, make sales and fund new ventures. At the same time, it notes that there has been a complete change in attitudes to entrepreneurship and small businesses and increased government support for small firms. Support includes:

   a) a new British Business Bank, which aims to increase the supply of finance to small businesses (but does not provide that finance directly)

   b) Start Up Loans, which provide advice, business loans and mentoring to start up businesses

   c) Growth Vouchers, which provide financial support for existing firms seeking strategic business advice

   d) a single procurement market place through Contracts Finder, which lets businesses search for information about government-related contracts worth over £10,000

   e) Employment Allowances, which give businesses and charities reductions on their National Insurance Contributions

   f) business rates support, which provides extra relief for small businesses

g) Apprenticeship Grants for Employers, 80 per cent of which have gone to employers with fewer than 25 employees – helping them to train their future workforce

h) reductions in the costs of domestic regulation

i) schemes for small businesses to manage their tax affairs more easily and cheaply.

What do you think?

The government believes that equipping young people with vital skills is a way of securing the future economic success of the UK. This is not just about developing the next generation of entrepreneurs, but about encouraging young people to develop valuable enterprise-related skills for their futures. Many schools offer a range of opportunities for students to develop their enterprise capability. These include Young Enterprise business projects, Tycoon Tenner activities, as well as a range of local business-related and start-up activities and opportunities.

How valuable has the enterprise education you have received been in developing your entrepreneurial skills?

The impact of UK and EU government policy related to the role of regulators

As mentioned earlier in this chapter, competition law in the UK is enforced by the Competition and Markets Authority (CMA). However, for a number of industries enforcement is carried out by industry or sectoral regulators. These sectors include: communication and postal services (Ofcom – regulator for the UK communications industries); gas and electricity (Ofgem – Office of the Gas and Electricity Markets); railways (ORR – Office of Rail Regulation); air traffic and airport operation services (CAA – Civil Aviation Authority); water and sewage (Ofwat – the Water Services Regulation Authority).

Regulators are appointed by the government. The role of regulators for industries where a few large firms dominate the market (such as those for gas and electricity and for water and sewage) usually involves:

- monitoring and regulating prices: regulators aim to ensure that companies do not exploit their monopoly power by charging excessive prices. In the past, the EU Competition Commission (an EU regulator) made a ruling on the 'roaming' charges of mobile phone operators in the EU and enforced a maximum price on such charges.
- maintaining high standards of customer service: companies that fail to meet specified service standards can be fined or have their franchise/license taken away. Regulators may also require that unprofitable services are maintained because of wider public interest. Examples include: BT keeping telephone booths open in both rural areas and inner cities; the Royal Mail being required by law to provide a delivery service at least once a day to all postal addresses in the UK.
- opening up markets to competitive forces: regulators are required to encourage competition by removing barriers to entry to their sectors.

An example of a regulator is Ofgem (Office of the Gas and Electricity Markets). Ofgem is the official regulating body for both the gas and electricity industries. Its primary objective is to protect consumers of gas and electricity services by: maintaining healthy competition between providers to ensure a choice of competitive prices are available; securing gas and electricity supplies for providers; preventing industry monopolies from occurring; regulating social and environmental outputs of gas and electricity products.

The Enterprise and Regulatory Reform Act 2013 placed a stronger obligation on sector regulators to use their competition powers where appropriate. The UK Competition Network has been established to improve co-ordination between the Competition and Markets Authority (CMA) and sector regulators.

Did you know?

Regulators exist in many sectors, not just those mentioned above. The following list includes examples of other regulators:

- Advertising Standards Authority (ASA)
- Care Quality Commission (CQC)
- Charity Commission for England and Wales
- Environment Agency (EA)
- Financial Conduct Authority (FCA)
- Food Standards Agency
- General Dental Council (GDC)
- General Medical Council (GMC)
- Health and Safety Executive
- Independent Press Standards Organisation (IPSO)
- Ofqual (Office of Qualifications and Examinations Regulation)
- Ofsted (Office for Standards in Education, Children's Services and Skills)
- Police Complaints Authority.

In addition, local authorities provide regulatory functions in a number of areas, and professional associations, such as The Law Society, act to regulate their members. The UK is also bound by a number of European regulators, such as the European Union Competition Commission.

Fact file

'Big six' energy firms face competition inquiry

In 2014, an Ofgem report criticised the effectiveness of competition in the electricity and gas industry. It suggested 'possible tacit co-ordination' on the size and timing of price rises among the 'big six' UK energy suppliers, but did not accuse them of colluding over prices. (The 'big six' UK energy suppliers are SSE, Scottish Power, Centrica, RWE Npower, E.On and EDF Energy. Together they account for about 95 per cent of the UK's energy supply market.) The report noted low levels of switching by consumers and the fact that the market shares of the big six suppliers had not changed significantly over time. It also said that profit increases and price rises had intensified public distrust in suppliers.

The report called for further investigation by the Competition and Markets Authority (CMA) 'to clear the air' and 'to consider once and for all whether there are further barriers to effective competition'. Some commentators suggested that the report indicated that Ofgem itself has not done enough to regulate the market it was responsible for.

The impact of UK and EU government policy related to infrastructure

Infrastructure spending can have a positive effect on economic growth by increasing productivity and attracting investment, as well as by providing short-term boosts to employment in construction and related industries. Evidence also suggests that failure to invest in the maintenance of infrastructure can have a significant negative impact on economic growth.

Some economic commentators suggest that UK infrastructure has suffered from historic underinvestment and has failed to keep up with demand. The UK was ranked 27th in the world in terms of overall quality of infrastructure in 2013, behind France (10th), Germany (11th) and the USA (16th).

Although the development and operation of infrastructure in the UK is largely the responsibility of the private sector, the government plays a role in infrastructure policy in the following ways:

● providing funding
● directing investment and support towards certain projects that the government considers valuable for the UK
● ensuring the development of coherent infrastructure systems that require strategic leadership and decisions.

In 2014, data indicated that 64 per cent of planned infrastructure investment was funded by the private sector, 23 per cent was publicly funded, and the rest was funded by a mixture of private and public investment. The Treasury estimates that total infrastructure investment is £47 billion per year. The government argues that a higher level of investment is needed if the UK is to have the infrastructure it needs. Measures the government has taken to increase infrastructure investment include:

● The UK Guarantee Scheme – which provides financial guarantees from the government for planned infrastructure projects while private sector investors are sought. Under this scheme, government expenditure is only necessary if private sector investment cannot be found.
● The Pensions Infrastructure Platform – which helps UK pension funds invest more in UK infrastructure assets. Traditionally, UK pension funds have invested little in UK infrastructure – only about 1 per cent of their total assets, which is low compared to overseas pension funds. (In Australia and Canada, an estimated 8–15 per cent of pension fund assets are invested in infrastructure.)
● Infrastructure UK – which is an organisation that advises the government on long-term infrastructure planning to facilitate private sector investment and provide commercial expertise.
● EU funding is another source of finance for UK infrastructure projects.

The government sets out its infrastructure priorities and approach in its annual National Infrastructure Plans. The three key criteria guiding the government in deciding which projects to invest in or support are:

● Projects must have high potential contribution to economic growth, with particular emphasis on increasing productivity and enabling innovation.
● Investments must deliver, enhance or replace infrastructure of national importance.
● Projects must attract significant private sector investment.

Fact file

HS2 – the high speed train – different perspectives on a current infrastructure project

The first phase of HS2 will be between London and Birmingham. Work is due to begin in 2017, with the line due to open in 2026. This will be followed by a V-shaped section from Birmingham to Manchester and to Leeds. Eventually further developments will be planned between towns in the north and to Scotland.

The expected impact of HS2 on journey times from London is as follows:

▼ **Table 4.1**

	Now	HS2	Saving
Birmingham	1 hr 21 mins	49 mins	32 mins
Nottingham	1 hr 44 mins	1 hr 08 mins	36 mins
Sheffield	2 hr 05 mins	1 hr 19 mins	46 mins
Leeds	2 hr 12 mins	1 hr 23 mins	49 mins
Manchester	2 hr 08 mins	1 hr 08 mins	60 mins

The government's view of HS2 is that it will have a 'transformational effect', rebalancing the economy, helping to secure future prosperity for the UK and providing high value for money to the taxpayer. The UK must have the proper infrastructure in place to compete. At the moment, people can travel by high-speed train from London to Paris or Brussels, but not to Manchester or Leeds. For the Midlands and the North to compete effectively with London requires better infrastructure to be in place; HS2 will contribute to this.

MPs on the Public Accounts Committee of the House of Commons are sceptical about whether the HS2 rail line will deliver value for money and whether it will be completed on time and on budget. Its expected cost is currently £50 billion. The Committee suggests this figure includes a 'generous contingency', which gives the government a good chance of delivering within budget, but could be used to mask cost increases rather than valid calls on the contingency fund element of the costing.

The high-speed line will cut a 45-mile track through rural Staffordshire as part of the western leg connecting Birmingham to Manchester. The government was originally going to confirm the final route of the Birmingham to Manchester and to Leeds leg by the end of 2014. That decision was then delayed until after the General Election on 7 May 2015. This left residents living along the proposed route through Staffordshire, including long-established farming and other businesses, facing months of waiting to find out how seriously their homes and businesses would be affected by the line.

▲ Not everyone supports HS2

Source: adapted from a range of articles and news items, including www.bbc.com, 16 January 2015 and the *Express* and *Star*, 3 January 2015

Author advice

The AQA specification indicates that an understanding of **the impact of UK and EU government policy related to the environment** is required. This has been discussed in the previous section of this chapter on the legal environment and also in Chapter 3 of Book 1.

The impact of UK and EU government policy related to international trade

International trade is vital for the UK's prosperity. Through its international trade policy, the government aims to help UK businesses succeed internationally and encourage overseas companies to work with the UK. International trade is measured and recorded in the balance of payments. The following Fact file provides an explanation of this account and the current position of the UK in relation to international trade.

Fact file

The balance of payments

The balance of payments is a record of transactions between one country and the rest of the world. It records exports and imports as well as transfers of income and assets.

An important part of the balance of payments is the current account, which includes:

- trade in goods (also known as the balance of trade or the visible balance), which records exports of goods minus imports of goods
- trade in services (or the invisible balance), which records exports of services minus imports of services
- the balance of income going to and coming from abroad, such as interest, profits and dividends, together with transfers such as UK government payments to the EU or gifts.

The current balance is the total of the current account. The UK usually has a deficit on its trade in goods (we import more goods in value terms than we export) and a surplus on its trade in services (we export more services in value terms, particularly financial services, than we import). However, the surplus in UK trade in services does not cancel out the deficit in UK trade in goods and the balance of income going to and coming from abroad tends to be a deficit. In 2013, the current account showed an overall deficit made up of the following figures:

Trade in goods	- 110,196 million
Trade in services	+ 78,096 million
Total trade in goods and services	- 32,100 million
Income going to/coming from abroad	- 40,296 million
Current account	- £72,396 million

Currently, the most important government policy in relation to international trade is the UK's membership of the European Union (EU).

The EU is in effect a single market that involves:

- common technical standards for EU products
- harmonised VAT and excise duties, so that there are no tax advantages resulting from locating in a particular EU country
- a free trade area with no trade barriers between member states and a customs union in the form of a common external tariff barrier (i.e. taxes on imports) levied on goods and services from non-member countries
- the free movement of people – EU citizens are allowed to travel, reside, study and work wherever they wish in the European Union
- the free movement of capital, making it possible to invest money anywhere in the EU.

Fact file

The European Union

At the time of writing (March 2015), 28 countries are members of the European Union (EU). Figure 4.1 shows the 28 members of the enlarged EU.

▲ **Figure 4.1** The 28 members of the European Union

Membership of the EU offers the following benefits to UK businesses:

- Access to a market of 500 million people, which is bigger than Japan and the USA put together.
- The large market provides opportunities for economies of scale, lower costs and increased specialisation.
- More competition may lead to improved efficiency and therefore lower costs.
- More intense competition can encourage innovation.
- Opportunities for more European mergers and joint ventures, resulting in synergy and improved efficiency.
- Encouragement for inward investment from non-EU countries, which increases employment, income and opportunities for supplier industries. The UK has been a major recipient of inward investment, with firms like Toyota in Derby and Nissan in Sunderland establishing themselves within the external tariff wall.
- Greater mobility of labour, giving firms a wider labour force to draw on.
- With firms more able to invest anywhere in the EU, there is greater mobility of capital.
- The free movement of factors of production makes it possible for existing EU and UK businesses to move to new EU countries where costs are often substantially lower.

Membership of the EU presents the following difficulties for UK firms:

- An increase in legislation and the need to meet common technical standards.
- Increased competition both in Europe and in the domestic market.
- Labour and capital may be attracted to other European countries.
- Low wage rates in Eastern European member countries make these member states fierce competitors for jobs, and they may attract inward investment that might previously have come to the UK.

Membership of the EU significantly increases Britain's trade with other member states. Britain is home to a larger stock of EU and US foreign direct investments (FDI) than any other EU economy and is the preferred location for investments from other leading markets.

Current debate is about whether Britain should leave the EU. If this were the case, some of the FDI would be threatened and British firms would lose access to the EU's single market. On the other hand, some argue that membership of the EU's customs union deters trade between the UK and non-EU countries. Similarly, some argue that membership of the customs union can divert trade from lower cost non-EU countries to higher cost EU countries. Britain's trade with countries outside the EU is growing, particularly with emerging (developing) economies.

In 2013, the UK's export of goods and services totalled £511 billion and imports totalled £543 billion. The EU accounted for 45 per cent of exports of goods and services in 2013 and 52 per cent of imports. Table 4.2 indicates the UK's major trading partners. The USA is the UK's most important export partner, followed by Germany, the Netherlands, France and Ireland. Germany is the UK's major import partner, followed by the USA, the Netherlands, France and China.

▼ **Table 4.2** UK's largest trading partners, 2013

Exports			Imports		
	£bn	% of total		£bn	% of total
USA	90.1	17.6	Germany	66.6	12.3
Germany	42.7	8.3	USA	48.7	9.0
Netherlands	35.6	7.0	Netherlands	41.4	7.6
France	32.2	6.3	France	36.6	6.7
Ireland	26.7	5.2	China	35.3	6.5
EU	228.0	44.5	EU	284.0	52.2
Non-EU	284.0	55.5	Non-EU	260.0	47.8
World total	511.0	100.0	World total	543.0	100.0

Source: Office of National Statistics, Pink Book, Table 9.3, 2014

Examples of the impact of changes in the political environment on business and on strategic and functional decision making

1. **Government policy relating to enterprise**: A more encouraging approach to enterprise enables more new businesses to set up and trade and ensures that existing businesses receive more support. Knowing that government policy favours enterprise encourages businesses to take strategic decisions that involve more risk taking and more innovative approaches.

2. **Government policy relating to regulators**: Industry or sector regulators ensure that strategic decisions taken by businesses in the relevant area are in the public interest and in the interests of fair competition. This in turn will mean that tactical decisions about, for example, pricing or relationships with suppliers, do not exploit a particular business's dominant position in a market. The more effective regulators are, the more likely they are to influence this type of decision making.

3. **Government policy relating to infrastructure**: Improved infrastructure will allow business to benefit in terms of faster and more efficient transport and communication links. This in turn will have an impact on costs and prices charged. Strategic decisions about location, for example, will be influenced by the quality of infrastructure provided and whether government policy is supporting the continuing improvement to this. In turn, tactical decisions about access to manpower and materials will be affected.

4. **Government policy relating to the environment**: The extent to which government policy protects the environment and promotes a green and an ethical approach to business will have a significant influence on the decisions made by business. The impact could be on decisions about waste management, about the polluting effects of business activity or about which fuel or other resources to use. For many businesses, ensuring that increased costs associated with producing products in an environmentally sound manner can be covered by prices that will attract consumers is a key challenge.

5. **Government policy relating to international trade**: Government policy, for example, on whether to continue membership of the EU, will have a significant impact on strategic and tactical decision making for businesses. For example, a non-EU business that has located in the UK because of its membership of the EU is likely to review its strategic decisions about its

location and its tactical decisions about where and how it wishes to sell its products. Similarly, UK businesses that currently sell most of their products in Europe may need to review their strategic decisions about which markets to trade in and tactical decisions relating to the pricing of goods if tariffs were to be imposed on sales in Europe.

Practice exercise 2

Total: 75 marks

1. Define the term 'enterprise'. (3 marks)
2. What is an entrepreneur? (3 marks)
3. Identify four characteristics of successful entrepreneurs. (4 marks)
4. Explain why the ability to take risks is important in developing a successful business. (4 marks)
5. Why are an enterprising culture and people with entrepreneurial skills important for the UK economy? (6 marks)
6. Explain three ways in which government policy supports enterprise and entrepreneurs. (9 marks)
7. Identify three industries in which regulators operate. (3 marks)
8. Explain three ways in which regulators intervene. (9 marks)
9. What does the term 'infrastructure' mean? (3 marks)
10. Why is a modern and effective infrastructure important for UK business and for the UK economy? (6 marks)
11. Explain three ways in which government policy tries to encourage improved infrastructure in the UK. (9 marks)
12. Explain two ways in which government policy tries to protect the environment. (6 marks)
13. How many countries make up the European Union (EU)? (1 mark)
14. Identify and explain three benefits of the EU for UK businesses. (9 marks)

Case study: Hardweave Fabrics

Hardweave Fabrics produces high-quality furnishing fabrics. Its factory is located just outside of Manchester and it has an office in London, near St Pancras, that is used as an administrative centre. The London office is used for meetings with customers because it is very convenient for those travelling to London by Eurostar. However, potential clients usually want to see the products and, although there is a small display of products in the London office, it is nothing like the extensive display available at the factory site. Approximately 75 per cent of Hardweave's products are sold in Europe, including 30 per cent being sold in the UK. The other 25 per cent is sold in America.

Questions

Total: 60 marks

1. Analyse the potential impact of HS2 for a business such as Hardweave Fabrics. (You may wish to refer back to the Fact file about HS2 on p. 92 of this chapter.) (9 marks)

2. Evaluate the value to Hardweave Fabrics of the UK's continuing membership of the EU. (16 marks)

Essay question

Total: 25 marks

Using examples of your choice, discuss the extent to which the political and legal environment influences strategic and tactical decision making in business.

(25 marks)

5

Analysing the external environment to assess opportunities and threats: economic change

The first part of this chapter considers the impact of changes in the UK and global economic environment on strategic and functional decision making. In doing so, it considers the following economic factors: GDP, taxation, exchange rates, inflation, fiscal and monetary policy, and more open trade versus protectionism. (Note: the discussion about taxation is included in the section on fiscal and monetary policy.) In explaining and considering these issues, a range of economic data is presented and questions are posed that require the interpretation of changes in economic data for the UK, the EU and globally, and the implications of such changes for business. The second part of the chapter considers the meaning of globalisation, the reasons for greater globalisation of business and the importance of globalisation for business. The chapter concludes with a discussion about the importance of emerging economies for business.

The impact of changes in the UK and global economic environment on strategic and functional decision making

Author advice

In order to provide context and background to the discussion about the UK and global economic environment, a brief explanation of macroeconomics and the circular flow is provided. This is not a specific requirement of the AQA specification, but a broad understanding of how the economy works provides a helpful background to the issues discussed in this chapter.

The study of macroeconomics is concerned with the total (or aggregate) level of spending (or demand) in the economy, the total (or aggregate) level of production (or supply) in the economy, national employment and unemployment levels, the general level of prices, and the rate of interest and the exchange rate. It is, in effect, concerned with making the most efficient use of an economy's resources.

The circular flow of income (Figure 5.1) illustrates the interrelationship between the main parts of the macroeconomy – that is, between producers (firms), consumers (households), the government and other countries.

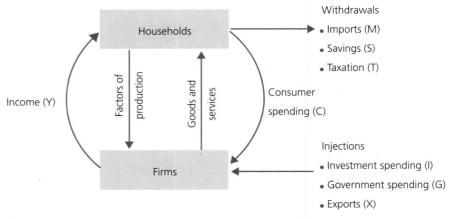

▲ **Figure 5.1** A simple circular flow of income

Firms receive revenue or consumer spending (C) in exchange for the goods and services that they provide. This revenue is used to pay incomes (Y) to workers and to other factors of production, in return for their contribution to the production of the goods and services available for sale.

The income of households (Y) is either spent on consumer goods and services that are produced by UK firms (C) or withdrawn from the circular flow. Income withdrawn from the circular flow is used to buy imported goods from abroad (M), is saved (S) or is paid to the government as taxation (T).

The revenue received by firms comes either from consumer spending (C), or from injections. Injections include investment spending by other firms (I) (e.g. when they purchase capital goods such as a digger or a lorry), government spending (G) (e.g. paying for the building of a new school or hospital) or export sales abroad (X).

Fact file

Index numbers

Many pieces of information, particularly sales records and economic data, are presented as index numbers. The use of index numbers simplifies comparisons between the different items over time. To demonstrate this, consider which of the products in Table 5.1 has experienced the fastest rate of growth in sales.

Sales of product C have declined, so it is clear that this has been the most disappointing product.

Sales of product B have increased by the greatest number, but does this mean that it has performed better than product A?

▼ **Table 5.1** Volume of product sales (units)

	Year			
	2013	2014	2015	
Product A	150	285	345	+195
Product B	600	780	990	+390
Product C	250	225	215	−35
Product D	40	70	120	+80
Product E	80	100	128	+48

Product A has more than doubled its sales in the two years, but product B has less than doubled its sales. In this respect, product A has performed better than product B if the firm's main objective is growth.

Index numbers are used to make it easier to compare numbers that would otherwise be difficult to compare. They are constructed as follows:

A base year is selected. The sales volume (or value) in this year is given an index number of 100 (a figure from which it is easy to calculate percentage changes).

Figures in later years are calculated as a percentage of the base-year figure.

The index number is calculated as follows:

$$\text{index number} = \frac{\text{actual sales volume in selected year}}{\text{actual sales volume in base year}} \times 100$$

Thus sales of product A were 150 units in 2013 and 285 units in 2014. The index number for 2014 is thus:

$$\frac{285}{150} \times 100 = 190$$

Similarly, the index number for product A in 2015 is:

$$\frac{345}{150} \times 100 = 230$$

This allows the percentage growth in sales between the base year and subsequent years to be calculated easily, as well as growth between any particular years. For product A, growth in sales between 2013 and 2014 was 90 per cent (actual growth/original figure × 100, i.e. 90/100 × 100); growth in sales between 2013 and 2015 was 130 per cent (130/100 × 100). Growth in sales between 2014 and 2015 was 21 per cent (40/190 × 100).

Completing the calculations for all of the products in years 2013, 2014 and 2015 gives the results detailed in Table 5.2.

At a glance it can be seen that product A has grown much faster than product B. It also shows that product D has had the fastest growth rate, and that the growth rate of product E is only slightly less than that of product B (although it was much less in terms of volume).

Index numbers are used where it is more important to compare percentage growth rates than the actual volume of change. They are often used to calculate and compare information on the business cycle, exchange rates and inflation rates.

▼ **Table 5.2** Index number of product sales

	Year		
	2013	2014	2015
Product A	100	190	230
Product B	100	130	165
Product C	100	90	86
Product D	100	175	300
Product E	100	125	160
Base year (2013) = 100			

Economic factors: Gross domestic product (GDP)

GDP statistics are usually presented in 'real' terms, that is they are adjusted to take account of changes in price levels. Growth in GDP is usually associated with higher standards of living. This is because increasing levels of production of goods and services allow incomes to rise, which in turn allow for higher levels of consumption.

GDP and the business cycle

The business (or trade) cycle is the regular pattern of ups and downs in demand and output within an economy, or of gross domestic product (GDP) growth over time. It is characterised by four main phases: boom, recession (or downturn), slump and recovery (or upturn) (see Figure 5.2).

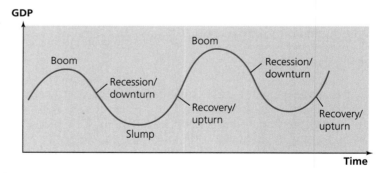

▲ **Figure 5.2** The business cycle

Some firms are more vulnerable to changes in the business cycle and GDP than others. Indeed, some are often known as cyclical businesses because demand for their products fluctuates very closely in line with the business cycle.

The extent to which a business is affected by the business cycle depends on the income elasticity of demand for its products: that is, how much demand for its products is influenced by changes in income. (Elasticity of demand was explained in Chapter 8 of the AQA A-level Business Book 1.) For example, the construction industry and firms producing machine tools and heavy capital equipment are very sensitive to changes in GDP, the demand for their products being highly income elastic. In a boom period, when incomes are high and rising, demand for consumer goods is high and this in turn generates a high demand for capital goods. Similarly, high incomes create more demand for house building. On the other hand, the demand

▲ High incomes create more demand for house building

for products that are relatively income inelastic (i.e. where demand does not change much when income levels change), such as flour, soap and paper, is unlikely to be much affected by the business cycle.

Fact file
GDP

GDP has grown considerably since the end of the Second World War. The value of goods and services produced in the economy is now approximately four times larger than in 1948 (the first year in which comparable statistics are available). This is the result of a range of factors including: population growth, which increases the amount of available labour in the economy; investment in capital, which improves labour productivity; technological improvement, which increases how much the economy can produce. The highest annual rate of growth was 7.4 per cent in 1973. Despite the considerable improvement since 1948, there have been periods when annual growth in output has fallen. The largest of these started in 2008.

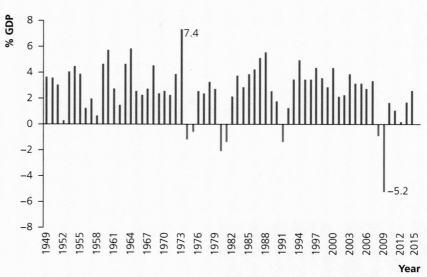

▲ **Figure 5.3** GDP, quarterly data, 1948–2012

Source: ONS

Figure 5.3 illustrates changes in GDP on a quarterly basis from 1948 to 2012. Although GDP on a quarterly basis rises and falls during a single year, GDP on an annual basis rose consistently from 1948 to 1973. Since 1973, there has been a significant fall in GDP once in each decade – in 1974/75, 1980/81, 1991, 2008/09. The 2008/09 economic downturn or recession was the most severe of the four. During this period, GDP fell overall by 7.2 per cent, compared to 4.6 per cent in the 1980s and 2.4 per cent in the 1990s.

Possible causes of the business cycle

- Changes in business confidence, which lead to changes in the level of investment in fixed assets. (Note: the term 'fixed assets' used in economic data means the same as the term 'non-current assets' used by accountants, and in the finance chapters of this book and Book 1.) If a business believes that its sales are going to increase, it will buy more fixed assets in order to produce more and, overall, this could mean a large increase in orders for the producers of fixed assets. The opposite applies if confidence is low, as businesses are likely to cancel orders to update fixed assets or to replace fixed assets that are about to wear out, and instead continue to use existing fixed assets.
- Periods of stock or inventory building and then de-stocking. Again, these depend on the confidence of a business in its ability to sell inventory.
- Irregular patterns of expenditure on consumer durables, such as cars, washing machines and televisions. These are influenced by the level of interest rates and consumer confidence in the economy, and by the need to replace old items.
- Confidence in the banking sector and its ability to make sound decisions about whom to lend money to. When banks have insufficient funds to meet the demands of their depositors, they are more likely to call in loans. This has a knock-on effect on business and consumers.

Did you know?

De-stocking is where a business attempts to reduce its holding of inventory by cutting orders of materials or by cutting production levels. This is usually undertaken by businesses at the beginning of a recession when orders begin to fall.

Phases of the business cycle

1. Boom: a period characterised by high levels of consumer demand, business confidence, profits and investment at the same time as rising costs, increasing prices and full capacity. A boom is likely to have the following effects on business:

- Consumer demand is likely to be greater than supply, creating excess demand, which is likely to lead to increases in the prices of goods.
- The shortage of resources relative to demand means that costs are likely to rise. For example, wages may have to increase in order to attract and/or keep skilled workers, which in turn may lead firms to increase their prices.
- Increased demand may result in firms utilising their production capacity to the full. Such high capacity utilisation may lead firms to consider expansion plans in order to increase output and meet demand.
- Increased demand and high prices may result in an overall increase in profits, allowing for high retained profits and dividends.

2. Recession: a period characterised by falling levels of consumer demand, output, profit and business confidence, little investment, spare capacity and rising levels of unemployment. The official definition of a recession is a fall in GDP for two consecutive quarters. A recession is likely to have the following effects on business:

- Falling demand and therefore excess stock may lead to reduced prices.
- Falling demand and reductions in output may lead to low profits or even losses being made and workers being laid off. On the other hand, firms producing inferior goods may benefit, as consumers switch from luxury items to low-priced alternatives.
- Liquidations or business closures, as a result of falling demand and losses, may result in fewer suppliers of certain products and fewer customers for other products.
- As businesses struggle with falling demand and individuals feel the effects of lower incomes, firms are likely to experience an increase in bad debts. To address this issue, firms may need to introduce tighter credit control procedures, which may lead to less trade.
- A strong balance sheet, sufficient liquidity and low gearing are important requirements for survival during a recession. High unemployment will lead to a drop in demand for some goods and a switch in demand to other (e.g. inferior) goods. This may lead firms facing falling demand to search for new markets. Indeed, one way to survive a recession for a producer of consumer goods is to diversify the product range. In this way the business is not too dependent for its profits on those products that are likely to experience wide variations in demand over the course of the business cycle.
- Low investment due to falling demand may lead to a decline in the output of firms producing capital goods.
- In order to survive during a recession, businesses need to operate as efficiently as possible. As a result, those that do survive may emerge stronger and better able to compete during the subsequent recovery stage.

▲ In a recession businesses may have to reduce their prices and may have to close

Author advice

Notice how the analysis of the effects of a recession tends to be circular. For example, falling demand leads to reductions in output, which results in redundancies and more unemployment, which leads to falling income, which leads to falling demand …

What do you think?

Read the descriptions of the businesses below – the year was 2008, a time of recession in the UK.

Nannies: The telephone at Bright Beginning Childcare Agency in York rang non-stop with calls from parents who needed nannies because they had to return to work. Profits were up and the business was growing. The daycare centre and the nanny agency saw a big increase in the number of people looking for part-time care.

Plumbers: Nick Chapman, a plumber, said: 'People are putting things on hold until they can see some light – their priority is to pay the mortgage.' Mr Chapman still had his job, but was aware that thousands in the construction and property industries had lost theirs as people resorted to DIY. 'It's better for me than for carpenters and decorators. People are wary of trying plumbing but they say any fool can paint.'

Cobblers: Martin Middleton, who ran the Greenmarket Cobbler business in Newcastle upon Tyne, said: 'People will always wear shoes.' Less expected, however, was the 40 per cent increase in business as a result of the recession. 'City types used to spend lots of money on a pair of shoes, wear them until they "died" and then throw them in the bin. Now, people are more willing to be seen having their shoes repaired.'

It is usually assumed that recession will have a negative effect on business. Why do you think the recession had a positive impact, or an impact that was less negative than expected, on these businesses?

Source: adapted from an article in *The Times*, 26 October 2008

Author advice

'Slump' is a rather vague term, sometimes used interchangeably with depression; essentially it means a very severe recession. A full-scale depression is much rarer – an example is the Great Depression of the 1930s.

3. Slump: a period characterised by very low levels of consumer demand, investment and business confidence, an increasing number of businesses failing and high unemployment. A slump is likely to have the following effects on business:

- The lack of demand means that firms are content to charge low prices, concentrating on sales volume rather than sales revenue. It is possible that deflation (falling prices) may occur across the whole economy.
- The low level of demand means that factories are likely to close, leading to large-scale unemployment.

4. Recovery (or upturn): a period characterised by slowly rising levels of consumer demand, rising investment, patchy but increasing business confidence and falling levels of unemployment. A recovery is likely to have the following effects on business:

- Increasing demand for consumer goods may lead to increased profits and to new businesses starting up.
- The pace of recovery will vary between firms. Some will benefit from the increasingly favourable conditions almost immediately; others will need to await the completion of capital investment before they begin to benefit.
- Business confidence is growing, which may mean more investment in fixed assets and more borrowing.
- To meet the increasing demand, existing spare production capacity will be used. However, one of the characteristics of a recovery is that shortages, which are almost inevitable as recovery kicks in, may lead to increased costs and potential bottlenecks.

Business confidence

Business confidence can be a key influence on the business cycle. Many commentators believe that a high level of business confidence can become a self-fulfilling prophecy – an optimistic outlook leads to higher levels of investment spending and stock building, which in turn cause the economy to grow. For this reason, governments often try to describe the economy in positive terms so that confidence will increase.

The government's Insolvency Service publishes data on company liquidations: that is, on the number of businesses that stop trading because of financial difficulties. These are used as a means of analysing business confidence because liquidations tend to rise during periods of recession and decrease during periods of economic growth. The liquidation rate peaked at 2.6 per cent or 24,400 companies in the year ending March 1993, over a year after the end of the 1990s recession. The next sustained increase in the liquidation rate coincided with the 2008–09 recession, when 0.9 per cent or 20,500 companies entered liquidation.

Implications for business and for its strategic and functional decision making of changes in the business cycle

The strategies a business might use in response to changes in the business cycle will depend on which phase of the cycle the economy is in. For example, during a recession, many businesses will suffer declining demand. As a result they will wish to reduce production and improve efficiency. For many, this will mean laying off workers in order to reduce costs and survive. Although this may be an appropriate strategy in the short term, in the longer term, losing experienced staff could become problematic, especially when demand begins to improve and experienced workers are difficult to find. The fact file on JCB suggests an alternative approach likely to retain the goodwill of the workforce and benefit the business in the longer term.

Fact file

JCB

During the last recession, in 2008, as growth slowed to its weakest level in many years, most economists predicted unemployment to be 2 million by the end of the year. Like many firms producing capital goods, JCB, maker of bright yellow diggers for muddy building sites, needed to cut jobs as a result of the recession. However, it came up with a more positive approach. In negotiation with the trade union, about 2,500 staff agreed to a four-day week and a £50-a-week pay cut. It was an unusual deal. Wages are usually assumed to be 'sticky' and resistance to cuts is normally severe, yet Keith Hodgkinson, of the

GMB union, declared: 'I am delighted we have been able to save 350 jobs.'

Source: adapted from an article in the *Independent*, 24 October 2008

Economic growth

The recovery phase of a business cycle is characterised by a period of economic growth in an economy. Economic growth is an increase in the level of economic activity or real gross domestic product (GDP); essentially the extent to which the volume of goods and services being produced increases over time. Figures for economic growth are based on the percentage increase in real GDP. (Where figures are quoted as GDP per capita, this means per head of population.)

The trend in UK annual economic growth as measured by changes in GDP is illustrated in Figure 5.3 (see page 103).

The level of economic growth in an economy is influenced by a number of factors. These include:

- The exploitation of valuable natural resources. For example, the extraction and sale of oil in the Middle East and in the North Sea has significantly increased economic growth in these areas.
- A well-educated and highly skilled labour force. This improves productivity and generates economic growth.
- Increasing investment and new technology. This enables firms to keep pace with other countries and so create economic growth.
- Government policy. Governments can adopt specific policies aimed at promoting economic growth by encouraging any or all of the above.

Implications for business and for its strategic and functional decision making of changes in the rate of economic growth

The effects of economic growth on business depend on whether the rate of economic growth is rapid, slowing down or actually decreasing, which reflects the various phases of the business cycle.

- Impact on sales. With higher levels of real GDP, real incomes in the economy are higher, which in turn is likely to lead to higher retail sales. Higher growth rates are usually recorded for non-food items than for food items. This is probably because many food items are income inelastic and therefore, despite higher consumer incomes, sales in these areas are less positively affected. In contrast, firms producing or selling income-elastic goods and services, such as DVD players, mobile phones and wide-screen televisions, are likely to see sales improve more significantly as real GDP increases. From a strategic point of view, this illustrates the need for businesses to consider the possibility of having some income-elastic products or services in their portfolio.
- Impact on corporate profits. Higher incomes lead to greater demand for goods and services, which provides opportunities for firms to generate higher profits. Not only are sales likely to increase, but in many cases higher demand should provide more opportunities to raise prices as well, helping to boost profit margins.
- Impact on investment. Higher demand for goods and services means that firms are more likely to invest in expanding their operations – for example, seeking larger premises or extensions to existing facilities, or planning to install extra machinery and equipment. Increasing demand is likely to be accompanied by rising share prices, which will make it easier for firms to raise funds, and higher profitability, which will mean more retained profits are available for reinvestment.
- Impact on employment. Businesses seeking to expand production may initially choose to make their existing labour force work harder, by offering overtime to employees, and only recruit more workers once they are convinced that the increase in demand for their products or services is sustainable. If businesses intent on expansion cannot find sufficient skilled employees to meet their demands, it may prevent such firms from growing as quickly as desired and may act as a brake on the rate of economic growth in the UK. Skills shortages can lead to higher wages,

▲ Oil extraction in the Middle East is a significant cause of economic growth in the region

Author advice

Notice how often elasticity – whether price elasticity of demand or income elasticity of demand – is relevant to the analysis of data on sales.

which present further problems. For example, if average earnings increase, firms will be faced with rising input costs due to rising wage rates. This leaves them with a dilemma: should they absorb the higher wage costs and squeeze their own profit margins, or should they pass these higher costs on to consumers in the form of higher prices?

- Impact on strategic and functional decision making. The impact of economic growth suggests that certain business strategies are better suited to an environment of economic growth.
  - Expansion. Rapid company expansion is more easily achieved during this period, as a firm may be able to expand production and sales without having to gain sales from rivals. However, expansion and a rapidly growing business can bring their own problems and test a firm's ability to cope in terms of organisational structure, personnel, technology, production capacity and finance.
  - New products. Economic growth provides new opportunities for firms to update or extend the range of products and services they offer. Thus, strategies based around launching new products have a greater chance of success, as rising consumer incomes lead to greater demand for new products and more willingness on the part of consumers to try them.
  - Repositioning. Firms intent on repositioning and changing their appeal may also find this policy easier during a period of rising economic prosperity. With higher incomes, consumers are more willing to consider new trends and fashions, which in turn are likely to shorten product life cycles. This has encouraged some companies to redefine their image as well as their product offerings, in effect repositioning their brands in the market.
  - In general, economic growth provides favourable trading conditions and new business opportunities. It means growth and possibly new markets for existing products and market opportunities for new products. High levels of income and spending may even encourage the introduction of what might otherwise have been seen as risky products or business ventures. Economic growth also offers more security and certainty to firms and therefore provides them with more confidence in planning for the future.

Practice exercise 1   *Total: 65 marks*

1. Explain the term 'GDP'.   *(3 marks)*

2. Explain the term 'business cycle'.   *(3 marks)*

3. Why might demand and output in the economy as a whole fluctuate in a cyclical manner?   *(5 marks)*

4. Which of the following is not associated with a recovery (or upturn) period in the business cycle?
   a) Rising levels of consumer demand
   b) Rising investment
   c) Rising levels of unemployment
   d) Increasing business confidence   *(1 mark)*

5. Explain two possible causes of the recession phase of the business cycle. *(6 marks)*

6. Analyse two effects of the boom phase of the business cycle on business. *(8 marks)*

7. Compare the different implications of a recession for a firm selling:
   a) an inferior good *(4 marks)*
   b) a luxury product. *(4 marks)*

8. Business confidence is a major factor in influencing the business cycle. Why is this the case and how might it be measured? *(8 marks)*

9. Define the term 'economic growth'. *(3 marks)*

10. Identify two determinants of economic growth. *(2 marks)*

11. Explain the possible impact of economic growth on the sales of goods with income-elastic demand. *(5 marks)*

12. Explain how investment in capital goods might be affected by a period of strong economic growth. *(4 marks)*

13. Why might skills shortages occur during periods of economic growth? *(3 marks)*

14. Explain two strategies that companies might adopt to benefit from a period of sustained economic growth. *(6 marks)*

Practice exercise 2   *Total: 50 marks*

1. Analyse the possible business opportunities available to a clothing retailer during an upturn or recovery in the business cycle. *(9 marks)*

2. Evaluate the implications for a manufacturer of kitchen equipment of the unpredictability of the length of the business cycle. *(16 marks)*

3. Refer back to Figure 5.3 on page 103. Discuss how changes in GDP in the period from 2005 to 2015 might have had an impact on the strategic and functional decision making of a business operating in the construction and building sector. *(25 marks)*

Practice exercise 3

Total: 20 marks

▼ **Table 5.3** GDP trends, 2004–13

YEAR	GDP at 2011 prices	Index number of GDP
	£ millions	Base year: 2004 = 100
2004	1,5071,91	100.0
2005	1,549,491	102.8
2006	1,596,628	105.9
2007	1,637,432	108.6
2008	1,631,995	108.3
2009	1,561,646	103.6
2010	1,591,494	105.6
2011	1,617,677	107.3
2012	1,628,338	108.0
2013	1,656,498	109.9

1. What is meant by the term 'index number? (3 marks)

2. What was the percentage change in GDP between 2004 and 2005? (2 marks)

3. What was the percentage change in GDP between 2008 and 2009? (2 marks)

4. Based on this data, explain whether the UK economy has recovered from the recession. (4 marks)

5. Analyse the implications of this data for UK retailers of household goods, such as electrical appliances and furniture. (9 marks)

Economic factors: exchange rates

Key term

Exchange rates The price of one country's currency in terms of other currencies.

There are **exchange rates** for pounds sterling against all other currencies, although the ones most commonly quoted are the rates against the euro and the US dollar and also against a 'basket of currencies' (an average of a number of major currencies). (Note: the official name for the UK currency is pound sterling, commonly known as the pound, but also as sterling.)

Trends in the annual average exchange rates of the pound against the euro and the dollar since 2006 are given in Table 5.4 and Figure 5.4. When examining this type of data, try to get a picture of what is happening over time and how data about exchange rates might be influenced by or linked to other data. For example, the rates of exchange in the table and in the graph below reflect patterns in GDP discussed in the previous section, in particular the recession of 2008–09.

▼ **Table 5.4** Trends in the €/£ and $/£ exchange rates, 2006–15

Year	Euro	US dollar
2006	1.43	1.74
2007	1.47	1.97
2008	1.26	1.99
2009	1.08	1.43
2010	1.12	1.52
2011	1.13	1.61
2012	1.20	1.60
2013	1.19	1.52
2014	1.21	1.67
2015	1.39	1.47

Source: ONS

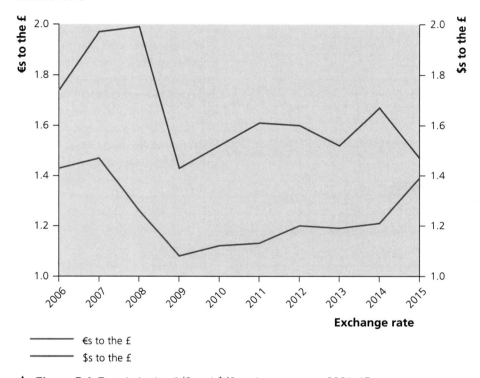

▲ **Figure 5.4** Trends in the €/£ and $/£ exchange rates, 2006–15

Exchange rate policies

Exchange rate policies are strategies that the government can adopt in order to determine the exchange rate of a country's currency.

● **Free exchange rates**: Free exchange rates are also known as floating exchange rates, freely floating exchange rates and flexible or fluctuating exchange rates. Under this regime, an exchange rate is determined by the demand for, and the supply of, the currency. As with any 'product', if lots of people want (demand) it, the price will go up. On the other hand, if there is too much available (being supplied), then the price will fall. The demand for pounds comes from those who wish to buy UK goods and services (i.e. from UK exports) or invest in the UK. The supply of pounds comes from those who need foreign currency in order to purchase foreign goods and services (i.e. from imports to the UK) or invest abroad. Thus the exchange rate is influenced by the level of demand for exports and imports and the level of foreign investment.

Did you know?

The foreign exchange market is a good example of a market situation known as perfect competition. The products are identical: for example, one dollar is exactly the same as another dollar. There are many buyers and sellers, all of whom are too small to influence the price on their own. Everyone buying and selling a particular currency knows the price, so sellers are unlikely to try to charge higher or lower prices than their competitors.

● **Fixed exchange rates**: Fixed exchange rates are when a government decides to fix the value of its currency permanently in relation to other currencies or to a single currency. A fixed exchange rate occurred for 11 European Union countries when they fixed their exchange rates in relation to each other's currency on 1 January 1999 in preparation for the introduction of the euro on 1 January 2002. Note that, once established, the euro became a freely floating currency, its value determined by the forces of supply and demand. (The euro is discussed in a Fact file below.) An example of a currency permanently fixed in relation to another currency is the Barbadian or Bajan dollar (BB$), which is fixed against the United States dollar (US$), with one BB$ being worth 0.5 US$.

Fact file

The single European currency: the euro

On 1 January 1999, the euro was introduced as the single European currency. On that date, the currencies of the 11 original EU member states who adopted the euro were fixed permanently to each other. At the same time as the single currency was introduced, the European Central Bank took control of interest rates across those countries that had adopted the euro (known as the Eurozone).

Today, the euro is used by more than 330 million Europeans in 19 countries of the EU. These countries are: Austria, Belgium, Cyprus, Estonia, Finland, France, Germany, Greece, Ireland, Italy, Latvia, Lithuania, Luxembourg, Malta, the Netherlands, Portugal, Slovakia, Slovenia and Spain. The UK and Denmark decided not to convert to the euro and Sweden is not a member. Other newer EU member countries are working towards becoming part of the Eurozone.

Adopting the euro and relinquishing their old currency involves countries in a number of short-term problems, such as the transition costs of new electronic tills, computer software and staff training.

However, a single currency and a common interest rate make trading within the EU much easier and cheaper. Other benefits include:

● no exchange rate transaction costs, that is commission charges when exchanging pounds for euros
● no uncertainty due to exchange rate changes (e.g. in relation to export earnings or costs of imported raw materials); this is likely to encourage trade and make financial forecasting more accurate
● no need to use expensive futures contracts to insure against exchange rate changes
● price transparency, making it easier for consumers and producers to compare prices within the Eurozone.

In addition:

● A single currency and common interest rates might encourage firms to operate in a wider market, with expansion bringing the benefits of economies of scale.
● New and improved sources of supply, previously considered too risky, might become viable once exchange rate fluctuations no longer occur.
● Investment from the rest of the world might increase as a single currency makes trade with a large market simple and relatively cheap.

The UK has a free exchange rate system, meaning that the exchange rate for the pound sterling is determined by the forces of demand and supply. However, if the exchange rate of sterling rises too high or falls too low, the government may request the Bank of England to intervene and 'manage' the exchange rate, by buying or selling pounds, until the rate reaches an acceptable level.

Exchange rate uncertainty

Because UK exchange rates are determined by supply and demand for the pound sterling, the rate can change from day to day. Firms that are exporting and importing on a regular basis find fluctuations in exchange rates a source of considerable uncertainty, making it difficult for them to predict the volume of overseas sales or the price they will receive from these transactions. Such uncertainty affects a firm's ability to plan ahead effectively. In some instances, it can be enough to stop firms developing export markets, especially at times when the exchange rate is rising rapidly, since the loss of competitiveness quickly erodes profit margins. To overcome some of this uncertainty, firms can make use of futures contracts, which are a form of insurance that enables them to buy currency in advance at a guaranteed fixed rate. This reduces the level of uncertainty and risk, but is expensive and may reduce profits. On a more practical level, for an exporting firm, unpredictable exchange rate changes create administrative and marketing problems, such as the costs and inconvenience of continually updating pricing and advertising literature for overseas markets.

Causes of changes in exchange rates

An *increase* in an exchange rate can result from any of the following:

- an increase in exports, which increases the demand for the currency
- a reduction in imports, which decreases the supply of the currency
- high interest rates, which attract savings from abroad and therefore increase demand for the currency
- if speculators expect a currency to increase in value in the future, this is likely to cause an increase in the demand for the currency now – then, when its value does rise, speculators will sell the currency and make a profit
- if foreign multinationals wish to invest in a country, they will need to buy its currency, which in turn will increase the demand for it
- the government may buy the currency in order to support its value.

A *decrease* in an exchange rate is caused by the opposite factors.

Impact of exchange rate changes on exporters and importers

Note: the figures used in these examples are for illustration only and are not intended to reflect the actual value of currencies or costs and prices.

Example 1: the effect of a change in the exchange rate on the price and competitiveness of an exporter

In this example, profit margins per unit remain fixed at £2,000, but the selling price abroad changes as the exchange rate changes.

Currently £1 = €1.60.

In the UK a car costs £8,000 to produce.

What do you think?

Over half of the UK's overseas trade is conducted outside the EU. This means that there are many firms which, if the UK adopted the euro, would not benefit from the reduced costs of trade with Europe, and which would still face exchange rate issues when they traded with countries outside the Eurozone.

Taking into account the advantages of adopting the euro outlined in the Fact file on page 112, and the point made about the proportion of UK trade that takes place with non-EU countries, how advantageous might the euro be to UK business?

It sells for £10,000 in the UK.

At the current exchange rate, it sells for €16,000 (10,000 × 1.60) in Spain.

Similar models in Spain sell for €17,000.

Therefore, the UK car is competitively priced.

If the value of the pound rises to £1 = €1.75, the UK car now sells for €17,500 (10,000 × €1.75) in Spain.

Therefore the UK car is no longer competitively priced.

If the value of the pound falls to £1 = €1.50, the UK car now sells for €15,000 (10,000 × 1.50) in Spain.

Therefore the UK car is very competitively priced.

Thus it can be seen that in this situation a *rise* in the value of the pound leads to a *less competitive* export price, while a *fall* in the value of the pound leads to a *more competitive* export price.

Example 2: the effect of a change in the exchange rate on the profitability of an exporter

In this example, selling price abroad remains fixed at $20,000, but profit margins change as the exchange rate changes.

Currently £1 = $2.00.

In the UK a car costs £8,000 to produce.

It sells for $20,000 in the USA (£10,000).

Therefore profit margin per car is £2,000.

If the value of the pound rises to £1 = $2.5, the revenue per car ($20,000) is now equivalent to £8,000.

Therefore the profit margin per car is 0.

If the value of the pound falls to £1 = $1.6, the revenue per car ($20,000) is now equivalent to £12,500.

Therefore the profit margin per car is £4,500.

In this situation, the *rise* in the value of the pound leads to a *smaller profit margin*, while a *fall* in the value of the pound leads to a *larger profit margin*.

Example 3: the effect of a change in the exchange rate on an importer of raw materials

Currently £1 = €1.60.

An importer buys 1,000 units of raw materials from France at a cost of €32,000 or €32 each. At the current exchange rate this is a total of £20,000.

If the value of the pound rises to £1 = €2, the UK importer will now need to exchange only £16,000 in order to get the €32,000 to buy the raw materials.

If the value of the pound falls to £1 = €1.28, the UK importer will now need to exchange £25,000 in order to get the €32,000 to buy the raw materials.

Therefore, the *rise* in the exchange rate has made it cheaper for the importer to buy raw materials and the *fall* in the exchange rate has made it more expensive for the importer to buy raw materials.

The impact for business and for its strategic and functional decision making of changes in exchange rates

The level of, and changes in, exchange rates affect businesses in different ways depending on whether they are:

- businesses that export their goods to consumers in other countries
- businesses that sell their goods in the UK, competing against foreign imports
- businesses that purchase imported fuel, raw materials and components to use in the production of their own goods.

Assuming that profit margins remain the same, an increase in the exchange rate may increase the price at which exports are sold abroad and reduce the price charged for imports in the UK. This in turn will affect revenue, competitiveness and profitability. The extent to which the changing prices of exports and imports will affect export sales and the purchase of imports depends on the price elasticity of demand.

If the price elasticity of demand for exports is inelastic, an increase in their price, due to a rise in the exchange rate, will have little effect on sales. Although it is likely to increase revenue substantially in terms of the foreign currency, when converted back to pounds sterling there will be a minimal effect. If, on the other hand, the price elasticity of demand for exports is elastic, an increase in export prices is likely to lead to a significant fall in sales volume and in sales revenue.

If the demand for imports is price elastic and their price falls due to a rise in the exchange rate, consumers are likely to purchase more of them, possibly substituting them for domestically produced goods. This will mean a reduction in demand for UK goods. If, on the other hand, the price elasticity of demand for imports is inelastic – often the case where firms purchase imported raw materials and components – the reduction in price will cause their costs to fall, which could lead them to reduce the price of their finished products or simply increase their profit margins.

The above analysis assumes that firms prefer to maintain their profit margins at the same level. If this were not the case – for example, if a firm were prepared to absorb the rise in the exchange rate and reduce its profit margins – it could leave prices unchanged.

It is important to note that the levels of export sales and import purchases are influenced not only by exchange rates, but also by a range of other factors, including reputation and quality, after-sales service, the reliability, design and desirability of a product, the overall packaging provided and

Author advice

Price elasticity of demand is an important concept in this area. Ensure that you understand the concept and the implications of different elasticities for a firm's revenue.

115

payment terms. Many firms have a competitive advantage based on these types of factors, which may override any adverse effects due to changes in the exchange rate or prices. In order to determine the most appropriate strategy, firms need to assess the price elasticity of demand for their products and also whether price or other factors are the most important influences on sales.

The strategies a business might deploy in response to changes in exchange rates will depend on whether exchange rates are rising or falling and what market a business operates in.

For a business that exports its goods to consumers in other countries, a rising exchange rate for the pound means that it must understand how higher prices will affect sales. If sales are likely to fall because foreign buyers switch to competing substitutes whose price has remained the same, it may be better to accept lower profit margins. Staying competitive when the exchange rate is rising is very difficult. Most big businesses want a stable, and low, exchange rate if export markets are important to them.

For a business that exports its goods to consumers in other countries, a falling exchange rate for the pound is a bonus. The value of its product in pounds will rise if the foreign currency price stays the same. It has a choice: it could leave prices the same and accept a higher profit margin, or it could cut the price in the hope of higher sales. The best strategy depends on the price elasticity of demand for its product. A high elasticity (greater than 1) means that a price cut will bring a more than proportionate increase in sales.

For a business that sells its goods in the UK in competition with foreign imports, a rising exchange rate for the pound will put it under added pressure to improve its efficiency. It may consider increasing investment in labour-saving machinery and reducing the workforce. It may introduce new technologies and organisational strategies. It is likely to increase its marketing efforts. The fight will be on just to maintain competitiveness.

For a business that purchases imported fuel, raw material and components to use in the production of its own goods, staying competitive is more complicated, especially if it then exports its final product, since it will need to think through each of these perspectives when deciding on its strategy.

Thus, for any firm, a decision to enter an export market is influenced by the potential exchange rate risk. A firm that is over-reliant on one foreign currency because a majority of its sales go to one country could find a rise in the value of the pound against that currency to be crippling. On the other hand, for many businesses, selling abroad is absolutely essential if they wish to expand their markets.

Practice exercise 4

Total: 60 marks

1. What is an exchange rate? *(3 marks)*

2. Explain how free exchange rates are determined. *(5 marks)*

3. State and explain three reasons why a currency might increase in value. *(9 marks)*

4. List two reasons that might cause a currency to fall in value. *(2 marks)*

5. Select one of the following statements to complete the sentences below:
   - If the value of the pound against the dollar rises ... *(1 mark)*
   - If the value of the pound against the dollar falls ... *(1 mark)*
     a) prices of exports to America and prices of imports from America rise.
     b) prices of exports to America rise and prices of imports from America fall.
     c) prices of exports to America and prices of imports from America fall.
     d) prices of exports to America fall and prices of imports from America rise.

6. When the exchange rate rises:
   a. How might a firm ensure that its prices abroad do not rise? *(4 marks)*
   b. Why might a firm not always choose to take the action you have indicated in your answer to 6a? *(4 marks)*

7. What is the effect of a fall in the exchange rate on the price of exports and of imports? *(6 marks)*

8. If a firm is dependent on imported raw materials, what is likely to be the impact of a fall in the exchange rate on its costs and pricing? *(6 marks)*

9. Why might fluctuating exchange rates cause difficulties for a firm involved in exporting or importing? *(5 marks)*

10. At an exchange rate of £1 = $1.50, a firm sells 10,000 units abroad at a price equivalent to £6.00. If the exchange rate rises to £1 = $2, what effect might this have on its sales revenue? Explain your answer. *(5 marks)*

11. The exchange rate of a currency rises by 10 per cent. Analyse how an exporter of goods with an elastic demand might be affected differently from an exporter of goods with an inelastic demand. *(9 marks)*

Practice exercise 5

Total: 45 marks

▼ **Table 5.5** Sterling exchange rates, 2006–15

Year	US dollar	Japanese yen	Euro
2006	1.74	204.27	1.43
2007	1.97	231.84	1.47
2008	1.99	198.31	1.26
2009	1.43	141.73	1.08
2010	1.52	141.84	1.12
2011	1.61	132.95	1.13
2012	1.60	132.70	1.20
2013	1.52	143.26	1.19
2014	1.67	171.77	1.21
2015	1.47	178.11	1.39

Source: ONS

Study Table 5.5 and answer the questions below.

1. Explain the key features of the changing value of the pound sterling against the three currencies given in Table 5.5. *(5 marks)*

2a. If a component purchased from Japan in 2006 cost 17,000 yen, how much would that have been in sterling? *(3 marks)*

2b. Assuming that the Japanese supplier did not alter the yen price of the component between 2006 and 2015, what would its sterling price have been in 2015? *(3 marks)*

3a. Assuming that in 2006, the price of a particular product in the UK was £500, what would its price have been in euros? *(3 marks)*

3b. Assuming that the sterling price of the product did not change between 2006 and 2015, what would its euro price have been in 2015? *(3 marks)*

4. Compare and contrast the impact of the exchange rate changes shown on the following firms:
    a) a UK business that exports to Germany and to the USA *(6 marks)*
    b) a UK business that sells its products worldwide on the basis of quality and service rather than price. *(6 marks)*

5. Discuss the possible impact of the changes in exchange rates shown in the table on a firm that imports essential components for production from Japan and sells its finished products mainly in Europe. *(16 marks)*

Practice exercise 6

Total: 30 marks

In Chapter 3 of Book 1, interest rates and their effect on business were explained. Read the following paragraph and use your knowledge of interest rates and of exchange rates to answer the questions below.

On 19 March 2015, sterling suffered its biggest one-day fall against the dollar for five years. Commentators suggested that the fall was due to an announcement that the Bank of England might cut interest rates further in the near future. The pound fell by 2.4 cents to $1.4716, a 1.73 per cent drop. At the time the Bank of England's base rate was 0.5 per cent.

1. Explain why an announcement that interest rates might be cut further might lead to a fall in the value of the pound.
(5 marks)

2. (Essay Question) Discuss the possible implications of both a drop in interest rates and a fall in the value of the pound for a business with a high gearing ratio that imports its raw materials from China and exports its luxury products to Europe and America.
(25 marks)

Economic factors: inflation

Data for the rate of **inflation** between 2006 and 2015 are given in Table 5.6.

> **Key term**
>
> **Inflation** An increase in the general level of prices within an economy. Inflation also means that there is a fall in the purchasing power of money. In contrast, deflation is a decrease in the general level of prices within an economy or a rise in the purchasing power of money.

▼ **Table 5.6** UK rates of inflation, 2006–15 (% January CPI inflation rate for each year)

2006	2007	2008	2009	2010	2011	2012	2013	2014	2015
1.9%	2.7%	2.2%	3.0%	3.5%	4.0%	3.6%	2.7%	1.9%	0.3%

Source: ONS

The rate of inflation is measured by using price indices. One way to understand a price index is to think of a very large shopping basket containing all the goods and services bought by households. The price index estimates changes to the total cost of this basket. In the UK the main measure of inflation is the Consumer Prices Index (CPI). CPI is a measure of consumer price inflation produced to international standards and in line with European regulations. It is the inflation measure currently used in the government's target for inflation. The CPI is also used for purposes such as up-rating pensions, wages and benefits.

The Chancellor of the Exchequer sets the inflation target for the UK, which, in 2015, stands at 2.0 per cent (CPI). The Bank of England's Monetary Policy Committee (MPC) is required to set interest rates in order to keep the rate of inflation at or below the target rate.

Fact file

CPI

The categories in the CPI by relative weight in 2015 are as follows:

- transport - 14.9 per cent
- recreation and culture - 14.7 per cent
- housing and household services – 12.8 per cent
- restaurants and hotels – 12.1 per cent
- food and non-alcoholic beverages – 11.0 per cent
- miscellaneous goods and services – 9.1 per cent
- clothing and footwear – 7.0 per cent
- furniture and household goods – 5.9 per cent
- alcoholic beverages and tobacco – 4.3 per cent
- communication – 3.1 per cent
- education – 2.6 per cent
- health – 2.5 per cent

Source: ONS

Fact file

Inflation

As noted in Table 5.6, inflation in January 2015 was only 0.3 per cent. At the time of writing, this was the lowest level of inflation on record in the UK and well below the Bank of England's target for inflation of 2 per cent.

Excluding certain goods with volatile price movements, such as food, energy, alcohol and tobacco, from the general CPI inflation calculation, gives a measure known as 'core' inflation. Historically, the rate of core inflation has been more stable than the overall CPI. The rate of core inflation in January 2015 was 1.4 per cent, 1.1 percentage points higher than overall inflation. This reflects that most of the downward pressure on inflation towards the end of 2014 and early in 2015 came from price movements for those goods excluded from the core calculation – mainly motor fuel, food and energy prices.

It is important to be able to distinguish between real and money or nominal values. Real income broadly measures what you can buy with your income. If prices increase by 2 per cent over a year (in other words, the cost of living rises by 2 per cent) and your money income or nominal income also increases by 2 per cent over the same period, then your real income (i.e. what you can buy with your income) has remained the same. Thus real income increases only if the nominal or money value of income rises by more than the rate of inflation over the same period. If money income rises by 10 per cent and prices rise by 3 per cent, then real income has risen, since you can now buy more with your income. But if money income rises by 2 per cent and prices rise by 5 per cent, then real income has fallen, since you can now buy less with your income.

Author advice

'Real' as opposed to 'money' changes should always be considered when analysing changes in the value of variables quoted in money terms. These variables include income, output, the amount of government expenditure and marketing budgets. Always consider the rate of inflation and how this has affected any increase or decrease in the value of these and other monetary variables.

▲ Inflation affects how much you can buy with your income, for example, groceries

Causes of inflation

In general, the causes of inflation can be divided into two types: cost-push and demand-pull. In addition, expectations can play a role in generating inflation.

- Cost-push inflation occurs when there is an increase in the costs of production (including wages, raw materials, fuel, taxation and interest rates) that forces firms to increase their prices in order to protect their profit margins. Cost-push inflation could be due to trade unions achieving wage increases that are greater than productivity increases, or it could be due to a massive increase in the price of an essential fuel, such as oil.
- Demand-pull inflation is the process by which prices rise because there is excess demand in the economy. Just as an increase in demand for a particular product might lead to an increase in its price unless there is a corresponding increase in supply, so demand-pull inflation can be explained as a situation when aggregate (or total) demand in the economy increases without a corresponding increase in the aggregate supply of goods and service in the economy. This leads to an increase in the general level of prices because aggregate supply cannot increase beyond the point where firms are working at full capacity.
- Inflationary expectations are views about what will happen to the rate of inflation in the future. As a result of inflationary expectations, people expect a period of rising inflation to continue into the future. For example, if the rate of inflation has risen from 1 per cent two years ago, to 2 per cent last year and then to 3 per cent this year, workers and their trade unions are likely to expect inflation to be 4 per cent next year. If this is the case, they may try to negotiate pay rises of 4 per cent in order to avoid a fall in their real income if inflation does rise to 4 per cent. If they are successful, this will add to costs and will help bring about a 4 per cent rate of inflation.

In practice, the causes of inflation are difficult to disentangle. As prices rise, for whatever reason, workers and their trade unions may try to negotiate wage increases to maintain their standards of living, anticipating future levels of inflation and thereby helping those levels to come about. An inflationary spiral is the way in which price rises in one sector of the economy cause price increases in another, in a continuous upward spiral. Pay increases become price rises, which in turn lead to demands for further pay increases, which cause further price rises, and so on.

Hyperinflation is a situation where the value of money decreases so quickly that people lose confidence in it. During hyperinflationary periods, people start to barter or to make use of other commodities, such as gold, which have their own intrinsic value, or to use an internationally dependable foreign currency such as the US dollar. There is no precise level of inflation that means it is hyperinflation. It is more the case that price rises become so rapid and uncontrollable that confidence in the currency is lost and people are reluctant to enter into transactions with it.

Hyperinflation has severe consequences for society because it not only affects people's willingness to enter into transactions, but also leads to a major redistribution of income in favour of those with debts and with non-financial assets, and against those dependent on fixed incomes, such as pensioners and those relying on their savings.

Did you know?

The best-known example of hyperinflation occurred in Germany in the 1920s, when prices were rising every day and paper money rapidly became worthless. By 1923 the annual rate of inflation had reached 7 trillion (7,000,000,000,000) per cent, and in 1924 the German currency was replaced by a new currency.

More recently, Zimbabwe experienced chronic hyperinflation. Inflation reached 624 per cent in 2004 and 1,730 per cent in 2006. The Reserve Bank of Zimbabwe revalued the currency in August 2006 at a rate of 1,000 old Zimbabwean dollars to 1 revalued Zimbabwean dollar. In June 2007, inflation reached 11,000 per cent. Zimbabwe's annual inflation was 231 million per cent in July 2008, in other words prices were doubling every 17.3 days. In August 2008, the Zimbabwean dollar was redenominated by removing ten zeros: 10 billion Zimbabwean dollars became 1 dollar after the redenomination. In January 2009, the Zimbabwean government introduced a range of trillion dollar bank notes; at the time, 100 trillion Zimbabwean dollars was estimated to be worth about £22. Anecdotes of the time suggest that a loaf of bread cost what 12 new cars did ten years earlier, and a small pack of locally produced coffee beans cost about 1 billion Zimbabwean dollars, which would have bought 60 new cars ten years earlier.

In 2009, Zimbabwe abandoned its currency. The South African rand, Botswana pula and US dollar were granted official status and the US dollar became the principal currency.

The impact of inflation on business and on strategic and functional decision making

- Inflation tends to encourage borrowing if interest rates are less than the rate of inflation. For highly geared firms and those with heavy borrowing, inflation reduces the real value of the sum they owe, making it easier to repay the loan towards the end of its life. For example, if a firm borrowed a large sum of money ten years ago, and if inflation has been increasing such that the average price level is double what it was then, it is likely that the firm's income or revenue has also doubled in this period, so the loan will be much easier to repay towards the end of the ten-year period.
- As inflation rises, so do property prices and the price of stock. Thus balance sheets tend to look healthier as rising property and stock values boost reserves.
- A firm will find it easier to increase the price of its own products when prices are rising generally, because cost increases can be passed on to the consumer more easily.
- Higher prices may mean lower sales, depending on the price elasticity of demand for particular products.
- The producers of major brands that tend to sell at premium prices may suffer as inflation makes consumers more aware of the prices of different products. This increased price sensitivity on the part of consumers may lead them to switch brands towards more competitively priced items. As a result, brand owners may either cut their price premiums or greatly increase their advertising expenditure in order to try to regain customer interest and loyalty.
- Just as consumers become more aware of prices, so workers become far more concerned about the level of their real wages because, unless they obtain a pay rise at least as high as the rate of inflation, their real income

will fall. Therefore industrial action often increases in inflationary periods as workers and trade unions negotiate hard for pay increases. As a consequence, industrial relations tend to deteriorate.

● Suppliers may increase prices for the goods and services they supply, adding further to a firm's costs and putting more pressure on a firm to increase its own prices.

● If inflation in the UK is relatively higher than inflation in other countries, the international competitiveness of UK firms may be reduced.

● As the future is uncertain, forecasts of sales revenue and profits will become very difficult to make, and planning will be less reliable. As forecasting is subject to greater uncertainty, firms will begin to want higher forecast average rates of return on any investments they undertake.

● If the Monetary Policy Committee (MPC) of the Bank of England (the institution that sets interest rates) takes action to reduce inflation by increasing interest rates, this is likely to reduce demand and sales, which will have an adverse effect on business.

● When prices are changing quickly, businesses find it more difficult to keep track of competitors' pricing strategies.

● Cash flow is squeezed as the costs of new materials and equipment rise.

The possible impact of a low rate of inflation

A low level of inflation, as experienced in the UK over recent years (see Table 5.6 on page 119) can have a number of effects on a business's strategic and functional decision making:

● Interest rates are likely to be low if the rate of inflation is low, which will benefit most businesses. However, low interest rates may cause the exchange rate to fall, with the consequences discussed in the previous section of this chapter.

● A low rate of inflation relative to other countries is likely to mean that firms become more competitive in their export markets and in their domestic markets against imports.

● In general, low levels of inflation create more certainty in the economy, which means that business is able to plan ahead because prices can be predicted more easily.

● Marketing and administrative costs will be lower, as there will be fewer price adjustments, for example, to price lists and advertising information.

● The fact that there is more certainty about short-term pricing decisions means that there should be more time available for long-term strategic decision making.

● Efficient firms survive and inefficient firms disappear. Continually rising prices mean that poorly performing firms can record increasing sales and profits in nominal terms. However, low inflation means that such firms cannot disguise poor sales performance and cannot easily raise prices to cover their own inefficiency.

The impact of deflation

While deflation might sound welcome, in fact it can be devastating to borrowers, banks and businesses. The Great Depression in the 1930s was

Author advice

Do not make the mistake of thinking that a fall in the inflation rate means a fall in prices. It simply means a slowing down of the rate at which prices are rising. Falling prices (or deflation) can only occur if the inflation rate is negative. In January 2015, inflation fell to 0.3 per cent and some commentators were predicting that deflation might occur later in the year.

accompanied by deflation of 10 per cent per year, reflecting the widespread lack of demand. As prices fell, consumers and businesses became less willing to spend and invest, thus worsening the economic downturn.

A sustained drop in prices can have a negative effect for the following reasons. Because consumers and businesses anticipate prices will continue to fall, they are likely to cut back on present spending and investment as they wait for prices to fall even lower. As spending dries up, the economy starts to shrink. As GDP shrinks, so do the businesses providing goods and services for consumers. As businesses shrink or close down, unemployment rises. Out-of-work consumers have less money to spend, which cuts deeper into the economy. Once the cycle takes hold, it is very difficult to stop.

Evaluating the impact of changes in inflation on business and on strategic and functional decision making

When evaluating the strategies a business might deploy in response to changes in the level of prices, it is important to consider whether inflation or deflation is occurring and, in the case of inflation, whether this is a low or a high rate. It is also important to consider the nature of the business and the goods or services it offers. For example, a luxury product with a high status and popular brand, and for which price is not a major factor in determining demand, may be able to maintain its high price even during a period of deflation. However, products in highly competitive markets, where price competition is of crucial importance in maintaining demand, are likely to be involved in extensive price cutting during a period of deflation.

During inflationary periods, it is usual for workers and their trade unions to try to maintain their real income by pushing for wage increases at least in line with price increases. In such situations, firms are generally able to pass on cost increases without affecting the demand for their products. However, when deflation occurs and prices are falling, a major issue is that wages tend to be 'sticky' and may not fall in line with general costs and prices. Strategies will also depend on what is happening to the price of the firm's supplies and the prices of its competitors both at home and abroad.

Practice exercise 7 — *Total: 30 marks*

1. Explain the term 'inflation'. *(3 marks)*

2. Distinguish between cost-push and demand-pull inflation. *(6 marks)*

3. If the rate of inflation in 2015 was 0.3 per cent and my annual salary in 2015 increased by 1 per cent, was I better off? Explain your answer. *(3 marks)*

4. Explain why inflationary expectations are likely to cause inflation. *(5 marks)*

5. Explain one benefit that inflation might have for firms. *(4 marks)*

6. Identify and explain three adverse effects of inflation on a firm. *(9 marks)*

Practice exercise 8

Total: 45 marks

▼ **Table 5.7** Inflation rates for selected countries, 2013–15 (%)

Country	2013	2014	2015
USA	1.6	1.6	−0.1
UK	2.7	1.9	0.3
France	1.0	0.9	−0.3
Germany	1.6	1.3	0.1
Japan	0.8	1.4	2.4
Australia	2.2	2.7	1.7

1. Refer to Table 5.7 above.
   a) Explain what the rates of inflation quoted for the USA and France for 2015 indicate about price levels in those countries. *(4 marks)*
   b) As a UK company selling goods in all of the countries mentioned in Table 5.7, discuss the possible implications of their differing inflation rates for the competitiveness of your product. *(16 marks)*

2. Refer to Table 5.6 (UK rates of inflation, 2006–15) on page 119.
   a) Consider the likely impact of inflation on a firm producing consumer durables such as televisions and other electrical goods between 2006 and 2015. *(9 marks)*
   b) Inflation in the UK has been low and stable in recent years. To what extent might a firm be adversely affected by such low inflation? *(16 marks)*

Economic factors: fiscal and monetary policy

(Note: this section includes a discussion about taxation.)

Macroeconomic policy is the government's attempt to influence the level of aggregate demand in the economy as a whole. It works primarily through **fiscal policy** (that is, the impact of government tax and expenditure changes) and **monetary policy** (such as the impact of interest rates). The choice of economic policies depends on the priorities of the government of the day and the particular objectives it wishes to pursue.

Fiscal policy

Taxation allows the government to raise revenue and to influence demand by placing a charge on goods, services or income. It is a withdrawal of money from the economy, in that it tends to reduce total spending and demand. In contrast, government expenditure is an injection of money into the economy and thus tends to increase total spending and demand. (Injections and withdrawals are part of the circular flow of income, which was discussed at the beginning of this chapter.)

> **Key term**
>
> **Fiscal policy** The use of taxation and government expenditure to influence the economy.
>
> **Monetary policy** Controlling the money supply and the rate of interest in order to influence the level of spending and demand in the economy.

Taxation

There are two main categories of taxation: direct taxation and indirect taxation.

- Direct taxes are taxes on incomes or profits. Individuals earning over a certain income level pay income tax, while businesses pay corporation tax. Direct taxes are usually levied as a proportion of income or profit, so as more income or profit is earned, proportionately more tax is paid.
- Indirect taxes are taxes on spending. Value added tax (VAT), at the rate of 20 per cent, is charged on most goods and services. Some goods and services, such as children's car seats and home energy, are charged at 5 per cent, and some are zero rated, including children's clothes and most food. (These rates were in place at the time of writing, March 2015.) Petrol, cigarettes and alcohol all have an additional tax, known as excise duty, imposed upon them by the Chancellor of the Exchequer.

What do you think?

In 1978, the highest rate of UK income tax was 83 per cent, levied on income above £24,000 a year. This meant that for people on the highest incomes, for every additional £1 they earned above £24,000, the government took 83p in income tax, leaving them with 17p.

What do you think might be the justification for such a high rate of income tax and what do you think the impact is likely to have been?

Because a tax increase effectively reduces the spending power of taxpayers, it can be used selectively to target particular groups of people or types of spending. For example:

- to increase incentives for people to set up their own businesses, corporation tax for small firms can be reduced
- to encourage consumer spending, the rate of VAT can be reduced, leading to a reduction in prices
- to deter people from using leaded petrol and thus to reduce environmental pollution, excise duty on leaded petrol can be increased, making it more expensive
- to redistribute wealth from the well-off to the less well-off, higher rates of income tax could be increased and the bottom rate could be reduced or the starting point for paying it increased.

Did you know?

Taxes can be proportional, progressive or regressive:

- A **proportional tax** is one that takes the same proportion of someone's income regardless of how much they earn.
- A **progressive tax** takes a larger proportion of someone's income the more they earn. Income tax is an example of a progressive tax because the rate levied on the lowest income levels is less than that levied on higher incomes. For 2015–16, individuals could earn £10,600 before paying income tax. Any income between £10,600 and £42,385 was taxed at 20 per cent, income between £42,385 and £160,600 was taxed at 40 per cent and income over £160,600 was taxed at 45 per cent.
- A **regressive tax** is one that takes a larger proportion of someone's income the less they earn. Flat-rate taxes, such as VAT, are regressive. For example, an individual earning £1,500 per month who purchases a television costing £400, on which £60 of VAT is added, is paying 4 per cent ($60/1500 \times 100$) of their monthly income in VAT. On the other hand, someone earning £6,000 per month who purchases the same product is paying only 1 per cent ($60/6000 \times 100$) of his or her monthly income in VAT.

Government expenditure

Government expenditure includes the financial assistance provided by government to, for example, housing, education, health and social security. In relation to business, government expenditure is often in the form of subsidies to support businesses that are important to the economy and that might otherwise fail, and to encourage business activity that would otherwise not take place. This might involve encouraging businesses to set up in areas of high unemployment or to encourage large infrastructure projects. For example, in March 2015, the government announced plans to build the world's first 'tidal lagoon' in Swansea Bay and to enter formal negotiations about subsidising the project. The £1 billion scheme, which will involve a six-mile sea wall with turbines to harness the power of the tide, will rely on subsidies funded by levies on consumer energy bills, with the level of subsidies to be decided through negotiations with government. A range of government grants and incentives for start-up businesses are detailed on page 88 of Chapter 4 in the section on enterprise. Government also provides subsidies to promote and encourage sporting, arts and cultural activities. (Lottery funding extensively supplements this.) In addition to UK government expenditure, the EU provides extensive subsidies to industry, in particular to agriculture.

Fiscal policy is also known as budgetary policy and is the responsibility of the Chancellor of the Exchequer.

- A budget surplus is where taxation is greater than government spending. Thus, more money is being withdrawn from the circular flow than is being injected into it. As a result, overall spending and demand in the economy will be reduced, leading to a fall in economic activity.
- A budget deficit is where government spending is greater than taxation. It means that overall spending and demand are likely to increase, leading to a rise in economic activity.

- A balanced budget is when taxation is equal to government spending. Overall spending and demand in the economy remain unchanged, although specific industries and areas may see changes in economic activity.

Initial changes in fiscal policy, such as a change in tax rates or a change in government expenditure, have further multiplier effects on business and the economy. For example, an increase in indirect taxation may lead to an increase in the price of goods and a subsequent reduction in demand. This in turn may lead to a cutback in production and, in the extreme, redundancies, triggering a further fall in demand. An increase in income tax will reduce disposable income and thus lower demand.

Governments use fiscal policy in various ways. For example, in a recession, government could try to boost demand in the economy by reducing taxes because this should leave firms and households with more money and so encourage spending. Alternatively, government spending could be increased, which will, in turn, increase demand for goods and services.

The impact of an increase in taxation depends on how much it has been increased, which taxes have been increased and whether consumers and firms are sensitive to such changes and react as expected. Taxes cannot be changed as often or as easily as interest rates, since tax changes are usually announced in the annual budget statement produced by the Chancellor of the Exchequer. However, compared with interest rates, taxation and government spending can provide the flexibility to target certain products or affect certain types of behaviour more specifically. In this sense, changes in tax and government expenditure can be a very effective way of influencing demand.

Monetary policy

Interest rates can be changed more easily and more quickly than rates of taxation, with decisions about interest rates being made each month by the Monetary Policy Committee of the Bank of England. Chapter 3 in Book 1 included a detailed discussion about the impact of changes in interest rates on demand and on business costs. Make sure that you are familiar with the content of that chapter before proceeding with this section.

Interest rates and quantitative easing (QE)

Changing interest rates is one of the main tools available to government to control growth in the economy. Lower interest rates encourage consumers and business to spend rather than save and higher interest rates tend to encourage the opposite. However, when interest rates are almost at zero (at the time of writing in March 2015, the interest rate set by the Bank of England was 0.5 per cent and had been at this rate since March 2009), central banks need to adopt different tactics. One of these is essentially pumping money directly into the economy. This process is known as quantitative easing or QE.

QE means that the central bank (in the UK, this is the Bank of England) creates new money (in the past by printing it, today by creating it electronically) and uses this money to buy bonds from investors such as banks or pension funds. This new money increases the amount of cash in the financial system, which then encourages financial institutions to lend more to businesses and individuals. This in turn should allow businesses and individuals to invest and spend more, hopefully increasing growth.

Did you know?

Bonds are essentially IOUs from governments and other very large organisations. They are offered at fixed interest rates and are guaranteed to be paid back at a fixed date in the future.

The Bank of England used QE during the 2008 and 2009 financial crisis in an attempt to stimulate economic growth. The Bank of England estimated that its QE during that period was 'economically significant' and that the £200 billion worth of bonds it bought between March and November 2009 helped to increase the UK's annual economic output by between 1.5 and 2 per cent.

Initial changes in monetary policy have multiplier effects on business and the economy. For example, increasing interest rates to slow the rate of inflation may cause the economy to go into recession. Falling demand will cause businesses to cut production. People may be made redundant and their incomes will then fall. They will spend less, which will cause demand to fall further in a downward spiral. Before long, the problem of inflation will give way to unemployment and slow or non-existent economic growth. Interest rates then need to fall in order to encourage spending.

Impact of fiscal and monetary policies on business and on strategic and functional decision making

The previous sections on fiscal and monetary policy both include discussions about how changes to fiscal and monetary policies influence the economy and thus the economic environment that businesses face. For example:

● During a period of recession, growth can be encouraged by allowing demand to increase. This can be done by lowering interest rates and introducing QE, both of which will encourage investment and consumer spending. Reducing taxation will give people more spending power and increasing government spending will have multiplier implications throughout the economy. For example, the building of a new hospital involves the employment of builders and eventually of medical staff, who have incomes that they will spend in the local economy. Suppliers of raw materials will receive additional demand that may have favourable effects on their financial position, and so on.

● When the economy is booming, symptoms of 'overheating' may start to appear, such as high inflation and shortages of skilled labour. Governments, faced with accelerating inflation and rising imports, want to reduce the rate at which demand is growing. They will focus on how to reduce the level of demand by restricting consumer and government spending. Reducing the level of demand to cut inflationary pressures can be done by increasing interest rates and/or increasing taxes and/ or reducing government expenditure. The danger here is that reduced demand and a cut in the level of spending may eventually lead to a reduction in investment, which, in turn, may reduce productivity and competitiveness. Reduced demand may also cause unemployment, meaning further reductions in income and spending and demand.

The above scenarios illustrate the impact of changes in fiscal and monetary policy on the economy. Businesses will need to respond to such changes by making decisions, at both strategic and functional levels, that enable them to survive, in the case of a recessionary situation, or to grow, in the case of a growth situation. Much will depend on the nature of the products being offered for sale and whether these are income or price elastic; whether the business operates in the home or international markets; whether it has a competitive advantage that it can maintain; whether it has spare capacity; what its financial standing is and whether it is efficiently run.

Practice exercise 9

Total: 65 marks

1. A tax that takes a higher percentage of income from the poorest citizens than from the richest is:
   a) a progressive tax
   b) a proportionate tax
   c) a recessionary tax
   d) a regressive tax. *(1 mark)*

2. Explain how monetary policy is used to influence the level of demand in an economy. *(4 marks)*

3. Explain how a fall in interest rates might affect business costs. *(4 marks)*

4. Explain how a change in interest rates might affect profit margins. *(4 marks)*

5. If interest rates fall, what might happen to the value of the pound? Explain your answer. *(6 marks)*

6. Analyse the likely impact of a reduction in interest rates on UK retailers of price- and income-elastic goods and services during a recession. *(9 marks)*

7. Explain how fiscal policy is used to influence the level of demand in an economy. *(4 marks)*

8. Explain how a rise in the rates of income tax, corporation tax and VAT might affect a business. *(9 marks)*

9. Assume that the government is using monetary and fiscal policy to bring the economy out of recession.
   a) Explain the actions the government is likely to be taking in relation to (i) monetary policy and (ii) fiscal policy. *(8 marks)*
   b) Discuss the likely impact of these actions on the strategic and functional decisions being made by a business that produces and sells consumer white goods. *(16 marks)*

Economic factors: more open trade versus protectionism

The government of any country must decide whether it wishes to trade with other countries openly and without restrictions or whether it wishes to protect its own industry by erecting barriers that prevent, limit or raise the price of goods and services from abroad. In doing the latter it is likely to face equivalent barriers when its own businesses wish to sell their goods and services abroad. Decisions to trade with other countries openly and without restrictions are usually made by groups of countries acting together.

More open trade

As noted in Chapter 4, the European Union is an example of a free trade area, that is, a group of countries that agree to trade with each other without erecting any barriers to trade. This encourages competition between firms in the different member countries and, as a result, fosters greater efficiency in the delivery of goods and services and lower prices for consumers. For more details on the benefits and problems of such a system, refer back to page 95 in Chapter 4.

As well as the EU, there are other free trade areas in the world, including ASEAN (Association of Southeast Asian Nations), AFTZ (African Free Trade Zone), NAFTA (North American Free Trade Agreement) and SAFTA (South Asia Free Trade Area). In addition to these well-defined areas of free trade, there are ongoing developments globally towards greater freedom of trade. The World Trade Organization (WTO) is a group of over 160 countries that are committed to the encouragement of free and fair international trade through the elimination of trade barriers. It aims to ensure that 'trade flows as freely as possible'.

Protectionism

The UK's position on **protectionism** is determined by its membership of the EU, which has a policy of free trade among member countries and a common external tariff barrier for goods and services coming from non-member countries.

A protectionist policy makes use of import controls to limit the number of overseas goods and services entering domestic markets. Import controls take a number of different forms:

> **Key term**
>
> **Protection (or protectionism)**
> The extent to which a government uses controls to restrict the amount of imports entering the country.

- Tariffs: Tariffs are taxes imposed on imported goods. In general, the imposition of tariffs leads to an increase in the price of the imported good and, depending on price elasticity of demand, may lead to a reduction in demand, making cheaper domestic goods more attractive to consumers. Two types of tariff can be levied:
  - an ad valorem tax, which is a percentage added to the price of the imported good, such as 10 per cent added to the price of all imported goods, regardless of whether they are priced at £10 or £1,000
  - a specific duty added to the price of the imported good, such as £2 per item added to the price of all imported goods, regardless of whether the good is valued at £10 or £1,000.
- Quotas: Quotas are a form of import protection that limits the sales of foreign goods to a specified quantity (e.g. 1 million pairs of shoes), value (e.g. £50 million worth of products) or market share (e.g. no more than 10 per cent of the total market for the imported good).
- Non-tariff barriers: Non-tariff barriers are more subtle controls that are imposed by governments because they wish to restrict imports without being seen to do so, perhaps because it would be contrary to international regulation under the World Trade Organization. Such barriers may take several forms, including:
  - constantly changing technical regulations, which make compliance difficult for importers
  - forcing importers to use specified points of entry where documentation is dealt with only slowly
  - introducing regulations that favour domestic production – for example, packaging and labels that conform to local language requirements.
- Embargos: An embargo is an order forbidding trade with a particular country, perhaps imposed by the United Nations against a country that has broken international laws or conventions.

Fact file

China

China is introducing a range of protectionist policies that will affect foreign technology companies selling their products to Chinese banks and financial organisations. These companies will have to give the Chinese government unusually high levels of access to information about their products, establish research centres in China and build facilities to enable Chinese government officials to manage and monitor data processed by them.

The policies will have a major impact because of the importance of the Chinese market. For example, foreign technology companies currently produce approximately 90% of the hardware used in China and, one of the major companies affected, Apple, currently sells more iPhones in China than in the USA.

Foreign businesses are critical of the policies because they are a type of protectionism that will make it more difficult for them to operate in China. On the other hand, such policies benefit Chinese companies, such as Apple's major Chinese rival, Xiaomi.

Impact of more open trade versus protectionism on business and on strategic and functional decision making

Whether international trade is more open or protectionist will have a significant impact on business. Even if a business does not sell its goods and services in overseas markets, it is still likely to encounter competition from overseas businesses when selling its goods in the UK. As discussed in Chapter 4 and in this chapter, open trade or free trade areas will make trading easier and cheaper. Protectionist policies, such as import tariffs, may make products from abroad less competitive on price compared to domestic products. However, tariffs on imported raw materials used in the production of UK goods will simply raise the costs of these goods, which may reduce their competitiveness.

Overall, the impact of open trade versus protectionism on a business's strategic and functional decision making will depend on a range of factors about the business and its markets. These will include whether it sells its products in the domestic market only or internationally; whether it uses imported raw materials in the production of its goods; whether it encounters competition from foreign goods in its domestic market; whether it competes on price or has a competitive advantage based on other aspects of its products; and where its production bases are located.

Practice exercise 10

Total: 30 marks

1. Explain the advantages of more open trade to
   a) a country   (4 marks)
   b) to businesses within that country.   (4 marks)

2. Define the term 'protectionism' in relation to international trade.   (3 marks)

3. Which of the following is not an example of a protectionist policy?
   a) Tariffs   b) Embargoes   c) Quotas   d) VAT   (1 mark)

4. Analyse the impact of the imposition of import tariffs on goods entering the UK from all other countries around the world on
   a) a business that only operates in the domestic market but buys raw materials from abroad   (9 marks)
   b) a business that sells its goods in the UK and abroad.   (9 marks)

Globalisation

Globalisation, linked to modern communication and the rapid spread of information technology (IT), is changing the way companies, whether manufacturing or service providers, organise their activities. Firms can now reduce their costs of production by manufacturing where it is cheapest in the world to do so, and can increase their revenue by selling anywhere around the world. Such developments allow a sportswear manufacturer, for example, to design its products in Europe, make them in Southeast Asia and sell them in the USA. More and more global production is carried out by big multinational companies that operate across international borders, locating manufacturing plants overseas in order to capitalise on cheaper labour costs or to be closer to their markets. Some multinationals, like Apple, have become 'virtual firms', outsourcing most of their production to other companies, mainly in Asia.

Reasons for greater globalisation of business

- The growth of free trade areas (also known as global trading blocs), such as the EU, NAFTA and ASEAN, have reduced barriers to trade within their groups and mean that individual economies are becoming more closely integrated with each other.
- Tariffs and other protectionist barriers have gradually been reduced in countries around the world, leading to an increase in world trade.
- The World Trade Organization (WTO) has been instrumental in bringing about a more integrated and interdependent global economy.
- Increased communication and improved transport have led to reduced barriers between countries. Improved transport makes global travel easier. For example, there has been rapid growth in air travel, enabling greater movement of people and goods across the globe. The introduction of containerisation has reduced the costs of goods transport, making trade cheaper and more efficient.
- The growth of large multinational firms creates increased opportunities for economies of scale, leading to lower prices for consumers. Multinational companies have huge power in the world today and have played a significant role in the growth of globalisation. It is estimated that the top 500 multinational companies account for about 70 per cent of world trade; a figure that has increased steadily over the last 30 years.

WORLD TRADE ORGANIZATION

▲ The World Trade Organization has increased the integration of world economies

- Improved technology makes it easier to communicate and share information around the world.
- Improved mobility of capital. In the past few decades there has been a general reduction in capital barriers, making it easier for capital to flow between different economies. This has increased the ability of firms to obtain finance. It has also increased the global interconnectedness of financial markets.
- Increased mobility of labour. People are more willing to move between different countries in search of work.

Note: some of the issues listed above as reasons for greater globalisation of business also illustrate the importance of globalisation for business.

Fact file

Trade organisations

- ASEAN is the Association of Southeast Asian Nations. It consists of ten member states, details of which are given in Case study 1 at the end of this chapter. ASEAN aims to promote collaboration and co-operation among member states, as well as to advance the interests of the region as a whole, including economic and trade growth. It has negotiated a free trade agreement among member states and with other countries such as China, as well as easing travel in the region for citizens of member countries.
- NAFTA is the North American Free Trade Agreement. It sets the rules that govern trade and investment between Canada, the United States and Mexico. The agreement was introduced in 1994 with the intention of systematically eliminating most tariff and non-tariff barriers to free trade and investment between the three countries.

The importance of globalisation for business

- **Comparative advantage**. Not all countries are good at producing all types of products. The idea of comparative advantage is that countries that are good at producing particular products are better off specialising in the production of those products and then exporting them to countries that are less efficient at producing them. Just as countries have comparative advantage, firms also benefit from specialising in products where they have a comparative advantage because this will enable them to reduce costs, charge lower prices and/or provide better quality – that is, be more competitive. This is linked to sectoral changes in an economy. Globalisation can cause the importance of different industrial sectors in an economy to change. For example, the UK no longer has a comparative advantage in industries such as textiles. Developing countries now have a comparative advantage in the manufacture of textiles because they have lower labour costs. Sectoral changes can lead to temporary structural unemployment in the economy, as happened in areas of the north of England when textile manufacturing declined. However, over the long term, these effects tend to be offset by specialisation in other areas of comparative advantage, for example in the UK this is the case in the banking and financial services sector.
- **Increased competition**. Globalisation means that domestic firms are likely to face more international competition. This is likely to improve efficiency and lead to reduced costs and prices, as well as providing more choice for consumers.

- **Migration**. Globalisation makes it easier for migrants to enter and work in the UK. This can help UK firms fill job vacancies, but it can also place greater stress on UK housing and public services.
- **Global economic cycles**. Closely linked economies tend to move together in trade cycles. A recession in one country tends to have an impact in other linked countries; the bigger the country and the more trading partners it has, the more world trade is affected. For example, a deep recession in EU countries or the USA will affect the UK because the EU and the USA are our main trading partners. Table 5.8 and Figure 5.5 illustrate the very similar pattern of GDP growth experienced by a range of countries over a nine-year period.

▼ **Table 5.8** Trends in GDP growth (%) across a range of countries

	2005	2006	2007	2008	2009	2010	2011	2012	2013
France	1.6	2.4	2.4	0.2	-2.9	2.0	2.1	0.3	0.3
Germany	0.7	3.7	3.3	1.1	-5.6	4.1	3.6	0.4	0.1
Japan	1.3	1.7	2.2	-1.0	-5.5	4.7	-0.5	1.8	1.6
UK	2.8	3.0	2.6	-0.3	-4.3	1.9	1.6	0.7	1.7
USA	3.3	2.7	1.8	-0.3	-2.8	2.5	1.6	2.3	2.2

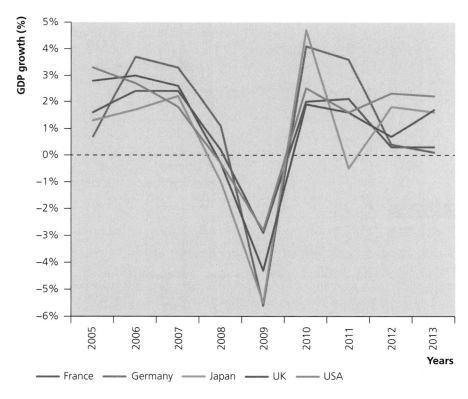

▲ **Figure 5.5** Trends in GDP growth (%) across a range of countries

Source: The World Bank

- Businesses that are successful in global markets have to be able to respond quickly to change, and sophisticated information systems are essential in such situations. The importance of technology, and particularly the internet, has revolutionised business by creating a whole new virtual marketplace that has expanded beyond physical and geographical boundaries. Any company with a website can now compete for customers internationally. In the same way, online work means people from many different countries can work together on particular projects. The internet has made it possible to access information and resources across the world – and to co-ordinate activities in real time. Banking and retailing are examples of business sectors that have adopted new technologies and illustrate aspects of globalisation. When you contact your bank, the person you speak to is often in a call centre many thousands of miles away in another country. When you buy books from an internet supplier like Amazon, the computers taking your order may be on a different continent to those processing your payment, while the books themselves might be stored somewhere else in the world – or they may arrive as a digital download.

● The growth of multinationals and the globalisation of their impact are related closely to the rise in the importance of the brand. Major global brands mean that the same products can just as well be sold in Mumbai or New York, regardless of cultural or socio-economic differences in these locations. Brands like Coca-Cola, Nike, Sony, Starbucks and Disney have become part of the fabric of people's lives. Some commentators suggest that the growth in the wealth and cultural influence of huge multinational businesses over the last 25 years can be traced back to a single idea – that to be very successful, businesses must primarily produce brands rather than products. Companies like those mentioned above spend huge sums of money on promoting and sustaining their brands rather than their individual products. This is often done to try to establish particular brands as an integral part of the way people understand, or would like to see themselves. This focus on the brand rather than the essential qualities of individual products is a huge advantage in terms of market development for these companies. However, it is also a huge risk. Damage to the brand can do significant harm to sales and profitability across a company's complete product range. For example, the Fact file on Nike in Chapter 3 of Book 1 is a classic example of where a brand becomes associated with the exploitation of workers.

Fact file

Starbucks as an example of the opportunities offered by globalisation

The original idea for Starbucks came from Italian coffeehouses. The first Starbucks opened in 1971 in Seattle. After refining the concept in America, the company opened its first international coffeehouse in Tokyo in 1996 and then began to expand globally. The company is now one of the world's best known brands, with more than 21,000 stores in over 65 countries. Starbucks has had an impact on consumers' behaviour around the world, changing the way they consume coffee and profiting by this at the same time. The company is also changing the way coffee is produced. By committing to purchase only Fair Trade Certified coffee beans, Starbucks is promoting ethical and environmentally sound approaches to coffee growing and processing policies in developing countries. At the same time, it is finding that 'doing good' in this sense is also good for business because it reinforces the value of Starbucks' brand.

Practice exercise 11

Total: 35 marks

1. Explain the term 'globalisation'. *(3 marks)*

2. Which of the following points is not a characteristic of globalisation?
   a) Greater free trade between countries
   b) Greater trade barriers between countries
   c) Greater movement of capital between countries
   d) Greater movement of labour between countries *(1 mark)*

3. Identify and explain two reasons for the greater globalisation of business. *(6 marks)*

4. Refer to Table 5.8 and Figure 5.5 (see page 135). Analyse the data and what it suggests about the likely impact on demand and profitability for companies trading in all the countries mentioned during the period 2007 to 2010. *(9 marks)*

5. Evaluate the importance of globalisation to a UK business that imports its raw materials and sells its products in many countries in addition to the UK. *(16 marks)*

The importance of emerging economies for business

Did you know?

'Advanced economies' or 'developed economies' are terms used to describe countries such as the UK, USA, Western European countries, Canada, Australia and Japan. 'Emerging economies' are also called 'developing countries', but should be distinguished from those developing countries that are sometimes called 'frontier markets'. These latter are less developed than emerging economies because their governmental infrastructure and economic and financial markets are not yet as fully formed as those of emerging economies. Frontier markets include countries such as Ukraine, Romania, Bulgaria, Kazakhstan, Lebanon and Jordan.

Key term

Emerging economies (also known as emerging markets) Developing countries that have the potential to grow and develop in terms of productive capacity and market opportunities; from an investment point of view they are seen as developing countries, in which investment would be expected to achieve higher returns but be accompanied by greater risk.

A frequently used acronym to describe some of the largest **emerging economies** is BRIC. This refers to the countries of Brazil, Russia, India and China, all of which have large populations and plentiful supplies of natural resources. Although much attention is given to the BRIC nations, there are many smaller emerging markets. An acronym for another group of emerging economies is Civets, which includes Colombia, Indonesia, Vietnam, Egypt, Turkey and South Africa. Many other countries besides these are emerging economies, including some of the countries of Eastern Europe.

Fact file
BRIC countries

While definitions and classifications of emerging economies vary, there is a general consensus about the role and prominence of the BRIC countries among emerging markets. For example, between 2004 and 2013, their economies doubled in size and now collectively account for 21 per cent of global GDP and 53 per cent of emerging market GDP; they have huge populations with steadily rising incomes.

Fact file

Central and Eastern Europe as an emerging market

The fall of the communist governments in Central and Eastern Europe (CEE) in the late 1980s and the 1990s had major implications for businesses in the UK and the rest of Europe. In most cases, new governments replaced the old centrally planned systems. As a result, many of these countries undertook extensive privatisation policies and, in the early years of this process, recruited experts from the UK and other Western economies to advise on the transfer of assets from the public to the private sector.

In many cases, the governments of these countries were keen to attract Western European businesses to locate in their economies. They did this by providing tax advantages and government funding. For example, in Estonia some company taxes were as low as 0 per cent in order to attract foreign investment, and in Slovakia, government subsidies of over £200 million were provided to US Steel when it located in the country.

Businesses in the EU sought to take advantage of the CEE markets in a number of ways:

- Joint ventures – where EU firms contributed cash, machinery and management skills, while the host country provided land, buildings and labour. As wages and rents were lower, and in some cases controls on production and pollution were less stringent, EU firms gained a low-cost means of production and access to a relatively untapped market.
- Technical co-operation, which allowed some co-production, short of a formal joint venture. Such agreements encompassed joint assembly of products or the creation of assembly plants in the host countries near to potential markets, as with Volvo cars in Hungary. This reduced production costs for Western producers, while offering domestic firms technical expertise.
- Selling technology and expertise to producers in CEE countries, often in the form of licences to produce particular products. For example, Coca-Cola granted a licence to allow manufacture in Bulgaria, which provided a cheap method of extending its market.

The advantages of the emerging markets in the CEE countries included new markets for goods and services, lower labour and other production costs such as land and rent, and less stringent government controls. However, there were risks involved. These included: lower levels of income in the CEE countries than in Western Europe, meaning consumers had far less income to spend on the products of Western European firms; political systems that were still immature and could be unstable, leading to unpredictable decision making and sudden changes to trading conditions; difficulties in raising finance because banking systems were less well developed; and relatively poor infrastructure in terms of transport and communication.

Key factors making emerging economies important for business:

- The rise of emerging economies and their markets has been a significant feature of the global economy. In 2000, emerging markets in total accounted for 37 per cent of global GDP; in 2013 this figure reached approximately 50 per cent. Growth in consumer spending in emerging economies has outpaced that of developed countries every year since 2000 and is expected to continue to do so. This indicates how strongly global economic growth is influenced by emerging economies. Data suggests they are growing about three times faster than developed countries. Figure 5.6 illustrates a clear strengthening in the growth rate of emerging economies since the late 1990s. Not only has the growth rate in advanced economies fallen relative to emerging economies since the late 1990s, it has actually fallen in absolute terms as well. If they continue to open their economies to trade, and continue their trend of growth and development, emerging economies are likely to continue to grow much faster than developed nations and established markets.

- Emerging economies provide huge market opportunities. They are home to 85 per cent of the world's population and 90 per cent of the under 30-year-olds. They are developing and growing rapidly. They have young and increasingly affluent populations who aspire to consume the same types of goods and services as in developed countries. Because of the growing needs of their consumers and their consumers' increasing wealth, they will require huge imports of consumer goods and also the development of infrastructure, which provides further business opportunities. In theory therefore, they are likely to provide enormous opportunities for companies to increase their profits and dividends rapidly – but in a highly competitive climate.

- Emerging economies are likely to have a major impact on the industrial structure of the world. As well as the enormous market opportunities, their population size and age structure mean they are also expected to supply huge numbers of productive, low-paid workers to the world market.

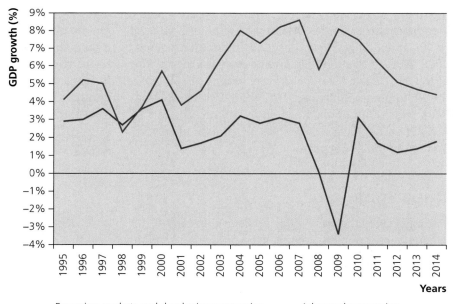

— Emerging markets and developing economies   — Advanced economies

▲ **Figure 5.6** Relative growth rates of advanced economies compared to emerging economies

Source: IMF

Practice exercise 12

1. Using examples, explain what an emerging economy is. *(4 marks)*
2. Identify and explain two possible reasons why UK business might want to do business in emerging economies. *(8 marks)*
3. Identify and explain two possible problems for UK firms attempting to do business in emerging economies. *(8 marks)*
4. What does Figure 5.6 on page 139 show about the growth rates of advanced economies compared to emerging economies over the period covered in the graph? *(5 marks)*

Case study 1: The middle class in emerging economies

Many consumer goods and services businesses planning a strategy to enter one of the emerging markets look at data about the consumer expenditure in terms of its total growth potential in that economy. This is not the best data to consider. Instead, consumer goods and services businesses should focus on the growth potential of non-essential purchases per person and per household. Doing this means paying close attention to what is happening to the middle classes in these emerging economies.

Estimates from The Boston Consulting Group and McKinsey & Company predict that the middle-class income group in the ASEAN (Association of Southeast Asian Nations) region will exceed 100 million people by 2020. ASEAN is a political and economic organisation of ten Southeast Asian countries: Indonesia, Malaysia, the Philippines, Singapore, Thailand, Brunei, Burma (Myanmar), Cambodia, Laos and Vietnam. The ten ASEAN states have a combined population of more than 600 million people.

Looking at the world's 20 largest non-BRIC emerging economies, the proportion of middle class households (middle class in this context is defined as those with a disposable income over US $10,000 – that is, over roughly £6,000) ranges from 99.5 per cent in the United Arab Emirates to 4.8 per cent in Kenya. Within these 20 countries, the middle classes earn from between US $3,000 and 6,000 (about £1,000–2,000) per household in Nigeria, to US $74,000–150,000 (about £50,000–100,000) in the United Arab Emirates.

Despite what may appear to be relatively low levels of middle-class income in some emerging economies, the middle classes remain an important consumer group. Engaging with these consumers at an early stage can be a smart strategy for building brand awareness and for creating and shaping the market for goods and services from the outset, all of which may lead to long-term rewards.

Source: adapted from Euromonitor International, '2015 Outlook for emerging market economies'

Questions

1. Analyse why the case study advises companies considering doing business in an emerging economy to 'focus on the growth potential of non-essential purchases per person and per household'. *(9 marks)*

2. To what extent does evidence in this case study and in this section on emerging economies suggest these markets provide good opportunities for businesses wishing to expand outside the UK? *(16 marks)*

Case study 2: Emerging economies tempt Tesco

Tesco is one of the world's largest retailers. It has 3,300 stores in the UK. In order to grow it had to look beyond the UK. Tesco began a rapid expansion in the late 1990s into emerging economies, focusing on Eastern Europe and Southeast Asia. It now has approximately 7,500 stores and operates in 12 countries. As well as the UK, it operates in China, Czech Republic, Hungary, India, Ireland, Malaysia, Poland, Slovakia, South Korea, Thailand and Turkey.

Many of these areas had relatively undeveloped grocery retail markets, but ones that were changing rapidly, offering Tesco major opportunities. Tesco managed to become among the top retailers in many of the countries in which it operates, giving its business a secure base.

The potential offered by the retail food sector in India is huge. However, the country's stringent rules on foreign direct investment (FDI) bar multinationals from entering in a manner of their choosing. For example, Tesco would have preferred to enter the Indian retail food sector by starting up or acquiring a consumer retailer. Instead, Tesco entered into an agreement with the huge Indian Tata group to provide backroom support and retail expertise for the expansion of Tata's Star Bazaar hypermarket chain. It provides 80 per cent of the stock sold by Star Bazaar, both food and non-food, all of which is sourced through its modern distribution centre in Mumbai. This distribution centre also provides wholesale products to traditional Indian retailers, restaurants and other businesses. This deal provides a platform for future growth and an opportunity to learn about the market, and enables Tesco to establish a supply chain in the country. By entering the wholesale market and forming links with Tata, Tesco may be setting the stage for future growth into the consumer retail market. Tesco estimates that within a decade, over half of its annual revenue will be generated outside the UK – this figure is currently about 35 per cent.

Emerging economies provide very attractive opportunities for retailers. Analysts suggest that size alone will not determine which businesses will be successful in today's global trading environment. To operate globally and successfully, retailers must be efficient, flexible and provide strong brand positioning. While emerging economies are not immune to global economic trade cycles, the pace of growth in these countries continues to outstrip that of the advanced economies (as indicated in Figure 5.6 on page 139).

Source: adapted in part from information on Tesco's website

Questions

Total: 45 marks

1. Explain why strong brand positioning might be important in establishing success in an emerging market. *(4 marks)*

2. Using Tesco as an example, analyse the link between the increasing globalisation of markets and the existence of emerging economies. *(9 marks)*

3. Discuss the benefits to Tesco of establishing supermarkets in emerging economies rather than in Western Europe or North America. *(16 marks)*

4. To what extent might Tesco's current developments in India contribute to its longer-term objectives of establishing itself as a consumer retailer in the Indian market? *(16 marks)*

Case study 3: Harewood Ltd

Tessa Harewood opened the newspapers excitedly. Following the takeover of T.J. Laing Ltd, she was now the chief executive of the UK's fifth-largest sports goods supplier.

It was a gamble. Harewood Ltd had built up a tremendous reputation for its sportswear, and sales were growing fast, helped by Tessa's decision to move all of the production of its sportswear to India. However, Tessa found it difficult to foresee a time when Harewood Ltd could displace some of the major international sportswear suppliers. On that basis the takeover made good sense.

T.J. Laing specialised in equipment manufacturing. However, the company had been plagued by problems. The fitness equipment was manufactured in a factory in Birmingham, but more and more competitors had moved production to Asia or Eastern Europe, where wage costs were lower. T.J. Laing had responded by specialising in the higher-quality, technically sophisticated end of the market, but the recession had hit sales of these products significantly.

The other division of T.J. Laing was racquet production. Production of racquets was based in China, but difficulties with quality and delivery had led to heavy financial losses.

Year 1

Tessa's first action was to start producing racquets in two more places. Harewood Ltd opened a new factory in Portugal. In Birmingham, Tessa used some of the spare capacity in the fitness equipment factory to produce racquets. Only 30 per cent of racquet production was left in China, with 60 per cent in Portugal. After delivery costs had been allowed for, the production in Portugal was only slightly dearer than China. The remaining 10 per cent was manufactured in Birmingham – mainly the more expensive racquets – but there was also scope to produce other racquets just in time, to meet sudden orders or shortages in the UK.

Gradually sales in all products improved, as the UK came out of the recession that had started just before the takeover. Sportswear recovered most strongly in the UK, but by the end of the year fitness equipment sales there were still at their lowest level for three years. Tessa was pleased that the business was not reliant on UK sales for the majority of its revenue from fitness equipment. The sales in Italy and France accounted for 65 per cent of the company's sales of fitness equipment and the T.J. Laing brand name was very strong in those two countries. Tessa's long-term strategy was to use the T.J. Laing brand name and reputation to sell its sportswear in Italy and France.

Year 2

As the business cycle moved from recession to recovery, sportswear sales grew quickly, but it took much longer for the fitness equipment sales to pick up. However, by the end of the year, the growth in orders for fitness equipment was so high that Harewood was forced to subcontract manufacturing to other companies in order to keep up with demand.

In the economy, borrowing had reached record levels. A mixture of major construction projects in the public sector and high consumer spending in the private sector led to a sudden rise in inflation. Tessa was not worried overall, but did have concerns that this would have a negative effect on some products. People did not seem to be too concerned about price when buying fitness equipment and most racquets, but some of the sportswear goods were price elastic in demand. By the end of the year, the company was achieving record

▶▶▶

profits and Tessa's main problem was finding ways of meeting the huge increase in demand for fitness equipment.

Year 3

The new factory in Wolverhampton opened at the beginning of the year. Unemployment was low in the economy overall. However, the Midlands had been hit by high levels of structural unemployment due to the decline in the metal manufacturing industry. As a consequence, it was relatively easy for Harewood Ltd to find both a suitable site and the necessary skilled labour to produce fitness equipment.

Sales (and prices) continued to grow. The announcement of a 1.5 per cent increase in interest rates in April took Tessa by surprise. Harewood Ltd had borrowed all of the money needed to open the new factory, hoping to benefit from the low interest rates at the time. All the same, the firm's cash flow was strong and all three product areas were producing high profits.

Tessa had expected some slowing in the rate of growth of sales, but she was shocked to see the order book at the end of June. Orders from shops for sportswear were down by 2 per cent and racquet sales had fallen by 5 per cent, but the biggest shock was fitness equipment – orders had decreased by 20 per cent. Tessa wondered whether she had been too hasty in agreeing to the new factory.

The increase in interest rates also coincided with an increase in the value of the pound against other currencies. Tessa wondered whether this was good news or bad news for Harewood Ltd.

Tessa was not the only person surprised by developments. By July the economy had lurched from a strong recovery back into a downturn. In August the Bank of England announced a reduction of 1 per cent in interest rates. By the end of the year, another cut (of 0.5 per cent) had been made and the threat of a recession seemed to have disappeared.

At the end of the year, Tessa was thinking about her new year's resolutions. She decided that from now on she would seek a clearer picture of future macroeconomic changes before making any strategic decisions. On 31 December she read the economics section of her daily newspaper carefully. It included a summary of the current year's (Year 3) economic data, with its predictions for the next 2 years (Years 4 and 5). This is provided in Table 5.9.

▼ **Table 5.9** The UK economy: current and forecast macroeconomic variables

Year	Change in GDP (%)	Unemployment (%)	Inflation (% change in CPI)	Value of the pound against other currencies*	Average interest rates (%)
Year 3 (actual)	+1.2	5.6	1.4	110	4.5
Year 4 (forecast)	+2.0	5.5	1.6	105	4.0
Year 5 (forecast)	+4.0	4.4	2.0	90	5.0

*base year: Year 2 = 100

Questions

Total: 100 marks

1. What does a rate of inflation of 1.4 per cent (Year 3 in Table 5.9) actually mean? *(3 marks)*

2. What does a forecast change in GDP of +4.0 per cent (Year 5 in Table 5.9) actually mean? *(3 marks)*

3. In relation to the data in Table 5.9, by how much is the value of the pound against other currencies expected to fall in value between Year 3 and Year 5?
   a) 10 per cent
   b) 15 per cent
   c) 18 per cent
   d) 20 per cent. *(1 mark)*

4. Define the terms 'recession' and 'recovery' in relation to the business cycle. *(6 marks)*

5. Outline two different ways in which the business cycle has influenced Harewood Ltd. *(6 marks)*

6. Explain why Tessa believed that inflation would not have the same effect on all of Harewood Ltd's products. *(6 marks)*

7. Why are the sales of goods that are price elastic likely to suffer during a period of high inflation? *(6 marks)*

8. Explain two ways in which a rise in interest rates might affect Harewood Ltd. *(6 marks)*

9. Explain how a rise in the value of the pound might affect Harewood Ltd. *(6 marks)*

10. If the government were to announce a rise in the basic rate of income tax, how might this affect a business such as Harewood Ltd? *(6 marks)*

11. Distinguish between fiscal policy and monetary policy. *(4 marks)*

12. Identify and explain two problems for Harewood Ltd of operating in global markets. *(6 marks)*

13. Analyse the implications for Harewood Ltd of the sudden and unpredictable fluctuations of the business cycle during Years 1 to 3. *(9 marks)*

14. How important are more open trade, globalisation and emerging economies in influencing the performance of Harewood Ltd? *(16 marks)*

15. Assess the extent to which the success of Harewood Ltd has been influenced by changes in the economic environment and how the forecast changes in macroeconomic variables are likely to affect the business in the future. *(16 marks)*

6

Analysing the external environment to assess opportunities and threats: social and technological

This chapter considers the impact of the social and technological environment on strategic and functional decision making. It focuses firstly on social change. In considering this it explores demographic changes and population movements such as urbanisation and migration; changes in consumer lifestyle and buying behaviour; and the growth of online businesses. The social environment and Corporate Social Responsibility (CSR) is then considered. Discussion about CSR includes the reasons for and against CSR; the difference between stakeholder and shareholder concepts in relation to CSR; and Carroll's Corporate Social Responsibility pyramid. The chapter then focuses on technological change, and in particular the impact of technological change on functional areas and strategy. The chapter concludes with a discussion of the pressures for socially responsible behaviour.

Social change

Social change means any significant change over time in behaviour patterns and cultural values and norms. Significant change implies change that leads to profound social consequences for individuals, for businesses and for society. Examples to be discussed in this chapter include the following:

● demographic change and population movements, which have resulted in changes in migration patterns and have led to increasing urbanisation, providing business opportunities in the UK and globally
● changes in, for example, work and leisure patterns that have led to changes in lifestyles and buying behaviour
● the internet and how it is used, which has led to significant changes in the way people communicate with each other and has provided opportunities for the growth of online businesses.

Social change involving demographic changes and population movements such as urbanisation and migration

Demographic changes and their impact on business costs and the demand for goods and services were discussed in detail in Chapter 3 of the AQA A-level Business Book 1. Ensure that you are familiar with the content of that section before proceeding with the next section of this chapter. In

▲ Businesses need to adapt to demographic change

Key terms

Urbanisation The increase in the proportion of people living in towns and cities.

Migration The permanent movement of people from one region to another; migration can be internal, that is within a country and for which urbanisation is an example, or international, that is between countries.

Book 1 it was noted that the UK population has grown in recent years, and, alongside this overall increase there have been changes to the geographical spread of the population, its ethnic balance, the size of households and the age distribution of the population.

Demographic change can be perceived as either an opportunity or a threat, and the response of a business to such change will largely determine which of these it is. Demographic change influences two important aspects of business: employees, and markets or customers. Opportunities therefore exist in relation to meeting the demand for goods and services of those demographic segments that are growing. Opportunities also exist as a result of the innovative potential of a diverse workforce. A growing body of evidence suggests that businesses that take a positive approach to diversity generally are likely to do better than their competitors.

Chapter 3 in Book 1 suggested that those businesses that take note of changes in demographic trends and adapt their businesses accordingly are more likely to be successful. It also notes that because demographic change happens slowly and can be anticipated, analysed and understood well in advance, changes can be predicted and prepared for much more clearly than is the case for changes that occur in other areas of the external environment.

Urbanisation and migration

As well as population movement to towns and cities, **urbanisation** is also characterised by a move away from employment in primary sectors and towards employment in secondary and then tertiary sectors. Urbanisation usually grows because of two distinct processes – the result of a natural increase in the number of people living in towns and cities, and the result of **migration** to towns and cities. Migration can take place for economic, social, political and environmental reasons.

In the developed world, urbanisation has taken place over hundreds of years. In the UK, this was largely following the Industrial Revolution in the late eighteenth and early nineteenth centuries. People were attracted to towns for employment and the range of services available and businesses were attracted by the infrastructure, workforce availability and consumer demand opportunities. In the developed world, growth in cities has largely stabilised or is, at least, more managed. Interestingly, more recently, the growth in car ownership, good transport links and the congested nature of many city centres have led to 'counter-urbanisation', where people prefer to live away from the city and where businesses, particularly retailers, move to 'out of town' sites. Technology plays an important role here. While people used to be attracted to cities because of employment opportunities, technological change and flexible working arrangements now mean that for many jobs this is no longer the case. Equally the growth of online business means businesses themselves can be located anywhere.

Urbanisation and the growth of cities is a more recent phenomenon in the developing world. Table 6.1 indicates the growing percentage of the population living in urban areas by world regions. The important point to note from this data is the rapid rate of growth in Africa and Asia compared to the rates of growth in North America and Europe. Such growth is partially the result of natural population growth, but mainly the result of massive movements of population from rural areas to cities.

▼ **Table 6.1** Percentage of population living in urban areas by world regions, 1970–2010

Region	1970	1980	1990	2000	2010
North America	67	70	73	75	78
Europe	67	70	73	77	80
Africa	23	28	34	41	47
Asia	24	26	34	43	50

Source: UN statistics

Positive aspects of urbanisation:

- cheaper and easier access to basic services and infrastructure, for example in relation to water and health
- more job opportunities, market opportunities and opportunities for external economies of scale
- higher incomes, better living standards, more stable economies.

Negative aspects of urbanisation:

- the urban poor are often dependent on casual, unskilled jobs or unregistered and illegal work, which weakens their rights and benefits and limits their ability to escape poverty
- global economic downturns are likely to increase the number of job losses among the urban poor
- slums, crime and pollution.

Fact file

Migration in the UK

ONS figures from 2014 suggest that over half a million people came to live and work in the UK in the year to June 2014. At the same time about 325,000 people left the UK over the same period. Net immigration (immigration – emigration) was 260,000. For the last 20 years, the UK has seen more immigration than emigration, reaching a peak in 2005. Net migration then began to fall as a result of the 2008 economic recession and government restrictions on the entry of some people from outside Europe. Net migration has been rising since 2012. Much of the increase is due to EU citizens coming to live and work in the UK. However, the number of people coming to live and work in the UK from the rest of the world exceeds those from the EU and has been increasing since 2013. Most migrants coming to the UK are looking for work, and those entering from the EU account for more than half of all the workers in the UK who are not British citizens.

Chapter 3 of Book 1 discussed the impact of migrant workers on business, including on wage costs, on filling skills gaps, on attitudes to work and on productivity and competitiveness. It also considered the geographical shift of the population to the southeast of England and the impact of this on business.

Impact of net immigration:

- an increase in the labour force and thus an increase in the potential output capacity of the economy
- an increase in total demand and real GDP as a result of an increase in spending power

- more flexibility in the labour market with, for example, more nurses from abroad and more skilled and semi-skilled workers, such as builders and plumbers, from Eastern Europe
- more demands on social services, including housing, education and health.

The above discussion about urbanisation and migration illustrates the fact that social change in relation to demographic issues brings major implications for businesses in terms of: the nature of their strategies for growth, both national and global; how they adapt their marketing and distribution to take account of an increasingly urban customer base with distinct needs and consumer habits; how and where to locate their business; and the nature and employment pattern of their workforce.

Social change leading to changes in consumer lifestyles and buying behaviour

Chapter 3 of Book 1 discussed how changes to the structure of the UK population were affecting the demand for goods and services, with an ageing population and the changing ethnic make-up of the population being two of the most influential factors discussed. This reflects changes to consumer lifestyles and buying behaviour, which firms need to take into account in order to be successful.

Chapter 9 in Book 1 discussed different marketing segments, including behaviour segments and lifestyle issues. Changes in consumer lifestyles and buying behaviour include a vast array of issues. Some of these, in relation to the UK, are identified below:

- an increasingly 'throw-away' society – for example, where clothing, shoes and accessories are bought as fashion items that are not expected to last beyond the current season
- an increase in the frequency with which people eat out and/or purchase ready meals, rather than cooking from scratch at home
- people taking more frequent holidays and travelling further
- people's attitudes to health and diet, joining fitness clubs and buying organic foods
- the increasing use of technology and social media for entertainment, communication and for business
- a 24/7 society where there is an expectation that retailers and other businesses and services will be open all day and every day, or can be accessed at all times online
- the fact that people feel more pressured for time, which in turn results in some of the issues already identified – more eating out and use of ready meals, more use of technology to organise their lives and make purchases
- a greater focus on ethical consumption, in terms of fair traded food products and clothing that use Fairtrade material and provide Fairtrade labour conditions.

All of these lifestyle changes cause changes to buyer behaviour, which in turn leads to changes in the demand for goods and services. Businesses need to be constantly aware of such changes in order to be able to respond quickly and effectively. If they do not respond quickly and effectively, consumers will go elsewhere.

What do you think?

The list on this page gives some examples of changes in consumer lifestyles and buying behaviour. There are many more.

What other changes in consumer lifestyles and buying behaviour can you identify and what impact are these likely to have on business?

Social change leading to the growth of online businesses

Discussion of online businesses – the reasons for their growth and the impact of such businesses – are considered in a number of different sections of this and Book 1. For example, it was considered in Chapter 10 of Book 1, where the growth in Tesco's online sales is discussed. The topic is linked to changes in consumer lifestyles and buyer behaviour in the previous section of this chapter and is also discussed later in the section on technological change. The topic is also considered in Chapter 14, when the greater use of digital technology is considered.

The significant growth in online businesses is a response to technological change that facilitates such a development and allows any business to sell to anywhere in the world at the click of a button. It is also a response to consumer demand and expectations about 24/7 access to the purchase of goods and services anywhere in the world. Online businesses can be small or large; size does not appear to affect the likelihood of success, nor does whether a business has a high street presence as well as an online presence. (The Fact files below illustrate these different types of businesses.) The most recent annual Royal Mail study of UK SME (small and medium enterprises) online retailers indicates that eight out of ten are targeting new international markets. Another report indicates that over half of all firms surveyed said that technology was a key driver for growth and sales and that websites and mobile apps were named by almost 70 per cent as the key. Creating a better website presence was a priority reflecting that retailers in particular are trying to satisfy customer demands in an increasingly global marketplace. For online businesses, delivery and the importance of a good returns policy for online shoppers were recognised as vital.

Commentators claim that the most successful businesses are using technology to ensure they understand their customers well and offer personalised service, whether face to face or online. In a recent survey of more than 300 executives across 11 countries by the International Data Group (IDG), 75 per cent of them said online sales represented at least half of their 2014 revenues. One executive said, 'Consumers are willing to spend their money with retailers who provide the best online experience. This expectation is regardless of where customers are geographically located.'

Did you know?

Analysts suggest that central shopping streets – high streets – are changing in nature as they recover from the economic downturn. They are complementing rather than competing with digital or online shopping through the rise of services such as 'click and collect' (ordering a good online and collecting it from a local store). Changes in consumer lifestyles and buyer behaviour are a major part of this change. Among these shifts in consumer behaviour is the rise of leisure services such as coffee shops. Consumers, apparently, value the presence of coffee shops and make shopping decisions according to which streets have them, boosting local high streets by not only increasing footfall but also the amount of time spent there.

Fact file

Two small companies trading successfully online

Wiggly Wigglers: Wiggly Wigglers is an example of a small company making it big online. It is a rural store specialising in garden equipment and worm composters. By using a website and social media, it has made rather boring products literally 'come alive'. As well as general sales information about products and prices, the site hosts video demos of their latest products, they have a regular podcast and they share specialist information and expertise. Their actions in relation to online and social media have established the company as an expert in its area and brought credibility to the brand.

Howies: Howies is a UK clothing company specialising in activewear. Using its website, Howies has succeeded in giving the brand a real personality by making sure visitors get to know the individuals within the company. The blog is regularly updated by staff members so that individual personalities shine through. The website and the company's presence on most social networks are helping Howies to connect people to the brand.

Fact file

Two large companies trading successfully online

Dunelm: In April 2015, Dunelm, the homewares retailer, reported a 40 per cent rise in home delivery sales, reflecting a strategy to increase its sales through a multichannel approach. In February 2015, in its half-year results report, it said that it aimed to grow its sales by 50 per cent over the medium term, with half of that growth coming from stores and half from its online home delivery channel. In March 2015, its online sales were up 60 per cent on the last year, with overall sales up by 13 per cent.

Marks and Spencer: M&S said e-commerce sales had grown by 14 per cent in the final quarter of the financial year to end of March 2015 compared to the same time last year. That contrasts with performance in the first three quarters, each of which was down on the previous year by 5–8 per cent. E-commerce sales in the third quarter were hit by problems at its distribution centre, which affected online sales and deliveries over Christmas 2014. M&S suggested it had 'experienced a period of transition' and 'massive amounts of change', but had now fixed the online distribution problem and customers were increasingly enjoying shopping on the website and were happy with the experience – as evidenced in the latest results.

Practice exercise 1

Total: 30 marks

1. Explain the terms 'urbanisation' and 'migration'. (6 marks)

2. Describe three significant demographic changes or population movements, other than urbanisation, that are affecting business in the UK. (9 marks)

3. Identify and explain two examples of how social change in relation to urbanisation and migration might affect business in the UK or globally. (6 marks)

4. Identify and explain three examples of how changes in consumer lifestyles and buying behaviour might affect business in the UK. (9 marks)

Corporate Social Responsibility (CSR) as part of the social environment

Business for Social Responsibility (BSR) is an organisation that helps companies achieve commercial success in ways that respect ethical values, people, communities and the environment. It defines **corporate social responsibility** as 'achieving commercial success in ways that honour ethical values and respect people, communities, and the natural environment'. It also says that corporate social responsibility means addressing the legal, ethical, commercial and other expectations that society has for business, and making decisions that balance the claims of all key stakeholders fairly.

Key term

Corporate social responsibility (CSR) The duties of an organisation towards employees, customers, society and the environment; companies that accept their corporate social responsibility usually do so by integrating social and environmental concerns into their business operations and their interactions with stakeholders.

Did you know?

There is historical evidence of firms accepting social responsibilities. For example, in the nineteenth century, religiously motivated firms such as Cadbury in Birmingham and Rowntree in York (chocolate and confectionery manufacturers, respectively) and Titus Salt, a woollen mill owner in Saltaire, Bradford, treated their workforce with respect, providing good working conditions, education, housing and a pleasant, communal environment.

Examples of activities that would be viewed as socially responsible are:

- using sustainable sources of raw materials
- ensuring that suppliers operate responsibly – for example, avoiding the use of child labour
- operating an extensive health and safety policy above the legal requirements, thereby protecting the well-being of employees
- engaging in a continuous process of environmental management and monitoring the effects of production on the environment
- trading ethically and taking account of moral issues.

Fact file

Business in the Community

Formed in 1980, Business in the Community (BITC) is the Prince's Responsible Business Network. It is a business-led charity which engages thousands of businesses through its programmes, driven by a membership of over 800 companies from small enterprise to global corporations. It created the Corporate Responsibility Index, which provides an insight into how leading companies are driving responsible business practice and which serves as a valuable self-assessment tool that helps companies benchmark their own activities and performance in this area.

Did you know?

Some companies report their corporate social responsibility performance in their annual reports, others provide this information in separate reports. Some companies call their CSR reports 'sustainability' reports or use similar terminology.

CSR reporting

CSR reporting, which is also known as social auditing, involves the following stages:

- identifying social objectives and ethical values
- defining stakeholders
- establishing social performance indicators
- measuring performance, keeping records and preparing social accounts
- submitting accounts for independent audit and publishing the results.

Did you know?

The role of an independent auditor is to form a view, on the basis of detailed and systematic investigation, as to whether the statements and claims made in the corporate social responsibility report are trustworthy and adequately supported by evidence. In doing this, they seek to apply the following three tests:

- Materiality. Is the information relevant to stakeholders' concerns and interests and will it help them make informed judgements about the company's performance?
- Completeness. Does the information provide sufficient evidence that the company understands all its significant social, economic and environmental impacts?
- Responsiveness. Does the report demonstrate the company's responses and commitment to improving its performance?

151

A CSR report, or social audit, results in the production of a set of social accounts that attempt to evaluate performance against a set of non-financial criteria. Just as financial ratios (explained in Chapter 2) allow a firm to judge and compare financial management and performance over time and within and between companies, social ratios can be used to examine how well a company is performing in relation to a range of 'social' issues.

Comprehensive CSR reports, or social audits, might include reference to each of the follow areas of an organisation's work:

- **The workplace** – how well it is treating its employees and how well it values them; how well it monitors health and safety-related accidents, and the strategies it has in place to reduce accidents; the range of salaries in the organisation; whether it is respecting human rights; the extent to which it is employing individuals from minority ethnic groups.
- **The marketplace** – the extent to which it is responding to its customers' needs; the extent to which it trades with ethically sound suppliers.
- **The environment** – the extent to which it is using renewable raw materials and recycling inputs; how effectively it is monitoring the pollution and emissions it creates and the waste it generates; whether it is setting targets in this area and the extent to which it is reaching them; whether it is talking to pressure groups.
- **The community** – the extent to which it is communicating with, helping and giving something back to the community.

Did you know?

Research suggests that graduates and, in particular, postgraduates with MBA (master of business administration) degrees, favour companies that are able to demonstrate high levels of corporate social responsibility.

What do you think?

How useful is a CSR report or social audit? Can a company such as BAT, (see Fact file on the right), which produces an arguably lethal product, be socially responsible? Is it possible for such a company to reconcile its business interests with accepting its corporate social responsibilities in relation to people's health?

Fact file

The 'ethics' of cigarettes

British American Tobacco (BAT), the major cigarette manufacturer, produces CSR reports. The anti-smoking group ASH calls the whole idea laughable. BAT's CSR report defines targets for reducing energy use, water consumption, carbon dioxide emissions and waste production, and commits itself to enlightened employment practices. This is at odds with what many see as BAT's ruthless marketing to entice young people to smoke. This was illustrated, in 2000, when BAT employees were caught on television handing out packets of Benson and Hedges cigarettes to teenage volleyball players in the Gambia. BAT helped to draw up the International Tobacco Products Marketing Standards, intended to bring worldwide marketing in line with UK restrictions. However, it does not fund, for example, anti-smoking campaigns among the young.

Fact file

The importance of CSR

'Issues that many managers think are soft for business, such as environment, diversity, human rights and community, are now hard for business,' said David Grayson, then a director of Business in the Community (BIC) and now Professor of Corporate Social Responsibility at Cranfield University. 'They are hard to ignore, hard to manage, and very hard for businesses that get them wrong. However, managed well, these issues can be a source of competitive advantage.'

▲ Reduction of pollution is a benefit of CSR

The reasons for and against CSR

Reasons for CSR

In most cases, businesses that accept their social responsibility benefit society and themselves.

Benefits for society:

- Problems such as unemployment and pollution are likely to be reduced.
- Quality of life is likely to be improved because decisions will be based on what is best for society rather than what is best for an individual firm.
- Society's long-term needs are likely to be considered rather than simply the short-term needs of a business.
- Life and business activity will be easier if everyone involved is working together for the common good rather than if one group is trying to exploit another for its own benefit.
- It can be argued that it is simply the right thing to do and that firms have a duty to be concerned with the wider impact of their activities.

Benefits for business:

- Improved financial performance. A recent US study showed that the overall financial performance of companies gaining awards in a league table for business ethics and citizenship was significantly better than that of other companies.
- Reduced operating costs. Some CSR initiatives can reduce operating costs. For example, many initiatives aimed at improving environmental performance – such as reducing gas emissions that contribute to global warming or reducing the use of agricultural chemicals – also lower costs. Many recycling initiatives cut waste-disposal costs and generate income by selling recycled materials.
- Enhanced brand image and reputation. Customers are often drawn to brands and companies with good reputations in CSR-related areas. A company considered socially responsible can benefit both from its enhanced reputation with the public and from its reputation within the business community, increasing the company's ability to attract capital and trading partners.
- Increased sales and customer loyalty. A number of studies have suggested that there is a large and growing market for the products and services of companies perceived to be socially responsible.
- Increased ability to attract and retain employees. Companies perceived to have strong CSR commitments often find it easier to recruit and retain employees, resulting in a reduction in staff turnover and associated recruitment and training costs, because employees feel happier working in such a business.
- Access to capital. The growth of socially responsible or ethical investing (e.g. the Co-operative Bank) means that companies with strong CSR performance have increased access to capital.

Author advice

When answering questions on this area, always try to see the big picture. Think of this topic in relation to everything else you know about business, so that you can really consider the implications. For example, review what you know about the functional areas of the firm (marketing, finance, people and operations) and think about how acting in a socially responsible manner might affect these areas.

Reasons against CSR

Some of the following statements are contentious, but they reflect the range of arguments against CSR.

- Efficient use of resources is likely to be reduced if businesses are restricted in how they can produce and where they can locate. This might lead to higher prices.
- Socially responsible policies can be costly to introduce. International competitiveness will be reduced if other countries do not consider externalities (explained opposite) and social responsibility, and therefore produce more cheaply.
- Stakeholder groups tend to have differing objectives (as discussed in Chapter 6 in Book 1) and they are therefore unlikely to agree on what is socially responsible behaviour.
- Social responsibility may be just a passing fashion and no one can be sure of the value to firms of being socially responsible.
- If the economy is generally doing well, managers feel able to look at intangibles such as social responsibility. During a recession, however, they will look more at profits and survival, even if this means taking little or no notice of social responsibility.
- If something is important to society at large, it can be argued that the government should pass laws to ensure that everyone acts responsibly.
- It can be argued that social responsibility is just an extension of firms being market orientated. In other words, because consumers want firms to act this way, firms respond in order to maximise their profits. According to this view, firms are cynically using the idea of social responsibility as a method of marketing their products, and will use the idea only for as long as it allows them to extend the product life cycle.

Although there is evidence that accepting social responsibility provides direct benefits to firms, in general the benefits tend to accrue to society as a whole or to the local community. In this sense, firms that accept their social responsibility create external benefits (explained below) for society. But equally, if society and/or the local community improve in terms of wealth, standard of living and quality of life, then in the longer term business will also benefit.

Did you know?

Business and external costs and benefits

Externalities are the environmental effects of a firm's activities. These may be positive (known as external benefits or positive externalities), such as job creation or providing a pleasing landscape around the factory. They may also be negative (known as external costs or negative externalities), such as polluting the atmosphere with fumes, polluting rivers with waste or congesting the roads with lorries.

Social costs are the total costs to society of a particular action – they include private costs (i.e. financial costs) and external costs.

Note: individuals also create external costs. For example, travelling to work by car rather than bus or train means an individual creates higher levels of pollution and congestion.

Negative externalities are external costs imposed on society by firms. Because these external costs do not directly affect a firm's profits (unlike financial costs that would reduce profit levels), there is no incentive for firms to minimise them. This situation is known as market failure (where the forces of demand and supply do not provide the best outcomes) and requires government intervention in order to influence the behaviour of firms. Types of intervention include:

● legislation to ban or control certain activities
● licences that allow a certain level of activity to be undertaken
● taxation to make the polluter pay and encourage firms and individuals to select options that have less impact on the environment
● fines to penalise those who carry out undesirable actions.

The extent to which a firm is concerned about the external costs it creates depends on the degree of government intervention, pressure group action and the extent to which the firm takes its environmental responsibilities seriously.

CSR and its link to the difference between stakeholder versus shareholder concepts

The difference between stakeholder and shareholder concepts was explored in detail in Chapter 6 of Book 1. Ensure that you are familiar with the content of that chapter before proceeding with this section.

In relation to social responsibility and ethics, businesses may take different stances in the way in which they perceive shareholders and other stakeholders. For example:

● They might view shareholders' or owners' short-term interests as their only responsibility. Such organisations are likely to meet only their minimum obligations in relation to other stakeholder groups and to the wider environment.
● They might recognise that well-managed relationships with other stakeholders bring long-term benefits to shareholders or owners. The approach of such organisations is not dissimilar to the previous stance, but in addition they realise that expenditure on welfare and other provision is sensible, while not seeing it as an ethical duty.
● They might include the interests and expectations of stakeholders in their mission. Organisations with this stance are likely to go beyond their minimum obligations. For example, they might avoid selling anti-social

products or making products in a manner that is considered unethical, and would be prepared to accept reductions in profitability for the social good.

● They might take an ideological approach and place financial considerations secondary. The extent to which this stance is viable depends on how accountable the organisation is to its shareholders or owners. It is probably easier for a private, family-owned organisation to be run in this way.

The previous section discussed CSR reporting, or social auditing. This process enables a business to assess the impact of the entire range of its activities on stakeholders and society in general. Businesses are becoming more aware of the need to try to meet the expectations of different groups of stakeholders. Although the various stakeholder groups tend to have different objectives and it may never be possible to reconcile all of their differences, CSR reporting, or social auditing, goes some way towards assisting businesses to address this issue and to meet their social responsibilities.

The process of CSR reporting, or social auditing, is part of the move towards more scrutiny of business practices and increased availability of information for stakeholders, whether employees, consumers, pressure groups, the local community or the government.

CSR reporting or social auditing, if done seriously and effectively, is beneficial both for business and for stakeholders.

● A social audit provides information to all the stakeholders of a business about the extent to which it is meeting its non-financial objectives. Evidence suggests that consumers increasingly prefer to purchase their goods and services from 'responsible' businesses. Social audits enable consumers to be more informed about which firms to purchase from and which firms to avoid. They enable pressure groups to gain access to valuable information, which may inform their campaign against a particular firm or minimise their complaints against it. They also assist government in monitoring the behaviour of firms and identifying the need for legislation or regulation in certain sectors of business.

● A social audit provides employees with information about the non-financial performance of the whole organisation rather than simply the department or office they work in. It ensures that senior management has a complete view of the impact of the organisation's activities on all of its stakeholders, thus identifying areas for improvement and encouraging more informed decision making. This is particularly important for large organisations and multinational companies, which have businesses in many different locations worldwide.

● By opening up its activities to public scrutiny, a social audit might deter future criticism of a firm, which in turn might reduce the actions of pressure groups. This is more likely to be the case if the social audit is carried out by independent consultants or is independently scrutinised and published in full.

● Of course, undertaking social audits may highlight areas that need improving. Firms may be reluctant to undertake these improvements if they are likely to incur high costs. However, pressure from stakeholders and more responsible competitors is likely to mean that, eventually, they will have no choice.

Carroll's Corporate Social Responsibility pyramid

In his 1991 article entitled, 'The Pyramid of Corporate Social Responsibility', Dr Archie B. Carroll, a business management author and professor, identified four areas of corporate social responsibility. He structured them as a four-tiered pyramid and called it the **CSR pyramid**, or pyramid of responsibilities. The four different tiers were: economic responsibilities, legal responsibilities, ethical responsibilities and philanthropic responsibilities. See Figure 6.1.

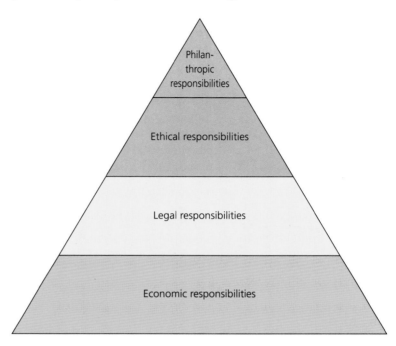

▲ **Figure 6.1** The Pyramid of Corporate Social Responsibility

The following provides an explanation of each tier:

- Economic responsibilities – this is the responsibility to be profitable: to maintain a high level of operational efficiency; to maximise sales and minimise costs; to make sound strategic decisions; to maintain a strong competitive position; to provide investors with adequate and attractive returns on their investments.
- Legal responsibilities – this is the responsibility to obey all laws and adhere to all regulations: this includes environmental and consumer laws, laws protecting employees, fulfilling contractual obligations and honouring warranties and guarantees; to provide goods and services that at least meet the minimum legal requirements.
- Ethical responsibilities – this is the responsibility to be ethical: to do what is right, just, and fair and to avoid or minimise harm to stakeholders (employees, consumers, the environment and others); to avoid questionable practices; to respond to the spirit not just the letter of the law.
- Philanthropic responsibilities – this is the expectation that businesses will be good corporate citizens: to contribute financial and human resources to the community and to improve the quality of life; to provide programmes supporting the community (in relation to education, health, human services, culture, arts, civics); to promote and engage in volunteerism.

Carroll said that the different types or kinds of obligations and responsibilities in the pyramid are in constant and dynamic tension with one another. He suggests that the most critical tensions are those involving the economic level. This is because this is the foundation upon which all the other responsibilities rest. Without successful economic responsibility, it is unlikely that a business would survive or be able to fulfil the other responsibilities. Carroll said the pyramid should not be seen as a sequential process, but should be viewed as a whole in assisting a business in its decisions, actions and policies.

Different stakeholders are affected by the different corporate social responsibilities identified in the pyramid. For example:

- if the business is not profitable, failure to fulfil economic responsibilities will directly affect employees and owners
- legal responsibilities are vital to the owners, but are also necessary for employees and consumers
- ethical responsibilities impact on all stakeholders, but most frequently they affect consumers and employees
- the major effect of the philanthropic responsibilities is on the community, but there is also an impact on employees because the company's philanthropic performance influences employees' morale.

Practice exercise 2   *Total: 65 marks*

1. What is corporate social responsibility (CSR)?   *(4 marks)*

2. What is the purpose of CSR reporting or social audits?   *(3 marks)*

3. Explain two examples of a firm acting in a socially responsible manner in relation to:
   a) an employee   *(6 marks)*
   b) its customers.   *(6 marks)*

4. Explain two reasons why a firm should act in a socially responsible way. *(6 marks)*

5. Explain two reasons why a firm might not wish to act in a socially responsible way.   *(6 marks)*

6. Identify two stakeholders (other than employees and customers), and for each, explain a business action that could be seen as socially responsible in relation to the particular stakeholder.   *(8 marks)*

7. Analyse why it might be difficult for a firm to act in a socially responsible way towards all of its stakeholders at the same time.   *(9 marks)*

8. Which of the following does not relate to a tier in Carroll's CSR pyramid?
   a) To be a good citizen
   b) To be profitable
   c) To be innovative
   d) To be ethical
   e) To obey the law   *(1 mark)*

9. Explain why the economic responsibilities tier in Carroll's CSR pyramid is considered to be the foundation of all the other tiers.   *(4 marks)*

10. For each tier in Carroll's CSR pyramid, explain how particular groups of stakeholders might be affected.   *(12 marks)*

Technological change and its impact on functional areas and strategy

Technological change occurs in all sectors of business. Examples in the primary sector are: specialist machinery such as combine harvesters, mining equipment, deep-sea oil rigs and computerised fish-locating equipment; genetically modified crops, fertiliser and pesticides. Examples in the secondary sector include: production-line equipment such as robotics and computer-aided manufacture (CAM); computer-aided design (CAD); research and development; stock control; and packaging. Examples in the tertiary sector include: communications; financial records and services (e.g. automated teller machines [ATMs]), logistics design and transport; internet shopping; and barcodes.

Technological change and information technology are reshaping the global economy, making the location of a business less relevant, levelling the playing field on which business operates and eliminating some barriers to participation. New business models involving integrated customer and supply chains, global product development and servicing all rely on information technology to create new ways of working. Used effectively, information technology enables organisations to make dramatic leaps in productivity and to redefine competition within whole sectors.

> ### Key terms
>
> **Technological change** Adapting new applications of practical or mechanical sciences to industry and commerce; it includes information and communication technology (ICT), which is the creation, storing and communication of information using microelectronics, computers and telecommunications.

> ### Author advice
>
> Technological change and its impact are covered in many chapters in both Book 1 and this book. For example, discussion about this in relation to specific functional areas was included in Chapter 8 of Book 1, where the value of technology in gathering and analysing data for marketing decisions is discussed; Chapter 10 of Book 1, where an understanding of the value of digital marketing and e-commerce was considered; and Chapter 13 of Book 1, which considered how to use technology to improve operational efficiency. In addition, Chapter 14 of this book discusses the use and importance of digital technology for the functional areas of business. A more strategic focus is provided in Chapter 12, in the discussion about the role of technology in terms of product and process innovation.

The impact of technological change

In Chapter 4, it was noted in the section on the impact of government policy on enterprise that the main factor encouraging enterprise and the growth in the number of small firms is the mass adoption of technology. Technology has lowered the barriers to entry, allowing people of all backgrounds and ages to make a business idea happen and to use mobile and digital devices to find customers, make sales and fund new ventures.

Benefits of technological change

Technological change offers several benefits to business, to consumers and to society. The following list identifies some of these benefits. Brackets indicate the specific functional areas within a business where such benefits are likely to have the greatest impact.

- Improved efficiency and reduced waste. Cost-effective use of resources benefits consumers and firms, and in the long term resources last longer, thus benefiting society in general. (Impact on operations and finance.)

- Better products and services. Consumers benefit from more choice, and if this leads to more demand, company profits are likely to increase. (Impact on operations and finance.)
- New products and materials. Needs and wants that were previously not satisfied or were even unknown can be provided for, as with the invention of the dishwasher, the bread maker and the electric toothbrush. (Impact on operations.)
- Advances in communication. Company efficiency is increased and consumer needs are met more directly. (Impact on all areas.)
- Improved working environment. Employees work in safer conditions and there are a greater number of jobs that are less physically demanding and more interesting. (Impact on human resources.)
- Wealth creation. Higher living standards are achieved.

Problems in introducing new technology

As well as significant benefits, the process of technological change can present problems, particularly for businesses. The following list identifies some of these problems. Brackets indicate the specific functional areas where such problems are likely to have the greatest impact.

- The cost of keeping up to date with the latest technology. The need to remain up to date in order to stay ahead of, or level with, competitors can lead to very high replacement costs that occur on a regular basis. (Impact on operations and finance.)
- Knowing what new technology to buy and when to buy it. In rapidly changing markets, an investment in technology that is becoming outdated can be a very expensive mistake. (Impact on operations and finance.)
- Industrial relations between employers and employees. As technology replaces jobs, there is a danger of resistance by workers and trade unions, and a consequent lowering of morale. (Impact on human resources.)
- Personnel issues. As technological change occurs, new skills are required and this has implications for recruitment, retention and training, and their associated costs. (Impact on human resources and finance.)

New technology and competition

The ability of firms to benefit from new technology depends on the competition they face. The following analysis demonstrates the possible costs and benefits of new technology to business in relation to both products and processes and illustrates its impact on functional areas and on strategy.

- New products. Price skimming can be introduced because consumers are often prepared to pay premium prices for unique products in the short term before competitors catch up. The high profits that result from such price skimming can be retained if a patent is gained that prevents competitors from copying the product. However, it is likely that copycat or 'me too' products will emerge that reduce the original uniqueness of the product. Firms might use the period before competition catches up to develop their next unique product. In monopoly markets (where there is only one firm, or where one firm has at least 25 per cent of the market), a lack of competition allows companies to continue to make high profits, thus limiting the incentive for them to introduce new, improved products. In some industries, the high cost of new technology acts as a barrier to entry, allowing existing organisations to maintain high profits in the long run.

- New processes. New technology can improve the efficiency of processes, which may help a company to increase its profit margins in the short term. However, in a competitive market, this advantage will soon disappear. More firms will begin to adopt these processes and prices will begin to fall, causing profit margins to fall. In the longer run, if prices fall and if demand is price elastic, profits may rise as a result of greater sales volume. Labour costs can also be reduced, which may be particularly important if companies in high-wage economies are to remain competitive.

Issues to consider when introducing new technology

The issues identified below impact variously on the strategic and functional decisions made by firms.

- The adoption of any new technology will be influenced by existing technology. For example, is the new technology compatible with the existing technology? Can the changeover from existing to new technology be managed effectively and efficiently?
- The reaction of the workforce to new technology is important, since their co-operation will be essential.
- In any given situation, there needs to be a reasoned judgement balancing the benefits of new technology (usually new markets and customers) against the problems created by new technology (usually personnel and operational issues).
- Potential short-term difficulties caused by the changeover must also be considered, such as possible cutbacks in production while old technology is being replaced.
- Finance is a major concern. It is likely that new technology will impose huge financial costs in the short term, but it may generate huge financial benefits in the long term.
- The reliability of forecasts and projections of costs, revenues, markets and technological developments need to be considered, since it is impossible to be totally sure of the impact of change. Firms need to be aware of, and have contingency plans for, when actual figures start to become significantly different from forecast figures.
- The use of IT within an organisation tends to reflect the prevailing management style and culture. A supermarket chain might collect vast quantities of data at shop-floor level and then transmit this to head office for analysis of the popularity of particular product lines and so on. In this way, those at the top of the management hierarchy are pulling information up and then passing decisions back down to local branches. Leadership with a more democratic approach might use computer networks to allow such information to flow more freely around the branches, which might empower local branch managers with the information needed for sound decision making.

▲ A business's use of IT will be influenced by its management style

161

Did you know?

Amazon is a striking example of a business that has used technology to reinvent entire categories of the retail business, including books, music and electronics. Its recommendation system – which uses vast amounts of data about customer behaviour to suggest the products that individuals might like to buy – has been fundamental to its success.

The pressures for socially responsible behaviour

The relationship between business and society is undergoing a dramatic change. Globalisation, ethical consumerism, environmental concerns and strict government regulation are all factors that are forcing businesses to reconsider their priorities.

Pressure for social and environmental responsibility comes from both internal and external sources.

Internal sources of pressure include:

- business leaders and decision makers – change will happen if these people are concerned with sustainability, with how to work with the local community, how to work in the most efficient way, and how to minimise the business impact on the environment
- shareholders – they may have a long-term view of the business and want it to do well and to prosper in its local community – or they may prefer a quick profit and be unconcerned with later developments
- employees – if the business is dependent on the need to recruit talented individuals who can be retained by the business over the long term, much will depend on their view of the importance of corporate social responsibility.

External sources of pressure:

- Legislation imposes minimum standards, for example in relation to employment contracts and the quality of goods produced. Most companies, especially if they have a reputation to protect, will seek to operate within the law.
- Industry pressure, including that from organisations focused on promoting CSR within business, such as Business in the Community and Business for Social Responsibility (both mentioned earlier in this chapter).
- Pressure group and stakeholder campaigns, which, with the right publicity, can create significant pressure to change a firm's behaviour (see page 163 for references to Nike and Wal-Mart).

Research by D.P. Baron in an article entitled 'The economics and politics of corporate social performance' (1993) said that businesses operate in three interrelated markets:

- the product market shaped by customers
- the capital market shaped by investors
- the market of social pressure in which government, activists and non-governmental organisations (NGOs) put demands on companies to increase their social performance. Pressure from these groups comes through actions such as regulatory enforcement, product boycotts, internet campaigns and statements to the press.

Research data in the article showed that the impact of social pressure was due almost entirely to 'private politics', that is actions by activists and NGOs rather than 'public politics' stemming from government action.

The research reached two important conclusions:

- Greater social pressure is associated with lower financial performance. Social pressure can hurt a company's reputation, brand image or productivity. If activists call attention to a company's poor environmental record, the pressure could dissuade consumers from buying its products, cause some investors to shun its stock, and reduce productivity by hurting employee morale and motivation.
- However, social pressure and social performance reinforce each other. Greater social pressure can result in better social performance. Firms step up responsible behaviour in response to pressure. Nike, mentioned previously, became an industry leader in promoting better working conditions in apparel and footwear factories in Asia and elsewhere after activities made the company a prominent target in the 1990s. (See the Fact file in Chapter 3 of Book 1.) Similarly, in 2005, Wal-Mart responded to critics by adopting more progressive employee, community and environmental practices, including initiatives to cut energy and require eco-responsibility among its suppliers.

Business ethics

Business ethics are the moral principles that should underpin decision making. Ethical behaviour involves actions and decisions that are seen to be morally correct (i.e. match the moral values or principles of the decision makers). An organisation may make a decision that it believes to be morally right rather than one that suits the needs of some of its stakeholders. Thus a decision made on ethical grounds might reject the most profitable solution for an organisation in favour of one of greater benefit to society as a whole, or to particular groups of stakeholders. Such ethical decision making is likely to distinguish a business that is behaving ethically from one focused on profit.

Ethical dilemmas

Firms are frequently presented with ethical dilemmas when making decisions. Typical ethical dilemmas facing businesses include the following:

- Should an advertising agency accept a cigarette manufacturer as a client?
- Should a producer of chemicals sell to an overseas buyer that it suspects will be using the goods to produce chemical weapons?
- Should a firm relocate to a country paying lower wages?
- Should a firm always pay suppliers on time or should it delay as long as possible?
- Should a manufacturer of military aircraft sell to a foreign government suspected of using force to maintain power?
- Should a firm try to minimise its production costs and its prices by using environmentally polluting processes?

Author advice

Business ethics is not a specific element of this or any section of the AQA specification. It is included here because the introductory note to the 'A-level only' section of the specification states the importance of considering 'the influences of CSR, ethical and environmental issues on strategic decisions'.

Author advice

Do not confuse ethical behaviour with behaviour that is within the law. Behaving in an ethical way is more than behaving according to the law. This point is implicit in Carroll's CSR pyramid model.

163

Fact file

Ethics at Texas Instruments

Texas Instruments (TI) prides itself on its ethical stance and is seen as a benchmark against which other firms can measure themselves. Since 1987 it has had a specific office dealing with ethics and an ethics director.

The company's approach to ethics is clearly and simply summed up as: 'know what's right', 'value what's right', 'do what's right'.

All employees are given a business card that carries TI's 'Ethics Quick Test':

- Is the action legal?
- Does it comply with our values?
- If you do it, will you feel bad?

- How will it look in the newspaper?
- If you know it's wrong, don't do it.
- If you're not sure, ask.
- Keep asking until you get an answer.

Source: www.texasinstruments.com

Did you know?

Ethical investment is stock market investment based on a restricted list of firms that are seen as ethically sound because, for example, they:

- do not finance weapons deals to oppressive governments

- do not make products involving tobacco, the fur trade, animal testing or exploitative factory farming
- act responsibly toward the environment
- are good employers.

Advantages of ethical behaviour

The advantages of ethical behaviour are similar to the reasons for CSR and include the following.

- As consumers become better informed and better educated about products, processes and companies, they demand products and services that do not pollute, exploit or harm. In order to be successful, companies need to respond positively to these demands.
- Ethical behaviour can give companies a clear competitive advantage on which marketing activities can be based. Indeed, some companies have developed their ethical behaviour into a unique selling point and base their marketing campaigns on these perceived differences: for example, by creating a caring image through its marketing, The Body Shop hopes to gain increased sales.
- Firms that adopt ethical practices may also experience benefits in relation to their workforce. They may expect to recruit staff who are better qualified and more highly motivated. Employees can be expected to respond positively to working for a business with a positive ethical image. Equally, employees may be less likely to leave. All of these factors can help to reduce the employment costs incurred by a business.

Problems with ethical positions

Problems with the ethical positions adopted by businesses are similar to the reasons against CSR and include:

- Effect on profit. An ethical choice can incur extra costs: for example, buying renewable resources from a less developed country or continuing extensive testing of a product before releasing it.

- What is ethical? People have different views on what is ethical and these views change over time. For example, in the past, few shops opened on Sundays because it was against many people's religious beliefs and was considered unethical. Now most firms open on Sundays and many would open for longer on Sundays if legislation did not limit their opening time (currently six hours in England).
- Communication of ethics within an organisation. In large organisations, it may be difficult to inform staff of the ethical policy or ethical code and to monitor adherence to it. At Texas Instruments (TI) (see the Fact file on page 164) an ethics booklet is issued to every employee. This booklet was first published in 1961, when TI's founders felt that the company was getting too large and the marketplace too complex to have ethical standards passed on simply by word of mouth. The booklet has been revised regularly to take into account expanding world markets, marketplace complexities, changing government regulations, and business growth and modifications.
- Delegation and empowerment. As empowered workers take more decisions, it becomes harder to maintain a consistent company policy on ethical behaviour.

Group exercise

Discuss each of the ten actions below and rank them in order, with the most ethical behaviour first and the least ethical last. Justify your choices to the rest of the class.

1. In order to prevent an epidemic, a drugs company releases a new drug before it has been thoroughly tested.

2. In order to increase public awareness of child poverty, a charity publishes unpleasant images of children that upset members of the public.

3. An animal rights pressure group frees animals that are being used for experiments on the effects of cosmetics.

4. A recycling plant dumps toxic waste in a deep trench in the middle of the Atlantic.

5. An armaments manufacturer saves 1,000 jobs by supplying arms to North Korea.

6. An animal rights pressure group frees animals that are being used for experiments that will save human lives.

7. A supermarket decides that it will open as normal on Christmas Day.

8. A farmer tips slurry into the river that adjoins his farm, killing all of the fish downstream for 10 kilometres.

9. In order to reduce its production costs, a sportswear business moves production of its trainers to a country that employs child labour.

10. A cigarette manufacturer aims its latest campaign at schoolchildren by concentrating on poster sites next to schools.

Practice exercise 3

Total: 50 marks

1. Identify and explain one example of the impact of technological change on each functional area within a business. *(12 marks)*

2. Identify and explain one example of the impact of technological change on business strategy. *(4 marks)*

3. Explain two benefits to consumers of the use of new technology. *(6 marks)*

4. Explain two benefits to firms of the use of new technology. *(6 marks)*

5. Explain two problems for business of introducing new technology. *(6 marks)*

6. Identify and explain four factors that illustrate the pressures for socially responsible behaviour. *(12 marks)*

7. What is meant by the term 'ethical behaviour'? *(4 marks)*

Case study 1: Corporate social responsibility at Starbucks and B&Q

Starbucks Coffee Co.

Starbucks defines corporate social responsibility (CSR) as conducting business in ways that produce social, environmental and economic benefits for the communities in which it operates. Starbucks has been widely recognised for its commitment to numerous stakeholders, including coffee growers, the environment, employees and communities, while simultaneously achieving rapid business growth. The company has a senior vice president of CSR who provides strategic development of policies, strategies, processes and tools to link corporate social responsibility with business success.

Since 1998, Starbucks has supported Conservation International's Conservation Coffee programme, which encourages sustainable agriculture practices and the protection of biodiversity through the production of shade-grown coffee and the institution of coffee-purchasing guidelines. The programme has resulted in a 60 per cent price premium being paid to farmers and a 220 per cent increase in the coffee-growing land preserved as tropical forests.

The company has been praised for its generous employee benefits and its commitment, unusual in the industry, to provide full benefits for both full- and part-time employees. Starbucks also has a number of programmes to help benefit the communities in which it has stores, as well as in the developing economies where its coffee is grown, harvested and processed.

B&Q

B&Q is a do-it-yourself retailer. It is the leading home improvement and garden centre retailer in Europe and the third largest in the world, with more than 60 stores opened internationally, including B&Q Beijing, which is now the largest B&Q store in the world. Currently, it has 350 stores in the UK and 8 stores in Ireland. About 22 per cent of B&Q's turnover is timber and timber-related products, and the company has worked to lessen its impact on forests and other environments since 1991. B&Q has monitored its suppliers' social and environmental practices, sourcing 99 per cent of wood-based products from independently certified, well-managed forests, becoming a model to other companies and encouraging change in its business partners. B&Q also managed to reduce environmental impact at its stores by minimising packaging, increasing recycling and improving energy efficiency and waste management.

More recently, B&Q has adopted a more holistic approach to corporate social responsibility through the theme of 'being a better neighbour': 'We believe sustainable development is about improving the quality of life for all the people we touch. This can only be achieved by striving to be a better neighbour, whether it is to our store or global trading neighbourhoods.'

The company has found that close monitoring of its suppliers and their sources helps to ensure healthy working conditions, maintain good environmental practices and increase its profits through improved brand loyalty and reduced costs. B&Q also aims to employ people of all backgrounds, particularly older workers, and tries to meet the needs of all customers, including the disabled. B&Q has awarded thousands of Better Community grants to local store-run community projects.

Source: adapted from information on www.bsr.org

Questions

Total: 25 marks

1. Analyse how stakeholders benefit from Starbucks' and B&Q's socially responsible approaches.

(9 marks)

2. Discuss the extent to which the focus on CSR activities by either Starbucks or B&Q, as indicated in the case study, influence the type of strategic and functional decisions they are likely to make.

(16 marks)

Case study 2: Improving business performance with barcode technology

One of the reasons for Tesco's success has been its investment in IT and particularly in barcode technology. By minimising the stock level of every item, shelf space is freed up, which allows it to expand its range of non-food items. Minimum stock levels mean it must replenish continuously, which it does by capturing in-store product data. As well as scanning barcodes at checkouts, staff monitor stock with handheld computers, which they use to scan barcodes on the shelves and check the quantity. Tesco's responsive supply chain then keeps the deliveries coming.

Even small companies can use barcodes to cut errors. A retailer asked its supplier of artificial flowers to put a barcode label on each bloom. Eighteen months later the three to five complaints the supplier used to receive every day (such as 'you sent five yellow and two white when I ordered two yellow and five white') had fallen to three a year – the packer scanned the barcodes before boxing the order and hence eliminated most of the errors. This simple system paid for itself in weeks by cutting the cost of errors.

Food-processing firms include barcodes in their pack designs. An in-line scanning system detects rogue items and stops the line, thus reducing the risk of loading the wrong material into the packaging machine. A well-known jam maker uses such a system to inspect 230 jars a minute to prevent raspberry jam going out as strawberry jam.

An engine manufacturer, with a £40 million annual turnover and a 350-strong workforce, used to check all of its stock manually. With over 25,000 stock locations, this was a very slow process. Even when the physical stock check had been completed, it would take up to two weeks for staff to input the data manually into an in-house computerised stock record. The solution was to add barcodes to products and locations, and introduce handheld computers for counting purposes. The benefits gained through this application were impressive. Payback was immediate. Man-hours were saved, costs were reduced and stock control procedures improved.

Source: adapted from information on www.codeway.com

Questions

Total: 25 marks

1. The article suggests that there are many benefits from adopting technology like barcodes, and few, if any, costs. Identify and explain three potential costs or problems a business is likely to encounter as a result of technological change. (9 marks)

2. Using the information in the case study and your own knowledge and understanding, evaluate the impact of technological change on different functional areas of a firm. (16 marks)

Essay questions

Total: 25 marks

Answer one of the following questions:

1. Discuss how the growth of online businesses and increasing urbanisation and globalisation are likely to influence the strategic and functional decisions made by a business of your choice based in the UK.   *(25 marks)*

2. Assess the effects on a business of your choice of changes in either the social environment or the technological environment and evaluate how both its strategic and functional decisions might change as a result.   *(25 marks)*

3. To what extent do all businesses face pressures to behave in a socially responsible manner?   *(25 marks)*

7

Analysing the external environment to assess opportunities and threats: the competitive environment

This chapter introduces **Porter's five forces** (also known as Porter's five competitive forces). The forces are: entry threat, including barriers to entry; buyer power; supplier power; rivalry (also known as jockeying for position); and substitute power. The chapter considers how and why these forces might change, and the implications of these forces for strategic and functional decision making and profits. It concludes with a consideration of how the five forces shape competitive strategy.

The competitive environment

Chapter 3 of the AQA A-level Business Book 1 introduced the idea of the competitive environment as part of the external environment in which businesses operate. It considers the impact of competition on business costs and demand for goods and services. Ensure that you review this information before continuing with this chapter.

Porter's five forces

The competitive environment in which firms operate means that some struggle to survive or are forced out of business, while others grow and become profitable. Michael Porter's model of five forces, also known as five competitive forces, provides a way of analysing the market conditions that determine how a successful firm might cope with the competitive environment it faces. These forces are shown in Figure 7.1.

> **Key term**
>
> **Porter's five forces (or competitive forces)** A model developed by Michael Porter to analyse the competitive environment in which a business operates; the five forces are: the threat of entry, buyer power, supplier power, competitive rivalry and substitute threat.

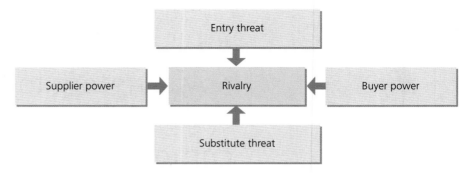

▲ **Figure 7.1** Porter's five competitive forces

The five forces and how/why they might change

The following section provides an explanation of each of the five forces and in doing so indicates how and why they might change.

- **Entry threat**, that is the threat of entry to the industry by new competitors. If new firms enter the market easily in response to high profits, the entry threat is likely to be high. If, on the other hand, there are significant barriers to entry, the threat is likely to be much lower. (Barriers to entry are explained below.) Just as important are the likely reactions to new entrants from existing competitors. If new entrants can expect serious retaliation from existing firms, they are less likely to pose a serious entry threat. The threat of entry changes as conditions change. For example, when patents expire, barriers to entering a market may fall. This happened when Polaroid's original patents for instant photography expired in the mid-1990s. Conversely, developments in automation, which increased the opportunities for economies of scale in the car industry, have raised barriers to entry and generally prevented new firms setting up in the industry.

- **Buyer power**, that is the power of a firm's buyers (or customers). If a firm sells to a single buyer such as a major supermarket chain, buyer power is likely to be high. If, on the other hand, it sells to a large number of individual customers, each of which buys only a very small proportion of the firm's total sales, buyer power is likely to be much lower. Buyers are also more likely to be powerful if the products they purchase from a firm are standard or undifferentiated. This is because they will be confident that they can always find alternative suppliers and may therefore play one supplier off against another. Changes to the power of buyers may come about because the number of buyers changes or the uniqueness of the products they purchase changes.

- **Supplier power**, that is the power of a firm's suppliers. If a firm gets most of its inputs from a single supplier, supplier power is likely to be high. If, on the other hand, it gets its supplies from a large number of competing suppliers, each of which supplies only a very small proportion of the firm's total supplies, supplier power is likely to be much lower. Suppliers will also be powerful if their products are unique or if they have built up switching costs. (Switching costs are the costs buyers face when changing suppliers.) Changes to the power of suppliers may come about because the number of suppliers changes, the uniqueness of the products they supply changes or there are changes to switching costs.

Key term

Rivalry The intensity of competition between firms in the industry – Porter called this 'jockeying for position'.

Key term

Substitute threat The threat to a firm's existing market share from substitute products that might be introduced by competitors.

Key term

Barriers to entry Factors that obstruct or restrict the entry of new firms into an industry or market.

- **Rivalry**, that is the intensity of competitive rivalry between firms in the industry. Porter called this force 'jockeying for position'. Rivalry often involves tactics like price competition, new product development and advertising campaigns. Intense rivalry tends to occur where: competitors are numerous or roughly equal in size and power; industry growth is slow so that if a firm wants to grow in size, it can only do so at the expense of other firms; the products lack differentiation, or switching costs are low or non-existent, meaning that customers are easily persuaded to buy the products of other firms. Changes to the extent of rivalry in an industry may come about because one firm becomes more dominant than the others, the number of firms changes, the rate of growth in the industry changes or the degree of product differentiation and level of switching costs change.

- **Substitute threat**, that is the threat from substitute goods or services. If a firm's product is unique and in high demand, the substitute threat is likely to be low. If, on the other hand, there are substitute products produced by other firms that consumers may be tempted to buy instead, the substitute threat is likely to be high. In Chapter 3 of Book 1, Waterman Pens was cited as an example of a business that defined its competitors not as other manufacturers of pens such as Parker and Bic, but as the producers of executive gifts such as Dunhill and Rolex. This illustrates the idea that the substitute threat comes not just from products of the same type. Changes to the substitute threat may come about because the uniqueness of the product changes or because alternative products become acceptable substitutes.

Barriers to entry

Barriers to entry include:

- The high capital costs required to set up a new business in markets in which existing firms are large and dominant; this is particularly risky if the capital is required for up-front advertising campaigns or research and development because it may not be recoverable.
- Patents that allow existing businesses to 'monopolise' the market legally (patents are discussed in detail in Chapter 12).
- The loyalty of customers to existing businesses; this is a barrier because to overcome such loyalty can mean huge spending on product differentiation, advertising and customer service.
- Economies of scale, gained through producing on a large scale; unless they can enter a market on a large scale, new entrants will have much higher average costs than existing firms and may be unable to charge a competitive price. (Economies of scale were discussed in Chapter 13 of Book 1 and are considered in Chapter 11 of this book.)

- Government policy and regulation; government can limit entry to industries with controls such as licence requirements or limits on access to raw materials; government can also play an indirect role by introducing regulations related to air and water pollution, waste disposal and health and safety, all of which add to business set-up costs.
- Access to resources and distribution channels; for example, to get shelf space in a large supermarket, a new food product must displace others; this means offering price discounts or mounting extensive promotions and persuading the supermarket chain that the new food product will sell better than other products.

Car manufacturing, for example, involves huge capital investment in manufacturing equipment, compliance with safety and emission rules and regulation, access to parts suppliers, the development of a network of car dealerships and huge marketing campaigns to establish new car brands with consumers. All of these represent signigficant barriers to entry for potential new businesses to the car industry.

The implications of the five forces for strategic and functional decision making and profits

All businesses need to be able to respond appropriately to the changing competitive environment in which they find themselves. To do this, they need to understand the nature of each of the five forces that face them and use their understanding to make strategic and functional decisions that enable them to maintain or increase their profits.

Entry threat

An entry threat occurs when a new business tries to enter an industry. In very competitive markets, such as those that can be described as monopolistic competition, new competitors enter all the time. For example, new hairdressers and new cafés regularly open on the high street. In order to compete and continue to make profits, existing businesses need to take decisions that ensure their goods or services are of an appropriate quality, are priced and promoted appropriately and have their own USPs. In some industries, barriers to entry prevent or deter new businesses from entering. They thus enable existing businesses to continue relatively unchallenged and, in effect, protect them from new entrants and allow them to earn higher profits than they might in a more competitive environment. This is the case in monopoly or oligopoly markets such as car manufacturers, supermarkets and banks.

The expectations of potential new entrants about the reaction of existing competitors will influence their decision about whether to enter a market or not. For example, if existing firms possess substantial resources to fight back, including cash, borrowing power and productive capacity, new firms are less likely to enter. If existing firms decide to cut prices in order to maintain their market shares, new firms are less likely to enter. If industry growth is slow, so that a new entrant would cause the financial performance of all firms involved to decline, retaliatory action from existing firms is likely to be stronger. Their motives are to maintain their market share and profit levels and to ensure these are not threatened by new firms.

Existing businesses need to consider the threat of competition from all sources and to constantly review their position in order to maintain their profit levels. New and often unexpected or, non-traditional, competitors can emerge and completely change the nature of a market. For example, supermarkets now sell perfume, books, electrical equipment and mobile phones – often massively undercutting the more traditional sources of such products. Jewellery and watches were once only sold through independent specialist retailers, but are now sold extensively in fashion shops, department stores and online.

Buyer power

The power of buyers (or customers) is related to their ability to influence the price that they pay or the quality of products they buy. A single customer in a large supermarket has little power because the value of any one customer's purchases is likely to be very small and hence is unlikely to have any influence on the supermarket's decision making. However, where the value of a customer's purchases is a huge proportion of a business's total sales, that customer is likely to be very influential and will have lots of buyer power. For example, if a small farm making its own sausages sells them all to a major supermarket chain, it will be in a highly vulnerable position. The supermarket chain, as the only buyer of its products, could insist on a price reduction or a longer credit period, and the small farm would have little option but to meet the supermarket's demands or lose the business and future potential profit. To overcome such a situation, the farm would need to take action to extend its customer base so that it is no longer dependent on a single buyer. This will involve strategic and tactical decisions about future marketing and placement of the product and possibly about costs and methods of production linked to its quality.

In addition to the actual number of customers, the economic climate can influence the buying power of customers. Recession and deflationary periods, such as in 2008–09, give customers stronger buying power and put them in control. The case study on the motor industry that is provided at the end of this chapter explains how in 2009, people who wanted to buy cars were in a strong bargaining position. Due to the recession and low levels of demand, dealers were prepared to reduce prices, massively because they needed to get rid of excess stock.

Improvements in information and communication technology have an influence on the power of buyers. The internet and general access to information mean that customers today are much more aware, much better informed and much more prepared, for example, to switch energy suppliers, phone networks or mortgage firms more regularly if it means getting a better deal. As a result, firms need to constantly review their strategic decisions to ensure they are not vulnerable to buyer power, which can reduce their profits.

Supplier power

The power of suppliers is related to their ability to influence the prices they will receive for their supplies or the quality of the products they supply. The more concentrated and controlled the source of supply, the more power an individual supplier is likely to wield in the market. An example of an industry facing a powerful supplier is the personal computer-making industry, which is supplied by the almost monopolistic operating system supplier, Microsoft.

▲ Suppliers who sell their product to only one supermarket are in a very vulnerable position

On the other hand, using the example of a small farm supplying sausages to a large supermarket chain, if the supermarket can get its supply of sausages from a large range of small farms, all of which are competing with each other for the supermarket contract, the power of any individual farm is likely to be weak. From the supermarket's point of view, its decisions will be about ensuring that the supply base for most of its products is broad and that it is not dependent on any one supplier. This will enable it to keep its costs down and profits up.

Suppliers can group together in order to wield more power. They can join together as a cartel, such as OPEC (the Oil Producing and Exporting Countries) to try to influence prices to their own advantage. Note, however, that in most countries cartels are illegal.

Rivalry

It is often assumed that more rivalry takes place in industries where there are more competitors fighting for a share of the market for a particular product. This is not necessarily the case because in these situations an element of monopolistic competition takes place. This allows each firm to capture a small section of the market, for example based on location, as is the case for a small local hairdresser or small local convenience store. Conversely, however, just because there are few rather than many firms in an industry does not mean that rivalry is reduced. For example, the car industry, the supermarket sector and the markets for breakfast cereals and soap powders, all of which have oligopolistic market structures, feature intense rivalry. For these types of businesses, decision making will be focused on differentiating products, building brand loyalty and, perhaps, developing switching costs for their products – all to prevent or deter consumers from purchasing the products of their competitors instead.

If a business has sufficient financial resources, it might decide to try to grow in size quickly by merging with, or taking over, another firm. (Mergers and takeovers are discussed in detail in Chapter 11.) This might enable it to become a large and dominant force in its industry, which will reduce the threat of rivalry. This in turn can have a significant impact on the competitive forces for other businesses that are now faced with a more powerful rival.

Substitute threat

The threat from substitute products is likely to be intense when a market is characterised by a large number of firms with very similar products, all competing for a share of the market. Each business must try to ensure that its product is the preferred product, whether on the basis of price or other characteristics, at least for a sufficient proportion of consumers, to allow the business to survive and make a profit.

Even where a market is characterised by a few large firms, such as the breakfast cereal market or car market, the threat of substitute products can be intense – the extensive and costly marketing campaigns for these products are evidence of this.

The substitute threat can also come from alternative products, not just different brands and versions of the same product. The previous section mentioned the case of Waterman Pens. Chapter 3 of Book 1 provided two further examples – that of British Gas competing not just with other suppliers in the gas provision market, but also with the suppliers of other types of fuel, including coal,

---

Author advice

Note how the extent of rivalry in a particular market is likely to influence and be influenced by the nature of the other forces – hence its place at the centre of Figure 7.1. For example: where a market begins to be characterised by fewer and larger firms, barriers to entry are likely to become more significant; where there are lots of substitute products that are relatively undifferentiated, rivalry is likely to be more intense.

electricity and oil – and that of the *Guardian* newspaper competing not just with other newspapers, but also with other news sources, including internet sites, radio and television. These examples indicate the need for businesses to be aware not only of competing products that are plainly evident now, but also developments that may increase the range of substitute products in the future. Well-judged, strategic decisions about how to cope with such developments and enable a business to remain competitive and profitable are vital.

Innovation and the continuing development of new products through research and development are key strategies in some industries, for example, pharmaceuticals. Because of the costly nature of such developments and the long lead time between the initial product development and the eventual launch of the product on the market, the threat of substitute products and what competitors might be planning are major considerations in their decision making. The use of patents provides protection against this, but inevitably rivals aim to develop their own versions and patent-related court cases are not uncommon. (See Chapter 12 for more detail on this aspect of business.)

Fact file

Concentration ratios

The market for a particular product could be supplied by many firms, but dominated by a few large firms, each of which has a significant market share. Such an industry would be described as 'highly concentrated'. This would be the case, for example, in an industry with 500 firms where the largest five firms have 90 per cent of the market.

The extent to which a few firms dominate an industry can be measured by concentration ratios. A five-firm concentration ratio identifies the total market share of the five largest firms in an industry, while a four-firm concentration ratio gives the market share of the largest four firms in an industry. The four-firm concentration ratio for the supermarket industry in October 2014 was just under 75 per cent. This means that 75 per cent of the total market share was controlled by four firms. These were Tesco (with a market share of approximately 29 per cent), Asda (17 per cent), Sainsbury's (16 per cent) and Morrisons (11 per cent).

(Market shares of the other large supermarket chains were as follows: the Co-op (6 per cent), Waitrose (5 per cent), Aldi (5 per cent), Lidl (4 per cent), Iceland (2 per cent).)

Market structures can be classified by their concentration ratios. For example:

- A perfectly competitive market will give a very low concentration ratio.
- A monopolistically competitive market will usually have a four-firm concentration ratio of less than 40 per cent.
- An oligopolistic market, like the supermarket sector, will usually have a four-firm concentration ratio of above 60 per cent.
- A monopoly market will have a four-firm concentration ratio of almost 100 per cent. (In practice, the definition of a monopolist is where one firm has at least 25 per cent of the market.)

As well as the intense competition between the largest firms in an industry, there is also likely to be a lot of competitive rivalry among the firms that are not among the largest. For example, there is significant competitive rivalry in the supermarket sector, with Aldi and Lidl jockeying for position against the likes of Waitrose as well as the other main supermarkets. Aldi and Lidl are examples of the success of new entrants to an established market structure, and of the cheaper substitute products they offer that are having significant success in changing consumer buying habits. Their success can be seen in the percentage change in their respective market shares between October 2013 and October 2014, which were as follows:

- Aldi — +27 per cent
- Lidl — +19 per cent
- Tesco — −4 per cent
- Asda — +1 per cent
- Sainsbury's — −3 per cent
- Morrisons — +2 per cent

Source: data on market shares from http://grocerynews.org

How the five forces shape competitive strategy

Because changes in the competitive structure of an industry can have a significant impact on the success of a business, it is vital that any business understands fully the competitive environment in which it operates and the opportunities and threats it presents. This means it should have good information about: the market in which it operates; the number and size of competitors; the nature of the product and the quality, availability and nature of substitute products; how easy it is for a new firm to set up in the industry; whether it has control over the price it charges (for example, is it a price setter or a price taker?); how important price and non-price competition are; how many and how powerful its suppliers are; and how many and how powerful its customers are.

By constantly assessing the changes that are taking place in its competitive environment, a business is able to introduce strategies that help it to create the right conditions for establishing a competitive advantage over its rivals. If, for example, a new competitor emerges in the market, a business might try to diversify into other markets or consider merging with or taking over another business in order to establish itself as a dominant business in the market. If a supplier has too much power over a business, one possibility is for the business to find alternative sources of supply. Equally, if a business currently sells to a single buyer, its strategy might be to find more buyers in order to reduce the power of any one buyer.

In trying to devise a competitive strategy to influence its future success and profitability, a firm needs to consider its current position and where it might be in the future. This will involve analysing the industry it is in and each of the five competitive forces it faces both now and in the future. For example, the solar power business in the UK is currently made up of several thousand small- and medium-sized companies, none with a major market position. Entry is easy, and competitors are battling to establish solar power as a good substitute for conventional methods of energy production. The future of this industry may look very different. It will depend, for example, on the nature and level of future barriers to entry, the industry's position relative to substitutes, the intensity of competition, and the power of buyers and suppliers. These characteristics will in turn be influenced by factors such as success in establishing brand loyalties, the extent of economies of scale, the rate of technological change and the level of fixed costs and capital requirements in relation to production facilities.

In developing a competitive strategy, a firm broadly has the following options:

- Attempting to position itself so that its capabilities, for example its competitive advantage or USP, provide the best defence against the five competitive forces. In pursuing this option it is likely to reduce the impact of rivalry, reduce the substitute threat and buyer power and raise barriers to entry.
- Influencing the balance of the five forces so that it improves its position, for example by ensuring that the power of its suppliers and buyers is reduced substantially or that it introduces innovations in marketing that raise brand loyalty, thus reducing the substitute threat and raising barriers to entry. In this situation a firm is devising a strategy that takes the offensive and alters the forces rather than just copes with them.

Theodore Levitt, in a classic article called 'Marketing Myopia' (1960, *Harvard Business Review*), argued against labelling a business simply in relation to the products it produces rather than on how it meets customer needs. Many other writers have stressed that firms need to look beyond the range of their current competitors and their competitors' products to the potential sources of future competition, in all its different forms. By only concentrating on their direct competitors in the fight for market share, businesses might miss other opportunities and threats. For example, they might fail to realise that they are also competing with their customers and their suppliers for bargaining power; they may fail to keep track of new entrants to the industry; or they may fail to recognise the subtle threat of substitute products of many different sorts. In this sense, Porter's model of the five forces is vitally important in shaping competitive strategy.

Remember that the competitive environment does not just refer to the home or domestic market; it includes the international competitive environment in which business operates. This was considered in Chapter 5 and is discussed further in Chapter 13.

Practice exercise 1 — *Total: 50 marks*

1. Identify Porter's five competitive forces. *(5 marks)*

2. For each of the five forces, identify and explain a reason that might cause them to change. *(15 marks)*

3. Select three of the reasons you identified in question 2 and explain how each of them might affect a business's ability to make or maintain profit. *(12 marks)*

4. Analyse how the threat of a new entrant to an industry that is not growing rapidly might influence the strategic and functional decisions made by an existing firm. *(9 marks)*

5. Analyse how the five forces might shape a business's competitive strategy. *(9 marks)*

Case study 1: The jewellery and watch market

Over time, the market for jewellery and watches has gained from its repositioning into the fashion market. This has led to consumers owning and buying a wider range of pieces, from costume jewellery to precious items. At the same time, it has opened up the market to new players and brands, including fashion and retail clothing labels. There has also been an increase in the number of retailers offering both fashion and real jewellery pieces.

Major developments in the market have included the successful introduction of branded jewellery ranges. As specialist retail jewellers have endeavoured to differentiate themselves from mixed retailers and other competitors, branding has been a key part of the package, with exclusive ranges and designs, such as Pandora, playing an important role. The market has also gained increasing transparency, owing to the development of online sales.

Women are the major buyers in the UK market and are more likely than men to buy either watches or jewellery. While the majority of women's purchases are for themselves, male buyers tend to buy jewellery as a gift. The men's jewellery market is continuing to develop, driven by younger consumers.

Between 2009 and 2013, the UK jewellery and watch industry experienced consistent growth, with the total market size increasing by about 10 per cent, driven primarily by high growth in the watches sector. Even during the recession of 2008–09, the market still saw some growth.

The jewellery sector is the larger of the two sectors, with just over 70 per cent of all UK sales of jewellery and watches in 2013. Despite this, the jewellery sector experienced slightly slower growth than watches in the period 2009 to 2013.

The jewellery sector consists of two subsectors – real jewellery (which includes items made in precious metals and set with precious gemstones) and costume and fashion jewellery. Real jewellery accounts for a much greater proportion of all jewellery sales in terms of value compared with sales of costume and fashion jewellery items. Despite this, real jewellery has increased at a slower rate than costume and fashion jewellery sales as consumers are increasingly purchasing low-cost, fast-fashion items.

The jewellery and watch market is highly competitive in terms of both manufacture and retail. Recent years have seen the emergence of several luxury-goods and high-fashion retailers in the market, with strong brands and substantial financial resources. This has had the effect of overcrowding the market – particularly in the watches sector – and is putting pressure on the small- and medium-sized operations that make up the majority of the UK industry.

This overcrowding has led to excess capacity in the industry as the number of manufacturers and retailers has increased at a faster rate than the demand for watches and jewellery. Analysts predict that some smaller firms will be forced out of the industry eventually, unless they can find a niche market for their products. The high-fashion conglomerates are able to purchase the more expensive locations in the high street and can afford to spend much more money on advertising in order to promote their brands and achieve brand loyalty.

In 2013, there were approximately 1,500 enterprises engaged in the manufacture of jewellery and watches in the UK. The vast majority of these were small companies generating low turnovers: 70 per cent of these manufacturing enterprises recorded a turnover of less than £250,000, with just 20 companies (2 per cent) generating a turnover of £5 million or more. Statistics on the number of retail outlets for jewellery and watches are more difficult to establish because of its repositioning in the fashion market and increasing competition for traditional jewellers from fashion stores, department stores and online retailers. However, approximately 4,000 dedicated retail jewellery and watches outlets are recorded.

The state of the industry is relatively dependent on the state of the overall economy. Jewellery and watches are considered to be discretionary items, and demand is reliant on the level of disposable income and consumer spending. Generally, in poor economic conditions, consumers are likely to reduce the frequency of and spending on these products or, as appears to have happened in this industry, trade down to cheaper jewellery. Despite this, the sales of luxury jewellery and watches appear to have been immune to the economic downturn.

Source: adapted from information on www.keynote.co.uk in 2008 and an article in *Professional Jeweller*, 18.07.2014

Questions

Total: 25 marks

1. Analyse why overcrowding in the industry might mean smaller firms may be forced out.   *(9 marks)*

2. Evaluate the market conditions for the jewellery and watch industry using Porter's five forces model.
     (16 marks)

Author advice

The following case study on the external environment and the car industry is provided to encourage you to consider the external environment in total (i.e. the issues covered in Chapters 4, 5, 6 and 7), how it might influence a major industry and how such an industry might respond. It is based on data and events in the period 2008–09, a time of major turbulence for all industries, and particularly the motor industry.

Case study 2: External influences and the car industry

The global picture

'The current economic climate is having an unprecedented impact on the car industry. The combination of evaporating consumer confidence combined with significant restrictions on available finance and credit, and overcapacity have created the car industry's "perfect storm"' (comment by a KPMG spokesperson in 2009).

In 2009, the global car industry had the capacity to make 94 million vehicles each year – an overcapacity of about 34 million, or the output of about 100 major factories. In other industries, merger and acquisition activity had removed excess capacity, but not in the car industry. As a result, predictions were that car-makers were likely to close down factories and lay off thousands of workers. The challenge for the industry was to cut production without losing the ability to increase it when people started buying cars again.

On the one hand, Japanese car-makers were closing production plants in Japan, where sales had slipped, but in North America, they were only slowing production, cutting contract workers, and postponing plans to open more factories because they were keen to grab market share once the US economy improved. The so-called Big Three American manufacturers (General Motors, Ford and Chrysler) did not have the same opportunities, and for them the cuts at home were significant. To become profitable, according to experts, US car-makers needed to close at least a dozen of their 53 factories in North America.

Nowhere was there greater overcapacity than in China, where local companies absorbed much of the pain, as the weakest players closed and large state-owned companies gobbled up the stronger ones. That was good news for foreign makers and their joint-venture partners. General Motors was closing plants at home in America, but not in China, where it was much easier

to lay off workers and rehire them when things picked up. Toyota actually expanded its Chinese operations. As in China, the global downturn hit car-makers in Russia and Eastern Europe hard. Sales by multinational car companies, which had captured about three-quarters of the Russian market, were hit by the downturn too. However, they were reluctant to pull back for fear of being unable to regain their previous strong position when the economic outlook improved.

Supporting this picture, the key findings of KPMG's 2009 survey of executives in the global automotive industry included the following:

● The profitability of the car industry was expected to decrease between 2009 and 2013 and there would be increasing risk of company insolvencies or bankruptcies.

● Overcapacity of 11–20 per cent was expected for the period 2010 to 2014, and high costs and declining demand would drive restructuring – including more mergers and acquisitions and alliances.

● Prospects in emerging markets were being scaled back, as consumers were expected to be hit by rapid credit contraction. However, demand for cars in emerging markets was still expected to grow faster than in all other regions. In addition to China and India, the biggest potential growth was expected in Central and Eastern Europe.

● Technology and innovation were keys to the future of the industry – with fuel efficiency, advanced fuel technologies and environmental pressures considered the most important trends.

● Consumers were becoming increasingly price sensitive. Lower fuel consumption would be the most important criteria in the next five years and affordability of vehicles was likely to be more important than quality.

- Chinese and Indian car brands were expected to significantly expand their market share between 2009 and 2013, while US manufacturers (GM, Ford and Chrysler) were expected to lose market share.

The UK picture

At the time, the UK was the third largest car market in the EU. Over 850,000 people were employed by the UK motor industry, which had a manufacturing turnover of £51 billion and exported 75 per cent of its manufactured vehicles.

The car industry is influenced by the business cycle because it produces durable goods, which are very sensitive to changes in income. As a result of the downturn in 2008, new car sales fell to their lowest level for 12 years. All parts of the market were hit, from Rolls-Royce and Bentley at the top end to the Nissan Micra at the other. Ford and Aston Martin sent staff home for an extended Christmas 2008 break, as plants closed temporarily in order to save money. Vauxhall offered workers sabbaticals of up to nine months on reduced pay, while Honda axed its Formula One racing team to lower costs. Nissan announced plans to cut a quarter of its 5,000-strong workforce at its Sunderland plant. It said the reduction was necessary to 'safeguard our long-term future' and 'ensure we are in a strong and viable position once business conditions return to normal'. These are 'extraordinary circumstances, not of our making'.

The chief executive of the Society of Motor Manufacturers and Traders (SMMT) said the announcement from Nissan emphasised how much the industry needed government support. 'Swift action is necessary to limit the extent of the damage and ensure we retain valuable industrial capability.' Lord Mandelson, the Labour government's Business Secretary at the time, outlined a package of government support for the car industry to ensure it survived the economic crisis and to influence manufacturers to produce more environmentally friendly vehicles. The package included government guarantees to support loans of up to £1.3 billion from the European Investment Bank, as well as a further £1 billion in UK government loans to fund investment in greener vehicles.

One of the few success stories of 2008 was the Smart car, which recorded a sales increase of more than 43 per cent to 7,526. Among the big losers were Aston Martin and Bentley, which saw sales down by more than a quarter in 2008, and Land Rover, where sales fell 30 per cent. A Ford spokesman said the number of small cars the company had sold had risen.

The slump in car sales was good news for those wanting to buy a new car, with dealers knocking thousands of pounds off vehicles in a desperate attempt to shift stock. Some of the biggest bargains involved 4x4s and other large cars that were deemed 'environmentally unfriendly' and which faced the threat of increased taxation by the government. Over the previous decade, car and fuel taxation and excise duties had been structured so as to encourage motorists to drive more environmentally friendly vehicles. In the 2008 Budget, plans were announced to increase vehicle excise duty on cars with high carbon dioxide emissions, and to apply this increased rate retrospectively to cars registered before March 2006. It was estimated that the proposed changes would affect 1.2 million motorists and cost them a total of £260 million.

The SMMT, reporting on environmental factors in its annual 'Sustainability Report', accepted the evidence of global warming and that increasing levels of carbon dioxide in the atmosphere, caused by non-natural sources, were to blame. As a result, improvements had been made in the environmental credentials of cars and their production sites. For example, from production sites across the UK, energy use and carbon dioxide emissions per vehicle produced, water use and waste to landfill had all been significantly reduced, and from products, average new car carbon dioxide emissions had dropped, thanks to investment in alternative fuel technologies.

Sources: adapted from information on www.businessweek.com, www.kpmg. co.uk and www.smmt.co.uk in 2008 and 2009

Appendix 1 UK economic growth, 2003–08 (%)

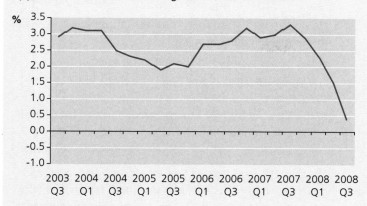

Source: www.statistics.gov.uk

Appendix 2 New car registrations

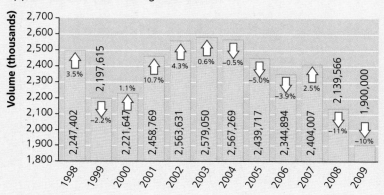

Source: www.smmt.co.uk

▼ **Table 7.1** Percentage change in new car registrations, May–November 2008

Month	Month-on-month
May	−3.5%
June	−6.1%
July	−13.0%
August	−18.6%
September	−21.2%
October	−23.0%
November	−36.8%

Source: www.smmt.co.uk

Appendix 3 Carbon dioxide emissions in the car industry

UK average new car carbon dioxide emissions

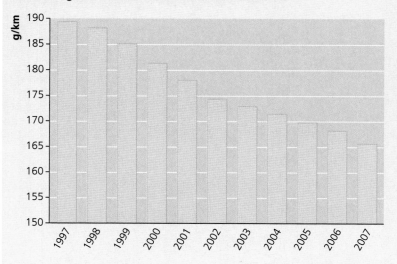

Source: www.smmt.co.uk

Carbon dioxide emissions from production and distribution

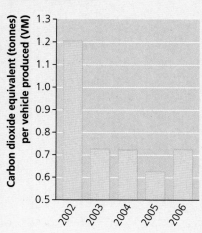

Questions

1. Which of the following are not aspects of the external environment?

   a) Competitive and technological issues

   b) Economic and environmental issues

   c) Marketing and financial issues

   d) Legal and social issues

   e) Political and technological issues *(1 mark)*

2. Explain each of the following three competitive forces from Porter's model of five forces – buyer threat, rivalry and substitute threat – in the context of the car industry in the period covered by the case study. *(15 marks)*

3. Using the information in the case study and the data in the appendices, analyse:

   a) the opportunities in the external environment that faced the car industry in the UK in the period 2006–09 *(9 marks)*

   b) the threats in the external environment that faced the car industry in the UK in the period 2006–09. *(9 marks)*

4. Discuss the likely impact on strategic and functional decisions that firms in the motor industry are likely to have made as a result of the opportunities and threats you have identified in question 3a and b. *(16 marks)*

8

Analysing strategic options: investment appraisal

This chapter considers financial methods of assessing an investment by introducing the concept of investment appraisal. It examines three quantitative methods of investment appraisal: payback, average rate of return and net present value. It shows how to complete the calculations for each of these methods and explains how the results of these calculations should be interpreted. The relative merits of each method of investment appraisal are briefly compared. The chapter also examines factors that influence investment decisions, including investment criteria, non-financial factors, risk and uncertainty. Finally, the concept of sensitivity analysis is explained and its value assessed.

Did you know?

Investment appraisal techniques are usually applied to capital investment projects, such as building a new factory, purchasing a new delivery van, relocating an office or installing a new piece of machinery. However, on occasions the techniques described in this chapter can be applied to revenue expenditure, such as putting resources into an advertising campaign or spending money on research and development.

Reasons why businesses invest

Investment or capital investment describes the process of purchasing non-current assets, such as new buildings, plant, machinery or office equipment. It considers the buying of any asset that will pay for itself over a period of more than one year.

Capital investment is undertaken for two main reasons:

- to replace or renew any assets that have worn out (depreciated) or become obsolescent (out of date)
- to introduce additional, new assets in order to meet increased demand for the firm's products.

Key terms

Investment decisions The process of deciding whether or not to undertake capital investment (the purchase of non-current assets) or major business projects.

▲ Businesses invest in research to produce new assets

Financial methods of assessing an investment

Major business projects involve decisions that incorporate more than just capital equipment. Setting up new factories or stores, introducing new products, setting up a research laboratory and relocating to a new country are all examples of major projects which businesses must analyse using rigorous, scientific techniques. **Investment appraisal** ensures that investment decisions are subject to rigorous scrutiny before agreement.

Investment appraisal is a **quantitative** (numerical) tool in the decision-making process. Any investment recommendations from numerical investment appraisal should be combined with an investigation of **qualitative** (non-financial) factors before a final decision is reached. These non-financial factors are considered later in the chapter.

The three investment appraisal techniques examined in this chapter base their recommendations solely on the following financial information:

- the initial cost of the investment
- the net return (revenue minus costs) per annum
- the lifetime of the investment.

Methods of investment appraisal

There are three main methods of investment appraisal:

- payback period
- average rate of return, or annual rate of return, or average annual rate of return (ARR)
- net present value (NPV).

Each method provides a numerical calculation of the financial benefits of an investment. This result can be compared with the investment criteria set by the business and/or the results of alternative investment decisions.

The following scenario will provide the background information for investment appraisal by each of these methods.

Key terms

Investment appraisal
A scientific approach to investment decision making, which investigates the expected financial consequences of an investment, in order to assist the company in its choices.

Author advice

Investment appraisal can be applied to any major business decision. A firm considering a takeover or a new marketing strategy can assess the financial implications by using investment appraisal.

Martin's Motors

Martin's Motors is a small garage on the outskirts of Basingstoke in Hampshire. The business offers servicing of certain makes of car for customers who do not wish to take their cars to the main dealerships.

Martin's key selling points are low overheads and a more flexible and personal service for customers, in comparison with local competitors. Most customers are recommended by friends, but in recent years a number of loyal customers have taken their cars back to the main dealers for their servicing. Martin has discovered that the main reason is the lack of certain technical equipment within his garage, as he is unable to afford the state-of-the-art machinery purchased by the large garages against which he is competing.

A particular weakness is the lack of a machine to recharge (service) the air-conditioning units in his customers' cars. He is looking at purchasing a Texa Konfort air-conditioning machine for carrying out this task. Martin has financial estimates based on prices in a Texa Konfort catalogue, comments from other garages, and his own estimates of the number of customers that he has lost through his failure to provide recharging of air-conditioning for his customers. These estimates are outlined below:

Initial costs:

Cost to purchase a Texa Konfort air-conditioning machine: £5,000

Cost of a one-off advert in the *Thomson Local* directory (to alert customers to the new service): £250

Initial costs = £5,000 + £250 = <u>£5,250</u>

Running costs:

Air-conditioning liquid:	£20 per treatment
Wages and other costs:	£5 per treatment
Price charged to customers:	£65 per treatment

Anticipated number of customers requesting the treatment:

Year 1: 60

Year 2: 45

Year 3: 39

Year 4: 34

Year 5: 30

Martin is expecting to make money by attracting back customers for a full service of their cars. However, he wants to take a pessimistic view, so he is basing his decision on whether the Texa Konfort will pay for itself by attracting customers who only wish to service their air-conditioning. Any additional revenue is seen as a bonus.

The expected lifetime of the machine is anticipated to be five years, although this is probably a pessimistic estimate. As competition for air-conditioning recharging increases, the selling price is expected to fall from £65 to £50 or £60.

Table 8.1 shows the expected revenue, costs and net return on the Texa Konfort over its expected lifetime, based on the estimated costs, charges and customer numbers. For example, in year 1, revenue is $60 \times £65 = £3,900$ and costs are $60 \times (£20 + £5) = £1,500$.

▼ **Table 8.1** Expected revenue, costs and return on the Texa Konfort

Year	Annual revenue (£)	Annual cost (£)	Net return (£)
0*	0	5,250	(5,250)
1	3,900	1,500	2,400
2	2,925	1,125	1,800
3	2,535	975	1,560
4	2,210	850	1,360
5	1,950	750	1,200
Cumulative total	**13,520**	**10,450**	**3,070**

*It is traditional to denote the year in which the initial cost of an investment is incurred as year 0.

Payback

Payback is calculated by adding the annual returns from an investment until the cumulative total equals the initial cost of the investment. The exact time at which this occurs is the **payback period**. It is often measured in years, but for some investments, months or weeks may be more appropriate. Firms will hope for as short a payback as possible, but the exact target will vary according to circumstances, with the payback criteria for major projects tending to be much longer than for smaller projects.

An example calculation based on Martin's Motors is shown in Table 8.2.

▼ **Table 8.2** Predicted payback period for a Texa Konfort air-conditioning system for Martin's Motors

Year	Annual revenue (£)	Annual cost (£)	Net return (£)	Cumulative returns (£)
0	0	5,250	(5,250)	(5,250)
1	3,900	1,500	2,400	(2,850)
2	2,925	1,125	1,800	(1,050)
3	2,535	975	1,560	510
4	2,210	850	1,360	1,870
5	1,950	750	1,200	3,070
Cumulative total	**13,520**	**10,450**	**3,070**	

The final column shows the running total of revenues minus costs. When this column reaches zero, payback has been achieved. By the end of year 2, £4,200 of the £5,250 has been repaid. During year 3 the net return is £1,560, leading to a surplus of £510 by the end of year 3. Thus, the payback occurs at some time during the third year.

In payback calculations, it is assumed that costs and income occur at regular intervals throughout the year. Therefore, the £1,560 net return in year 3 is spread evenly over the 52 weeks of the year. This means there are net returns of £1,560/52 = £30 per week. At this rate it will take exactly

Key terms

Payback period The length of time that it takes for an investment to pay for itself from the net returns provided by that particular investment.

£1,050/£30 = 35 weeks of year 3 to reach payback. Thus, the payback point is 35 weeks after the end of year 2: that is, 2 years 35 weeks.

An alternative way to calculate the final part is to work out the fraction of the year that elapses before payback is reached. In the above example, £1,050 is still needed to reach payback after the end of year 2. The net return for year 3 is £1,560. Therefore, the payback point is reached 1,050/1,560 of the way through the year. This is 0.673 of a year. Thus the payback period is 2.673 years.

A simpler result is achieved by calculating in weeks:

number of weeks before payback is achieved during

the third year $= \dfrac{1,050}{1,560} \times 52 = 35$

Therefore, the payback period is 2 years 35 weeks.

Average rate of return

Firms want to achieve as high a percentage return as possible. A benchmark that is often used to set the criteria for an acceptable **ARR percentage** is the interest rate that the firm must pay on any money borrowed to finance the investment. If the percentage return on the project exceeds the interest rate that the business is paying, the project is financially worthwhile.

An example calculation based on Martin's Motors is shown below:

$$\text{ARR(\%)} = \frac{\text{total net return or surplus from a project/no. of years}}{\text{initial cost}} \times 100$$

Calculations for the Texa Konfort air-conditioning machine:

$$\frac{£3,070/5}{£5,250} \times 100 = \frac{£614}{£5,250} \, 100 = 11.7\%$$

At current interest rates, this ARR would mean that it is financially worthwhile to purchase the air-conditioning equipment.

Net present value

Given a choice between £1 now and £1 in the future, a rational individual (or firm) will choose £1 now. Implicitly, this suggests that money today has a greater value than money in the future. This arises because of the **opportunity cost** of the money. For example, £100 received today could be invested at, say, 10 per cent and would be worth £110 in a year's time. Thus, in these circumstances, the **present value** of £110, receivable in one year's time, is £100.

The **net present value** method of investment appraisal takes this factor into consideration.

Any receipts (or payments) in the future are considered to be worth less than the equivalent sum received (or paid) today. In effect, future sums are **discounted** (reduced) by a certain percentage to reflect their lower value. In our example, a 10 per cent discount rate would be appropriate. A commonly used discount rate is the current rate of interest, as this is the opportunity cost of using money for a particular investment. The opportunity cost (next best alternative) is assumed to be the return that the firm could have made by just saving the money involved.

Key term

Average rate of return % (ARR%) Total net returns divided by the expected lifetime of the investment (usually a number of years), expressed as a percentage of the initial cost of the investment.

Author advice

When using ARR% to assess whether a project is financially worthwhile, a business will select a target interest rate that the project should match or exceed. The interest rate chosen is likely to be the rate of interest that the business would be charged if it borrowed the money to finance the project. Currently, interest rates are very low and so a target interest rate might be about 5 per cent. The project would be worthwhile if its ARR% exceeded 5 per cent.

Key term

Net present value (NPV) The net return on an investment when all revenues and costs have been converted to their current worth.

Discounted cash flow

The payback and average rate of return methods assume that the exact timing of the payments and receipts is not important. They ignore the **time value of money**. However, the net present value method of investment appraisal includes this factor in its calculation.

There is no single agreed percentage by which future values should be discounted, as companies face different circumstances. If a company can find a very profitable immediate use for its cash, it will place a much higher value on money in the present (as the opportunity cost of waiting will be the lost opportunity to make a high profit). Paradoxically, a firm suffering from cash-flow problems will deem a high discount rate appropriate: money received in the present may be necessary to keep the business operating. Conversely, a business that is secure but less profitable might consider a low discount rate to be valid.

Whatever the financial situation of a firm, the current market interest rate can be earned if money is received immediately. This acts as a guide to the loss or discount that should be applied to money in the future.

The process of reducing the value of future sums is known as **discounted cash flow**. As time progresses, the 'present' value of a given future sum declines. The higher the discount rate, the lower the value. Exact values can be determined from a 'present value' table.

Table 8.3 shows the present value of £1, based on four different discount rates.

The choice of discount rate may be critical in an investment appraisal. It can be seen that £1 received in five years' time is equivalent to £0.784 (78.4p) today, if a discount rate of 5 per cent is applied, but only 62.1p (£0.621) if 10 per cent is used and as much as 90.6 p (£0.906) if a 2 per cent discount rate is used.

Two example calculations based on Martin's Motors are shown in Tables 8.4 and 8.5.

▼ **Table 8.3** Present value of £1 at selected discount rates

	Discount rate			
Year	2%	5%	7%	10%
0	1.0	1.0	1.0	1.0
1	0.980	0.952	0.935	0.909
2	0.961	0.907	0.873	0.826
3	0.942	0.864	0.816	0.751
4	0.924	0.823	0.763	0.683
5	0.906	0.784	0.713	0.621

Author advice

Do not try to remember discount tables. Discount rate tables will be provided if you need to calculate net present value. Use information on current interest rates or the firm's targeted percentage return on its investments when assessing investment appraisal results.

▼ **Table 8.4** Net present value of a Texa Konfort air-conditioning system for Martin's Motors, using a 5 per cent discount factor

Year	Net return (£)	Discount factor (5%)	Present value (£)
0	(5,250)	1.0	(5,250)
1	2,400	0.952	2,284.8
2	1,800	0.907	1,632.6
3	1,560	0.864	1,347.84
4	1,360	0.823	1,119.28
5	1,200	0.784	940.8
Total	**3,070**		**2,075.32**

Net present value gives a definite recommendation. The criteria used are that if the NPV is positive, it is financially justified; if the NPV is negative, the project is not worthwhile. The net present value of the investment above is +£2,075.32. **On financial grounds alone**, the project is worthwhile. However, the firm may wish to include other factors in its decision. These will be discussed later.

Note how the actual net return on this investment is +£3,070. However, the net present value is only +£2,075.32. This is because the main costs are incurred in year 0, whereas the returns are in the future when we are assuming that money is less valuable.

Table 8.4 uses a 5 per cent discount factor. If Martin's Motors could earn a 10 per cent return on its money, then a 10 per cent rate might have been selected. Would the project still be worthwhile?

Table 8.5 shows that, at a 10 per cent discount rate, the net present value is +£1,264.04. This is much lower than the net present value at 5 per cent (+£2,075.32), but it is still a positive return and therefore the investment is worthwhile.

▼ **Table 8.5** Net present value of a Texa Konfort air-conditioning system for Martin's Motors, using a 10 per cent discount factor

Year	Net return (£)	Discount factor (10%)	Present value (£)
0	(5,250)	1.0	(5,250)
1	2,400	0.909	2,181.6
2	1,800	0.826	1,486.8
3	1,560	0.751	1,171.56
4	1,360	0.683	928.88
5	1,200	0.621	745.2
Total	**3,070**		**1,264.04**

Fact file

Zero discount rate

Since 1999, interest rates in Japan have tended to be 0 per cent, in order to encourage spending and discourage saving. At the time of writing, UK interest rates have fallen to 0.5 per cent. It is therefore possible, in some circumstances, for a zero discount rate to be the most appropriate discount factor to use when calculating NPV.

In the Martin's Motors NPV calculation the net return column shows the present value if a 0 per cent discount factor is used, and so NPV at 0 per cent discount is +£3,070. When the discount factor is 0 per cent, any project that provides a positive return is financially worthwhile.

Fact file

Tesco cost-cutting

Investment appraisal is not necessarily a comparison of costs and revenues. In January 2015, Tesco's new Chief Executive, Dave Lewis, announced plans to close the company's headquarters in Cheshunt. For this decision, the initial costs are the high levels of redundancy payments and potential loss on the value of the property, which is on an industrial estate and therefore unlikely to attract high offers. In future years, the benefits will take the form of reduced costs. This decision will reduce head office costs by 30 per cent and is part of a plan to cut costs by £250 million a year.

Lewis's plans also include the closure of 43 Tesco stores, some of which are reputed to be profit-making.

However, investment appraisal of these stores indicates that the decision to close the store will prove to be financially worthwhile because some customers are expected to use alternative Tesco stores instead. For example, the Tesco Metro store in Bootle, which is closing, has two other large Tesco stores within just over a mile, while the Kensington Express Store in Liverpool has 15 other Tesco stores within two miles. Bicester, a town of 30,000 people, is losing a Tesco Metro, but will still have a Tesco superstore and four Tesco Expresses. In these cases, the appraisal suggests that the closures are worthwhile because the reduction in future revenue is expected to be less than the savings on costs.

Source: article entitled 'Analysis: Why has Tesco chosen to shut these 43 stores?' by Matthew Hopkinson in *CityA.M.*, 29.1.15 and other sources

Comparing the different methods of investment appraisal

The three methods of investment appraisal outlined above use very different approaches in deciding whether an investment is worthwhile. Each method can also be used to compare alternative investments, where a firm has to decide between different projects. The methods have various strengths and weaknesses, as described below.

Payback

Advantages

- The payback period is easy to calculate. If many projects are being considered, this may save valuable time.
- The concept of payback is easy to understand – it is how long it takes to get the money back.
- The payback method emphasises cash flow by focusing only on the time taken to return the money. As a result, it is a particularly relevant approach for organisations that have some cash-flow difficulties.
- By emphasising the speed of return, the payback period is popular with firms operating in markets that are experiencing rapid change because estimates for years in the distant future are going to be less reliable than those for the near future.

Disadvantages

- The calculation of payback ignores any revenues or costs that occur after the point at which payback has been reached. This means that it does not consider the overall net return from a project. As profit is usually considered to be the main aim of most businesses, this is a major weakness. The payback method may lead to a business ignoring the most profitable investment, simply because it takes slightly longer to achieve that profit.
- It is very difficult to establish a target payback time. Some major investments, such as a new factory, will take many years to pay for themselves. However, investment in a marketing campaign or a new record download will pay for itself in months or not at all.
- Payback values future costs and revenues at the same value as current costs and revenues. Thus it does not consider the time value of money in the way that net present value does.
- By focusing on payback, the business may be encouraged towards short-termism. A firm using the payback method would fail to look at the long-term consequences of an investment.

Average rate of return

Advantages

- The result (a percentage calculation) can be easily compared with the next best alternative (the opportunity cost), such as the percentage interest earned from a savings account.
- The average rate of return shows the true profitability of the investment. It is the only method that takes into consideration every item of revenue and expenditure at its face value.
- Percentage returns, such as the average rate of return, are usually understood by non-accountants.

Disadvantages

- The average rate of return is harder and more time consuming to calculate than the payback method, so it may use valuable company time in compiling shortlists of potential investments.
- It considers all income and expenditure as equal in value. Thus, projections a long time into the future are given the same importance as predictions of present costs and incomes.

Net present value

Advantages

- Net present value is the only method that considers the time value of money. By discounting future figures, NPV recognises that people and organisations place a higher value on money paid/received now than in the future.
- As sums of money far into the future are discounted more heavily, this approach reduces the importance of long-term estimates. As long-term estimates are probably the least reliable predictions, NPV helps to make the conclusions more accurate.
- Net present value is the only method that gives a precise answer. A positive NPV means that, on financial grounds, the investment should be undertaken. A negative NPV indicates that the project should be rejected.

Disadvantages

- Net present value is time consuming and more difficult to calculate than the other methods.
- It is more difficult to understand than the other approaches. This may mean that decision makers distrust any conclusions drawn using this method.
- The calculation of net present value is based on an arbitrary choice of percentage discount rate. Although the method is calculated scientifically, the final conclusion often relies on the discount rate used.

Although each method of investment appraisal can be criticised, investment appraisal in general is still a worthwhile process. It encourages organisations to research and evaluate carefully the possible financial consequences of potential investment decisions. A careful evaluation can help an organisation to avoid expensive mistakes or alert it to projects with tremendous potential.

Factors influencing investment decisions

When making an investment decision, businesses usually consider a variety of factors. The key factors are:

- investment criteria
- non-financial factors
- risk and uncertainty.

Investment criteria

Investment criteria are based on the overall objectives of the business and the objectives of functional areas involved in the actual investment. Very few decisions are taken purely on financial grounds, although the specific

Key term

Investment criteria The ways in which a business will judge whether an investment should be undertaken.

investment appraisal targets, such as a three-year payback or a 10 per cent, average rate of return, could be deemed to be investment criteria.

Other investment criteria that a business might consider are:

- Strategic fit – is the investment consistent with the corporate strategy that the business is pursuing?
- Cash-flow implications – is the investment going to place the business into liquidity problems in the short run?
- Prestige – will the investment enhance the reputation or image of the brand/business?
- Market conditions – is the market expected to grow or decline and how might this affect the success of the project?
- Competition – how competitive is the market?
- Change – will tastes change or technological progress negate the potential benefits of the project?
- Impact on stakeholders – will the investment impact favourably or unfavourably on different stakeholders.
- Strengths – does the investment play to the strengths of the business or might it expose weaknesses?

The choice of investment criteria will depend on the business's circumstances. If cash flow is absolutely vital, then the payback method is more likely to be used. For medium-term projects which are relying on borrowed money, the ARR percentage is often deemed to be the most appropriate method. For long-term projects, when some income may be received a long time in the future, the net present value is used. As all three methods use the same data, it is easy to calculate all three and so it is common practice for businesses to use all three criteria to support their investment decisions.

However, few investments are taken purely on the basis of financial factors. Non-financial factors and the level of risk and uncertainty can be crucial also.

Non-financial (qualitative) factors

It is vital that decisions are not based solely on numerical (quantitative) factors. A business needs to consider the level of uncertainty in its financial forecasts. Furthermore, it is crucial that non-financial (qualitative) factors are taken into account in its decision making. With a thoughtful blend of numerical and non-numerical analysis, investment appraisal will help an organisation to make sound investment decisions.

The qualitative factors to be considered, and their relative importance, vary according to circumstances. Some of the key factors are described briefly below, but these are only an indication of some of the issues that may apply. Every investment project will raise its own issues to consider.

- **The aims of the organisation**. A profit-making firm will emphasise the quantitative (numerical) results of an investment appraisal, and is therefore likely to accept its results. However, a firm that places a high value on social issues might reject a profitable investment that might exploit its workforce or damage the environment.
- **Reliability of the data**. Future costs and incomes rely on the accuracy of market research and an ability to predict external changes. For the more original investments and those of a longer duration, predictions may be wildly inaccurate, undermining the use of investment appraisal techniques.

Key term

Risk and uncertainty The probability of unforeseen circumstances that may harm the success of a business decision.

▲ Demand for the London Eye surpassed expectations

- **Personnel**. Will the new equipment or method suit the company's staff? The ease of use; the level of training needed; the safety of machinery; the impact on the number of staff employed – are all factors that should be considered.
- **The economy**. Economic forecasts (for example, predicting a recession or boom) must be considered in the predictions of future costs and revenues.
- **Legal requirements**. Does the project enable the business to meet current (or planned) legal requirements?
- **Subjective criteria**. All investment decisions are taken by individuals who have their own personal preferences. Sometimes a manager may have a 'gut feeling' or intuition that an investment will benefit the business. (This was referred to in Chapter 5 of the AQA A-level Business Book 1.)

Risk and uncertainty

High-return projects often involve high risk, but the potential to make high profits might be seen as being worth the risk. However, some firms may prefer to choose a project with a lower, but more certain, return.

For many major projects it is very difficult for a firm to estimate the anticipated costs and revenue. The construction costs for the London Olympics were budgeted at £2.4 billion in 2005, but its eventual costs were £8.8 billion. The British Library was budgeted to cost £74 million but the actual cost was £511 million.

The major government project at present is HS2 (the High Speed rail links between London, the Midlands and Leeds/Manchester). Its original budget was £33 billion, but this has already increased to £43 billion. Early signs are not promising. Some initial consultancy work has already been completed for the HS2 project at a cost that exceeded the budget allowed for it by 86 per cent. HS2 is an example of three major difficulties that often occur in investment appraisal:

- The project is a unique piece of construction, so it is difficult to draw on previous experience to get accurate financial estimates.
- With any major project there is the chance that business logic may not prevail, as the decision makers may wish to make their mark by providing a grand project.
- Predicting revenue is often very difficult. The longer the project takes, the harder it becomes to gauge consumer demand. For example, the Millennium Dome (O2 Arena) did not attract the revenue that had been forecast, despite being built on time, whereas the popularity of the London Eye surpassed even the most optimistic forecasts, despite the delay in its completion.

Firms usually take the following actions to allow for risks and uncertainties in their investment appraisals:

- Build in allowances or contingencies in case problems occur. Of course, this can lead to investments being unexpectedly cheaper than the budgeted costs if the project runs smoothly.

- Use sensitivity analysis to calculate alternative results. Often three scenarios will be calculated: the expected outcome, the best-case scenario and the worst-case scenario.
- Set more demanding targets, such as a short payback period or a high ARR. By setting a more challenging target, the business is, in effect, allowing for risks and uncertainties.

The other uncertainty that may occur is the market. Most appraisals cover a period of years. Even in stable markets it is difficult to foresee the future. In rapidly changing markets, estimates may be no more than guesswork. Thorough market research, close scrutiny of similar investments in the past, and benchmarking data with other companies are all methods that can reduce the uncertainty.

Fact file

Investment decisions and cost escalation

Any organisation must monitor its proposed investments closely and be prepared to modify its decisions if changes occur. In December 2002 the government announced plans for a 2 kilometre tunnel that would take the A303 trunk road away from its current proximity to Stonehenge. The forecast cost of this project was £183 million. Over the next five years, the  estimated cost of the project increased to £540 million. In December 2007 the government announced that it was abandoning the planned tunnel as the high costs meant that it was no longer feasible on financial grounds. In December 2014 the tunnel project was approved again. Its budgeted cost is now £1.2 billion.

What do you think?

For many government projects, such as road-building, there is no direct source of revenue. Therefore, when government departments use investment appraisal, they use an approach known as cost–benefit analysis (CBA). This compares the cost of the road-building with an estimate of the financial benefits of the road to society. Most of these financial benefits are the journey times saved. Business time (such as road use by lorries) is valued much more highly than leisure time (such as a visit to a tourist attraction). This may be one reason why the A303 Stonehenge project has still not been completed.

Is this a fair method of measuring the benefits of a road? What do you think?

The value of sensitivity analysis

Investment appraisal criteria, such as payback and NPV, are usually calculated on the basis of the **expected outcome**. In doing so, the financial outcome could be argued to be the most likely one to occur. However, sensitivity analysis allows businesses to predict other outcomes, if the expected outcome does not occur. Sensitivity analysis is often referred to as 'What if?' analysis. By using sensitivity analysis to calculate alternative results, the level of uncertainty can be considered and the level of risk identified.

Sensitivity analysis often uses three scenarios and calculates: the expected outcome, the best-case scenario and the worst-case scenario. These different scenarios may be combined to look at the overall risk.

For further information on sensitivity analysis, please read the two Fact files in Chapter 5 in Book 1.

Example

An investment appraisal involves assessing a new production line that will lead to cost savings. The business uses payback to assess its investments. The project will be accepted if its payback is less than 5.5 years.

Sensitivity analysis reveals the following possible outcomes:

▼ **Table 8.6** Expected outcomes of investment

	Expected financial outcome for:		
	Best-case scenario	Expected outcome	Worst-case scenario
Initial cost of project (£000)	100	120	160
Annual cost saving (£000)	60	40	20

▼ **Table 8.7** Payback (in years) for each combination of scenarios

	Payback period (in years)		
Annual cost savings	Best-case scenario	Expected outcome	Worst-case scenario
Best-case scenario	1.7 years	2.0 years	2.7 years
Expected outcome	2.5 years	3.0 years	4.0 years
Worst-case scenario	5 years	**6.0 years**	**8.0 years**

Result of sensitivity analysis: For seven of the nine combinations, the payback is acceptable (less than 5.5 years). The two situations in bold show the circumstances in which the target payback will not be met.

Conclusion: The key strategy is to try to avoid the worst-case outcome for annual cost savings (where there are two entries in bold). If planning can prevent this scenario occurring, the business will achieve its target payback – although it will be certain to achieve its target if the initial project cost is the best-case scenario (where there are no entries in bold).

Practice exercise

Total: 70 marks

1. A project has an initial cost of £10,000 and then annual revenue of £5,000 and annual costs of £3,000. What is its payback?
   a) 50 per cent
   b) 20 per cent
   c) 2 years
   d) 5 years. *(1 mark)*

2. A discount rate of 10 per cent means that £100 next year has a present value of £91. A project that costs £100 now but brings in a return of £100 in a year's time has a net present value of:
   a) –£9
   b) 0
   c) + £9
   d) + £9. *(1 mark)*

3. What is meant by the term 'investment appraisal'? *(3 marks)*

4. What is meant by the term 'sensitivity analysis'? *(3 marks)*

5. Identify the two main reasons for capital investment. *(2 marks)*

The table below shows the financial details of a new investment. Based on this data, answer questions 6, 7 and 8.

Year	Income (£)	Costs (£m)	Annual net return (£m)	Present value of £1 at a 5% discount rate
0	0	50	(50)	1.0
1	30	20	10	0.952
2	40	20	20	0.907
3	50	20	30	0.864

6. Calculate the payback period. *(3 marks)*

7. Calculate the average rate of return. *(5 marks)*

8. Calculate the net present value based on a 5 per cent discount rate. *(6 marks)*

9. On the basis of your answers to questions 6, 7 and 8, advise the business on whether it should go ahead with the new investment. Justify your decision. *(4 marks)*

10. Explain two advantages of using the average rate of return method of investment appraisal. *(8 marks)*

11. Explain two problems of using the net present value method of investment appraisal. *(8 marks)*

12. Explain two reasons why it is difficult to provide reliable forecasts for major investment projects. *(6 marks)*

13. Explain how a business can reduce the risk of inaccurate forecasts. *(6 marks)*

14. Explain two reasons for choosing payback as a method of investment appraisal. *(6 marks)*

15. Explain two non-financial factors that might be considered in assessing an investment. *(8 marks)*

Case study 1: Maize mazes

Farmers and theme parks, predominantly in the UK and USA, are using maize mazes as tourist attractions. A specialist firm designs a maze and in the spring the maize is planted in accordance with its instructions. Once the maize is fully grown, it forms a maze that can be used from July to September. The following year a revised design can be created to present a new challenge to visitors. Because of the short lifespan of the maze, the field can be used to cultivate a winter growing crop and generate more profit.

Paul Swaffield, a Dorset farmer, is one individual who has been won over by the idea. The maize maze on his farm brought in 25 times as much revenue as the crop that he usually grew in that field. Furthermore, at the end of the summer the maize was used as cattle feed, providing additional revenue.

Jowett House Farm in Cawthorne, Yorkshire, is a farm that has taken advantage of this new source of revenue. The year 2014 marked its fourteenth maize maze. The maze is open for 53 days in the summer. The average ticket price is £5.75 per visitor and the maze is expected to receive an average of 220 visitors per day. However, the vast majority of these visits occur at weekends and heavy rainfall has a big impact on sales revenue.

A typical maize maze costs £30,000 to make, although running costs vary. For a maze such as the one at Cawthorne, where a 'Maze Master Team' is employed to help visitors, the running costs can amount to £160 per day. At the end of the summer, the maize is used to feed the cows in the farm's dairy herd.

Questions

Total: 30 marks

1. Calculate the payback period of the Cawthorne maze, based on the figures in the case study.
   (4 marks)

2. Sensitivity analysis suggests that heavy rainfall in the summer could reduce the average visitors to 120 per day. Explain one benefit and one limitation of using sensitivity analysis to decide whether to construct a maze at the farm. *(10 marks)*

3. Discuss possible reasons why the average rate of return and net present value methods of investment appraisal are not as suitable as the payback method in assessing the Cawthorne maize project.
   (16 marks)

Case study 2: Managing the prison estate

In 2012, the government completed the construction of two new prisons in order to improve the management of prisons in the UK. A third large prison in Wrexham is due for completion in 2017. Thirteen prisons were closed between 2010 and 2013.

The government's prison estate strategy has two main aims:
● to reduce costs
● to improve quality and performance in terms of: security, safety, decency and providing 'purposeful activity' for prisoners. Purposeful activity is primarily education and training suited to life after prison.

Between 2012 and 2015, the government's strategy has focused on cost reduction. Despite this, the National Audit Office indicates that 44 per cent of the closures are 'high performing prisons', in terms of their cost-effectiveness and quality and performance. However, the prison service's ability to respond to sudden changes in prisoner numbers has been a particular success of the recent strategy.

Table 8.8 summarises the expected financial outcomes of this strategy of replacing older prisons with larger new prisons. Larger prisons cut costs, but smaller prisons perform better in terms of non-financial factors. Following the initial cost of £372 million in 2012 (Year 0), the strategy leads to cost savings in future years. Each of these savings is shown by a + because the cost savings are expected to pay for the initial cost of the strategy.

In recent years, temporary accommodation has been used to cope with rising prisoner numbers. The new prisons being built are of a significantly higher quality than older prisons, and include better safety features and facilities, such as cells with integrated toilets and showers. The accommodation has a planned lifespan of 60 years. However, 12 per cent of the accommodation is designed for prisoners to share cells, which is against the United Nations and Council of Europe guidelines.

The new accommodation provides better security, but it lacks the facilities for 'purposeful activities' for prisoners.

Overall, the average cost of holding a prisoner is £28,000 a year. However, in the new Thameside prison, the average cost of holding a prisoner is over £50,000 a year. This is partly due to its location in London, an area with a shortage of prison spaces (one aim is to try to limit travelling distances for relatives of prisoners).

The current prison population is about 84,000 people. Many people believe that a reduction in prisoner numbers is the best solution, as a cut of 1,000 prisoners will save £28 million per year.

▼ **Table 8.8** Financial outcomes of the prison estate strategy

Year	Effect on costs (£ millions)	Present value of £1 at a 5% discount rate
0 (2012)	(372)	1.0
1 (2013)	zero	0.95
2 (2014)	+44	0.91
3 (2015)	+70	0.86
4 (2016)	+70	0.82
5 (2017)	+70	0.78
6 (2018)	+70	0.75
7 (2019)	+70	0.71
8 (2020)	+70	0.68

Source: National Audit Office

Questions

Total: 35 marks

Based on the data in Table 8.8, answer the following three questions.

1. Calculate the payback period for the new prison estate strategy. *(4 marks)*

2. Calculate the average rate of return, over the eight years of the project, for the prison estate strategy. *(6 marks)*

3. Calculate the net present value of the strategy over the eight years from 2012 to 2020, based on a discount rate of 5 per cent. *(9 marks)*

4. Basing your decision on **both** of the overall aims of the government's prison estate strategy, evaluate whether the new prison strategy is likely to succeed in achieving its aims. *(16 marks)*

Strategic direction: choosing which markets to compete in and what products to offer

This chapter introduces the concept of strategic direction and the factors that influence how a business chooses which markets to compete in and which products to offer. The use of Ansoff's matrix in order to decide between market penetration, (new) product development, market development and diversification is explained. The chapter concludes by demonstrating how Ansoff's matrix can be used to show the reasons for choosing, and the value of, different options for strategic direction.

Factors influencing which markets to compete in and which products to offer

In Chapter 1 of this book we saw that strategy is the medium- to long-term plans that will allow a business to achieve its objectives. Such plans include details about what is to be done and the financial, production and personnel resources required to implement the plans. Strategies should not be considered until corporate objectives have been agreed.

Once corporate objectives have been agreed, the business should follow the stages outlined in Chapters 2 to 8 in this book, by:

● analysing the existing internal strengths and weaknesses of the business (both financial and non-financial), so that any strategy is based on strengths or so that strategies to overcome the weaknesses can be implemented (these topics were covered in Chapters 2 and 3);
● analysing the external environment to assess opportunities and threats that face the business, such as political and legal change, economic change, social and technological change, and changes in the competitive environment (these topics were covered in Chapters 4 to 7);
● applying investment appraisal, where appropriate, of planned strategic options, in order to assess their financial viability (see Chapter 8).

Once this process has been undertaken the company should have the information needed to decide its **strategic direction**.

If a business's long-term objective is primarily to increase profitability, then its strategy will be the methods through which this fundamental objective will be achieved. For example, an organisation such as Coca-Cola might aim to achieve this objective through a strategy of building brand loyalty through marketing; AstraZeneca might aim to achieve this objective through the development and patenting of new products; whereas Apple

> ### Key term
> **Strategic direction** Describes how a business plans to get to where it wants to be in the long term.

will focus its strategy on ensuring that products are well designed and suited to customer needs.

In each of these cases the strategy is based around a business's strengths. However, it may be possible that a business will need to adopt a strategy of strengthening areas that are presently weaknesses in order to achieve its objectives. In all cases, an awareness of potential changes in the external environment is crucial if the business is to move forward in the right direction.

Fact file

Apple's strategic direction

In 2015, Apple's high profits were attributed to the success of its iPhones. Apple has always been prepared to change its strategic direction according to changes in the internal and external market. Its original focus was on a niche (design) within the market for computers, before internal research and development led to a shift in towards music through the iPod. Having then shifted its direction largely towards the mobile phone market, the introduction of the iPad appeared to be taking it in yet another direction. However, the growth in mobile technology appears to be taking Apple back to the iPhone, but adapting it as a fully flexible method of mobile communication.

Key term

Ansoff's matrix A strategic or marketing planning model that can be used to help a business decide its strategic direction in terms of its product portfolio and target markets.

Author advice

In looking at the strategic directions available in Ansoff's matrix, draw upon your understanding across all of the functional areas and external influences. Try to take an integrative view of business when using Ansoff's matrix because the best direction may depend on the strengths and weaknesses of each functional area and/or the opportunities and threats resulting from external changes.

In most cases strategic direction is concerned with a business using its understanding of its internal and external environments in order to choose:

- the products it should produce
- the markets in which to sell those products.

The most well-known model used to decide on strategic direction is **Ansoff's matrix**.

Ansoff's matrix

Ansoff's matrix is a decision-making tool for marketing planning and developing a suitable business strategy. It was created by Igor Ansoff and first published in his article 'Strategies for diversification' in the *Harvard Business Review* in 1957. Ansoff's matrix provides a useful framework for analysing a range of strategic directions in relation to risks and rewards.

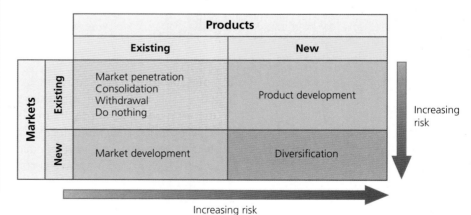

▲ **Figure 9.1** Ansoff's matrix

Ansoff's matrix consists of four cells that provide a company with a range of options or strategic choices, each with a different degree of risk attached (see Figure 9.1). We will examine each of these choices in turn.

Existing products, existing markets

In this situation, the company has the choice of whether to penetrate the market further, consolidate its present position, withdraw from the market altogether or simply do nothing. Providing existing products in existing markets is a low-risk strategy because the firm is working in areas in which it has both knowledge and experience.

- **Market penetration** – promoting growth in existing markets with existing products. Several different tactics can be employed: increasing brand loyalty in order to reduce customers' purchases of substitute products; encouraging customers to use the product more often, and therefore make more frequent purchases; or encouraging customers to use more of the product on each occasion – for example, by promoting the sale of larger packs. In highly competitive markets, taking customers from rivals may result in short-term gains, but competitors are likely to fight back. As a strategy, market penetration has its limits and once the market approaches saturation, another strategy must be pursued if a firm is to continue to grow.

Fact file

Classic toys: a case of market penetration

Makers of traditional toys such as teddy bears and board games (e.g. Monopoly) have been facing tough competition in a world where children are more interested in playing computer games than spending their time with a more 'passive' toy or taking hours playing a time-consuming game.

Both types of organisation have used marketing strategies that fit into Ansoff's matrix. Teddy bear makers such as Deans, Merrythought and Steiff have started to market nostalgia more aggressively and to aim their products at grandparents, who are buying more toys for their grandchildren. For Christmas 2014 Merrythought released a Christmas Teddy, while in 2013 a limited edition bear was launched to celebrate the birth of Prince George.

There is now a niche market among adults for 'collections' of bears, particularly from manufacturers with a long

tradition, such as Deans and Steiff. Some toys, such as Hornby Trains, are targeted directly at the older consumer. 'People are retiring earlier, going back to their old hobbies and renewing their interest in toy trains and Scalextric sets. They are the ones with the disposable income.'

Board game manufacturers, such as Monopoly, Scrabble and Trivial Pursuits, have also responded by adapting their games so that new versions allow the games to be completed more quickly.

Source: adapted from *Business Review*, April 2005 and company websites

- **Consolidation** – concentrating activities on those areas where the firm has established a competitive advantage or competence, and focusing its attention on maintaining its market share. If this strategy is prompted by falling profits, then some form of **retrenchment**, such as redundancies or the sale of assets, might be needed. (Retrenchment means cutting back on activities in order to save costs.)
- **Withdrawal** – through the sale of all or part of the business. This might be appropriate if there is an irreversible decline in demand or the firm cannot match new competitors.
- **Doing nothing** – that is, continuing with the existing strategy. This might be appropriate in the short term when the environment is static or the firm is waiting to see how a situation develops, but it is not realistic or beneficial in the long term.

Existing products, new markets

Here the strategy of **market development** is followed to extend a product's market into new areas. Examples are seeking new geographical territories, promoting new uses for the existing product, or entering new market segments. The development of new markets for the product is a good strategy if a firm's core competences are related more to the product than to its experience with a specific market segment. Market development is more risky than market penetration because the firm will not be familiar with the needs and wants of the new market.

Fact file

Market development at Starbucks

Opened in Seattle in 1971, Starbucks (at the time of writing – December 2014) has 21,878 stores in 65 different countries, three times as many stores as it had in 2007. In the USA, it has ten times the number of stores of its nearest competitor, and this market has now reached saturation point. In Seoul, the capital of South Korea, it has 284 stores.

In terms of Ansoff's matrix, Starbucks has pursued a strategy of market development and its growth has been based on a number of factors. It has a powerful brand name that is recognised around the world, and it has sought to ensure customer satisfaction by speeding up service and introducing a range of new drinks. But the main reason for the company's growth has been its ability to repeat a winning formula throughout the world, with stores from Chile to China and Hong Kong to Hawaii. Although the economic downturn in 2008 led to store closures in many countries, overall numbers have continued to grow.

Fact file

Market development at Costa Coffee and Caffè Nero

Costa Coffee and Caffè Nero have also built their success around a strategy of market development. Costa Coffee has developed a successful store model, with Costa stores in partner outlets, such as Homebase, WH Smith and Waterstones. Meanwhile, Caffè Nero expanded by opening stores in suburban high streets and city centres and inside department stores, such as Selfridges. In 2014 it opened a joint venture with House of Fraser, in Cambridge. The outlet has House of Fraser tablet computers to allow customers to purchase goods while enjoying their coffee. Opening coffee shops within existing retail outlets is a good way of keeping overhead costs down – particularly the cost of city-centre rents – in order to remain competitive.

New products, existing markets

Here a **product development** strategy is followed, which may involve substantial modifications or additions to a product range in order to maintain a competitive position. This strategy is particularly useful in competitive markets where firms need to maintain product differentiation. In some instances, products are changed completely, while in other cases, 'spin-offs' are developed, such as Mars Ice Cream and KitKat Kubes.

This strategy might need extensive research and development funding, but a firm has the advantage of operating from the security of its established customers. Product development is appropriate if a firm's strengths are related to its products. Like market development, product development is more risky than simply trying to increase market share.

New products, new markets

The strategy of launching new products in new markets is known as **diversification**. It is a high-risk strategy because it requires both product and market development and may be outside the core competences of the firm. Despite this, it may be the right choice if high risks are balanced by the chance of a high rate of return. Diversification could take place by means of organic growth, or it could involve a move into new but related markets by vertical or horizontal integration, or into new and unrelated markets by conglomerate integration. Nokia moved from being a producer of car tyres in the early 1990s to become a major player in the mobile phone market ten years later.

(Diversification and other growth strategies, such as vertical or horizontal integration, are considered in detail in Chapter 11 of this book.)

Ultimately, the effectiveness of an option for strategic direction will be judged by the extent to which the achievements of the business match its corporate objectives. However, it is only possible to recognise whether the objectives have been achieved after the strategy or strategies have been implemented.

The reasons for choosing and value of different options for strategic direction

As indicated, Ansoff's matrix can be used to assess the degree of risk involved in a particular strategy. In general terms, market penetration or consolidation is the least risky option when considering the four quadrants of Ansoff's matrix. Product development and market development increase the level of risk facing a business, and diversification (that is, new products in new markets) is considered to be the most risky strategy of all.

However, Ansoff's matrix can oversimplify the level of risk. Diversification into a new market with similar features to an existing market, and selling a new product that is slightly modified from the original, may not present a huge risk for a business.

Reasons for choosing and value of a strategy of market penetration

A business will use a strategy of market penetration if one or more of the following conditions prevails:

- There is growth in the existing market.
- There is scope to encourage greater frequency of use among existing customers.
- Some consumers may be encouraged to put an existing product to different uses, thus increasing demand.
- By modifying its marketing mix, there may be potential to attract customers away from competitors, thus increasing the business's market share.

The value of market penetration as a strategy is based on the following benefits. Firstly, there is limited risk because the business is continuing with its existing product in its existing market. Secondly, costs of implementation are likely to be low, because the business is only slightly modifying its existing strategy. Thirdly, the business is likely to be playing to its strengths, because it is already operating in this market. Fourthly, this strategy is likely to lead to higher volume and therefore greater scope for internal economies of scale and reduced costs. This, in turn, will lead to higher profit margins.

Reasons for choosing and value of a strategy of product development

A business will use a strategy of product development if one or more of the following conditions prevails:

- There is scope to adapt the quality of a product in order to appeal to different market segments.
- An existing product is becoming obsolete or out of date and needs to be replaced in order to avoid the loss of market share.
- An existing product has created a need or desire for complementary products.
- Research and development within the business has led to the creation of a new innovative product.
- Market researchers reveal the potential for a new product that would serve previously unrecognised customer needs.

The value of product development as a strategy is based on the following benefits. Firstly, it enables a business to stay competitive in a rapidly changing market. Secondly, it can allow a business to build a product portfolio on the strength of existing brands. Thirdly, new products developed through research and development may often gain patent protection and therefore give the business monopoly power within that market for 20 years. (Patents are described in more detail in Chapter 12 of this book.) Fourthly, it can enable a business to compete effectively in markets that are becoming increasingly segmented.

Reasons for choosing and value of a strategy of market development

A business will use a strategy of market development if one or more of the following conditions prevails:

- There are market segments that do not currently buy an existing product in significant numbers, but that the business believes has the potential to buy more of the product.
- There is scope to enter new markets, such as overseas countries.
- New markets/market segments can be reached easily using the business's existing channels.
- The business has spare capacity and high fixed costs and therefore it would be cost-effective to increase levels of production.
- The business's greatest strength is the reputation of its existing products.

The value of market development as a strategy is based on the following benefits. Firstly, the popularity of its products may make it easy to enter new markets successfully. Secondly, the business is not changing its core function, but merely extending its marketing to different countries. Thirdly, the product has already proved it has the potential to be successful. However, if the culture in its new markets differs from its existing markets, then this can cause marketing difficulties.

Did you know?

Sometimes diversification may be a defensive strategy. In recent years shopping habits have changed. Skilled craftsmen from Eastern Europe have lowered the cost of home improvements and so demand for DIY (do-it-yourself) products has declined. Similarly, the traditional weekly grocery shopping trip to the supermarket has declined. This has led to a lot of spare capacity in large stores for businesses such as B&Q, Homebase, Tesco and Sainsbury's. These stores are responding by diversifying their product ranges, such as clothing and homeware. They are also offering spaces in their stores to other retailers, such as Argos (in Sainsbury's) or coffee shops.

Reasons for choosing and value of a strategy of diversification

A business will use a strategy of diversification if one or more of the following conditions prevails:

- Its existing products and/or markets are in decline and likely to remain so.
- Its existing markets are saturated and therefore there is no scope for expansion within them.
- Senior managers of the business want to avoid complacency and so wish to give the business a new challenge.

Diversification is considered to be significantly the most risky strategy outlined in Ansoff's matrix and therefore most businesses treat this strategy with considerable caution. However, it does have potential to bring benefits. The main potential benefits are as follows:

- It can enable a business to grow when its market is saturated.
- It can spread risks when a business faces potential decline (for example, the Case study on HMV in Chapter 3 of the AQA A-level Business Book 1 showed how HMV failed to diversify sufficiently when the market for CDs started to decline).
- It can create synergy where two different businesses may still gain some benefits from being united. For example, Unilever plc is very diverse, but many of its cleaning products are sold in the same retailers as its food products, and so transport deliveries can be organised more cost efficiently.

On occasions, diversification occurs because a business is undervalued and so a takeover by another firm producing different products becomes financially beneficial. Many venture capital organisations manage a wide range of diversified businesses because they recognise the potential opportunity of buying a business when its share price is low.

These instances describe situations in which a business might benefit from diversification.

Fact file

Unilever and diversification

Unilever is an Anglo-Dutch company that is one of the largest companies quoted on the UK stock exchange. It sells its products in more than 180 countries of the world, and uses more than 400 brand names. In any given day, over 2 billion people use its products. Some examples of Unilever brands are: Marmite, Wall's ice cream, Lynx, Persil, PG tips and Flora.

After operating many divisions with high levels of independence, Unilever is now trying to encourage the public to recognise the diversified nature of its business by encouraging use of the 'Unilever' company brand alongside its product brands, many of which were the identities of companies that Unilever took over in the past.

Ansoff's matrix is a useful tool for deciding on strategic direction, but it does not take account of what competitors are doing or what they are planning for the future; nor does it take account of how competitors will react to the selected strategy, or in what timescale. Therefore, it should be used alongside other information when deciding on the strategic direction of a business.

Practice exercise 1

Total: 40 marks

1. Before deciding on its strategic direction, a business should examine each of the following, apart from one. Identify that one.
   a) Strengths and weaknesses
   b) Opportunities and threats
   c) Corporate objectives
   d) Functional tactics   *(1 mark)*

   Options a–d are the four quadrants of Ansoff's matrix. For each of questions 2, 3 and 4, select one of these for your answer.
   a) Market penetration
   b) Product development
   c) Market development
   d) Diversification

2. Retrenchments and withdrawal are possible approaches to: *(1 mark)*

3. A computer manufacturer intending to sell computers overseas is pursuing a strategic direction of: *(1 mark)*

4. Unilever produces a wide range of products, including washing powder, food and beverages in 180 different countries. This is an example of: *(1 mark)*

5. What is meant by the term 'strategic direction'?   *(3 marks)*

6. Distinguish between the market development and product development strategies in Ansoff's matrix.   *(4 marks)*

7. Explain one benefit of the diversification strategy in Ansoff's matrix. *(4 marks)*

8. Which strategic option from Ansoff's matrix is a risk-averse firm likely to follow and why?   *(5 marks)*

9. Explain one weakness of Ansoff's matrix in helping a firm to develop a successful strategy.   *(4 marks)*

10. Explain two situations that might encourage a business to choose market penetration.   *(8 marks)*

11. Explain two benefits to a car manufacturer of a strategy of product development.   *(8 marks)*

Case study: Stagecoach: a history

Stagecoach was founded by Brian Souter and his sister, Ann Gloag, in Perth, Scotland, in 1980. The business started with just two buses.

1980s: transport deregulation

Stagecoach was one of the first companies to take advantage of transport deregulation in the UK in 1980. In the early years of the decade it operated coach services in Scotland, as well as longer-distance links to London.

The Transport Act of 1985 deregulated bus services, which had previously been owned and operated by councils and local transport authorities. In the late 1980s, Stagecoach borrowed heavily and bought a number of former National Bus Company businesses, including Hampshire, Cumberland,

United Counties, East Midlands, Ribble and Southdown.

Stagecoach was one of the first major transport operators to expand overseas and this period saw it run its first services outside the UK, after buying UTM, the major bus company in Malawi.

Early 1990s: expansion in the UK and overseas

Expansion continued at a rapid pace in the early 1990s as Stagecoach bought further bus operations in Scotland and England.

Stagecoach continued to develop its overseas portfolio, adding to its operations in Africa and moving into New Zealand in 1992.

The floatation of Stagecoach on the London Stock Exchange in 1993 valued the company at £134 million, and provided a basis for the company to grow significantly in the mid to late 1990s.

Major overseas bus operations were bought in Portugal, Sweden and later Hong Kong. Stagecoach has since moved out of all of its overseas markets except North America.

Mid-1990s: diversifying into rail

After the UK network was privatised in 1995, Stagecoach put in bids for all 25 rail franchises. Its founder, Brian Souter, was described by Richard Branson as 'a maverick, like me' because of his willingness to take risks. Two of the 25 bids were successful and, as a result, Stagecoach took over South West Trains, the UK's biggest rail franchise. It was also successful in winning the UK's smallest railway, Island Line, on the Isle of Wight.

In 1996, Stagecoach bought Porterbrook, a company that leases trains and rolling stock to rail franchises, but it sold this business to Abbey (Santander) Bank in 2000, making over £100 million profit from the deal.

In 1997 it moved into trams, purchasing Sheffield Supertram. Within six months, the company had announced a tie-up with Sir Richard Branson's Virgin Group as it took a 49 per cent stake in Virgin Rail Group, the operator of the Cross Country and West Coast inter-city rail franchises.

For a few years, Stagecoach also had an interest in air travel after buying Prestwick International Airport in 1998. This business was later sold.

Late 1990s: new markets in Asia and North America

The year 1998 was one of the busiest periods for acquisitions in the company's history, as it added bus operations and ferries in Auckland to the New Zealand business and purchased Citybus in Hong Kong – businesses that were later sold.

However, Stagecoach's biggest deal took place in North America the following year with the purchase of Coach USA, the largest bus and coach operator in the States, which also included services in Canada.

From 2000: new millennium, a new approach

Stagecoach is now focused on market consolidation and market penetration in the UK and USA, with smaller complementary acquisitions.

In 2005, Stagecoach sold its New Zealand operations in order to fund the acquisition of other UK bus companies. Overall Stagecoach had experienced mixed fortunes in its overseas activities, and this decision left North America as its only remaining international operation.

Stagecoach Group was awarded the new East Midlands rail franchise in June 2007 and it became the UK's biggest tram operator in July 2007 when it took over the contract to operate and maintain the Manchester Metrolink tram network.

Since 2007 it has mainly prioritised the renewal of existing rail and bus franchises, with some expansion of the latter. However, in February 2015 it was awarded the major East Coast franchise on a joint venture, using the Virgin brand, but with Stagecoach being the major owner.

The company's focus is now on innovations within its existing products and markets. Since the millennium it has introduced the UK's first web-based low-cost inter-city travel service, megabus.com, which now serves more than 30 major cities across the UK. It has also piloted demand-responsive taxibus services. Recent projects have focused on introducing biodiesel buses, fuelled by cooking oil, in order to reduce carbon emissions, to provide a carbon-neutral bus network.

Market share information for Stagecoach's UK bus and UK rail services are provided in Figure 9.2. It should be noted that Stagecoach owns 49 per cent of Virgin Rail Group, which has a 5 per cent market

share. The East Coast franchise will increase its market share by about 7 per cent. Although its market share in the USA is only 1 per cent, it is a significant transport provider in a country with 5,000 operators, where the average market share per operator is only 0.02 per cent.

Source: www.stagecoachplc.com and other sources

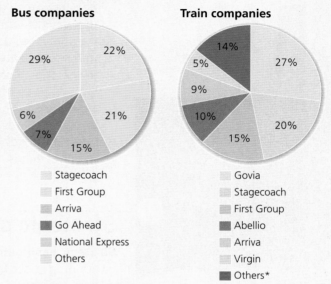

* Includes East Coast line (8%) which will transfer to Stagecoach in 2015

▲ **Figure 9.2** Market share information for UK bus and rail markets

Questions

Total: 40 marks

1. In the mid-1990s, Richard Branson described Brian Souter, the co-founder of Stagecoach, as a risk-taker. Using Ansoff's matrix, evaluate the extent to which Stagecoach's strategy from 1980 to the mid-1990s supports Richard Branson's opinion. Justify your view. *(20 marks)*

2. In terms of the level of risk being taken, to what extent has Stagecoach's strategic direction changed since 1995? *(20 marks)*

Strategic positioning: choosing how to compete

In this chapter the concept of strategic positioning is introduced. The ways in which firms compete in terms of benefits and price are analysed, using two models: Porter's low-cost, differentiation and focus strategies, and Bowman's strategic clock. Influences on the choice of positioning strategy are considered and the value of each of the different strategic positioning strategies is explained. The chapter concludes by linking the concept of competitive advantage to strategic positioning and explaining the causes and benefits of competitive advantage and the difficulties firms face in maintaining a competitive advantage.

Strategic positioning

Strategic positioning is primarily determined by the business itself. This positioning arises from the planned activities of the business, based on its own perception of its strengths and weaknesses and its view of the opportunities and threats arising from the external environment. It can be influenced by internal factors, such as poor quality control of products, or by factors outside the business's control, such as unexpected changes in consumers' tastes.

A more detailed analysis of the factors influencing a business's choice of positioning strategy is provided later in this chapter.

Strategic positioning can describe the business's niche within its market or markets. It has been described as the essence of a business.

A key feature of strategic positioning is that it should provide a sustainable competitive advantage. A position that can be easily replicated by competitors is not strategic positioning, because any advantage derived from that particular position is soon eroded. Thus strategic positioning involves adopting a strategy that is based on the specific strengths of the business, but which other businesses are unlikely to possess to the same degree.

In most cases strategic positioning is based on two key factors:

- costs – enabling a business to offer a competitive price to consumers
- differentiation – enabling a business to offer unique benefits to consumers.

The concept of strategic positioning originated in work conducted by Michael Porter. His 'generic' strategies explain how a business could use positioning strategy in order to achieve a competitive advantage over its rivals.

A number of other business writers have developed strategies relating to positioning, most of them extending Porter's original work. In this chapter we will also consider one of these models: Bowman's strategic clock.

Key term

Strategic positioning The view people take of a business that results from the business's strategic decision making.

How to compete in terms of benefits and price

In this section we will explain strategic positioning through two separate, but related, models:

- Porter's low-cost, differentiation and focus strategies
- Bowman's strategic clock.

Porter's low-cost, differentiation and focus strategies

If a successful firm's winning formula is easy to copy, its superior returns will not last long. Rivals will offer either a better price or a better product, and profitability will be driven downwards. Only if the winning formula is 'special' in some way, and difficult to imitate, will superior profitability be sustainable. A formula of this kind represents a competitive advantage.

Every business strategy needs to find a basis for competitive advantage that can be defended against the forces of competition. This means that business strategy must involve the analysis of **Porter's five competitive forces** (discussed in detail in Chapter 7). Five forces analysis considers the following factors:

- new entrants
- substitute products
- the power of buyers
- the power of sellers
- the level of competition between firms.

Thus, if customers can see acceptable alternatives from new entrants or existing competitors, or if suppliers can find alternative markets, the firm's competitive advantage will be weak. However, if the firm is a major buyer of its materials, or if there is limited competition in the market, then the firm's advantage will be strong.

Relevant questions for a firm to consider include: Is this an attractive industry in which to compete? How can we protect ourselves from the threat of these forces? How can we build our competitive advantage so that it will be resilient in the face of such threats? Successful companies build highly distinctive products and services for which there is no ready substitute. The perils of a business strategy that ignores competition may seem obvious, but established companies such as Marks and Spencer, Sainsbury's and WH Smith have lost ground as a result of complacency and a failure to maintain competitive advantage.

Michael Porter's work suggests that firms that achieve 'sustainable competitive advantage' do so through one of three generic strategies – cost leadership, differentiation and focus (see Figure 10.1) – each of which is explained below.

▲ W H Smith have failed to maintain a competitive advantage

		Strategic advantage	
		Low producer cost	High customer value
Strategic target	Mainstream market	Cost leadership	Differentiation
	Niche market	Focused cost leadership	Focused differentiation

▲ **Figure 10.1** Porter's generic strategies

Low cost/cost leadership

By pursuing a strategy of low cost (or cost leadership), a firm sets out to become the lowest-cost producer in its industry. It does this by producing on a large scale and gaining economies of scale. Its products will tend to be standard and mass produced.

A low-cost strategy may arise because a business identifies an opportunity to reduce costs. This may result from a number of sources:

- the introduction of a new method of production
- discovery of a new source of supply that is cheaper than that available to competitors
- new technology allowing a business to cut costs
- a new method of distribution that lowers costs of transportation or rental payments
- improvements in productivity that reduce unit costs.

However, it is likely that competitors will be able to copy these ideas in the medium term. **Permanent** cost leadership is difficult to achieve, but it may be created by:

- a patent on the process that allows a business to reduce unit costs
- achievement of economies of scale by the business as a result of its scale
- creating barriers to entry that prevent competition from eroding its market.

Examples of firms pursuing permanent cost leadership are B&Q, Wilkinson and Asda.

Differentiation

In order to compete in a mass market, a firm needs to make sure that its product is different from competitors' products. If consumers value this difference, it will benefit the firm in two ways:

- increased sales volume
- greater scope for charging a higher price.

Product differentiation, also known as **value leadership**, can be based on a number of characteristics, such as:

- superior performance
- product durability
- after-sales service
- design, branding and packaging to improve the attractiveness of a product
- clever promotional and advertising campaigns to boost brand image and sales
- different distribution methods.

Avon cosmetics differentiated itself by selling cosmetics directly to the customer; Amazon differentiated itself through internet selling, without the use of a traditional shop outlet.

In addition, examples of firms following this strategy of differentiation are Nike and BMW.

▲ Wilkinson pursues a cost leadership strategy

Key terms

Product differentiation The degree to which consumers see a particular brand as being different from other brands, for example because of a unique selling point/proposition (USP). A USP is a feature of a product or service that allows it to be differentiated from other products.

212

What do you think?

Are Nike sportswear and trainers of better quality than their competitors, or are they just marketed more effectively? Is their success due to their distribution and their ability to get shelf space in shops?

Focus

Cost leadership and differentiation have so far been applied to firms in mainstream mass markets. Porter also identified the comparable approaches of firms operating in niche markets, where a strategy of focus on one or more market segment is applied. This focus may depend on cost leadership or on differentiation, and is the basis of success for most smaller and medium-sized enterprises.

By pursuing focus as a strategy, a firm picks a segment of the market that is poorly served by the main players in the industry and then adopts either a cost leader strategy or a differentiation strategy to target the segment or niche.

Porter suggests that a firm must make a conscious choice about the type of competitive advantage it seeks to develop. If it fails to choose one of these strategies, it risks being stuck in the middle, trying to be all things to all people, and ends up with no competitive strategy at all (see Figure 10.2).

Bowman's strategic clock

Some commentators have criticised Porter's model of low-cost, differentiation and focus strategies, arguing that they provide a range of strategic positions that is too limited. A model that extends Porter's ideas in order to consider a broader range of strategic positioning is Bowman's strategic clock.

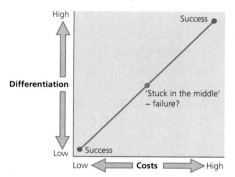

▲ **Figure 10.2** Porter's generic strategies and firms that are 'stuck in the middle'

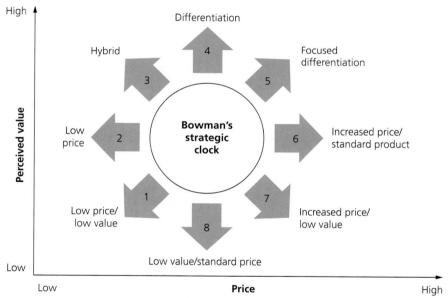

▲ **Figure 10.3** Bowman's strategic (or strategy) clock

Source: C. Bowman and D. Faulkner, *Competitive and Corporate Strategy*, Irwin, 1996

Figure 10.3 shows Bowman's model of strategic positioning. The vertical axis measures the perceived value of the product to consumers; the horizontal axis measures the price of the good being sold.

In Bowman's clock, there are eight choices of positioning strategy, although Bowman considers three of these positions to be undesirable strategic positions. These eight positions are as follows:

1. Low Price/Low Value: In general, this is a strategic positioning that businesses would wish to avoid. It represents a situation in which the business is perceived to be selling goods of low value at low prices.

These goods are likely to be inferior goods and so there is a risk that as people's incomes increase, sales will diminish. However, it is a sustainable position if a business is able to achieve significant economies of scale and is therefore able to offer prices that are lower than those of its competitors. Profit will be earned through volume rather than added value. Examples of this positioning are Poundland, Poundstretcher and many charity shops.

2. Low Price: This position represents businesses that are low-cost leaders in a market in which the products themselves are not seen to be inferior goods. The strategy of such businesses is to cut costs and operate at low profit margins. Their low prices enable them to achieve very high sales volumes and thus it can be a sustainable market position, especially if competitors are unable to match the economies of scale that the low-cost leaders possess. Profit is earned through sales volume rather than high added value on each product. Examples of low-price positioning are Lidl, Aldi and Asda.

3. Hybrid: Hybrid positioning represents a moderate price with a moderate level of differentiation between the business's products and those of its competitors. Customers will tend to be attracted to this hybrid positioning if they do not aspire to the highest priced products, but wish to be reassured that the product is likely to be reliable and of sound quality. Consequently, a loyal customer base can be established using this positioning strategy. Examples of hybrid positioning include Next, Vauxhall and Peugeot.

4. Differentiation: Differentiation means that the customers perceive they are gaining high value from the product but paying a mid-level price. In some circumstances, differentiated positioning can enable a business to charge a higher price and accept lower sales volume, or charge a lower price and generate very high sales volume. However, the essence of differentiation is that the product is considered to have high value, usually in a mass market. Businesses will strive to achieve sustainable differentiation, so that they can maintain the high levels of profit that this positioning is likely to create. Some examples of differentiation are those listed in Porter's model – Nike and BMW.

5. Focused Differentiation: Focused differentiation tends to apply to niche markets in which products are perceived to be very high value and have very high prices. In general, this positioning is achieved by brands that have excellent reputations for quality. Even where new products are launched, consumers tend to assume that these will be of the same perceived high quality and are therefore prepared to pay high prices. Examples of focused differentiation are Rolls-Royce, Porsche, Rolex and Gucci.

6. Increased Price/Standard Product: This strategic position is likely to exist only in the short term, and possibly arises from the business having an exaggerated view of the perceived value of its product. It may also exist if a business launches a new product and believes that it will be more popular than it eventually is. Finally, it can occur if a business has successfully achieved focused differentiation with a product, but persists with that product after competitors have introduced new products that have greater appeal to the customers in that market. This strategy yields high profit margins, but this can be deemed risky because sales volume is likely to be very low, and it can damage the image of the business.

Author advice

Strategic positions 6, 7 and 8 are included in Bowman's clock so that all combinations of perceived value and price are included in the clock. However, these three combinations are considered to be undesirable strategies, because they can only succeed in the short term in certain circumstances. They are not regarded to be long-term strategic positions.

7. Increased Price/Low Value: Increased price and low value is unlikely to be a successful combination. This position in Bowman's strategic clock is often described as monopoly pricing because it is a combination that can only really exist if a business has no competition. If there are barriers to entry into an industry then this strategy can be sustained, but in a competitive market, any business using this strategy is likely to fail.

8. Low Value/Standard Price: This strategy is associated with the loss of market share. If a product has low value it is likely to be cheap to produce, and therefore it is probable that competitors will be able to offer this product at a low price. Any business offering a low value product at a standard price will lose sales to businesses that are prepared to offer low value products but who only expect low prices in return.

What do you think?

The examples given in positions 1 to 5 all feature companies rather than products. This is because strategic positioning is based on a company's strategic decision making. However, the classification of companies in this way is a matter of debate and may well change over time. Furthermore, businesses may use different strategic positioning for different products in order to appeal to a wider market. For example, Vauxhall is identified as a business adopting a hybrid positioning. However, its premium performance car – the Vauxhall VXR8 – is priced at £56,000 and would be classified as a 'focused differentiation' positioning.

How often do companies occupy different market positions with different products? Can you think of other examples?

Influences on the choice of a positioning strategy

A business's choice of strategic positioning is affected by many factors. Because strategic positioning is a long-term aspect of a business, these influences are generally factors that will remain in place over a long period of time.

Strategic positioning is based on two core concepts: the perceived value of a product and the price of that product. Consequently, the key influences on a positioning strategy relate to either or both of these concepts.

Some of the key influences on the choice of positioning strategy, and the key questions to address, are as follows:

- The scale of the business. Is it large enough to sustain cost leadership over a long period of time?
- The strategic capability and strengths of the business. Will its production processes and sources of materials enable it to continue to keep its costs low? Does it have popular appeal to certain market segments? Does the business's workforce possess any unique qualities?
- Customer perceptions. Is brand loyalty sufficient that it will enable the business to offer high perceived value in comparison to the costs of production?

- Customer base. Is it a narrow focus that will require focused differentiation or is it broad-based so that wider appeal such as differentiation or cost leadership can be targeted?
- The values of the customer base. What are their key requirements? Can the business meet those requirements more effectively than its competitors?
- Sustainable differentiation. What are the business's core competences? Does the business possess advantages, such as patents or copyright, which will enable it to maintain its difference against its competitors?
- Market factors. Are there developments within the market that the business has anticipated, thus giving it scope to gain first-mover advantage and the benefits that follow from the reputation it may then acquire?
- Competitor analysis. What are the strengths of competitors? In which markets are competitors least capable of matching the business's strengths?
- PESTLE factors. Are there any political, economic or other external changes that might provide opportunities for new strategic positioning for the business?
- Stakeholders. Would the majority of stakeholders support and assist efforts to achieve a particular strategic positioning or would this positioning cause conflict between stakeholders?

The value of different strategic positioning strategies

By identifying a specific strategic positioning strategy a business will send a clear message to its customer base. It is also likely to be able to establish a consistent reputation and therefore build brand loyalty, whether that brand loyalty is based on the quality of the product or on the low prices provided. Each of the different strategic positioning strategies offers its own advantages and disadvantages and so a brief summary of the advantages and disadvantages of each positioning strategy will be outlined below.

This analysis will be based on Bowman's strategic clock because it incorporates each of the elements of Porter's model. Table 10.1 summarises the overlap between the two models.

▼ **Table 10.1** Summary of the overlap between Bowman's strategic clock and Porter's generic strategies

Bowman's strategic clock	Porter's generic strategies
1. Low price/low value	(Focus*)
2. Low price	Low cost
3. Hybrid	
4. Differentiation	Differentiation
5. Focused differentiation	Focus*

NB: Three strategies noted in Bowman's clock (increased price/standard value; increased price/low value; and low value/standard price) are NOT included in this table because they are undesirable strategies.

* In Porter's model, 'focus' takes two different forms – a focus on a differentiated product and a focus on low prices.

1. **Low cost, low value (focus on cost leadership)**: The key to success with this strategic positioning is to achieve the lowest price in the industry, and so it is essential that costs are kept very low. In this way a business can achieve a small profit margin on each product sold. This strategy also requires very little marketing effort, which will again keep costs low. However, the strategy does not require particular qualities and therefore it is easy to copy. Consequently, if there is profit it is likely to encourage competitors. This will then erode the profit that is being made. If competitors are able to reduce their costs to match the firm's levels then it has lost all of its advantage. This position is likely to be a market niche, although during the recession it was a large niche in many markets.

2. **Low price**: The key to success with this strategic positioning is to achieve the lowest costs in the industry, but with prices that are close to the industry average. In this way a business can achieve a good profit margin on each product sold, but still achieve a high level of sales volume. This positioning strategy is likely to be in a mass market and therefore volume should be high. A problem with this strategy occurs if customers perceive the quality/value of products to be lower than that of competitors, which may then force the company to reduce prices and thus profits. Moreover, if competitors are able to reduce their costs to match the firm's levels, cost leadership will be lost.

   Both of these low-cost strategies are likely to appeal to price-sensitive customers who elect not to buy better quality goods or who cannot afford them. However it does tend to avoid competitors, as there is very little profit to attract them into the market. The disadvantage of these low cost/price strategies is that the low profits mean there is little money to reinvest in order to improve the business.

3. **Hybrid**: The hybrid strategy requires a business to achieve differentiation and low prices, relative to its competitors. This can be a difficult balancing act for a business to achieve, as any efforts to achieve differentiation are likely to cost money and therefore make it more difficult to achieve low costs and thus low prices. The main advantages of the hybrid strategy is that it can achieve very high sales volume in a mass market, as the ideal scenario for many customers is a combination of reasonable quality goods at reasonable prices. In some cases this hybrid approach may be achieved by selecting aspects of the business's activities that will not adversely affect customers' perception of quality. The business can then focus its cost savings on those activities without endangering popularity of its products.

4. **Differentiation**: Pursuing a policy of differentiation can add value by creating a unique selling point/proposition (USP). This may be real, such as a different design or different components, or it may be based on image and branding.

   The key to success with this strategy is to try to reduce costs in areas that do not affect the uniqueness of a product and to identify the features that add value to a product without leading to significant increases in costs.

   In order to maintain the advantages of differentiation, a business must ensure that it understands its customers. This may mean considerable focus on market research and data collection. It must also be aware of the key reasons for differentiation so that it can ensure that competitors cannot match the qualities that it offers its customers. Given the scope for high profits, competitors will be keen to enter this market and so a business must constantly identify the strengths of its competitors, as well as its own strengths.

Differentiation can also cause tensions within larger businesses which, by necessity, are likely to have to appeal to some customers who will not wish to pay high prices. This may make it more difficult for a business to persuade customers that it can provide the quality required to justify high prices on some of its product ranges.

5. **Focused differentiation (focus):** This strategy offers the greatest scope for high profit margins, as it is possible for the market leader to dominate a niche market. If a business bases its focused differentiation on a well-established brand name, it can make it even more difficult for competitors to achieve success. However, the limited scale of the markets may mean that overall profit is lower with focused differentiation than it is with a successful differentiation strategy in a mass market. In some cases, products benefiting from focused differentiation may be fashion items. Therefore a business may find it hard to sustain differentiation, as customer views of what is necessary to give them high value are constantly changing.

6. **Increased price/standard product.**

7. **Increased price/low value.**

8. **Low value/standard price.**

   Collectively, these three positions are known as failure strategies. The major disadvantage of them is that the price charged is likely to significantly outweigh the value that they provide the customer. Consequently, none of them is likely to attract customers. However, if there is a customer base – perhaps because the organisation is a monopoly – then this disadvantage is turned into an advantage, because the lower value is like to be a reflection of the low costs required to provide this product. Consequently, if customers do buy any of these products then there will be a significant profit margin on each product sold by the business.

Conclusion

Bowman's clock extends Porter's generic strategies, but as three of these strategies are deemed to be unviable, there is little difference between the two ideas. Porter's low-cost and differentiation strategies are repeated in Bowman's strategic clock. Furthermore, the idea of focus is common to both models; the main difference is that Porter divides focus into two elements – focus on low costs and focus on differentiation through value.

Another difference between the two models is the hybrid classification used by Bowman. Bowman's model sees this as a viable strategic positioning, and there is a lot of empirical evidence to suggest that many businesses exist in this position in the market. However, Porter regarded this hybrid approach as a potential course of failure – arguing that any business using this strategic positioning was likely to get 'stuck in the middle' and therefore would find it difficult to establish a clear positioning identity to its consumers. This potential cause of failure is illustrated in Figure 10.2 on page 213.

With the exception of this hybrid positioning, both Porter's and Bowman's models draw the same conclusion: the ideal strategic positioning is either offering high perceived value through differentiation or offering a low price advantage to customers. These two approaches are those most likely to give a business of **competitive advantage** that is sustainable.

Competitive advantage

Competitive advantage can be derived from many sources; these are explained in the next section, alongside the benefits they bring. However, in essence there are two main types of competitive advantage:

- **Comparative advantage**. This is also referred to as cost advantage. It describes the business's ability to produce a good or service at a lower cost than its competitors. This lower cost of production enables that firm to either gain more sales by charging a lower price or generate a higher profit margin on each item sold.
- **Differential advantage**. This arises from a business's ability to differentiate goods and services from its competitors in a way that enables them to be seen as superior to the competition. As with comparative advantage, this should lead to either greater sales volume or higher profit margins, although the latter will be achieved through high prices rather than low costs.

The benefits of having a competitive advantage

The benefits of competitive advantage are essentially those identified in the paragraphs on comparative and differential advantage above. Accessible strategic positioning enables a business to achieve low costs or a high selling price. Both of these advantages enable the business to either widen its profit margin or to maintain a lower profit margin but achieve much greater sales volume. It can be seen that the benefits of competitive advantage link very closely to strategic positioning.

Comparative and/or differential advantage can be gained in many ways, some of which are more sustainable than others. Some of these approaches may provide other benefits, such as brand loyalty and monopoly status. The main approaches and their benefits are described below.

Fact file

The UK government's Competitiveness Unit

The UK government has set up a special Competitiveness Unit to examine ways in which UK firms can improve their performance both domestically and in overseas markets. One of the key conclusions of the Competitiveness Unit was that the government should increase competition within markets, to ensure that businesses become more efficient. For individual firms, the Competitiveness Unit believes that the following four factors are the most critical determinants of competitive advantage:

- Investment in new equipment and technology
- Staff skills, education and training
- Innovation through investment in research and development
- Enterprise.

These and other determinants of competitive advantage are considered below.

Determinants of competitive advantage and the benefits they bring

- **Investment in new equipment and technology**. Machinery and computers can improve the speed, reliability and quality of products, and still provide flexibility. Labour and other costs can be reduced. Advanced technology can also enable a business to provide unique products that are highly valued by consumers. If the technology can be patented it can lead to an advantage that can be guaranteed for 20 years, after which the brand's reputation should be sufficient to ensure an even longer-term sustainable advantage. New technology is a critical determinant of competitive advantage because it can achieve long-term lower costs and higher added value, along with benefits, such as greater flexibility so the business can cope with changes in the market.

- **Staff skills, education and training**. A skilled and educated staff will be more adaptable and flexible, able to cope with change more readily, and possess more creativity and innovative talents. From a production perspective, these skills are likely to lower costs; however, they can also increase customer satisfaction and therefore enable the business to differentiate its goods and services from those of its competitors.

- **Innovation through investment in research and development**. The pace of change requires companies to update and broaden their product range constantly. Product life cycles are becoming shorter, and new ideas must be incorporated into products. Even where patents are acquired businesses must keep innovating in order to keep pace with changing customer demand. According to the Competitiveness Unit, this is an area in which UK firms perform poorly in comparison to most other advanced economies.

- **Enterprise**. The entrepreneurial skills of owners of business start-ups and their desire to become their own bosses create a culture of independence, hard work and flexibility, which helps to supply the needs of larger organisations while also providing alternative products and services. In larger firms, owners try to encourage the development of an entrepreneurial approach by rewarding innovation and risk-taking. The growth of outsourcing and sub-contracting in recent decades has meant that there are much greater opportunities for small, entrepreneurial businesses to find a market niche which they can exploit.

- **The effectiveness of a business's marketing**. A well-planned marketing mix, suited to the needs of a business, can greatly improve its competitive advantage and therefore its ability to gain greater sales volume and charge higher prices in the face of competition. Market research can benefit a business by helping it to develop a product that satisfies the needs of its target market. Once the product has been produced, the promotional mix will be geared towards the interests of the target market in a cost-effective way, to maximise the profitability of the process.

- **Improving quality**. As living standards have improved, quality has become more important to consumers. Improving quality can help a business to increase both sales volume and the selling price of its products and services. This is because high quality will provide

▲ Innovation through research and development can give a firm a competitive advantage

much greater customer satisfaction and help to create a USP. Quality improvements can also take place in the production process itself. This will help to reduce waste and make the production process more cost-effective, thus increasing profit margins.

- **Effective human resource management**. This can take different forms, such as effective recruitment, high-quality training, an efficient organisational structure and appropriate use of incentives in order to motivate workers. A well-organised and motivated workforce that is well-educated and trained can provide a number of different benefits. Greater labour productivity can be achieved, thus reducing the cost of goods or services. Well-trained staff are more likely to identify innovative ways of making a product and are more likely to be able to produce high-quality products and identify defective ones, thus preventing flawed products from reaching the consumer. Finally, a well-educated workforce tends to be more flexible and adaptable. In the modern business world, where change is becoming increasingly rapid, this can be a significant asset for a business that is trying to stay ahead of its competitors.

- **Efficient operational procedures**. Improvements to factors such as factory layout, capacity utilisation, the location of the organisation, inventory control and the processes used in the factory or outlet can all reduce unit costs. These changes will improve both the profitability and the competitiveness of a firm.

- **Financial planning and control**. A well-organised finance department can ensure that clear targets are set, challenging managers and their subordinates to improve their efficiency. Furthermore, effective monitoring of progress can also improve efficiency by making sure that any problems are quickly detected and rectified.

The difficulties of maintaining a competitive advantage

In competitive markets all firms will be trying to secure the features that will distinguish them from their competitors and give them a competitive advantage. However, markets are always changing, with constantly evolving consumer tastes being the driving force behind these changes. Consequently it can be very difficult to maintain a competitive advantage.

For each of the factors providing a competitive advantage there may be problems that make it difficult to maintain a competitive advantage.

- **Investment in new equipment and technology**. This is an expensive undertaking, particularly if technology is changing rapidly and requiring constant renewal of equipment. If investment appraisal suggests that certain examples of new technology are not expected to be profitable, possibly because a company has too little time in which to regain the initial cost, then the company must accept that it cannot constantly improve its products and processes. In some fast-moving industries businesses may allow a certain level of technology to be skipped, temporarily losing some of their competitive advantage, so that they can control their costs of updating technology.

- **Staff skills, education and training**. Some of the problems associated with this method of improving competitive advantage are: skilled workers are likely to require high wages; training costs may not be recovered, particularly if labour turnover is high; and in some fast-moving technology-based industries, skills become outdated so quickly that training costs may not be recoverable.
- **Innovation through investment in research and development**. Research and development (R&D) is not an exact science and it does not guarantee financial returns. Successful R&D can create very high profits, but if no new invention or innovation is achieved, it can be a very expensive process that damages the company's profitability. In times of difficult economic circumstances many companies cut back on R&D because it is seen to be a relatively high-risk strategy.
- **Enterprise**. Entrepreneurial skills often focus on identifying opportunities in a market. For this reason they involve a higher element of risk than many other approaches to improving competitive advantage. Many entrepreneurs who have developed very successful enterprises have struggled to maintain the quality of their ideas throughout their careers.
- **The effectiveness of a business's marketing**. Unless a business has developed a very high level of brand loyalty, marketing is not likely to help achieve sustained competitive advantage. This is because the successful strategies used by a business's marketing department are easily copied by competitors. Consequently, marketing tends to provide short-term rather than sustained competitive advantage.
- **Improving quality**. Improving quality is a key factor in creating product differentiation. However, as with marketing, the techniques used are easily imitated. Furthermore, improving quality can increase costs, as more expensive procedures and materials are required. It is feasible that the price charged for a differentiated product is not sufficiently high to cover the additional costs incurred in creating the high quality.
- **Effective human resource management**. Because a business does not own its human resources in the same way as its capital equipment or brand, it can be difficult to maintain an advantage through its personnel. High quality staff can easily be 'poached' by competitors, allowing competitors to benefit from the training and skills that the workforce has developed. This can lead to an erosion of the original business's competitive advantage.
- **Efficient operational procedures**. Unless aspects of the operational procedure have been patented it is difficult to sustain competitive advantage in this way, because competitors can erode the advantage by copying it.
- **Financial planning and control**. Although high-quality financial planning and control helps competitive advantage, it is unlikely to be a key factor in its creation. Furthermore, businesses need to be cautious that they do not devote too many resources to planning and monitoring, and thus divert resources from the activities that create the competitive advantage.

Group exercise

Select one business that has recently experienced a change (improvement or deterioration) in its competitiveness. Investigate the main factors that appear to have led to the changes in its competitiveness.

Practice exercise 1

Total: 55 marks

1. Which one of the following strategic positions is not one of Porter's generic strategies?
   a) Differentiation
   b) Focus
   c) Hybrid
   d) Low cost   *(1 mark)*

2. Value leadership can be achieved through all of the following approaches, except:
   a) after-sales service
   b) design
   c) low price
   d) superior performance   *(1 mark)*

3. The following strategic positions are all taken from Bowman's strategic clock. Which is the only one that is deemed to be viable?
   a) Low price/low value
   b) Increased price/standard product
   c) Increased price/low value
   d) Low value/standard price   *(1 mark)*

4. Define the term 'strategic position'.   *(3 marks)*

5. What is meant by the term 'product differentiation'?   *(3 marks)*

6. What is meant by the term 'competitive advantage'?   *(3 marks)*

7. Why does Porter suggest that 'being stuck in the middle' of the generic strategies model is likely to lead to failure?   *(5 marks)*

8. Explain the difference between 'differentiation' and 'focused differentiation'.   *(5 marks)*

9. Explain **two** factors that might influence a firm's choice of strategic positioning.   *(8 marks)*

10. Explain two possible benefits of competitive advantage to a firm. *(8 marks)*

11. Explain why it is difficult to maintain a competitive advantage. *(8 marks)*

12. Porter's generic strategies model is a tool for assisting business to identify strategic options. Explain his three recommended strategies.   *(9 marks)*

Case study: Ryanair and Starbucks

Ryanair

In the early 1990s, the Ryan family was considering closing down the loss-making Irish airline, Ryanair. As a last resort, a new young chief executive, Michael O'Leary, was hired and sent to the USA to see how Southwest Airlines was becoming a rising star. O'Leary learned well, and returned to Ireland convinced that the Southwest Airlines approach was right – a focus solely on minimising costs in order to deliver the lowest possible price, and set up routes going directly from point to point, so that people do not need to change flights.

O'Leary, as a graduate of business studies, understood that the underlying strategy was to take Ryanair out of the centre ground of the Ireland–UK market. Instead it would be positioned as the lowest-cost operator in a niche market. From then on, every aspect of the Ryanair operation was geared to minimising costs – to provide enormous pricing flexibility. The success of this approach is shown in a few figures. Whereas British Airways needs a capacity utilisation level of 75–80 per cent to break even on a flight, Ryanair needs less than 60 per cent – yet Ryanair's actual utilisation rates are currently 88 per cent.

O'Leary set about the task of building up Ryanair's position in a number of ways:

- Extreme minimisation of overhead costs; staff work in cramped surroundings and are expected to work extremely hard.
- Minimising aircraft costs (depreciation and interest charges) by purchasing second-hand Boeings or buying them when world prices are low.
- Minimising maintenance costs by buying just one model (the Boeing 731), so that inventories of spares are minimised and the maintenance staff know the planes backwards and can therefore service and repair them quickly.
- Minimising landing charges: that is, the price that airports charge to allow a plane to land and to 'rent' time on the ground at the stand, waiting to take off again. Ryanair pioneered the use of secondary airports, flying from Stansted to unheard-of airports such as Alghero (Sardinia) and Dinard (Brittany). Airports keen to build business were willing to offer cheap deals to an airline that could bring in so many passengers.
- 'Sweating' the key asset – the planes – by ensuring that they operate many more times per day than rivals. The key is the turnaround time. Ryanair takes little more than 20 minutes to get passengers off the plane, clean it, refuel it and get new passengers seated. So the plane spends the maximum time in the air – earning revenue.
- 'Sweating' the staff. Ryanair has achieved this partly through ruthless treatment of unions; the compensation is that it pays well and gives staff share options that have proved very valuable as its share price has risen. Minimising staffing (Ryanair is famous for its minimal customer service department) also cuts costs.

Ryanair's marketing mix has also been rooted in cost minimisation. O'Leary learned from Southwest Airlines that low airline prices are newsworthy – they can be showbusiness. So Ryanair launched by painting its telephone ticket sales number in huge letters on the planes, refused to sell through travel agents (saving 10–15 per cent) and relied on news reports of its unprecedented low prices and word-of-mouth advertising from customers.

O'Leary's other ace was to follow Richard Branson's example by manipulating the media. He staged stunts such as an 'attack' on easyJet's Luton headquarters. O'Leary hired a tank, dressed himself and other staff in army uniform, and drove up to the easyJet HQ waving banners saying 'Ryanair blasts 50% off easyJet's fares'. The newspapers and television cameras lapped up the story, giving Ryanair masses of free promotion.

The basic marketing rule for airlines has always been to encourage repeat business by looking after the passengers. Ryanair, by contrast, lays down rules that it will not break, such as 'no refunds'. If you are booked on to a Ryanair flight and are rushed into hospital that morning, do not waste time asking for a refund. It has turned this into a marketing advantage by assuring other customers that this keeps their prices low.

Part of the company's cost-cutting approach is that there is minimal spending on customer service.

Ryanair has a much stronger balance sheet than BA, meaning that there is no possible threat from a price war or even from excessively rapid growth. Ryanair's low-cost strategy has worked during periods of economic growth, because it has helped to make a former luxury (air travel) more widely available.

Since the recession, Ryanair has struggled in comparison to easyJet, as the latter has gained a reputation for higher quality which has enabled it to set higher prices. Losses in early 2014 triggered a change in strategy for Ryanair. The key features of this strategy were:
● better customer service
● allowing customers to purchase allocated seating (a revenue earner, but one that may slow down the turnaround time between flights)
● a more relaxed baggage policy – this had been a major cause of customer complaints.

These changes were intended to improve customer perception of the Ryanair brand, which had been ranked as the second worst brand in the world for customer service. Early signs of this new process are promising; Ryanair has been able to increase its prices by 5 per cent and profits have increased by 32 per cent.

According to Michael O'Leary: 'Being nice to our customers is a new winning strategy for Ryanair. Our service left something to be desired 12 months ago.'

Source: *Business Review*, November 2003 and various other sources

Starbucks

After three decades of unprecedented growth, Starbucks began to struggle during the recession. Losses in major markets, such as the USA, UK and Australia, have led Starbucks to re-examine its marketing strategies in the last year.

Starbucks' rapid growth, from its foundation as a coffee bar in Seattle, USA, was a classic example of differentiation. Starbucks' strength lay in delighting customers with little touches that differentiated it from its rivals, such as free Wi-Fi, comfy seats, newspapers to read, cheerful welcomes and great tunes. These touches created a sense of occasion when customers visited Starbucks, encouraging repeat custom and brand loyalty.

Starbucks has become a victim of its own success. It has widened high-street interest in the coffee shop and, in doing so, has helped to increase consumer interest in coffee. Its place at the high-quality end of the coffee market is being displaced by more specialist coffee shops focusing on the quality of the coffee, rather than the wide range of differentiated 'touches' provided by Starbucks. High-quality coffee customers are looking towards some of the new competitors entering the market.

The atmosphere of Starbucks has been copied by many of the new competitors, but as it has grown Starbucks has found it difficult to maintain the consistency and quality of its stores.

Management at Starbucks believe that there are other aspects to include in a new marketing strategy, and university sites. It has also responded to health concerns related to the calorie content of some of its products, particularly its focus on large sizes of milky drinks. Until recently, Starbucks has relied on word-of-mouth advertising. For the first time it is now running a national advertising campaign to promote its Vivanno™ range of products.

In some markets Starbucks is experiencing market saturation, which has made it difficult for the company to continue the pace of growth it enjoyed in the past. Starbucks has expanded throughout the world to such an extent that Seoul, in South Korea, is the city with the most Starbucks stores.

Starbucks' new approach is based on extending its differentiation through strategies such as:

- training and developing staff, so that they can provide superior customer service
- extending the product range so that customers visit Starbucks and purchase its products more evenly throughout the day, rather than peaking at specific times
- using digital mobile media to encourage closer engagement with customers
- using the brand to develop new products, most notably aiming for leadership in the tea business through its Teavana brand. Having taken over the Teavana shops that sell loose tea in the USA, Starbucks is using the brand to build a chain of tea bars. Its initial aim is to open 1,000 Teavana bars in the next five to ten years, with a long-term aim for Teavana bars to rival Starbucks coffee shops in number.

Source: Starbucks' annual reports and other sources

Questions

Total: 40 marks

1. Explain two possible reasons for Ryanair's change in strategic positioning. *(8 marks)*

2. Evaluate the main factors influencing the success of Ryanair's low-cost strategy. *(16 marks)*

3. To what extent have Starbucks' recent difficulties been the result of its inability to retain its level of differentiation and competitive advantage? *(16 marks)*

Assessing a change in scale

The chapter begins by identifying the reasons why businesses grow or retrench. The difference between organic growth and external growth is then explained. The chapter goes on to discuss how to manage and overcome the problems of growth and retrenchment. In relation to this, the following issues with growth are considered: economies of scale (including technical, purchasing and managerial) and diseconomies of scale; economies of scope; the experience curve; synergy; and overtrading. This section includes an explanation of Greiner's model of growth. The impact of growth or retrenchment on the functional areas of business is then discussed. The chapter ends with an assessment of methods and types of growth. Methods of growth considered include mergers, takeovers, ventures and franchising; types of growth considered include vertical (including backward and forward), horizontal and conglomerate integration.

The reasons why businesses grow or retrench

For most businesses, growth is an important objective, and is sometimes the only way to ensure that a firm survives in the long term. Growth is usually seen as a natural development for a business, providing benefits and opportunities for the business and for its stakeholders. At a basic level, growth enables a company to reach breakeven and make profit. It provides more opportunities for a company to take advantage of economies of scale (which were explained in Chapter 13 of the AQA A-level Business Book 1 and are reviewed again later in this chapter), and a growing and dynamic company is more likely to remain competitive. Growth by diversification allows a company to spread risks, and a large company with plenty of assets and diversified activities will find it easier to cope with recession and fluctuations in the business cycle.

Growth may be due to increased demand for a business's products following the successful exploitation of a competitive advantage. A strong economy where living standards are rising is likely to lead to increased demand for goods and services and thus provide opportunities for businesses to expand to meet demand. The identification of new markets for existing products or new products in existing markets can also lead to business growth.

Conversely, poor performance or poor economic conditions may cause a business to decline in size (or **retrench**). For example, weak demand due to recession might cause a business to concentrate production on

Key term

Retrenchment The cutting back of an organisation's scale of operations.

a narrower range of products or in fewer locations. Strong competition from rival businesses may mean a business loses market share and has to close down production facilities. Sometimes a business that has diversified too much may retrench because it decides to refocus on a narrower range of activity so that it can reap the benefits of greater specialisation. General Electric (GE) is an example of this and is included in a Fact file towards the end of this chapter in the discussion about conglomerates.

The difference between organic and external growth

Growth can be achieved either internally (known as organic growth) or externally. The choice of which type of growth is best suited to a particular organisation depends on a trade-off between the costs involved, the level of risk and the speed of each method of development.

Organic (internal) growth

Organic growth is usually pursued because a firm wishes to grow in a steady and closely managed way. This is likely to be the case where:

- a firm's product is in the early stage of its life cycle and is not yet fully established in the marketplace
- a firm's product is highly technical and the firm needs to gain experience of dealing with it, ensuring that any problems can be ironed out
- the costs of growth need to be spread over time.

For some firms, organic growth is the best option because there are no suitable opportunities for external growth available.

Finance for investment and expansion accompanying organic growth usually comes from the retained profit resulting from existing activities, from borrowing or by attracting new investors. As a result, this process of growth tends to be relatively slow, but less risky than external growth.

External growth

External growth tends to be via the **integration** of two or more companies and can occur by **merger** or **takeover** (acquisition). Mergers occur when two businesses believe and jointly agree that they can increase their combined profit, or achieve other objectives, by merging their businesses. Takeovers (acquisitions) are accomplished by the acquiring firm offering cash or shares (or both) to the shareholders (i.e. the owners) of the firm that is being taken over. External growth is usually the fastest way to achieve growth, but given the problems of integrating two separate organisations, it can be risky.

External growth, whether by merger or takeover, can be classified into three broad types of integration – vertical, horizontal and conglomerate. Mergers and takeovers and the different forms of integration are discussed in the final section of this chapter.

Key terms

Organic (internal) growth
When a firm expands its existing capacity or range of activities by extending its premises or building new factories from its own resources, rather than by integration with another firm.

External growth When a firm expands by integrating with another firm as a result of either a merger or a takeover (also known as an acquisition).

Integration The coming together of two or more businesses via a merger or takeover.

Merger Where two or more firms agree to come together under one board of directors.

Takeover (acquisition) Where one firm buys a majority shareholding in another firm and therefore assumes full management control.

▲ Mergers happen when two or more firms come together

Alternative Networks plc (part one)

Alternative Networks plc is a leading technology and telecommunications service provider for UK businesses. It has grown organically and through the acquisition of companies with appropriate criteria.

To ensure it continues to grow organically it focuses on:

- gaining clients in the SME (small, medium enterprise) sector
- improving profitability by cross-selling and up-selling
- innovating and developing its product range to meet the needs of its customers.

Its criteria for deciding on companies to acquire are that they must:

- be profitable, successful, growing businesses
- provide cross-selling opportunities
- be able to demonstrate increased earnings in the first year following acquisition.

Source: adapted from www.alternativenetworks.com

Did you know?

Cross-selling means encouraging existing customers to buy related products. Up-selling means encouraging customers to buy more expensive products, upgrades or add-ons. Both are done in order to make more profitable sales.

How to manage and overcome the problems of growth and retrenchment

Managing and overcoming the problems of growth

Topics covered later in this section explain a range of growth-related issues that highlight some of the problems of growth and how these can be overcome. For example:

- Economies and diseconomies of scale. As the scale of its production increases, a business benefits from falling average costs as its takes advantage of economies of scale. However, it must ensure that close attention is given to appropriate organisational structures and communication systems to ensure that diseconomies of scale do not emerge.
- Economies of scope. A firm can gain cost advantages as it grows by diversifying its product range. This is because it can benefit by using the same facilities, equipment, labour and technology. This depends significantly on how diversified the product range becomes. For example, in the case of conglomerates, which usually have very different products in their portfolio, this is less possible.
- The experience curve. This indicates that the more experienced a business gets at making a product, measured by the cumulative volume of production since it began producing, the better, faster and cheaper it is likely to be at producing the product. If a firm does accrue benefits due to the experience curve effect, the fact that it is growing and therefore increasing its cumulative volume of production should bring benefits.
- Where growth is via external means, the integration of two businesses can produce synergy because the new integrated business produces, for example, better profits and revenues than the sum of profits and revenues of the two individual firms. However, there is extensive evidence to suggest that to be successful, in relation to mergers and takeovers, the two firms need to plan effectively for the process of merging different cultures and have realistic expectations of what they can achieve.
- Overtrading. Overtrading is a common reason for business failure. To avoid it, businesses need to plan carefully to manage growth, for example, in terms of increased orders, by ensuring sufficient working capital.

● Greiner's model of growth. The model provides a clear picture of the phases of growth, the problems that are likely to emerge and how these can be dealt with in order to allow a business to move to the next stage.

Without strong and effective management, growth can result in a loss of direction and control. The demands placed on leaders or managers in relation to managing and motivating a large team require very different skills from those needed to manage and motivate a relatively small team. Introducing an appropriate organisational structure, having an effective management team and carrying out detailed financial and operational planning and forecasting are vital.

Additional organisational issues to consider when a business grows include:

● Management structures and hierarchies will need to change so that the business is better positioned to achieve its objectives. A medium-sized business may replace its simple and clear functional structure with a complex matrix structure or, depending on the nature of the business, a product-based or region-based structure. Spans of control are likely to increase and new layers of authority and departments will need to be created. The whole process of management becomes more complex. In most instances, the expertise to build and manage that structure will come from outside the business. A bigger company needs managers to take control of departments and a hierarchy that has the expertise and the time to drive it forward. The Fact file on Alternative Networks (below) and the Case study of Friends Reunited at the end of this chapter provide examples of how growing businesses can benefit from outside expertise.

● There will be more delegation. The original owners are likely to lose much of the direct contact they had with customers, suppliers and staff, and will take on more of a managing and leading role. Professionals in finance, marketing and personnel will need to be recruited to take on growing specialist responsibilities, and an effective management team will need to be created.

▲ Management structures will have to change as a business grows

Fact file

Alternative Networks plc (part two)

Alternative Networks plc, the UK technology and telecommunications service provider mentioned in the last Fact file, was established in 1994. When James Murray, co-founder, wanted to expand the business he had little time to do so. 'As a board we were getting to the size where we needed a senior management team to deal with day-to-day issues. The board had five members which, with eight departments to look after, were spread too thinly and getting bogged down by nitty-gritty activities. We weren't getting the opportunities to look away from the business and work on strategy. We needed to bring people in to look after these areas and then report to the board,' says Murray. In support of its corporate objective to double its sales within two years, Alternative Networks appointed an HR director, a head of IT, a finance controller, a head of marketing and a client management director. While still being fully integrated into the company, Murray claims, the board benefited from its new management structure. 'It allowed the board to focus on new ideas, new products, strategy, acquisitions and the overall direction of the business.'

Since 1994, Alternative Networks plc has achieved a track record of consistent profitability. It now employs 600 people across six offices in UK.

Source: adapted from www.alternativenetworks.com

● Staff responsibilities will need to change. As the business and workload grows, employees will need to focus on what they do best; jobs will become more clearly defined, with job descriptions, training and development plans, and appraisal systems being introduced.

● Staff motivation may decline, at least in the short term, as the changes that result from growth begin to have an impact. This may in turn affect customer service. For example, in the past employees may have been used to dealing directly with the owner/boss of a business, and the additional layers of management that will be introduced as the business grows may be resented. Managing and motivating a larger team successfully is likely to require a democratic leadership and management style, which may be very different to the previous style.

What do you think?

Michael Dell, of Dell Computers, once said: 'If you limit a company by its structure or by the people in the company, you will, by definition, limit the full potential of that business.'

Do you agree?

Author advice

Most of the issues discussed above were explored in various chapters in Book 1. For example, organisational structure, span of control, levels of hierarchy, job descriptions, training, appraisal and motivation were covered in Chapters 20–24 and leadership styles were covered in Chapter 4. Ensure that you are familiar with these areas before proceeding further with this chapter.

Fact file

From private to public limited company

For many firms, problems arise when growth involves changing from private to public limited company status. Going from a private limited company to a public limited company usually means floating shares on the stock market. Companies join the stock market all the time, and the more optimistic the economic climate, the more new issues of shares there are. The value of a stock market listing is that a company has a higher profile and access to a large pool of capital. This can provide a more balanced capital structure, especially for highly geared firms.

A drawback of flotation is that public companies are answerable to their shareholders, and investment analysts will scrutinise the company prospectus closely. Once the company is floated on the stock market, shareholders may simply be interested in generating quick profits at the cost of longer-term success. The shareholders of a private company tend to be 'in it for the long run', for example, happy to agree to high levels of research spending and accepting relatively low dividend payouts. However, once the shareholder base is widened, the firm comes under severe pressure to generate record levels of profit year by year, even if the 'right' thing to do is to spend heavily on research in the hope of generating future success.

Managing and overcoming the problems of retrenchment

Just as a business must manage and overcome the problems associated with growth, it must do the same when retrenchment takes place, that is when it reduces the scale of its operations.

The main problems that are likely to occur when any form of retrenchment takes place include:

● damage to employee morale due to job losses
● damage to the relationships with customers and suppliers if they are affected by reductions in products available for sale or by reductions in the purchase of supplies
● general reputation among stakeholders who may be adversely affected
● loss of corporate knowledge when experienced employees leave.

Retrenchment can be managed in a number of different ways, each of which is likely to have both positive and negative effects on a business and on its various stakeholder groups. These include:

- Reducing the workforce gradually by freezing recruitment or offering early retirement or voluntary redundancy. Using this strategy might lessen the feelings of job insecurity among existing employees because any changes to their employment status would be voluntary. On the other hand, staff who choose to retire early or take voluntary redundancy may be key people in the organisation and, if they leave, their skills and experience disappear. Cutting back in this way may provide less opportunity for the organisation to introduce change and to restructure.

- Delayering, which means removing a layer of management from the organisational hierarchy. This has less impact on operations at shop-floor level and hence on production. It may empower or enrich jobs at the lower levels of management because these jobs will now have more responsibility allocated to them. However, the workload of the remaining management team will increase, which can add to stress levels and reduce motivation. Motivation might be further affected due to the loss of promotion prospects when a layer of opportunities vanishes.

- Closing a factory, outlet or division of a business. This will reduce overall fixed costs and hence a business's breakeven point. In addition, and depending on the nature of the closure, capacity utilisation may rise in other factories, outlets or divisions. The problem with this strategy is that it is almost impossible to reverse if there is an upturn in the economy. In addition, closure will mean a loss of many staff with valuable skills.

- Making targeted cutbacks and redundancies throughout a business. This strategy should allow a business to reorganise in order to meet objectives – for example, putting more emphasis on e-commerce. It also enables a business to get rid of less productive staff, which might improve the overall performance of all staff. It may, however, create feelings of job insecurity and lack of trust among the remaining staff.

Poor performance may also lead to a change in ownership of the business or changes in its leaders and senior managers. Much will depend on the context of the business. For example, a business that is not performing well and whose share price is falling may be an attractive proposition for another business considering a takeover. It might be that a business is not performing as well as it could be because the original management did not have the necessary skills or experience. In this case, new leaders might be brought in.

Private investors and venture capital firms evaluate management structures and expertise before committing funding, and often insist on recruiting new or interim management. This can be seen as a way of taking control away from the founder, but it is often a means of protecting any investment by ensuring that skills gaps are plugged and that the necessary structures and experience are in place.

Did you know?

Interim managers are employed for a specific task or set period. They can oversee a period of development or the setting up of a new structure, or can come in to run departments until existing members of staff have developed the skills to take over.

Fact file

Management buyouts (MBOs)

A management buyout (MBO) is where the managers of a business buy out the existing shareholders in order to gain ownership and control of the business or part of the business.

Reasons for buyouts

- A large company might sell off a small section to raise cash, refocus the business or get rid of an unprofitable activity – all forms of retrenchment. The management team of the parent company's unwanted section might feel it could be successful with a different approach or more finance.
- Owners of a family business who wish to retire might prefer to sell to the management team in the hope of maintaining employment and continuity in the community.
- A business might be in the hands of the receiver, who must try to keep it going in order to raise money to pay off creditors. One way of doing this is to sell part of it to the management team.

Finance for buyouts

Finance for management buyouts can come from managers' personal funds, bank loans and investment funds obtained by selling shares to employees. However, more often it comes from either venture capitalists or private equity firms. Venture capitalists and private equity firms work by lending the MBO the cash it needs and by taking a stake in the company for a return that usually exceeds 20 per cent on their investment over three to five years.

Benefits of buyouts

- Management and employees have more motivation and responsibility.
- Objectives may be clearer because there is no owner–manager conflict.
- There is likely to be less bureaucracy in the form of a head office that might hinder progress.
- Profits will not be diverted to another part of the organisation.
- If successful, the possibility exists of floating the company on the stock market or selling shares in a takeover offer.

Risks of buyouts

- If unsuccessful, personal losses are felt by the new owners or investors.
- The original owners might have been correct in assessing that the business was fundamentally unprofitable.
- There may be little access to capital.
- They often involve considerable rationalisation and job losses, with adverse effects on staff morale.
- Managers have to learn a whole range of new skills immediately, particularly if they have bought out from a large company. Suddenly, they have to do everything that before they took for granted, such as looking after the IT infrastructure, human resources and payroll.

Are buyouts a good thing?

- According to figures from the Centre for Management Buy-Out Research at Imperial College Business School, the value of buyouts shows a cyclical trend. From £16 billion in 2003 to a peak of £47.3 billion in 2007, value then fell consistently to 2010; since then it has risen steadily to £16.6 billion in 2014. The actual number of buyouts reflects the same picture, with 672 recorded in 2007 and 400 in 2014.
- Some institutional investors are critical of such deals, suggesting that if management sees value in a business, it should deliver this value to existing shareholders of the plc and not wait until the division has been hived off in a buyout before exploiting such value. Historically, the main method for management to realise investments in a buyout was to float it on the stock market again.
- Some commentators argue that workers may be more at risk with a management buyout than if the company had been purchased by a large organisation. If the company is not successful, workers and managers share the loss, but if the company is successful, it is really only the managers who benefit. Others argue that managers are the real risk takers and that workers' jobs might have disappeared if there had been no management buyout.

Fact file

From public to private limited company

A number of companies change from public to private limited companies. Sometimes this is due to retrenchment because the company is less successful than previously. However, this is not always the case. Private limited company status has the advantages of more privacy and less pressure on management resulting from share price movements. This allows management to take a longer-term view. Firms go private because, in general, there is a lack of interest in private firms. In such instances, the benefits of being listed are outweighed by the cost of meeting regulatory requirements and by the amount of time that needs to be spent with analysts and fund managers and generally communicating with the market.

Issues involved with managing growth include:

Economies of scale and diseconomies of scale

As a business expands, it may experience economies of scale. Economies of scale are the advantages a business gains, usually in terms of reduced average (unit) costs of production, due to an increase in its size. However, if a business grows too large, it may suffer disadvantages that lead to a lowering of efficiency and higher unit costs of production. These are known as diseconomies of scale.

Economies of scale and diseconomies of scale were covered in detail in Chapter 13 of Book 1. The AQA specification for the 'Strategic methods: how to pursue strategies: Assessing a change to scale' part of the course requires students to understand three specific types of economies of scale – technical, purchasing and managerial economies. Each of these, in addition to other economies of scale and diseconomies of scale, were explained in Chapter 13 of Book 1. Ensure that you review that chapter before proceeding further with this chapter. Additional points about the three economies of scale identified in the specification are included below.

Technical economies of scale

Technical economies of scale focus mainly on capital inputs, workforce specialisation and the law of increased dimensions. The first two are more often seen in very large, mass-production businesses. Capital inputs include capital investments in specialised equipment or machinery that increase productivity, or cutting-edge technology that improves internal control and reduces related costs such as transportation and distribution. Workforce specialisation creates efficiency by breaking down large, complex tasks into small, simple tasks performed in a mass production-line environment – the result is a reduction in average costs. The law or principle of increased dimensions applies mainly to transportation and distribution industries. It means that, for example, doubling the height and width of a warehouse or container leads to a more than proportionate increase in the cubic storage capacity of the warehouse or container. This again results in a reduction in average costs.

Key term

Technical economies of scale
The lower unit costs that arise because larger firms are able to use more efficient techniques of production and to benefit from the law or principle of increased dimensions.

Purchasing economies of scale

Firms purchasing supplies on a larger scale should be able to bulk-buy them and thus reduce average costs. They may be able to cut out wholesalers by buying direct from producers, thus reducing costs further. If purchases of supplies are in sufficiently large quantities, this might give the firm more buyer power and enable them to make very specific demands about product quality, specifications, service, and so on, so that supplies exactly match their requirements. **Purchasing** (or buying) **economies of scale** can also refer to the fact that a large firm wishing to borrow a large amount of money may be able to do so at a lower interest rate than firms borrowing smaller amounts.

Fact file

Wal-Mart and Asda

In his book *The Wal-Mart Effect* (2006), Charles Fishman notes how purchasing economies of scale can have a huge impact on costs. Apparently, prior to the takeover of Asda by Wal-Mart, Asda used to pay $14 per metre for 50,000 metres of material to make men's jeans. After the takeover, purchasing rose to 6 million metres per annum and the price fell to $4.77 per metre. Asda also benefited from technical economies when the Wal-Mart takeover took place. Analysts at Deutsche Bank estimated that Asda saved £150 million when it linked into the Wal-Mart IT system.

Managerial economies of scale

Larger firms can afford to employ specialist managers for the different functional areas or to lead specific projects within a business. This means more specialisation and greater knowledge and understanding of these functional areas/projects, which should increase productivity and lower average costs.

Economies of scope

Economies of scope enable an organisation to lower its average unit costs by using the same facilities, equipment, labour force and technology to produce or provide a range of different products.

Economies of scope exist if a firm can produce several product lines at a given output level more cheaply than a combination of separate firms each producing a single product at the same output level. Economics of scope differ from economies of scale in that a firm receives a cost advantage by producing a complementary variety of products with a concentration on a core competency. While economies of scope and economies of scale are often positively correlated and interdependent, the benefits from economies of scope have little to do with the actual size of output.

Economies of scope are sometimes termed 'economies of diversification'. This occurs when a firm builds on or extends existing capabilities, resources or areas of expertise for greater competitiveness.

The motivation for mergers and takeovers is sometimes an attempt to create economies of scope. Evidence suggests that mergers and takeovers that extend or enhance a company's product portfolio succeed more often than mergers and takeovers undertaken to increase size. Pharmaceutical companies, for example, frequently combine forces to share research and development costs and bring new products to market.

Examples of the economies of scope include:

- Extending the product range to benefit from the value of existing brands. For example, Amazon expanding into selling toys and sports goods or McDonald's expanding its range of food products to include salads and healthy foods.
- Using a specialist expertise or competency to benefit a range of different products. For example, Proctor & Gamble, which produces hundreds of products from razors to toothpaste, can afford to hire expensive graphic designers and marketing experts who will use their skills across all the product lines. Because costs are spread out, this lowers the average unit cost of production for each product.
- A drinks maker, such as Coca-Cola, using its current equipment, facilities, technology, distribution channels and labour to produce a wider range of drinks (Sprite, Fanta, Minute Maid as well as the range of Coca-Cola branded drinks). As a result it is able to diversify and lower costs.
- Fast food outlets have lower average costs producing a wide range of different food products than would separate firms specialising in each individual food product, because the provision of multiple food products shares storage, preparation and customer service facilities.
- Banks offering a variety of financial services, such as retail banking and investment services through a single service infrastructure that is likely to include branches, ATMs and internet sites. The costs of providing each service separately would be much greater than the costs of using a single infrastructure to provide multiple services.
- Flexible manufacturing, where a producer can manufacture multiple products with the same equipment. If the equipment provides the flexibility to change as market demand changes, the manufacturer can add a variety of new products to their current line quickly in response to consumer preferences.
- A company like the Kleenex Corporation, which manufactures a wide range of paper products for a variety of end users, including hospitals and healthcare providers, infants, children, families and women, benefits from economies of scope. Its brands include Kleenex, Huggies, Pull-Ups, Kotex, New Freedom and Litedays. All of their product lines utilise similar raw material inputs and/or manufacturing processes, as well as distribution and logistics channels.

Economies of scope (or scope economies) can increase a firm's value and lead to increases in performance and higher returns to shareholders. Building economies of scope can also help a firm to reduce the risks inherent in producing a single product or providing a service to a single industry.

▲ Kleenex has economies of scope

The experience curve

The experience curve is based on the idea that the more 'experienced' a firm is at making a product, the better and faster it becomes at making it and therefore the cheaper it is able to make it. As a result, it is able to fulfil demand better than its rivals.

The experience curve is a graphical representation of a phenomenon explained in 1966 by Bruce D. Henderson, founder of the Boston Consulting Group (BCG). It refers to the fact that firms learn from doing and, as a result, the higher the cumulative volume of production, the lower the direct cost per new unit produced. The cumulative volume of production is the quantity produced from the first unit, when the firm began operations, to the last unit, that is where it is at this point in time. In the 1960s, BCG's work with a wide range of companies suggested a consistent relationship between the cost of production and the cumulative production quantity. Its data revealed that product costs declined by 20–30 per cent for each doubling of cumulative production quantity and that this was a fairly constant and predictable movement.

In Figure 11.1 direct costs per unit are measured on the vertical axis and the cumulative volume of production is measured on the horizontal axis. When the firm begins production, direct costs per unit are high, but as it gains more experience of producing the product and its cumulative production level increases, direct costs per unit fall, as indicated by the experience curve (EC).

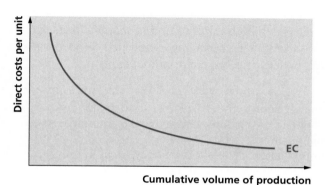

▲ **Figure 11.1** The experience curve

The implication for business strategy is that if a firm is able to gain market share leadership over its competitors, it can develop a cost advantage because its cumulative level of production will be greater and therefore its direct unit costs will be lower. Limitations to an experience curve-based strategy include the fact that:

- competitors may also pursue this strategy, which will reduce the returns to all firms because high levels of competition will limit a firm's cumulative production and so limit the cost savings arising from its experience
- competitors that copy the leading firm's manufacturing methods may achieve even lower production costs by not having to recover R&D investments
- technological change may enable even bigger experience curve effects, particularly for later entrants to an industry, for example because they build new plants that take advantage of the latest technologies and offer a cost advantage over the older plant of the leading firm.

The experience curve was a popular and relevant concept in the 1960s and 1970s when the general business environment was relatively stable and technological change and new product developments were relatively infrequent, compared to today.

In 2013, BCG undertook an evaluation of the experience curve concept and suggested that its original idea about the experience curve needed supplementing. It suggested that today most companies need two types of experiences. As consumer tastes and product generation change even more rapidly, experience in *fulfilling demand* (the ultimate outcome of the experience curve concept) alone is no longer sufficient to sustain a competitive advantage. An additional type of experience – experience in *shaping demand* – becomes necessary as well. The latter experience must be acquired through new and different means that can sometimes be in direct conflict with the current means an organisation employs to acquire experience. The Fact file on Facebook and Netflix illustrates these ideas. The two companies, in different ways, have focused on excellence in both fulfilling and in shaping demand, which has allowed them to thrive, often overtaking established competitors – a phenomenon that the traditional experience curve cannot explain.

Synergy

In a technical context, **synergy** is the fact that the value added by the system as a whole is beyond that contributed independently by the parts (whether the parts are people, hardware, software, facilities or policies) and is a result of the relationship among the parts and how they are interconnected.

In terms of organisational behaviour, synergy can be seen when a team of people working together is able to outperform what even its best individual member can do. Teams that are successful in this way have been observed to engage in productive disagreement in order to arrive at the best solutions that all agree upon. In contrast, less successful teams have been observed to arrive at a common view quickly, focusing on completing tasks and avoiding disagreement. In a business context therefore, synergy means that teamwork can produce an overall better result than if each person within the group were working toward the same goal individually.

Synergy is often claimed as a potential advantage of mergers and takeovers. Two firms join together and the resulting outcome is expected to be much better than the two individual companies working alone. Some of any subsequent improvement is the result of economies of scale and the reduction

> **Key term**
>
> **Synergy** The whole is greater than the sum of the parts; synergy is sometimes summarised as '1 + 1 = 3'.

in costs due to the integration of two previously separate operations – a single head office instead of two, a single board of directors instead of two, a single HR department instead of two, and so on. Some is the effect of corporate synergy, that is that the separate parts fit together so well that the integrated organisation is more productive, exploits opportunities more effectively and is thus more successful and more profitable than the two individual companies working alone. The AB InBev Fact file below provides a good example of synergies resulting from the merger of two firms.

Fact file

AB InBev

AB InBev, the world's largest brewer, was created from the merger in 2008 of Anheuser-Busch and InBev. AB InBev produces some of the best-known beer brands, including Stella Artois, Budweiser and Corona. At the time of the merger, AB InBev announced anticipated synergies that were higher than could be expected from the economies of scale that would result from two large organisations joining together. But these synergies were realised because the two companies entered the merger with a track record of successful previous mergers and a solid plan of action to ensure their predictions would be realised. On average, the integration of two consumer products companies results in an increase in target sales of about 3 per cent but in the case of the AB InBev merger, there was an improvement of almost 17 per cent over a three-year period following the merger. Analysts suggest that its success is based on the fact that there was a clear focus from the start on managing the changes required to fully integrate the two companies. In addition, appropriate targets and standards were set across the organisation based on the best approaches. These included standards and benchmarks for best brewing operations, and standardised sales and delivery routines to increase efficiency.

Despite the positive impact synergy can have, evidence suggests that synergy is achieved less often than is claimed and that mergers and takeovers often result in what some commentators call 'negative synergy', that is reduced efficiency of operations. Some of the Fact files later in this chapter illustrate this point. A 2012 survey of 300 global executives by Bain and Company (a global business consulting firm), indicated that overestimating synergies was the second most common result for disappointing mergers and takeovers. This is because companies often set overambitious targets to justify the mergers or takeovers they are about to enter into. In addition, most companies do not have a clear understanding of the level of synergies they can expect through increased scale following a merger or takeover.

Overtrading

Overtrading was explained in Chapter 19 in Book 1. Refer back to this before proceeding with this rest of the chapter.

Overtrading usually takes place when a business is attempting to grow too quickly. In such situations, a business accepts work and tries to complete it, but finds that to meet its customers' demands requires more working capital (net assets) than is available. The case study later in this chapter illustrates this situation.

Overtrading often results in the closure of a business but can usually be avoided by the careful management of cash. This means ensuring that

Key term

Overtrading Takes place when a business grows too quickly without organising sufficient long-term funds to support the expansion. This puts a strain on working capital.

the timing of payments for deliveries from suppliers and the timing of payments for orders from customers are negotiated and regulated to ensure that there is always sufficient working capital available in the business.

Greiner's model of growth

Greiner's model of growth was first published in L.E. Greiner's 1972 article, 'Evolution and Revolution as Organisations Grow' in the *Harvard Business Review* and was reprinted in a revised version in 1998.

The model includes five key dimensions, as follows.

1. The age of the organisation is measured on the horizontal axis. As an organisation develops over time its organisational practices change.
2. The size of the organisation is measured on the vertical axis. A company's problems and solutions tend to change as its size increases.
3. The stages of evolution. As both age and size increase, evolutionary growth may occur. Greiner used the term 'evolution' to describe prolonged periods of growth where no major upheaval occurred in organisational practice. He suggested that periods of evolutionary growth might last between three and eight years, depending on the nature of the industry.
4. The stages of revolution. Greiner used the term 'revolution' to describe periods of substantial turmoil in organisations, when, for example, serious upheaval of management practices took place.
5. The growth rate of the industry is influenced by the particular market environment. For example, a company in a rapidly expanding market will find that the speed with which it experiences evolution and revolution is different to a more established and slow-growing industry.

Figure 11.2 illustrates these key dimensions.

Key term

Greiner's model of growth
A model describing different phases of company growth, each of which includes calm periods of evolutionary development and growth that ends with a period of crisis and revolution.

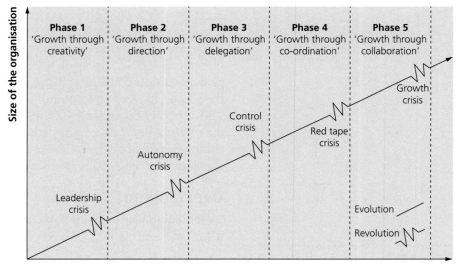

▲ **Figure 11.2** Greiner's model of growth

Greiner's model of growth identifies five phases of growth, that is five specific phases of evolution and revolution. Figure 11.2 illustrates that each evolutionary period is characterised by a dominant *management style* used to achieve growth, while each revolutionary period is characterised by a dominant *management problem* or crisis that must be solved before growth can continue. The phases of growth and development are explained below. Table 11.1 summarises the key characteristics of each phase.

Phase 1 – Growth through creativity

- This phase is characterised by: founders who are individualistic, entrepreneurial and focused on the product and the market rather than management activities; communication among employees that is frequent and informal; long hours and modest salaries that reflect the commitment of founders and employees; the business being very responsive to feedback from the marketplace.
- As the business grows, more effective management is required, larger numbers of employees mean more formal structures and communication systems are required. It is at this point that a *leadership crisis* can occur and the onset of the first revolution when a strong business manager is required, who is often not one of the original founders. (See the Fact file on Friends Reunited for an example of this aspect of growth.)

Phase 2 – Growth through direction

- Those companies that survive the first phase by installing a capable business manager usually embark on a period of sustained growth under strong directional leadership that improves the efficiency of operations. Characteristics of this phase include: a centralised and functional organisation structure; systems and procedures such as standards and cost centres; formal communication structures and hierarchies and centralised direction from the top; management rewards that emphasise clear salary structures and increases based on merit.
- Eventually however, the *autonomy crisis* occurs. The strong directive approach ensures employees are more efficient. However, as people's specialist expertise increases, they want more autonomy. At this revolutionary stage, some companies flounder because they stick to centralised methods, mainly because some managers find it difficult to give up being directional and some employees find it difficult to take responsibility. The solution adopted by successful companies is to introduce more delegation.

Phase 3 – Growth through delegation

- Those companies that survive phase 2 do so because they introduce a successful decentralised organisation structure. Its characteristics include: more responsibility being delegated; incentives such as bonuses used to encourage motivation; expansion of the market by mergers and takeovers; communication from the top being infrequent and brief; senior managers exerting control by the regular request for progress reports and the use of profit centres.
- Decentralised systems give managers greater authority and incentives to expand markets, respond to customers more quickly and develop new products. However, this results in the *control crisis* because senior management begins to realise that it is losing control over a highly decentralised structure. The phase 3 revolution sees senior managers trying to regain control by returning to centralised management systems, which often fail because of the huge scale of the operations.

Phase 4 – Growth through co-ordination

- Those companies that survive phase 3 do so because they use special co-ordination techniques. These include consolidating the organisation by merging decentralised units into product groups, each of which is treated as an investment centre, with the return on investment being an important criteria for allocating funds; formal planning procedures; numerous staff hired for the head office to initiate companywide programmes of control and review and to act as watchdogs; stock-options and profit sharing to encourage staff to identify with the firm. Such systems enable the company to achieve growth through the more efficient allocation of its limited resources.

- Managers still have much responsibility, but they have to justify their actions very carefully to head office. This leads to the *red tape crisis*, which is the result of a lack of confidence between staff in the decentralised units and those in head office. Managers in decentralised units resent the heavy direction from staff at head office who know nothing about local conditions. Staff at head office complain about managers and staff in the decentralised units being unco-operative. Both groups criticise the bureaucratic systems and procedures that have evolved and are taking precedent over problem solving, and discouraging innovation. The phase 4 revolution is underway because the company has become too large and complex to be managed through formal programmes and rigid systems.

Phase 5 – Growth through collaboration

- Phase 5 emphasises a more flexible and participative approach to management, with the following characteristics: solving problems through teamwork and a greater emphasis on innovation; teams combined across functions in a matrix structure; previous formal systems being simplified and a control system involving mutual goal setting being introduced; economic rewards being geared more to team performance than to individual achievement.

- Companies realise that there is no internal solution, such as new products, for stimulating further growth. Thus the revolution is triggered by a *growth crisis*.

Phase 6 – Growth through alliances

- Growth may continue through merger, outsourcing, networks and other solutions involving other companies. The challenge facing companies in this phase is how to access the external support and expertise required for the development of effective alliances and networks.

Author advice

Note that phase 6 was discussed by Greiner in his 1998 update to his original 1972 article but was not incorporated into his diagrammatic or tabulated representations. Hence it is not included in Figure 11.1 or Table 11.1.

▼ **Table 11.1** Organisational practices in the five phases of growth

Category	Phase 1	Phase 2	Phase 3	Phase 4	Phase 5
Management focus	Make and sell	Efficiency of operation	Expansion of market	Consolidation of organisation	Problem solving and innovation
Organisational structure	Informal	Centralised and functional	Decentralised and geographical	Line-staff and product groups	Matrix of teams
Top management style	Individualistic and entrepreneurial	Directive	Delegative	Watchdog	Participative
Control system	Market results	Standards and cost centres	Reports and profit centres	Plans and investment centres	Mutual goal setting
Management reward emphasis	Ownership	Salary and merit increases	Individual bonus	Profit sharing and stock options	Team bonus

Source: adapted from L.E. Greiner's, 'Evolution and Revolution as Organisations Grow', *Harvard Business Review*, 1998

It is important to note that each phase is both an effect of the previous phase and a cause of the next phase. For example, the evolutionary management style in phase 3 is delegation. This emerges out of, and becomes the solution to, the demands for greater autonomy in the phase 2 revolution. The style of delegation in phase 3, however, eventually provokes a revolutionary crisis that is characterised by attempts to regain control because of the inconsistency and variety of approaches, resulting from too much delegation.

Greiner's model of growth demonstrates the paradox that success creates its own problems. As a company grows, it faces new crises. Each crisis, in turn, requires management to make adjustments to organisational design.

Key criticisms of Greiner's model include the following:

- It implies there is a logical, sequential development path for company growth; this is not the case in reality because companies may move forwards and backwards along the growth curve.
- It assumes that all growth occurs in discrete phases, when in fact a company may experience two phases simultaneously or miss one phase.
- It has limited value in predicting when transition points, between phases or between evolution and revolution periods, will occur and thus provides no advice for planning ahead.
- It is difficult to understand precisely where a large company is on the growth curve at any one time because different parts of a large organisation may be at different stages.

However, the model does illustrate clearly that not all companies are successful at responding to the various crisis points, with the result that some businesses fail to grow or fail completely.

Author advice

Earlier in this chapter, it was explained that diseconomies of scale would not be considered formally at this point in this book because the topic had been considered in detail in Chapter 13 of Book 1. You may need to refer to pages 260–262 in Chapter 13 of Book 1 in order to answer question 8 in Practice exercise 1.

Practice exercise 1

Total: 90 marks

1. Explain two types of retrenchment. *(6 marks)*

2. Identify and explain one reason why a business might grow and one reason why a business might retrench. *(6 marks)*

3. Explain one positive and one negative effect of retrenchment on an organisation or its stakeholders. *(6 marks)*

4. Distinguish between organic growth and external growth. *(6 marks)*

5. Analyse the issues that a business needs to consider in managing and overcoming the problems of growth and retrenchment. *(9 marks)*

6. Explain two problems that may occur for a growing firm that changes from private limited to public limited company status. *(6 marks)*

7. Explain, with an example, each of the following economies of scale – technical, purchasing, managerial. *(9 marks)*

8. Identify and explain three diseconomies of scale. *(9 marks)*

9. Distinguish between economies of scope and economies of scale. *(6 marks)*

10. What does 'the experience curve' illustrate? *(3 marks)*

11. Explain the difference between falling average direct costs due to the experience curve effect and falling average total costs due to the effect of economies of scale. *(6 marks)*

12. Explain the term 'synergy'. *(3 marks)*

13. What does 'overtrading' mean? *(4 marks)*

14. Which one of the following is not a phase of Greiner's model of growth?
    a) Collaboration
    b) Communication
    c) Creativity
    d) Delegation
    e) Direction *(1 mark)*

15. Which of the following is not one of the crisis factors in Greiner's model of growth?
    a) Autonomy
    b) Control
    c) Growth
    d) Leadership
    e) Retrenchment *(1 mark)*

16. Analyse the characteristics of businesses in phase 1 of Greiner's model of growth and how these lead to a crisis of leadership. *(9 marks)*

Essay questions

Total: 25 marks

Answer one of the following questions.

1. Using examples of businesses you are familiar with, assess the implications for a business of organic growth as compared with external growth. *(25 marks)*

2. To what extent does Greiner's model of growth suggest that success at one stage of a company's development is unlikely to last? *(25 marks)*

Case study 1: Overtrading

Josh has a small business that has been in operation for four years. His working capital has been adequate to facilitate the steady growth that has taken place over these four years. His turnover is £250,000 p.a. and his profits are £22,000 p.a. An opportunity to bid for a contract with ABC plc comes up. The contract is to supply products worth £50,000 every two months for two years. Josh thinks this would help his business to grow more quickly – extra turnover of £300,000 p.a. He puts in a bid and is successful, agreeing to payment being made three months after delivery of the goods. Josh agrees an increase in his overdraft with the bank from £30,000 to £40,000. His bank suggests that he might be overstretching himself with such a large contract and will not increase the overdraft to the level Josh requests. Josh thinks he will manage.

He contacts his suppliers and orders sufficient supplies to fulfil the first few orders and asks that delivery is made as soon as possible. The contracts with his suppliers require him to make payment six weeks after delivery.

At the start things go well. ABC plc is pleased with the products they receive. The only problem is that Josh is at the limit of his overdraft because of the additional funding he needs to pay for the supplies he has bought and the wages of employees he has had to employ to meet the orders. He makes sure he can fund his employees' wages, but begins to fall behind with payments to suppliers.

At first he does not worry about the developing situation. As far as he is concerned he has the huge contract to supply ABC plc and that means a lot of additional revenue coming in. ABC plc makes the first payment on time and things ease temporarily. However, the next payment they make is late. Some of Josh's suppliers refuse to supply until they receive payment and some threaten legal action. Josh has gone over his agreed overdraft limit without permission and the bank is now refusing to honour any more payments to suppliers. The bank demands that the overdraft is paid in full within ten days. Josh cannot fulfil any more of the orders for ABC plc or for any of his other customers. The business has to close because he has no money to pay his workers or to buy supplies.

Questions

Total: 15 marks

1. Explain what a cash flow forecast is and how it can assist a business to manage its operations. *(6 marks)*

2. Analyse how Josh could have avoided the problem of overtrading and thus benefited from the growth his business experienced due to the huge order he gained. *(9 marks)*

The impact of growth or retrenchment on the functional areas of the business

The impact of business growth or retrenchment on the functional areas of business includes many of the concepts and topics studied in the chapters on the various functional areas in Book 1. Ensure that you take an integrated approach when considering this area of the specification and be familiar with the financial, marketing, operational and human resource issues covered in Book 1. In addition, relevant issues have been discussed in the earlier part of this chapter, including the impact of growth on leadership and human resources arrangements, and the financial and operational aspects of an organisation. The following is therefore just a summary of some of the key issues to consider.

The impact of growth or retrenchment on the functional areas of a business are likely to be extensive and will vary depending on the nature of the business, its current size and, in the case of a multi-product business, whether all areas are growing or retrenching or just some. The impact will also depend on the external environment of a business. For example, if a business is growing and requires additional funding for capital investment, the level of interest rates may be a key consideration in assessing the investment viability; if a business is considering expansion by entering markets abroad, the exchange rate might be a key consideration when setting prices. For any business the impact will mean leaders and managers have to constantly review the situation to ensure that their decisions are appropriate for the context and must anticipate and plan rather than simply react. The following lists provide some examples of key areas of decision making within each functional area that will need to be kept under review during a period of growth or retrenchment.

Marketing

- Decisions about the most appropriate marketing objectives given the changing nature of the business, for example whether the business should focus on particular product areas because they show improving/declining markets
- Decisions about whether to increase/decrease the resources allocated to marketing and how to deploy those resources
- Decisions about how the marketing mix should be allocated to achieve the changing objectives resulting from growth or retrenchment.

Operations

- Decisions about capacity and whether it needs to be increased/decreased given the changing circumstances of the business
- Decisions about the extent to which changes in technology are required to meet the changing operational situation
- The extent to which the business is able to exploit economies of scale, economies of scope and the experience curve effects as the business grows and how well it deals with potential diseconomies of scale
- Decisions about the business's current practice in relation to outsourcing and other arrangements to facilitate efficient operations as the business grows or retrenches.

Finance

- Ensuring that there is sufficient working capital to support the business as it grows
- Ensuring that sources of funding are available to enable the business to achieve its growth potential, and that the cost of funding is appropriate
- How to manage declining revenues and meet business costs during retrenchment
- How to manage shareholder expectations if retained profits need to increase, for example to support research and development, and dividends need to fall.

Human resources

- Decisions about the most appropriate organisational structure to manage the change from a smaller to a larger business or to manage the impact of retrenchment
- Decisions about job responsibilities, pay and reward structures, and approaches to motivation will be needed to ensure staff are contributing fully and remain committed
- Decisions about recruitment and selection and training to ensure workforce planning meets the needs of the business as its situation changes.

Assessing methods and types of growth

Methods of growth

Methods of growth include mergers, takeovers, ventures and franchises. Each method is explained below, together with assessments of their advantages and disadvantages.

Mergers

Mergers were introduced at the beginning of this chapter as a method of external growth. Because they involve the mutual decisions of two companies to combine to become one business, they are usually viewed as mergers of 'equals'. As a result, typical mergers usually involve two companies of relatively equal size that combine to become a single business with the goal of producing a company that is worth more than the sum of its parts – that is to reap the benefits of synergy as well as the economies of scale of operating on a larger scale. See the Fact file on AB InBev in the section on synergy earlier in this chapter for an example of such a merger. As mentioned in the section on synergy, many mergers have overambitious expectations about what they can achieve. The Case study on Hewlett Packard (HP) and Compaq at the end of this chapter, and the Fact file on the merger of Chrysler and Daimler Benz below, provide examples of high expectations that were not realised in practice.

Fact file

Daimler-Chrysler

In 1998, the American car maker, Chrysler Corporation, merged with the German car maker, Daimler Benz (famous for Mercedes cars), to form Daimler-Chrysler. At the time, this merger appeared to have all the makings of a merger of equals. The chairmen of both organisations became joint leaders of the new organisation. The two businesses appeared to complement each other because they operated in different segments of the car market and were prominent in different geographical markets – Chrysler was bigger in the US market, while the German firm had much more presence in Europe and Asia. The merger was therefore thought to be beneficial to both – giving Chrysler an opportunity to reach more European markets and Daimler Benz a greater presence in America. When the merger was announced, analysts, and the companies themselves, spoke highly of the synergies that would result and the fact that integrating the companies would strip out $8 billion in what were called 'redundant' costs.

Despite the hype, the resulting merged organisation struggled to blend the contrasting business cultures of the two businesses and the deal failed to produce the transatlantic automotive powerhouse that was anticipated. Some of the reasons were, with hindsight, obvious. Prior to the merger, Chrysler had systematically simplified its design and assembly processes. As a result, it had cut its design cycle from five to two years (compared to about six years for Daimler Benz) and could design a car at one-fifth of the overhead cost of Daimler Benz. This allowed Chrysler to introduce a series of very popular cars at prices that enabled it to consistently increase its market share. When Daimler Benz absorbed Chrysler's resources (including brands, dealers, factories and technology) into its own operations, the real value of Chrysler, in terms of its speedy processes and lean profit formula, disappeared, and with it the basis for Chrysler's success. Differences between the companies included their level of formality, philosophy on issues such as pay and expenses, and operating styles. The German culture became dominant and employee satisfaction levels at Chrysler fell significantly. Daimler Benz would have done far better preserving Chrysler's business model as a separate entity.

The merged company made continuous losses of billions of dollars and, in 2007, Daimler-Chrysler sold Chrysler to a private equity organisation.

Takeovers

Takeovers (acquisitions) were introduced at the beginning of this chapter as a method of external growth. Unlike mergers, they are often, but not always, characterised by the purchase of a smaller company by a much larger one. This combination of 'unequals' can produce the same benefits as a merger, but it does not have to be a mutual decision.

Takeovers can be hostile or friendly. A hostile takeover is where the attention of the predator company (the company wishing to take over the other company) is not welcome. The company being targeted recommends that its shareholders do not accept the bid. This was the case in the successful bid by Kraft for Cadbury in 2009 (see the Case study at the end of this chapter) and the unsuccessful bid made by Pfizer for AstraZeneca (see the Fact file below). In contrast, a friendly or recommended takeover is where the company being targeted welcomes the takeover and recommends shareholders to accept the bid. In 2006, the Walt Disney Corporation bought Pixar Animation Studio in a friendly takeover where Pixar's shareholders all approved the decision to be acquired.

Fact file
Pfizer/AstraZeneca takeover bid

The American pharmaceutical giant, Pfizer, launched a hostile takeover bid for the UK pharmaceutical firm, AstraZeneca, in May 2014. Its offer of £69 billion was rejected by AstraZeneca for being at least £5 billion pounds too low. Pfizer offered £55 a share, but AstraZeneca said this price would need to be at least £58.85 a share, to be considered. The proposed takeover would have been the largest ever of a UK firm by a foreign company. As well as the synergies of the combined strengths of the two businesses and cost-cutting benefits, analysts suggest that a strong motive for Pfizer's bid was a desire to move its headquarters to the UK in order to reduce its tax liability in the USA.

The proposed deal was heavily criticised in the UK by scientists, trade unions, investors and MPs, who feared it would lead to significant job losses, particularly in the life science industries. The boss of AstraZeneca argued that the business had 'attractive prospects' and would be better off on its own. He promised investors that their shares would eventually be worth more than what Pfizer offered, without the risks of the disruption caused by the takeover. He indicated that the company expected revenues to increase significantly by 2023, but that they would rise only slowly to 2017 as the company lost patent protection for some of its most lucrative products. AstraZeneca is now under pressure from shareholders to show that it can prosper as an independent business – its share price in April 2015 was £47.50 – well below the price offered in Pfizer's bid.

Under UK takeover panel rules, following its initial bid in May 2014, Pfizer was unable to make a further bid for six months (known as the cooling-off period), that is until November 2014. Since then, US tax rules have been tightened such that the tax benefits Pfizer anticipated in moving its headquarters to the UK are much less attractive. Pfizer did not make another bid for AstraZeneca following the end of the cooling-off period.

Fact file

Merger and takeover statistics

Table 11.2 indicates that total mergers and acquisitions (takeovers) involving UK companies fell in 2014 to lower levels than experienced during the 2008–09 economic downturn. The total value of the 173 acquisitions of UK companies by other UK companies in 2014 was £8 billion. Of the 98 mergers and acquisitions in the UK by foreign companies in 2014, 37 per cent involved US companies, 28 per cent involved EU companies and 35 per cent involved companies from the rest of the world. Of the 105 mergers and acquisitions abroad by UK companies in 2014, 28 per cent involved US companies, 31 per cent involved EU companies and 45 per cent involved companies from the rest of the world. (Where figures do not add up to 100 per cent, this is due to rounding up.)

▼ **Table 11.2** Merger and acquisition statistics for the UK

2011	2012	2013	2014
Total number of acquisitions of UK companies by other UK companies			
373	266	238	173
Total mergers and acquisitions in the UK by foreign companies			
237	161	148	98
Total number of mergers and acquisitions abroad by UK companies			
286	122	58	105

Source: ONS

Did you know?

- In a merger of two companies, the shareholders of each usually have their shares in their old company exchanged for an equal number of shares in the merged company.
- In a takeover, or acquisition, the acquiring firm usually offers a cash price per share to the target firm's shareholders or the acquiring firm's shares in a specified conversion ratio (for example, two new shares for one old share).

Did you know?

Whenever the shares of a company are bought or sold on the stock market, this results in a change in the ownership of that company. Such changes to ownership are usually very minor and rarely affect the overall control of the company. If, however, an individual or organisation buys up at least 51 per cent of shares in a particular company, this means they will be able to win all votes taken at an annual general meeting (AGM), and thus obtain control of the company. In practice, control can be gained with ownership of much less than 51 per cent of shares because most shareholders, probably owing to inertia, do not attend AGMs and do not vote.

Motives for mergers and takeovers

- A large company entering a new market may not have the necessary technical expertise and may thus acquire smaller companies with that expertise. In the mid-1990s, Sony did this when it entered the entertainments industry with its PlayStation. While it had the ability needed to produce the hardware, it did not have sufficient software programmers. Its purchase of smaller software producers allowed it to gain a suitably skilled workforce. See the Fact file on page 250 on Apple for a similar situation.
- The costs of acquisition or integration may be more favourable than the costs of internal growth, and the speed of growth might be a high priority.
- Brands are expensive to develop, in terms of both time and money, and therefore acquiring companies with prominent brand names is a way to avoid such expense. This was one of the main reasons for Nestlé's takeover of Rowntree and was an important factor in Kraft's takeover of Cadbury (see the Case study at the end of this chapter).
- The resulting organisation can exploit any patents owned by the company it has acquired. This is particularly important in takeovers in the pharmaceutical and computing industries.

Fact file

Apple

Apple's $278 million purchase of chip designer P.A. Semi in 2008 is an example of a takeover motivated by a desire to acquire necessary technology and talent. Apple historically had procured its microprocessors from independent suppliers. As competition with other mobile-device makers increased the competitive importance of battery life, it became more difficult to improve power consumption unless the processors were designed specifically for Apple's products. This meant that to maintain its quality and sustain its price premium, Apple needed to purchase the technology and talent to develop in-house chip design capability, which it did by acquiring P.A. Semi.

▲ Shareholders fail to benefit in 65 per cent of mergers and takeovers

- An organisation may have identified that the market value of a particular company is considerably less than its asset value. Once the company has been acquired, its valuable assets can be sold and the loss-making aspects of the business wound up. This technique is known as asset stripping.
- The benefits of synergy can be exploited. See the section earlier in this chapter on this topic.

Do mergers and takeovers work?

Theory suggests that growth via mergers and takeovers will produce synergies, economies of scale, economies of scope, the experience curve effect, higher profit levels and increased market share. However, research in the UK and the USA tends to suggest that most takeovers lead to disappointing results.

The previous section on synergy referred to the impact of 'negative synergy' because firms overestimate the benefits of joining together. Studies show that many takeovers damage the interest of the shareholders of the acquiring company, while rewarding the shareholders of the acquired company, who receive much more for their shares than they were worth before the takeover was announced. Professor Mark Sirower, an adviser to the Boston Consulting Group, in his book *The Synergy Trap: How Companies Lose the Acquisition Game* (1997), says that surveys have repeatedly shown that approximately 65 per cent of mergers and takeovers fail to benefit the acquiring company, whose shares subsequently underperform in their sector. His observations have been supported by numerous later studies and surveys.

The majority of failed mergers and takeovers suffer from poor implementation and the fact that, in a significant proportion of cases, senior management fails to take account of the different cultures of the companies involved. Merging corporate cultures takes time, which senior management does not have, particularly immediately after a merger or takeover. The nature of the problem is not so much that there is direct conflict between the two sides, but that the cultures do not merge quickly enough to take advantage of the available opportunities.

Many consultants refer to how little time companies spend before a merger or takeover thinking about whether their organisations are compatible. The benefits of mergers and takeovers are usually considered in financial or commercial terms rather than human and organisational terms. The Fact file on Daimler-Chrysler and the Case study on Hewlett Packard (HP) and Compaq illustrate this.

If 65 per cent of mergers and takeovers fail to benefit shareholders, what are the conditions that allow the remaining 35 per cent to be successful? Analysts suggest that the combined organisation has to deliver better returns to the shareholders than they would separately – the synergy element. In addition, the merging companies need to agree in advance which partner's way of doing things will prevail – the culture element. Finally, the combined organisation must generate advantages that competitors will find difficult to counter.

Key term

Ventures The term is used for a range of different arrangements between two or more firms; most usually involve companies in the early stage of development with high growth potential; venture capitalists or larger companies invest in these companies knowing that the risk is high but the rewards are equally high.

Ventures

The role of **venture** capital and venture capitalists in funding and supporting growing businesses was explained in Chapter 18 in Book 1. Ensure you are familiar with this before continuing with this chapter.

The key issue is that such funding is provided to support companies that are often in the early stages of their development, have little track record of profitability, are cash hungry and are high risk. Venture capitalists are prepared to invest in and support them, often with technical and managerial expertise, because they are assessed as having long-term growth potential coupled with the potential to earn above-average returns.

Corporate venturing is a type of venture capital. It is essentially where a large company takes an equity stake in a smaller company. Often this type of venture provides a strategic alliance for the large company and supports the smaller company by helping it to develop products that will generate income or cost savings for both parties. Motives for large companies investing in this way include the opportunity to gain from innovation without actually paying high R&D costs or incurring too much risk. An example of a corporate venture is provided in the Fact file below on Unilever Ventures.

Fact file

Unilever Ventures

Unilever Ventures is the venture capital and private equity arm of Unilever. It invests in small, new companies that have the potential, with support provided by Unilever, to grow and become profitable, established companies. In supporting such companies, Unilever usually becomes an active minority shareholder with a seat on the board.

Examples of Unilever's ventures include:

- Froosh, a fast growing, independent Swedish company that makes 100% fruit smoothies.
- SNOG pure frozen yoghurt Ltd, a chain of retail stores, mostly in London, selling SNOG frozen yoghurt.
- Brainjuicer, a marketing and brand consultancy with market research solutions based on the principles of behavioural science.

Source: adapted from www.unileverventures.com

Franchising

Franchising is a method of organic or internal growth for the franchisor. Someone with a successful business format (the franchisor) is able to expand the business by getting other people (the franchisees) to replicate the format in other areas, while allowing the franchisor to maintain a level of control and benefit financially from this growth. Well-known UK

Key term

Franchise When a business (the franchisor) gives another business (the franchisee) the right to supply its product or service.

businesses that offer franchises include Burger King, Clarks Shoes, KFC, McDonald's, Pizza Hut, Reeds Rains (estate agents), Subway, Starbucks, Sweet Factory, Thorntons and Toni&Guy.

Formation and operation of a franchise

The most common form of **franchise** arrangement is known as a 'business format franchise'. This is when the owner of a business (the franchisor) grants a licence to another person or business (the franchisee) to use their business idea. The franchisee sells the franchisor's products or services, trades under the franchisor's trademark or trade name, and benefits from the franchisor's help and support. In return, the franchisee usually pays an initial fee to the franchisor and then a percentage royalty on sales. The franchisee owns the outlet he or she runs, but the franchisor maintains control over how products are marketed and sold, and how their business idea is used.

▲ Clarks offer franchises

Fact file

Franchising survey

The British Franchise Association (BFA) indicates that the sector has shown considerable growth during periods when other business formats have struggled. From 2008 to 2013, while the UK economy shrank by 2.5 per cent, revenue for franchises overall increased by 20 per cent, the number of franchised businesses increased by 7 per cent and 11 per cent more brands used franchising as the method of growth.

In conjunction with NatWest bank, the BFA produces an annual survey about UK franchising. Its 2013 survey provides the following statistics about the UK franchise industry:

- annual turnover: £13.7 billion
- number of franchisor brands operating in the UK: 930
- number of franchised outlets: 39,000
- number of people employed in franchising: 561,000
- percentage of units profitable: 92 per cent.

This indicates significant growth over the last 20 years. In 1993, annual turnover was just over £5 billion, there were 379 different brands and 18,300 franchised outlets.

Source: www.thebfa.org

Fact file

Other types of franchise

Other types of sales relationship may sometimes be referred to as franchises. These include:

- Distributorship and dealership, where the franchisee sells the products but does not usually trade under the franchise name. In this case, the franchisee has more freedom over how his or her business is run. This is common in car sales, where a particular showroom may be the main dealership for a particular make of car (e.g. Toyota).
- Agency, where the franchisee sells goods or services on behalf of the supplier (the franchisor).

- Licensing, where the franchisee has a licence giving them the right to make and sell the licensor's product. As in distributorships and dealerships, there are usually no extra restrictions on how the business is run.

Key reasons for this method of growth and benefits of operating a franchise for the franchisor

Franchising is a means of growing the original business established by the franchisor. The key reasons why this form of growth is selected include the following:

- The franchisor receives a regular reward for the value of the intellectual property and concept that has been developed, while the franchisee provides the capital for expansion into other sites and locations, and takes on the risk involved.
- Rapid expansion is easier to achieve with franchising than it is with the more traditional company-owned expansion. The franchisor does not need to invest in additional premises or staff, and can instead focus on developing the business idea.
- By speeding up expansion, franchising enables the franchisor to achieve higher economies of scale earlier, stronger brand awareness and a larger share of the market more quickly. It may also allow the franchisor to establish market leadership more easily than if they had used a non-franchising format.
- Unlike licensing and other distribution agreements, the franchisor retains control over the quality of the products, and the way they are marketed and distributed. Under the franchise agreement, the franchisee is required to maintain a specified standard of service, which can be monitored through mystery shoppers, client feedback and field visits.

Factfile

McDonald's franchise

When brothers, Mac and Dick McDonald opened their first restaurant in 1940 in San Bernardino, California, they could never have imagined the phenomenal growth that their company would enjoy. From extremely modest beginnings, they hit on a winning formula of selling high-quality food cheaply and quickly. However, it was not until Ray Kroc, a Chicago-based salesman with a flair for marketing, became involved, that the business really started to grow. In 1955, Ray Kroc realised that the key to success was rapid expansion. The best way to achieve this was through offering franchises. Today over 80 per cent of McDonald's restaurants worldwide are run on this basis. In the UK the first McDonald's restaurant opened in 1974 and the first franchised McDonald's restaurant opened in 1998. There are now over 1,200 McDonald's restaurants in the UK, employing more than 85,000 people; about 50 per cent are operated by franchisees.

McDonald's is an example of brand franchising. McDonald's, the franchisor, grants the right to sell McDonald's branded goods to someone wishing to set up their own business (the franchisee). Under a McDonald's franchise, McDonald's owns and leases the site and the restaurant building. The franchisee buys the fittings, the equipment and the right to operate the franchise for 20 years. To ensure uniformity around the world, all franchisees must use standardised McDonald's branding, menus, design layouts and administration systems. The licence agreement also insists the franchisee uses the same manufacturing or operating methods and maintains the quality of the menu items.

In addition to benefits for the franchisor, there are also benefits of operating as a franchise for the franchisee who is wishing to establish a business of their own. These benefits mean that franchising is a popular business format, which, in turn, helps the franchisor to grow their business. Benefits for the franchisee include the following:

- They involve the least amount of risk for a start-up business and, as a result, a high percentage of them are successful.
- Franchise businesses usually have established brand names, which mean the franchisee is investing in a business with a proven track record of success.
- Financing the business may be easier because banks are often more willing to lend money to someone wishing to buy a franchise with a proven reputation than to an unknown, new business.
- The franchisee is likely to incur lower advertising and promotional costs, as the business is likely to benefit from national advertising or promotion by the franchisor.
- The franchisee usually has exclusive rights in his or her area, as the franchisor will not sell any other franchises in the same region.
- Relationships with suppliers are likely to have been established by the franchisor.
- The franchisor offers support and training, usually funded by an ongoing management service fee paid by the franchisee. The franchisor helps in setting up the business, including putting together the business plan, assisting the franchisee in gaining suitable funding for the business, selecting a site, and giving operational and technical support where relevant. As franchisees gain more experience, they usually require less advice and guidance from the franchisor. As a result, many franchisors provide intensive initial support followed by more general ongoing support and advice once the business is up and running successfully.

Possible pitfalls of operating as a franchisor

- Considerable capital is required to build the franchise infrastructure and to pilot the operation to ensure its success. At the beginning of the franchise programme, the franchisor is required to have all the appropriate resources in place to recruit, train and support franchisees – this could be a huge undertaking.
- If the franchisor does not have rigorous systems in place to select the right candidates as franchisees from the start, they could find that, at the beginning of the franchise programme, there is a risk that the brand name might be spoiled by an unsuitable franchisee.
- There is a risk that franchisees exercise undue pressure over the franchisor in order to implement their own style of policies and procedures.
- The franchisor has to disclose confidential information to franchisees about the nature of the business – recipes, business approaches, and so on – and this may constitute a risk to the business, if they subsequently leave.

Franchisees also face problems in running a franchise. These are identified below. The problems for franchisees can have a negative impact on the franchisor and the success of the franchise. For example, if franchisees are unsuccessful in running a franchise, this could reduce market share and profits for the franchise and may therefore limit its growth opportunities.

- There is always a possibility that the franchisor has not researched the business carefully, and has not tackled teething problems, set up robust systems and procedures, or built a sufficiently strong brand image.
- Costs may be higher than expected. As well as the initial costs of buying the franchise, a franchisee must pay ongoing royalties to the franchisor in the form of a percentage of turnover, and may have to agree to buy all its supplies from the franchisor. This will limit a franchisee's ability to earn high profits.

- Other franchisees could give the brand a bad reputation and this may have an adverse impact on all franchisees.
- The franchise agreement usually includes restrictions on how the business should be run. Therefore, a franchisee may not be able to make changes to suit the local market or, in general, use their initiative in making decisions as much as an independent business could.
- Franchisees are required to sign non-competition clauses, agreeing not to set up competing businesses in the franchisor's industry for a significant period after the end of the franchise agreement.
- Franchisees must be approved by the franchisor, so an existing franchisee may find it difficult to sell the franchise.
- If the franchisor goes out of business or changes the way it does things, this will have a direct impact on the franchisee's business.

Types of growth

Types of growth include vertical (backward and forward), horizontal and conglomerate integration. Each type is explained below, together with assessments of their advantages and disadvantages.

Vertical integration

> **Key term**
>
> **Vertical integration** The coming together of firms in the same industry but at different stages of the production process; vertical integration can be backwards of forwards.

Vertical integration can occur by one firm integrating backwards. A manufacturer might integrate with the supplier of its raw materials or components: for example, a car assembler owning a component supplier or an oil distribution company owning oil wells. On the other hand, vertical integration can also occur by one firm integrating forward: for example, where a manufacturer integrates with a retailer that sells its finished product.

An example of a firm using vertical integration is BP, which has grown by integrating with firms at all points in the chain of production, from oil exploration, extraction and refining, to distribution and retailing via petrol stations. A further example is American Apparel, a fashion retailer and manufacturer that actually advertises itself as a vertically integrated industrial company. The brand is based in Los Angeles, where the dyeing, finishing, designing, sewing, cutting, marketing and distribution of the company's products take place. The company makes and distributes its own advertisements, often using its own employees as subjects. It also owns and operates each of its retail locations as opposed to franchising. According to its management, the vertically integrated model allows the company to design, cut, distribute and sell an item globally in the span of a week. Zara is another example of a vertically integrated company. (See the Case study on Zara at the end of this chapter.)

Backward vertical integration means that the resulting organisation is in a position to control the supplies of raw materials and components in terms of price, quality and reliability, while forward vertical integration means that it is able to control the marketing and sale of products to the final consumer. In both cases, integration:

- enables internal planning and co-ordination of processes to overcome the uncertainty of dealing with external suppliers and retailers
- facilitates cost savings in both technical and marketing areas
- builds barriers to entry for new competitors
- enables the resulting organisation to absorb the profit margins of suppliers and/or retailers.

▲ BP has used vertical integration

▲ Morrisons' took over Safeway in 2004

In practice, mergers or takeovers designed to achieve vertical integration are relatively few in number; the vast majority are designed to achieve horizontal integration.

Horizontal integration

Firms involved in **horizontal integration** are usually potential competitors. Classic examples include Wal-Mart's takeover of Asda in 1999, EasyJet's takeover of the airline Go in 2002, Morrisons' takeover of Safeway in 2004, Lloyds TSB's takeover of HBOS in 2008, and Virgin Active's purchase of Esporta gyms in 2011 (see the Fact file below).

Horizontal integration is likely to create significant economies of scale, resulting in lower unit costs because duplicate and/or competing facilities can be closed down. However, diseconomies are possible if the integration results in poor communications and co-ordination. Equally, a failure to plan how the integration will actually work can lead to an unsuccessful outcome, as was illustrated in the Fact file about Daimler-Chrysler earlier in this chapter.

Horizontal integration reduces the amount of competition in the market and thus means that the resulting organisation has an increased market share. But if, as a result of the takeover, market share is likely to reach or exceed 25 per cent, it might be referred to the Competition and Markets Authority (CMA), which may either ban the takeover or set various conditions.

Fact file

Virgin Active and Esporta

Virgin Active agreed to pay £77.5 million to buy 55 Esporta gyms in 2011, adding to its own 71 gyms across the UK. Virgin said that this would give it a much wider spread of clubs around the UK and would also mean that it could offer a wider range of activities in their clubs.

The move nearly doubled Virgin Active's size in the UK. Important issues were the strategic rationale behind the takeover, the advantages of economies of scale and market share/market leadership potential resulting from the integration.

Virgin Active did not open any new clubs in 2010 and yet, in 2011, it passed the milestone of having 1 million members in its clubs. This suggests that, at the time, it was able to increase its membership without expanding the number of locations. The additional capacity provided by the acquisition of Esporta should enable further growth to take place.

Conglomerate integration

Conglomerate integration results in diversification and thus helps the resulting organisation spread its risks, which is in the long-term interest of both shareholders and employees. It can also lead to a sharing of good practice between different areas of business. However, in some instances, management may have little or no expertise in the newly acquired business area. Studies of corporate growth through conglomeration seem to indicate that unrelated diversification is the fastest route to the growth of sales, but not to the growth of profits. The latter is more likely to come through growth in existing fields.

Examples of UK-based businesses that have grown by conglomerate integration include:

- Virgin Group – established in 1970. Its activities include air travel, rail travel, holidays, leisure clubs, financial services and telecommunications.
- EasyGroup – founded in 1998. Its activities include airlines, bus services, car hire, internet and hotels.
- The Co-operative Group – established in 1863. Its activities include travel agencies, farming, banking, food stores, chemists, financial services, insurance services, legal services and funerals. It is the UK's largest farming operation, largest funeral service provider and fifth largest grocery retailer.
- The Swire Group – founded in 1816. Its activities include transport, deep-sea shipping, agricultural activities, cold storage and aerospace.

Conglomerates, by buying up companies, can grow to giant proportions. However, the popularity of the conglomerate form of growth has declined and there have been a number of demergers of conglomerate divisions, often as a result of unsuccessful takeovers and the subsequent need for companies to focus more clearly on their core activities.

Fact file

The General Electric Company conglomerate

The General Electric Company (GE), founded by light bulb inventor Thomas Edison in 1878, is a conglomerate. Throughout the 1980s and 1990s, it transformed itself from a simple maker of electrical appliances into a giant global conglomerate with interests in sectors from aircraft engines and power generators to financial services, medical imaging, television programmes and plastics. It did this through a process of strategic acquisitions, innovations and reorganisations. That strategy has now been abandoned because it has not provided the returns anticipated.

In April 2015, General Electric announced plans to sell off most of its GE Capital unit (essentially a huge commercial property and finance business) in order to create a 'simpler, more valuable company' focused on its core industrial operations. This decision is the latest in a series of sell-offs by the company. In recent years it has sold off its appliances division, its stake in broadcasting and its plastics business. It now says that it only wants to be in businesses where it can have a significant market share and meet its profit margin targets. The latest announcement resulted in a rise of nearly 11 per cent in GE's share price.

257

Practice exercise 2   *Total: 70 marks*

1. Identify and explain one example of the impact of growth and one example of the impact of retrenchment on each of the following departments of a business:
   a) marketing   *(6 marks)*   c) finance   *(6 marks)*
   b) operations   *(6 marks)*   d) human resources.   *(6 marks)*

2. Explain the difference between a merger and a takeover.   *(6 marks)*

3. What are 'ventures'?   *(4 marks)*

4. Explain what a franchise is.   *(4 marks)*

5. Identify and explain two advantages of franchising as a method of growth for a business.   *(6 marks)*

6. Explain one problem of franchising as a method of growth for a business.   *(4 marks)*

7. Distinguish between vertical and horizontal integration.   *(6 marks)*

8. Explain the term 'conglomerate integration'.   *(3 marks)*

9. Explain one possible motive for each of the following types of external growth:
   a) horizontal integration   *(3 marks)*
   b) forward vertical integration   *(3 marks)*
   c) backward vertical integration   *(3 marks)*
   d) conglomerate integration.   *(3 marks)*

10. Which of the following options completes the sentence correctly? A chain of yoghurt bars in the South East of England that merges with a dairy farm in the South West of England and another chain of yoghurt bars in the North East has undertaken:
    a) backward vertical and conglomerate integration
    b) horizontal and forward vertical integration
    c) horizontal and conglomerate integration
    d) backward vertical and horizontal integration.   *(1 mark)*

Essay questions   *Total: 25 marks*

Answer one of the following questions:

1. Research indicates that 65 per cent of mergers and takeovers fail to benefit shareholders. Discuss why the other 35 per cent are likely to be successful.   *(25 marks)*

2a. With reference to a company of your choice, evaluate the methods and types of growth it has undertaken to arrive at its present situation.   *(25 marks)*

   or

2b. Panda Ltd sells clothing made only from bamboo cotton. It has been in operation for three years. During this time it has expanded so that it now has four stores in the North West of England from which it sells its goods. It gets most of its supplies from China. Although there is a lot of competition in the form of other clothes retailers, some of which sell a small range of bamboo cotton items – usually socks – it has not yet come across another retailer specialising in bamboo cotton. Evaluate the most suitable methods and types of growth that Panda Ltd should consider. *(25 marks)*

Case study 2: Friends Reunited

Steve Pankhurst and Jason Porter, founders of Friends Reunited, realised they had a business with plenty of potential, but without the expertise to exploit it. 'We quickly became aware of the true value of the company, but we were ideas people and developers who, all of a sudden, had this massive company on our hands. We had a go at growing it ourselves and had taken on ten people who were mostly friends and family, but we were struggling. We knew we were missing opportunities, such as global expansion, where we simply didn't have the experience.'

Friends Reunited's appointment of a new management team to drive the expansion came from an assessment of their long-term objectives for the business. They received a number of takeover offers. 'The offers we received were tempting and we listened to what they had to say. But it became clear that by selling or giving away some of the company, the site would have become over-commercialised and lost its core values. We didn't want that, so decided to keep control and bring someone in who shared our beliefs.'

Pankhurst and Porter appointed former *Financial Times* chief operating officer Michael Murphy as chief executive. 'We liked him because he was down-to-earth and shared our entrepreneurial feelings about not over-commercialising the site, and he had the experience to grow the site internationally. Michael then brought in someone to take care of the marketing side of the company and made several other management appointments.'

The founders suggested that bringing in management allowed them to step away from the running of the business. At the same time, it helped stabilise the business and 'took it to the next level'.

The founders suggest that although the introduction of a management team went smoothly, it wasn't without its teething problems. 'When Michael came in we were still a bit hands-on, particularly on the technology side, and we were the only people who knew how certain things ran. Initially, Michael wanted to change things, such as the design, and when you've got so close to something, you can become blinkered and defensive about it. It can be difficult to accept criticism about a business you've sweated blood over building. You have to learn to take a step back and accept that's why you've brought these people in.'

ITV bought Friends Reunited in 2005 for £120 million and sold it to the publisher DC Thornton for £25 million in 2009. DC Thornton introduced a revised version of Friends Reunited in 2012 with a focus on nostalgia. This was not successful. The growth in popularity of Facebook and other social media sites, such as Pinterest, have taken away further market opportunities. Despite this, a spin-off, Genes Reunited, is popular and successful.

Source: adapted from a range of articles and news stories and www.friendsreunited.co.uk

Questions

Total: 25 marks

1. The original owners received a number of takeover offers in the early stages of the business and then eventually sold the business to ITV in 2005. Analyse the possible benefits and problems that a takeover can bring to the firm that is taking over another firm. *(9 marks)*

2. Use Greiner's model of growth to assess what phase of development Friends Reunited was in at the time described in the case study and what the implications of this might have been for the business. *(16 marks)*

Case study 3: Hewlett Packard (HP) and Compaq merger

In 2001, the struggling computing giant, Hewlett Packard, announced it would merge with a similarly struggling competitor, Compaq. The merger was controversial. Critics questioned how the HP engineering-driven culture based on consensus, and the sales-driven Compaq culture based on rapid decision making could be successfully integrated.

Carly Fiorina, the chief executive officer (CEO) of HP in 2001, was said to have 'aggressively' pushed for the merger with Compaq. News reports at the time suggest there was a battle with shareholders, and particularly those who were members of the families of the founders. One is quoted, in a letter to other shareholders, as describing HP's investment in Compaq as 'disastrous'. Michael Dell, of Dell computers, described the merger as the 'dumbest deal of the decade'.

In proposing the merger in 2001, the CEO said: 'In addition to the clear strategic benefits of combining two highly complementary organisations and product families, we can create substantial shareowner value through significant cost structure improvements and access to new growth opportunities. At a particularly challenging time for the IT industry, this combination vaults us into a leadership role with customers and partners – together we will shape the industry for years to come.'

In explaining the preparation for the merger, she said: 'We have done comprehensive integration planning and have clear metrics* to drive our success. We are committed to achieving the synergies we have identified while maintaining our competitive position and momentum in the marketplace.'

Carly Fiorina left three years after the merger took place and HP has had a range of other CEOs since. The poor cultural fit commented on by critics resulted, apparently, in years of bitter infighting in the merged company, and resulted in a huge loss in market capitalisation and in sales that regularly failed to meet targets. In 2012, Hewlett-Packard decided that it would split into two separate, and more flexible, companies, eliminating 5,000 jobs in the process. HP realised that it had to be ready to adapt to the constantly changing technology market, which it could not do with its previous unwieldy corporate structure.

*Standards of measurement by which efficiency and performance can be evaluated.

Source: adapted from a wide range of newspaper, online and other news media over a period of time

Questions

Total: 30 marks

1. Identify and explain three benefits the CEO of HP expected growth via a merger to bring. *(12 marks)*

2. Analyse possible reasons why these benefits were not realised. *(9 marks)*

3. Analyse the possible impact of the merger and the subsequent splitting up of the company on the human resource area of HP. *(9 marks)*

Case study 4: Vertically integrated Zara

In the distant past, it made more sense for clothing and fashion retailers to make their own clothes. Labour was cheap, the high street was not so competitive and merchandising was less of an art form. How that has changed. The days when UK clothing retailers manufactured their own garments are long gone. The UK textiles industry crumbled because of high production costs and increased competition. Today, vertically integrated retailing is seen as detrimental to flexibility, in terms of the cost of the supply chain and adapting quickly to new styles. Apart from the cost of labour, when a business owns its own factories, it also has to worry about keeping the factories and the staff occupied during quiet periods.

In Europe there is one exception to the rule that vertically integrated retailing does not work – Zara, the cutting-edge Spanish fashion chain and the major division of the Spanish retailer, Inditex. Like many UK retailers, Zara was a clothing producer long before the first store opened in 1975. But, unlike its UK rivals, Zara managed to transform its manufacturing arm into a highly efficient machine, able to cater to the needs of customers.

The company manages all design, warehousing, distribution and logistics functions itself with highly sophisticated technological and capital-intensive systems to ensure maximum efficiency. Owning its in-house production means Zara can be flexible in the variety, amount and frequency of the new styles it produces. Its in-house production enables it to have a rapid product turnover because its production runs are limited and its inventories are strictly controlled: 50 per cent of its products are manufactured in Spain, 26 per cent in the rest of Europe, and 24 per cent in Asia and Africa. Zara makes its most fashionable items – about half of all its merchandise – at a dozen company-owned factories in Spain and Portugal, particularly in Galicia and northern Portugal, where labour is cheaper than in the UK and most of Western Europe. Clothes with a longer shelf life, such as basic T-shirts, are outsourced to low-cost suppliers, mainly in Asia and Turkey.

In contrast, because production is highly labour intensive, most of its competitors outsource all their production, usually to Asia, and focus on distributing and retailing those goods.

Zara has become the leader in the rapid development of fast-changing fashions. Designers develop new models daily – sometimes three or four a day – which are then reviewed and put into production. New fashion designs are shipped at a rapid rate. Zara claims that it can translate a catwalk design into quality high-street fashion within three weeks, which means that the company does not have to second-guess what will be fashionable up to nine months ahead. There is a much-quoted story that when Madonna played a series of concerts in Spain in 2005, people attending the final performance were able to wear a Zara version of the outfit she had worn at the first concert.

The secret of its fast fashion retailing is its ability to generate a quick turnover of merchandise in its stores. Customers know they should buy an item they like when they see it in store – because it will not be there for long – part of the company's approach is to create a climate of scarcity and opportunity for the clothes in its stores. Its success is evident – over 2,000 stores located across 88 countries.

Horizontal integration is more common in the clothing retail sector. Examples include the Arcadia Group and Gap Inc. The Arcadia Group is the result of a series of horizontal integrations, bringing together Burton, Topshop, Topman, Outfit, Miss Selfridge, Evans, Dorothy Perkins and Wallis. The GAP Inc. retail clothing corporation integrated horizontally to control three distinct companies, Banana Republic, Old Navy and the GAP brand itself.

Questions

Total: 30 marks

1. How might a 'climate of scarcity and opportunity' in Zara's stores encourage sales? *(5 marks)*

2. Analyse the possible reasons the Arcadia Group and Gap Inc. chose to expand through horizontal rather than conglomerate integration. *(9 marks)*

3. To what extent is Zara's vertically integrated approach something that clothing retailers in the UK could successfully adopt? *(16 marks)*

Case study 5: Kraft and Cadbury – hostile takeover

In 2009, US food company, Kraft Foods, launched a hostile takeover bid for Cadbury, the UK chocolate maker. At the time of the offer for Cadbury, Kraft was the world's second-largest food conglomerate. Cadbury, founded by John Cadbury in 1824 in Birmingham, had also grown through mergers.

The challenge for Kraft was how to buy Cadbury when it was not for sale. Not only was Cadbury not for sale, but it actively resisted the Kraft takeover. The chairman of Cadbury said that the 745 pence-per-share offer was 'unattractive', and that it 'fundamentally undervalued the company'. He advised shareholders to reject the offer. He made it clear that even if the company had to succumb to an unwanted takeover, almost any other confectionery company (citing Nestlé and Ferrero) was preferable to Kraft. This was because if the deal went ahead, the chocolate company would be absorbed into Kraft's 'low growth conglomerate business model' – an unappealing prospect that contrasted sharply with Cadbury's strategy of being a specialist confectionery company.

Despite this and following lengthy negotiations, a deal was made early in 2010 at 840 pence per share, which was approved by 72 per cent of Cadbury's shareholders.

Kraft wanted Cadbury and its portfolio of brands in order to assist its plans to move into the emerging markets of India, Asia and South America, where Cadbury already had strong links. The addition of Cadbury strengthened Kraft's existing range of iconic products and brands, including Kenco, Terry's Chocolate Orange, Dairylea and Toblerone. Kraft also saw the takeover as the 'logical next step' in its transformation to a 'high-growth, higher-margin company' and a 'global powerhouse in snacks, confectionery and quick meals'.

Following the takeover, despite Cadbury helping to boost sales, Kraft's profits fell due to costs associated with integrating the UK business into the expanded Kraft business. However, Kraft believed that by the end of 2012, it would be able to make 'annual synergy savings' of at least $675 million.

In March 2011, Kraft caused outrage when it closed a Cadbury factory near Bristol and eventually sold it for £50 million. Production was immediately outsourced to Poland. This was despite Kraft publically promising, during the takeover negotiations, that production in the UK would continue. Interestingly, prior to the takeover, Cadbury had already spent £100 million building manufacturing facilities in Poland, intending to move the operation there. Kraft said that it felt that progress with this move was too far down the line to halt.

What Cadbury's management did not know at the time of the takeover, and what they were not told, was that Kraft was intent on getting rid of its conglomerate structure and becoming more focused and therefore able to create more value for its shareholders. It intended to do this by splitting into two companies, but wanted Cadbury on board first to help it establish itself in emerging markets.

In August 2011, Kraft Foods Inc. announced plans to split into two independent companies. Mondelez International is the name of the high-growth global snacks business and Kraft Foods Group is the name of the high-margin North American grocery business. Cadbury now belongs to Mondelez International.

Source: adapted from a wide range of newspaper, online and other news media over a period of time

Questions

1. The case study indicates that Kraft is focused on increasing value for its shareholders. What evidence is there to suggest that it might not be as concerned about other stakeholders? *(6 marks)*

2. The takeover of Cadbury was part of Kraft's growth strategy. Analyse the reasons for Kraft's focus on external rather than organic growth. *(9 marks)*

3. Analyse possible reasons why Cadbury's chairman did not want the company to become part of a conglomerate. *(9 marks)*

4. Evaluate, using examples to illustrate, what Kraft is likely to mean by the 'annual synergy savings' it expected after 2012. *(16 marks)*

12

Assessing innovation

This chapter introduces the concept of innovation and the pressures for innovation. It explains the different types of innovation, with particular emphasis on product innovation and process innovation. The value of innovation, its benefits and the problems arising from it, are then studied in depth. The focus of the chapter then moves on to the ways in which an organisation can become more innovative. Four alternative ways are considered: kaizen, research and development, intrapreneurship and benchmarking. The chapter then goes on to explain how a business can protect innovation and intellectual property, primarily through the use of patents and copyrights. The concluding section of the chapter studies the impact of an innovation strategy on the functional areas of a business.

The pressures for innovation

Key terms

Innovation The successful exploitation of new ideas. Innovation enables businesses to compete effectively in an increasingly competitive global environment.

Product innovation The creation and launch of a good or service that is new, or a significant change to an earlier good or service.

Process innovation The creation of a new way of making, providing or delivering a particular good or service.

What is innovation?

The government department responsible for **innovation** is the Department for Business, Innovation and Skills (BIS). The department conducts an innovation survey every two or three years. It defines a business as 'innovation active' if it is engaged in any of the following:

- The introduction of a new or significantly improved product (good or service) (**product innovation**).
- The introduction of a new process for making or supplying a product (**process innovation**).
- Spending in areas such as research and development, linked to innovation activities.
- Training or the acquisition of external knowledge that is linked to innovation activities.
- The introduction of new machinery and equipment for the purpose of innovation activities.

Based on the definition above, 44 per cent of UK enterprises surveyed were 'innovation active'.

Research and development (R&D), which is an element of innovation, will be explained later in this chapter. Training and new machinery may also be classed as innovation, but only if they are part of the successful exploitation of new ideas. In many cases these activities are just supporting existing (non-innovative) products or processes.

BIS also recognises an additional form of innovation: **strategic innovation**. Strategic innovation takes place when a business undertakes major changes in its management practices, business structure, organisational structure or marketing strategy in order to improve its competitiveness.

Table 12.1 shows the percentage of UK businesses that fall into these categories of innovator.

▼ **Table 12.1** Main types of innovation in the UK, 2008–13

Type of innovation	Percentage of UK businesses* engaged in innovation		
	2008 %	2011 %	2013 %
Innovation active of which:	64	37	44
Product innovator	22	19	18
Process innovator	12	10	10
Other innovator	55	31	37

*Figures and sub-totals do not add up to 100% because businesses may fit into more than one category.
Sources: BIS, Persistence and Change in Innovation, December 2008 and BIS, Proportion of firms who are innovation active, October 2014

Innovation activities

As indicated earlier, a variety of activities are recognised by BIS as examples of innovation. Figure 12.1 provides a more detailed breakdown of the main innovation activities by type.

Figure 12.1 shows that innovation in the UK is dominated by computer software and hardware manufacturers. Although internal research and development (R&D) is the third most prominent activity, in many of the UK's competitors R&D spending is much higher than UK spending on R&D. Globally the UK tends to be focused more on computing, workforce training, innovative marketing and design as the key components of its innovative activities. Countries such as South Korea and Germany are much more likely to focus on R&D, new products and product design.

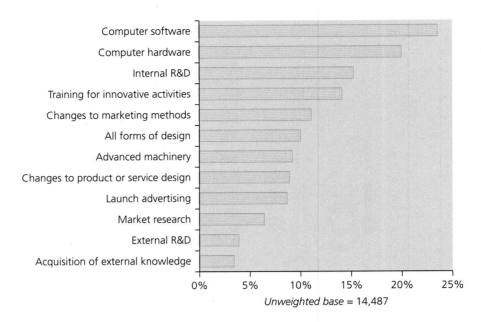

| Computer software |
| Computer hardware |
| Internal R&D |
| Training for innovative activities |
| Changes to marketing methods |
| All forms of design |
| Advanced machinery |
| Changes to product or service design |
| Launch advertising |
| Market research |
| External R&D |
| Acquisition of external knowledge |

0%   5%   10%   15%   20%   25%

Unweighted base = 14,487

▲ **Figure 12.1** Innovation activities by type
Source: BIS

Note: internal R&D is carried out by the business; external R&D is subcontracted to another business.

Fact file

The world's most innovative companies

The UK's low labour productivity is sometimes blamed on low innovation, particularly with respect to scientific-based innovation arising from research and development. In 2014 the Boston Consulting Group (BCG) – the organisation that formulated the Boston Matrix – compiled a list of the 50 most innovative companies in the world. Only one UK company was placed in the top 50 – Unilever, which spends over £1 billion a year on R&D, was placed 49th. The top three innovators were Apple, Google and Samsung.

BCG believes that innovative companies are those that:

- use internal and external sources of knowledge
- have a specified budget for innovation

- focus on customer needs, not their production capabilities
- are prepared to take risks.

Google

A similar list is compiled by Thomson Reuters. This ranks companies according to a formula based on patents granted. No UK company reached their list of the world's top 100 innovators.

The pressure for innovation comes from the need to compete. As markets have become more competitive globally, with fewer restrictions imposed by governments, opportunities have arisen for businesses to expand from domestic markets to global markets. This development provides greater opportunities to businesses that can come up with new ideas through innovation, because they can now exploit these innovations on a worldwide scale. However, if businesses that might previously have dominated their domestic market are complacent, they are likely to lose their market to innovative companies from other countries.

Further pressure arises from other external factors, such as changes in technology leading to a firm's existing product becoming out of date, changes in customers' tastes, and the need to meet the requirements of government legislation and health and safety standards.

Internal factors can also lead to a pressure for innovation. If a firm prides itself on the quality and range of its products, there will therefore be a constant need to ensure that these factors are enhanced in order to continue to attract customers. Shareholders will want high added value and in a competitive market this can only be achieved by keeping up with, or ahead of, competitors (to achieve differentiation) or by reducing costs (to achieve low-cost leadership). Finally, both internal and external pressures may lead to a desire within a business to improve the environmental impact of the business's activities.

These pressures are most evident in the most recent UK government Innovation Survey, as outlined in Table 12.2. This table shows the percentage of large businesses citing a particular reason or benefit as being of 'high' importance when making decisions to support innovation.

▼ **Table 12.2** Main purposes and benefits of innovation for UK firms

Reason for innovation	% of large firms stating this factor is of 'high' importance 2013
Improve quality	43
Increase market share	39
Replace outdated products or processes	31
Increase product range	31
Increase value added	31
Meet regulations	29
Reduce costs	28
Enter new markets	23
Improve flexibility	20
Increase capacity	20
Improve health and safety	20
Reduce environmental impact	19

Sources: BIS, UK Innovation Survey, 2013

The value of innovation

Innovation brings many benefits to businesses and the UK economy as a whole. However, innovation does not guarantee positive results as it is considered a relatively high-risk strategy, largely because the nature of innovation involves moving into new or unknown territory. Consequently, it can bring problems. The overall value of innovation, to both a business and a country, can be assessed by comparing benefits and problems related to products or processes.

Table 12.2 provides a useful checklist of the main benefits of innovation.

Benefits of innovation

- **Improve quality**. Innovation may help a business to develop higher-quality products that will be more attractive to consumers, leading to increased sales and a better reputation.
- **Increase market share**. Innovation can help a business to improve its core competences and strategic position. A new innovation may enable a business to gain a reputation for possessing a particular competence. Product innovation can help a business to achieve differentiation from its competitors; process innovation may cut costs and lead to low-cost leadership in a market.
- **Replace outdated products or processes**. As the pace of change increases, product life cycles tend to fall dramatically. In order to retain competitive advantage in a market, a business must anticipate products and processes that are likely to become outdated and undertake innovation. This allows the business to ensure that these products or processes are replaced before they endanger the competitiveness of the business in that particular market.
- **Increase product range**. Innovation can allow a business to update its product range continually and stay ahead of competitors. In rapidly changing, technologically advanced industries, innovation is vital in presenting new products to the market. In addition, innovation enables firms to balance their product portfolio through the creation of new growth products to take over from those that have reached the decline stage of the product life cycle.
- **Increase value added**. Innovation helps firms to develop goods or services that have a unique selling point (USP), allowing them to achieve a higher degree of product differentiation. Products with a USP usually sell in higher quantities and their uniqueness tends to lead to more inelastic demand, allowing firms to increase prices and so earn higher profit margins. In addition, if innovation uncovers a new invention, this can be patented, giving the firm a guaranteed monopoly of manufacture for a number of years. Analysis by the UK and US governments shows a high correlation between the increase in sales achieved by a firm, its level of innovation spending and the number of patents that the firm acquires. This in turn allows a business to achieve higher value added.
- **Meet regulations**. Innovation enables a business to respond to changes in UK and EU laws that necessitate changes to products and production methods. UK businesses expanding beyond the EU may need to make changes in accordance with the legislation of the countries in which they are trading.
- **Reduce costs**. Innovation is often designed to improve processes: that is, to improve the efficiency of production methods through process innovation. Innovative ways of producing goods reduce the average cost of production and help competitiveness.
- **Enter new markets**. Innovation can help businesses to enter new markets. It is a key element of product portfolio planning and enables businesses to identify opportunities in new markets through a combination of product-based and market-based innovation.
- **Improve flexibility**. Greater flexibility is now an expectation of most customers, particularly in b2b (business-to-business) transactions. As a consequence, a great deal of innovation is designed to find ways of enabling a business to adapt quickly to changing circumstances.

▲ Innovation helps businesses improve existing products and develop new ones

- **Increase capacity**. High capacity utilisation helps a business to maintain a reputation for good customer service while controlling its fixed costs. Consequently, a business might need to introduce innovative new products to use more of its capacity. In 2013, 20 per cent of firms surveyed cited the need to increase capacity as a reason for innovation.
- **Improve health and safety**. Innovation, particularly process innovation, often incorporates ways of improving health and safety. Innovative production techniques can improve the safety of the working environment, thus reducing days lost through accidents or illnesses. It can also help add value and sales volume by improving the safety of consumers when they use the products.
- **Reduce environmental impact**. The environment is considered to be a stakeholder of any business, so a business may innovate in order to reduce any negative environmental effects of its activities.
- **Provide a stimulating working environment**. The opportunity to create new products and ideas provides a stimulating working environment and therefore motivates employees. This may improve labour productivity, reduce turnover and make it easier for a business to recruit workers. Businesses such as Google and Apple find it easier to attract workers because of the excitement created by an innovative atmosphere.

Problems of innovation

Although innovation brings many benefits, businesses need to be aware of the risks and potential pitfalls.

- **Uncertainty**. There is no guarantee that innovation and R&D expenditure will lead to new products and processes. Some projects, such as research into the common cold, have still not generated successful outcomes. The level of uncertainty in R&D in particular makes it much more difficult to justify the high levels of spending that are often needed.
- **Operational difficulties**. These are common with new products, processes and ideas. Companies often suffer setbacks when new products are released or innovative processes introduced, particularly if they are in a hurry to release them and have had to rush their testing processes. In industries where product safety is vital, a hasty action can destroy a firm's reputation and the trust of its customers.
- **Competition**. Innovation spending may encourage rivals to undertake similar activities. This will merely lead to increased costs for both firms, but with no competitive advantage being gained.
- **Generic products**. In industries such as pharmaceuticals, there is a growing tendency towards generic products. These 'copies' are produced cheaply as soon as the patent expires. In industries where patent protection is more difficult to achieve, this can negate the benefits of innovation. A company may spend millions developing an innovative product, only for a rival to market a similar product at a much cheaper price because the rival has not had to spend so much money on innovation.

In addition to these problems, businesses may choose not to innovate because they believe that innovation has a limited chance of success. The UK government's most recent survey (in 2013) identified nine main factors that were likely to limit innovation. For large firms, they are listed in order of importance:

1. Innovation costs
2. Excessive risk
3. Costs of finance
4. Availability of finance
5. Government and EU regulations
6. Market dominated by established businesses
7. Uncertain demand
8. Lack of information on technology
9. Lack of information on market.

However, no single factor was identified as a problem by more than 17 per cent of the companies surveyed, and only factors 1 to 4 affected more than 10 per cent of firms.

Conclusion

Overall, the benefits of innovation depend on external circumstances. Table 12.1 shows how innovation declined during the recession of 2008–09. In 2008, 64 per cent of UK businesses were 'innovation active'. This fell to 37 per cent in 2011 and had only risen to 44 per cent by 2013. The success of innovation depends on the markets within which businesses operate. Fast-changing markets provide much greater opportunities for innovation; although too rapid change can undermine the long-term profitability of innovation. Innovation is also influenced by culture and being prepared to take risks. With certain exceptions, UK businesses tend to avoid risk more than their counterparts in other countries and so gain less value from innovation. According to BIS, UK businesses are more likely to work co-operatively with organisations from other countries on innovative projects. However, UK businesses are less likely than businesses in other leading economies (except Russia) to devote resources to their own innovation activities. Again, Table 12.1 shows the low level of innovation in the UK, with only 44 per cent of all businesses engaging in innovation activities in 2013.

Although many firms elect not to innovate because of the potential risks, there are ways of improving the chances of successful innovation so that the benefits are more likely to outweigh the problems. Some of these approaches are outlined below.

Did you know?

Have you ever dreamed of owning Harry Potter's invisibility cloak but thought it was a technical impossibility? Think again. Scientists in Japan have developed an invisibility cloak.

The cloak has cameras built into the back and front of the garment. The material acts as a screen and the image from the cameras at the front of the cloak is projected on to the rear of the cloak and vice versa.

The only problem is that passers-by see a disembodied head. The scientists are working on an invisibility balaclava to overcome this problem.

Unfortunately, commercial applications have not yet been identified.

Fact file

Wiggly Wigglers

Wiggly Wigglers started in 1990 when Heather Gorringe, a farmer's wife from Herefordshire, decided to use worms to create compost from kitchen waste. Heather's creativity has created a £2 million business that has diversified into 700 natural products. Wiggly Wigglers' core values mean that it focuses on providing natural products, sourcing supplies and labour from the local area. However, as with any innovative business, Wiggly Wigglers has seized opportunities as they arise. Although it is focused on environmentally friendly products, it has embraced new technology too. Online orders enable the business to monitor changing tastes and ensure delivery of products within 48 hours. The company has also introduced podcasts, reaching thousands of listeners every week.

Source: Wiggly Wigglers website, www.wigglywigglers.co.uk

The ways of becoming an innovative organisation

There are different ways of becoming an innovative organisation. As indicated earlier, it may be achieved through a change in company culture, usually involving a willingness to take greater risks and welcoming the opportunities offered by change. Four specific ways of becoming innovative are:

- kaizen
- research and development
- intrapreneurship
- benchmarking.

These ways will each be considered in turn.

Kaizen (continuous improvement)

Kaizen can operate through individuals or by using **kaizen groups** or **quality circles** – groups designated to identify potential innovations or productivity and quality improvements. It is considered to be a cost-effective means of steady improvement because all employees of an organisation support its aims.

The key features of kaizen are as follows:

- It relies on many small steps, rather than on fewer, more significant, changes, such as happens with research and development.
- It uses everyday ideas on innovation from ordinary workers rather than major technological or dramatic innovative changes.
- It usually focuses on methods rather than outcomes, assuming that improved methods and approaches will guarantee a more effective outcome.
- It employs the talents of the workforce rather than using expensive consultants, and encourages staff to use their talents to seek improvements.

Kaizen is based on two main principles:

- **Gradual change**. Kaizen relies on many small changes rather than sudden leaps. Britain's Industrial Revolution in the nineteenth century was characterised by a number of dramatic leaps forward, caused by major inventions or innovations such as the Spinning Jenny (textiles) and the steam engine. In contrast, the kaizen approach concentrates on finding lots of small innovations which, over time, will lead to significant improvements and can result in major advances.

Key term

Kaizen (or continuous improvement) A policy of implementing small, incremental changes in order to achieve innovation, better quality and/ or greater efficiency. These changes are invariably suggested by employees and emanate from a corporate culture that encourages employees to identify potential improvements.

- **Staff suggestions**. Because continuous improvement relies on staff identifying ways in which efficiency can be improved, it is more likely to be successful if staff are given opportunities and encouraged to express their opinions. It also works better if the workforce is more educated and skilled, and thus able to recognise potential new approaches or weaknesses in the firm's existing approach.

What do you think?

Kaizen at Toyota

Toyota is the company most closely associated with kaizen. In Europe its materials handling section receives 3,000 suggested improvements each year. In Japan, Toyota gets an average of over 20 written suggestions per annum from each employee. In the UK, the average number in all industries is estimated to be one idea every six years.

Why is there such a difference between the two countries?

Did you know?

Twitter is an example of an innovation that arose from kaizen. The idea was formulated by Jack Dorsey and developed through a series of suggestions by fellow co-founders Biz Stone and Evan Williams.

Did you know?

Amazon's senior management team are required to work at least one day a year in customer services so that they have direct contact with customers and can therefore understand their needs. This fits in with the management approach of Amazon's CEO, Jeff Bezos, who is a firm believer in the use of kaizen to drive innovation. Front-line workers in customer services are encouraged to use their daily contact with customers to find and suggest new ways in which Amazon can appeal to its customers. Product innovations, such as the Kindle, have been developed by Amazon as a result of their understanding of customer needs. Process innovations can also be introduced through kaizen. Warehouse workers are encouraged to make suggestions on how to improve the materials handling aspect of their jobs.

Research and development

Key term

Research and development (R&D) The scientific investigation necessary to discover new products or manufacturing processes, and the procedures necessary to ensure that these new products and processes are suited to the needs of the market.

Author advice

Do not confuse research and development with market research. Market research involves finding out what consumers want and developing a product to meet that need. R&D, which often starts in a laboratory, means that the product or process is invented or discovered and then its commercial applications are investigated. As a consequence, products developed from market research are often described as 'market led', while those arising from R&D are 'product led'.

How research and development (R&D) contributes to innovation

R&D serves a number of purposes, most of them leading to innovation. These innovations improve the business's performance and therefore are a motive to devote resources to R&D. The specific benefits of R&D are:

- It helps businesses to invent new products and thus achieve a distinctive competence and unique selling point.
- Unique ideas can be patented and therefore companies investing in R&D usually benefit as they can have a monopoly of a product for 20 years. After 20 years, other companies are allowed to produce similar, 'generic' products.
- New inventions and patents help businesses to achieve on a large scale. Consequently they can benefit from economies of scale and achieve lower unit costs than their competitors, even after the patent has expired.
- R&D that improves production processes can lead to higher profit margins because it lowers costs.
- R&D can improve the durability and reliability of a product and also enhance its appearance, all of which will contribute to higher sales.
- The creative nature of R&D can excite and motivate the workforce, and therefore improve the efficiency of a business's human resources.

Fact file

R&D for tea

Even the humble cup of tea is subject to rigorous research. Unilever, producer of PG Tips, undertook R&D to establish the ideal shape a teabag should be to give a great cup of tea. This R&D project, which took 4 years to complete, led to the introduction of the pyramid teabag.

Unilever is the world's biggest tea company. It carries out research at its R&D Centre of Excellence for Drinks at the Colworth Science Park in the UK.

Unilever's successful R&D activities have supported the rise of Lipton to become the world's number one tea brand and PG tips to become the UK's number one tea brand.

Other drinks innovations resulting from its R&D activities include:

- Ready-To-Drink teas
- tea products for slimmers
- natural leaf tea that brews in cold water, so that consumers can make fresh ice tea without having to wait hours for it to cool down
- Flora cholesterol-lowering milk and yoghurt drinks
- Knorr Vie fruit and vegetable mini-drinks, and
- the soy-based fruit juice Adez.

Source: adapted from website www.unilever.com

Fact file

R&D spending in the UK and overseas

Some 40 per cent of R&D in the UK is undertaken by the pharmaceutical and biotech sectors. However, in recent years a major increase in R&D has taken place in computer software.

Overall, the UK still lags behind other countries in terms of R&D spending.

▼ **Table 12.3** Spending on R&D as a percentage of GDP

Country	2000	2006	2012
South Korea	2.3	3.0	4.4
Finland	3.4	3.4	3.5
Japan	3.0	3.4	3.3
Germany	2.5	2.5	2.9
USA	2.6	2.5	2.7
France	2.2	2.1	2.3
China	0.9	1.4	2.0
UK	1.8	1.7	1.7
Russia	1.1	1.0	1.1

Source: BIS

Low investment in R&D also applies to the UK's major firms, which invest less than 2 per cent of their sales revenue in R&D, compared with 5 per cent for similar firms in the USA.

▼ **Table 12.4** Annual R&D spending by companies, 2014

UK top 5	R&D spending (£bn)	International top five	R&D spending (£bn)
GSK	6.1	Volkswagen	13.5
AstraZeneca	4.8	Samsung	13.4
BAE Systems	1.2	Intel	10.6
BT	1.1	Microsoft	10.4
Unilever	0.9	Roche	10.0

Source: Company reports, www.themanufacturer.com and www.fortune.com, November 2014

Fact file

UK pharmaceuticals

The pharmaceutical industry is an exception to the rule that UK firms spend little on R&D. The three major UK businesses that spend the highest percentage of their sales revenue on R&D are all pharmaceutical companies. Ironically, although GSK and AstraZeneca are the UK's two biggest R&D spenders, their smaller rival – Shire plc – is the large UK company that spends the highest percentage of its sales on R&D.

GSK's £6.1 billion of R&D spending is 15.2 per cent of its sales revenue. AstraZeneca spends 18.6 per cent of its revenue on R&D. In first place is Shire plc, with 20.6 per cent of its sales revenue spent on R&D.

Key term

Intrapreneurship Acting like an entrepreneur within a large organisation.

Intrapreneurship

Successful entrepreneurs usually possess characteristics such as creative ability and a willingness to take the initiative and take risks. **Intrapreneurship** occurs when a large business encourages its employees to demonstrate these traits within the working environment. The major difference between entrepreneurship and intrapreneurship is that the rewards from intrapreneurship tend to go to the business, rather than the intrapreneur. However, the entrepreneur, who is usually the founder of the innovative business and the major shareholder, is likely to be rewarded for successful innovation and, in some businesses, can gain high rewards.

The term 'intrapreneurship' is credited to Steve Jobs of Apple. In an article in 1985 he stated: 'the Macintosh team was what is commonly known as intrapreneurship … a group of people going, in essence, back to the garage, but in a large company'.

Some very large businesses tend to develop bureaucracies, where rules, systems, procedures and hierarchies become very important. Bureaucratic businesses can be very results-driven and therefore tend to reward safe decisions rather than risky decisions that might lead to significant losses. To encourage intrapreneurship requires a particular culture and approach within a large business.

Some of the necessary requirements for successful intrapreneurship are:

● **Support from senior managers**. This can range from mentoring and training of intrapreneurs to the allocation of specific resources for intrapreneurial activity. In many businesses time will be set aside for intrapreneurship.
● **Excellent two-way communication**. There must be the ability for intrapreneurs to express their ideas to senior managers, and senior managers to indicate possible lines of activity to intrapreneurs.
● **An innovative working environment**. A business needs to ensure that there is an atmosphere of creativity and support for people with new ideas and innovations.
● **Rewards**. It is vital that successful intrapreneurship is linked to rewards. These rewards might be in the form of recognition and promotion prospects as well as financial rewards. Financial pressures, such as the need to repay student loans, can make it difficult for many young creative employees to set up their own enterprises. Consequently, a large firm may provide a secure environment within which they can flourish. However, a failure to reward their creativity is likely to lead to high labour turnover among young creative staff. It is vital that firms try to keep their creative talent.
● **Ownership of projects**. Employees with innovative ideas should be allowed to see them through to their natural conclusion. Not only will this maintain their motivation and commitment, but also, by giving them a sense of ownership, their ideas may lead to greater success for the business.

Intrapreneurship is credited with a number of significant product innovations. 3M developed post-it notes, and the 'like' button on Facebook originated from intrapreneurship. Google encouraged intrapreneurship through its '20 per cent time', which gave employees one day a week to devote to any ideas that they wished to pursue. Google's programme of intrapreneurship is directly linked to the introduction of some of its products – notably Google News, AdSense and Gmail. However, since 2011 stricter controls have been introduced at Google and employees can only work on innovative projects if they are approved by managers. LinkedIn allows employees to suggest one innovative idea every three months. They can then get a development team together and present their idea to the senior managers. Teams whose ideas are approved are allowed a further three months to turn the idea into a product or change that will benefit the business.

Sir Richard Branson is a big fan too: 'Virgin could never have grown into the group of more than 200 companies it is now, were it not for a steady stream of intrapreneurs who looked for and developed opportunities, often leading efforts that went against the grain. Perhaps the greatest thing about intrapreneurship is that often everyone becomes so immersed in what they're doing that they feel like they own their companies.'

> **Fact file**
>
> *W.L. Gore*
>
> W.L. Gore, the manufacturer of Gore-tex waterproof fabrics, allow their employees 10 per cent 'dabble time' for their own projects. An employee, Dave Myers, identified that one of their products could make the use of guitar strings more comfortable. This was only marginally the case, but unexpectedly the product enabled the strings to retain their tone for much longer than conventional guitar strings. W.L. Gore launched the product under the brand name 'Elixir' strings. It is now the number one selling acoustic guitar string.

Benchmarking

The benchmarking process

The **benchmarking** process involves the following stages:

1. Select the processes and/or activities to be benchmarked.
2. Identify the firm that is best in class, against which to benchmark.
3. Gather data from both firms and analyse any performance gaps.
4. Establish reasons for these gaps and set targets for improvement.
5. Agree and implement new strategies and review the results.
6. Continue the process. Benchmarking should be seen as a never-ending process.

Benefits of using benchmarking to enhance innovation

- A firm can gauge what it is possible to achieve and compare this to its own level of performance. This process will help the firm to recognise how much potential for greater innovation exists.
- Data from other firms can provide ideas and inspiration to help a firm to improve the quality and efficiency of its innovation. Often, these ideas can be applied to many areas of a firm, besides the one involved in the original comparisons.
- It can identify areas of a firm that are not keeping pace with innovation in competitors. This will enable it to pay more attention to improving areas of the firm that are restricting innovation.
- Cost advantages achieved through process innovation, and thus more efficient methods and reduced wastage, can improve a firm's competitiveness.

Although these benefits can be achieved through other methods, the main benefit of benchmarking is that it tends to highlight areas that need improving and may indicate how improvements might be made.

> **Key term**
>
> **Benchmarking** The process of setting competitive standards, based on the achievements of other firms, against which a firm will monitor its progress. The benchmarking firm tends to focus on the companies that are best in its industry ('best in class'), but for specific functions a company may compare itself with firms in other industries.

Possible reasons why benchmarking may not lead to innovation

- It may encourage a firm to just copy ideas from other firms. This will be counterproductive because the firm will not be innovating in the true sense of the word. Its achievements are unlikely to match those of the firm that originally developed the innovation.
- It may not be possible to introduce an innovation that has been successful in another firm, especially as the firm with the innovative idea may have protected it from being copied by taking out a patent or gaining copyright.
- There may be a lack of belief by staff, who may be demoralised by the challenge of achieving a level of innovation that they consider to be unrealistic. Targets for innovation should be agreed and not just based on those achieved by the best competitor.
- There can be difficulties in gathering reliable information – in particular, other firms may be reluctant to share their data. Benchmarking is more likely to succeed if firms share each other's data, but innovative firms are likely to be very secretive.

Internal benchmarking

It is not necessary for benchmarking to involve comparisons with outside firms. Because of the limited competition in its market, National Express Coaches decided to benchmark itself against one of its own subsidiaries – the rail company c2c. c2c achieved the highest punctuality record among train operating companies and scored highly in customer satisfaction surveys. These results coincided with growing demand. The lessons learned have helped National Express to record increased customer satisfaction in many other areas of its operations in recent years.

What do you think?

Benchmarking is used in many aspects of business performance. In this chapter it is used to compare levels of innovation with other companies. However, it can be used in any aspect of business management. Areas in which the use of benchmarking is commonplace are: quality, financial management, motivation of staff and operations procedures.

Many people believe that benchmarking is not a good way of encouraging innovation. This view is based on the belief that by encouraging comparisons with existing activities, business will be less likely to develop brand new, innovative ideas. Genuine innovation may make comparison impossible.

Is benchmarking a help or a hindrance to innovation? What do you think?

How to improve the chances of successful innovation

In addition to the ways of becoming innovative explained above (i.e. Kaizen, R&D, etc.) a business can improve its chances of successful innovation by taking the following actions:

- **Protection**. Make sure that any results are protected as soon as possible and in as many countries as possible through the use of copyrights, trademarks and patents. This protection will give the firm sole ownership of the idea and will also give it time to refine the product. This topic will be dealt with in more detail later in this chapter.

- **Early planning**. Plan projects early rather than late. A business should be aware of its existing products, particularly those that are approaching (but not yet in) the decline stage of their life cycles. At this point, the business should undertake innovation so that it always has a product in the maturity stage of the product life cycle.
- **Developing a supportive culture**. Create a business culture that is supportive of innovation and encourages all employees to use their initiative. Quality circles are a classic Japanese approach to innovation, encouraging lots of small changes rather than relying on a major discovery. This culture must include the management of finance. In times of difficulty, innovation is often the first area of spending to be cut because of the uncertainty of returns. However, successful innovation can be the ideal way to overcome problems.
- **Maintaining secrecy**. Attempt to maintain high levels of secrecy so that ideas cannot be copied. This will often involve signing confidentiality agreements with suppliers and other business partners.
- **Remembering the consumer**. Pay careful attention to the attractiveness of the idea to consumers. Many inventions have not been developed further by their inventors because they did not recognise the potential or were unable to persuade consumers to buy the product.

How to protect innovation and intellectual property

Key term

Intellectual property Any intangible assets that arise from human knowledge and ideas.

Intellectual property includes the business's name, logo, designs and inventions. All businesses have some form of intellectual property, which is likely to be a valuable asset that can:

- set the business apart from competitors
- be sold or licensed, forming an important source of income
- offer customers something new and different
- form an essential part of marketing or branding.

Intellectual property tends to arise from innovation. Innovation is more likely to benefit an organisation if competitors cannot copy the ideas generated through the innovation process. 'Protection' of these ideas can be achieved primarily through **patents** and **copyrights**. Innovation that arises through marketing and brand image may be protected by **trademark**.

Key term

Patent An official document granting the holder the right to be the only user or producer of a newly invented product or process for a specified period.

Patents

If an individual invents a new process, piece of equipment, component or product, he or she may apply for a patent in order to prevent other people copying the invention and then making, selling, importing or using it without permission. To register a patent, the inventor must provide full drawings of the invention for the UK Intellectual Property Office (UK-IPO), demonstrate that the ideas have original features, and promise that the ideas are his or her own. The Copyright, Designs and Patents Act 1988 gives patent holders the monopoly right to use, make, license or sell the invention for up to 20 years after it has been registered.

The following issues need to be considered in relation to patenting an idea:

- Holding a patent allows the product or process to be developed further, to be positioned in the market, and to reap benefits in terms of revenue and profits.

- Having a patent means that the invention becomes the property of the inventor, which means that it can be bought, sold, rented or licensed – and can therefore be a useful bargaining tool when trying to persuade manufacturers and investors to help the business.
- Purchasing a small business that has an existing patent might be an attractive proposition for a large business, simply in order to obtain the patent.
- Although a patent can be a valuable asset for a business, taking a patent application through to completion can be a complex and expensive process. As a result, the cost of effectively developing and launching a product for which a patent is held may be too high for a small business and the business may sell the patent. Although the initial costs of filing an application for a patent are low, the process takes a long time, and where disputes are involved the cost of hiring the services of a patent agent can be expensive. Moreover, if a business is planning to sell its product abroad, the cost will be much higher because patent protection may need to be applied for in a number of other countries. Once granted, renewal fees must be paid to renew the patent every year after the fifth year for up to 20 years' protection.
- Although a patent grants the inventor rights that can be valuable, there is no agency for enforcing patents. Therefore, the holder has to be willing to take those who infringe the patent to court (see the Fact file on *Dyson* v. *Hoover*). An individual inventor is unlikely to be able to afford the legal costs and hence new patents are often sold on to larger businesses.

Fact file

Samsung's patents

Patents can be a major influence on a firm's competitiveness. Companies apply for patents on many products and processes and it can be difficult to establish where a specific idea or design originated. In the four weeks ending 12 March 2015, Samsung was granted 852 patents by the US Patent Office. Each year they expect to gain 8,000 patents in the USA alone.

There has been a series of high-profile law suits between Apple and Samsung in recent years, with both companies claiming that the other has infringed some of its patents. In 2012 a court in California awarded damages of $1 billion to Apple arising from a ruling that Samsung had infringed six of its patents. Samsung has countered by arguing that Apple has infringed some of *its* patents.

The growing number and complexity of patents has led to courts facing difficulties in enforcing patent laws.

Fact file

Dyson v. Hoover

In 2000, the inventor who sparked the vacuum cleaner wars with his revolutionary bagless machine won a multimillion-pound court battle against Hoover and its Vortex 'triple cyclone' machine. Hoover was found guilty of stealing ideas from James Dyson and of infringing the patent on bagless cleaners. Dyson claimed that it was a blatant copy of the cleaner he had spent 20 years developing. After the judgment in his favour was made, Dyson said: 'I spent 20 years developing the technology and I am very pleased to see Hoover, who made a lot of false claims about their product, have been found guilty of patent infringement.

I am also pleased on behalf of other small businesses and inventors, who should be encouraged to take out patents by the result of this case.'

However, in October 2011, Dyson lost a legal battle with Vax over the design of the Vax Mach Zen, which he claimed they had copied from Dyson's first bagless vacuum cleaner. In a statement, James Dyson accused Vax of 'cashing in' on Dyson's success. He said: 'We've invested decades, not to mention millions, in creating better technology. And sadly we waste millions more in cases like this. We need to better protect British design.'

Source: adapted from articles in *The Times*, October 2000 and *Which?*, October 2011

Fact file

Virgin v. Contour

In the cut-throat battle for business-class airline passengers, any competitive advantage is jealously guarded – even the shape of the seats. Virgin Atlantic started legal proceedings in 2007 to protect the design of its Upper Class seat after competitors started to roll out suspiciously similar seats. Sir Richard Branson's airline sued Contour (now Zodiac), a Wales-based seat manufacturer, for breach of patents. Virgin spent £50 million developing the herringbone shape and layout for its Upper Class seat, based on an idea put forward by one of Virgin's intrapreneurs – a young designer named Joe Ferry.

Business-class tickets (Upper Class seats, in the case of Virgin), which generate most of an airline's profits, are sold on features such as the flattest bed and best in-flight entertainment. The largest airlines develop their own seats in order to have a unique sales proposition. Virgin had two patents covering the shape and configuration of the seats and the technology used to lower the seat into a bed. Contour built Virgin's seats and also supplied herringbone-shaped seats to Delta, Cathay Pacific, Air Canada and JetAir.

The battle between Virgin and Contour was finally resolved in July 2013. Diagrams pre-dating Virgin's patent were discovered that suggested that Contour may have come up with the same design independently and before the Virgin patent was finalised. Virgin had asked for damages of £49 million, but the Supreme Court ruled in favour of Contour, arguing that these diagrams invalidated the patent.

Source: adapted from Robertson, D. (2007) 'Airliners in the hot seat over Virgin's Upper Class patents'; *WIPR*, July 2013

Key term

Copyright Legal protection against copying for authors, composers and artists.

Author advice

Think of patents and copyright as barriers to entry: that is strategic tools that protect businesses from possible competitors entering the market.

Copyright

If a business creates or employs someone to create an original piece of literary, dramatic, musical or artistic work, it automatically holds the **copyright** on the work. The material could range from books, information leaflets and films, to computer programs and sound recordings. The material cannot then be copied without permission from the owner of the copyright. The law allows the owners of the copyright to decide whether it can be copied and adapted, and allows them to charge a royalty or licence fee.

Copyright protection for literary, dramatic, musical and artistic works, including sound recordings, lasts until 70 years after the death of the creator. Unlike patents, there is no requirement to register an author's copyright. The law on copyright is governed by the Copyright, Designs and Patents Act 1988. Copyright is indicated by the symbol ©.

Fact file

Changes to laws on digital copying

In October 2014, legislation was introduced allowing UK residents to copy digital items, such as music, e-books and DVDs. However, people are not allowed to sell the original version if they have taken and stored a copy.

The government argued that this change would bring greater flexibility and accessibility to the use of creative works. It also brought the UK into line with many other European countries. However, authors, musicians and songwriters contested this view, arguing that it would damage creativity if they did not benefit financially. In other European countries there is a tax on items such as blank DVDs and media players. The revenue received from this tax is used to compensate producers of digital materials.

The UK government argued that the financial effect on composers and singers would be negligible. This new law was challenged by the Musicians' Union, UK Music, and the British Academy of Songwriters, Composers and Authors. They estimated that the new law would lead to a loss of income of £58 million a year for people in the creative sector of the economy.

In July 2015, this challenge was considered by the High Court which ruled that the government was legally incorrect when failing to introduce compensation for lost earnings for songwriters, composers and authors.

Key term

Trademark Signs, logos, symbols or words displayed on a company's products or on its advertising, including sounds or music, which distinguish its brands from those of its competitors.

Trademarks

Trademarks can be powerful marketing tools, helping customers to recognise the products of a business, and distinguishing them from those of competitors. In order to prevent rivals from copying a symbol or style of wording, the trademark must be registered at the UK Intellectual Property office (or UK-IPO). Once the trademark has been registered, the company has exclusive rights to its use. Trademarks are indicated by the symbol ®.

Did you know?

The phrase 'Have a break, have a KitKat' was first used in a television advert in 1957. Despite the popularity of the slogan, Nestlé, the chocolate bar's Swiss maker, was refused a trademark for it in May 2002. The case then went to the High Court, where it was decided that the slogan 'Have a break' on its own was not distinctive enough. The High Court therefore decided that Nestlé could not claim that it owned the phrase. This meant that Nestlé's rival, Mars, was free to begin a confectionery war by launching its own new product called 'Have a Break'.

However, Nestlé has won a trademark battle against Cadbury and succeeded in stopping rivals from copying the shape of the four-fingered chocolate bar. The four-fingered shape of KitKat, which was created in 1935, was registered as a trademark by Nestlé in 2006. Cadbury appealed unsuccessfully against the application.

Source: adapted from an article in *Metro*, December 2002 and *Mail* Online, March 2013

The impact of an innovation strategy on the functional areas of the business

Innovation is organised in different ways in different businesses. In general, process innovation is the responsibility of the operations department, as it is their job to produce goods and services cost-effectively. However, product innovation may arise from the operations department identifying new product opportunities (product-led innovation) or it may arise from the marketing department's understanding of changes in consumer tastes (market-led innovation). Because of its strategic significance, the driving force behind innovation is very often the senior management team of the business, rather than the functional areas. However, an innovation strategy will have a significant impact on each of the four functional areas. This impact is described below.

Finance

Innovation tends to be an expensive undertaking. For this reason the finance department must be aware of, and in agreement with, any plans for new innovation. It is almost certain that new sources of finance will be needed to support the innovation process.

The finance department will carry out investment appraisals in order to assess the likely results of innovation. If an innovation or R&D project is approved by the finance department, there are still major repercussions for cash flow. In some industries, such as motor vehicles and pharmaceuticals, it can take as much as eight years of innovation before a product is launched. However, these returns can be very impressive. In 2014 Shire plc, a pharmaceutical company, achieved an operating profit from its normal activities of $1.7 billion from sales of $6 billion because many of its products are protected by patents.

Marketing

In the case of product innovation, the marketing department will be affected in two ways. First, market research will be needed to ascertain whether the innovation project is likely to appeal to customers. Second, innovation is often linked to the product life cycle, so the operations and marketing functions must co-operate. The experience of these two functional areas will help a firm to ascertain the normal time that it takes to modify a product or develop and release a new one. With this information, firms can plan the timing of extension strategies and new product launches.

Figure 12.2 shows the link between R&D and extension strategies. The company forecasts that, at point A, sales of its existing product will reach the decline stage of the product life cycle. The dotted line AB shows the

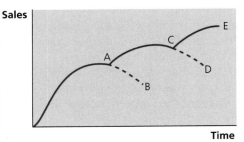

Sales

Time

▲ **Figure 12.2** R&D and product life cycle extension

forecast sales of the original product. Careful timing of an R&D programme will allow the firm to create a modified version of the product that will revitalise sales, keeping the product in the maturity stage. The line AC shows the sales of the modified product.

Again, at C a further modification is introduced in order to prevent sales falling (as shown by the line CD). This modification again prolongs the maturity stage of the product life cycle, allowing sales to grow from C to E.

Human resource management

Typically, the role of HRM in the innovation process has been to recruit and train suitable employees and then to ensure that the business retains their services. Successful innovation can also lead to the growth of a business and this may require additional recruitment and training. In its workforce planning, the HR department must ensure that the impact of innovation and research and development are taken into consideration.

Recently, much greater emphasis has been placed on the creative aspects of the innovation process, focusing on activities such as restructuring the organisation, instilling a corporate culture that supports innovation and creativity, introducing greater flexibility, and changing processes as well as the goods and services provided.

These changes require much greater involvement from HRM, in providing training and creating more autonomy within the workforce so that ideas for change can be provided by the workforce itself. If a business is using intrapreneurship to encourage innovation, then the responsibility for changing the business's culture is likely to fall on business leaders and the human resource management division. The HR department will need to organise training to develop intrapreneurship skills across the workforce and develop appropriate reward systems.

Operations

In most cases operations management will be the department most affected by a business's innovation strategy. Product-led innovation will be planned by the operations management division of the business and any R&D activities are likely to be a part of operations management. Investigating the feasibility of putting new ideas into practice will also be undertaken by operations management, as they would need to ascertain whether the business is physically capable of producing any new, innovative goods.

Process innovation will also be centred on operations management, because it is their responsibility to improve the efficiency of production methods. The operations management department will need to work closely with finance to enable the business to discover whether an innovation is likely to bring financial success.

The different ways of becoming innovative tend to be within the remit of operations management. Kaizen activities tend to be the responsibility of operations management, working alongside human resource management. R&D activities are often a part of the overall production/operations department, even where the original ideas for R&D are generated elsewhere within the business. Finally, benchmarking activities are also usually led by operations management, as they tend be centred on production of the good or service.

Practice exercise 1

Total: 75 marks

1. Innovating by comparing your approach to that of other companies is an example of:
   a) benchmarking
   b) intrapreneurship
   c) kaizen
   d) research and development. *(1 mark)*

2. The idea of 'continuous improvement' is most closely associated with:
   a) benchmarking
   b) intrapreneurship
   c) kaizen
   d) research and development. *(1 mark)*

3. The successful outcome of scientific research and development will usually be protected by:
   a) copyright
   b) intellectual property
   c) patent
   d) trademark. *(1 mark)*

4. What is meant by the term 'intrapreneurship'? *(3 marks)*

5. What is meant by the term 'intellectual property? *(3 marks)*

6. Explain one problem with using benchmarking as a way of achieving innovation. *(5 marks)*

7. What is the difference between product innovation and process innovation? *(5 marks)*

8. Distinguish between the terms 'innovation' and 'research and development'. *(6 marks)*

9. Explain how a business might use 'kaizen' to help it to innovate. *(6 marks)*

10. Analyse the benefits of innovation for a car manufacturer, such as Ford. *(9 marks)*

11. Analyse the problems that a car manufacturer, such as Ford, might experience in its innovation. *(9 marks)*

12. Analyse how a business might benefit from patents or copyright. *(9 marks)*

13. Explain two problems that might occur if innovation is not linked to other functional areas of the business. *(8 marks)*

14. Analyse how an innovation strategy would impact on the human resource function of the business. *(9 marks)*

Case study 1: Small business innovation: Martek Marine Ltd

Martek is a world leader in providing marine safety and environmental monitoring systems, most notably an engine efficiency optimisation system that allows ship owners to make significant fuel savings and reduce vessel downtime. It was established in 2000 with £6,000 capital. In 2015 it achieved its 20:15 target, that is the ratio of a 20 per cent profit on a turnover of £15 million a year.

▶▶▶

The challenge for Martek was to improve its human and technical support, as the market required 24-hour service throughout the world. The solution was based on communications technology – the company adopted a teleworking strategy with staff being provided with access to the company's communication network from home. Offices were also opened in the USA and in Singapore, eight hours behind and eight hours ahead of Greenwich Mean Time respectively. This enabled Martek to provide a 24-hour service effectively.

Another key element was the human resource strategy – Martek needed to recruit, train and encourage the right staff to work in a dynamic and empowered working environment. Martek's focus on technology and the achievement of work–life balance (staff in all three offices work, in effect, from nine to five in their respective countries) has paid dividends in terms of staff retention, which is almost 100 per cent. The CEO, Paul Luen, believes that the single biggest indicator of the success of its approach is its labour productivity – its 47 workers achieve an annual sales turnover of £15 million.

Questions

Total: 30 marks

1. Calculate the average labour productivity at Martek Marine Ltd, based on its annual sales revenue. *(3 marks)*

2. Calculate Martek Marine's profit for 2015. *(2 marks)*

3. Analyse the ways in which technology has assisted innovation at Martek Marine Ltd. *(9 marks)*

4. To what extent does Martek's success show the importance of integrating R&D with the other functional areas of the business, such as marketing, finance and HRM? *(16 marks)*

Case study 2: Innovation through research and development at AstraZeneca

AstraZeneca is one of the world's leading pharmaceutical companies and the UK's second biggest spender on research and development.

The company's R&D takes place in eight countries, but is mainly concentrated in Sweden, the UK and the USA. Its employee base is worldwide with over 57,000 employees (35 per cent in Europe, 30 per cent in the Americas and 35 per cent in the rest of the world, mainly in Asia). Production takes place in 16 different countries.

In the 'noughties' AstraZeneca faced a 'patent cliff'– a period in which many patents were expiring. AstraZeneca's reaction was to increase its R&D efforts even more (its R&D spending has grown by 140 per cent in the last seven years). It also took over some smaller pharmaceutical companies with expertise in its target areas, and a 'generic' drugs company in China which specialises in producing cheap 'generic' drugs, based on patents that have expired. In this way it can reclaim some of the sales lost by the expiry of its patents. As a result of these changes, the number of drugs under development (in the 'pipeline') has grown steadily and stands at 133 different drugs at present (2015).

However, although AstraZeneca's success rates are above average for pharmaceutical firms, not all of these drugs will become government-approved treatments. In 2014, 33 of the company's pipeline drugs are in the final stages of completion, but 9 projects were discontinued.

People are naturally cautious about new drugs, so pharmaceutical companies face greater risks than firms in other industries. However, these risks can be offset by successes, although the nature of successes in this industry is that they become the high-risk products when patents expire. Crestor, its cardiovascular treatment, is a world-leading drug and provides sales of over £5.5 billion a year. Currently, it accounts for 21 per cent of AstraZeneca's sales revenue. Unfortunately, AstraZeneca faces another 'patent cliff' because patents on Crestor are expiring over the next five years (AstraZeneca organises its patents on a particular product between different countries so that they do not all expire at the same time).

One consolation is that drugs companies can plan ahead. The Crestor manufacturing plant in Bristol is due to close in late 2016 or early 2017. However, this

➤➤➤

decision was made in 2008 and the company plans to relocate staff to other plants, where possible.

AstraZeneca's strategic plan to offset the forecast loss of sales arising from the loss of patents on Crestor, and some other drugs, consists of a number of elements:

- It has identified three treatments that offer growth opportunities. These are Brilinta (a treatment for heart attacks and angina); and treatments for diabetes and respiratory problems.
- It has targeted two markets for growth – emerging markets and Japan.
- It has identified oncology (cancer treatment) as an area of expertise to be developed.

	Sales revenue: 2014	Growth (%)
Brilinta	$476m	70
Diabetes	$1,870m	139
Respiratory	$5,063m	10
Emerging markets	$5,827m	12
Japan	$2,227m	(3)*
Oncology emerging as sixth growth platform		

Growth rates at constant exchange rate (CER)
*Including impact from mandated price cuts

▲ **Figure 12.3** AstraZeneca's growth platforms

It can be seen that Brilinta and the treatment for diabetes have provided very high levels of growth in 2014. Respiratory drug growth is also contributing well, especially as the scale of this area of treatment means sales growth in excess of $500 million in one year. Emerging markets are also growing well, but sales in Japan have fallen. The success of the 'Oncology' platform will depend on the success of the company's R&D.

Sources: AstraZeneca website and an article by Dan Stanton in www.inPharmaTechnologist.com, 8 December 2014

Questions

Total: 50 marks

1. Analyse two types of risk that AstraZeneca might experience through its R&D activities. *(9 marks)*

2. Examine the reasons why a company such as AstraZeneca focuses most of its research and development in 3 countries and yet has production bases in 16 different countries. *(9 marks)*

3. Analyse the reasons why a drugs company such as AstraZeneca is more likely to use R&D rather than other ways of innovation, such as kaizen, intrapreneurship and benchmarking. *(12 marks)*

4. On the basis of the evidence provided, evaluate whether AstraZeneca has benefited from its decision to put more resources into research and development (R&D) in the twenty-first century. *(20 marks)*

13 Assessing internationalisation

This chapter begins by considering the reasons for targeting, operating in and trading with international markets. The factors influencing the attractiveness of international markets are identified. The reasons for producing more, and sourcing more, resources abroad are then considered, decisions about which include off-shoring and re-shoring. The chapter then discusses ways of entering international markets and the value of the different methods that can be used. Methods considered include: export, licencing, alliances and direct investment; targeting overseas markets by becoming a multinational is also discussed. Influences on buying, selling and producing abroad are identified. Managing international business is then discussed, including pressures for local responsiveness and for cost reduction. This section includes an explanation of Bartlett and Ghoshal's international, multi-domestic, transnational and global strategies. The chapter concludes with a discussion of the impact of internationalisation on the functional areas of the business.

Reasons for targeting, operating in and trading with international markets

Author advice

The final section of Chapter 5 discusses the reasons for greater globalisation of business and the importance of globalisation and emerging economies for business. Ensure your knowledge of these issues is secure before proceeding with this chapter.

Key term

International markets Geographically, markets outside the international borders of a company's home country; the opposite of an international market is a domestic market, which is the geographic region within the national boundary of a company's home country.

Targeting, operating in and trading with **international markets** are essentially the different ways in which a particular business might participate in such markets. For example:

- If wishing to sell its products abroad, it will need to target, or decide to focus on, particular countries' markets or segments of those markets.

- It may wish to operate in international markets by having physical bases in those countries, whether in the form of offices, factories or retail outlets.
- It may trade with other countries by selling its products abroad and/or by purchasing supplies from abroad.

Increasingly companies are choosing, or are being forced by market conditions, to sell their products in international markets rather than just their domestic markets. The boundary between a company's domestic market and its international markets is getting blurred because the internet and online buying mean easy access to a worldwide market for both consumers and producers. As the global economy becomes more interrelated, many companies have recognised that international opportunities can make the difference between success and failure. In addition, reductions in trading barriers in the European Union and internationally, and the opening up of extensive markets, for example, in Eastern Europe, India and China, have increased competition in world markets and therefore have increased the need for UK firms to be internationally competitive.

Did you know?

'The world is getting smaller', McCarthy and Perreault say in their book, *Basic Marketing* (1990). They go on to say, 'Advances in communications and transportation are making it easier to reach international customers ... Around the world there are potential customers with needs and money to spend. Ignoring those customers doesn't make any more sense than ignoring potential customers in the same town.'

Some reasons for targeting, operating in or trading with international markets are strategic in nature, while others are more reactive. Examples of strategic motives include to take advantage of opportunities in emerging markets or to acquire new knowledge. Examples of more reactive motives include the need to supply a large established customer that has itself expanded abroad, or sales that result from unsolicited orders from consumers abroad.

Reasons for targeting, operating in and trading with international markets are identified and explained below.

1. **Avoiding the risks of operating in a single market**. Although moving into an international market can be seen as a risky proposition, it may also reduce a firm's dependence on a single market. There is potential that a business operation might fail if a firm is completely dependent on a market in a single country as negative events in that country could ruin the firm. For example, the earthquake and tsunami that hit Japan in 2011 could have had much more significant financial effects on Japanese car manufacturers such as Toyota, Nissan and Honda if the only markets for their cars had been their home country. Because these firms operate in many countries, they were not dependent on the Japanese market and therefore were protected from being ruined by the natural disaster in Japan. Companies may decide to target international markets to reduce their exposure to potential economic and political instability within one particular country. For example, if a severe recession occurs in one market, a business operating in a number of different

international markets is likely to be able to balance such a downturn with more positive economic conditions in another international market. By expanding into other international markets, businesses are less vulnerable and less dependent on their domestic markets and any intense competition that might be present in these markets.

Just as the Boston Matrix (discussed in Chapter 10 of the AQA A-level Business Book 1) indicates the need for a range of products at different stages of their market development, so a company considering targeting international markets will need to ensure these markets are in different stages of development for the company to remain profitable over time.

Fact file

The tobacco industry

The tobacco industry includes some of the largest and most powerful multinational companies in the world. These include the American cigarette company, Philip Morris, and the British company, British American Tobacco (BAT). Tobacco use in America and in Western Europe is declining as more laws are passed that ban smoking in public areas and in restaurants, and as people become more aware of the risks of lung cancer. In response, since the early 1990s, cigarette makers have attempted to increase their operations within countries where smoking remains popular in order to remain profitable over time. For example, in 2006 Philip Morris purchased a controlling interest in an Indonesian cigarette maker. Taking advantage of opportunities in Indonesia was attractive because nearly two-thirds of men (in its population of about 230 million at the time) were smokers, and smoking among women was on the rise. Similarly, BAT adopted a policy of market development to deal with the decline in UK demand for tobacco products. In 2013, it set up a joint venture with the world's largest tobacco company, China National Tobacco Corporation (CNTC), both to help it access the Chinese market and to provide a Chinese manufacturing base.

2. **Taking advantage of economies of scale and the experience curve effects**. By producing and selling on a much larger scale, a business is able to reap the benefits of economies of scale and thus reduce its average costs of production and increase its profit margins. (Economies of scale were discussed in Chapter 13 of Book 1 and also in Chapter 11 of this book.) Countries with large domestic markets, such as China and India – each with populations in excess of 1 billion people – provide their industries with great potential growth opportunities. This enables companies in these countries to achieve greater economies of scale, which in turn allows them to lower their unit costs and improve their competitiveness. A UK firm trying to match these economies of scale will need to enter international markets in order to produce on an equally large scale and lower its unit costs. For example, Samsung is a South Korean company that has been able to achieve massive economies of scale by becoming a worldwide brand.

By producing for a huge international market, experience curve effects (explained in Chapter 11) are likely to be realised more quickly, thus helping to reduce costs further.

3. **Boosting profitability**. Profitability might increase because of cost advantages other than economies of scale. Many firms operate in international markets in order to achieve cost reductions. Western economies, in particular, can benefit from much lower wage and land costs by relocating to countries in Eastern Europe or Asian countries such as China and India. Over 60 per cent of UK businesses that move abroad indicate that cost reduction is the main motivate for relocating internationally. Dyson's move to Malaysia, where production costs were reported to be 30 per cent lower, is an example of this.

a) Profitability might increase because of price advantages in international markets. A company's products may be more profitable abroad because of the nature of a particular overseas market. For example, car prices in the UK have traditionally been higher than those in most of Europe. This market feature has encouraged Japanese car manufacturers to target the UK car market in order to boost their profitability.

b) Profitability might increase because of operational advantages in international markets. A business may wish to enter international markets in order to be closer to supply sources, or to gain flexibility in the sourcing of its products.

c) Profitability might increase because of the ability to exploit marketing advantages across international markets. A company may target international markets in order to exploit a distinctive asset such as a brand or a patented product. The Fact files on McDonald's and Crocs later in this chapter provide examples of the successful exploitation of brands in international markets.

d) Profitability might increase because there is greater opportunity to exploit the advantages of patents. Companies in the pharmaceutical industry are good examples of the exploitation of patented products. Such companies usually spend years developing patented drugs and require huge international markets in order to recover research and development costs and make profit.

4. **Competing against international firms in order to safeguard domestic markets**. Even if a company decides to concentrate on its domestic market, it is unlikely to be able to pursue its objectives unhindered. The ability of a business to compete successfully in its domestic markets is likely to depend upon its ability to match the resources and competences of other international companies that are likely to be competing for market share in its domestic market. As a result, a company may have no choice but to enter international markets in order to maintain its market share and profitability.

5. **Increasing market share and achieving business growth**. Increasing market share enables a business to increase its scale and reap the benefits of economies of scale, economies of scope and the experience curve effects (each of which is discussed in Chapter 11). The UK domestic market is relatively large compared to most countries, but very small compared to the largest international markets, as indicated in Table 13.1. With a population of about 65 million, many UK firms have been able to produce on a large scale, achieving substantial economies of scale, just by focusing on the domestic market. However, many businesses find that it becomes difficult to sustain growth in

What do you think?

Small- and medium-sized enterprises (SMEs) involved in internationalisation tend to do better than those not involved. However, research about the reasons for this is inconclusive. Some research suggests that internationalisation may encourage improved business performance because international SMEs transfer best practice developed internationally to their overall business. Other research suggests that SMEs that expand internationally are more likely to be ambitious and more likely to take advantage of opportunities abroad.

Why do you think international SMEs are likely to be more successful than other SMEs?

Fact file

P&G and Unilever

Both Proctor and Gamble (P&G) and Unilever set themselves ambitious goals in 2010. P&G's was to add one billion new customers by 2015, a 25 per cent increase. Unilever's was to double its revenues by 2020. Both firms made clear that growth in emerging markets was crucial to achieving these goals.

Author advice

The discussion in Chapter 9 about strategic direction and the use of Ansoff's matrix as a guide to determining which markets to compete in is relevant to the discussion in this section. Ensure that you are secure in your knowledge of Ansoff's matrix.

the domestic market. This may be due to the level of competition or the existence of a relatively limited customer base. Many supermarket chains, such as Tesco, began to operate in international markets because their domestic markets were saturated. What they looked for were international markets with large populations, high population growth rates, increasing income levels and a low supermarket presence – elements which provided these companies with a strong likelihood of success – particularly if they could become established before a rival company tried to enter these international markets.

The size of a market is a major factor in deciding whether to target a particular international market. Table 13.1 indicates that almost 19 per cent of the world's population live in China and over 17 per cent in India. It is no surprise therefore that many firms are encouraged to locate there, particularly as the population of Asia as a whole is expanding rapidly. In addition to population levels, the wealth of particular countries will determine whether there is a sufficient market available. Table 13.2 shows the world's largest markets in terms of total GDP and GDP per capita. Note that despite its much greater population size, China is still, economically and financially, a much smaller market than the USA.

▼ **Table 13.1** Population data for a range of countries (2015 projections)

Rank	Country	Population size	% of world population
1	China	1,369,610,000	18.90
2	India	1,270,580,000	17.50
3	USA	320,912,000	4.43
4	Indonesia	255,461,700	3.53
5	Brazil	204,249,000	2.82
9	Russia	146,267,288	2.02
10	Japan	126,910,000	1.75
16	Germany	81,083,600	1.12
20	France	66,121,000	0.91
22	UK	64,800,000	0.89

Total world population is 7,246,613,756.

Source: Department of Economic and Social Affairs, United Nations

▼ **Table 13.2** Top ten leading economies by total GDP 2013 (GDP per capita is also provided for each of these countries)

Rank	Country	Total GDP ($ trillion)	GDP per capita ($)
1	USA	16.8	53,042
2	China	9.2	6,807
3	Japan	4.9	38,633
4	Germany	3.7	46,251
5	France	2.8	42,560
6	UK	2.7	41,781
7	Brazil	2.3	11,208
8	Italy	2.2	35,686
9	Russia	2.1	14,612
10	India	1.9	1,498

Source: World Bank

Fact file

McDonald's

By the end of 2014, the US fast-food company, McDonald's, had been in business for more than 70 years and had 36,258 restaurants worldwide. Its success is heavily reliant on sales outside the USA. In 2006, the USA accounted for 34 per cent of McDonald's total revenue, while Europe accounted for 32 per cent and 14 per cent was generated across Asia, the Middle East and Africa. By 2014, of its $27.44 billion total revenue, Europe provided the largest share at 40 per cent, the US share had fallen to 32 per cent, and the collective contribution of Asia, the Middle East and Africa had increased to 23 per cent. With less than one-third of its sales being generated in its home country, McDonald's is a very good example of a business that could not have achieved the success it has without targeting a whole range of international markets.

Fact file

Crocs

Crocs, an American company, is the fast-growing maker of brightly coloured, plastic footwear. Since its inception in 2002, Crocs has sold more than 200 million pairs of shoes in more than 90 countries around the world. Crocs has steadily expanded the availability of its shoes internationally, adding Europe, China, India and Brazil as target markets, so that now the US market represents less than a third of its sales.

When Crocs was launched on the US stock market in 2006, just four years after it began selling the colourful foam clogs, sceptics suggested that it was only a matter of time before the 'fad' for its shoes disappeared and the company would begin to fail. However, by expanding its footwear product line (today clogs account for less than half of all sales) and targeting international markets, Crocs has become a very successful company.

6. **Better serving key customers located abroad**. In some industries, customers or buyers want their suppliers to have international presence so that they can contribute in most of the markets where the buyer is operating. For instance, a multinational business is likely to choose an advertising agency that has a presence in all the markets where the multinational sells its products. This means the multinational does not have to hire separate advertising agencies for each of its international markets. Similarly, a multinational company seeking materials and equipment for its various manufacturing sites around the world is likely to want a supplier that can supply to all of its international manufacturing locations. If the supplier wants the business, they may be required to develop competences and resources in each of the different international locations in order to be able to serve the international manufacturing locations of its buyer.

7. **Developing market knowledge and expertise**. Sometimes a company might decide to enter an international market in order to learn more about that market. See the Fact file on Koç.

Fact file

Koç

Founded in 1926, Koç Holding is one of the largest and most successful groups of companies in Turkey. Its website says that its growth and success have been due to 'staying one step ahead of change' and that the Koç Group is 'constantly moving toward its objective of duplicating its success in Turkey' on a global scale. The German market is regarded as the world's leading market for dishwashers, refrigerators, freezers and washing machines in terms of consumer

sophistication and product specification. The consumer product division of Koç decided to enter the German market. In doing so, it recognised that its unknown brand would struggle to gain much market share in this fiercely competitive market. However, Koç took the view that, as an aspiring global company, it would benefit from participating in the world's toughest market because its own product design and marketing would improve and this would enable it to perform better around the world. This in turn would allow it to achieve its aim 'to be one among the community of the leading companies in the world'.

▲ The UK government provides incentives for businesses to trade abroad

8. **Making a competitive move**. A business might enter an international market because a major competitor has already entered that particular market or is about to do so. This might mean that the competitor would gain a major advantage if it were allowed to operate alone in that market. Such a reason for entry to international markets is likely to be most common in industries that are heavily concentrated or duopolistic industries. For example, the consumer goods industry, and particularly the detergents sector, is dominated by two companies – Proctor and Gamble and Unilever. These two giant companies endeavour to compete in the same international markets to ensure that neither gains a competitive advantage over the other.

9. **Taking advantage of government incentives**. The UK government provides a range of incentives to encourage UK firms to trade with international markets. This usually involves offering companies help and support to enter export markets and to find overseas contracts.

Factors influencing the attractiveness of international markets

A range of factors influence the relative attractiveness of different international markets. These include:

1. **The size of a potential market and its expected growth**. This will determine whether it is worth pursuing this particular market. The potential market needs to be sizeable enough to be profitable given a firm's operating costs. Even if a market is small, it may be profitable if there are indications that it will grow significantly. For example, the middle class in India is growing rapidly, making it a very attractive market for consumer products companies. Similarly, the population in China is growing richer so that the proportion of people who can afford cars is growing significantly. See the Fact file below.

Fact file

Analysing data

The World Bank provides data on the proportion of the population owning a car in a range of countries. Current data indicates the following:

- USA   809 cars per 1,000 population; i.e. 81 per cent
- UK   519 cars per 1,000 population; i.e. 52 per cent
- China 101 cars per 1,000 population; i.e. 10 per cent

Based on percentages, it might seem that the Chinese market is small compared to that of the USA and UK.

However, taking into account population sizes in each country gives a very different picture of the size of the market. Table 13.1 indicates the following population sizes:

- China   1,369,610,000
- USA   320,912,000
- UK   64,800,000

Based on these two sets of data, car ownership in actual numbers is likely to be about:

- USA   259,938,720 (81 per cent of 320,912,000)
- China   136,961,000 (10 per cent of 1,369,610,000)
- UK   33,696,000 (52 per cent of 64,800,000)

This illustrates the fact that a small percentage market could still be huge in terms of potential for a business to exploit. In the case of China, factoring in improving standards of living, the percentage car ownership figure will only increase over time.

2. **The accessibility of the international market**. Issues to consider when reviewing the accessibility of a market include geographic accessibility as well as political, legal, technological and social barriers. For example, to overcome geographic barriers, the consumer products company Unilever hires about 50,000 'shakti' (meaning 'strength' or 'power' in Hindi) women in India to sell its products in remote villages to rural consumers who lack access to shops. This initiative provides Unilever with access to all the rural consumers in India that it could not otherwise reach, while the women get a source of income. As well as difficulties in the physical transportation of products over much greater distances, additional challenges can include international laws relating to exporting and importing and documentation required by foreign governments.

3. **Compatibility or alignment of the market**. This is essentially how well the international market fits with a company's objectives, mission and image. The Fact file on Sainsbury's venture into Egypt later in this chapter indicates the potential problems that can occur if the market is incompatible.

4. **Availability of financial and other resources**. Resources to consider include: skilled personnel, raw materials, components, general labour, technology, quality of local and national infrastructure supporting services and appropriate location sites.

5. **The competitive environment**. If a market is already swamped by competitors it is unlikely to be attractive unless a firm has found a way to stand out by having a strong USP. The nature of the competitive environment can be analysed using Porter's five forces model, which was considered in Chapter 7. Review this chapter to ensure you are secure in your knowledge of the five forces model.

6. **The external environment**. The external environment and the various influences on it were considered in Chapters 4, 5 and 6 of this book and Chapter 3 of Book 1. Ensure you are familiar with the content of these chapters and secure in your understanding of the external environment and the different elements of the PESTLE framework.

   a) Political influences. Political influences include systems of government in countries abroad, how politically stable they are and the extent to which they welcome foreign business activities, the potential for government upheaval or interference with business to harm an operation within a country.

      i. A business considering entering international markets will normally seek advice from UK authorities to establish the level of political risk involved in transactions in particular countries. On a practical basis, it is unlikely that a business will be able to get insurance for transactions in countries, such as Somalia, that represent extreme political risk. Relatively high levels of political risk are present in several of the world's important emerging economies, including India, the Philippines, Russia and Indonesia. This creates a dilemma for firms because these relatively risky settings also offer enormous growth opportunities if risks do not emerge. An extreme example was the period known as the 'Arab Spring' in 2011, which was a time of upheaval and unrest in countries such as Tunisia, Egypt, Libya, Bahrain, Syria and Yemen.

The operations of foreign firms doing business in these areas were suddenly, and severely, affected by a lack of supplies or inability to continue production.

ii. Governments can become hostile to foreign businesses and impose stringent taxes and new regulations on them. In some cases governments have forcibly taken control of, or acquired controlling interests in, private-sector companies, particularly those in essential industries such as oil and steel. This is usually done as part of a political policy to improve social and economic well-being by extending state control, as has been the case in a number of South American countries, including Venezuela, in recent years.

b) **Economic influences**. Economic prosperity and economic stability are important factors to consider in deciding on the attractiveness of international markets. A range of economic variables needs to be considered to evaluate this. These include income and expenditure trends, interest rates and levels of inflation, currency stability and the degree of trade protection in the form of import controls.

i. For example, multinational car manufacturers can be severely hit by changes in interest rates in the countries in which they sell their cars – simply because most cars are bought using some form of credit or loan.

ii. As well as analysing national indices of GNP and per capita income, important factors to consider are whether enough people have enough disposable income to buy the products a company proposes to sell.

iii. Exchange rates can have a huge impact on the profitability of international markets. For example, during the recession of 2008, the value of the pound (sterling) fell from $1.98 in January to $1.50 in December. This change meant that UK exports to the USA were a lot cheaper in December than in January of that year. For example, a product priced at £100 in the UK might have sold for $198 in the USA in January, but $150 in December. A firm may have decided not to move into the US market in January because it judged the high exchange rate meant the price of its goods in the USA were too high to generate sufficient demand. The same firm might have had a very different view about prices in the USA in December. The level of the foreign exchange rate is often seen as one of the crucial factors in the success of companies competing internationally. This is not always the case. Successful exporting countries and companies appear to perform well despite high and rising exchange rates, suggesting that the price of goods is not always the main determinant of competitiveness. Germany and Japan, for instance, have thrived through well-designed, high-quality products such as BMW cars and Sony televisions, for which consumers are willing to pay a price premium.

iv. Whether an international market is within a free trade area, such as the EU, will be a factor to consider as this will enable a business to avoid protectionist policies and trade barriers that might limit its ability to compete effectively. For example, many US, Japanese and Korean companies have set up bases in the UK so that they can access the EU market. Chapter 5 discussed the arguments for more open trade versus protectionism. Ensure that you are familiar with the various protectionist policies explained in Chapter 5 before proceeding with the rest of this chapter.

c) **Social and cultural influences**. Social and cultural influences include general education levels, language, religion, ethics, social values and cultural norms and lifestyles, as well as demographic influences, including population size, growth and geographical distribution. A business must recognise cultural differences when dealing with people from other countries and when trying to appeal to customers in other countries. For example, the structure of family life, the roles of males and females, lifestyles of different age groups and religious beliefs can all vary considerably between countries. The Fact file on Sainsbury's later in this chapter illustrates how cultural and religious issues can influence the attractiveness of international markets. Chapter 16 discusses the work of Hofstede on national cultures and the importance these can have on business practices.

d) **Technological influences**. Not only are there differences in cultures and languages between countries, technical aspects may also differ in terms of standards, measurement systems, materials and regulations.

e) **Legal and environmental issues**.

   i. Legal influences include import and trading regulations, tax and employment laws, patent and trademark laws, health and safety and consumer protection laws, plus the extent to which contracts can be rigorously enforced. While the UK has similar laws to other EU countries, there can be considerable differences in legislation for a business that is seeking to market its products beyond the EU.

   ii. Laws related to environmental considerations and general expectations and standards of behaviour in relation to environmental issues may be very different and may make an international market more or less attractive.

Fact file
Sainsbury's in Egypt

In 1999, Sainsbury's made a disastrous attempt to go into the supermarket business in Egypt. It went into a joint venture with the Egyptian Distribution Group, buying an 80 per cent stake in the group for £100 million. By joining forces with an established domestic partner that had extensive local knowledge and operated about 100 stores, it seemed that Sainsbury's had prepared itself well for entering a new and unknown market. However, the move failed for a number of reasons. Firstly, Sainsbury's faced stiff opposition from local rivals. It also found it difficult to adapt to the shopping habits of Egypt, which at the time had no tradition of Western-style supermarket shopping. It was also heavily affected by inaccurate rumours, apparently encouraged by local shopkeepers, that Sainsbury's owners had connections with Israel. (In the year 2000 there was a Palestinian uprising against Israeli occupation.) In 2001, Islamic activists organised a boycott of Sainsbury's stores in Cairo and Giza. This led to angry mobs throwing stones at some outlets and Muslim preachers advising consumers that it was 'sinful' to shop at Sainsbury's. Thus, only 18 months after entering the market, and incurring £10 million of operating losses, Sainsbury's withdrew from the Egyptian market and sold its shares back to the Egyptian Distribution Group.

Source: Adapted from range of news stories in the press and other media in April 2015

Did you know?

The 2014 Engineering Employers' Federation (EFF) survey found that 51 per cent of companies had some production overseas, a slight increase from 48 per cent in 2004. It also noted that the proportion of work for individual companies that was carried out abroad had also risen.

Key term

Off-shoring Where companies outsource or subcontract business activities overseas, largely because labour and other production costs are much cheaper there; also known as outsourcing off-shore.

Reasons for producing more, and sourcing more, resources abroad; off-shoring and re-shoring

Chapter 15 in Book 1 explained the nature of outsourcing, the factors influencing the decision to outsource and the advantages and disadvantages of outsourcing. Ensure you review this information before proceeding with this chapter.

There are a number of reasons why firms will choose to produce more, and source more resources, abroad. Some of these reasons have been identified and explained in the first section of this chapter on 'Reasons for targeting, operating in and trading with international markets'. The most common reason is the relocation of a business activity to another country to reduce costs. Many UK companies have closed down operations at home in favour of creating new operations in countries such as China and India that offer cheaper labour and other production costs. Such a move is known as **off-shoring**.

Chapter 15 in Book 1 defined outsourcing as the transfer of activities that were previously conducted in-house, to a third party, outside the business. Thus outsourcing and off-shoring are similar processes, although outsourcing can apply to the subcontracting of activities to other firms within the UK, while off-shoring is specifically focused on subcontracting activities overseas.

Fact file

Off-shoring at Rolls-Royce

In March 2015, Rolls-Royce was accused of off-shoring engineering jobs via the backdoor when it emerged that the company plans to open a new design facility in India. Five hundred new CAD specialists will be recruited to handle both domestic and international projects at the new site in Bangalore. The announcement coincides with a global restructuring exercise by Rolls-Royce, which is expected to result in the loss of 2,600 jobs worldwide. The restructuring exercise has already led to the proposed closure of its precision manufacturing facility in Derby and the turbine machining facility in Ansty, Warwickshire, leading to warnings from the trade union, Unite, that vital skills would be lost to the UK economy. A trade union official said that the UK workforce is world class, has proved time and again to be at the cutting edge of engineering and has shown their loyalty in building up Rolls-Royce over time. Rolls-Royce said that it was increasing capacity in India to better position itself for new business opportunities and to be closer to customers in the region. It already operates two engineering centres in Bangalore. It indicated that more than half of the work they plan to do in India is currently provided by outsourced providers and agency contractors.

Reasons for off-shoring

- As mentioned, many businesses decide to produce more, and source more of their resources, abroad because in general costs are much lower. For example, manufacturing costs in Western Europe are about 15 times higher than in China. Cost differences involve higher energy and labour costs and the costs associated with the burden of regulations that face businesses operating in the UK. Insurance, utilities and maintenance costs are often cheaper in other countries.
- A lack of investment in manufacturing for many years in the UK means that for certain business sectors, off-shore factories are often more likely to have the most up-to-date machinery and CAD/CAM systems, and thus provide a reason for businesses to produce more abroad.
- As well as the availability of low-paid, unskilled workers, some countries have large pools of skilled, specialist, but relatively low-paid workers, which can attract businesses to move production abroad, particularly when similarly skilled workers are not available in sufficient quantities in the UK.
- Multinational companies may already have capacity and capability abroad and may prefer to improve their efficiency by utilising that rather than producing in the UK – as illustrated in the Fact file on Dunlop below.
- It can be far easier to establish manufacturing operations abroad. In some instances, the addition of a production unit abroad provides a business with more flexibility to meet customers' needs – as the Fact file on Cricket, below, indicates.
- Off-shoring production facilities can allow business leaders to focus on what they do best. When manufacturing is done locally, many business owners find themselves spending a lot of time overseeing operations rather than focusing on key strategic issues related to the future direction of their business.
- Depending on the nature of a business and what it produces, key resources and inventory may be more abundant or cost-effectively accessible abroad.
- Free trade areas, such as the EU, can be a key factor in moving production abroad or in sourcing resources from abroad. Similarly governmental incentives can be a reason to increase links abroad. For example, when US Steel bought its plant in Slovakia in 1999, not only did it benefit from lower costs available in Slovakia, but the deal included government subsidies worth £240 million over 10 years.

Fact file
Flamagas

Flamagas, the Spanish maker of Clipper cigarette lighters, operates three factories – one in Spain, one in India and a third in China. Flamagas' labour costs in Spain are much higher than in India or China, but its unit costs of production in Spain are lower than in China because the Spanish plant has been fully automated. Flamagas' maintains its plant in China because when customers need to order customised lighters – for example, lighters carrying a corporate logo – production lines must be retooled, and it is cheaper to retool in China where the lines are not automated. The China plant therefore gives the firm the flexibility it needs to meet customers' needs more effectively.

Fact file
Dunlop

The tyre manufacturer Dunlop (owned by Goodyear and formally known as Goodyear Dunlop) left its famous factory landmark – the towering Fort Dunlop – in Birmingham in 2014, making 240 employees redundant. The manufacturer had operated in Birmingham for 125 years. Dunlop's management suggested that, although there were new location sites available in Birmingham and elsewhere in the UK, pursuing these would have involved building a brand new factory, which would take time and involve huge costs. The company already had two other factories with capacity and capability in France and Germany.

Fact file
Cost competitiveness by country

The risk analytics company, Verisk Maplecroft, produces a Labour Costs Index that enables companies to identify and compare the cost-competitiveness of workforces in 172 countries. The index measures a combination of wages, employment regulations, social security contributions and labour productivity.

Western Europe makes up the majority of the highest-cost countries in the index. In 2014, the ten most costly countries were: (1) Italy; (2) France; (3) Belgium; (4) Spain; (5) Finland; (6) Slovenia; (7) Luxembourg; (8) Austria; (9) Iceland; (10) Greece. High average wages, expensive redundancy systems and high employer social security contributions contribute to these positions in the index, and thus to reducing the attractiveness of Western Europe as a location to employ staff.

China, which is ranked 64th, has seen costs in the labour market rise rapidly in line with the country's strong rate of economic progress. By contrast, key sourcing destinations that are increasingly replacing Chinese manufacturers in global supply chains perform very well in the index, with Myanmar (Burma) ranked 171, Bangladesh 170 and Cambodia 169. However, the cost-competitiveness of international markets where labour costs are the lowest could be offset by the risks of poor working conditions and high levels of child labour and trafficking. As a result, countries at the bottom of the index are rated as 'extreme risk' to ensure firms investigate them thoroughly before doing business in them.

▲ Cambodia is one of the cost-competitive locations that are replacing China as a location for manufacturing

Source: www.maplecroft.com

What do you think?

Should UK companies, like Rolls-Royce and Dunlop (see Fact files), be allowed to move jobs to low-wage countries, even if it means job losses at home that can devastate local communities?

Problems with off-shoring

Despite the popularity of producing abroad and sourcing resources abroad, many firms have encountered problems with their experiences of off-shoring. Most problems relate to some of the following issues:

- additional business risks associated with contractual issues, political instability and natural disasters, which can disrupt business continuity
- increased additional costs, including managing the transition abroad, ongoing management and supervision costs, transport, delivery and insurance costs
- how off-shoring, particularly to developing countries, affects a company's image and its reputation for corporate social responsibility (CSR) (see Chapter 6 for more details on CSR)
- currency fluctuations that can affect profit margins
- difficulties in controlling the quality of goods produced or services provided – and the fact that quality issues are much harder to address when there are the additional barriers of distance, time zones and cultural differences
- communication, including language differences, particularly for highly technical products
- logistics, including transportation, delays in deliveries, the responsiveness of suppliers and their ability to get products to market quickly enough.

The shift to re-shoring

The problems encountered with off-shoring have led to more UK companies returning their production and service provision to the UK. This is known as **re-shoring** or on-shoring.

According to the Engineering Employers' Federation (EET), in its 2014 survey of employers, one in six manufacturers that moved production away from the UK had re-shored back to the UK during 2014. General reasons were improved production quality and reduced lead times. This represents a significant shift from 2009, when the focus was on moving to the Far East because of cheaper production costs.

Fact file
Re-shoring ATMs

NCR Corporation is a global technology company. It had been making ATMs (automatic teller machines – that dispense cash) and self-service checkout systems in China, Hungary and Brazil. These machines can weigh more than a ton, and NCR found that shipping them from overseas plants back to the United States was extremely expensive. NCR decided to move production of ATMs and check-out systems to a plant in America, employing over 800 workers in the process. 'Our decision to bring our North American ATM manufacturing in-house was driven by our belief that as self-service ATM technology became more innovative and strategic to financial institutions, the ability to control manufacturing in key markets became a core and competitive advantage to our growth strategy,' said the Vice President of Global Operations at NCR. 'By in-sourcing the production of our ATMs, we will decrease time-to-market, improve our internal collaboration, and lower our current operating costs.'

Source: www.ncr.com

Re-shoring is increasing and is driven by the following factors:

- shifting consumer preferences, for example the added value that a 'Made in the UK' brand has, and the desire to respond more quickly to consumer preferences and thus develop greater competitive advantage
- a reduction in the wage gap with emerging economies
- fluctuating exchange rates

- the difficulties of dealing with changing international transport costs, import duties, potential transport disruptions and supply chain risks
- a desire to improve cash flow by reducing the levels of inventory that need to be held
- a desire to improve the quality of products and components; this was cited by 35 per cent of employers in the EEF survey
- a desire to reduce the production-to-market lead time so that companies are able to react more effectively to demand
- a desire for a solid legal framework and a predictable regulatory system.

Did you know?

David Cameron discussed re-shoring opportunities for the UK at the 2014 World Economic Forum in Davos. He suggested that, because of the increased amount of re-shoring activity and the positive benefits of re-shoring for the UK economy (see the Fact file below), there was a possibility of the UK becoming the 'Re-Shore Nation'. He also launched the government's 'Reshore UK' initiative, a service to help companies considering moving operations back to the United Kingdom.

Fact file

Advantages to the UK economy of re-shoring

It is estimated that around 1,500 manufacturing jobs, which were moved off-shore to cut production costs, have been brought back to the UK since 2011. A study by PricewaterhouseCoopers (PWC) forecasts that between 100,000 and 200,000 jobs could be created as a result of re-shoring in the next decade, boosting GDP by between £6 billion and £12 billion. The UK manufacturing industry stands to benefit most from re-shoring, particularly the textile and machinery sectors, as the demand for products with a 'Made in Britain' label, seen as a badge of reliability and quality, continues to grow. Re-shoring is also expected to benefit the services sector, particularly in research and development, back-office services and telecommunications sectors.

Fact file

Re-shoring Raspberry Pis and Trunkis

The Raspberry Pi Foundation is a registered educational charity based in the UK. Its goal is to advance the education of adults and children in the field of computers, computer science and related subjects.

The Raspberry Pi is its low-cost, credit-card-sized computer that plugs into a computer monitor or TV and uses a standard keyboard and mouse. It is capable of doing everything one would expect a desktop computer to do. It enables people of all ages to explore computing and to learn how to program. Its various models, at the time of writing, cost less than £25.

The Raspberry Pi Foundation transferred production from China to South Wales in 2012. The chief executive of the Raspberry Pi Foundation said the decision 'was quite simply a matter of cost' and that building the computers in the UK was cheaper than building them elsewhere. This was in part due to a thorough review of how the computer was built, which led to more automation in order to reduce production costs as much as possible.

Magmatic, maker of the famous Trunki children's wheeled suitcase, moved all its production to a British manufacturer. A company spokesman said that if its intention had been to simply produce a standard product in large quantities, off-shoring operations would have continued to be cheaper and more appropriate. Its move back to the UK was because it wanted to introduce more differentiation into its product range.

Both Raspberry Pi and Magmatic are benefiting from the opportunity that re-shoring gives to bring their research and innovation teams physically closer to their actual production processes. At Raspberry Pi, this has allowed them to introduce greater levels of automation and continual technical updating. At Magmatic, this has allowed them to respond more effectively to the demands from buyers for greater variety and customisation, making it cheaper to produce new designs and upgrades more quickly. It has apparently reduced its lead time (i.e. the time from receipt of a customer order to getting the finished product to the customer) from 120 days to 30 days.

Fact file

Other companies that re-shored in 2014

- Jaeger, the 129-year-old British fashion brand, restarted UK production for the first time since 2000, seeking the benefit of fewer supply chain problems and shorter and more flexible lead times as production is moved closer to its Western European markets.
- Hornby, the maker of model railway sets, relocated the making of model aircraft kits from India to East Sussex.
- WedgeWelly, a business that makes wellington boots aimed at music festival goers, decided to relocate its production from China to Leicester. The decision was motivated by a bid to shorten lead times from five months in the Far East to six weeks in the UK. This allows the company to respond to market demands more quickly and to take advantage of market opportunities more effectively.

Ways of entering international markets and the value of different methods of entry

There are several ways of entering international markets. The entry methods discussed in this chapter are **export**, **licensing**, **alliances** and **direct investment**. In addition, the activities of multinationals in targeting overseas markets are also considered. In explaining each method, consideration is also given to its relative value to a business.

Export

For many businesses, exporting is the least risky strategy, as it incurs relatively few additional costs. Furthermore, if a business is unable to sell its products in international markets, it can often consolidate by selling the same products in its home country (unless the product has been specifically modified to suit the needs of the overseas market).

The vast majority of UK exports are services rather than goods. With technological advancement many of these services, such as banking and insurance, can be provided through the internet at similar costs to their provision for the domestic market. This has allowed many UK businesses to move into export markets at very little cost.

Achieving export sales can be accomplished either directly or indirectly.

- Direct exporting means the exporting company is marketing and selling its products on its own behalf. This gives it greater control over its brand and its operations overseas.

- Indirect exporting usually involves selling products to agents with local knowledge based in the export market abroad or to other retailers in those export markets. A disadvantage of this arrangement is that control of the marketing of the product is lost. Indirect exporting is particularly suitable for companies with little international experience since almost all international operating functions are borne by the agent. However, in addition to the low level of control, a number of other disadvantages exist. Agents tend to operate on the basis of economies of scope (explained in Chapter 11); seeking to act as intermediaries for many different companies that want to export their products – and thus not giving complete attention to the products of any one exporter. In addition, some agents operate on a commission basis, rather than actually buying the products themselves, which means that credit and cash-flow risks remain for the exporter.

Summary of advantages and disadvantages of exporting

Advantages:

- reduces risk and little investment is required
- speeds up entry to international markets
- makes use of existing facilities and therefore increases economies of scale.

Disadvantages:

- may face import tariffs and other trade barriers
- incurs transport costs
- limits access to local information about the international market, particularly in the case of indirect exporting.

Licensing

Licensing normally applies to manufacturing industries. Permission to make a product in a certain country is given in the form of a licence granted by the original manufacturer to a manufacturer in another country. Licensing is a common method of entry to international markets for companies with a distinctive and legally protected asset, which is a key differentiating element in their marketing offer. This might include a brand name, a technology or product design, or a manufacturing or service operating process.

Licensing is particularly useful for businesses in which both the cost of transportation and the cost of establishing a foreign base would be high. Brewers, such as Carlsberg, and soft-drinks makers, such as Coca-Cola, frequently use licences in order to sell their products in other countries. High transport costs and potential quality problems arising from long-distance transport make licensing an ideal solution in these circumstances.

Licensing offers a particularly effective way of entering foreign markets because it is low risk and means products can be adapted to local requirements. Disney's licensing arrangements in China allow its characters to adorn clothing or toys suited to local taste in terms of colour, styling or materials. This is because the local licensee has considerable autonomy in designing the products into which it incorporates the licensed characters.

Another advantage of licensing is that the licensee tends to be a local business and thus any import barriers that the country erects against

Key term

Licensing A business arrangement whereby one company gives another company permission to manufacture its goods, offer its services, and use its technology, brand or expertise for a specified fee or royalty.

incoming products do not apply. However, although licenses facilitate the creation of localised products, the approach is characterised by very low levels of marketing control for the company aiming to enter the international market. Another potential problem is that licensing runs the risk of creating future local competitors. This is particularly true in technology businesses, in which a design or process is licensed to a local business, thus revealing 'secrets' in the shape of intellectual property that would otherwise not be available to that local business. In the worst-case scenario, the local licensee can end up breaking away from the international licensor and quite deliberately stealing or imitating the technology. Participation in international markets via licensing is therefore best suited to firms with a stream of technological innovation, because these firms will continuously introduce new products or services that retain a competitive advantage over imitations.

Did you know?

Franchising, which is considered in Chapter 11, is similar to licensing. If a business wishes to retain some control of its international marketing, while limiting its financial commitment, franchising offers a good solution. Firms such as McDonald's (see the Fact file earlier in this chapter) and Papa John's Pizza have used franchising to assist rapid expansion. Franchising reduces risk to the franchisor because, if the business gets into difficulties in another country, it is the franchisee that suffers most of the financial loss. However, a badly managed franchise may damage the reputation of the franchisor, so there is some risk involved.

Summary of advantages and disadvantages of licensing

Advantages:

- reduces risk and little investment is required
- speeds up entry to international markets
- avoids import tariffs and other trade barriers
- makes use of existing facilities and therefore increases economies of scale.

Disadvantages:

- lack of control over marketing of products
- licensee may become a competitor.

Alliances

A strategic alliance is less involved and less permanent than a joint venture, with the companies involved remaining independent and separate. A joint venture usually involves two companies pooling resources to create a separate business; each company maintains its autonomy but owns a proportion of the new business.

Small- and medium-sized businesses in search of growth often favour alliances because such arrangements can quickly and inexpensively provide a company with access to technology, expertise, marketing, production, distribution and other capabilities. Some studies suggest that businesses that participate in alliances grow faster, increase productivity faster and report higher revenues than those that do not.

Key term

Alliances Agreements between two or more companies to combine their strengths and expertise in order to undertake a mutually beneficial project – in this context, involving entry to an international market; alliances can include strategic alliances and joint ventures.

Synergy (discussed in detail in Chapter 11) is a key benefit most alliances seek. In international alliances, one company can provide local market skills while another supplies imported products or technologies. Alliances can also be an effective way to spread investment costs in new technologies and manage the risks associated with doing business in emerging markets.

One of the most important elements companies involved in alliances need to take into account is the potential conflicting interests and objectives of themselves and their partners. In some cases there is a danger that a partner company may eventually become a competitor. Research suggests that about three out of four corporate alliances disappoint, producing higher costs or lower returns than expected.

Joint ventures occur when two or more companies agree to act as one organisation in launching a product or providing a service. Joint ventures are popular with businesses trying to enter emerging markets, such as India and China. Businesses in emerging markets may lack the technology and financial resources but possess a much greater understanding of local market conditions and distribution channels. In these circumstances, a joint venture can prove to be a very effective combination of strengths. However, joint ownership of a new business by two existing businesses can lead to conflict and communication problems.

Author advice

Note how the problems of strategic alliances and joint ventures mentioned here are similar to the issues discussed in Chapter 11 about why mergers and takeovers do not always work as well as expected.

Fact file
Entering new markets

- In 2007, Virgin entered the Indian mobile phone market through a 50-50 joint venture with the Tata Group, the largest industrial group in India. The venture was named Virgin Mobile and targeted India's fast-growing youth market, which accounts for almost half of the country's mobile phone market.

- In 2010, Royal Dutch Shell and the Russian company, Gazprom, formed a strategic alliance. The deal paved the way for two of the world's biggest gas companies to deepen co-operation in Russia and work together in other countries. The agreement indicated recognition by Gazprom that it needed foreign allies to help globalise its gas business and expand further into oil.

Summary of advantages and disadvantages of alliances

Advantages:

- combines the resources and strengths of two or more companies
- potential for learning and benefiting from each other
- less investment required than going it alone.

Disadvantages:

- can be difficult to manage
- less control than going it alone
- greater risk than exporting and licensing
- partner in alliance may become a competitor.

Direct investment

A business may prefer to own manufacturing operations in a foreign country by directly investing in manufacturing in the country with which it intends to trade. Capital requirements associated with this method generally mean that large businesses are far more likely to use this

Key term

Direct investment The taking of a controlling ownership in a company in one country by a company based in another country; this can be via organic growth or by the takeover of a foreign business; sometimes known as foreign direct investment.

▲ Several Japanese car manufacturers have factories in the UK

Author advice

The issues discussed here about the types and methods of growth in international markets reflect the same general issues discussed in Chapter 11 about methods and types of growth.

alternative. This method allows a business to avoid high import taxes, reduce transportation costs, utilise cheap labour, and gain increased access to raw materials.

A key benefit of this way of entering an international market is that the business becomes localised – it manufactures for customers in the market in which it trades. It will gain local market knowledge and will be able to adapt its products to meet the needs of local consumers. However, the business also takes on all the risk associated with operating a business in that particular international market. Another key issue is the difficulties of managing businesses abroad, including taking appropriate account of any cultural differences.

Over the last few decades there has been a rapid expansion in the number of multinational businesses that keep greater control of their international activities by having bases in many different countries. Overseas bases can be formed in one of two ways:

- Organic growth by establishing an overseas factory or outlet. In the motor industry, this strategy has been used often by Japanese manufacturers such as Honda, Nissan and Toyota, all of which have set up factories in countries such as the UK.
- The takeover of a foreign business. An example is the Bank of Santander entering and expanding in the UK through the takeover of Abbey, Alliance and Leicester, and Bradford and Bingley's branch network. Another example is Tata's acquisition of Jaguar Land Rover.

Strategically, direct investment comes in three types:

- Horizontal: where a company directly invests in plant that carries out the same activities abroad as at it does at home; for example, Toyota assembling cars in both Japan and the UK.
- Vertical: when different stages of activities are added abroad. Forward vertical direct investment takes a firm nearer to the market; for example, Toyota acquiring a car distributorship in America. Backward vertical direct investment is where international integration moves back towards raw materials; for example, Toyota acquiring a tyre manufacturer.
- Conglomerate: where a direct investment is made in an unrelated business abroad. This is the most unusual form of foreign direct investment because it involves overcoming two barriers simultaneously – entering a new international market and entering a new industry.

Summary of advantages and disadvantages of direct investment

Advantages:

- greater knowledge of local markets
- opportunities to make better use of specialist skills
- retains knowledge of production and markets within the company.

Disadvantages:

- higher level of risk than other methods
- requires huge resources and long-term commitment
- requires well thought-out strategy for managing local plants and resources, including overcoming cultural barriers.

▲ Shell's stores at petrol stations compete with other multi-nationals as well as local shops

▲ Kellogg's alter various aspects of their product to appeal to the different markets they operate in

Targeting overseas markets may include becoming a multinational

International trade is dominated by **multinationals**. Multinationals compete with other multinationals as well as with small and medium-sized businesses. For example, all types of retail stores now compete with multinationals like Shell and BP with their 24-hour stores at petrol stations.

Although multinationals, by definition, are involved in direct investment as a means of entering international markets, this is not the only method they use. Examples were provided earlier of Coca-Cola and Carlsberg using licensing agreements and of Tata using joint ventures.

Multinationals pursue a range of strategies to ensure they maintain their global brands and also cater for local needs in their international markets. For example:

- Global brands, such as Kellogg's, while maintaining their famous branding, change product content, packaging, size and price in order to enhance their attraction to retailers and consumers in these markets.
- Introduced by Coca-Cola in Japan in 1975, Georgia Coffee is Japan's top ready-to-drink cold and hot coffee brand. It simultaneously enables Coca-Cola to meet local consumer tastes and to take advantage of the economies of scope from all of its sales and distribution investments in the country.
- Some multinationals undertake extensive development of infrastructure in new markets that later provide them with a strong competitive advantage. Proctor and Gamble (P&G) used this approach in certain Eastern European markets. Distribution systems in these former communist states were very poor. P&G recognised that high quality distribution systems were essential if the market for their consumer goods was to develop. It therefore invested substantial sums in developing its own distribution network prior to entering the market. This produced a significant competitive advantage over both international and local competition.

A later section in this chapter considers different types of multinational companies in detail.

Summary of the value of different methods of entering international markets

The previous explanations of each method of entry to international markets include analysis of their value. Mostly value is analysed in terms of the balance between the risks of each method and the amount of control each method allows over quality, systems and marketing.

Low-risk methods include exporting and licensing. However, these methods tend to minimise control. More control is present in alliances, and direct investment tends to allow almost complete control. However, there is more risk in these methods, in particular in direct investment. In general, control in international markets only comes from involvement in them, and this usually means some level of investment in international markets. The desire for increasingly greater control over a business in an international market in many ways explains the pattern of development of most multinationals.

Practice exercise 1

Total: 75 marks

1. Identify and explain two reasons for targeting, operating in or trading with international markets. *(8 marks)*

2. Identify and explain three factors, related to the external environment, that influence the attractiveness of international markets. *(9 marks)*

3. Identify two internal factors that influence the attractiveness of international markets. *(6 marks)*

4. Distinguish between outsourcing and off-shoring. *(4 marks)*

5. Explain three reasons for off-shoring. *(9 marks)*

6. Define the term 're-shoring'. *(3 marks)*

7. Analyse why more companies are now re-shoring to the UK. *(9 marks)*

8. Explain each of the following methods of entry into international markets:
   a) export *(3 marks)*
   b) licensing *(3 marks)*
   c) alliance *(3 marks)*
   d) direct investment. *(3 marks)*

9. What is a multinational company? *(3 marks)*

10. Select two methods of entry into international markets and identify and explain one advantage and one disadvantage of each method. *(12 marks)*

Case study 1: Call centres – off-shoring and re-shoring

The financial services sector led the trend for UK call centres to relocate to countries such as India. Among the businesses that decided to locate their call centres in India were HSBC in 2002 and Prudential in 2003. For example, Prudential transferred 850 jobs from its call centre in Reading to Mumbai in India. On average, call centre costs in India, at the time, were 35–40 per cent lower than in the UK, with nearly all of the savings coming from lower wage levels. Other destinations also became popular, with more off-shoring going to Malaysia and China, where costs were often lower than in India.

A particular problem in call centres in both the UK and India has been the high rate of labour turnover. Across the entire industry, call centres replace about 26 per cent of staff annually. Actual rates vary by sector and by the nature of an employee's contract, with turnover for part-time employees being about 33 per cent annually. However, the average staff turnover in India is over 50 per cent. Many call centre employees in India are graduates who are only willing to stay in a job for an average of 11 months before moving on.

Indian call centres also experience recruitment difficulties and high absence rates, blamed primarily on antisocial hours and abusive customers. The cost of replacing people – in both the UK and India – and the fact that new employees are less effective during the early period of their employment, adds to costs and inefficiencies. High turnover rates and the difficulties in recruiting staff in India are leading to gradual increases in salaries in order to attract and retain suitable staff.

▶▶▶

Organisations such as HBOS, Nationwide and the Co-operative Bank all ruled out going abroad. Nationwide's chief executive, Philip Williamson, said that he received letters from new customers stating that they had switched accounts to his organisation because their previous bank had transferred jobs overseas.

A number of companies that relocated call centres to Asia complain about bad communication, rapidly increasing wages, high labour turnover rates and lower customer satisfaction than expected, all of which effectively add to the costs of operating abroad. As a result of such problems, a number of firms are re-shoring call centres back to the UK. For example,

Santander UK closed its call centre operations in Bangalore and Pune in India in 2011 and re-routed calls to centres in Liverpool, Leicester and Glasgow, creating 500 new jobs. A spokesman said that the company was responding to the preferences of customers who had made clear that they prefer UK-based call centres. New Call Telecom, which competes with BT and Sky to offer home telephone services, broadband and low-cost international calls, closed its call centre in Mumbai in 2011 and opened a call centre in Burnley, Lancashire. It was attracted by low commercial rents, cheap labour costs and loyal staff. Staff in Burnley are paid the minimum wage, but costs have been cut because the average amount of time taken to deal with customer enquiries is less.

Questions

Total: 25 marks

1. Evaluate the reasons why so many companies in the financial services and other sectors decided to off-shore their call centre activity. *(16 marks)*

2. Analyse the main reasons why some companies are making the decision to re-shore their call centre activity. *(9 marks)*

Case study 2: Dell

Dell has wholly owned subsidiaries in a number of countries, including Brazil, Malaysia, China and Ireland, in addition to its operations in America. Each of these plants is large enough to serve a regional market and provide economies of scale. Each plant uses the same supply-chain management techniques that led to Dell's domestic success.

Dell uses wholly owned subsidiaries because the firm wants to ensure that its methods are followed exactly, and also to reduce the risk of losing know-how to a partner that may then use the knowledge to compete against Dell.

Prior to 2010, Dell's sales in India were weak compared to its competitors. Indian customers had to wait up to a month for delivery while the computers were manufactured in Dell's factory in Malaysia. In 2007, it sold just fewer than 80,000 computers in India. In 2010,

it sold over 1.1 million, beating all of its competitors. It achieved this by setting up a factory in India. By manufacturing locally, it cut delivery time by almost 50 per cent, reduced waiting time to less than eight days and improved profitability.

Questions

Total: 25 marks

1. Analyse why Dell appears to have preferred a direct investment approach to entering international markets. *(9 marks)*

2. With reference to firms of your choice, discuss the potential value of two different methods of entering international markets. *(16 marks)*

Influences on buying, selling and producing abroad

Most of the influences on buying, selling and producing abroad have already been discussed in earlier sections of this chapter, particularly in the section on the 'Factors influencing the attractiveness of international markets'.

In general, factors influencing decisions about buying abroad will include unit costs, price, quality, the promptness and reliability of delivery and after-sales services.

Influences on firms selling and producing abroad will include the extent of their own financial and other resources and capabilities, and whether they have a competitive advantage that will enable them to be successful. A competitive advantage could be in terms of their market knowledge, their technology or their portfolio of products. Other important influences will be their cost structures, the reliability of their partners (if they are in alliances) or agents and licensees, and the skills and experience, including knowledge of foreign markets, of their own staff.

Operational issues will include the suitability of locations abroad, infrastructure, distribution systems, distance, time zones, climatic features, access to resources, technology and quality issues.

In order to succeed in markets abroad, companies and products must meet customer needs. With the exception of products that sell simply because they are famous imported brands, most products and the associated marketing need to be tailored to meet the needs of markets abroad. Assuming that marketing materials simply need to be translated into the local language is not enough. For example, when Kelloggs first tried to sell its breakfast cereals to the mass market in India it was unsuccessful. It based its marketing campaign on the same message it conveys in the West, that is, speed and convenience. This did not work in India, where most people prepared a traditional breakfast each morning or bought biscuits and tea at roadside tea stalls.

Did you know?

McDonald's is far from being a global seller of just American-style burgers. Instead it offers different menus in different countries, meeting the requirements of different international cultures, tastes and markets. For example, it offers a McBaguette in France (with French baguette and Dijon mustard), a Chicken Maharaja Mac and a Masala Grill Chicken in India (with Indian spices), a Mega Teriyaki Burger (with teriyaki sauce) or Gurakoro (with macaroni gratin and croquettes) in Japan. In addition, in Arabic and Muslim countries its ingredients are certified halal.

311

The external environment (introduced in Chapter 3 of Book 1 and in Chapters 4 to 6 of this book) and the competitive environment (discussed in Chapter 7 of this book) provide significant influences on buying, selling and producing abroad, in particular because of the added uncertainty of dealing with international markets. These influences were discussed earlier in this chapter in the section on 'Factors influencing the attractiveness of international markets'. Ensure you are familiar with the content of these chapters and the earlier section of this chapter before continuing.

Did you know?

There is potential for a company's operations in a country to struggle because of differences in language, customs, norms and customer preferences. The history of business is full of what, with hindsight, are amusing examples of cultural differences undermining company performance. For example, an advertising campaign for Tide, a laundry detergent brand owned by Proctor and Gamble (P&G), was launched in the Middle East. The company was surprised at the weak sales because they had tried to avoid any language barriers by using picture-only hoardings. The hoardings included three frames. In the first frame, a frowning woman holds up a dirty shirt. The second frame shows her placing the shirt into a washing machine and loading it with Tide detergent. The third frame shows her smiling and holding up the now-clean shirt. Unfortunately, what P&G's marketing specialists were not aware of was that in Arabic-speaking countries both text and images are read right to left, rather than left to right. To consumers, the implication of the advertisement was that the detergent made clean clothes dirty.

Source: Blunders in International Business, Ricks, 1993

What do you think?

Hiam and Schewe in their book, *The Portable MBA in Marketing* (1998), say that 'cultures differ in their values and attitudes toward work, success, clothing, food, music, sex, social status, honesty, the rights of others, and much else'. They also note how business practices vary between countries. 'For instance, haggling is never done by the Dutch, often by Brazilians, and always by the Chinese.'

Do you think most companies thinking of buying, selling or producing abroad, spend as much time exploring social and cultural issues as they do exploring financial issues? If not, why not?

Any analysis of influences on buying, selling and producing abroad is further complicated if a firm buys its raw materials and components from one or more countries abroad, manufactures its products in another country and then sells the finished products in still other countries abroad. In such a situation, it is important to consider all of the different possible influences on all aspects of the firm's operations.

Managing international business including pressures for local responsiveness and pressures for cost reduction

Managing an international business is a constant balance between keeping costs down and being responsive to local customer needs and demands – both of which enable a business to remain competitive. The balance of these two competing pressures will dictate the nature of the strategy adopted by a business, that is, the actions it takes in order to achieve its goals. This is similar to the ideas raised in Porter's low-cost, differentiation and focus strategies, which were discussed in detail in Chapter 10.

Pressures for local responsiveness

Pressures to be locally responsive mean a company needs to cater for the different lifestyles and expectations of consumers in different countries. This is likely to require a company to differentiate its products and marketing strategies from country to country. This approach is likely to raise costs of production.

Sources of pressure to be locally responsive are likely to emerge:

- where consumer tastes and preferences differ significantly between countries; this is likely to mean that products and marketing messages have to be customised for local tastes and preferences
- where there are differences in infrastructure, business operations and practices and distribution channels between countries
  (For an international business, the above two sources of pressure to be locally responsive are likely to lead to the delegation of production and marketing functions to foreign subsidiaries.)
- where economic and political demands are imposed by a country's government, for example in relation to protectionist policies, the possibility of a government wanting to take over part or full ownership of a business, or strict regulations about products being made using local resources.

Pressures for cost reduction

Pressures for cost reduction come from greater international competition and mean a company must try to minimise its unit costs. This is likely to mean offering a standardised product to the global market so that a company can benefit not only from economies of scale but also from experience curve advantages as quickly as possible. (Experience curve effects are discussed in Chapter 11.) It is also likely to mean locating production facilities where costs are lowest.

Sources of pressures for cost reductions are likely to emerge:

- where the product in question is either a commodity (that is, products like oil, gas, grain and cement, which are virtually the same regardless of which company produces them) or is very similar to those produced by other firms; because of the lack of differentiation for these products, price competition is the main strategy
- where major competitors are based in low-cost locations
- where there is persistent excess capacity, which means downward pressure on prices
- where consumers or buyers are powerful and face low switching costs. (This refers to the buyer element of Porter's five forces model, discussed in Chapter 7.)

What do you think?

Some observers claim that consumer demands for local customisation of products are on the decline worldwide because modern communications and transportation technologies have led to a convergence of tastes and preferences. The result is the emergence of enormous global markets for standardised consumer products.

Do you think that this is the case? If so, what evidence would you use to support your view?

Fact file

Vodafone KK

Vodafone's experience with Vodafone KK, the mobile phone it launched in Japan in 2005, is an example of how an international business can fail if it does not achieve a good balance in relation to the pressure for cost reduction and for local responsiveness. The company admitted that its biggest mistake was its decision to offer Japanese customers handsets that were identical to those released in 13 other countries at the same time. By offering the same phones Vodafone hoped to reduce costs and keep prices low. This approach might work in some international markets, but it did not work in Japan. Features that were acceptable in Europe and the USA were not acceptable in Japan. In Japan technological products are often available well before being launched in the rest of the world and, as a result, Japanese consumers are much more sophisticated in their expectations of such products. As a consequence, in the first half of 2005, Vodafone lost 200,000 subscribers.

Source: adapted from a range of articles in the media in 2005

▲ Vodafone found the technology market in Japan was more sophisticated than in Western Europe

Bartlett and Ghoshal's international, multi-domestic, transnational and global strategies

In their book, *Managing Across Borders: The Transnational Solution* (1989), Bartlett and Ghoshal identify four distinct types of multinational corporations (MNCs) with different strategies towards managing their subsidiaries. These strategies are linked to how MNCs balance the pressures for cost reduction and for local responsiveness. Figure 13.1 provides a matrix illustrating how different ways of balancing the pressures for cost reduction and local responsiveness can lead to different strategies.

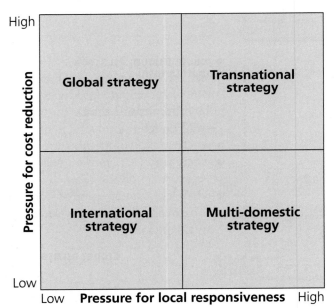

▲ **Figure 13.1** Bartlett and Ghoshal's matrix of international, multi-domestic, global and transnational strategies

Key term

Bartlett and Ghoshal's international strategy
Involves taking products first produced for the domestic market and then selling them internationally with only minimal local customisation; it is most appropriate when pressures for cost reduction and for local responsiveness are low.

Firms that pursue an **international strategy** tend to centralise product development functions at home, but establish manufacturing and marketing functions in each major country they trade in. They undertake limited local customisation of products and marketing strategies. An international strategy can be very profitable if a company has a valuable distinctive competency (i.e. valuable knowledge/skills/products) that competitors in its international markets lack, and if the pressures for local responsiveness and cost reductions are relatively weak. However, when pressures for local responsiveness increase, companies pursuing an international strategy lose out to companies that customise products to meet local needs. In addition, because they must duplicate manufacturing facilities, international companies suffer from high operating costs.

Like firms that pursue an international strategy, firms that pursue a **multi-domestic strategy** transfer their distinctive competency, developed at home, to foreign markets. However, unlike international companies, multi-domestic companies extensively customise both their products and their marketing strategies, usually because of substantial differences in consumer tastes and preferences between their international markets.

The structure of this type of MNC is likely to be similar to that of a group of autonomous national companies, because multi-domestic companies tend to establish a complete set of operational activities in each major national market in which they do business. Because of this structure, multi-domestic companies are unable to benefit from extensive experience curve effects, location economies and other economies of scale, which means they tend to have a high cost structure. A further danger for multi-domestic companies is that they may become too decentralised. If this happens they are likely to lose the ability to transfer knowledge, skills and products (their distinctive competency), between subsidiaries effectively.

> **Key term**
>
> **Bartlett and Ghoshal's multi-domestic strategy** Focuses on increasing profitability by customising a firm's products so that they provide a good match to tastes and preferences in different international markets; most appropriate when there is high pressure for local responsiveness and low pressure for cost reduction; this is sometimes known as a localisation strategy.

> **Key term**
>
> **Bartlett and Ghoshal's global strategy** Focuses on increasing profitability by benefiting from cost reductions that come from economies of scale, experience curve effects and location economies; it is most appropriate when there is high pressure for cost reduction and low pressure for local responsiveness; this strategy is sometimes known as a global standardisation strategy.

Author advice

The term 'location economies' means the cost reductions that a firm benefits from as a result of locating in an area where it reduces both its procurement costs and its distribution costs. Procurement costs are those costs associated with all the activities and processes involved in acquiring suppliers and resources, including the transportation of raw materials. Distribution costs are those costs associated with transporting and distributing goods and services to retailers and consumers.

> **Key term**
>
> **Bartlett and Ghoshal's transnational strategy** Tries simultaneously to achieve lower costs through location economies, economies of scale and experience curve effects and to differentiate products across different international markets; most appropriate when there are high pressures for cost reduction and for local responsiveness.

Firms pursuing a **global strategy** are usually aiming to be cost leaders and use aggressive pricing techniques. The production, marketing and R&D activities of companies pursuing a global strategy tend to be concentrated in a few favourable locations. Global companies do not customise their products and marketing strategy to local conditions because such customisation raises costs, instead they market a standardised product worldwide. These conditions prevail in many industrial goods industries, but are not as common in consumer goods.

Each of the three previous strategies has some serious drawbacks. Increasingly, companies must be both low cost and differentiated in order to compete, especially in industries with intense international competition. A **transnational strategy** allows companies to pursue both goals simultaneously. It does this by encouraging and sharing the best practice in any particular section of the organisation or its international markets with all other sections and markets. It allows knowledge, skills and products, that is distinctive competency, to flow in both directions between the home country and foreign subsidiaries in a process referred to by Bartlett and Ghoshal as 'global learning'. However, this strategy is not an easy one to pursue, because pressures for local responsiveness and cost reductions place conflicting demands on a company. In addition, there are difficulties in ensuring that an MNC has an organisational structure that enables different parts of the business, involved in different functions and located in different parts of the world, to communicate effectively and learn from each other.

To deal with cost pressures, some transnational companies redesign their products so that they use identical components even though the final product is differentiated for different markets. Others invest in a few large-scale manufacturing plants sited at favourable locations around the world, and then have assembly plants in each of their major markets that allow for customisation of the finished product to local needs.

Table 13.3 summarises some of the key issues related to each of the strategies discussed in this section.

▼ **Table 13.3** Summary of key issues related to Bartlett and Ghoshal's strategies

Organisational characteristics	International	Multi-domestic	Global	Transnational
Structure	Product development and overall control centralised; other functions may be decentralised	Decentralised and nationally self-sufficient	Centralised	Dispersed, independent and specialised
Role of overseas units	Adapting and exploiting parent company's abilities	Sensing and exploiting local opportunities	Implementing parent company's strategies	Differentiated contributions by overseas units to integrated worldwide operations
Development and sharing of knowledge and skills	Knowledge developed at centre and transferred to overseas units	Knowledge developed and retained within each overseas unit	Knowledge developed and retained at the centre	Knowledge developed jointly and shared worldwide

In summary

Because the competitive forces of almost every industry are increasing as a result of globalisation, Bartlett and Ghoshal suggest that many MNCs will eventually have to adopt a transnational strategy, which means they must focus on cost reduction and local differentiation to maintain their competitive edge.

Based on Bartlett and Ghoshal's analysis:

● an international strategy may not be viable in the long term
● to survive, firms may need to shift to a global strategy or a transnational strategy before competitors do
● a multi-domestic strategy may give a firm a competitive edge, but if the firm is also facing aggressive price competition, it may also have to reduce its unit cost, and the only way to do that is to move towards a transnational strategy.

Table 13.4 summarises the advantages and disadvantages of the four strategies discussed in this section. Although a transnational strategy appears to include the advantages of each of the other strategies without their disadvantages, it raises difficult organisational issues.

▼ **Table 13.4** Advantages and disadvantages of each of Bartlett and Ghoshal's strategies

Strategy	Advantages	Disadvantages
International	• transfer of knowledge and skills/distinctive competency to foreign markets	• lack of local responsiveness • inability to gain location economies or benefit from experience curve effects
Multi-domestic	• ability to customise products and marketing to meet local differences	• inability to gain location economies or benefit from experience curve effects • failure to transfer distinctive competency to foreign markets
Global	• ability to exploit experience curve effects, location economies and economies of scale	• lack of local responsiveness
Transnational	• ability to exploit experience curve effects, location economies and economies of scale • ability to customise products and marketing to meet local differences • gaining the benefits of global learning	• difficulties in implementation because of organisational problems

The impact of internationalisation for the functional areas of the business

Did you know?

Globalisation and **internationalisation** are terms that are often used interchangeably. However, there are slight differences in their meanings. Internationalisation refers to the increasing importance of international trade and alliances between or among nations. However, the basic unit remains the nation. Globalisation refers to the gradual economic integration of national economies into one global economy, mainly by free trade and free capital mobility. It is the effective removal of national boundaries for economic purposes.

The impact of internationalisation for the functional areas of a business has been touched on many times in the previous sections of this chapter. The impact is extensive, but depends very much on the nature of a particular business's involvement in the internationalisation process. For example, the impact on a business will be different if it is simply exporting its products abroad or purchasing supplies from abroad compared to if it is manufacturing and selling abroad.

As discussed in the last section, a critical challenge of managing international businesses is the need to achieve a best fit in relation to the competing demands of co-ordination and integration of international sites, cost reduction and local responsiveness (known as the 'global versus local debate'). The same challenge faces each of the functional areas of a business, and in general it is these aspects that have the greatest impact on functional areas.

In addition to this general impact, the following includes a summary of some of the key aspects of the impact of internationalisation on each functional area of a business:

Marketing:

- Maintaining international competitiveness means a need to increase marketing efforts and ensure that strategies are appropriate to each of the overseas markets in which a firm operates. This means adapting the marketing mix so that it caters well for social and cultural expectations in different countries.
- The marketing function is likely to increase substantially in scale and complexity to cope with increasing sales and the opening of new international markets.

Operations:

- In order to improve its international competitiveness, a business might need to reduce unit costs and increase the quality of its products. This could mean introducing more capital-intensive means of production and new technology, and generally ensuring that the production process is as efficient as possible in order to increase the rate of productivity.
- Ensuring efficient systems are in place to cope with increasing productive capacity – and decisions about whether this should be centralised in the home country, to achieve greater economies of scale, or decentralised to plants in a range of different countries.
- Quality assurance issues across a range of different international sites may need to be developed, including arrangements to ensure that the quality of off-shored production meets required standards. Quality assurance issues are much harder to address when there are additional barriers of distance, time zones and cultural differences.
- Adapting products to meet local responsiveness issues will mean the need for more flexible approaches to production.
- Decisions about the suitability of locations abroad, coping with different standards in relation to infrastructure, transport and distribution systems and technology will all need to be dealt with.
- Sourcing of materials and services to take advantage of price differences between countries may become a more important and wide-ranging activity.
- Developing know-how and technology competences through technical co-operation with partners in an alliance may become more common.

Finance:

- A stronger focus on cost reduction issues across all international areas, including off-shored activity, will become a key issue.
- The challenge of maintaining control of the financial performance of a complex organisation with a range of activities across a range of different countries.

Human Resources (HR):

- A vital factor for the HR function is the impact of different national cultures on views about appropriate management styles, organisational processes, team working, motivation, training and reward strategies.
- Evidence from cross-cultural research, such as that by Hofstede (which is discussed in detail in Chapter 16), shows significant variations in perspectives among managers from different countries.
- Recruiting, training and rewarding labour forces abroad, taking into account different cultures and expectations and different employment laws will be an important factor in the HR function's work.
- Appropriate strategies will need to be introduced to deal with the inevitable redundancies that off-shoring is likely to bring.

Practice exercise 2   *Total: 55 marks*

1. Identify and explain three influences on buying, selling or producing abroad.   *(12 marks)*

2. In relation to managing international businesses, explain the pressures for local responsiveness and the pressures for cost reduction.   *(8 marks)*

3. Match the following strategies to the correct balance of pressures for local responsiveness and for cost reduction:
   a) international strategy   *(1 mark)*
   b) multi-domestic strategy   *(1 mark)*
   c) global strategy   *(1 mark)*
   d) transnational strategy.   *(1 mark)*
   i) Low pressure for local responsiveness and low pressure for cost reduction
   ii) Low pressure for local responsiveness and high pressure for cost reduction
   iii) High pressure for local responsiveness and low pressure for cost reduction
   iv) High pressure for local responsiveness and high pressure for cost reduction

4. What does the term 'internationalisation' mean?   *(3 marks)*

5. Identify and explain one example of the impact of internationalisation on each of the functional areas of a business, that is on marketing, finance, operations and human resources.   *(12 marks)*

6. Discuss Bartlett and Ghoshal's view that if multinational companies are to remain successful over time, they are likely to have to develop a transnational strategy.   *(16 marks)*

Case study 3: Clarks

Clarks, the shoemaker, traces its history to 1825 when Quaker brothers, Cyrus and James Clark, began making shoes in Street. By the 1850s, Clarks employed a third of the population of Street.

Products such as the 'Desert Boot' and the 'Wallabee' heralded the company's golden years in the 1960s and 1970s. In its prime, and with over 20 UK factories employing tens of thousands of people, C&J Clark International Ltd, trading as Clarks, was one of the UK's biggest manufacturers, exporting shoes throughout the Commonwealth. However, in the early 1980s, competition from cheap imports took its toll, sales began to fall and profits slumped, leaving Clarks vulnerable to takeover.

After deciding to retain its status as a private limited company, Clarks set about aggressively cutting costs by closing factories and shifting production to cheaper overseas locations, including China, India, Vietnam, Romania, Brazil and Portugal.

Once costs were under control and the company was confident about the quality of products made outside of the UK, it was ready to compete in international markets. Clarks set about giving itself a younger, 'trendier' image. It had been best known for children's shoes, but the image lost favour and the brand became associated with dull, chunky designs. With its aim to reduce the age of the typical Clarks buyer from the late 50s to 35–45, it embarked on multimillion-pound advertising campaigns, including 'Act your shoe size, not your age' and 'Enjoy every step', and a revamping and rebranding of its stores.

The company still employs about 1,200 people at its headquarters in Street, near Glastonbury. Shoemaking ended there in 1992 and most of the head office jobs are in distribution, IT, accounts and marketing.

Former factory buildings were sold and, in 1993, these were turned into Clarks Village. This is a retail village of restaurants and shops, including a Clarks' shoe shop. Clarks Village is one of the leading free attractions in the West Country, drawing over 4 million visitors each year. It also attracts bus-loads of Chinese tourists. Apparently Chinese tourists like to buy Chinese-made European 'labels' in Europe! So the Chinese fly to the UK, visit the site where Clarks used to make shoes, and buy shoes, actually made in China, in the Clarks shop – an interesting example of globalisation.

Today, new technology, state-of-the-art facilities and a strong commitment to its products mean that Clarks is now the number one shoe brand in the UK. With continuing growth in North America, Europe, India and China, it is also the world's largest casual and smart shoe company and the fourth largest footwear company in the world.

Some of its subsidiary companies abroad are run by agents on behalf of Clarks, but most are run by distributors. Many of the factories have been purpose-built for Clarks. It aims to have reliable delivery services that ensure it gets products to customers across the world within 48 hours, to provide free returns and offer a 24-hour helpline.

Increasingly sales are made via the internet. Clarks has created a worldwide (English language) website and localised sites for France, Germany, the Netherlands, India, Spain, the UK, Australia and the USA. This is part of its plan to become a leading multi-channel retailer within the footwear market. To create and maintain these sites, Clarks employs native speakers to ensure the messages are appropriate for each international market. It uses data from the sites to analyse national differences in buying behaviour so that it can more effectively cater for their preferences. For example, its data suggests that customers in Germany plan well ahead and are always the first to make purchases for the coming season – so for example, they are likely to buy sandals in February in readiness for the summer season. French customers on the other hand are usually the last to buy for the coming season – buying sandals just before or at the beginning of summer.

All of these features enable the company to remain competitive.

Source: adapted from www.clarks.co.uk and a range of media articles over a number of years

Questions

1. Why might a company like Clarks decide to retain its private limited company status rather than becoming a public limited company? *(5 marks)*

2. Discuss the main influences that are likely to have led Clarks to move all of its production abroad. *(16 marks)*

3. Analyse how Clarks is managing the pressures for cost reduction and for local responsiveness. *(9 marks)*

4. As an international business, identify which of Bartlett and Ghoshal's strategies are likely to apply to Clarks and explain why. *(6 marks)*

5. Identify and explain three examples of the possible impact on Clarks' functional areas of its decision to move all of its production abroad and focus its attention on international markets. *(9 marks)*

Case study 4: IKEA

IKEA, the household goods and home furnishings retailer, was established in Sweden in 1943. IKEA's international expansion began in 1974, and today the firm generates only 8 per cent of its sales in Sweden. It now operates over 300 stores in over 40 countries. IKEA has grown to be one of the world's largest furniture retailers.

IKEA's strategy is the same in every country where it does business – selling furniture and household items that reflect Swedish style at low prices. Its huge sales volume enables the firm to benefit from significant economies of scale and volume discounts from its suppliers. IKEA tries to avoid high shipping costs by working with suppliers in each of its big international markets, at the same time as gaining efficiencies by concentrating production of certain items in markets like China. IKEA relies on a network of 1,300 suppliers located in 53 countries.

IKEA began its globalisation efforts with a pure international strategy in which products that were designed for Swedish customers were sold to buyers around the world. This strategy worked well because Swedish furniture design is admired by many for its simplicity and stylishness. The fact that the company pays close attention to price, quality and design, which are its core principles, is reflected in its products worldwide.

However, when the firm entered the North American market in 1985, its stores were not immediately profitable. This was because American tastes and requirements differed significantly from Swedish preferences and European requirements. For example, its dinner plates and glasses were too small for American tastes. In addition, it had not taken account of the fact that beds and bedding made for the European market were not the right sizes for the American market and curtains were too short. US kitchen appliances did not fit into the IKEA's kitchen cabinets and drawers. These issues took some time to resolve, but eventually IKEA began to tailor products to American needs, and since then sales have taken off.

While similar product lines are sold everywhere, the company does now adapt to meet the needs of consumers in different markets. In addition to the changes made to products sold in America described above, IKEA was also keen to understand the range of American customers. For example, in California, it felt it needed to meet the needs of the large Hispanic population and thus visited the homes of Hispanic staff members to observe their style and taste in home furnishings. The result was more large-scale furniture, more bold colours and more elaborate picture frames than the usual IKEA offering. In China, the company is designing its store layout to reflect the style of Chinese apartments, and is including a balcony section because most Chinese apartments have balconies.

Analysts suggest that IKEA has had to change to something like a transnational strategy, in which it centralises some tasks, but also provides opportunities to learn from its regional bases around the world.

Questions

1. Explain why managing an international business like IKEA is likely to involve responding to pressures for cost reduction and for local responsiveness.

   (8 marks)

2. Explain the impact of internationalisation on the marketing, operations and human resource functions of a business like IKEA. Use a different example to illustrate the impact on each of the three functions.

   (9 marks)

3. Some analysts suggest that IKEA is moving towards a transnational strategy. Discuss the evidence for this and the value of such a strategy for a business like IKEA.

   (16 marks)

4. In addition to a transnational strategy, Bartlett and Ghoshal identify three other strategies available to business operating in many international markets. Identify and explain each of these three other strategies.

   (12 marks)

14

Assessing greater use of digital technology

This chapter introduces the concept of digital technology. The pressure to use digital technology to improve business performance is examined through a consideration of e-commerce, big data, data mining and enterprise resource planning (ERP). The chapter then assesses the value of digital technology, before concluding with analysis of how digital technology has impacted on each of the functional areas of a business – operations management, marketing, finance and human resource management.

The pressures to adopt digital technology

Digital technology contrasts with analogue technology which uses electronic signals to transmit data. Digital technology enables a greater volume of data to be stored and processed.

Traditionally broadcast media used analogue technology, but over time most uses of analogue technology have been replaced by digital technology.

Digital technology has helped businesses and individuals to utilise the internet more fully for commercial purposes, through e-commerce (and more recently, through m-commerce). Mobile communication has changed the way in which people organise their lives, providing new opportunities to businesses (and threats to those that are slow to adopt new technology).

The greater efficiency of digital technology in comparison to other technologies has created pressures on businesses to adopt digital technology in their operations. It has also encouraged a more unified approach to technology, so that each functional area of business can integrate its activities more easily with the activities of other functional areas. In fact, digital technology has led to the breaking down of some of the barriers between the traditional functional areas of a business.

Some of the major aspects of the use of digital technology to improve business performance are evident in the following aspects of business:

- e-commerce
- big data
- data mining
- enterprise resource planning (ERP).

Key term

Digital technology Electronic technology which uses binary numbers (1 or 0) to store, generate and process data.

Key term

E-commerce The buying and selling of goods and services and/or the transmission of funds or data, using an electronic network, such as the internet.

E-commerce

Initially **e-commerce** described transactions using internet access through desktop computers. However, more and more transactions are now being undertaken through mobile communication, known as m-commerce. M-commerce is the buying and selling of goods and services and/or the transmission of funds or data using an electronic network that is accessed through a mobile device, such as a mobile phone or tablet.

Fact file

E-commerce and m-commerce – country comparisons

In 2014, UK online retailing sales grew by 15.8 per cent. Online retailing's sales represented 13.5 per cent of UK retail sales in 2014 and are expected to reach 15.2 per cent in 2015. The UK is further advanced in the use of online retailing than other European countries, with Germany (10.0 per cent) and Sweden (7.6 per cent) the next largest in terms of the market share of e-commerce. Although the USA is the country in which online retailing sales are highest, e-commerce's market share of retailing in the USA is lower (at 11.6 per cent) than it is in the UK.

In the UK e-commerce has grown rapidly in the twenty-first century. From negligible sales in the year 2000, online sales grew steadily over the next seven years, reaching 3.7 per cent of all retail sales in 2007. In the next seven years it grew much more rapidly, reaching 13.5 per cent of all retail sales in 2014. Growth is expected to continue, albeit at a lower rate, so that online retailing is expected to account for about 23 per cent of retail sales by 2021.

Figure 14.1 shows the percentage market share of online sales as a percentage of retail sales in 2014, with projected figures for 2015.

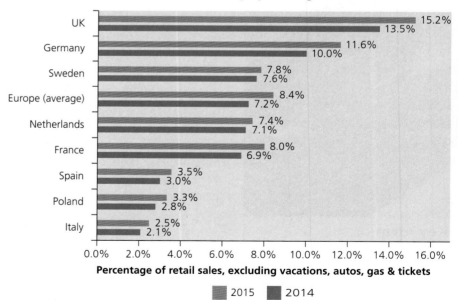

Percentage of retail sales, excluding vacations, autos, gas & tickets

▓ 2015 ▓ 2014

▲ **Figure 14.1** Online percentage market shares, Europe, 2014 and 2015

Table 14.1 shows the breakdown of online sales between PCs and mobile devices (including smartphones and tablets, i.e. m-commerce). In 2014, m-commerce represented 19 per cent of online sales but is expected to reach 29 per cent in 2015. Mobile communications are expected to account for over half of all online transactions by 2017. Research in March 2015 suggested that the 29 per cent forecast has already been surpassed.

▼ **Table 14.1** Online sales: e-commerce and m-commerce

	2014				2015			
	PC	Tablet	Smartphone	Total mobile	PC	Tablet	Smartphone	Total mobile
UK	81.3%	8.0%	10.7%	18.7%	71.4%	12.1%	16.5%	28.6%
Germany	83.2%	7.2%	9.6%	16.8%	72.3%	11.5%	16.2%	27.7%
France	88.2%	5.8%	6.0%	11.8%	80.8%	8.1%	11.1%	19.2%
Spain	90.6%	3.8%	5.6%	9.4%	84.4%	7.5%	8.1%	15.6%
Italy	92.9%	3.0%	4.1%	7.1%	89.9%	5.0%	5.1%	10.1%
Netherlands	88.8%	4.8%	6.4%	11.2%	81.7%	8.7%	9.6%	18.3%
Sweden	83.2%	7.4%	9.4%	16.8%	73.8%	11.7%	14.5%	26.2%
Poland	92.0%	3.4%	4.6%	8.0%	86.1%	6.1%	7.8%	13.9%
Europe	87.5%	5.4%	7.1%	12.5%	80.0%	7.5%	12.5%	20.0%
USA	81.3%	8.4%	10.3%	18.7%	73.2%	12.4%	14.4%	26.8%
Canada	88.7%	4.9%	6.4%	11.3%	83.8%	7.5%	8.7%	16.2%

NB: 2014 – actual; 2015 – projected

Source: RetailMeNot, France

E-commerce and m-commerce have both grown dramatically because of the benefits they bring to both businesses and customers. However, both groups need to recognise the potential disadvantages too. These advantages and disadvantages are summarised below.

Advantages of e-commerce to business

▲ E-commerce can result in substantial savings for businesses

- **Cost-effectiveness**. E-commerce allows businesses to cut certain costs – most notably the major expense of owning or renting shops in expensive city or town centre locations. It may also allow a business to save money by using more flexible staffing. Retail outlets must base their staffing on 'push techniques', using the estimated numbers of customers expected to visit a store on a particular day. This can lead to over-staffing and consequently high wage costs. However, online retailing uses 'pull' techniques, with customer orders dictating how many staff are needed to process and service their orders. Consequently, staff on flexible contracts can be called into work in accordance with the number of known orders received online. With online shopping, customers do not expect immediate receipt of goods that they order, whereas customers do expect the store to have sufficient inventory to meet their needs when they are shopping in the high street.
- **Flexibility**. Retailers can provide greater flexibility by storing all of their goods in one particular factory or warehouse and delivering them to customers in accordance with orders from the customers. This overcomes the problem of having inventory held in the wrong shops. With 'click and collect' deliveries online customers are able to visit the store knowing the good is available for collection, although in fact, it may have been transferred from another store in response to an online order.
- **Increased demand**. The advantages of e-commerce to customers (outlined on page 327) mean that firms can benefit because they may experience greater demand for their products. Online retailing increases the customer base of a business, to the extent that, in theory, any business can enter global markets. Using the internet is particularly useful for customers with mobility difficulties, and can also save expenses by reducing transport costs and time, because comparing alternative online retailers is a much simpler process than comparing

physical shops in a town centre. If a business has a unique selling point or competitive advantage, online retailing allows this to be shown to a much greater range of customers.

- **Improved efficiency**. Because online retailing tends to be based on specific orders, businesses are more likely to be able to organise their production to match demand. Consequently, there is less waste and so average (unit) costs of production should fall.

- **Greater profit margins**. Manufacturers can enjoy greater profit margins as a result of e-commerce. Traditionally manufacturers would sell their products to retailers at relatively low prices, because the retailers would then run the risk of not being able to sell the products if consumer tastes were not as expected. However, e-commerce allows manufacturers to sell directly to customers, because deliveries can be made directly from the factory. Thus the profit that was previously made by the retailer is now taken by the manufacturer. Furthermore, for bulky goods the transport costs may be cheaper because goods may be delivered directly from the factory to the customer. Previously, goods would be delivered from manufacturer to retailer and then from retailer to customer.

- **Impact on marketing**. E-commerce gives businesses a much greater understanding of the individual requirements of their customers and also the ability to tailor-make promotions to specific individuals. As a consequence, marketing should be much more cost-effective and successful in achieving greater sales, although the scope to sell more may be negated by the fact that competitors also have this benefit.

Disadvantages of e-commerce to business

- **Greater competition**. Because of the ease of entry to online markets, existing firms may find their market becoming much more competitive. This can lead to a fall in demand in the short term, as market share is spread between a wider range of businesses. In the long term this may lead to some businesses being forced to exit the market, particularly if they have been slow to adapt to e-commerce.

- **Costs of new technology**. Although digital technology tends to save costs in the long run, it can involve considerable expense in establishing the systems required to operate online selling. To attract customers, the design of the website must be user-friendly and be able to attract potential customers through search engines. Search engines tend to require payment for the most prestigious placings on their websites and so many smaller businesses are becoming harder for customers to find through online searches. More significantly, businesses require a distribution network and this can involve considerable expense and reliance on external organisations. However, the competitive nature of the distribution industry in the UK does tend to keep down distribution costs.

- **Lack of tactile experience for customers**. For many customers the ability to experience the physical qualities of a product is vital, particularly for items such as clothing and fragrances. Although online retailing gives visual clues, it is unable to match shops in offering this more direct contact with, or experience of, a product.

Although the growth of e-commerce is largely attributable to its benefits to business, a key influence on its growth is the impact that it has on customers. The impacts are summarised below.

▲ When shopping for certain products, for example, perfume, the customer is likely to want to visit a store to try it

Advantages of e-commerce to customers

- **Wider choice of products**. Goods and services are no longer limited to the retail outlets that a customer can visit. This means that customers are more likely to be able to purchase their preferred product.
- **Greater convenience**. Shopping can be conducted at any time of day and from any place, particularly with the growth of mobile commerce. This is particularly advantageous to people who work during the hours that most stores are open. Deliveries can be made directly to the customer's home.
- **Improved information**. Websites and related support systems allow customers to get much greater information about products, although this might not match the quality of information provided from a visit to a specialist retailer. This information can also include better access to customer reviews. These reduce the risk of customers making a poor choice when buying a new product.
- **Lower prices**. As indicated earlier, businesses can reduce costs through online retailing. It also encourages competition between businesses, which can drive down prices for customers. These two factors should lead to reduced prices for consumers.

Disadvantages of e-commerce to customers

- **Security**. Online retailing relies on secure payment systems. There have been a number of instances where personal financial details have been accessed by 'hackers' and instances where payments have been taken but no goods delivered.
- **Lack of tactile experience**. For some customers, and for some products, the lack of ability to experience the product before purchasing it can be a major issue.
- **Impersonal**. Many consumers would perceive the lack of human interaction during a commercial transaction as a particular disadvantage.
- **Faulty products**. Returning faulty goods can be a time-consuming and possibly costly activity, although in most cases any costs would be incurred by the supplier. It is usually much more convenient to return goods to a retailer.

What do you think?

UK shop numbers are expected to decline by 20 per cent over the next ten years. However, this is part of a trend that commenced in 1950. In 1950 there were 580,000 retail outlets in the UK, but the emergence of large-scale chain stores and supermarkets led to a change from a large number of small shops to fewer, but larger, retailers. By 1980 there were only 340,000 stores. Numbers declined slowly to 280,000 in 2009, but the recession and move to e-commerce have led to a rapid fall. The forecast for 2020 is that there will be only 200,000 retail outlets in the UK.

In many cases this decline will be a reduction in the number of stores of leading brands. In 2005, it was estimated that a retailer needed 200 stores to maintain a 'national presence'. With e-commerce leading to more direct selling to customers, retail analysts now consider that 75 stores are sufficient for a retailer to have a 'national presence'.

In contrast, many online businesses are seeking to establish town centre outlets, in part so that they can offer collection points for online sales. Some retail analysts believe that empty shops will be turned into residential accommodation, entertainment and leisure outlets, and services such as offices, doctor's surgeries and meeting rooms.

What changes do you believe will happen to traditional shopping centres over the next few years?

Big data

The rapid growth of the use and analysis of data by businesses is often expressed in terms of its high volume (quantity), high velocity (speed of transmission) and variety (the range of different data).

In 2001, business analyst Doug Laney introduced the idea of defining **'big data'** in terms of the three 'V's:

- **Volume**: This refers to the quantity of data being produced for business analysis. Businesses have always generated data, but have tended to lack the ability to interpret its meaning. In many cases businesses also experienced difficulties in storing high volumes of data. Furthermore, the relevance of some data was not recognised. However, the costs of data storage are now lower and analytical software enables businesses to discover relationships and correlations arising from their data.
- **Velocity**: The speed with which data can be recorded has increased dramatically. In addition, analytical software allows it to be interpreted much more quickly too. This has increased the usefulness of big data because much of the information is very up to date and therefore conclusions based on this information are likely to be more reliable indicators, even in markets in which there is rapid change.
- **Variety**: Traditionally businesses relied on structured numerical data in databases, with most of this data being based on output, sales levels and financial information. Big data provide the opportunity for more unstructured information, such as e-mails, qualitative customer feedback and social media comments.

Some people have added a fourth 'V' – veracity – to describe the level of reliability of business data. According to IBM, one-third of US business leaders do not trust the information they use to make decisions, and 27 per cent of managers surveyed were unsure about the accuracy of the data they were using.

Fact file

Volume of data

According to IBM, 90 per cent of the data in the world has been created within the last two years. In the future, this figure may well increase. It is estimated that 43 trillion gigabytes of data will be created by 2020.

Uses of big data

The uses of big data can vary considerably and depend on the particular needs of the business and, sometimes, on the data available for analysis. Some examples of big data usage are as follows:

- **Analysis of operations**. The growing use of computerised machinery, sensors and meters has led to increased data on the performance of a business's operations. In particular, the speed with which data can be gathered enables businesses to correct errors in their operations, such as quality defects, much more rapidly. Often the equipment is also easily and remotely adjustable, so that action can be taken to ensure that problems do not continue. This analysis can register factors such as speed of production, accuracy of specifications and customer experience.

Combining this data with data such as costs of manufacturing and levels of repeat purchases can enable a business to recognise the level of financial benefits that arise from rectifying different problems, so that priorities can be established.

- **Marketing information**. The data allows a business to gather much more detailed information on its customers so that they can understand their needs. Data from loyalty cards, websites, credit cards and other payment systems and customer feedback may enable the business to ascertain levels of brand loyalty of individual customers, key factors that influence their buying habits, how they are likely to react to different forms of promotion and price changes, how and where they prefer to shop and possible clues to changes in their future buying habits.
- **Improving decision making**. The analysis of internal data may be used to ascertain the effectiveness of new strategies introduced into a business and the consequences of decisions made by managers within a business. By analysing this data, a business should be able to recognise its successes and failures, and so recognise its strengths and minimise the impact of its weaknesses. This data can then be linked with other data that might be able to explain the reasons for success or failure, in order to improve future decision making.
- **Improving security**. Security issues are a major threat to the growing use of data in business. Analysis of customer records from the business itself and from external sources can enable a business to reduce its risks of fraud or customer default. The technology may also help a business to develop systems that are more secure and thus prevent the possibility of security breaches in future.

Issues involving the use of big data

Although big data provides many advantages to businesses, there are certain factors that need to be considered in its use. Firstly, data protection legislation prohibits the use of data when the person, usually a customer, has not agreed to its use. Although most big data is considered to be gathered legally, the level of data gathering is so high that it is difficult for a business to be sure that this is in fact the case. Secondly, the reliability of the data can be questionable, particularly if it is from external sources or opinions. If the data is unreliable, then any analysis based on it is likely to be incorrect. Consequently, incorrect conclusions are likely to be drawn. Finally, although data analysis can be conducted much more effectively, it can still use a lot of resources. The big data market is predicted to grow to a market worth $16.9 billion in 2015. The global business consultancy, Gartner, expects this industry to produce 4.4 million jobs globally, with each IT job created by big data likely to generate three more non-IT jobs. However, this huge expansion in job opportunities will only occur if businesses can be sure that the benefits of big data outweigh the costs of using it.

Examples of users and their uses of big data

- **Online retailers**: retailers are able to get much better data from their online customers than from those that use shops. Retailers can track the behaviour of online customers by observing what they buy, but also by noting what other products they looked at. It is also possible to observe features such as how consumers navigate a website, to what extent they are influenced by promotions and reviews, and the impact

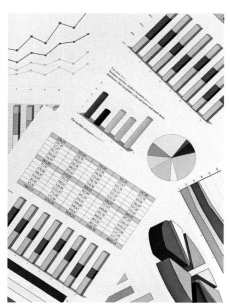

▲ Businesses have access to more data than ever before

▲ Big data has allowed more accurate scheduling for airports, ensuring staff are in the right place and saving the airports money

of page layouts on their behaviour. As a consequence, retailers are often able to predict what products a consumer would like and what they are likely to want in the future, through noting their reactions to different information and promotions. To businesses such as Amazon big data is a source of competitive advantage.

● **Transport scheduling**: airports have been particular beneficiaries of big data. Previously they relied on estimated times of arrival from pilots, 10 per cent of which were incorrect by more than ten minutes in US airports. This meant that staff, such as baggage handlers, were in the wrong place at the wrong time. However, analysis of big data provided by computer programs, which incorporate factors such as localised weather conditions, has led to much greater accuracy of arrival times. PASSUR, the software provider, estimates that each airport in the USA has saved several million dollars a year through the system, which reduces idle time for airport staff.

● **More personalised marketing**: by centralising all data on sales and inventory holdings a business can match the availability of products to the likely demand, the latter being based on their improved observations of consumer behaviour. This matching automatically creates instructions to increase (or run down) inventory levels where the availability does not match the anticipated demand. In traditional organisations, these items of data would be held by different departments, and so this type of co-ordination would have been difficult to achieve.

What do you think?

The growth of big data has led to businesses accumulating significant levels of information on customers, much of which is not recognised by those customers. In many cases, the use of this data is 'agreed' by the customer when visiting a website or completing a transaction. However, the level of information given in these conditions is so high that it is unlikely that most customers fully understand the nature of the agreement. Is it ethical for businesses to use information collected in this way? Just because it gives businesses a better understanding of their customers' needs, is it always beneficial to customers? What do you think?

Did you know?

Business analysts at McKinsey & Company and the Massachusetts Institute of Technology undertook research to test the hypothesis that 'data-driven' companies that use big data perform better than other companies. Measures of performance were based on financial information and operations data. The research concluded that businesses that consider themselves to be major users of big data were 6 per cent more profitable than their competitors and 5 per cent more efficient in their production.

Many of these businesses regard their use of 'big data' as a source of competitive advantage when comparing themselves to their competitors.

Source: *Harvard Business Review*

Data mining

Much of **data mining** is based on statistical techniques. However, whereas statistical analysis was often based on sampling in order to prove (or disprove) ideas, the volume of data now available is likely to lead to more certainty in the conclusions and predictions that arise from analysing the data.

Because of the sheer volume of data available, businesses in the past had to prioritise the data that they elected to retain and analyse. Big data uses the analytical tools provided by software to enable a business to not only store more information, but also to allow their computing facilities to generate a multitude of connections between different data. For example, it has been found that the background colour of a website may have a significant influence on consumer reactions to the content of the website. This type of connection between data would not have been analysed in the past, but data mining allows computer programs to analyse random connections, such as the impact of different colours, and present the results of these connections where there appears to be some connection present. It is then left to the skill and intuition of business analysts to decide whether this connection is causal or merely coincidental.

The ability to analyse data is a key growth area for employment and is vital to the successful use of data mining. Data mining can take many forms and its precise use depends on the type of analysis required by a business. Examples of types of data mining are outlined below. Most of these examples describe the use of statistical information in business decision making and, as such, are dealt with in more detail in other parts of the A-level Business course.

Examples of data-mining techniques

- **Data counting and analysis**: Data mining allows a business to compile data that can be used to improve performance. The calculation of average sales revenue per day can inform a business of how much production they should plan each day. The data may also allow them to recognise the likely extent of variations from an average so that the likely maximum and minimum sales revenues can be known. Probability data enables businesses to estimate the chances of events occurring so that they can create decision trees to improve their planning and decision making. The use of decision trees was covered on pages 82–87 of Chapter 5 of the AQA A-level Business Book 1.
  (Data mining will have also provided the business with analysis of the likely impact of these events on the business's performance.)
- **Clustering/grouping**: Clustering is the grouping of similar data. The basis of clustering can take many different forms, and the form or forms chosen will depend on factors such as the nature of a business, its products, its customers or other relevant characteristics. In Book 1, Chapter 6 showed how 'Stakeholder mapping' could be used to recognise the needs of different stakeholders so that a business could satisfy those needs. Also in Book 1, Chapter 8 introduced the concept of 'Market mapping', which enables businesses to recognise the key characteristics that influence a product's popularity and the way in which different products or businesses are perceived in regard to those characteristics. Data mining allows a business to broaden the number of possible clusters to see if there are characteristics whose importance the business did not recognise.

Probably the most widely used form of clustering in data mining is market segmentation, targeting and positioning. These topics formed the basis of Chapter 9 of Book 1. Data mining allows a business to correlate sales of a product to a wide range of different characteristics in order to discover those characteristics that have the biggest influence on demand for a product. Data mining also allows this information to be constantly updated, so that changes in consumer opinions are immediately recognised.

● **Correlation and regression analysis**: Data mining improves the efficiency of traditional statistical techniques such as correlation and regression analysis. In Book 1, Chapter 8 dealt with the interpretation of marketing data through correlation and regression. Regression techniques enable a business to forecast the influence of a factor (such as advertising) on another variable (such as sales revenue). Correlation allows the business to recognise the reliability and consistency of this relationship, as few statistics provide absolute certainty in their projections. With improved data and more detailed analytical techniques a business can discover the most important factors that influence its sales revenue and also quickly recognise any changes in these relationships. Chapter 8 of Book 1 also introduced the concepts of price elasticity of demand and income elasticity of demand, which explained the relationship, respectively, between the quantity demanded of a good and its price and the quantity demanded of a good and the level of consumer income. Elasticity of demand calculations are based on regression techniques.

● **Decision trees**: Decision trees are another decision-making technique that can be enhanced by data mining. You are advised to re-visit Chapter 5 of Book 1 if you want to remind yourself of this topic. In essence the data for decision trees comes from data mining. Statistical analysis, based on historical decisions, enables a business to discover the probabilities of different outcomes arising from particular decisions. This analysis can also enable a business to recognise the costs involved in the decision and the payoffs arising. This set of data is constantly updated as new decisions are made, thus enhancing the likely accuracy of any decision trees. Applying this data to a decision tree will help a business to make the decision that provides the most favourable outcome.

● **Network analysis/critical path analysis**: In Chapter 17 of this book, we will examine network analysis (critical path analysis). This is a technique used in both strategic management and in operations management. The technique allows a business to plan projects in the most efficient manner possible. Data from past experiences will help a business to recognise the different stages required to complete a particular project, the resources needed at each stage and the time taken to complete each stage. This information then helps a business to more accurately plan projects – a vital business tool when customers require accurate information on how long a project will take to complete.

▲ A business's ability to analyse the data it collects is key to its success

Fact file

Cloud computing

Cloud computing has allowed businesses to expand their data collection to much greater levels. This has facilitated the use of big data and enabled businesses to establish statistical connections that provide useful insights to help improve their performance.

Enterprise resource planning (ERP)

The core business processes that tend to be automated are activities such as processing customer orders, keeping inventory records, scheduling operations such as production and delivery, and maintaining records of financial transactions.

ERP operates through business software that brings together the activities needed to satisfy customer orders and to monitor the performance of those activities so that they are performed cost-effectively and to the customer's satisfaction. ERP software can be used within a business, but where activities are outsourced, it is typically shared with suppliers and sub-contractors so that a business can be sure that their activities are conducted to the standards required by the business.

The activities automated through ERP may include all of the following:

- Order processing: Taking orders, checking customer credit ratings and ensuring that delivery meets the procedure agreed with the customer.
- Manufacturing: Production planning, monitoring the flow of production, and quality assurance of finished products on the production line.
- Supply-chain management: Ordering and handling of materials and ensuring cost-effectiveness and quality of components.
- Inventory control: Managing inventory of raw materials and finished products in a way that balances the needs of keeping costs low but availability high.
- Sales and customer service: Ensuring that all activities are suited to the needs of the customer and that the customer has a direct point of contact within a business.
- Human resource management: Managing human resources through recruitment, training, payroll and benefits and incentives.
- Financial accounting. Dealing with payables and receivables and managing cash flow.

The main benefits of Enterprise Resource Planning (ERP) are:

- Integration of all business processes so that all aspects of a business work towards the same goals. Usually one individual is responsible for a particular customer and their orders so that consistent messages are conveyed to customers. ERP links together all of the functional areas of a business so that each area is working towards meeting the needs of the customer rather than its own specific targets.
- Greater efficiency from automation. The automation of these processes reduces the possibility of human error and provides better co-ordination, so that time management is more effective, thus cutting costs.
- Closer scrutiny of all activities. Because ERP tends to be integrated with suppliers and other external organisations, it tends to mean that the business has a much clearer picture of all of the activities being undertaken in the production and delivery of its goods.
- Reports. ERP software analyses the effectiveness of the performance of the various activities that it co-ordinates and provides reports to management. This enables managers to identify the strengths and weaknesses of their activities and to take appropriate action to improve efficiency.

Fact file

Benefits of ERP

A survey by the Aberdeen Group in 2010 revealed that businesses that successfully used enterprise resource planning (ERP) recorded the following benefits:

- 22 per cent reduction in operating costs
- 20 per cent reduction in administrative costs
- 19 per cent improvement in on-time deliveries to customers
- 17 per cent improvement in the completion of production on schedule
- 17 per cent reduction in inventory levels.

Why do businesses use enterprise resource planning (ERP)?

The benefits outlined in the previous section provide reasons for businesses to choose to use ERP. A survey in 2010, the results of which have been confirmed by subsequent surveys, confirms that cost reduction is the main motivation behind the adoption of ERP by a business.

The key factors leading to its adoption are:

- to reduce costs
- to make a business more accessible for other businesses to do business with
- to efficiently manage future growth
- to manage growth expectations in a co-ordinated manner
- to improve customer response times
- to overcome difficulties in co-ordinating activities taking place in different locations
- to help innovation in order to increase added value.

Figure 14.2 shows the relative importance of these reasons, based on a survey of small and medium-sized enterprises.

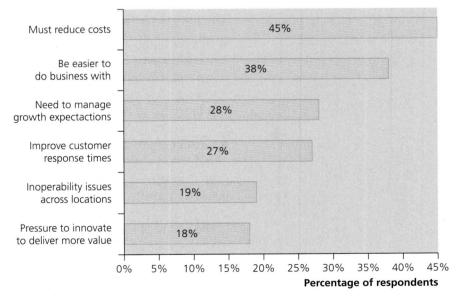

▲ **Figure 14.2** Factors driving ERP adoption

Source: Aberdeen Group

The value of digital technology

Digital technology provides many benefits, although these vary according to the way in which digital technology is being used. Many of these benefits have been described earlier in this chapter. The list below provides an overview of the key benefits of digital technology.

- Higher living standards. Digital technology has improved the efficiency with which businesses can provide goods and services, and this has led to improvements in wealth creation throughout the world.
- Greater competition. By improving communications and creating global markets, digital technology has been a key factor in reducing the barriers to entry in many industries, consequently leading to more intense price competition and lower prices for customers.
- Improved efficiency and reduced waste. Cost-effective use of resources benefits consumers and firms, and in the long term resources last longer, thus benefiting society in general.
- Advances in communication. These advances have allowed businesses to improve their efficiency, customers to have their needs met more fully, and society to benefit from a much wider choice of goods and services. Improved communications have given people a much better understanding of their world, and mobile communications in particular have greatly assisted people in keeping in contact with each other.
- Better quality products and services. Consumers benefit from more choice, and if this leads to more demand, company profits are likely to increase.
- New products and materials. Needs and wants that were previously not satisfied can be provided for, such as mobile communication.
- Advances in communication. Company efficiency is increased and consumer needs are met more directly.
- Improved working environment. Employees work in safer conditions and there are a greater number of jobs that are less physically demanding and more interesting.

When assessing the overall value of digital technology, some of the issues arising from its use can have negative repercussions and so must be considered too. These issues are listed below. However, on balance the benefits certainly seem to outweigh the problems generated by these issues.

- **Stress**. People are often concerned by change and digital technology has led to more rapid change than earlier technological developments.
- **Lower morale**. Digital technologies give greater power to people who have the skills to benefit from it. However, there are suggestions that unskilled workers are being left behind. Furthermore, digital technology has allowed businesses to delayer their organisational structures, leading to significant losses in middle-management roles. These changes may further exaggerate the social divisions within society.
- **Costs of introducing and updating digital technology**. For many businesses, the most significant problem is the cost of new technology. Not only is it expensive to introduce, but it also needs regular updating and servicing. In some situations, it may be more cost-effective to employ less advanced techniques, to avoid constant expenditure on updating technology. For some organisations, the cost of technology can make the business uncompetitive and thus threaten its survival. Staff will also have to undergo frequent training, again adding to costs and threatening efficiency if a business is unable to keep up with the pace of change.

- **Possible higher barriers to entry**. Although lower barriers to entry are a potential benefit of digital technology, there are some markets, such as telecommunications, where large firms have been able to use digital technology to gain a competitive advantage. It has thus become more difficult to enter these markets and so existing businesses have been able to achieve high added value, potentially at the expense of consumers who are paying higher prices for goods and services.
- **Digital technology is changing the global competitive environment**. Developing countries, particularly in Asia, have adapted to digital technology more rapidly than European countries, particularly those in southern Europe. This has led to a shifting of the balance of economic power away from Europe, to a significant extent.

The impact of digital technology on the functional areas of the business

A key feature of digital technology is that it has led to much greater levels of integration between the different functional areas of business. The impact has also not necessarily been spread evenly between the different departments or functional areas.

The main impacts of digital technology on the functional areas of the business are described below.

The impact of digital technology on operations management

Some of the key effects are:

▲ Robots are increasingly used to carry out production activities

- **Robotic production**: Digital technology has improved robot technology, so that robots can be programmed to carry out both routine and increasingly complex activities. Some of the main applications of robotics are handling operations, manipulating materials and components into position, in order for other production activities, such as welding, to take place. Robots can also be programmed to undertake welding, painting, precision cutting and assembling. Finally, robots can be used to measure, inspect and test finished products with much greater accuracy than people.
- **Automation**: Digital technology is important in several aspects of automation:
  - Production planning, using digital technology to construct and manipulate networks on computers. Programs can use 'what if?' analysis to examine the implications of any modifications to the network. By using this approach for all of its activities, a business can plan the use of resources more effectively. Once the production line is up and running, any variations to the planned schedule can also be monitored by computer and, if necessary, remedial action taken to modify the approach used.
  - Digital technology can also be useful in the design and manufacturing process. In CAD (computer-aided design), designs can be formulated from other data and quickly modified. Two-dimensional figures can be easily transformed into 3D layouts to give a clearer picture of the final product or design. In CAM (computer-aided manufacture), the use of robots and fully automated production lines, controlled by computers, has increased productivity and reduced the problems arising from human error. With greater use of miniaturisation in production, many components are now too small for human beings to manipulate. Flexible programming also allows a fully automated line to produce different varieties of a product.

▲ Organisations can use digital technology to establish the locations where stock is being held

- Quality assurance can be achieved through digital technology because, once the manufacturing process begins, the product and the efficiency of the process are scrutinised constantly. Maintaining control of the process through computer-based quality assurance systems can overcome the possibility of human error and also provide more rigorous scrutiny of quality.
- **Inventory control**: This was one of the first aspects of operations management to be transformed by digital technology. This is aided by technology in the following ways:
  - Computer programs linked to statistics on patterns of consumer purchases allow firms to anticipate changes in stock levels more accurately. This reduces the possibility that a business will run out of stock or build up unnecessarily high levels. Firms are now able to operate with lower levels of inventory and so reduce their costs.
  - Computerised systems allow organisations to access instantly their current stock levels, reducing the need for time-consuming manual checks (although these will still be needed on occasions to cover for problems such as pilferage).
  - Retailers are able to link their tills to stock control through EPOS (electronic point of sale) systems. Every time an item is sold, the EPOS system adjusts the stock level. These systems can also order new stock from suppliers automatically when a particular item has fallen to a certain level (known as the re-order level).
  - Organisations with many branches can also use technology to establish the locations where stock is being held, so that, in emergencies, stock can be moved between branches.

In operations management, digital technology has led to:

- reduced costs and greater productivity
- improved quality
- better co-ordination
- greater innovation
- higher levels of flexibility
- reduced waste.

The impact of digital technology on marketing

Digital technology has had a significant impact on marketing departments in recent years. It has led to the creation of a whole new category of business (e-commerce companies) and brings a number of specific advantages to the marketing function:

- It can reduce or eliminate the need for expensive high-street premises. Operations can be moved to places where costs such as rent and wages are considerably lower.
- It can reduce the need to employ marketing staff. Organisations such as insurance companies no longer feel the need for a sales force, while other businesses, such as estate agents, rely more on websites to promote their services.
- Digital technology has added flexibility to marketing activities, which no longer have to fit in with traditional business structures. For example, 24-hour opening is possible and decisions such as credit card approval can be made on the basis of information that is accessible via computer.

- Data can be stored more cheaply and accessed at greater speed, and so businesses have a much greater understanding of their customers. They are also able to access previous communications instantly, so that customer enquiries can be handled quickly and efficiently. Marketing decisions can be taken with a much greater level of understanding of a business's customer base.
- Digital technology has enabled the growth of social media, which has become a major force in the promotion of brands by marketing departments. This has totally transformed the nature of marketing, as businesses must react quickly to business-related items that are trending on social media, such as Twitter, in order to take advantage of the marketing opportunities offered. Tried and tested marketing campaigns are becoming the exception rather than the norm.
- Digital technology offers much greater scope for added value because it enables businesses to get a much better understanding of their customers, and therefore tailor-make products to meet the needs of individual customers.
- Greater use of digital marketing has led to significant cuts in marketing expenditure as customers can be accessed much more cheaply. In 2015 digital marketing is expected to account for 50 per cent of all UK advertising expenditure, with the traditional market leader – television advertising – accounting for less than a quarter of advertising expenditure. (See the Did you know? on the left.)

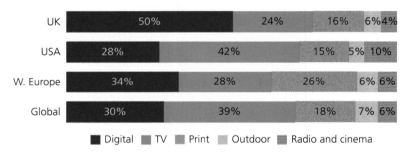

▲ **Figure 14.3** Share of advertising spending by media type, 2015

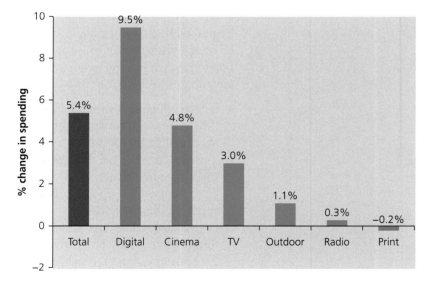

▲ **Figure 14.4** Annual change in UK advertising spending by media type, 2015

Fact file

Online gambling

One industry that has been transformed by the internet is gambling. Two major beneficiaries are, coincidentally, based in the same office block in Gibraltar. 888 Holdings plc was launched in 1996 and in 2007 was valued at $65 million. Its rival, iGlobalMedia, has also been successful. Launched in 1997, its www.partypoker.com and related websites helped it to increase its value to $75 million by 2007. When it floated on the London Stock Exchange, it immediately entered the FTSE 100 as one of the Stock Exchange's top 100 most valued companies. However, both companies were badly hit by a loss of customers in the USA, where their method of internet gambling was declared illegal. Despite this, global growth has continued and, in 2015, 888 Holdings plc was valued at $185 million while iGlobalMedia was worth $680 million.

The impact of digital technology on financial management

On the whole, financial management benefits from digital technology because it is able to identify deficiencies and inefficiencies at an early stage. Some examples of processes used are outlined below.

- **Financial monitoring**. Digital technology greatly improves the budgeting process. The speed of processing data and the ability to access more information directly enable businesses to plan their budgets more rigorously. Alternatives can be scrutinised to make sure that the budgets are allocated efficiently. Perhaps the greatest benefit to the budgeting process is in budgetary control. With every item of expenditure being recorded, it is possible to monitor actual expenditure against the budget in order to identify areas of inefficiency. This helps a firm to take prompt action to resolve any problems.
- **Financial management of projects/activities**. Improvements to the level of data collected enable businesses to more closely monitor the financial performance of projects, such as a new building, or activities, such as a marketing campaign. Rather than await the results of these projects, early signs of errors can be detected and actions taken to improve financial performance.
- **Accounting ratios**. Typically, businesses tended to analyse their overall financial performance on an annual basis. Difficulties in collecting and collating all the necessary data meant that at times this analysis was performed sometime after the end of the financial year. As a consequence, this financial analysis tended to show strengths or weaknesses after the event. As a result of data mining many businesses analyse their accounts more frequently, usually on a quarterly basis. This means that problems can be detected within the first few months of the year, and therefore any remedial action taken may lead to an improvement in that year's performance, rather than having to wait until the following year for improvements to take effect.

The impact of digital technology on human resource management

Digital technology is having a significant impact on the nature of jobs and the ways in which human resources are managed.

The pace of technological change has meant that new skills are required and this has considerable implications for recruitment, retention and training, and their associated costs. Employment has been affected in several ways by the introduction of technology. Traditional workforce skills, such as printing, have been replaced by tasks requiring computer operators, and a number of new jobs requiring data handling have been introduced. The 'communication age' has increased the demand for data and has been instrumental in shifting the balance of employment in the UK from the secondary sector to the tertiary (service) sector. Even in manufacturing companies themselves there has been a shift towards more tertiary jobs, as computers have led to automated production lines that require fewer manual employees.

The job market has also changed, with digital technology providing much higher levels of control and monitoring. It has also improved internal communications within businesses and therefore enabled businesses to give managers wider spans of control. This has reduced the number of layers within a business and also the number of managerial and supervisory positions. However, it has opened up significant opportunities for data analysis, as digital technology only provides the data – it requires human interpretation for conclusions to be drawn on the significance of this data for a business.

Digital technology also allows businesses to benefit from the multi-skilling of staff, creating jobs that are less rigidly defined and adaptable to changes in the workplace. It has also been a key factor in the development of many small businesses operating from home or small premises. It also offers greater flexibility to both businesses and employees in terms of the place of employment. It is encouraging teleworking (i.e. people working from home and other locations, and keeping in contact through digital technology). Some small businesses are utilising public areas, such as coffee shops, as meeting places and carrying out the rest of their work from home. Occupations such as market research, design and software development can all be based away from the office. This can motivate staff by giving them more independence and responsibility, while reducing Herzberg's hygiene factors such as travel time and expense. However, projections that the typical office will cease to exist are probably unrealistic, as many teleworkers find that they miss the social aspects of working alongside colleagues. Moreover, some teleworkers find it difficult to separate work from leisure – a major factor in causing stress.

Internal information can be processed and amended more quickly. By keeping employees up to date and facilitating two-way communication, ICT improves the efficiency and motivation of staff. Company intranets enable employees to access company information at any time. Individuals are not always aware in advance of their information requirements, so a system that provides data at the press of a button saves a considerable amount of time, improving the efficiency of staff.

Digital technology increases the speed of communication and gives employees more scope for individuality and the taking of greater responsibility. This also allows companies to delayer and operate wider spans of control.

Industrial relations between employers and employees can be damaged. As technology replaces jobs, there is a danger of resistance by workers and trade unions, and a consequent lowering of morale. However, morale can be improved by the greater scope for profit and financial or non-financial rewards, and also by increased opportunities for employees to achieve as individuals.

Digital technology also facilitates better working conditions. It can regulate the working environment, through factors such as reductions in the level of noise and greater control over temperatures in the work area, thus improving the welfare of employees.

Big data enables businesses to maintain much better records of both their staff and applicants. Consequently, recruitment may be improved because a business has a much better understanding of its potential workforce. Many firms use social media to gain some understanding of the background of potential employees, as this is information that may give a clearer picture of the character of the employee, but is not information that the employee would provide directly to a potential employer.

Practice exercise 1

Total: 50 marks

1. Electronic technology which uses binary numbers to store data is known as:
   a) analogue technology
   b) big data
   c) data mining
   d) digital technology. *(1 mark)*

2. Which one of these European countries had the highest level of online sales as a percentage of total retail sales in 2014?
   a) France
   b) Germany
   c) Sweden
   d) UK *(1 mark)*

3. Which one of these terms is **not** one of the three Vs of big data?
   a) Variety
   b) Velocity
   c) Vitality
   d) Volume *(1 mark)*

4. Which one of the following is **not** an example of a data-mining technique?
   a) Correlation and regression
   b) Decision trees
   c) Network analysis
   d) Qualitative analysis *(1 mark)*

5. What is meant by the term 'e-commerce'? *(3 marks)*

6. What is meant by the term 'data mining'? *(3 marks)*

7. State three activities that can be automated through enterprise resource planning. (*3 marks*)

8. Explain one way in which 'clustering' can help a firm's marketing. (*4 marks*)

9. Explain one disadvantage to customers arising from e-commerce. (*3 marks*)

10. Explain two benefits to businesses arising from e-commerce. (*6 marks*)

11. Explain two possible uses of big data to improve business performance. (*6 marks*)

12. Analyse possible problems for businesses as a result of the growth of digital technology. (*9 marks*)

13. Analyse ways in which digital technology can help to improve the performance of the human resource management function of a business. (*9 marks*)

Case study: Digital technology at Amazon

Amazon epitomises the movement towards greater use of digital technology. Founded by Jeff Bezos in 1994, it began operating as an online bookshop in 1995. Amazon was able to offer a wider range of books than established bookshops because, in effect, it was using the warehouses of the book publishers to store the books that it would sell. In the first two months of business Amazon sold books to more than 45 countries, with sales figures reaching $20,000 a week.

By 2000, annual e-commerce sales had reached $2.5 billion. By 2007, the year in which the iPhone enabled m-commerce sales to commence, Amazon's e-commerce sales had reached $13 billion. In 2014, Amazon recorded annual sales of $89 billion, of which $17 billion were mobile (m-commerce) sales.

Amazon is the largest online retailer in the USA, but in 2014 Alibaba, the Chinese e-commerce giant, became the world leader. Both businesses are based on offering a wide variety of online goods and services at low prices. However, Alibaba operates as an open marketplace where buyers and sellers can meet, more akin to the eBay model of selling. As Alibaba sells no products directly to customers it does not own any warehouses or employ distribution staff. Therefore the revenue it receives provides Alibaba with a high (40 per cent) profit margin (Amazon's profit margin tends to fluctuate between 1 per cent and 4 per cent). In contrast, Amazon owns large warehouses and sells the majority of its products directly to customers. It also manufactures its own brands of smartphones and tablets. However, Amazon's model does enable it to accumulate vast quantities of data.

One of Amazon's competitive strengths was its personalised recommendation system. Using data mining to establish customers' wants enabled it to target customers with offers that were designed to meet their specific needs. Amazon's data system has become so sophisticated that it has patented a system designed to deliver goods to customers before they have decided to buy them. This 'predictive despatch' demonstrates the confidence Amazon has in the quality of its big data and data mining.

One of the key strengths of Amazon's use of data mining is that much of Amazon's data is related to people's spending. This contrasts with data held by social media, such as Facebook, which shows considerable insight into the character of people, but not necessarily in a way that can be exploited commercially.

Amazon is now in direct competition with Google. Both companies are offering other companies access to their databases and to the analytical tools they use for data mining. Unlike businesses such as Apple and Nike, which attempt to shape consumer tastes, Amazon is intent on discovering consumer tastes and shaping their goods and services to those tastes.

Amazon is a major user of enterprise resource planning (ERP). Its warehouse operations are designed to ensure that inventory is managed in a way that reduces costs but allows the business to meet orders promptly. Another priority is minimising the time taken for staff to carry out different operations. Items are scanned on arrival and popular items are kept on pallets for quick placement on lorries. Inventory is located close to other items that may be purchased together. At peak times the most popular items are stored in multiple locations to avoid bottlenecks when employees are 'picking' supplies. Amazon uses an algorithm to decide the best shipping route and delivery for each product, to enable the company to meet its delivery objectives.

Questions

Total: 45 marks

1. What is meant by the term 'enterprise resource planning'? *(3 marks)*

2. Calculate Amazon's m-commerce sales as a percentage of its total sales in 2014. *(2 marks)*

3. Calculate Amazon's growth rates:
   a) from 2000 to 2007
   b) from 2007 to 2014.

   Show your working. *(5 marks)*

4. State two examples of data-mining techniques used by Amazon. *(2 marks)*

5. Explain one advantage and one disadvantage of Alibaba's approach to e-commerce. *(8 marks)*

6. To what extent is Amazon's use of digital data the most important reason for its rapid growth since 1994? *(25 marks)*

15

Managing change

This chapter begins by discussing the possible causes of, and pressures for, change. In doing so, it considers different types of change, including internal change, external change, incremental change and disruptive change. In discussing the management of change, Lewin's force field analysis is explained. The value of change is then considered, followed by the value of a flexible organisation. In discussing flexible organisations, the following aspects are considered: restructuring, delayering, flexible employment contracts, organic versus mechanistic structures, and knowledge and information management. The value of managing information and knowledge is then discussed. Barriers to change are considered, and Kotter and Schlesinger's four reasons for resistance to change are explained. The final section of the chapter reviews how to overcome barriers to change, and discusses Kotter and Schlesinger's six ways of overcoming resistance to change.

Causes of and pressures for change

Causes of and pressures for change emanate from both the internal and the external environment of a business.

Internal environmental causes of and pressures for change have been discussed throughout this and the AQA A-level Business Book 1. They include, for example:

- issues about the current technology in a business, including the state of plant, machinery and tools, and whether this performs as well as it could to enable a business to remain competitive
- issues about the nature, quality and sufficiency of human resources in a business. For example, whether there are enough skilled staff available to enable the business to meet its objectives, or whether payment and reward systems enable a business to motivate its staff and ensure that they meet expected performance targets
- issues about the organisational structure of a business, including lines of communication, managerial hierarchies and co-ordination and co-operation between departments or divisions, and whether these are suitable to support a business in meeting its objectives
- the profitability of a business and whether it is looking to grow in size or to retrench
- the objectives and vision of business owners and key stakeholders, and how they wish a business to develop.

The main pressure for change is usually external, because business has to be prepared to face the demands of a changing external environment. Causes of and pressures for change in the external environment can come from political, economic, social and cultural, technological, legal and environmental sources, or from sources within the competitive environment of a business. These areas have been considered in detail in previous chapters of this and Book 1 (external environmental influences in Chapter 3 of Book 1 and Chapters 4–6 in this book, and competitive environmental influences in Chapter 7 of this book). Ensure that you are familiar with all of these areas before proceeding with this chapter.

Change is a constant feature of business activity. The key issues are whether potential change has been foreseen by a business – and therefore planned for – and whether it is within a business's control.

Planned change may result, for example, from a strategy to bring about a significant increase in sales and the size of a business. This is likely to require new management structures, more layers of hierarchy and new divisions or departments. Although these changes may have been planned for, other, unforeseen consequences may emerge that lead to further unplanned changes. For example, the changes to organisational structure may lead to a business becoming very bureaucratic, which in turn may cause able and creative staff to leave. Alternatively, increased delegation to divisions or departments may have adverse effects on managers as they struggle to live up to their new responsibilities and fail to meet targets.

Unforeseen change is more of a problem. If a small business provides a service that suddenly becomes very popular, it may find it is unable to get the resources needed to support the increased business activity adequately. Management, in turn, may begin to lose control unless it is well prepared. For example, managers may be unable to delegate because of a lack of appropriate staff, or may be unwilling to delegate effectively because of an inability to 'let go' of power and to trust others. Appropriate planning could have improved the situation – by controlling the rate of growth, by creating an organisational structure that meets the needs of such growth, by developing a leadership style that encourages delegation, and by training staff to take on responsibility.

Kotter and Schlesinger (whose ideas on barriers to change and how to overcome them are explained later in this chapter) note that most organisations are likely to have to undertake moderate change once a year, and major changes every four or five years.

There are several types of change.

Internal change

Internal change refers to changes that occur within a business. This type of change has been the focus of many of the chapters in this and Book 1 – particularly those chapters related to the different functional areas of a business. For example, internal change could involve the introduction of new technology, the decision to outsource production, changes to employee reward systems, changes to the organisational structure, or changes because of new owners or new leaders.

External change

External change refers to changes in the external environment of a business or in its competitive environment. These changes, in turn, have consequences for, and lead to subsequent changes in, a business.

While a business has a great deal of control over internal change, it is likely to have little or no control over external change. For example, an average business has little control over changing tastes or fashions, the introduction of new laws or taxes, or the number of competitors in its market. Despite this, a very large and powerful business may have some influence over tastes and fashions, may be successful at lobbying government about business and economic policies, and may be able to prevent new competitors setting up in its industry.

If a business cannot influence external change, it must ensure that it is prepared to respond quickly and appropriately when external change happens that impacts directly or indirectly on it. This could mean, for example, ensuring that its financial and HR departments are always up to date and aware of government plans to introduce new employment legislation or business taxes, and are ready to implement such changes when they occur. Contingency planning helps a business by ensuring it has plans in place to deal with unexpected events. (Contingency planning is considered in Chapter 18.)

Incremental change

> **Key term**
>
> **Incremental change** Small adjustments made, usually over a long period of time, towards a desired end result; it usually does not alter current working practices in any significant way.

Incremental change means introducing many, small, gradual (and often unplanned) changes in order to reach a particular goal. For example, a manufacturer producing a product that requires a lot of different components, such as a car, wishes to cut costs and improve the quality of its product over time. Incremental change might involve it in gradually improving the quality and efficiency of each component so that, bit by bit, the quality of the overall product improves and costs fall. This may not be planned in any structured way, but happens gradually with little or no impact on workplace practice.

The alternative to incremental change is radical change (sometimes called step change). Using the above example, the manufacturer could achieve the same goals of reduced costs and improved quality by a well-planned process of introducing part or complete automation of its plant. This would achieve the goals in a much shorter time period, but would have significant and long-term effects on workplace practice.

Incremental change, as opposed to radical or step change, typically requires less management of the change process because employees are not being asked to make a big leap from what they know and are comfortable with. Radical change, on the other hand, usually requires careful management of the change process. This is because the future state is unknown and because radical change can have a significant and distressing impact on employees, many of whom may feel threatened by change. Their feelings of distress and uncertainty, in turn, can have serious repercussions for a business.

> **Fact file**
>
> *The Toyota Way*
>
> Toyota's success is tied up with its well-known business model – the Toyota Way – which focuses on incremental process improvements that are linked to its quality operations and production management. In contrast, Google grew rapidly because of its radical innovation in redefining the use of the internet and completely changing the way people use information and networking.
>
>

Did you know?

Disruptive innovation helps create new markets and disrupts existing markets. The term is used in business and technology to describe innovations that improve a product in ways that the market did not expect. In contrast, sustaining innovation does not create new markets, but helps to develop existing ones by allowing firms in the market to compete against each other's continuous improvements to existing products and processes.

Disruptive change

Disruptive change is characterised by a shift in the underlying forces of an industry or segment of an industry. Examples of industries where disruption has occurred include computing, telecommunications and retailing. It occurs when change leads to completely different methods of operating or products being produced.

When disruptive change occurs, the future that was expected ceases to exist. Businesses respond in a range of different ways. Some thrive, some continue as before but struggle, and some close down or are swallowed up by more successful firms.

Examples of disruptive innovation include:

- the internet for accessing information on anything and, more specifically, Wikipedia as a replacement for the traditional hard-copy encyclopaedia market
- the telephone replacing the telegraph (see the Did you know? box below)
- the computer industry, which is a classic example of ongoing disruptive innovation – from mainframe computers to mini-computers, to personal computers, to laptops, to tablets …
- data storage, which is another example of continual disruptive innovation – from filing cabinets to hard disc drives, to floppy disc drives, to CDs, to USBs.

Did you know?

Western Union, an American financial services and communication company, was established in 1851. In 1876, Western Union is said to have declined to purchase Alexander Graham Bell's telephone patents for $100,000. Its reason was because Western Union's most profitable market, at the time, was long-distance telegraphy and telephones were only useful for very local calls. The company dismissed the telephone as a 'useless toy that would never amount to anything'! Clearly Western Union could not imagine a future without the telegraph and could not imagine that the telephone would become the important instrument of communication that it is.

Managing change and Lewin's force field analysis

The management of change, known generally as 'change management', is a structured approach to moving individuals, teams and organisations from a current state to a desired future state. It can be applied to situations such as managing the growth or retrenchment of an organisation or introducing new technologies. It is an organisational process aimed at helping employees to understand, commit to and accept changes in their current business environment. It also aims to minimise the impact of any unintended negative outcomes on people and processes.

Key term

Lewin's force field analysis

The 'force field' consists of two opposing forces – one set of forces, the driving forces, are working for change, and the other set, the restraining forces, are working against change; change occurs when the driving forces are stronger than the restraining forces.

K. Lewin, in his book, *Field Theory in Social Science* (1951), introduced the idea of **force field analysis**, which is widely used in the management of change. Lewin wrote that: 'An issue is held in balance by the interaction of two opposing sets of forces – those seeking to promote change (driving forces) and those attempting to maintain the status quo (restraining forces).'

Before a change takes place, the 'force field' is thought to be in equilibrium or balance between those forces favourable to change (driving forces) and those resisting it (restraining forces). For change to occur, the equilibrium must be upset – either by adding or strengthening the forces favourable to the change or by reducing or weakening the resisting forces. Lewin suggested that whenever driving forces are stronger than restraining forces, the equilibrium will be upset and change will occur. Successful change is therefore achieved by either strengthening the driving forces or weakening the restraining forces.

A field force analysis (FFA) is a way of identifying and evaluating the key driving and restraining forces in order to devise a strategy to bring about successful change. In its simplest form, it involves the following steps:

- Describe the current situation. For example, the current organisational structure and the problems it creates for communication, management responsibility and motivation.
- Describe the desired situation when change has occurred successfully. For example, a new organisational structure and a clear analysis of the benefits it will bring in terms of communication, management responsibility and motivation.
- Identify and evaluate the strength of each driving force and determine which are critical. For example, faster decision making, clearer allocation of responsibilities, improved job satisfaction and increased efficiency. Assign a ranking to them in relation to the extent to which they can influence the eventual outcome (for example 1 = very weak; 5 = very strong).
- Identify and evaluate the strength of each restraining force and determine which are critical. For example, long-serving managers' reluctance to change their roles, resistance from staff who are likely to be downgraded, uncertainty from staff about their lack of training, and the finance director's concern about the capital investment required. Assign a ranking to them (as above).
- Chart the forces – see Figure 15.1 for an example of a force field chart.
- Develop a strategy to strengthen the key driving forces and/or weaken the key restraining forces. For example, a strategy might include providing more information about the benefits of the change and the implications it will have for the profitability and future stability of the organisation, offering high-level training for all staff, offering long-serving managers early retirement with enhanced pension rights, and making a commitment to maintain current salaries for a year for those who are to be downgraded.

Figure 15.1 provides an example of a force field analysis chart using the examples mentioned in the force field analysis above. The driving forces push the likelihood of change away from the current equilibrium towards the 'Desired State'. The restraining forces provide the pressure to keep the organisation at its current equilibrium – the 'Current State'. The chart shows the most important driving and restraining forces and their respective rankings. Increased efficiency is clearly a driving force judged to have a very strong influence on the decision to change. The reluctance of managers to change their role and the resistance from staff likely to be downgraded are important restraining forces, but not the most important. The total of the individual rankings indicate that overall, the driving forces are stronger than the restraining forces, and thus there is every likelihood that change will occur and the organisation will move to the 'Desired State'. To ensure that this happens smoothly, the organisation will need to minimise the impact of restraining forces, for example by introducing the strategies noted in the last bullet point above.

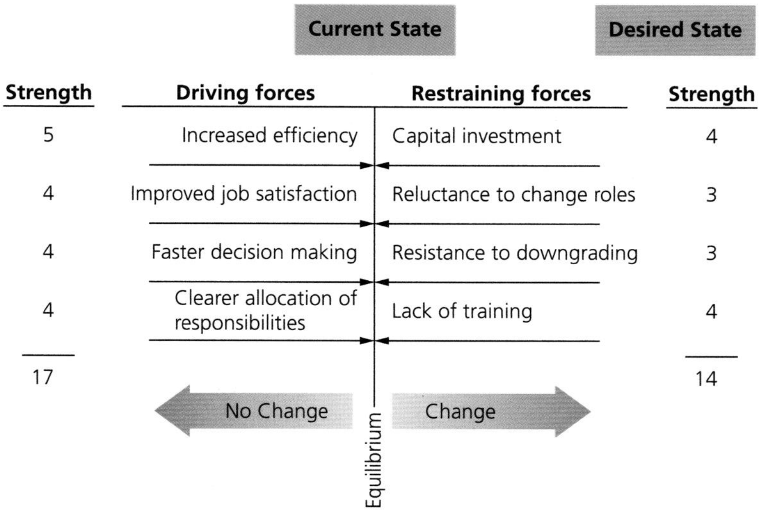

	Current State	Desired State	
Strength	**Driving forces**	**Restraining forces**	**Strength**
5	Increased efficiency	Capital investment	4
4	Improved job satisfaction	Reluctance to change roles	3
4	Faster decision making	Resistance to downgrading	3
4	Clearer allocation of responsibilities	Lack of training	4
17	No Change	Change	14

Equilibrium

▲ **Figure 15.1** Lewin's force field analysis

The value of change

Organisations need to change in order to respond and adapt to the continual pressure of internal and external developments.

Some of the reasons why change is valuable are identified below:

- Without change, businesses are likely to lose their competitive edge and fail to meet the needs of their customers.
- Without change, businesses would not have taken advantage of developing technologies – whether in terms of administrative processes or manufacturing tasks. The case study on HMV in Chapter 3 of Book 1 provides a good example of the consequences of failure to take advantage of new technologies. Similarly, the Did you know? box about Western Union and telephones in the earlier part of this chapter is another example of a failure to foresee future change and its value.
- Customers' needs change, creating demands for new types of goods and services – opening up new areas of opportunity for businesses that are prepared to change in order to meet these needs.
- Change has led to improved working conditions and job satisfaction for employees, which in turn lead to improved productivity. Change enables organisations to provide opportunities for employees to learn new skills, explore new opportunities and exercise their creativity in ways that ultimately benefit the organisation through new ideas and increased commitment.

- Change enables a business to grow and compete in its markets more effectively. If growth is likely to be better via merger or takeover, the resulting change may create a larger and more successful company.
- Change helps an organisation cope with globalisation, with changes to market opportunities, legislation and other elements from the external environment. For example, the ability to respond effectively to changing economic conditions enables a business to maintain a strong brand and strong relationships with its customers.
- Some companies initiate change in order to improve organisational culture and thus to improve efficiency and productivity. Effective organisational cultures attract new customers, increase employee and customer satisfaction, reduce costs of production and improve labour retention. (Organisational culture is considered in Chapter 16.)

The value of a flexible organisation

In a dynamic business environment, organisations need to be flexible and have structures in place that enable them to respond quickly to the continual changes taking place in the external environment. This includes: suitable organisational structures that encourage the most efficient and effective flow of communication and flexibility to respond to change; an appropriate range of employment contracts, including flexible working options, to meet the needs of employees and of the business; and effective knowledge and information management systems to ensure knowledge and information is effectively shared throughout an organisation. Each of these elements is considered below.

A **flexible organisation** that functions successfully can provide many benefits to a firm. For example:

- it can respond more quickly to market conditions by expanding or contracting capacity
- it can make more efficient use of resources by directing them to the organisation's priorities or strengths
- it is able to cut down on costs – particularly labour, which for most businesses is their major cost; this in turn leads to increased productivity
- it can make more effective and efficient use of specialists
- it can attract better quality job applicants and thus improve the quality of a firm's labour force
- it can lead to improved customer service by meeting customer needs more effectively, for example on a 24/7 basis
- subcontracting and outsourcing non-essential functions can enable an organisation to concentrate more on its core competence and therefore use its resources more efficiently
- it can make savings on business premises because technology enables more workers to either work remotely (usually from home) or to 'hot-desk' (see the What do you think? box below)
- by working from home, employees remove the need to travel, in itself a great saving in time, making them more productive, less stressed and happier, especially if they have family commitments; this can motivate staff by giving them more independence and responsibility and, at the same time, reducing the impact of Herzberg's hygiene factors
- employees who are given the option of working flexibly not only improve their work–life balance, but are likely to be more committed to their employer and less likely to take time off work due to sickness or stress.

Key term

Flexible organisation An organisation that can respond quickly to changes taking place in the external environment; includes a flexible workforce structure that allows capacity to be increased or reduced quickly and easily in response to external pressures.

▲ Offering employees the option to work remotely can improve staff morale

What do you think?

'Hot desking' means the practice of allocating desks, in an office, to workers when they are required, rather than giving each worker their own permanent desk. It usually means that all information and documentation (electronic and hard copy) is stored centrally at the end of each day so that all desk space is clear in readiness for other users the next day.

● How do you think employees feel about 'hot desking', that is, not having their 'own' desk to go to whenever they are in the office?
● What do you think are the advantages and the disadvantages for employees and for organisations of 'hot desking'?

What do you think?

An employee survey carried out for the Chartered Institute of Personnel and Development (CIPD) found that 'workers on flexible contracts tend to be more emotionally engaged, more satisfied with their work, more likely to speak positively about their organisation and less likely to quit'.

Why do you think this is the case?

Author advice

Try to relate these ideas to your knowledge of motivation theories, which were explained in Chapter 23 in Book 1.

Did you know?

A 2014 YouGov survey of directors of companies with flexible working policies, noted the following:

● 27 per cent reported that the flexibility helped to increase productivity.
● 28 per cent reported that it reduced staff sickness and absence.
● 42 per cent reported that it created higher staff morale.
● 63 per cent reported that employees enjoyed a better work–life balance.

Despite these valuable features, flexible organisations can face problems. The challenges most organisations encounter when introducing more flexible approaches include:

● overcoming concerns about operational pressures and meeting customer requirements with a more flexible structure
● dealing with the negative attitudes toward flexible working of some employees, including managers
● handling concerns that employees might have about the impact other people's flexible working might have on them
● how to measure or evaluate employees' performance by their output – rather than by hours worked – because they are no longer always on the premises
● being dependent on other organisations and agencies, to which they have subcontracted or outsourced, and that are outside their direct control
● downsizing and focusing on core activities, which may mean there are fewer opportunities for future expansion because workers' skills and experience will be lost
● ensuring that employees who work from home maintain a sensible work–life balance and have access to support and interaction with colleagues; research suggests that some teleworkers (i.e. people who work from home using computers and other telecommunication devices) find it difficult to separate work from leisure (which is a major factor in causing stress), and miss the social aspects of working alongside colleagues
● the fact that a successful flexible organisation approach is likely to require a significant culture change. The topic of organisational culture is considered in detail in Chapter 16.

Issues to consider in relation to flexible organisations

Restructuring

Restructuring in the context of a flexible organisation means designing an appropriate organisational structure to meet the needs of a more flexible approach to the employment of staff and of their work practices.

A flexible organisation aims to respond to changing circumstances quickly and easily. To do this, it requires an appropriate organisational structure. For many organisations this is likely to mean a significant restructuring. Certain organisational structures facilitate change more effectively than others. The section below on organic versus mechanistic structures explores this in more detail.

A key feature of most flexible organisations is the shift that has taken place in the structure of the workforce. For many organisations, restructuring has entailed a move to a system of core workers who are permanent, full-time and salaried, supported by other peripheral, temporary or part-time workers. The core group of workers are difficult to replace because they have specific skills and experience. The activities and responsibilities of this group are central to the organisation, and such workers are likely to be fully committed to the aims and objectives of the organisation. Peripheral workers, on the other hand, are likely to be engaged in activities that are additional to the main purpose of the organisation. This group consists of employees who could easily be replaced or are only needed in the organisation for either peak periods or specific tasks. Their jobs are less secure and they are less likely to be committed to the organisation's aims and objectives.

Fact file

The shamrock organisation

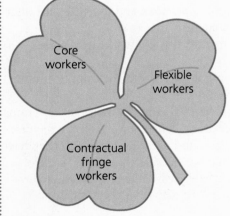

▲ **Figure 15.2** The shamrock organisation

Charles Handy, in *The Age of Unreason* (1990), developed the idea of core and peripheral workforces further. He suggested that modern firms would increasingly be composed of three elements: the core, the contractual fringe and the flexible or contingent workforce. He called this the 'shamrock organisation' (see Figure 15.2).

- The core includes professional, permanent employees who are essential to the organisation's continuity and have detailed knowledge of the organisation and its aims. They have the skills to move the organisation's core capabilities forward. They have to work hard and give commitment, but, typically, are very well paid.
- There has been a strong trend for organisations to outsource their non-critical work to independent contractors, so that the organisation can concentrate on its core competences. Handy suggests that the contractual fringe element of the shamrock is made up of both individuals and organisations of self-employed professionals or technicians. These independent contractors are project experts who may be used, for example, for advertising, R&D, computing, catering and mailing services. They are rewarded with fees rather than with salaries or wages. Their contribution to the organisation is measured in output rather than in hours, in results rather than in time. Management chooses not to add these people to its permanent payroll and benefits plan, thus achieving a significant cost saving.
- The third element of Handy's shamrock organisation is the flexible workforce, sometimes known as the contingent workforce. This comprises part-time, temporary and seasonal workers. These people are brought in from outside to do individual, low-level, temporary tasks.

▲ Fruit picking is seasonal work and employees will only be needed for a certain period of time

For many firms, the emphasis on being responsive to the external environment has led to a decline in the size of the core group of workers. Almost all functions other than those directly concerned with the organisation's primary business activity begin to take on a support role and are therefore candidates for outsourcing. This includes the bulk of the operations, administration, finance, personnel, legal, property and IT functions.

Subcontracting or outsourcing certain activities to other firms is the most usual method of achieving a flexible workforce structure. Outsourcing gives a firm the opportunity to use expertise not otherwise available in the organisation, to offload low-level administrative work, to free employees to undertake more interesting work and to reduce costs. (Outsourcing was discussed in detail in Chapter 15 of Book 1, and outsourcing off-shore was discussed in Chapter 13 of this book.) Outsourcing is linked to the issue of 'downsizing'. Downsizing means reducing the size of a firm to make it more responsive to market conditions – for example, by removing 'back room' activities such as office functions and call centres or the production and assembly of parts, which are then contracted out to other agencies. Recruitment is an area of work that is often outsourced. This is particularly the case in relation to the initial stages of dealing with enquiries and applications, and carrying out standard assessment. Training and payroll activities are also often outsourced. Such activities can then be increased or decreased at short notice, according to demand, without the need for expensive recruitment and selection processes or the difficult and expensive process of redundancies.

Delayering

In a dynamic environment, businesses need to be able to respond quickly and effectively to changes. A very tall management structure is unlikely to be as responsive as a flatter structure. (See the discussion below about organic versus mechanistic structures.) Many organisations have realised that the way to ensure they respond swiftly to change is to flatten or shorten their management structure by **delayering**.

The advantages and disadvantages of delayering are similar to those for a flat hierarchical structure with a wide span of control. (A detailed consideration of this was provided in Chapter 22 of Book 1 – ensure you are secure in your knowledge of these arguments before proceeding with the rest of this chapter.) However, delayering is often done in order to cut costs by making people redundant. A real problem with this kind of delayering is that the organisation loses many of its very experienced managers and thus, what is sometimes called its 'corporate memory' or 'corporate knowledge'. 'Corporate memory/knowledge' is essentially the knowledge of its history, past events, situations and contacts – much of which can be extremely valuable in dealing with the present. The sections below on 'Knowledge and information management' and on 'The value of managing information and knowledge' consider this issue further.

Flexible employment contracts

Flexible employment contracts can include:

- Part-time working: work is generally considered part-time when employers are contracted to work anything less than full-time hours.
- Term-time working: a worker remains on a permanent contract, but can take paid/unpaid leave during school holidays.
- Job-sharing: a form of part-time working where two or more people share the responsibility for a job between them.
- Flexitime: allows employees to choose, within certain set limits, when to start and finish work each day – as long as they are present at core times and work a required number of hours over a given period of time.
- Compressed hours: compressed working weeks (or fortnights) do not necessarily involve a reduction in total hours, but usually mean working fewer but longer blocks during the week – for example, working the same number of hours over four days rather than five days.
- Annual hours: the total number of hours to be worked over the year is fixed, but there is variation over the year in the length of the working day and week.

Key terms

Delayering The removal of one or more layers of hierarchy from the management structure of an organisation; it leads to a flatter hierarchical structure with a wider span of control.

Flexible employment contracts Working arrangements that give some degree of flexibility about how long, where, when and at what times employees work; the flexibility can be in terms of working time, working location or the pattern of working.

Author advice

Flexible working arrangements can be formal or informal. Some organisations choose to amend their employment contracts to include flexible working arrangements. Others maintain standard employment contracts with flexible working arrangements (such as working from home) being offered informally, on the basis of an agreement with an employee's line manager.

What do you think?

Although exclusivity clauses have now been banned, zero hours contracts have not. Should they be?

- Mobile working/teleworking/working from home: this permits employees to work all or part of their working week at a location remote from the employer's workplace (often from home), usually, but not always, making use of a range of computer and other telecommunication devices.
- Career breaks: career breaks, or sabbaticals, are extended periods of leave – normally unpaid – from a few months to a few years.
- Zero hours contracts: an individual has no guarantee of a minimum number of working hours; they can be called upon as and when required by the business and paid just for the hours they work.

Did you know?

Zero hours arrangements have proved controversial. There is some doubt as to whether, in legal terms, they constitute a form of employment contract at all. They are, in effect, 'on-call' arrangements. A relationship is entered into between an employee and an employer, but the employer is not obliged to find work and the employee is not obliged  to accept what is offered. Some employers have a pool of temporary workers employed on this basis. In this situation, some employers pay employees retainers to cover periods when no work is allocated and also provide benefits such as training, the use of facilities or the provision of discounts.

For some people zero hours contracts provide them with the flexibility they need – to earn money while studying, travelling, pursuing other careers such as acting, enjoying retirement, and so on. However, for people who depend on their zero hours contract for their whole income, there is no security of hours and therefore no security of income.

Some employers included 'exclusivity clauses' in their zero hour contracts, which prevented people working elsewhere. However, the Small Business, Enterprise and Employment Act, which became law in March 2015, banned this practice.

The Office of National Statistics (ONS) data indicates that about 6 per cent of employment is through zero hours contracts. According to ONS surveys, two sectors account for more than half of all UK zero-hours contracts – accommodation and food (which includes hotels, restaurants and catering at events), and administrative and support services (which includes cleaning and office support).

Fact file

Flexible working

The 'right to request flexible working' which had historically applied to parents and certain other carers, was extended from 30 June 2014 to include all employees with at least 26 weeks' continuous employment, regardless of parental or caring responsibilities. Employers have a duty to consider a request in a reasonable manner and can only refuse a request for flexible working if they can show that one of a specific number of grounds apply. These include, for example, the fact that extra costs will be incurred that will damage the business.

The growing use of flexible workforce structures, and of homeworking in particular, has had a significant impact on management and on HR departments. For example, managers need to be properly trained in how to manage homeworkers because different skills are required. HR departments need to ensure that all their policies are as robust for those employees who do not work regularly in an office as they are for those who do.

Key terms

Organic structures Features include flat organisational structures; horizontal communication and interactions; low levels of specialisation because knowledge resides wherever it is most useful; decentralisation involving a great deal of formal and informal participation in decision making.

Mechanistic structures
Features include hierarchical and bureaucratic organisational structures; highly centralised authority; formalised procedures and practices; highly specialised functions.

Knowledge and information management (KIM) The practice of organising, storing and sharing vital knowledge and information, so that everyone in an organisation can benefit from its use.

Organic structures versus mechanistic structures

Organisational structures fall into a spectrum with **organic structures** at one end and **mechanistic structures** at the other end. The features of each are as follows:

- Organic structures (also known as flat structures) are typified by wide spans of control, decentralisation, low specialisation and formalisation, and loose departmentalisation. The chain of command, whether long or short, can sometimes be difficult to decipher.
- Mechanistic structures are typified by narrow spans of control, high centralisation, specialisation and formalisation, as well as by rigid departmentalisation. The chain of command could be long or short but would always be clear.

Mechanistic structures represent the traditional top-down approach to organisational structure. Organic structures represent a more collaborative, flexible approach.

Mechanistic structures apply to most business structures, but are particularly apparent in manufacturing. Organic structures are best applied to businesses with a more open structure, such as online business platforms. Google and Facebook are reported to have organisational structures that could be defined as organic.

Knowledge and information management

The difference between **knowledge and information management** is linked to the differences between data, information and knowledge (see the Did you know? box below). Information management is the provision of the right information to the right people at the right time. Knowledge management goes beyond this and provides not just information, but insight, guidance, experience and know-how, for the purpose of decision making and effective action. In this context, knowledge is the ability to make effective decisions and take effective action. Knowledge is a lot harder to manage than information because it is mainly stored in

Did you know?

Words like 'data', 'information' and 'knowledge' are often used interchangeably. But there are important differences:

- Data is a specific fact or figure, without any context. For example, the name Joshua Bicknell and the number 160. Without anything else to define them, these two items of data are of little use.
- Information is data that is organised. For example, Joshua Bicknell is one of the founders of a small business and 160 is the number of international fellows.

- Knowledge builds on the information to give context. For example, knowledge is the fact that Joshua Bicknell is one of the founders of a small business called Balloon Ventures (www.balloonventures.com), which has organised programmes for 160 international fellows (young people from around the world) to work with and support budding entrepreneurs in Kenya.

▲ Google has offices that lend themselves to collaborative and flexible working

people's heads rather than on discs or in documents. However, effective knowledge management needs to be built on a foundation of good data and information management.

The value of managing information and knowledge

Information and knowledge are important elements of an organisation's key assets – as valuable as its human resources, financial resources, customers and brand. Just as financial and human resources need to be managed effectively if they are to contribute positively to an organisation's success, so information and knowledge need to be managed effectively.

More and more organisations and their leaders are being brought to task over their failure to retrieve documentation and data relating to key decisions in the past. Many organisations repeat past mistakes because new management teams choose not to, or are unable to, access critical information and knowledge from the past. This can affect performance and profits and it can also reflect on a firm's ability to be transparent when subject to public scrutiny and accountability.

Increasingly, therefore, strong management of information and knowledge is seen as a vital activity in an organisation. Its value is evident in terms of:

● the fact that information and knowledge have become the new keys to sustainable competitive advantage; some analysts suggest that the ability of a company to exploit its intangible information and knowledge-based assets may be more decisive than its ability to exploit its physical assets
● sharing information and knowledge between employees so that it is not lost, and can still be used even if someone is on holiday, absent due to illness, or has left an organisation
● the fact that it can result in substantial savings to an organisation because strong management of information and knowledge means people are more easily brought 'up to speed' with valuable knowledge; in turn, this means time and money is not lost as a result of people having to learn new information from scratch
● ideas being shared easily, which may increase innovation and help create better customer relationships
● if a company has a global team, good management of information and knowledge can create a more powerful workforce because the strengths of different cultures are bought together and shared
● employees being provided with the knowledge they need to do their jobs better, which makes them more productive, less prone to leave or be absent
● better and faster decisions being made by tapping into the experience of employees, avoiding previous pitfalls, sharing solutions and making the right decisions, first time, more often.

The majority of challenges a business faces are not new to its long-established teams of employees. It is likely that someone, somewhere in an organisation, has already solved most of the problems currently being faced. If there is knowledge in an organisation, it is important to get hold of it and use it when and where appropriate. Lord Brown, an ex-CEO of BP, said, 'Most activities or tasks are not one-time events. Whether it's drilling a well or conducting a transaction at a service station, we do the same things repeatedly. Our philosophy is fairly simple: Every time we do something again, we should do it better than the last time.' He might have added, as part of good management of information and knowledge – by learning from the last time we did it.

Fact file

Vision statements

The following list includes examples of information and knowledge management vision statements:

- 'Samsung's vision is to provide the best possible IT service to our customers. This best service can only be created via our know-how, which is produced by freely sharing our best practice, knowledge and experience from every area within the company.' (Samsung)
- 'The culture and tools are in place to make the appropriate sharing of knowledge the norm.' (British Airways)
- 'We know what we know, learn what we need to learn, and use knowledge for sustained competitive advantage.' 'Anyone in the organisation who is not directly accountable for making a profit should be involved in creating and distributing knowledge that the company can use to make a profit.' (BP)
- 'To create a world class knowledge-sharing culture and environment that contributes to Accenture's success.' (Accenture)

What do you think?

In the Fact file above, part of BP's information and knowledge management vision statement states: 'Anyone in the organisation who is not directly accountable for making a profit should be involved in creating and distributing knowledge that the company can use to make a profit.' To what extent might such a requirement ensure that everyone in the organisation contributes fully to the achievement of its primary objective of making a profit?

Barriers to change and how to overcome them

Barriers to change

Barriers to implementing successful change include:

- a lack of clear objectives or sense of mission or purpose in relation to the change process
- inappropriate and insufficient resources (including human, financial and physical resources, such as machinery and plant) to assist the change process
- inappropriately trained staff with expertise that is not relevant to the change process.

In addition to the above, the following factors also limit the success of the change process:

- Resistance to change, which can impede the ability of a business to serve its customers, to innovate for the future, or to capitalise on a new initiative.
- The impact of change on people employed in a business, and how a business deals with this; for example, different people react differently to change because for some it involves a loss of status, income, friends, and so on; how a business deals with such issues will determine how successful change is likely to be.

- The nature of an organisational structure – a flat structure is often most appropriate for implementing and managing change successfully.
- External factors, such as the impact of a competitor's actions or changes in the economy; for example, the recession of 2008–09 caused many businesses to cancel their plans for expansion.

No matter how successfully planned a proposed change might be, the influence of individuals in an organisation is likely to be disruptive. People differ in their perceptions of, and resistance to, change – some embrace it and some fight it. Resistance to change is in fact resistance to the loss of something that is valuable or simply the loss of the known and fear and uncertainty about the unknown. Resistance to change can range from passive resignation to deliberate sabotage. It can manifest itself in different ways, including grievances, high labour turnover, low efficiency and reduced output and aggression towards management.

Kotter and Schlesinger's four reasons for resistance to change

Kotter and Schlesinger, in their article, 'Choosing strategies for change', published in the *Harvard Business Review* in 1979, identify what they suggest are the four most common reasons for resisting change. These are:

- **Parochial self-interest**. A desire not to lose something of value. Some people are only concerned with the implications of the change from their own perspective and how it affects their own interests, rather than considering the effects of the change on the success of the business.
- **Misunderstanding and lack of trust**. A misunderstanding of the change and its implications, which is often as a result of communication problems or inadequate information. People often resist change when they do not understand its implications and perceive that it might cost them more than they will gain. Such situations often occur when trust is lacking between the person initiating the change and the employee.
- **Different assessments**. Where employees assess the situation differently from their managers or those initiating the change, and see more costs than benefits, not only for themselves but also for the business. This is the belief that the change does not make sense for the business. This reason is not the same as the first point above about self-interest.
- **Low tolerance for change**. People resist change because they fear they will not be able to develop the new skills and behaviours that will be required of them once the change is complete. Some people need security, predictability and stability in their work and react very negatively to change. If the changes are significant and an individual's tolerance for change is low, they might begin to actively resist change. People also sometimes resist change in order to 'save face', because to go along with change would be an admission that their previous decisions were wrong. Other people might resist change because of peer group pressure or because of a supervisor's attitude.

How to overcome barriers to change

The effective management of change is based on a clear understanding of human behaviour in organisations. It involves being able to deal with people's reactions, for example of uncertainty, frustration, fear, feeling threatened and disoriented – all of which are likely to lead to people exhibiting defensive and negative attitudes to change and thus resisting initiatives to change.

The reason why many organisations fail to accomplish change successfully is associated with underestimating the influence of change on individuals. Successful management of change means assessing how the various groups of individuals involved are likely to be affected by a change so that an appropriate way or ways to overcome resistance can be introduced.

Kotter and Schlesinger's six ways of overcoming resistance to change

Kotter and Schlesinger, in their article, 'Choosing strategies for change', published in the *Harvard Business Review* in 1979, identify six ways of overcoming resistance to change. These are:

- **Education and communication**:
  - This can involve one-to-one discussions, presentations to groups or memos and reports. It can be an appropriate approach when resistance is based on inadequate or inaccurate information and analysis, especially if initiators need the help of resistors in implementing change.
  - One of the most common ways to overcome resistance to change is to educate people about it beforehand. Communication of ideas helps people to see the need for and the logic of a change and helps to reduce the impact of the grapevine effect or inaccurate rumours. Once persuaded, people will often help with the implementation of change.
  - This approach requires good relationships between initiators and resistors or the latter may not believe what they hear. It also requires time and effort, particularly if a lot of people are involved.
- **Participation and involvement**:
  - This approach is useful when the initiators of change do not have all the information they need to design changes effectively, and the information, knowledge and skills that others have can be used positively for the change process rather than as a source of power to resist.
  - If the initiators involve the potential resistors in some aspect of the design and implementation of the change, they can often reduce or eliminate resistance. The more people are involved in the actual process of change, the more likely they are to 'buy in' to the change rather than resist it. Active involvement is likely to lower resistance and increase acceptance. Much research indicates that participation leads to commitment, not just compliance.
  - However, participation can lead to a poor solution if the process is not carefully managed. It can also be very time consuming. If change needs to be made quickly, involving others may take too long.
- **Facilitation and support**:
  - This involves providing emotional and material support to help people deal with the anxiety and uncertainty (what Kotter and Schlesinger call 'adjustment' problems) caused by change. This process might include training in new skills or giving employees time off after a demanding period of change, or simply listening and providing emotional support, including offering them mentoring and counselling services.
  - By being supportive of employees during difficult times, managers can prevent potential resistance. Kotter and Schlesinger suggest that no

> **Key term**
>
> **Kotter and Schlesinger's six ways of overcoming resistance to change** Education and communication; participation and involvement; facilitation and support; negotiation and agreement; manipulation and co-optation; explicit and implicit coercion.

> **Author advice**
>
> Kotter and Schlesinger use the following terms in their analysis:
>
> Initiators – these are managers who decide on, introduce and implement change; they are Kanter's strategists and implementers.
>
> Resistors – these are employees who are affected by change; they are Kanter's recipients.

359

other approach works as well with 'adjustment' problems. This approach is most helpful when fear and anxiety lie at the heart of resistance.

 – However, it can be time consuming and expensive.

● **Negotiation and agreement**:
 – This involves giving resistors incentives to either adapt or leave an organisation. This could be done by agreeing to certain of their demands regarding aspects of the planned change process they feel are threatening. It could involve agreeing a higher wage rate to prevent industrial action being taken. It could involve offering some individuals enhanced pension benefits in return for them taking early retirement.
 – This is a useful approach when someone or some group may lose out because of a change, and where that individual or group has considerable power to resist. Negotiated agreements can be a relatively easy way to avoid major resistance.
 – However, they can be expensive, particularly if they encourage other groups to want to negotiate for incentives to reduce their resistance to change.

● **Manipulation and co-optation**:
 – Co-opting an individual, or the leader of a group, involves giving them a desirable role in the design or implementation of the change. This is not the same as participation because the initiators do not want the advice of the co-opted member, they only want their endorsement. In this sense, co-option involves engaging people for the sake of appearances rather than for their ability to contribute.
 – In some situations, co-optation can be a relatively inexpensive and easy way to gain an individual's or a group's support – cheaper than negotiation and quicker than participation.
 – If, however, these people feel they are being tricked, they are likely to increase resistance even further. Difficulties can also arise if the co-opted member uses their ability to influence the design and implementation of change in ways that are not in the best interests of the organisation.
 – Manipulation usually involves the selective use of information and the conscious structuring of events in order to lead people to behave or make decisions in a certain way.
 – Despite its unethical nature, manipulation is often used successfully, particularly when all other tactics have failed. Not having enough time to educate, involve or support people, and without the power or resources to negotiate, coerce or co-opt them, managers have resorted to manipulating information channels in order to scare people into, for example, thinking there is a crisis coming that can only be avoided by change.
 – However, if a manager develops a reputation as a manipulator, it can undermine their ability to use other approaches in the future.
 – Both manipulation and co-optation are useful where other tactics will not work or are too expensive.

● **Explicit and implicit coercion**:
 – Managers can force employees into accepting change by suggesting that resisting change can lead to, for example, the loss of their jobs, being transferred to another site or being denied promotion. Whether

Author advice

Co-optation is a term that means managing opposition by co-opting someone onto a group because of their particular status rather than because they are expected to contribute to the action of the group. Co-optation is a form of manipulation.

Did you know?

Co-optation could involve getting the leader of a group of employees, who are particularly resistant to change, involved in meetings to discuss and plan the change process. The aim of this action would be to reduce the intensity and pressure of resistance from this group. Co-optation could also involve getting a senior executive to be involved in meetings about the change process. The purpose of this would be to enhance the importance of the change process within the organisation by sending a message that it is supported by senior executives.

this is explicit or implicit coercion depends on if these threats have been clearly stated or just implied and understood but not clearly stated. Coercion is the 'big stick' approach where speed is essential. As a result, it is a strategy of last resort, and only to be used if the initiators have the power to follow through with their explicit or implicit threats.

- Where speed is essential and where change will not be popular, regardless of how it is introduced, coercion may be the only option.
- Coercion is a short-term strategy that will do much to damage trust in an organisation. The negative effects of using coercion include frustration, fear, revenge and alienation, which may in turn lead to poor performance, dissatisfaction and high labour turnover. As with manipulation, coercion is a risky process because people strongly resent being forced.

Kotter and Schlesinger's analysis of ways to overcome resistance to change can be summarised in Figure 15.3, their strategic continuum. The features of this continuum are:

● At the left end of the continuum, the change strategy calls for a very rapid implementation, a clear plan of action and little involvement of others. This strategy aims to overcome any resistance to change.
● At the right end of the continuum, the strategy calls for a much slower change process, a less clear plan and involvement of many people in the change process. This type of strategy is designed to reduce resistance to change to a minimum.
● The further to the left, the more ways of overcoming resistance to change are likely to be coercive and manipulative. The further to the right, the more ways of overcoming resistance to change are likely to be educational and participative.

Fast	Slower
Clearly planned	Not clearly planned at the beginning
Little involvement of others	Lots of involvement of others
Attempt to overcome any resistance	Attempt to minimise any resistance

▲ **Figure 15.3** Kotter and Schlesinger's strategic continuum

Kotter and Schlesinger suggest that where an organisation uses inconsistent strategies, it is likely to encounter problems. For example, if change is not clearly planned in advance but is implemented quickly, it will encounter lots of unanticipated problems. Equally, if change involves a large number of people but is implemented quickly, the process will usually stall and eventually become less participative. They also suggest that a common mistake managers make is to move too quickly and involve too few people without having all the information they really need to design and implement change effectively.

Practice exercise 1

Total: 90 marks

1. Identify and explain two causes of, or pressures for, change in an organisation. *(6 marks)*

2. Explain each of the following terms:
   a) internal change *(3 marks)*
   b) external change *(3 marks)*
   c) incremental change *(3 marks)*
   d) disruptive change. *(3 marks)*

3. Distinguish between Lewin's driving forces and restraining forces. *(5 marks)*

4. What must happen to the balance between driving forces and restraining forces for a desired change to occur? *(2 marks)*

5. Identify and explain two issues that illustrate the value of change for an organisation. *(6 marks)*

6. Identify and explain two issues that illustrate the value of flexible organisations for employees and for business. *(6 marks)*

7. What is delayering and how does it affect an organisation? *(5 marks)*

8. Identify and explain three different flexible employment contracts. *(9 marks)*

9. Distinguish between organic and mechanistic organisational structures. *(6 marks)*

10. What is meant by knowledge and information management? *(5 marks)*

11. Identify and explain two examples of the value of managing information and knowledge for an organisation. *(6 marks)*

12. Identify each of Kotter and Schlesinger's four reasons for resistance to change. *(4 marks)*

13. Explain each of Kotter and Schlesinger's six ways of overcoming resistance to change. *(18 marks)*

Practice exercise 2

Total: 20 marks

For each of the following statements, decide which of Kotter and Schlesinger's ways of overcoming resistance to change is the most appropriate and explain why.

1. If resistance stems from employee's lack of information. *(4 marks)*

2. If an organisation wants resistors to become more committed to the change. *(4 marks)*

3. If employees fear they cannot make necessary adjustments. *(4 marks)*

4. If powerful people or groups are resisting because they will lose out as a result of the change. *(4 marks)*

5. If speed is essential. *(4 marks)*

Case study: Resistance to change

Management at Rockcliffe Marketing Consultancy face a dilemma. They need to change their marketing systems or risk losing their competitive edge. This means that all marketing executives have to learn how to use a new computer system to handle the various accounts they work on. The additional training will require them to attend a series of workshops in the evenings or on Saturdays over a six-week period so that the company can be ready to roll out the new system later in the year. The consultancy is prepared to pay marketing executives for their time in attending these out-of-hours sessions or offer them time off in lieu.

Management is very enthusiastic about the new system, but the marketing executives are not. They are resisting putting in the extra time to train, and this attitude is gradually resulting in them becoming generally resistant to change anything about their jobs.

Management has explained the reason for the change clearly. Change will allow the consultancy to remain competitive. Without change, the consultancy's profit objective will not be met and jobs are likely to be cut.

Up to now, marketing executives at Rockcliffe have been used to a fairly relaxed environment. Most have been with the company for several years and consider their positions secure. They are a tightly knit group. The most successful of the marketing executives tend to be very influential with the group and it is these individuals who are most resistant to the change and to attending the training. They want to maintain the status quo.

Questions

Total: 15 marks

1. Identify three driving forces and three restraining forces in relation to the change in systems that management at Rockcliffe Marketing Consultancy wish to introduce. *(6 marks)*

2. Analyse the types of actions that management might take to either strengthen the driving forces or weaken the restraining forces. *(9 marks)*

Essay questions

Total: 25 marks

Answer one of the following questions:

1. Assess the various causes of, and pressures for, change and how these contribute to the value of change for an organisation. *(25 marks)*

2. Evaluate the characteristics of flexible organisations that are likely to contribute to improving an organisation's productivity and efficiency. *(25 marks)*

3. Discuss how Kotter and Schlesinger's ways of overcoming resistance to change can be applied to the reasons they identify for resistance to change. *(25 marks)*

Managing organisational culture

This chapter begins by considering the importance of organisational culture. It goes on to explain two particular cultural models – Handy's task culture, role culture, power culture and person culture; and Hofstede's national cultures. Influences on organisational culture are then explained. The chapter concludes with a discussion about the reasons for, and the problems of, changing organisational culture.

The importance of organisational culture

Author advice

Many of the issues raised in this chapter – for example, hierarchical structures, centralised and decentralised structures, delegation and leadership style – relate to topics about organisational structure and leadership considered in the AQA A-level Business Book 1. Ensure your understanding of all of these areas is secure before proceeding with this chapter.

Just as societies have cultures that define the way people interact with each other and what constitutes acceptable behavior, so too do organisations.

Culture is often described as 'the way that we do things around here', meaning the type of behaviour that is considered acceptable or unacceptable, and that is a result of tradition, history and structure. Most of us are very sensitive to **organisational culture**; for example we are cautious when joining a new school, college or employer because we want to see 'how they do things around there'.

Key term

Organisational culture The unwritten code that affects the attitudes and behaviour of staff, approaches to decision making and the leadership style of management; the shared values of an organisation, including the beliefs and norms that affect every aspect of work life, from how people greet each other to how major policy decisions are made.

Every organisation has its own unique culture. It will have been created unconsciously, based on the values of the founders, senior managers and core people who built and now direct the organisation. Over time, the culture may change as new owners and senior managers try to impose their own styles and preferences on the organisation, or because of changing marketplace conditions.

A key role of organisational culture is to differentiate an organisation from others and to provide a sense of identity for its members: 'who we are', 'what we do' and 'what we stand for'. It is an acquired body of knowledge about how to behave, and the shared meanings and symbols that help everyone interpret and understand how to act within an organisation. An organisation's culture shows what it has been good at and what has worked in the past. Culture will therefore be influential when it comes to developing an organisation's mission statement.

Culture influences, and is influenced by, the decision-making processes, styles of leadership and management and what everyone sees as success. Interpreting and understanding organisational culture is therefore a very important activity for managers because it affects strategic development.

Just as there is no ideal style of leadership or organisational structure, so there is no preferred culture. What is important is that the culture is suited to the environment in which the organisation operates, allowing it to react appropriately to market and other changes.

The culture of an organisation will also affect the amount of resistance to change and therefore the ability of new management to impose its style or decisions on subordinates.

Culture influences the extent to which a business is centralised or decentralised and whether it has a narrow or tall hierarchical structure.

By affecting leadership styles in a business, culture will have a major effect on the degree of, and effectiveness of, delegation and consultation. However, as well as influencing organisational structure, culture will be influenced by the structure in place.

Organisational culture is important because it determines how firms respond to changes in their external environment. Though intangible, culture has an important bearing on an organisation's behaviour and performance. A production- or engineering-based culture can lead to a neglect of marketing skills and financial controls. Similarly, an over-concern with financial controls can undermine product development, leaving a firm increasingly exposed to competition from products that are technologically superior.

When mergers and takeovers occur between firms operating in similar markets and with similar technologies, the very different cultures of the firms involved often lead to managerial confusion and failure (see Chapter 11 and later in this chapter for examples of this). Such differences in culture can be an important explanation of why so many seemingly promising mergers and takeovers fail.

Culture is an important ingredient of effective company performance. The stronger a company's culture and the more clearly it is accepted by staff, the more likely a company is to be successful. Where the organisational culture is clearly understood by staff at all levels in a company, the less likely is the emergence of an alternative and disruptive culture. When culture in terms of common values, beliefs and attitudes is accepted by all staff, issues such as leadership, decision making, motivation and management control become more effective.

In summary, organisational culture performs a number of important functions:

- It creates distinctions between one organisation and another.
- It conveys a sense of identity for members of the organisation.
- It helps to generate commitment to something larger than an individual's own self-interest.
- It helps to hold organisations together by providing appropriate standards for what employees should say and do.
- It guides and shapes the attitudes and behaviour of employees by defining 'the rules of the game'.

A strong culture that all employees understand and are committed to is particularly important because organisations increasingly: have flatter structures and wider spans of control; place more emphasis on teams and less emphasis on formality; and seek to empower employees more. The 'shared meaning' provided by a strong culture can, in this context, ensure that everyone is aiming for the same goals.

Cultural models

Cultural models are the different ways organisational culture can be classified. At the simplest level, it is possible to distinguish between a 'them and us' culture in an organisation, where strict divisions exist between managers and workers. In comparison, a more equitable culture tries to reduce barriers and places emphasis on teamwork and more equal treatment of all.

The AQA specification requires a focus on two specific cultural models – Handy's task culture, role culture, power culture and person culture; and Hofstede's national cultures. Each of these is considered below.

Handy's cultural model

Charles Handy, in his book *Understanding Organisations* (1976), identified four different types of organisational culture: task culture, role culture, power culture and person culture. Each culture is determined by different assumptions about the basis of power and influence in an organisation, what motivates people, how people think and learn, and how change should occur.

Key term

Task culture Power is derived from the expertise required to complete a task or project; it is usually associated with a small team approach or small organisations co-operating to deliver a project; the emphasis is on results and getting things done.

Key term

Role culture Power is hierarchical and clearly defined in a company's job descriptions; a person's power derives from their place or role within a highly structured organisation; detailed rules indicate how people and departments interact with each other, customers and suppliers.

Key term

Power culture Power is concentrated in a small group or a central figure, who determines the dominant culture.

- **Task culture**: Individuals are empowered with independence and control over their work. Organisations with a task culture tend to be flexible and adaptable. This culture emphasises talent and ideas, and involves continuous team problem solving and consultation. Teams are formed to take advantage of individuals' expertise. As a result, the skills of the individuals are highly valued in a task culture. Professional services, such as accounting, law and consulting firms, have task cultures. Employees move frequently from one project or group to another. Additionally, these cultures often feature the multiple reporting lines seen in a matrix structure. This culture is very responsive to environmental and competitive developments.

- **Role culture**: An organisation with a role culture is often referred to as a bureaucracy. Such organisations are controlled by procedures and role descriptions. Co-ordination is from the top and job positions are central. Such organisations value predictability and consistency, and may find it hard to adjust to change. Such a culture creates a highly structured, stable organisation with precise job descriptions, and is often based on a single product. Policies and procedures are formalised into operating manuals so that interactions are ritualised. This means that roles are well defined. The advantages of role culture organisations are their stability, certainty and continuity. However, they may have trouble adapting to, or generating, change. The role culture is typified in government departments, local authorities, public utilities and large, well-established businesses like insurance companies and banks.

- **Power culture**: Power cultures are often evident in small, entrepreneurial companies, where power derives from the founder or top person, and a personal relationship with that individual matters more than any formal title or position. It can also be reflected in small or large family-owned businesses, where family members are the key figures. Power cultures are also found in some large companies where a charismatic leader is in place, such as Virgin's Richard Branson, and Apple under Steve Jobs. There are few rules and not much bureaucracy in a power culture because whatever the boss says, goes. Fashion, publishing and film tend to be sectors with power cultures, and investment banks and brokerage firms often reflect the characteristics of power culture. The advantage of a power culture is that decisions can be made very quickly. The ability of the power culture to adapt to changes in the environment is very much determined by the perception and ability of those who occupy the positions of power within it.

Did you know?

Some ex-employees of Apple shared details about their experience of the company under the leadership of Steve Jobs on the question and answer website, Quara. One of the posts suggested that like most companies, Apple had its fair share of red tape that could frustrate employees. If a particular project or issue did not involve or interest Steve Jobs, it could 'take months of meetings to move things forward'. If, on the other hand, 'Steve wants it done, it's done faster than anyone thinks is humanly possible. The best way to get any cross-departmental work done is to say it's for Steve and you'd probably have it the same day.'

● **Person culture**: Those involved in a person culture tend to have strong values about how they will work, and can be very difficult for an organisation to manage. Person cultures are typically found in professional partnerships such as accountancy and legal firms and in universities. Some professional partnerships operate well as person cultures, because each partner brings a particular expertise and clientele to the firm. Barristers' chambers, architects' partnerships and small consultancy firms often have this person orientation.

Person cultures differ from power cultures in that an organisation with a person culture involves a collection of individuals each with their own expertise and power, who are not organised into a single hierarchy. Organisations which portray this culture reject formal hierarchies for 'getting things done' and exist solely to meet the needs of their members.

Fact file

Handy's four cultures

In his 1978 book, *The Gods of Management*, Charles Handy classified the four organisational cultures in terms of gods. He had no preference for any of the four cultures and said that they co-exist in most organisations. To reflect his point of view, he named the four cultures after ancient Greek gods who were worshipped simultaneously. These gods and diagrams to illustrate each of the cultures are included below:

Task culture = Athena. The culture is represented by a net or lattice work, as illustrated in Figure 16.1, because there is close liaison between departments, functions and specialities.

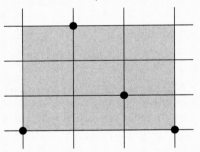

▲ **Figure 16.1** Handy's task culture lattice

Role culture = Apollo. The culture is represented by a Greek temple, illustrated in Figure 16.2. The apex of the temple is where the decision making takes place; the pillars of the temple reflect the functional departments of the organisation that have to implement the decisions from the apex.

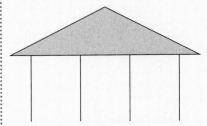

▲ **Figure 16.2** Handy's role culture Greek temple

Power culture = Zeus. Power culture is like a web with a ruling spider, illustrated in Figure 16.3. Those in the web are dependent on a central power source. Rays of power and influence spread out from the central figure or group.

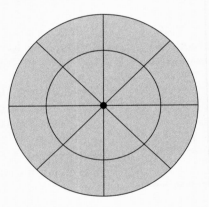

▲ **Figure 16.3** Handy's power culture web

Person culture = Dionysius. The organisational structure is as minimal as possible; the individuals are clustered together, like a 'galaxy of individual stars', as in Figure 16.4.

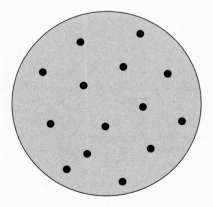

▲ **Figure 16.4** Handy's person culture cluster

Did you know?

In the 1990s and 2000s, many organisations made a determined effort to move from tall, narrow to wide, flat organisational structures. This process is known as 'delayering' or 'flattening' the organisation. A tall, narrow hierarchical structure will usually imply a role culture with great emphasis on control, symbols, titles and strict power relations. In contrast, a wide, flat structure will more often imply a task culture with little emphasis on symbols of hierarchy, more participative decision making and fewer controls. Centralisation means that most decision making is retained at the top of an organisation, and this implies a power culture. Decentralisation means that decision making is passed down through the group and may lead to more of a task culture.

Key term

Hofstede's national cultures A model of cultural dimensions that distinguishes one country's culture from another; the model measures and compares the cultural dimensions of different countries and demonstrates that there are national and regional cultural groupings that affect the behaviour of organisations.

Hofstede's national cultures

In the 1970s, psychologist Dr Geert Hofstede had access to a large database of over 100,000 questionnaires about the values and sentiments of people in about 50 countries. All these people worked in the subsidiaries of IBM, a large multinational company. From this data he developed a model of cultural dimensions that has become an internationally recognised standard. His findings were first published in his book, *Culture's Consequences: International Differences in Work-Related Values* (1980).

He initially identified four distinct dimensions that served to distinguish one culture from another. Later he added a fifth dimension and then a sixth dimension. He repeated the questionnaire on 400 management trainees, unrelated to IBM, across 30 countries, and came up with similar findings. His findings have also correlated with findings from other researchers.

He scored each country using a scale of 1 to 120 for each dimension. The higher the score, the more that dimension is likely to be exhibited in that country.

Hofstede's research showed that cultural differences matter and that managers in international organisations, especially those who are nationals of the country in question, tend to operate according to their country's values, rather than to the organisation's culture. His findings suggest that cultural awareness can lead to greater success in international business ventures. It indicates that there is not one set of principles that are universally applicable and confirms that there are multiple ways of structuring organisations and institutions.

Hofstede defined organisational or corporate culture as an idea system that is largely shared between members of an organisation. By filtering out IBM's dominant organisation culture from his data on IBM's employees in international subsidiaries, Hofstede was able to statistically distinguish cultural differences between countries. Hofstede's dimensions of culture are:

- **Power distance (PD):** This dimension is related to the different solutions to the basic problem of human inequality. It covers the extent to which power is distributed equally within a society and the degree that society accepts this distribution. A high PD culture prefers hierarchical bureaucracies, strong leaders and has a high regard for authority. Subordinates expect to be told what to do in this culture. A low PD culture tends to favour flatter organisations, personal responsibility and

autonomy. Subordinates expect to be consulted and involved in decision making in this culture. According to Hofstede's model, high PD countries include Malaysia (with a score of 104) and other Asian countries.

- **Individualism (versus collectivism) (IDV):** This refers to the strength of the ties people have to others within the community. In countries with a high IDV score there is a lack of interpersonal connection, and little sharing of responsibility beyond family and a few close friends. People's time and their need for freedom are valued highly and there is an expectation of rewards for hard work. A society with a low IDV score has strong group cohesion; work is more likely to be done for intrinsic rewards; harmony is often more important than honesty; tradition, age and wisdom are all respected; and change is introduced slowly. Hofstede's model suggests that Central American countries, such as Panama and Guatemala, have very low IDV scores (11 and 6, respectively).

- **Masculinity (versus femininity) (MAS):** This refers to how much a society sticks with, and values, traditional male and female roles. High MAS scores are found in countries where men are expected to be 'tough', to be the provider, and to be assertive and there are well-defined distinctions between men's work and women's work. In a low MAS society, women and men work together equally across many professions. Men are allowed to be sensitive. Powerful and successful women are just as admired and respected as powerful and successful men. Hofstede's model suggests that Japan has a high MAS score (95), whereas Sweden has the lowest score (5).

- **Uncertainty avoidance index (UAI):** This relates to the degree of anxiety that people feel when in uncertain or unknown situations. High UAI scores indicate societies that are governed by rules and order; tight organisational structures are valued and differences are avoided. Low UAI scores indicate that a society enjoys novel events and values differences. There are few rules, business attitudes are informal, and change and risk are accepted as routine aspects of business life. According to Hofstede's model, Belgium has a high UAI score (94).

- **Long-term orientation (LTO):** This refers to how much society values long-standing traditions and values. This is the fifth dimension that Hofstede added in the 1990s, after finding that people in Asian countries, with a strong link to Confucian philosophy, acted differently to those in Western cultures. In countries with a high LTO score, meeting social obligations and avoiding 'loss of face' are considered very important. Family is the basis of society, parents and men have more authority than young people and women, levels of respect for traditions and perseverance are strong, and loyalty and commitment are rewarded. In countries with low LTO scores there is greater promotion of equality and more emphasis on creativity and individualism. Self-actualisation by individuals is sought and change is not feared. According to Hofstede's model, the USA and UK have low LTO scores.

- **Indulgence versus restraint (IVR):** This is related to the gratification of, versus the control of, basic human desires. Indulgence sees freedom of speech and leisure as important. Restraint sees freedom of speech and leisure as of lower importance. Indulgence tends to prevail in South and North America and in Western Europe. Restraint prevails in Eastern Europe, in Asia and in Muslim countries.

Critics of Hofstede's conclusions about national cultures say that:

- they generalise about an entire national population on the basis of the analysis of a few questionnaire responses by certain categories of employees in an IBM subsidiary in that country
- there is no evidence that the sample questioned in each country was representative of the people in that country.

They also query:

- how accurate the data is
- how well designed the questionnaires were
- how up to date the data is and how much the culture of a country might change over time as a result of either internal or external influences.

Fact file

Hofstede's national culture values

Table 16.1 provides Hofstede's national culture scores for a range of countries.

▼ **Table 16.1** Hofstede's national culture scores from selected countries

Country	PD	IDV	MAS	UAI	LTO	IVR
China	80	20	66	30	87	24
France	68	71	43	86	63	48
Germany	35	67	66	65	83	40
Japan	54	46	95	92	88	42
UK	35	89	66	35	51	69
USA	40	91	62	46	26	68

Source: http://geert-hofstede.com

Applications of Hofstede's national cultures model

- **International communication.** Cross-cultural communication, for example in relation to negotiations about contracts, requires being aware of cultural differences because what may be considered perfectly acceptable and natural in one country, can be confusing or even offensive in another. All types of communication are affected by cultural dimensions: verbal (words and language), non-verbal (body language, gestures), etiquette dos and don'ts (clothing, gift-giving, dining, customs and protocol), and written communication.
- **Operational issues such as outsourcing.** Outsourcing is a very important strategic issue for most of the world's leading companies. Outsourcing, however, is much more complex than just taking advantage of low wages in some emerging countries. Companies need to plan it carefully and take into account national cultures. What may be an effective and efficient way of co-ordination in one country may prove to be ineffective, inefficient or even counter-productive in another.
- **Marketing and customer service.** Most aspects of consumer behaviour are culture-bound and therefore understanding national cultures is important to ensure the success of global marketing. For example, marketing a car in a country where the uncertainty avoidance index (UAI) is high, might mean emphasising safety issues as the most important

feature, whereas in other countries, emphasising social image may be more important. Evidence suggests that a lack of understanding of different cultures constitutes one of the most important reasons for failure when establishing customer service centres across geographical borders.

- **Leadership**. National cultures indicate that people have very different views on what a good boss is or on how teams should be led. Management techniques or leadership styles that work in one national culture do not necessarily work elsewhere. This is especially relevant for businesses that grow and set up new divisions in other countries. Most new and emerging markets tend to be in countries characterised by hierarchical cultures. For many US and Western European companies, the leadership styles they have been practising at home might not be suitable for these cultures.
- **Recruitment and HR**. For international organisations, recruiting the right people is crucial to their success. HR departments develop job specifications that identify relevant skills and character traits required for jobs in their organisations. However, they rarely consider the fact that the degree to which skills and traits are desirable differs from one country to another. Virtual working is increasingly the norm in many sectors. National culture has a big impact on this, because often a virtual team is also a cross-cultural team.

Other classifications of culture

In addition to the two cultural models specified by AQA, other classifications of culture exist. These include the following.

Bureaucratic culture

The characteristics of a bureaucratic culture are similar to Handy's role culture. They include: an emphasis on roles and procedures; behaviour that is risk averse and anxious to avoid mistakes; precisely defined responsibilities and roles; and a hierarchical structure

In general, these characteristics result in organisations: that survive for long periods of time; whose staff are unsuited to a dynamic environment; and which often have a culture where making the right decision is less important than making decisions in the right way. Bureaucratic cultures tend to be found in large, mature businesses or public sector organisations, such as the civil service. Such organisations are likely to discourage risk taking and even penalise managers who introduce unsuccessful projects. As a result, individuals will fear failure and seek to minimise its occurrence. Such behaviour may lead to the rejection of interesting or exciting projects because they are judged too risky or uncertain.

Entrepreneurial culture

Organisations with entrepreneurial cultures have characteristics similar to Handy's power culture. These include: an emphasis on results and rewards for individual initiative; risk taking; a flatter and more flexible organisational structure that gives more local control.

An entrepreneurial culture often applies to businesses in their early years of development, such as small start-up businesses. Such organisations encourage risk taking and the acceptance of occasional failure, on the basis that large gains may be achieved when there is success. As a result they are less likely to survive in the long term.

The influences on organisational culture

The formation of 'culture' will depend upon a whole host of factors, including company history, ownership, leadership style, organisational structure, technology, important business incidents and the external environment.

The cultural web

Johnson and Scholes in their book, *Exploring Corporate Strategy* (1988), identified a cultural web. This is illustrated in Figure 16.5. The cultural web consists of the factors that influence organisational culture and are the source of organisational culture.

▲ **Figure 16.5** The cultural web

- **Symbols and titles**. These include visual representations of an organisation, including logos, how people dress and how they address and speak to each other. For example, in the professions, the language or jargon that is used can effectively exclude others and thus reinforce professional cultures. Other examples include: the range of pay scales, from the highest to the lowest, which indicate status within the organisation; the size and location of managers' offices and whether they have their own PAs (personal assistants); and whether there are separate canteens, entrances and car parks for managers and workers.
- **Power relations**. The power structure is the interrelationship between individuals or groups who take decisions about how an organisation's resources are allocated. Power relations are about whether the power structure is autocratic or participative. For example, in some organisations, challenging managers' views is encouraged; in others, this would be considered disloyal. Some organisations encourage co-operation between

different groups, while others encourage a level of competitive rivalry. In some organisations real power may lie with just one or two key senior leaders; in others it may lie with a whole group of executives, or even with a particular department. The key is that these people will have the greatest amount of influence on decisions, operations and strategic direction.

- **Organisational structure**. This is about the way management is organised both vertically, by layers of hierarchy, and horizontally, by functional areas or by geographical or product categories. Some organisational structures are decentralised and emphasise delegation; others are more hierarchical and centralised. This aspect of the cultural web includes the structure defined by the organisation chart as well as the unwritten lines of power and influence that indicate whose contributions are more valued or are more influential – as indicated in the power relations section above.

- **Control systems**. This is about the way that an organisation is controlled, including financial systems, quality systems and pay and reward systems, and whether it is highly centralised or decentralised. Formal controls are the rules and procedures governing employee actions. In some organisations, employees have autonomy and independence, and entrepreneurial activity is encouraged, in others, employees are expected to follow procedures closely.

- **Rituals and routines**. These are signs of what is considered appropriate behaviour in an organisation and the way everyday decisions and tasks are undertaken. They determine what is expected to happen in given situations, and what is valued by leaders and managers. For example, in some organisations, managers regularly walk around and talk to staff; in others, managers are rarely seen. In some organisations, managers communicate and consult with their staff on a routine basis; in others staff are only informed once decisions have been made.

- **Myths and stories**. These are the things that are repeated, within the organisation and by others outside the organisation, about its history, its founders, other significant people in the organisation and about important events – for example, stories about how the founders built up the business or about when an organisation won an important client. Who and what an organisation chooses to immortalise says a lot about what it values.

- **Organisational assumption (paradigm)** – the six elements of the cultural web discussed above help to make up what Johnson and Scholes call the 'paradigm'. This is the set of assumptions about the organisation, which is held in common and taken for granted in the organisation, that is, its culture.

374

Did you know?

Nike's myths and stories

Apparently a Winnebago RV (a Winnebago is a type of large campervan and RV stands for recreational vehicle) is parked in the middle of the Innovation Kitchen (what Nike calls its sports research lab) at the Nike headquarters in Oregon, USA. The Nike team purchased it to use as a conference room, even though there is plenty of meeting space elsewhere. Legend has it that Nike co-founder, Phil Knight, first sold shoes in the back of an RV like this one. Apparently Nike's campus is full of odd objects like this, making it a sort of living museum of legends and oral history about the company. For example, the waffle iron that Nike co-founder, Bill Bowerman, is reputed to have ruined in making rubber soles in the 1970s, is also enshrined on the campus.

Other influences on organisational culture include:

- the nature of the markets served by a business: for example, banks have different cultures from breweries
- the developmental stage of a business: for example, startups are unlikely to have the formal roles, policies and procedures evident in long established companies
- the degree of regulation imposed on a business: for example, the need to meet a range of government regulations and standards, including relevant inspectorate requirements, will have a significant influence on the culture of some organisations, such as the civil service, financial institutions, hospitals and schools
- the finance available: cash-starved startups will have different cultures to high-flying social network companies
- the history of an organisation: the reasons it was formed, its age, the philosophy and values of its founders, the key events in its history, such as whether it was the result of a merger or takeover; this is linked to the myths and stories element of the cultural web
- its primary function and its technologies: the range and quality of its products, the importance of its reputation, the type of customers it serves and the nature of the technologies it uses
- its size: the larger the organisation, the more it will tend to have formal structures and a culture that matches that; the larger an organisation, the more likely it is to have separate departments and split sites, which can cause communication problems and rivalries, both of which may cause different cultures to emerge; this is linked to the organisational structure element of the cultural web
- the location of an organisation: whether it is in an urban or rural location might influence the type of customer and the type of staff attracted to work there, both of which can influence culture; the cultures in organisations in international locations will be influenced by the national cultures of the countries – as noted by Hofstede
- management and staffing: top managers and founders have considerable influence on culture, for example Richard Branson at Virgin and Steve Jobs during his time at Apple; this is linked to the power relations element of the cultural web; culture is also determined by the nature of staff employed and whether they truly accept management's philosophy and policies or just pay lip service to them.

Fact file

IKEA

The source of IKEA's culture is founder Ingvar Kamprad, who grew up in a poor farming area in Sweden where people worked hard and lived frugally. Kamprad combined the lessons he learned while growing up with his vision of creating a better everyday life for people by offering them affordable, functional, well-designed furniture. He named his company IKEA by combining his initials with the first letters of Elmtaryd and Agunnaryd, the farm and the village where he grew up. IKEA's success in expanding to 301 stores in 37 countries stems from Kamprad's vision and his continued influence as an active senior adviser to the company.

The reasons for and problems of changing organisational culture

Changing organisational culture is not easy to achieve and requires significant investment in effective training and communication if it is to be successful. It can be particularly difficult to change in large organisations that have a great deal of internal momentum (i.e. a powerful tendency to continue moving in the direction they are already moving). The size of an organisation and the strength of its culture are the biggest contributors to cultural inertia (or resistance to change).

A change in the external environment may mean profound changes are required in the way things are done within an organisation. For example, if the market becomes more competitive, an organisation's values may no longer be appropriate. They may hinder the ability of an organisation to adapt, and thus a change in culture might be needed in order to change the organisation's approach and, ultimately, its performance. However, an existing organisational culture can be a barrier to change, and when it is challenged this can produce strong resistance within the organisation because the fundamental values of staff are under threat.

Cultural change will be necessary when two companies come together because of a merger, takeover or joint venture. However, one corporate culture cannot simply suppress and replace another. A consensus has to be reached and the foundation for a new culture, based on elements of both cultures involved, has to be developed carefully. The many problems that can result are evident in the Fact files and Case studies in this chapter and in Chapter 11.

Fact file

The 2001 merger of America Online (AOL) and Time Warner

In 2001, this merger was one of the largest in corporate history. It was not a success and the clash of cultures between the two organisations was said to be the major problem. One commentator said, 'There were open collars and jeans at AOL', while Time Warner 'was more buttoned down'.

Rapid expansion or retrenchment can create a need for cultural change. As organisations grow, cultural change can be problematic because senior managers have less time to devote to ensuring a strong culture is established. The vision of the organisation, while still clear to senior managers, may be less clear to employees lower down the hierarchy and to new employees, which in turn is likely to weaken an organisation's culture. As departments or divisions increase in size and power, they may begin to look after their own interests rather than those of the organisation as a whole. They may begin to develop cultures of their own, which may not always be in tune with the dominant organisational culture and which prevent or impede the organisation's ability to meet its objectives. When organisations retrench, staffing will change substantially, key people will leave, different objectives may be introduced, a sharper and more streamlined organisational structure is likely to be introduced – all of which indicate the need to change the existing culture. In this situation, problems are likely to emerge as people try to adapt to a new way of doing things in a highly uncertain environment.

A change in strategy or objectives, as a result of a change in size or for other reasons, will often mean that the organisational culture needs to change to fit. For example, if an organisation wanted to change its generic strategy from cost leadership to differentiation, this would almost certainly require a culture change. The survival of some organisations is threatened by clinging to a culture that is no longer appropriate.

Implementing culture change is likely to involve some or all of the following stages:

- Analysing elements of the cultural web. This can assist leaders and managers in evaluating what is working, what is not working and what needs changing.
- Ensuring clarity in the strategic vision. This means making sure that the mission statement, vision statement and overall strategy work together to create a strong culture statement.
- Leading by example. Senior leaders and managers need to exhibit the kinds of values and behaviours that they want to see in the rest of their organisation. Leaders and managers are role models. If they say one thing and do the opposite, no one will take the culture change seriously and it will quickly lose credibility.
- Reviewing the organisational structure. The organisational structure and control systems need to match and support the new culture. Where an organisational structure acts as a barrier to change – for example, where a hierarchical structure may constrain entrepreneurial flair and risk taking – management can restructure the business to help bring about the change in culture. This includes altering employee handbooks, pay and reward policies, the hierarchical structure, decision-making authority and other elements of organisational structure.
- Ensuring recruitment strategies attract the right type of people who will adopt, and fit in with, the desired culture.
- Ensuring that the ethical and legal implications of the new culture are understood, planned for and in line with corporate ethics and that training materials emphasise this.
- Because the preparation and implementation of change is highly culturally sensitive, the importance of national cultural dimensions (see the earlier section on Hofstede) needs to be taken into account for businesses that operate internationally.

Practice exercise 1

Total: 70 marks

1. What is meant by the term 'organisational culture'? *(3 marks)*

2. Analyse why an organisation's culture is important to its success. *(9 marks)*

3. Which of the following is not an element of Handy's cultural model?
   a) Creative culture
   b) Person culture
   c) Power culture
   d) Role culture
   e) Task culture *(1 mark)*

4. Identify and explain Charles Handy's four different cultures. *(12 marks)*

5. Identify and explain two ways in which Handy's different cultures link to organisational structure. *(8 marks)*

6. Which of the following is not one of Hofstede's national cultures?
   a) Power distance
   b) Uncertainty avoidance
   c) Individualism
   d) Innovation
   e) Masculinity *(1 mark)*

7. Identify three aspects of business where Hofstede's national cultures might be important and explain why. *(9 marks)*

8. Identify and explain four influences on organisational culture. *(12 marks)*

9. Explain three reasons why a change in organisational culture might be necessary. *(9 marks)*

10. Explain two problems an organisation might encounter in trying to change its organisational culture. *(6 marks)*

Case study 1: A cultural web

Read the following statements that illustrate elements of the cultural web in a car maintenance business.

Myths and stories

'We are known for having a high level of customer complaints and for doing shoddy work.'

Staff members talk about the owner starting the business with a £5,000 lottery win.

'We have a reputation for doing things as cheaply as possible.'

Rituals and routines

'Our time cards are checked thoroughly every day to ensure we only get paid for the precise time we put in.'

'Whatever job we do, we always have to make sure we use the cheapest parts and complete it in the quickest time possible.'

'The boss is always talking to us about money.'

Symbols and titles

The business uses yellow vans.

The business offers yellow courtesy cars that are small, economy models.

The owner wears overalls rather than a suit on most days.

Organisational structure

The structure is flat and consists of three layers – the owner, the head mechanic and other mechanics.

Mechanics work on jobs independently and there is little or no team work.

Control systems

Costs are tightly controlled, and customers are billed for every part used and every minute of a mechanic's time.

Getting the work done on time and at the lowest cost are more important than the quality of the work done.

If it takes mechanics 15 per cent or more time to do a job than the estimate suggested, a deduction is made to their pay.

Power structures

The owner pursues a low-cost, high-profit approach to the business, even if this means losing repeat customers.

The threat of pay deductions ensures mechanics work as expected by the owner.

The receptionist is the owner's wife. She informs him immediately if customers complain about a mechanic's work.

Questions

Total: 10 marks

1. Identify and explain two of the common themes that come through about the culture of this organisation.

   (6 marks)

2. Explain which of Handy's organisational cultures appears to be most dominant in this organisation.

   (4 marks)

Case study 2: Bonobos

The company

Andy Dunn founded Bonobos (pronounced 'bu-NO-bos') in 2007 as an online-only male clothing company. Its 'Guideshops' are men's clothing stores where customers can try clothes on for size, put outfits together and get advice from salespeople. But if they want to buy the clothes, they have to order them on the Bonobos website.

The approach is similar to Apple's approach with its stores, which changed their focus from buying to trying. According to a recent survey by IBM, nearly half of all online shoppers use this technique of trying first and then buying online. It provides an example of how retail is changing. Instead of a place where you buy things, a shop or store is becoming a place where you are able to experience things. Andy Dunn says that 80 per cent of the people who come into the stores actually go back and purchases the clothes online.

'We founded Bonobos to really create a better shopping experience for men. Initially, we thought we could do it purely on a website, but we realised from talking to our customers that actually some of them like to try on the clothes.'

Bonobos opened its first Guideshop in May 2012 in New York and now has locations in other US cities.

379

Its culture

The founder, Andy Dunn, worked at creating an appropriate culture for the company.

1. In its early days, he identified five core human values evident in the best people the business hired. These became the company's core virtues – self-awareness, positive energy, empathy, intellectual honesty and judgement. They became the key factors that the business looks for when they hire people. The founder says that when hiring people, it is tempting to employ someone who has done the job before, but he suggests that this type of experience-based hiring leads to bringing in those who have the right credentials, but not necessarily the right 'fire in their soul'.

2. Once the business had identified its mission – essentially to solve the problem of ensuring that men's trousers fit well – this enabled it to hire the right technology leader – someone who loved technology and clothes – and then build a highly effective software engineering team.

3. People are only part of culture. The other part is the context in which they operate, which is influenced by a range of things, including objectives, feedback, promotions, pay and rewards, seating arrangements, what is celebrated and what is left unsaid. The company has focused on positive feedback to create motivation. It has made company-wide recognition a core part of every team meeting. Regular use is made of handwritten notes and emails to honour people when they have done well.

4. The company recognised that if it wanted employees to think and act like owners, in the sense of being totally committed to the mission and objectives of the business, they needed to become owners. By having a stake in the ownership of the company in terms of shareholding, employees are more committed and more focused on the company's objectives. The founder says that this feature is unusual in the clothing business, and as a result is an important source of competitive and cultural advantage for the company.

Source: https:// bonobos.com and an article on www.businessoffashion.com

Questions

Total: 15 marks

1. Using Handy's cultural model, analyse the type of culture that is likely to be evident at Bonobos.
   (9 marks)

2. Explain two problems related to its culture that a company like Bonobos is likely to encounter as it grows.
   (6 marks)

Case study 3: Daimler-Chrysler – a culture clash

Author advice

This Case study develops material included in the Fact file on Daimler-Chrysler on page 247 in Chapter 11 of this book. Read the Fact file before continuing with this Case study.

In May 1998, Daimler Benz and the Chrysler Corporation, two of the world's leading car manufacturers, agreed to combine their businesses in what they claimed to be a merger of equals. The merger resulted in a large automobile company, ranked third in the world in terms of revenues, market capitalisation and earnings, and fifth in terms of the number of units sold. German and American styles of management differed sharply. To minimise this clash of cultures, the Daimler Chairman decided to allow both groups to maintain their existing cultures.

In an interview with the *Financial Times* in early 1999, the Daimler Chairman admitted that the deal was never really intended to be a merger of equals and claimed that Daimler Benz had acquired Chrysler. Chrysler reported a huge loss in 2000 and its share value slipped by more than half its 1999 value. A number of Chrysler's key players had left the corporation and the remaining employees were demoralised and demotivated. Within 19 months, two American CEOs were dismissed and German management took over.

Daimler Benz had tried to administer the Chrysler division as if it were a German company. In September 2001, *Business Week* wrote: 'Daimler-Chrysler have combined nothing beyond some administrative departments, such as finance and public relations.'

Daimler-Chrysler was a cross-cultural merger that failed. Daimler Benz was a conservative, rigidly structured company. Chrysler was a much more informal and outward-focused company. These distinct organisational cultures were not addressed properly during the merger process. As a result, the expected and wished for synergy effects never materialised. Instead of gaining the competitive advantage that they anticipated, the merger caused the two car producers to move ever deeper into crisis.

Table 16.2 provides Hofstede's cultural dimensions scores for the USA and Germany.

▼ **Table 16.2** Hofstede's cultural dimension scores for the USA and Germany

	Germany	USA
Power Distance (PD)	35	40
Individualism (IDV)	67	91
Masculinity (MAS)	66	62
Uncertainty Avoidance Index (UAI)	65	46
Long-term Orientation (LTO)	83	26
Indulgence (IVR)	40	68

Source: a range of newspaper articles from 1998 to 2001, and http://geert-hofstede.com

Questions

Total: 25 marks

1. Using Hofstede's cultural dimensions scores for the USA and Germany, analyse the likely differences between each country's national cultures from a business perspective. *(9 marks)*

2. Evaluate the importance of culture in the context of the Daimler-Chrysler merger and the potential problems in trying to change culture. *(16 marks)*

Essay question

Total: 25 marks

Answer either of the following questions.

1. (Refer back to the discussion of mergers and takeovers in Chapter 11.) Surveys show that about 65 per cent of mergers and takeovers fail to benefit the acquiring company. To what extent might conflicting organisational cultures play a part in the failure of mergers and takeovers to achieve their expected success? *(25 marks)*

2. XYZ is a relatively new company that is highly innovative. Its organisational structure involves a relatively flat hierarchy and a democratic leadership style. It is beginning to enter European and Asian markets and is in negotiations to set up a base in Malaysia. Discuss how the cultural models of Handy and Hofstede might assist the company in ensuring that it has an appropriate organisational culture in place as it moves forward. *(25 marks)*

17 Managing strategic implementation

The focus of this chapter is managing strategic implementation. It begins by considering how to implement strategy effectively. In doing so it considers the value of leadership and communication in strategic implementation. The importance of organisational structure in strategic implementation is then discussed. In this context, organisational structures include functional, product-based, regional and matrix structures. The final part of this chapter considers the value of network analysis (often known as critical path analysis) in strategic implementation. The creation and amendment of network diagrams are explained, and the interpretation of key information such as the critical path and total float time is considered. The chapter concludes by identifying the benefits and problems of network analysis.

How to implement strategy effectively

Author advice

Chapter 1 defines strategy as the medium- to long-term plans through which an organisation aims to attain its objectives. In the section on 'Links between mission, corporate objectives and strategy' in Chapter 1, a detailed explanation of the corporate planning process is included. It identifies the various stages of the corporate planning process, including the strategic implementation stage. Ensure you are secure in your understanding of this area before proceeding with this chapter.

Key term

Strategic implementation The stage when a strategic plan is put into effect in order to achieve the objectives for which it has been designed; the stage where strategies are translated into policies, rules, procedures and operational targets within the different functional areas.

Strategic implementation involves creating a framework for carrying out the agreed strategy at both corporate and functional levels by assigning responsibilities and operational targets.

Author advice

Most of the chapters in this book contribute information needed to implement strategies effectively. Chapters 1–8 discuss issues relating to analysing the strategic position of a business. Chapters 9 and 10 cover issues relating to choosing strategic direction. Chapters 11–14 cover issues relating to strategic method and how to pursue strategies. The rest of the chapters, including this one, concern managing strategic change. Try, therefore, to see all of these topics in an integrated way based around how a business: sets objectives; reviews its internal and external environment; devises a strategy or plan to achieve its objectives; and implements its strategy or plan at the corporate and functional level.

While most organisations create a strategic plan, not all are successful in implementing it. Research suggests that about 70 per cent of strategic plans and strategies are never implemented effectively. In one study of 200 companies, 80 per cent of directors said they had the right strategies, but only 14 per cent thought they were implementing them well. In the same study, 97 per cent of directors said they had a 'strategic vision', but only 33 per cent reported achieving 'significant strategic success'.

Understanding which factors, whether external or internal, have the greatest impact on the effective implementation of a strategy allows a business to respond more quickly and effectively if these factors change. The impact of external and internal factors on effective implementation of strategy are explained in the next two sections.

External factors and the effective implementation of strategy

▲ Firms must be aware of changes in the external environment in order to compete successfully

- **Changes in a firm's external environment**. The external environment was considered in Chapters 4, 5 and 6. Changes in the external environment may affect strategic plans and their implementation. For example, a firm that makes and fits windows may have a strategy to increase its sales in different geographical regions by developing links with building firms in different regions. The effective implementation of this strategy will be strongly influenced by the state of the building industry and house building, which in turn will be influenced by the state of the economy and interest rates. Understanding this will allow the business to ensure estimates about demand in its market are realistic and that implementation of related plans are more effective.

- **Changes in a firm's competitive environment**. When designing a new strategy it is important to take into account how effectively a competitor is likely to respond to it. For example, Firm A's strategy might be to reduce price in order to gain sales. However, if a more powerful firm in the market is likely to reduce its own prices even further in order not to lose sales, the price reduction strategy of Firm A is unlikely to be a successful one. Thus it is important for a business to understand its competitive environment. Chapter 7 discusses the features of the competitive environment.

Being prepared to change strategy or key aspects of the implementation plan, if the external or competitive environments change significantly, is an important feature of a flexible and successful organisation.

Internal factors and the effective implementation of strategy

- **Leadership**. Strong leadership and appropriate styles of leadership that fully support a company's strategy and how this is to be implemented are vital if objectives are to be achieved. Leaders need to introduce actions that are well planned and coherent so that, for example, the tactics of the various functional areas are aligned well with the overall strategy, and functional targets contribute effectively to the overall objective. The value of leadership in strategic planning is considered in more detail in the next section of this chapter.

- **Organisational structure**. An organisation's structure must be appropriate for the effective implementation of its strategy. The value of organisational structure in strategic implementation is discussed later in this chapter.

- **Organisational culture**. A supportive culture is a key influence on effective strategy implementation. Organisational culture is discussed in detail in Chapter 16. The extent to which strategy implementation is effective will be linked to how well a planned strategy matches the culture of an organisation. In some cases, in order to introduce a new strategy, organisational culture needs to change. See the Fact files on Apple and on Samsung to illustrate how different cultures influence strategies and their implementation.

Did you know?

A 'blue ocean' strategy is one where a business works in a market that is virtually free of competition because it systematically tries to create 'blue oceans' of uncontested market space in order to grow. A 'blue ocean' strategy contrasts with 'red ocean' conditions, where businesses compete intensely for a share of a market.

Fact file

Samsung as a 'fast market follower'

Samsung has for a long time used a strategy of a 'fast market follower' – it carefully studies a market and if an innovative product emerges, it quickly copies it, then develops its own, often higher quality, product, and captures the market. The strategy Samsung employs is based strongly on an organisational culture of operational excellence.

Samsung was not always focused on delivering superior quality, but has developed this culture over time. In 1995, Samsung's chairman, Lee Kun-hee, organised a bonfire of 50 million dollars' worth of what he saw as low-quality Samsung phones, TVs, fax machines and other equipment. He did this in front of 2,000 factory employees to reinforce the message that superior quality, 'Quality First', was an absolute requirement. A dramatic way of trying to influence an organisation's culture and get a message across!

Samsung has realised that the 'fast market follower' strategy does not always work and that it needs to be more innovative in its own right. However, developing 'disruptive' products requires an extremely innovative culture, which may not come easily for Samsung. The South Korean organisational culture tends to favour strong hierarchies and formal organisational and leadership structures – which can limit an organisation's ability to innovate.

- **Communication**. Good communication is an important feature of effective strategic implementation. The value of communication in

Author advice

Chapter 9 discusses how businesses choose strategic direction, including which markets to compete in and what products to offer. Chapter 10 discusses how businesses decide on their strategic positioning, that is, how to compete. These chapters are relevant to the discussion here, so ensure you are confident in your understanding of these issues.

strategic implementation is discussed later in this chapter. In addition, Chapter 15 considers the issue of employees' resistance to change and how communication can be a very important means of overcoming such resistance. Equally important is involving employees in the process of change. Not all strategies are popular, but involving employees in the decision making and implementation process means that they are more likely to be positive about any changes.

- **Timing and distinctiveness**. Some strategies, while seemingly well researched and appropriate at the time of planning, may be ineffective when implemented because: a rival beats a company to market with a similar idea or strategy; or the strategy leaves a company undistinguished in the market because others are pursuing the same one.
- **Providing adequate resources**. Some strategies fail because not enough resources are allocated to their implementation. Adequate resourcing means having sufficient financial, human and other resources available for the implementation of the planned strategy.
- **Network analysis**. Network analysis is an important means of planning how to complete a complex project efficiently. It is therefore a useful tool in the design of strategic implementation. Its value is considered in the final section of this chapter.
- **Monitoring and accountability**. Effective implementation requires continual monitoring of, for example: progress in implementing the strategic plan; the competitive environment; the external environment; levels of customer satisfaction; financial returns generated by a strategy; levels of employee resentment. Monitoring must be accompanied by accountability for it to be of value. This means that managers in the various functional areas are responsible for ensuring that the effective implementation of strategy in their particular area meets targets.
- **Reviewing and evaluating**. If monitoring systems indicate that strategic implementation is not going to plan, further review and evaluation may be needed and a range of alternative options considered. These may include: changing the timing of activities (which might involve modifying the planned schedule in network analysis), changing the tactics (for example, deciding not to introduce straight price reductions but instead to provide 'three for two'-type offers), changing the strategy itself (for example, if the objective is to increase sales over the next two years and the strategy is to encourage more sales in the UK, to consider pushing sales in Europe instead) and, as a last resort, changing the objectives.

The value of leadership in strategic implementation

Leaders are likely to be involved in setting strategy, communicating the strategy, implementing the strategy through their staff and getting the results. While in practice a lot of leadership time is spent on setting strategy, a new strategy will not bring results if leaders do not invest enough of their effort in communicating the strategy and leading its implementation. This applies whether the strategy is about entering a new market or introducing new systems of working.

Implementing change or any new strategy within a company requires a feeling of urgency on the part of the entire company. It is the job of management to create that urgency by explaining to employees why the implementation is

Author advice

Chapter 4 of the AQA A-level Business Book 1 discussed the different styles of leadership and the role of leaders in setting objectives, analysing, making decisions and reviewing, that is, in determining strategy and in managing and leading its implementation. Ensure you review the content of that chapter before continuing.

necessary. Leaders need to help employees understand how their company benefits from the change and the problems of not making a change.

For strategic implementation to succeed, leaders must demonstrate their commitment to it. Samsung's chairman, Lee Kun-hee, is an example of a leader who has been instrumental not just in determining strategy but in ensuring its effective implementation. (See the Fact file on Samsung in the previous section of this chapter.)

A key task for leaders in relation to strategic implementation is to ensure it is well planned at both corporate and functional level, with appropriate individuals and groups being accountable for meeting targets.

The value of communication in strategic implementation

In most cases, strategies are developed by a few senior leaders and remain something that only the CEO and the management team understand. This becomes a challenge because, although strategy is developed by 'a few', it must be implemented by everyone. This is why communication in relation to strategic implementation is so important.

Regardless of how far-seeing and meticulously planned a strategy involving organisational change may be, it will not be effectively implemented unless it is communicated to employees in such a way that resistance is overcome, fears are eased, confusion is minimised and commitment to change is secured.

Effectively communicating the key features of a strategy at every level of an organisation using a range of different media is vital to ensure effective implementation. This should allow all staff to understand the reasons for the changes that are happening, how they will be affected, what their roles are and what is expected of them. Communication needs to occur at every level. Samsung's chairman, Lee Kun-hee, ensured that in communicating the new 'Quality First' approach (mentioned in the Fact file on Samsung earlier in this chapter) to all employees, simplistic cartoon-style versions of the information about the strategy were produced for those employees who were not sufficiently literate to read the standard versions.

An essential part of the communication process is that leaders in an organisation must behave in ways that are consistent with the vision they are promoting: communication regarding any change should occur not only via words, but also via deeds – the dramatic action taken by Samsung's chairman noted in the Fact file earlier in this chapter is an example.

▲ Samsung's chairman Lee Kun-hee has been a very effective leader

▲ Effective communication to staff is a key part of effective strategic implementation

The importance of organisational structure (including functional, product-based, regional and matrix structures) in strategic implementation

Organisational structure refers to the hierarchy within a business, how employees are grouped in relation to job tasks and activities, the authority lines within the business, as well as how groups interact and communicate with one another.

▲ Comet failed to react to the growth of online sales

Author advice

Organisational structure was considered in detail in Chapter 22 of Book 1. That chapter includes explanations of functional, product-based, regional and matrix organisational structures. (Note that regional structures were called geographical structures in Chapter 22 of Book 1.) In addition, organisational structure, in relation to the management of change, is discussed in Chapter 15 of this book. Ensure you refresh your knowledge of this topic before proceeding with this section.

Each organisation has a different structure, which is likely to be determined by the strategies implemented in the past, the size of the business, how it grew (for example, whether organically or by merger or takeover) and its leadership style. Although there is no single ideal organisational structure, the structure in place does need to be responsive to new strategies, which in turn should be responsive to changes in the external environment and the market. Recent history is littered with examples of firms that failed to reshape their organisational structures in a way that effectively delivered their strategic ambitions. For example, Comet's failure to recognise the growth of online sales meant that its organisation was structured with a heavy focus on sales via retail parks. This was a poor choice and resulted in an uncompetitive organisation characterised by falling sales and poor performance.

Structure is not simply an organisation chart. It is about all the people, positions, procedures, processes, culture, technology and related elements that comprise an organisation. It defines how all the pieces, parts and processes work together. This structure must be totally integrated with strategy for the organisation to achieve its mission and goals. For example, a marketing department may have been expanded in order to implement a strategy to increase profits by increasing sales. The strategy may have been successful in generating sales. However, if the rest of the organisation has not been expanded and restructured to cope with the increased work in, for example, order processing, customer support and manufacturing, there are likely to be a lot of unhappy customers and profits are unlikely to rise.

The structure of a business is an important factor to consider when implementing new strategies because structure plays a role in how strategies are converted into actions, who is responsible for monitoring and evaluating such actions, as well as how effectively the strategies and actions are communicated to the rest of the organisation.

Overall strategic plans will be broken up into functional plans, such as a marketing plan, an operations plan, an HR plan, and so on. The detail of each of these will be determined within the functional areas and implemented within these areas. In this sense, a clear functional organisational structure will assist the process of strategic implementation.

Where strategic implementation requires a focus on products or on geographical regions, product-based or regional organisational structures may be more appropriate. For example, the strategic focus of a transport business that operates coach tours, bus services and train services, might only be on its coach tours business. Strategic implementation might then be more effective if the organisational structure was product-based so that all functional elements within the coach tours section of the business could be considered more coherently. Similarly, in the case of a business operating in a number of different countries, a regional organisational structure might encourage more effective strategic implementation. For example, strategy might be focused on developing business operations in, say, Italy, and implementation would then be focused on all functional aspects of the business in Italy.

Where strategic implementation involves a more flexible approach that cuts across traditional functional boundaries, a matrix organisational structure might be more appropriate. For example, strategic implementation might involve a range of new product developments and teams of employees consisting of engineers, marketing personnel, designers and accountants.

Fact file

Restructuring at Lloyds

Early in 2015, Lloyds banking group announced that it was to restructure its operations. The decision to cut 9,000 jobs and close 150 branches across its UK network was evidence of a significant change to the way it conducted its business. Given improvements to the housing market, consumer confidence, a stable GDP and falling unemployment, at the time one might have expected banks like Lloyds to be expanding their workforces as they geared up for economic recovery. But the important point was not how many jobs were being cut, but where they were being cut. What is apparent is that Lloyds and other high street banks have seen a growth in workers in their digital and remote services sections at the same time as the numbers of their branch employees are falling. The way in which consumers access banking services is changing rapidly, with an emphasis on smartphone and mobile banking. Thus a restructuring of Lloyds' organisational structure was required in order to maintain customer service levels and effectively meet this developing demand – in this case the external market provoked an internal change in organisational structure.

Source: adapted from 'Restructuring for success' by Ryan Cook in *Business Review*, April 2015

Throughout business history, companies have attempted to improve their performance by matching their organisational structures to their strategies.

As mass production developed in the nineteenth and twentieth centuries, companies generated economies of scale by centralising key functions like operations, marketing, HR and finance, thus adopting functional organisational structures.

In the twentieth century, as firms diversified their product ranges and/or moved into new geographical regions, they created business units structured around products and geographic markets – the development of product-based organisational structures and regional organisational structures. These smaller business units sacrificed some of the economies of scale associated with functional organisational structures, but were more flexible and adaptable to local conditions. These three organisational structures – functional, product-based and regional – have been the most popular structures for a long time.

As competition intensified in the last quarter of the twentieth century, problems with the above three structures became apparent, and companies searched for new ways to organise themselves to improve their performance. Many large companies, including multinationals, adopted a matrix organisational structure in the belief that they could retain both the economies of scale of functional organisational structures and the flexibility of product-based and regional organisational structures. However, matrix organisational structures are often difficult to co-ordinate and staff often find themselves with two masters, which can lead to conflict and delay.

The opportunities and challenges that globalisation brings are forcing companies to revisit many assumptions about the control and management of both their physical and their intangible assets, including knowledge. For example, today a computer company can manufacture components in China, assemble them in Malaysia, ship them to Europe, and service its customers' queries from a call centre in India. This type of development creates demands for new structures. Chapter 13 discusses Bartlett and Ghoshal's ideas about strategy and structure in international businesses, including the move to transnational strategies and structures.

Practice exercise 1

Total: 50 marks

1. Identify and explain one factor in the external environment and one factor in the competitive environment that might influence the effectiveness of strategic implementation. *(8 marks)*

2. Identify and explain three internal factors that might influence the effectiveness of strategic implementation. *(9 marks)*

3. Give two examples of the value of leadership in strategic implementation. *(8 marks)*

4. Analyse the value of communication in strategic implementation. *(9 marks)*

5. Explain each of the following organisational structures:
   a) functional *(3 marks)*
   b) product-based *(3 marks)*
   c) regional *(3 marks)*
   d) matrix. *(3 marks)*

6. Give one example of why organisational structure is important in strategic implementation. *(4 marks)*

Case study 1: Anson Engineering Ltd

Anson Engineering Ltd was experiencing problems implementing its strategy to develop two new products within six months to enable the business to widen its market and increase profits.

The initial idea for the strategy came from the managing director and was supported by the marketing and human resource directors. However, not all members of senior management were fully committed to the project, in particular the production and finance directors.

The company did not have a specialist research and development department or a dedicated research and development team – simply because they had not been involved in new product development before.

Pressure from the finance director about the need to keep firm control of the company's finances led to the decision to give the company's engineering team the job of new product development. The main function of the engineering team was to keep the factory running smoothly. The production director saw this as their key role, regardless of whatever else they were asked to do. As a result, the engineers were not given dedicated time and no plans or interim targets were produced so that their progress in developing the products could be checked.

The engineers were not aware that the time scale for completion was six months and neither did they know how important the project was for the future success of the company. In fact no one except the directors was aware that without being able to compete in a wider market, the company's future survival might be in question.

Over time, the engineers kept getting pulled off their 'new products' project in order to provide manufacturing support for the factory. As a result, by the end of the six-month period, no new products had been developed.

Questions

Total: 20 marks

1. Explain the meaning of the term 'strategic implementation'. *(4 marks)*

2. To what extent might Anson Engineering Ltd have improved the implementation of its strategy to develop two new products if it had given more attention to leadership, communication and organisational structure? *(16 marks)*

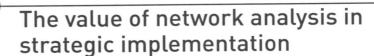

The value of network analysis in strategic implementation

Background

The roots of **network analysis** or **critical path analysis (CPA)** lie in aircraft use. During the Second World War, the US Air Force recognised that an aircraft on the ground was both ineffective as a fighting weapon and more vulnerable to attack. Consequently, critical path analysis techniques were employed to ensure that planes were serviced and overhauled as quickly as possible.

> ### Key terms
>
> **Network analysis** A method of planning business operations in order to identify the most efficient way of completing an integrated task or project. The main form of network analysis is critical path analysis.
>
> **Critical path analysis (CPA)** The process of planning the sequence of activities in a project in order to discover the most efficient and quickest way of completing it.
>
> **Critical path** The sequence of activities in a project that must be completed within a designated time in order to prevent any delay in overall completion of the project.
>
> NB: A critical activity is any activity on the critical path.

Ironically, one of the latest converts to CPA is the airline industry. Southwest Airlines in the USA and Ryanair in Europe used CPA to excellent effect to reduce the turnaround time on a plane (the time between it touching down and taking off again) to 25 minutes – initially this was half the time of rivals such as British Airways. This increases the number of journeys that a plane can make.

Network analysis (critical path analysis) is widely used in industries such as construction, in which it is possible to operate a range of activities in parallel. By mapping out the network of different activities, a firm is able to see which activities can run concurrently (at the same time), in order to save time and thus complete complex projects as quickly as possible. CPA also allows a firm to identify those activities that cannot be delayed without holding up the overall project.

▲ The airline industry uses CPA to reduce flight turnaround times

Features of network analysis/critical path analysis

Networks in critical path analysis are constructed in a specific way (see Figure 17.1). The features of a network are identified below:

- **Nodes**. These are circles representing a point in time, identified by the completion or start of an activity. Nodes are split into three. The left half of the node contains the **number of the node**. This serves to provide a unique identity for each node. The right half of the node is split into two. The top segment shows the **earliest start time (EST)** that an activity can commence, and depends on the completion of the previous activity. For the opening activity or activities the EST is always zero. The bottom segment shows the **latest finish time (LFT)** of the previous activity, or can be seen to represent the **latest start time (LST)** at which the next activity can commence without delaying the overall project.
- **Activities**. These are events or tasks that consume time and are shown as lines that link the nodes on the network diagram. Most network diagrams show activities moving from left to right, but for clarity, arrows are usually shown on the lines to indicate the direction and sequence of activities. A letter (or description of the activity) is placed above the line that represents that activity.
- **Duration**. This is the length of time that it takes to complete an activity. Depending on the nature of the project, the duration may be measured in months, weeks, days, hours or minutes. The duration is shown as a number below the line that represents that activity.
- **Prerequisite**. This is the activity (or activities) that must be completed before our selected activity can commence. For example, 'reading the questions' should be a prerequisite of 'starting to answer questions in an examination', and 'getting dressed' should be a prerequisite of 'catching the bus in the morning'.
- **Dummies**. These are activities that do not consume time, but are incorporated into a network to show the true sequence of events. (Dummy nodes and activities may also be used to show more clearly the ESTs and LSTs/LFTs of non-critical activities.)

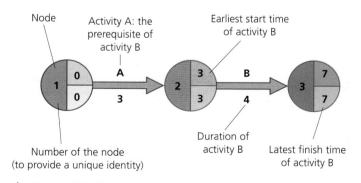

▲ **Figure 17.1** Features of network analysis

Constructing a critical path network

Table 17.1 shows a series of activities that form a network. This table lays out the prerequisites for each activity, that is the logic behind the sequence of activities that make up a project.

▼ **Table 17.1** Activities in a network

Activity	Duration (days)	Prerequisite(s)
A	6	–
B	7	A
C	5	A
D	3	C
E	8	C
F	4	B, D
G	2	E, F

Once a table of this type has been constructed, the network is laid out by following the approach outlined below.

1. Draw a node (circle) to represent the start of the network. (All networks must start and end at a single node.) See node 1 (the first node on the left) in Figure 17.2. Number each node as it is drawn.

2. Identify any activities that have no prerequisite. Draw lines from left to right, starting from the original node, for the activities that have no prerequisite. Do not draw any nodes at the right-hand end of these activity lines at this stage. See activity A in Figure 17.2.

3. Identify the activity line by placing a description of it immediately above the line in the diagram (either the letter or activity description). See activity A in Figure 17.2.

4. Put the duration of the activity immediately under the line. Activity A is represented by a 6, showing that it takes 6 days to complete.

5. Move on to the first activity that has a prerequisite (activity B in this example). Place a node (circle) at the end of the line that represents the prerequisite activity, as this activity must be completed before the next activity can begin. Draw a line starting at the node that you have just drawn to represent the new activity (see activity B in Figure 17.2). Do not place a node (circle) at the end of this line at this stage. If a new activity has two or more prerequisites, the lines representing these prerequisite activities must be drawn in such a way that they both lead into the same node. This node therefore represents the point in time at which both of the prerequisites have been completed and the new activity can begin. See activities F and G in Figure 17.2 for examples of activities that have more than one prerequisite.

6. Repeat stages 3 and 4 for activity B.

7. Continue this process until every activity has been completed. (At this point there will be at least one line that has not been completed by a node.)

8. As all of the network's activities have now been plotted, bring any remaining lines together into a final node. This node represents the completion of the project that has been planned by the network. See node 6, the last node on the right, in Figure 17.2.

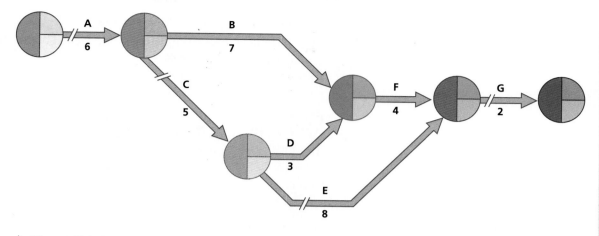

▲ **Figure 17.2** A network showing the activities described in Table 17.1 and the critical path

Completing the earliest start times

Once the outline diagram has been completed, work forward (from left to right) to calculate the earliest start times (ESTs). The EST in the first node (the EST of activity A) is shown as a zero.

For subsequent activities, the EST is found by adding the sum of the durations of activities on the path that leads up to the node that represents the start time of that activity. For example, the EST in node 3 is 6 + 5 = 11 (see Figure 17.3). Thus both D and E cannot start before day 11 because activity A takes 6 days and activity C takes 5 days to complete.

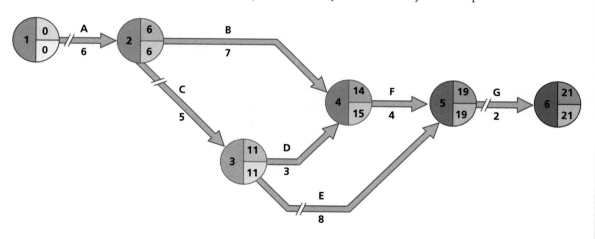

▲ **Figure 17.3** The completed network including all timings, the ESTs, LFTs and the critical path

If there is more than one path to a node, the highest total is taken as the EST. For example, activity F cannot begin until A and then B are completed (6 + 7 = 13 days). However, activity F also cannot start until activities A, C and D have been completed. These three activities take 6 + 5 + 3 = 14 days to complete. Therefore, the EST for activity F is 14 days rather than 13 days.

Insert the EST in the top right-hand corner of the node at the start point of that activity. The EST in the final node represents the earliest completion time for the project.

Completing the latest finish times (LFTs)

Once the ESTs have been completed, work backwards from right to left to calculate the latest finish times (LFTs). The LFT in the final node must equal the EST because a final activity must be on the critical path. Place the LFT in the bottom right-hand quadrant.

Moving from right to left, deduct the duration of the activity in order to calculate the LFT of the previous activity. Keep moving from right to left, inserting the LFTs in the bottom right-hand quadrants. For example, the LFT for activity F, shown in node 5, is 19. This figure is calculated by taking the LFT in node 6, 21, and deducting the 2 days that it will take to complete activity G: $21 - 2 = 19$.

Be cautious where there are nodes that lead on to more than one activity. For example, the bottom right-hand sector of node 2 shows the number 6. This is because by working backwards from right to left on the path G to E to C, we arrive at a figure of 6 as the LFT for activity A ($21 - 2 - 8 - 5 = 6$). Thus the LFT shown in node 2 is 6. However, by moving backwards from right to left along the path G to F to B we also arrive at node 2. The calculation for the LFT via this path is $21 - 2 - 4 - 7 = 8$. *If there is more than one path working backwards to a node, the lowest total is taken as the LFT.* In effect, the digit 6 in the bottom right-hand quadrant of node 2 means that the latest finish time for activity A is 6 days, if activity C is to be started on time. However, it is possible to start activity B on day 8 without delaying the overall project.

Plotting the critical path

The critical path is the sequence of activities that cannot be delayed without delaying the overall completion of the project. It is represented by those activities that:

● have LFTs identical to their ESTs
● represent the path that takes the most time between the nodes.

In Figure 17.3 the sequence A–C–E–G represents the critical path. For these critical activities, the ESTs and LFTs in each node are the same.

Non-critical activities are those that can be delayed without extending the completion time of the project. In Figure 17.3, these are activities B, D and F. Although both node 2 and node 3 show identical ESTs and LFTs, these arise because activities C and E are both on the critical path. We have seen already, by working back from right to left, that activity B can be delayed by 2 days without delaying the overall completion of the project. Similarly, activity D can be delayed by 1 day because the working-back process gives a figure of 12 for node 3.

In Figure 17.3, the critical path is shown by the symbol //. This is common practice, but the critical path may be shown in other ways, such as through the use of a highlighter or colour.

We can therefore see that, although individually the seven activities in Table 17.1 take a total of 35 days, by careful planning the project can be completed in 21 days.

Float times

Float time is the amount of time that non-critical activities within a project can be delayed without affecting the deadline for completion of the project as a whole.

The float times for each activity can be derived from the network. These are set out in Table 17.2.

▼ **Table 17.2** Float times

Activity	Total float (days)
A*	0
B	2
C*	0
D	1
E*	0
F	1
G*	0

*Critical activity

Key terms

Total float for an activity The number of days that an activity can be delayed without delaying the project.

Total float for an activity is measured by the formula:

total float for an activity is = LFT – EST – duration of the activity

Thus activity D can be delayed by 15 – 11 – 3 = 1 day, without delaying the project.

Similarly, the Total float for Activity B = 15 – 6 – 7 = 2 days.

Amending a network/critical path diagram

Network analysis is based on predicted timings. Consequently the network will need to be changed if circumstances (or predictions) change to take into consideration new information. For projects of a long duration, the network may be updated regularly. This is particularly the case in industries such as construction, where the complexities of the project, and the vagaries of the British weather, are likely to lead to a need to change predicted timings. In many instances these changes may only have a minor effect on timings; in other cases they may lead to a change in the critical path of the activity.

Figure 17.3 is based on the data in Table 17.1. What happens if one of the timings in Table 17.1 needs to be changed? For example, let us suppose that the expected timing of Activity F needs to be changed as follows:

- The duration of Activity F changes from 4 days to 7 days.

We will consider the impact of this change on the network and critical path.

- Activity F takes 7 days instead of 4, and so Activity F will be completed after 14 + 7 days = 21 days. Thus the EST for Activity G is now 21 days.
- G still takes 2 days and so the earliest that the project can be completed is now 23 days.
- Working backwards, the LFT for G is now 23 days.
- Subtracting the 2 days for G from 23 means that the LFT for Activities E and F is now day 21.
- Because Activity E has an EST of 11 days and takes 8 days, it can be completed by day 19. Consequently there is a 2-day float (21 – 19) for Activity E and so it is no longer on the critical path.
- Subtracting the 7 days for F from 21 means that Activities B and D must be completed by day 14.
- Path A to B takes 6 + 7 = 13 days. Therefore there is one day of float after B has been completed.
- Path A to C to D takes 6 + 5 + 3 = 14 days. Therefore there is no float as each of these activities must be completed on time. Thus they are on the critical path.
- The new critical path is now ACDFG. ACEG is no longer the critical path. The only non-critical activities are now B and E.
- Activity B could be delayed by 1 day without affecting the duration of the project (LFT – EST – duration = 14 – 6 – 7 = 1).
- Activity E could be delayed by 2 days without affecting the duration of the project (LFT – EST – duration = 21 – 11 – 8 = 2).

The amended timings and new critical path are shown in Figure 17.4.

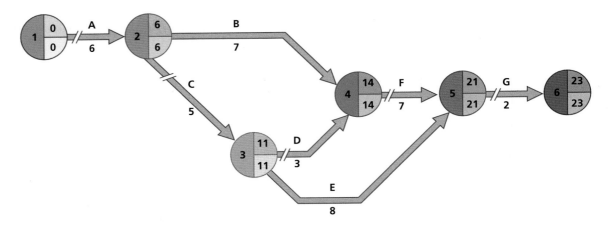

▲ **Figure 17.4** New critical path

Constructing a critical path network from descriptive information

In real life, managers will not be given a table of activities with their prerequisites neatly defined. The first step in compiling a real network is to work out the logic behind the project in order to identify sequences of events.

The following activities represent the steps needed to introduce a new product that has just completed its design stage:

A   Brief advertising agencies – 1 day

B   Await ideas from agencies – 15 days

C   Select advertising agency – 2 days

D   Prepare advertising materials for launch – 40 days

E   Order new production machinery – 3 days

F   Await delivery of machinery – 20 days

G   Install machinery – 12 days

H   Production run for initial launch – 15 days

I   Recruit production workers – 21 days

J   Off-the-job training of production workers – 6 days

K   Launch product – 1 day

Activities A to D form a logical sequence of events in the marketing department, with A being the first stage. Activities E to H are the sequence of production department activities, with activity E being able to start at the beginning of the network. Activities I and J are human resource management roles. Activity I can start at the beginning of the project and is the prerequisite of activity J. However, J must be completed before activity H, as this stage requires trained workers. Once all the marketing and production activities have been completed, the final activity (K) can take place.

The sequence of events based on the logic described above is shown in Table 17.3.

▼ **Table 17.3** Network of activities needed to launch a new product

Activity	Duration (days)	Prerequisite(s)
A	1	–
B	15	A
C	2	B
D	40	C
E	3	–
F	20	E
G	12	F
H	15	G, J
I	21	–
J	6	I
K	1	D, H

Figure 17.5 shows the network based on these data. The critical path is A–B–C–D–K.

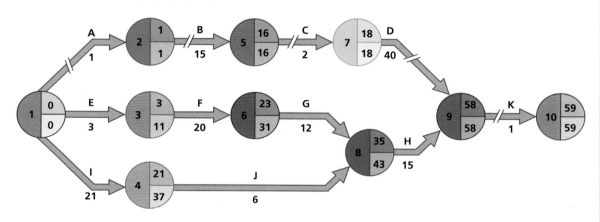

▲ **Figure 17.5** Network of activities needed to launch a new product

Assessing the value of network analysis in strategic implementation

Network analysis is a valuable tool in ensuring that strategic implementation is managed effectively. It can assist a business in planning a new strategy in the most cost-effective and timely way. Furthermore, close monitoring of the progress of a project can ensure that modifications are made to the network in response to any internal and external changes. However, its value may be reduced if certain problems occur. The potential benefits and problems that can influence the overall value of network analysis are explained below.

Benefits of network analysis (critical path analysis)

Use of network analysis brings many advantages to a business, if the system operates smoothly.

● Network analysis allows a business to improve the efficiency of its resources. If a business can reduce the time taken to complete a project, it can translate these savings in time into cost savings. In turn, this will

Author advice

Note that, although the sequence of events in the network may not change, the critical path can change because it is dependent on the timings of the activities. For example, in Figure 17.5 an increase in the duration of F from 20 days to 30 days will lead to a change in the critical path (from A–B–C–D–K to E–F–G–H–K). Overall, the duration of the project will increase from 59 days to 61 days.

increase the competitiveness of a business, particularly if cost or speed of completion is a vital factor in the eyes of the customers.

- The process lets a business know precisely when activities are scheduled to take place. This assists a business in its resource planning and stock ordering. This should improve the efficiency of resources, such as labour, as it enables a business to make sure that the use of labour corresponds to the available supply.
- If necessary, a business can use critical path analysis (CPA) to investigate changes in resources or sequencing that would improve efficiency. For example, additional resources can be transferred from a non-critical activity to one on the critical path. This will reduce the time taken on the critical path and therefore reduce the overall duration of the project.
- CPA can be used to help control and review. Monitoring of progress against the original plan will identify any delays and allow a business to take steps to rectify the problem.
- Network analysis forces managers to engage in detailed planning. This helps a business to reduce the risk of delays.
- A business's relationships with its customers can be improved, as CPA can provide detailed information on the schedule for completion of a project.
- During the operation of the project, CPA can be used to calculate the likely impact of any delays that are unavoidable.
- Critical path analysis helps a firm to estimate the minimum time within which it is possible to complete a project (through identifying the critical path).
- By identifying the (critical) activities that cannot be delayed without delaying the completion of a project, CPA gives a firm the opportunity to focus its attention on the more 'important' tasks.
- The network helps an organisation to calculate the extent to which other (non-critical) activities can be delayed. This reduces the possibility of a project failing because a delay in a non-critical activity suddenly becomes significant and causes that activity to be on the critical path.
- Critical path analysis allows a firm to plan when it needs particular resources. This means that the firm can avoid holding unnecessary stock.

Fact file

Critical path analysis at Unilever

Unilever is a company that has benefited from using CPA to obtain an integrated view of its projects. A network constructed to plan the release of a new food product shows that, at different stages of the network, the critical path activities are, on the whole, marketing department responsibilities. However, at particular points of time, production, packaging and distribution activities are on the critical path. Consequently, Unilever managers know when it is most vital to monitor the progress of particular departments.

Problems of using network analysis (critical path analysis)

Although CPA is a useful tool, its use can lead to difficulties:

- It can encourage rigidity. On paper, CPA works best with fixed times for each activity and a fixed sequence of activities. This may encourage managers to see these timings and this sequence as unchangeable, so

they may miss opportunities to reduce the overall time of a project by failing to identify the scope for flexibility.

- As every activity in a network is strictly timetabled, it can lead to greater inefficiency if a crucial activity is delayed. This can happen in projects such as the construction of a building, where subcontractors and suppliers will plan their workloads around the original network. Any delay can lead to the project coming to a halt because, for example, the crane hire company has agreed to hire its crane to another company or the electricians are working on another firm's building.
- Complex activities may be difficult to represent accurately on a network. (In practice, businesses use computer modelling to construct highly complex networks, but these need to be understood by the manager.)
- CPA relies on estimates of the expected duration of activities. If these are inaccurate, the whole process may break down. As major projects, such as the Channel Tunnel or the proposed HS2 train link, are often one-offs, it is possible that the firm has no prior experience in this particular field. Consequently, the probability of producing an accurate forecast of timings is low.
- CPA encourages businesses to focus on the speed of completion of a project, rather than other elements such as quality and flexibility in meeting customers' needs.

Practice exercise 2

Total: 35 marks

1. What is meant by the term 'network analysis'? (3 marks)

2. What is meant by the term 'critical path'? (3 marks)

3. In a network, what is represented by:
   - a) a node (circle)? (2 marks)
   - b) a line? (2 marks)

4. Distinguish between the EST and the LST. (3 marks)

5. What is a prerequisite? (2 marks)

6. What is meant by the term 'float'? (2 marks)

7. Explain three advantages to a business of using critical path analysis. (9 marks)

8. Explain three problems that may arise as a result of using critical path analysis. (9 marks)

Practice exercise 3

Total: 45 marks

The table shows a network of activities.

Activity	Duration (days)	Prerequisite(s)
A	5	–
B	4	–
C	5	A
D	8	B
E	3	D
F	3	D
G	6	C, E
H	5	F

The project is complete when both activities G and H are finished.

1a) Draw a fully labelled network diagram of the activities described in the table, including the numbered nodes, the duration of each activity, the earliest start times (ESTs) and the latest finish times (LFTs).   *(12 marks)*

1b) Show the critical path.   *(2 marks)*

2. Based on the original network in each case, describe how the critical path and overall duration of the project will be affected by the following changes in the duration of individual activities:
   a) Activity F increases from 3 days to 6 days   *(3 marks)*
   b) Activity D decreases from 8 days to 4 days   *(3 marks)*
   c) Activity C increases from 5 days to 12 days.   *(3 marks)*
   The following diagram shows a sample network. Questions 3 and 4 are based on this network.

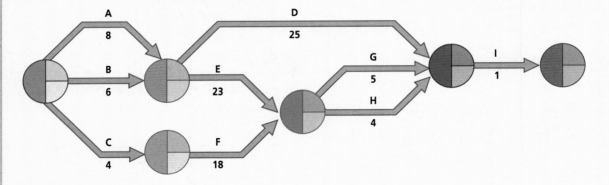

3. Complete the nodes, showing the earliest start times (ESTs) and latest finish times (LFTs), and show the critical path.   *(6 marks)*

4. Copy the table below and complete the prerequisites column, based on the network shown in the diagram in question 3.   *(6 marks)*

Activity	Duration (days)	Prerequisite(s)
A	4	
B	3	
C	5	
D	6	
E	2	
F	4	
G	1	
H	4	
I	6	
J	3	

5. Complete a network and show the critical path for the following project:

Ingredients are mixed for 15 minutes and then weighed (1 minute). At the same time, the container is cleaned for 5 minutes and then labelled (2 minutes) before being transported to the production line (6 minutes).

Once all of the above processes have been completed, the ingredients are placed in the container (7 minutes). The finished product is then simultaneously checked for defects (2 minutes) while being placed on a conveyor belt that puts the containers into boxes of a dozen products (4 minutes). The finished products then take 3 minutes to be loaded on to pallets, ready for delivery. *(10 marks)*

Case study 2: Critical path analysis at Balfour Beatty

The construction industry is a major user of critical path analysis. In order to improve efficiency, construction firms use CPA to plan the most efficient method of construction and to monitor progress.

Balfour Beatty is a major construction company that uses CPA. In one project, the use of CPA enabled the company to design and build a new road within the budget of £35 million considerably quicker than customer expectations. The customer requested completion in 124 weeks, but through careful planning using CPA, Balfour Beatty was able to plan the project for completion in 79 weeks.

Moreover, through close supervision and teamwork with its subcontractors, the company was able to take advantage of favourable external factors and complete the project 9.5 weeks earlier than its own estimate, despite some changes that increased the scope of the project.

Construction companies face particular problems in planning projects because they rely on other companies (subcontractors) to complete certain tasks. Furthermore, expensive earth-moving equipment is hired and any delays (or even improvements) in the schedule can make it difficult to acquire resources at the time they are needed. For this reason, companies tend to build large margins of error into their project timings.

A further complication that is often faced by construction companies is the need to keep existing facilities open. The building of new roads or shopping centres can cause tremendous disruption to existing businesses. Most contracts now reward construction companies for planning projects that minimise disruption to existing facilities.

A project in which this was an important element was the construction of Birmingham's Bull Ring Shopping Centre. Balfour Beatty was involved in this project, supporting the main contractor, Sir Robert McAlpine.

The following list gives the estimated timings of certain key aspects of the completion of the Bull Ring between 2000 and 2003:

A Demolition of old Bull Ring – 8 months

B Planning of new Bull Ring – 6 months

C Agreement reached with key retailers – 4 months

D Construction of West Mall – 25 months

E Construction of East Mall – 23 months

F Construction of 'flagship' stores – 18 months

G Food Court constructed – 5 months

H External work on Rotunda – 4 months

I Completion of works – 1 month

These are represented in the critical path network shown in Figure 17.6.

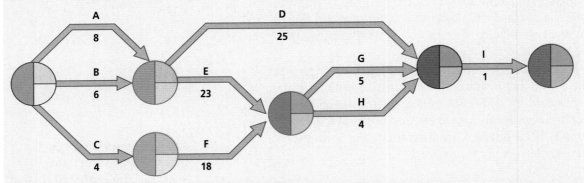

▲ **Figure 17.6** Critical path network for the new Bull Ring shopping centre in Birmingham

Sources: Highways Agency website, www.highways.gov.uk; Balfour Beatty website, www.balfourbeatty.com; Bull Ring website, www.bullring.co.uk

Questions

Total: 45 marks

1. Copy and complete the network for the construction of the new Bull Ring and use your completed diagram and timings to identify the following:

   a) the earliest start time for activity *(1 mark)*

   b) the latest finish time for activity *(1 mark)*

   c) the 'float' time for activity *(2 marks)*

   d) the critical path *(2 marks)*

   e) the prerequisites of activity. *(2 marks)*

2. Based on your network, briefly indicate the implications of a delay of six months in the completion of activity D. *(5 marks)*

3. Evaluate the benefits to Balfour Beatty of using critical path analysis in order to plan its construction projects. *(16 marks)*

4. Evaluate the main difficulties faced by Balfour Beatty and other construction companies in their use of CPA to plan their projects. *(16 marks)*

Problems with strategy and why strategies fail

This chapter begins by considering the difficulties of strategic decision making and implementing strategy. Planned and emergent strategies are then explained and reasons for strategic drift are identified. The possible effect of the divorce between ownership and control is considered, including the issue of corporate governance. Evaluating strategic performance is then discussed. The value of strategic planning is assessed. The chapter concludes by assessing the value of contingency planning.

Difficulties of strategic decision making and implementing strategy

Chapter 1 explained the various stages of a corporate planning process and the role of strategic choice or strategic decision making and strategic implementation within that process. (Review your understanding of this before proceeding with this chapter.)

Strategic decision making

The strategic choice stage of the corporate planning process identifies the range of options available to a business in order to gain competitive advantage. It is at this stage that strategic decisions are made resulting in medium- to long-term plans through which a business aims to achieve its objectives. Strategic decision making concerns the general direction and overall policy of an organisation. A range of approaches to decision making can be used at this stage – these were detailed in Chapter 5 of the AQA A-level Business Book 1 and Chapters 9 and 10 of this book. (Ensure you are secure in your understanding of the topics covered in these chapters: decision making, choosing strategic direction and choosing strategic positioning.)

Strategic decisions can be high risk because the outcomes tend to be unknown. Strategic decisions often involve moving into new areas and this requires additional resources, new procedures and retraining. For example, they may involve plans for a business to expand by acquisition or organic growth (considered in detail in Chapter 11) in order to achieve its corporate goal of, say, market dominance. They might also be about how a business will compete in a way that distinguishes it from its competitors – for example, on the basis of quality and uniqueness or in terms of cost leadership and low prices.

Chapter 1 discussed the fact that decisions are usually constrained by both internal and external factors – for example, by the finance available, the skills of the workforce, competitor activity or government policy. Most decision making includes an element of risk and this is certainly the case with strategic decisions. However, just because something is risky does not mean that it should not be pursued. It does mean, however, that careful analysis of the balance of risk and reward should be carried out.

Implementing strategy

Strategic implementation is the stage in the corporate planning process when the agreed strategy is put into effect, creating a framework of action plans and targets at a functional level. Chapter 17 considered this stage in detail, including the difficulties of implementing strategy and the key factors that improve the effectiveness of this stage. Ensure your knowledge of these issues is secure before proceeding.

Many analysts report that a key difficulty that firms encounter in relation to strategic decision making and strategic implementation is the transition phase from the decision-making process to implementation of plans. Much evidence suggests that those individuals who are given the main responsibility for the bulk of implementation tasks are often left out of the initial decision-making discussions. This means they are not as well informed as they might be about the rationale and logic behind the strategic decisions, the plans for implementation, and how this links to overall objectives. Previous chapters have discussed the importance of good communication and the value of involvement and participation in decision making, which would assist this process.

In summary, a range of factors make the process of strategic decision making and implementing strategies difficult. They include:

- whether the agreed strategy is in fact the right plan for the business in its present circumstances
- whether there are adequate financial, human and production resources to implement the plan
- the probable actions and reactions of competitors
- how changes in the external environment are likely to affect the plan and the business.

All of these factors have been considered in detail elsewhere in this book and Book 1.

Planned versus emergent strategy

Planned strategy

Planned strategy is the strategy that an organisation hopes or intends to implement. Such strategies are described in detail in an organisation's strategic plan. The usual approach to planned strategy involves the following steps: strategic analysis, strategic choice and strategic implementation. (Each of these is a stage in the corporate planning process described briefly in Chapter 1 and in more detail in subsequent chapters.) If planned or intended strategy is successfully implemented, the result should be an outcome that matches the original objectives for which the strategy was formulated.

> **Key term**
>
> **Planned strategy** Where the main elements of the strategy have been planned in advance and implementation involves putting the precise plan into effect in order to achieve the previously agreed objectives; also known as intended strategy.

Planned strategy has benefits for a business. For example:

- it can provide a structured means of analysis and thinking about complex strategic problems
- it can encourage a longer-term view of strategy than might otherwise occur
- it can be used as a means of control by regularly reviewing performance and progress against agreed targets
- it can be a useful means of co-ordination, for example by bringing together the various functional strategies within an overall corporate strategy, or by ensuring that resources within a business are co-ordinated to put the strategy into effect
- it can be used as a way of involving people in strategy development, therefore perhaps helping to create 'ownership' of the strategy
- because it is fixed and known, it can be communicated simply and effectively to employees.

For an example of successful planned strategy, see the Fact file below on FedEx.

Fact file

FedEx – planned strategy

For one of his assignments as an undergraduate student at Yale University in 1962, Frederick Smith had to complete a business plan for a proposed company. His plan described an overnight parcel delivery service that would gain efficiency by routing parcels via a central hub and then on to their final destinations, making use of overnight flights when airports were not congested. In 1971, Smith founded Federal Express (FedEx), a company whose strategy followed closely the planned strategy included in his university assignment. In 2014, Frederick Smith's personal wealth was more than $2.3 billion. His business, FedEx, delivered more than 10.2 million parcels daily throughout 220 countries and was ranked 12th among *Fortune* magazine's World's Most Admired Companies.

Source: adapted from a variety of articles in Forbes magazine, www.forbes.com

When an organisation's environment is stable and predictable, planned or intended strategy will be appropriate for it to achieve the objectives it was designed to achieve. In such an environment, an organisation can be more confident that its plans will not be undermined by changes over time. However, very few organisations operate in a stable or predictable environment. Change, whether internal or external, affects the strategies of almost all organisations. As a result, an organisation's actual or realised strategy can be very different from the original planned or intended strategy.

Emergent strategy

Several management theorists have identified problems with the rather static approach of planned strategy. In particular, they suggest that it does not reflect reality because businesses are unable to control the variables that affect business decisions. As a result, overly detailed plans are more likely to fail, particularly if they base assumptions on how external factors, such as the competitive environment or political and economic conditions, will develop over time.

Critics of planned strategy believe that strategy is a dynamic and interactive process. Henry Mintzberg introduced the idea of **emergent strategy** in his book, *The Rise and Fall of Strategic Planning* (1994). He argued that strategy emerges over time as 'intentions collide with, and accommodate, a changing reality', rather than being due to a deliberate planning process. An emergent strategy develops when an organisation takes a series of actions that, with time, turn into – 'a realised pattern [that] was not expressly intended' in the original planning of strategy – and which are not included in the strategic plan. Mintzberg also suggested that emergent strategy implies that an organisation is continuously learning what it is that works in practice, and is constantly adjusting its plans in light of its learning.

Most writers suggest that emergent strategy seems more relevant to the world today. This is not to say that planning is not useful. However, the days of highly detailed five-year or even two-year plans have begun to decline. Emergent strategy is the reality in most industries today because most firms need to adapt more flexibly to changes in their market conditions and in the general external environment.

Sometimes emergent strategies result in failure; sometimes they result in success. See the Fact files below on FedEx and on Southern Bloomer Manufacturing Company.

> ## Key term
>
> **Emergent strategy** Unplanned strategy that emerges in response to unexpected opportunities and challenges; a response to internal and external changes that were not envisaged at the time of the original planned strategy.

Fact file

FedEx – emergent strategy

In 1984, FedEx deviated from its planned strategy's focus on parcel delivery to capitalise on, what was at the time, an emerging technology – facsimile (fax) machines. FedEx developed a service called ZapMail that involved documents being sent electronically via fax machines between FedEx offices and then being delivered to customers' offices. This was before fax machines became generally available for home and business use. FedEx executives assumed that ZapMail would be a success because it reduced the delivery time of a document from overnight to a few hours. However, the ZapMail system encountered many technical problems and, more importantly, FedEx had failed to anticipate that many businesses would eventually purchase their own fax machines. ZapMail was a commercial failure and closed in 1986. By moving away from its planned strategy of overnight parcel delivery and pursuing emergent strategy, FedEx lost about $320 million.

Source: adapted from S. Godin, *Survival Is Not Enough: Shift Happens*, 2002

Fact file

Southern Bloomer

Southern Bloomer Manufacturing Company was founded in 1978 to make underwear for use in women's prisons and mental institutions. Its underwear was made of heavy cotton fabric to withstand the mass laundering required in the institutions in which they were worn.

A consequence of the success of its underwear sales was that it created a vast amount of scrap material. This was both wasteful and costly. As a result of the scrap material, an unexpected opportunity led the company to pursue an emergent strategy quite different from its planned strategy of selling durable underwear to institutions.

In 1983, co-founder, Don Sonner, visited a gun shop. He noted that the fabric patches the gun shop sold to clean the inside of gun barrels with were of poor quality. He thought the scrap material his firm produced as waste would do a much better job. The patches quickly became popular with the military, police departments and individual gun enthusiasts. A casual trip to a gun store unexpectedly gave rise to a lucrative emergent strategy.

Source: adapted from www.southernbloomer.com and an article in the *Wall Street Journal*, 1 April 1999, www.wsj.com

▲ The American military use Southern Bloomer material

At one extreme, a pure planned strategy means no learning is taking place in an organisation because no account is being taken of changing circumstances; at the other extreme, a pure emergent strategy means that there is no control or focus. Mintzberg suggests that few strategies are purely planned (or intended) or purely emergent and that most are a mixture of the two. The fact that most strategies are a mixture of the two means that in most organisations control is exercised over the strategic process and at the same time processes encourage learning in response to internal and external changes.

Realised and unrealised strategy

A realised strategy is the strategy that an organisation actually follows. Realised strategies are a product of a firm's planned (intended strategy); parts of the intended plan that an organisation continues to pursue over time and its emergent strategy (i.e. what the firm actually did in response to unexpected opportunities and challenges). In the case of FedEx, the planned strategy devised by its founder many years ago — fast parcel delivery via a centralised hub — remains a primary element of its realised strategy. For Southern Bloomer Manufacturing Company, realised strategy has been shaped greatly by both its intended and emergent strategies, which centre on the production and sale of underwear and of gun-cleaning patches.

In other cases, firms' original planned strategies are forgotten or abandoned because events develop in unexpected ways. They become unrealised strategies. This could be due to:

- a firm's underlying assumptions about a market turning out to be invalid because the pace of development in a market overtakes the pace at which a particular firm is working
- of changes in an organisation's external environment, such as the nature of the competition it faces or changes to the state of the economy
- of changes in a firm's internal environment, such as new managers.

Fact file

Facebook

The following example of how Facebook developed illustrates just how different planned strategies can be from emergent and realised strategies.

Did Harvard University student, Mark Zuckerberg, set out to build a company worth over $200 billion in 2015, and with more than 936 million daily active users? As shown in the 2010 film, *The Social Network*, Zuckerberg's original concept in 2003 had a less than ethical intent. After being 'dumped' by his girlfriend, a bitter Zuckerberg created a website called FaceMash where the attractiveness of young women could be voted on. This evolved first into an online social network called Thefacebook, which was for Harvard students only. When the network became popular, it then changed into Facebook, a website open to everyone. Ironically, Facebook's emphasis on connecting with existing and new friends is rather different to Zuckerberg's original concept. Zuckerberg's emergent and realised strategies turned out to be far nobler than his planned strategy.

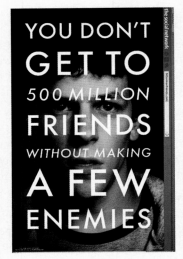

Key term

Strategic drift A situation where a company responds too slowly to changes in its external and competitive environments; a company continues with a strategy that may have served it very well in the past but is no longer suited to the current circumstances.

Reasons for strategic drift

Strategic drift is the situation where successive strategies fail to address the issues a company faces and its performance gradually deteriorates.

There are many examples of companies that continue to persevere with their once successful business strategies even when it is overwhelmingly evident that these are increasingly inappropriate in terms of current and future trends. The Fact file on page 409 and the Case study on Kodak at the end of the chapter provide examples of such companies.

There are a number of reasons for strategic drift. These include situations where:

● changes in the external and competitive environment are greater than the incremental changes being made in an organisation's strategy (incremental change was explained in Chapter 15)

● organisational culture restricts the ability of an organisation to change at a rate that is necessary to cope with external changes or to maintain its performance. Organisational culture is a key reason for strategic drift. This is particularly the case in organisations with cultures that focus on the past to formulate strategies for the future and that place too much emphasis on traditional methods of planning and execution, without taking account of changes occurring in the environment

● leaders of an organisation continue to persevere with obsolete or largely redundant policies and practices and are not prepared to, or do not see the need to, change

● an organisation simply reacts to changes in its external and competitive environments rather than innovating in a proactive way

● the strategic plan is not reviewed regularly to check that it is aligned well with what is happening in the external and competitive environments. (this links with the previous discussion about the relative merits of planned and emergent strategies)

● an organisation is not keeping up with, or adapting quickly or appropriately enough to, changes in technology.

A strategic plan is developed on the basis of the information available at the time, as well as assumptions and expectations prevailing at the time. It is therefore vital to constantly monitor, review and evaluate changes in the external environment and ensure that these changes are reflected appropriately in strategic plans.

Fact file

Examples of strategic drift

The business world is full of examples of businesses that have failed because of strategic drift. Some of these are identified below.

- HMV – the Case study on page 57 of Chapter 3 in Book 1 indicated the refusal of leaders in HMV to recognise the impact of new technology and to change their strategy appropriately and quickly.
- Blockbuster – the Fact file on page 39 of Chapter 3 in Book 1 indicated that the business closed because it was too slow to adapt to changing technology in the form of developments in film downloading being introduced by companies such as Netflix.
- Jessops – the Fact file on page 39 of Chapter 3 in Book 1 indicated the decline of the business due to its failure to keep pace with changing technological developments in the camera industry.
- MySpace – from being a pioneer of online social networking, it failed to respond to changes in its external environment and failed to innovate and meet consumers' expectations as well as Facebook.
- Nokia – after dominating the mobile handset market for more than a decade, the company failed to monitor and understand the changing expectations of consumers, who wanted to do more with their mobile phones than just make calls and send text messages. The advent of smartphones resulted in the gradual erosion of the market share of Nokia in the mobile handsets segment.

Note: Both HMV and Jessops have since been rescued and are undergoing a process of tranformational strategic change to their structures and business operations.

Planned strategic change, often of a transformational nature, is the main means of overcoming strategic drift. Transformational change in this context means a shift in organisational culture that includes a change in the underlying strategy and processes that an organisation has used in the past. A transformational change is designed to be organisation-wide and takes place over a period of time. It should address all of the reasons identified above that cause strategic drift.

The stages associated with the development of strategic drift and eventual failure or transformational change are illustrated in Figure 18.1.

The following briefly explains each phase illustrated in Figure 18.1.

- Phase 1: The firm makes incremental changes that are part of its planned strategy to change in line with external or competitive environmental changes and thus to remain ahead of the market and develop or retain a competitive advantage.

- Phase 2: The rate of change in the external or competitive environment speeds up, but the firm's approach of incremental change means that the strategic drift begins and the firm starts to get left behind.
- Phase 3: Leaders recognise the decline in their performance and the gap between what the market expects and what they are providing. They try to extend the market for their business by repeating what it already does and has always done. As a result strategy development is likely to go into a state of flux. This is a period when strategies change, but in no clear direction, when there is disagreement about what the right strategies are and when performance deteriorates. The strategic drift increases.
- Phase 4: At this stage, the business either fails completely and the firm closes or, if it survives, this is because it undergoes transformational change to align its strategies with the market it is in, and begins to operate successfully again.

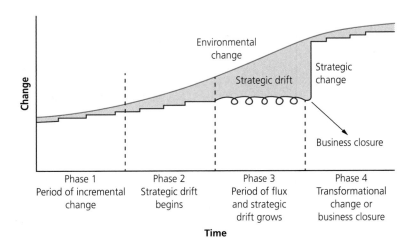

▲ **Figure 18.1** Strategic drift (adapted from Johnson and Scholes, *Exploring Corporate Strategy*, 2007)

The possible effect of the divorce between ownership and control

Chapter 2 of Book 1 explained the different forms of business, including what a public limited company is and the role of shareholders in it. Ensure that you are confident in your knowledge and understanding of these issues before proceeding with this section.

Traditionally, entrepreneurs have two functions – ownership and control. In a sole trader business, the owner and director/manager are likely to be the same person, so these functions remain with that one person, the entrepreneur. However, in public limited companies, the owners (shareholders) vote for a board of directors to control the business, and they in turn appoint managers to run the business on a day-to-day basis. In this case, the two functions of ownership and control are separated or divorced.

The possible effect of the **divorce of ownership and control** in public limited companies tends to centre on the tension between the objectives of owners (shareholders) and those in control (directors).

Key term

Divorce of ownership and control Separation of the two functions of ownership and control in public limited companies; ownership entails providing finance and therefore taking risks; control involves managing the organisation and making decisions.

- Public limited companies attract millions of shareholders, many of whom may only be interested in the dividends they can earn on their shares or in the capital gain they can make from buying and selling shares. They often have little or no real interest in the management of the company, its long-term performance or the impact of its actions on other stakeholders. (Stakeholders were discussed in detail in Chapter 6 of Book 1.) As a result of this, shareholders can put pressure on directors to opt for 'short-termist' decision making.

- The fact that directors and shareholders become more separated as a company grows in size can mean that shareholders find it more difficult to access the information they need to challenge or judge the quality of managers' decisions. The more autonomy directors have, the more likely they may be to pursue objectives that benefit themselves rather than shareholders. Their objectives could be furthering their own careers and the power they wield as individuals, for example, by pursuing business growth even if this is at the expense of ethical behaviour, efficiency or profitability.

Figure 18.2 illustrates the tensions between the owners of a business (the shareholders) and those in control of a business (managers).

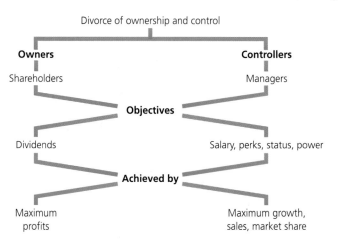

▲ **Figure 18.2** Divorce of ownership and control

Corporate governance

Corporate governance refers to the systems and mechanisms established by a company to protect the interests of its owners (shareholders). In theory, a board of directors is elected to represent shareholder interests, determine strategy and ensure that a company acts legally.

What do you think?

Given that most of the information shareholders receive about their company will be from directors themselves, how do shareholders make sure that directors actually do a good job?

411

The challenge of making sure that companies are run in the best interests of their owners is a complex one. Shareholders do not want or need to know everything that happens in their company – this would simply lead to information overload and directors must be given the freedom to do their jobs. On the other hand, shareholders are the owners of their company and so should be kept informed of relevant issues. While there is no doubt that an independent, questioning approach is desirable to keep a check on a company's actions, there is also a need for strong leadership and able directors who have a deep inside knowledge of the business.

The UK Corporate Governance Code, first issued in 1992 and revised every few years, sets out standards of good practice in relation to leadership by boards of directors and effectiveness, remuneration, accountability and relations with shareholders. Companies are required to report on how they have applied the code in their annual report and accounts.

The delicate relationship between shareholders and directors has been reviewed in the UK several times at the request of the government. The Cadbury Report (1992), the Hampel Report (1998) and the Higgs Report (2003) made numerous recommendations for UK companies, most of which have been incorporated into the Corporate Governance Code. Recommendations often focused on the need for public limited companies to have more non-executive directors, that is directors who do not have a full-time job in the business. The argument is that non-executive directors will be more independent and provide a better check on managers' behaviour than executive directors, who are in effect checking on themselves. However, the Case study at the end of the chapter on governance at Tesco raises questions about the effectiveness of non-executive directors.

Much greater pressure is now being put on directors to be more accountable to their shareholders. However, owners (shareholders) still cannot always be sure that their money is being used in the way they want or that the power of those in control (directors) is not being abused.

Evaluating strategic performance

Chapter 1 provides an explanation of the corporate planning process and indicates that the final stage in the process is control and evaluation. This stage allows managers to assess the appropriateness of current strategies and the extent to which they are still appropriate given any changes in the external or competitive environment.

The process of evaluating strategic performance is likely to involve:

- regular performance measurement against benchmarks or planned targets
- ongoing monitoring and reviewing of internal and external issues that might affect strategic plans and their implementation
- continual corrective actions to ensure that strategy is appropriate to current conditions and is on track to enable a business to meet its objectives.

Effective evaluation should indicate whether modifications need to be made to implementation strategies, the strategic plan itself and ultimately the initial objectives themselves.

Strategic evaluation is therefore not only a stage to review and evaluate the strategic process and how effective it is in enabling a business to achieve its objectives, it is also a means of continuous improvement.

Management thinkers tend to suggest that the evaluation process is most effective when it causes firms to think hard about what they are actually doing regarding the scope of the strategy being implemented, the choices that lie behind it and the process used to develop it. A failure to rigorously evaluate strategic performance is more likely to mean a business will experience strategic drift, which was explained in the previous section of this chapter.

The value of strategic planning

Chapter 1 explained the various stages involved in the corporate or **strategic planning** process. In turn, other chapters in this book have discussed each of the stages in the strategic planning process.

> **Key term**
>
> **Strategic planning** The process of determining an organisation's long-term goals and then devising a plan (strategy) to achieve them.

To summarise, strategic planning involves the following stages:

- Defining an organisation's mission and objectives.
- Analysing an organisation's internal strengths and weaknesses and its external opportunities and threats in the form of a SWOT analysis.
- The SWOT analysis informs the strategic choice stage. This is when an organisation decides on the various options available to enable it to meet its objective. Once options have been determined, the broad corporate level plans will begin to be interpreted into appropriate functional level plans and targets.
- Strategic implementation when plans are put into practice.
- Control and evaluation to determine how successful the plan and its implementation are and whether they are in need of revision because, for example, the external environment has changed.

Management thinker, Henry Mintzberg, who identified the idea of emergent strategies (discussed earlier in this chapter), disagrees with the traditional ideas about strategic planning explained above. He has labelled the term 'strategic planning' an oxymoron. (An oxymoron is a figure of speech that combines two apparently contradictory terms.) He suggests that real strategy is made informally and cannot be planned in the way suggested.

Other writers suggest that formal planning can be a real source of competitive advantage, but that it does not have to be done in a rigid series of stages as suggested in the process summarised above. These writers suggest, for example, that the SWOT analysis stage should be a fairly continuous process to ensure business leaders are fully informed at all times of the changing nature of the business environment they face. Equally, the evaluation phase, although it can only be done when implementation has started, is also something that should be ongoing so that strategy can be constantly reviewed and updated as the environment changes. These ideas link back to the issues raised in the earlier discussion about planned and emergent strategies. Thus rather than saying that strategic planning is not valuable, these writers suggest that the process of strategic planning is a valuable 'learning tool' for managers. This is because the business environment is mostly unpredictable. For example, two competitors merge, another develops a new technology, the government issues new regulations, or market demand swings in a different direction.

It is mostly during these 'real-time' developments and changes that a company's most important strategic decisions are made. Business managers who are not well prepared are unlikely to respond effectively to uncertainty in the business environment.

The value of strategic planning can be summarised as follows:

● By following a strategic planning process, an organisation can improve business outcomes and avoid taking on unanticipated risks due to lack of foresight.
● Strategic planning provides direction for an organisation, and ensures that everyone in the organisation knows where it is heading and how it intends to get there.
● Leaders have a solid understanding of their organisation, share a common understanding of the business environment it operates in and how that environment is changing.
● The process of strategic planning is a valuable learning tool for managers that ensures they are very well informed and able to make decisions about required changes to strategy quickly and appropriately.

The value of contingency planning

In a business context, a crisis is any unexpected event that threatens the well-being or survival of a firm. It is possible to distinguish between two types of crisis: those that are fairly predictable and quantifiable, and those that are totally unexpected and have massive implications for business. This is the difference, for example, between regular fluctuations in exchange rates and natural disasters such as the Japanese tsunami of 2011. The former can be dealt with by contingency planning and the latter must be dealt with by crisis management.

Examples of different types of crises affecting business include:

● physical destruction due to a natural disaster, such as the earthquakes in Nepal in 2015
● environmental disasters, such as the BP oil spillage in the Gulf of Mexico in 2010
● the impact of foot and mouth disease on the farming industry
● fraudulent activities of employees in financial services organisations
● major customers withdrawing their custom or going into liquidation – for example, the impact on component suppliers of the closure of a car manufacturer
● pressure group activities or unwelcome media attention, such as revelations about child labour used in the production of products for high-profile companies such as Nike (see the Fact file on page 56 of Chapter 3 in Book 1)
● faulty or dangerous products, such the recall of cars by Nissan, Honda and Toyota because of faulty airbags
● strikes by workers meaning orders cannot be satisfied or services provided
● machine failures causing massive reductions in production capacity
● competitors launching new products
● a severe recession or changes in exchange rates.

▲ Crisis management would be used to deal with the impact of a natural disaster

In the list above, the unexpected crises are towards the top, and the more predictable and quantifiable risks are at the bottom.

Contingency planning aims to minimise the impact of foreseeable yet non-critical events. In relation to such events, an organisation usually has weeks in which to prepare and respond. Contingency planning normally involves gathering detailed information on predictable situations and using computer models that provide systematic opportunities to ask and answer 'what if' questions.

Crisis management, on the other hand, is about responding to a sudden event that poses a significant threat to an organisation. Crisis management normally involves damage limitation strategies and places a heavy emphasis on public relations (PR) and media relationships. It emphasises the need for a flexible response to any situation and the selection of a crisis team to deal with situations as they arise.

Key term

Contingency planning Planning for unexpected and, usually, unwelcome events that are, however, reasonably predictable and quantifiable; the objective is to reduce the risks and costs of such events on an organisation.

Fact file

Thomas Cook

In 2006, two British children died from carbon monoxide poisoning while staying in a bungalow on a Thomas Cook package holiday in Corfu. The cause turned out to be a poorly maintained gas water heater. Thomas Cook's handling of the affair prompted a private tragedy to develop into a national scandal.

Thomas Cook has a policy of not using rooms with standalone gas heaters. As it turned out, the management of the accommodation had misled the staff of Thomas Cook about the safety of the setup in the bungalow. Thomas Cook denied liability for the deaths of the children from the start and its CEO refused to accept responsibility. Lawyers have suggested that there is good reason for denying liability, including protecting staff from prosecution. However, there are more sensitive and less sensitive ways of doing this.

A Greek criminal court convicted three people of the manslaughter of the children in 2010 – none of them were employees of Thomas Cook. However, in May 2015, an inquest in the UK found that the company had 'breached its duty of care'. The media interest intensified when it was learned that Thomas Cook and its insurer received £3 million compensation from the Greek hotel operator for legal expenses and lost revenue – far more than the compensation offered to the family. Rather belatedly, the company donated half of this to the children's charity, UNICEF.

A lawyer said that this type of situation was an all too common instance of senior management failing to see the bigger picture, in particular failing to understand what customers and stakeholders expect from them.

A reputation management lawyer said at the time, 'Managing the reputation of corporations in cases such as this is quite a delicate exercise, especially when the issues involved are as emotive as this. If you make the wrong call at the beginning, you can be perceived as just trying to cover your backside.'

Press reports following the inquest suggest that Thomas Cook is in the midst of a public relations disaster that could seriously damage its brand, which has been around for centuries. It is facing a customer boycott and a sell-off of shares. Approximately £75 million was wiped off the value of the company's shares as investors, horrified at the damage to its reputation, tried to sell their shares. The chief executive eventually apologised publicly to the parents of the children.

Thomas Cook's handling of the tragedy has been condemned by legal experts and by crisis management consultants. One said, 'I've watched this play out like a slow motion train crash ... It's impossible to overvalue the importance of reputation to a company like this.'

The Association of British Travel Agents (ABTA) said that it has a number of measures in place to help minimise the risks of such occurrences.

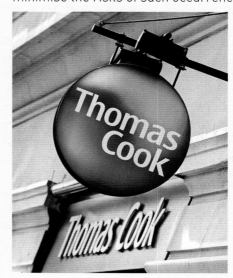

Source: adapted from a variety of media sources in May 2015

415

Crises of all types are likely to have effects on each of the functional areas of a business, and each function needs to be able to respond and manage the situation. For example:

- **Marketing**. When a firm's public image is under threat, successful PR often forms a major part of managing a crisis.
- **Finance**. Crisis management usually requires immediate cash expenditure – for example, on advertising campaigns or environmental clean-up campaigns.
- **Operations**. Contingency planning is important in this area, so that customers' needs can be met, especially if the company uses just-in-time production systems.
- **Human resources**. A crisis usually requires direct, authoritarian-type leadership in order to issue instructions and make quick decisions. In addition, effective communication systems are required. Internal communication should be direct, rapid and open; external communication should be informative, truthful and controlled.

Stages in contingency planning

If a firm is prepared for a crisis, it should be in a better position to deal with it. Contingency planning involves the following steps:

- Recognising the need for contingency planning. Without such recognition, a firm is unlikely to be prepared to deal with a crisis.
- Distinguishing between issues that are critical for the future of a firm and those that are not critical but will still have an adverse impact. In relation to the former, a firm has no choice but to do everything possible before the issues arise. For the latter, it is likely that these problems will be dealt with as and when they occur. For example, if the crisis is a computer crash, banks cannot risk losing records of customer accounts and hospitals cannot close down intensive care facilities; hence, both need back-up facilities at all times. On the other hand, disruption to computerised invoice systems may hit cash flow, but is not as critical and could be resolved in the short term by correcting mistakes by hand.
- Listing all possible crisis scenarios and then using sensitivity analysis (see the Fact file on page 417) and 'what if' questions: for example, 'What if the workforce does not accept the pay offer and decides to take industrial action?', 'What if a machine failure causes a 35 per cent reduction in capacity and cannot be fixed for the next 12 hours/12 days/12 weeks?', 'What if our largest competitor launches a new product that is more attractive than ours?', and 'What if our firm is the target of a hostile takeover bid?'
- Searching for ways to prevent each crisis: for example, where faults in products have severe repercussions, having extra quality checks, or relying less on a single supplier.
- Formulating plans for dealing with each crisis. This should include planning access to the necessary resources – human, financial and physical – and the establishment of a contingency fund. This is often known as business continuity planning or disaster-recovery planning (see the Fact files on page 417).
- Simulating each crisis and the operation of each plan. This is usually a computer-based activity, but it can also take the form of role-play exercises.

Did you know?

Disaster recovery planning refers to having the ability to restore the data and applications that run a business should the data centre, servers or other infrastructure get damaged or destroyed. One important disaster recovery consideration is how quickly data and applications can be recovered and restored. Business continuity planning refers to a strategy that lets a business operate with minimal or no downtime or service outage.

Fact file

Sensitivity analysis

Sensitivity analysis is a technique used to try to reduce uncertainty in decision making. It takes the estimates used in the decision-making process and considers what would happen if the figures were different. It enables managers to evaluate how sensitive the calculations are to changes affecting the inputs to a decision. It asks the question: 'What if?'

Two main methods of applying sensitivity analysis are used. The first asks the question: 'How will the results be affected by a change in each of the variables?' For example, how much will a 10 per cent reduction in sales or a 20 per cent increase in raw material costs affect the expected results?

The second method asks the question: 'What change in the variables will result in the project becoming unacceptable?' This method looks at each of the variables within the calculation and works out how much each of these would have to change to make the project unacceptable. The percentage change in value that makes the project unacceptable is called the sensitivity margin. For example, in an investment appraisal (considered in Chapter 8), a firm might calculate how much costs and revenues would have to change in order to reduce the net present value (NPV) of a particular project to zero.

Sensitivity analysis is a valuable tool in contingency planning. It gives managers more information to aid decision making, enables them to take a wider view of the risks and to be more prepared for changes. It helps to quantify some of the uncertainties that inevitably accompany business decisions. Sensitivity analysis was introduced on page 87 of Chapter 5 in Book 1.

Fact file

Disaster-recovery planning

When arsonists destroyed the head office of a field marketing agency, its owner ensured the 75 employees were re-housed and the business fully operational within three working days.

Having a disaster-recovery plan, which helped to relocate the entire business within days, sent out a strong, positive signal to customers that work would continue as usual. A lot of time was spent making sure that customers' confidence remained strong. Members of the management team held several informal meetings with customers to share ideas and resolve any residual problems. This demonstration of commitment showed that the firm was very much back in business and valued its customers' needs above everything else. The company's contingency planning routines meant that its data were backed up off site, so it knew this was safe.

Fact file

Business continuity planning

This is the term that is used to describe the process of planning for the unexpected. An effective plan will provide a business with procedures to minimise the effects of unexpected disruptive events. The plan should enable a business to recover quickly and efficiently, with the minimum of impact on its day-to-day activities.

Business continuity is particularly important for businesses that are reliant on IT systems, as they provide a process to counteract systems failure. If the IT systems in a business fail or are unavailable, it is likely to have a significant impact on the whole business.

Business is fraught with risk, and rehearsing the many ways in which things can go wrong is an important management activity. From small startups to established global corporations, all companies have to incorporate risk management in every aspect of their business or run the risk of ruin. The Federation of Small Businesses (FSB) notes that about 60 per cent of the small businesses questioned in a recent survey did not have a plan in place to deal with disasters such as floods and other extreme weather conditions.

Once a company's reputation has been damaged, it can take years to restore it because a snowball effect exaggerates the problem. Talented people are less likely to apply for jobs or remain loyal to the company and, as a result, management and morale may suffer. Low staff morale can lead to poor customer service. All of this can have adverse effects on company profits. As a consequence, large companies make risk management a priority.

In summary, the value of contingency planning to a business is that it helps to:

- minimise the impact of risks and limit the damage caused by business crisis – this could be in terms of reputational damage and its impact on share prices, access to finance, the recruitment of staff, morale of the workforce, and ultimately profits
- reduce the impact on customers and thus minimise the potential loss of business due to a crisis.

Despite the value of contingency planning to a business, it is a costly activity. In large firms, it can involve huge numbers of highly qualified staff in assessing risk and planning what to do if things go wrong. Like any other form of insurance, it reduces risk but may seem like a waste of money if nothing ultimately goes wrong.

Practice exercise 1   *Total: 80 marks*

1. Identify and explain two factors that make the process of strategic decision making and implementing strategies difficult.   *(8 marks)*

2. Distinguish between planned and emergent strategies.   *(6 marks)*

3. Explain the term 'strategic drift'.   *(3 marks)*

4. Analyse the main reasons for strategic drift.   *(9 marks)*

5. Who owns a plc and who controls a plc?   *(2 marks)*

6. What does the 'divorce of ownership and control' in a plc mean?   *(4 marks)*

7. What is corporate governance?   *(4 marks)*

8. Analyse how corporate governance affects the issue of divorce of ownership and control of a business.   *(9 marks)*

9. Explain what evaluation of strategic performance might involve.   *(4 marks)*

10. What is strategic planning?   *(4 marks)*

11. Explain two factors that illustrate the value of strategic planning to a business. *(6 marks)*

12. How might each of the different functional areas of a business be involved in contingency planning? *(12 marks)*

13. Identify three steps in the contingency planning process. *(3 marks)*

14. Explain two factors that illustrate the value of contingency planning to a business. *(6 marks)*

Case study 1: Kodak and strategic drift

Kodak was in business for about 110 years, and yet its demise was not a surprise to many commentators in the industry. Despite the fact that Kodak transformed the nature of photography in the twentieth century, its experience in the digital age of the twenty-first century provides a clear example of strategic drift.

Before Kodak, photography was mostly confined to professionals who took formal portrait-type pictures. Kodak transformed the industry and made photography and photographs part of family life. It focused, in particular, on wives and mothers as being the ones who recorded 'the family history' and preserved precious moments in photograph albums and picture frames. One of their most successful advertising campaigns was about recording the 'Kodak moment'. As a result, women became their most lucrative market. One of the Kodak CEOs called them the 'soccer moms' – mothers wanting to record and display photographs of their children's sporting successes.

The advent of digital technology did not cause a significant change in Kodak's strategy. Commentators at the time suggest that Kodak's senior management did not really grasp the significance of the digital revolution and how it might affect Kodak's market. For example:

- They clung on to their assumptions about who took pictures and when (the 'soccer moms') even though the main market was shifting to men – and, in general, men are not interested in storing and displaying photographs.
- They thought people would always want hard-copy prints and failed to realise that with digital photography, pictures would be viewed on cameras, phones or computers.

- They did not recognise that digital cameras were more of an electronic gadget, like other gadgets, and would eventually be sold in electronic retail stores alongside other electronic products.
- They allowed their brand to that of remain associated with traditional photography rather than digital photography.

Kodak's approach was similar to that of many companies facing technological change. First they try to ignore it, hoping that it will go away. Then they try to deride it, for example in terms of quality, speed, complexity, and so on. Then they try to enhance and prolong the life of their existing technology. Unfortunately all of these approaches simply increase the extent of strategic drift and reduce the performance of a business further. The next step is either the end of the business, as was the case with Kodak, or a transformational change that brings a business back on track.

Source: adapted from a variety of articles in the media at the time of Kodak's demise in 2012

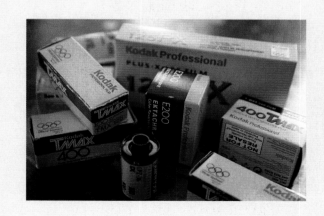

Questions

1. What is transformational change in this context? *(4 marks)*

2. Discuss the reasons why Kodak developed strategic drift. *(16 marks)*

Case study 2: Contingency planning at Heathrow's Terminal 5 (T5)

The £4.3 billion Terminal 5 (T5) at Heathrow airport was opened by The Queen on 14 March 2008. Its first day of operations on 27 March was catastrophic.

British Airways chief executive, Mr Willy Walsh, and bosses at airport operator, BAA, were grilled by MPs from the Commons Transport Committee in May 2008 about the T5 fiasco, which led to hundreds of flights being cancelled and tens of thousands of bags going missing.

Mr Walsh's statement to the committee included the following: 'We let our customers down. We could have done better and should have done better ... We believed that T5 was ready to open and we believed we had prepared sufficiently. With the benefit of hindsight, it was clear we made some mistakes ... We compromised on the testing ... because of delays in building the terminal ... We didn't supply staff with sufficient training and familiarisation. If we did it again, we would do things differently.'

He admitted that the opening of T5 had been 'a disaster' and added: 'I take responsibility for the issues that went wrong ... The decisions taken ultimately rest with me. I am prepared to be held responsible.'

Reviewing the press coverage of the situation suggests that there had been a huge failure of planning. For example, no dress rehearsals took place to iron out basic operational problems. As a result, on the day of opening, many staff could not find their car parks, could not get through security and could not find where they were meant to work. Other basic operational problems appear to have been the result of a lack of basic planning. There can be no excuse for assuming that just because the baggage system worked with one bag, it would work when loaded with 40,000, or that an escalator that glides smoothly when empty will work when full. It was this attention to detail that seems to have been missing. It was in fact a basic failure of management and a failure of the most basic management.

Source: House of Commons Transport Committee: the opening of Heathrow Terminal 5 (2008) (minutes and televised viewing)

Questions

1. Explain the term 'contingency planning'. *(4 marks)*

2. To what extent might effective contingency planning have averted, or at least minimised, the impact of the 'disaster' that took place at T5? *(16 marks)*

Case study 3: Corporate governance and Tesco

In September 2014 a bombshell hit the stock market when Tesco announced that its half-year profit had been overstated by £250 million. As the profit had totalled £1,100 million, this was an admission that the half-year figures had been overstated by more than 25 per cent.

Following this revelation by an internal whistleblower, four senior Tesco managers were suspended and the non-executive Chairman, Richard Broadbent, left the company. In the week after the announcement of the exaggerated profit, the value of Tesco's shares fell by 16 per cent (£3 billion).

There were warning signs. The BBC's Kamal Ahmed reported that:

'Investors say that Tesco has had multiple warnings ... An analyst report dated June 2010 ... said that "Tesco's accounting is consistently aggressive, and that if it had more standard" accounting methods its profit before tax would fall by £64 million'.

Serious though the technical issues were regarding the profit overstatement, other commentators pointed to a separate factor; no one on the Tesco board had any experience of retailing. This means that the people tasked with giving the right strategic advice and responsible for the culture and standards within the business could have no real insight into the day-to-day running of Tesco plc. See Table 18.1 for a summary of the Tesco board members in September 2014.

Corporate governance in the UK requires that the posts of chairman and chief executive should be held by different people, suggesting that no one person at the top should be too dominant. Despite this, problems have arisen when a chief executive's reputation or charisma gives them too much power – the chairman gives way to the person he or she is supposed to be supervising. This was the problem with several of the UK's biggest banks in the lead-up to the 2008 banking crisis. Arguably, it was also the problem for Tesco under the leadership of Terry Leahy.

Another concern is the issue of the balance between executive and non-executive board members. The usual expectation is for parity between the two. Executive directors have insights from their day jobs, perhaps as a marketing director or an operations director. Non-executive directors have independence thanks to not working within the culture of the organisation. At Tesco, the lack of executive directors on the board surprised commentators. If the board is made up of mainly non-executives, there are too few insiders to give variety to the debates that the directors are supposed to be having. The danger is that it becomes a talking shop dominated by the only person who really understands the business – the chief executive. With rewards of £100,000 plus for attending perhaps a meeting a month, it is easy to see why non-executive directors might feel quite happy lying low. In the long run, ethical and operational standards are helped if the board of directors is a robust debating chamber that scrutinises current performance and future plans.

Source: adapted from 'Governance' by Ian Marcousé, *Business Review*, February 2015

▼ **Table 18.1** Tesco plc board of directors in September 2014

Director	Title	Main career focus	Remuneration 2013–14	Retail experience
Richard Broadbent	Non-executive chairman	Deputy chairman, Barclays plc	£706,000	None
Dave Lewis	Chief executive	Whole career at Unilever plc	Only just appointed (basic salary of £1.25m)	None
Patrick Cescau	Senior independent director	Chief executive, Unilever	£132,000	None
Stuart Chambers	Non-executive director	Chief executive, Pilkington Glass	£195,000	None
Olivia Garfield	Non-executive director	Chief executive, Severn Trent Water	£62,000	None
Ken Hanna	Non-executive director	Chief financial officer, Cadbury	£126,000	None

Director	Title	Main career focus	Remuneration 2013–14	Retail experience
Mark Armour	Non-executive director	Chief financial officer, Reed Elsevier paper and publishing	£36,000	None
Gareth Bullock	Non-executive director	Standard Chartered Bank	£165,000	None
Deanna Oppenheimer	Non-executive director	Head of Barclays retail banking	£230,000	None
Jacqueline Tammenoms Bakker	Non-executive director	Ministry of Transport, Netherlands	£104,000	None

Source: Tesco accounts 2013–14

Questions

Total: 25 marks

1. Analyse why corporate governance is important to any business. *(9 marks)*

2. Discuss how well the board of directors at Tesco demonstrated good practice in their corporate governance in the period covered by the case study. *(16 marks)*

Essay questions

Total 25 marks

Answer one of the following questions:

1. Discuss the type of problems a business might encounter in developing its strategy and why its strategy might fail. *(25 marks)*

2. Discuss how each stage of the strategic planning process contributes to the overall process of strategic planning and how this overall process in turn contributes to the success of a business. *(25 marks)*

3. Discuss whether a traditional approach to strategic planning is likely to be most effective for the long-term success of a business. *(25 marks)*

4. Evaluate the factors that a business might consider before committing itself to a contingency plan that will cost £1 million to implement. *(25 marks)*

Acknowledgements

The Publishers would like to thank the following for permission to reproduce copyright photographs:
Photo credits: **p.3** © Roberto Herrett / Alamy Stock Photo; **p.5** *t* © moodboard - Thinkstock/Getty Images; **p.5** *b* © Fuse - Thinkstock/Getty Images; **p.14** © Andrew Paterson / Alamy Stock Photo; **p.18** © Topfoto / ImageWorks; **p.19** © Ingram Publishing - Thinkstock/Getty Images; **p.20** © vallefrias - Fotolia; **p.23** © Jupiterimages - Pixland - Thinkstock/Getty Images; **p.25** © michaeljung - iStock - Thinkstock/Getty Images; **p.30** © photocreo - Fotolia; **p.31** © Courtesy of Kolossos via Wikipedia Commons (https://en.wikipedia.org/wiki/GNU_Free_Documentation_License); **p.35** © Tinatin1 - iStock - Thinkstock/Getty Images; **p. 37** © Maira Brzoslowska - Fotolia; **p.40** © Newscast / Alamy Stock Photo; **p.41** © ezoom – Fotolia; **p.44** © Yuanyuan Xie - Hemara - Thinkstock/Getty Images; **p.45** © Mark Richardson / Alamy Stock Photo; **p.46** © Serghei Velusceac – Fotolia; **p.48** © Obak – Fotolia; **p.51** © bradcalkins – Fotolia; **p.64** © imageBROKER / Alamy Stock Photo; **p.71** © PA / PA Archive/PA Images; **p.75** © Ivo_Eterovic - iStock - Thinkstock/Getty Images; **p.79** © omgimages - iStock - Thinkstock/Getty Images; **p.80** © Edler von Rabenstein – Fotolia; **p.86** *l* © Tim Whitby/Getty Images; **p.86** *r* © Mike Marsland /Getty Image; **p.86** *c* © Ken McKay/ITV/REX/Shutterstock; **p.87** © Innocent Drinks, www.innocentdrinks.co.uk; **p.92** © mattphoto / Alamy Stock Photo; **p.95** © DutchScenery - iStock - Thinkstock/Getty Images; **p.102** © monkeybusinessimages - iStock - Thinkstock/Getty Images; **p.104** © Marco Rosario Venturini Autieri - iStock - Thinkstock/Getty Images; **p.106** © Fuse - Thinkstock/Getty Images; **p.107** © bomboman - iStock - Thinkstock/Getty Images; **p.112** © sirichai_ec2 - iStock - Thinkstock/Getty Images; **p.116** © NikWaller - iStock - Thinkstock/Getty Images; **p.120** © Dušan Zidar – Fotolia; **p.122** © Reserve Bank of Zimbabwe via Wikimedia Commons (Copyright Act of Zimbabwe, Chapter 26:1, states this image is in the public domain); **p.126** © RTimages / Alamy Stock Photo; **p.133** *t* © Stockbyte - Thinkstock/Getty Images; **p.133** *b* © World Trade Organization; **p.136** © Sue Cunningham Photographic / Alamy Stock Photo; **p.141** © Keith Douglas / Alamy Stock Photo; **p.142** © Andres Rodriguez – Fotolia; **p.143** © NatashaPhoto - iStock - Thinkstock/Getty Images; **p.146** © Mark Bowden - iStock - Thinkstock/Getty Images; **p.151** Business in the Community, The Prince's Responsible Business Network; **p.153** © AwaylGl - iStock - Thinkstock/Getty Images; **p.154** © James Lee - iStock - Thinkstock/Getty Images; **p.161** © moodboard - Thinkstock/Getty Images; **p.164** © Jason Janik/Bloomberg via Getty Images; **p.173** © sytnik - iStock - Thinkstock/Getty Imges; **p.175** © Mark Richardson / Alamy Stock Photo; **p.178** © michaeljung – Fotolia; **p.180** © Nataliya Hora - Fotolia.com; **p.184** © kasto80 - iStock - Thinkstock/Getty Images; **p.185** © Monkey Business – Fotolia; **p.188** © artisteer - iStock - Thinkstock/Getty Images; **p.193** Courtesy of www.khamtran.com via Wikipedia Commons (http://creativecommons.org/licenses/by-sa/3.0/); **p.194** © Mavratti via Wikipedia Commonsv(public domain); **p.197** © Bethany Clarke - Thinkstock/Getty Images News; **p.198** © jesse Karjalainen/iStockphoto.com; **p.202** © Graham Oliver / Alamy Stock Photo; **p.203** © Trevor Pearson / Alamy Stock Photo; **p.208** © Richard Naude / Alamy Stock Photo; **p.211** © incamerastock / Alamy Stock Photo; **p.212** © Mick Sinclair / Alamy Stock Photo; **p.220** © Tsyhun - iStock - Thinkstock/Getty Images; **p.224** © Isopix/REX Shutterstock; **p.225** © Matthew Horwood / Alamy Stock Photo; **p.228** © jonasginter – Fotolia; **p.230** © DigitalVision - Thinkstock/Getty Images; **p.231** © Chris Ratcliffe/Bloomberg via Getty Images; **p.234** © lee avison / Alamy Stock Photo; **p.235** © AKP Photos / Alamy Stock Photo; **p.236** Finnbarr Webster / Alamy Stock Photo; **p.238** © Netflix; **p.239** © Helen Sessions / Alamy Stock Photo; **p.247** © imageBROKER / Alamy Stock Photo; **p.248** © Astrazeneca; **p.250** © Scanrail – Fotolia; **p.252** *t* © ZealPhotography / Alamy Stock Photo; **p.252** *b* © TOYOTA (GB) PLC; **p.255** © TomasSereda - iStock - Thinkstock/Getty Images; **p.256** © Robert Convery / Alamy Stock Photo; **p.259** © Friends Reunited; **p.260** © Hewlett Packard; **p.261** © CFimages / Alamy Stock Photo; **p.263** © Chris Ratcliffe/Bloomberg via Getty Images; **p.266** © Google; **p.269** © KaYann – Fotolia; **p.272** © Twitter; **p.273** © Steve Stock / Alamy Stock Photo; **p.281** © Vigin Atlantic; **p.282** © Geoffrey Kidd / Alamy Stock Photo; **p.290** © Rob Wilkinson / Alamy Stock Photo; **p.292** © Matthew Horwood / Alamy Stock Photo; **p.293** © Art Directors & TRIP / Alamy Stock Photo; **p.294** © Gavin Hellier / Alamy Stock Photo; **p.297** © DAJ - Thinkstock/Getty Images; **p.298** © Art Kowalsky / Alamy Stock Photo; **p.300** © JasonKSLeung - iStock - Thinkstock/Getty Images; **p.301** Trunki image supplied by Alamy, picture © WENN Ltd / Alamy Stock Photo; **p.303** © Jeff Dalton / Alamy Stock Photo; **p.304** © Convery flowers / Alamy Stock Photo; **p.308** *t* © Jack Sullivan / Alamy Stock Photo; **p.308** *b* © studiomode / Alamy Stock Photo; **p.309** © Purestock - Thinkstock/Getty Images; **p.310** © Dell; **p.314** © Robert Harding World Imagery / Alamy Stock Photo; **p.320** © wda bravo / Alamy Stock Photo; **p.321** © Helen Sessions / Alamy Stock Photo; **p.339** © M4OS Photos / Alamy Stock Photo; **p.346** © Toyota; **p.347** © ClassicStock / Alamy Stock Photo; **p.350** © Siri Stafford - Digital Vision - Thinkstock/Getty Images; **p.352** © hemeroskopion - iStock - Thinkstock/Getty Images; **p.354** © Peter Marshall / Demotix / Demotix/Press Association Images; **p.356** © VIEW Pictures Ltd / Alamy Stock Photo; **p.355** © Balloon Ventures, www.balloonventures.com, a social enterprise tackling poverty in the developing world through entrepreneurship.; **p.357** © Charles Polidano / Touch The Skies / Alamy Stock Photo; **p.367** © Sipa Press/REX Shutterstock; **p.370** © shironosov - iStock - Thinkstock/Getty Images; **p.372** © Hewlett Packard; **p.372** © Nike; **p.374** © Nike; **p.375** © Helen Sessions / Alamy Stock Photo; **p.383** © jamesdavidphoto - iStock - Thinkstock/Getty Images; **p.386** *t* © Sipa Press/REX/Shutterstock; **p.386** *b* © Cultura Creative (RF) / Alamy Stock Photo; **p.387** © Convery flowers / Alamy Stock Photo; **P.390** © Ian McKinnell / Alamy Stock Photo; **p.399** © Fuse - Thinkstock/Getty Images;

p.401 © Topham/PA; **p.405** © Kristoffer Tripplaar / Alamy Stock Photo; **p.407** © zabelin - iStock - Thinkstock/Getty Images; **p.408** © c.Col Pics/Everett/REX/Shutterstock; **p.409** © Kevin Britland / Alamy Stock Photo; **p.414** © EnryPix – Fotolia; **p.415** © PhotoEdit / Alamy Stock Photo; **p.418** © David Levenson / Alamy Stock Photo; **p.419** © Scott Olson/Getty Images; **p.420** © Dan Kitwood - Thinkstock/ Getty Images News; **p.422** © Andrew Melbourne / Alamy Stock Photo; **1 & 16 & 57 & 74 & 99 & 145 & 169 & 183 (chapter openers)** © claudiodivizia - iStock - Thinkstock/Getty Images; **200, 210 (chapter opener)** © Danicek – Fotolia; **227, 264, 288, 323, (chapter opener)** © tr3gi – Fotolia; **344, 364, 382, 403 (chapter opener)** © visdia – Fotolia; **p.2** © Ryan McVay - Photodisc - Thinkstock/Getty Images; **p.61** © miflippo - iStock - Thinkstock/Getty Images; **p.62** © Fuse - Thinkstock/Getty Images; **p.62** © Digital Vision - Thinkstock/Getty Images; **p.70** © Zoonar RF - Thinkstock/Getty Images; **p.325** © anyaberkut - iStock - Thinkstock/Getty Images; **p.326** © kasto80 - iStock - Thinkstock/Getty Images; **p.329** © didecs - iStock - Thinkstock/Getty Images; **p.330** © Ryan McVay - Photodisc - Thinkstock/ Getty Images; **p.332** © shironosov - iStock - Thinkstock/Getty Images; **p.336** © gerenme - iStock - Thinkstock/Getty Images; **p.337** © Digital Vision - Thinkstock/Getty Images.

Every effort has been made to trace all copyright holders, but if any have been inadvertently overlooked the Publishers will be pleased to make the necessary arrangements at the first opportunity.

Index